STUDY GUIDE for use with McConnell, Brue, and Flynn MACROECONOMICS

Nineteenth Edition

WILLIAM B. WALSTAD
PROFESSOR OF ECONOMICS
UNIVERSITY OF NEBRASKA–LINCOLN

The McGraw-Hill Companies

Study Guide for
Macroeconomics, Nineteenth Edition
Campbell R. McConnell, Stanley L. Brue, Sean M. Flynn, and William B. Walstad

Published by McGraw-Hill/Irwin, a business unit of The McGraw-Hill Companies, Inc., 1221 Avenue of the Americas, New York, NY 10020.

1 2 3 4 5 6 7 8 9 0 QDB/QDB 1 0 9 8 7 6 5 4 3 2 1

ISBN 978-0-07-733796-4
MHID 0-07-733796-4

www.mhhe.com

About the Author

William B. Walstad is a professor of economics at the University of Nebraska-Lincoln, where he has been honored with a Distinguished Faculty Award from the College of Business Administration. Professor Walstad also has been recognized with the Henry H. Villard Research Award for his published research in economic education by the National Association of Economic Educators and the Council for Economic Education. He is the editor of the *Journal of Economic Education* and was a former chair of the Committee on Economic Education of the American Economic Association. He is a co-editor and contributor to *Teaching Innovations in Economics: Strategies and Applications for Interactive Instruction.* Professor Walstad received his Ph.D. degree from the University of Minnesota.

To

Tammie, Laura, Kristin, Eileen, Clara, and Martha

Contents

How to use the Study Guide to Learn Macroeconomics ix

PART ONE
Introduction to Economics and the Economy

1	Limits, Alternatives, and Choices	1
	Appendix: Graphs and Their Meaning	11
2	The Market System and the Circular Flow	19

PART TWO
Price, Quantity, and Efficiency

3	Demand, Supply, and Market Equilibrium	29
	Appendix: Additional Examples of Supply and Demand	40
4	Elasticity	45
5	Market Failures: Public Goods and Externalities	55

PART THREE
GDP, Growth, and Instability

6	Introduction to Macroeconomics	67
7	Measuring Domestic Output and National Income	75
8	Economic Growth	87
9	Business Cycles, Unemployment, and Inflation	97

PART FOUR
Macroeconomic Models and Fiscal Policy

10	Basic Macroeconomic Relationships	107
11	The Aggregate Expenditures Model	119
12	Aggregate Demand and Aggregate Supply	131
	Appendix: The Relationship of the Aggregate Demand Curve to the Aggregate Expenditure Model	143
13	Fiscal Policy, Deficits, and Debt	147

PART FIVE
Money, Banking, and Monetary Policy

14	Money, Banking, and Financial Institutions	159
15	Money Creation	169
16	Interest Rates and Monetary Policy	179
17	Financial Economics	193

PART SIX
Extensions and Issues

18	Extending the Analysis of Aggregate Supply	203
19	Current Issues in Macro Theory and Policy	215

PART SEVEN
International Economics

20	International Trade	225
21	The Balance of Payments, Exchange Rates, and Trade Deficits	239
22W	The Economics of Developing Countries **(WEB CHAPTER, www.mcconnell19e.com)**	251

Glossary 261

How to Use the Study Guide to Learn Economics

This *Study Guide* should help you read and understand the McConnell, Brue, and Flynn textbook, *Macroeconomics*, 19th edition. If used properly, a study guide can be a great aid to you for what is probably your first course in economics.

No one pretends that the study of economics is easy, but it can be made easier with this *Study Guide*. Of course, it will not do your work for you, and its use is no substitute for reading the text. You must first be willing to read the text and work at learning if you wish to understand economics.

Many students, however, do read their text and work hard on their economics course and still fail to learn the subject. This problem occurs because economics is a new subject for these students. They want to learn economics, but do not know how to do it because they have no previous experience with the subject. Here is where the *Study Guide* can help students. Let's first see what the *Study Guide* contains and then how to use it.

■ WHAT THE *STUDY GUIDE* IS

This *Study Guide* contains 21 chapters to support your learning of each of the 21 textbook chapters in *Macroeconomics*. There is also one more Study Guide chapter that fully supports the ***Web Chapter*** for *Macroeconomics*. In addition, the *Study Guide* has a ***glossary.*** This *Study Guide* should give you a complete set of resources to advance your learning of principles of economics.

Each *Study Guide* chapter has 11 sections to give you complete coverage of the textbook material in each chapter. The first five sections help you to ***understand*** the economics content in each chapter.

1. An ***introduction*** explains what is in the chapter of the text and how it is related to material in earlier and later chapters. It points out topics to which you should give special attention and reemphasizes difficult or important principles and facts.

2. A ***checklist*** tells you the things you should be able to do when you have finished the chapter.

3. A ***chapter outline*** shows how the chapter is organized and summarizes briefly the essential points made in the chapter, including the Last Word.

4. Selected ***hints and tips*** for each chapter help you identify key points and make connections with any previous discussion of a topic.

5. A list of the ***important terms*** points out what you must be able to define to understand the material in the chapter. Each term is defined in the glossary at the end of the *Study Guide*.

The next six sections of the *Study Guide* allow you to ***self-test*** your understanding of the chapter material.

6. ***Fill-in questions*** (short-answer and list questions) help you learn and remember the important generalizations and facts in the chapter.

7. ***True-false questions*** test your understanding of the material in the chapter.

8. ***Multiple-choice questions*** also give you a chance to check your knowledge of the chapter content and prepare for this type of course examination.

9. ***Problems*** help you learn and understand economic concepts by requiring different skills—drawing a graph, completing a table, or finding relationships—to solve the problems.

10. ***Short answer*** and ***essay questions*** can be used as a self-test, to identify important questions in the chapter and to prepare for examinations.

11. ***Answers*** to fill-in questions, true-false questions, multiple-choice questions, and problems are found at the end of each chapter. References to the specific pages in the textbook for each true-false, multiple-choice, and short answer or essay questions are also provided.

■ HOW TO STUDY AND LEARN WITH THE HELP OF THE *STUDY GUIDE*

1. ***Read and outline.*** For best results, quickly read the introduction, outline, list of terms, and checklist in the *Study Guide* before you read the chapter in *Macroeconomics*. Then read the chapter in the text slowly, keeping one eye on the *Study Guide* outline and the list of terms. Highlight the chapter as you read it by identifying the *major and minor* points and by placing *Study Guide* outline numbers or letters (such as I or A or 1 or a) in the margins. When you have completed the chapter, you will have the chapter highlighted, and the *Study Guide* outline will serve as a handy set of notes on the chapter.

2. ***Review and reread.*** After you have read the chapter in the text once, return to the introduction, outline, and list of terms in the *Study Guide*. Reread the introduction and outline. Does everything there make sense? If not, go back to the text and reread the topics that you do not remember well or that still confuse you. Look at the outline. Try to recall each of the minor topics that were contained in the text under each of the major points in the outline. When you come to the list of terms, go over them one by one. *Define or explain each to yourself and then look for the definition of the term either in the text chapter or in the glossary.* Compare your own definition or explanation with that in the *text or glossary.* The quick way to find the definition of a term in the text is to look in the text index for the page(s) in which that term or concept is mentioned. Make any necessary correction or change in your own definition or explanation.

3. *Test and check answers.* When you have done the above reading and review, you will have a good idea of what is in the text chapter. Now complete the self-test sections of the *Study Guide* to check your understanding.

In doing the self-test, start with the *fill-in, true-false, multiple-choice,* and *problems* sections. Tackle each of these four sections one at a time, using the following procedures: (1) answer as many self-test items as you can without looking in the text or in the answer section of the *Study Guide*; (2) check the text for whatever help you need in answering the items; and (3) consult the answer section of the *Study Guide* for the correct answers and reread any section of the text for which you missed items.

The self-test items in these four sections are not equally difficult. Some will be easy to answer and others will be harder. Do not expect to get them all correct the first time. Some are designed to pinpoint material of importance that you will probably miss the first time you read the text and answering them will get you to read the text again with more insight and understanding.

The *short answer and essay questions* cover the major points in the chapter. For some of the easier questions, all you may do is mentally outline your answer. For the more difficult questions, you may want to write out a brief outline of the answer or a full answer. Do not avoid the difficult questions just because they are more work. Answering these questions is often the most valuable work you can do toward acquiring an understanding of economic relationships and principles.

Although no answers are given in the *Study Guide* to the short answer and essay questions, the answer section does list text page references for each question. You are *strongly* encouraged to read those text pages for an explanation of the question or for better insight into the question content.

4. *Double check.* Before you turn to the next chapter in the text and *Study Guide*, return to the checklist. If you cannot honestly check off each item in the list, you have not learned what the authors of the text and of this Study Guide hoped you would learn.

■ WEB CHAPTER FOR *MACROECONOMICS*

The *Study Guide* fully supports the Web-based chapter in *Macroeconomics:* Economics of Developing Countries (Chapter 22W). This chapter is located at *www.mcconnell19e.com*. The *Study Guide* includes full content and self-test materials for this chapter.

■ GLOSSARY

All of the important terms and concepts in *Macroeconomics* are defined and described in the glossary. It is included in the *Study Guide* for easy reference when you see a term or concept you do not know. It will also aid your work on self-test items in the *Study Guide.*

■ SOME FINAL WORDS

Perhaps the method of using the *Study Guide* outlined above seems like a lot of work. It is! Study and learning requires work on your part. This fact is one you must accept if you are to learn economics.

After you have used the *Study Guide* to study one or two chapters, you will find that some sections are more valuable to you than others. Let your own experience determine how you will use it. But do not discontinue use of the *Study Guide* after one or two chapters merely because you are not sure whether it is helping you. ***Stick with it.***

■ ACKNOWLEDGMENTS

Special thanks are due to Sharon Nemeth for her hard work in preparing the electronic versions of this *Study Guide.* I am also indebted to Stan Brue, Campbell McConnell, and Sean Flynn for their on-going support during the development of this *Study Guide.* While I am most grateful for all these contributions, I alone am responsible for an errors or omissions. You are welcome to send me comments or suggestions.

William B. Walstad

CHAPTER 1

Limits, Alternatives, and Choices

Chapter 1 introduces you to economics—the social science that studies how individuals, institutions, and society make the optimal best choices under conditions of scarcity. The first section of the chapter describes the three key features of the **economic perspective.** This perspective first recognizes that all choices involve costs and that these costs must be involved in an economic decision. The economic perspective also incorporates the view that to achieve a goal, people make decisions that reflect their purposeful self-interest. The third feature considers that people compare marginal benefits against marginal costs when making decisions and will choose the situation where the marginal benefit is greater than the marginal cost. You will develop a better understanding of these features as you read about the economic issues in this book.

Economics relies heavily on the **scientific method** to develop theories and principles to explain the likely effects from human events and behavior. It involves gathering data, testing hypotheses, and developing theories and principles. In essence, economic theories and principles (and related terms such as laws and models) are generalizations about how the economic world works.

Economists develop economic theories and principles at two levels. **Microeconomics** targets specific units in the economy. Studies at this level research such questions as how prices and output are determined for particular products and how consumers will react to price changes. **Macroeconomics** focuses on the whole economy, or large segments of it. Studies at this level investigate such issues as how to increase economic growth, control inflation, or maintain full employment. Studies at either level have elements of **positive economics,** which investigates facts or cause-and-effect relationships, or **normative economics,** which incorporates subjective views of what ought to be or what policies should be used to address an economic issue.

Several sections of the text are devoted to a discussion of the **economizing problem** from individual or society perspectives. This problem arises from a fundamental conflict between economic wants and economic resources: (1) individuals and society have *unlimited* economic wants; (2) the economic means or resources to satisfy those wants are *limited.* This economic problem forces individuals and societies to make a choice. And anytime a choice is made there is an opportunity cost—the next best alternative that was not chosen.

The economizing problem for individuals is illustrated with a microeconomic model that uses a **budget line.** It shows graphically the meaning of many concepts defined in the chapter: scarcity, choice, trade-offs, opportunity cost, and optimal allocation. The economizing problem for society is illustrated with a macroeconomic model that uses a **production possibilities curve.** It also shows graphically the economic concepts just listed, and in addition it can be used to describe macroeconomic conditions related to unemployment, economic growth, and trade. The production possibilities model can also be applied to many real economic situations, such as the economics of war, as you will learn from the text.

■ CHECKLIST

When you have studied this chapter you should be able to

☐ Write a formal definition of economics.
☐ Describe the three key features of the economic perspective.
☐ Give applications of the economic perspective.
☐ Identify the elements of the scientific method.
☐ Define hypothesis, theory, principle, law, and model as they relate to economics.
☐ State how economic principles are generalizations and abstractions.
☐ Explain the "other-things-equal" assumption (*ceteris paribus*) and its use in economics.
☐ Distinguish between microeconomics and macroeconomics.
☐ Give examples of positive and normative economics.
☐ Explain the economizing problem for an individual (from a microeconomic perspective).
☐ Describe the concept of a budget line for the individual.
☐ Explain how to measure the slope of a budget line and determine the location of the budget line.
☐ Use the budget line to illustrate trade-offs and opportunity costs.
☐ Describe the economizing problem for society.
☐ Define the four types of economic resources for society.
☐ State the four assumptions made when a production possibilities table or curve is constructed.
☐ Construct a production possibilities curve when given the data.
☐ Define opportunity cost and utilize a production possibilities curve to explain the concept.
☐ Show how the law of increasing opportunity costs is reflected in the shape of the production possibilities curve.
☐ Explain the economic rationale for the law of increasing opportunity costs.

☐ Use marginal analysis to define optimal allocation.
☐ Explain how optimal allocation determines the optimal point on a production possibilities curve.
☐ Use a production possibilities curve to illustrate unemployment.
☐ Use the production possibilities curve to illustrate economic growth.
☐ Explain how international trade affects a nation's production possibilities curve.
☐ Give other applications of the production possibilities model.
☐ Identify the five pitfalls to sound economic reasoning (*Last Word*).

■ CHAPTER OUTLINE

1. ***Economics*** studies how individuals, institutions, and society make the optimal or best choices under conditions of *scarcity,* for which economic wants are *unlimited* and the means or resources to satisfy those wants are *limited.*

2. The ***economic perspective*** has three interrelated features.

a. It recognizes that scarcity requires choice and that making a choice has an ***opportunity cost***—giving up the next best alternative to the choice that was made.

b. It views people as purposeful decision makers who make choices based on their self-interests. People seek to increase their satisfaction, or ***utility,*** from consuming a good or service. They are purposeful because they weigh the costs and benefits in deciding how best to increase that utility.

c. It uses ***marginal analysis*** to assess how the marginal costs of a decision compare with the marginal benefits.

3. Economics relies on the ***scientific method*** for analysis.

a. Several terms are used in economic analysis that are related to this method.

(1) A *hypothesis* is a proposition that is tested and used to develop an economic *theory.*

(2) A highly tested and reliable economic theory is called an ***economic principle*** or *law.* Theories, principles, and laws are meaningful statements about economic behavior or the economy that can be used to predict the likely outcome of an action or event.

(3) An economic *model* is created when several economic laws or principles are used to explain or describe reality.

b. There are several other aspects of economic principles.

(4) Each principle or theory is a generalization that shows a tendency or average effect.

(5) The ***other-things-equal assumption*** (*ceteris paribus*) is used to limit the influence of other factors when making a generalization.

(6) Many economic models can be illustrated graphically and are simplified representations of economic reality.

4. Economic analysis is conducted at two levels, and for each level there can be elements of positive or normative economics.

a. ***Microeconomics*** studies the economic behavior of individuals, particular markets, firms, or industries.

b. ***Macroeconomics*** looks at the entire economy or its major ***aggregates*** or sectors, such as households, businesses, or government.

c. ***Positive economics*** focuses on facts and is concerned with what is, or the scientific analysis of economic behavior.

d. ***Normative economics*** suggests what ought to be and answers policy questions based on value judgments. Most disagreements among economists involve normative economics.

5. Individuals face an ***economizing problem*** because economic wants are greater than the economic means to satisfy those wants. The problem can be illustrated with a microeconomic model with several features.

a. Individuals have limited income to spend.

b. Individuals have virtually unlimited wants for more goods and services, and higher-quality goods and services.

c. The economizing problem for the individual can be illustrated with a budget line and two products (for instance, DVDs and books). The ***budget line*** shows graphically the combinations of the two products a consumer can purchase with his or her money income.

(1) All combinations of the two products on or inside the budget line are *attainable* by the consumer; all combinations beyond the budget line are *unattainable.*

(2) To obtain more DVDs the consumer has to give up some books, so there is a *trade-off;* if to get a second DVD the consumer must give up two books, then the *opportunity* cost of the additional DVD is two books.

(3) Limited income forces individuals to evaluate the marginal cost and marginal benefit of a choice to maximize their satisfaction.

(4) Changes in money income shift the budget line: an increase in income shifts the line to the right; a decrease in income shifts the line to the left.

6. Society also faces an economizing problem due to scarcity.

a. ***Economic resources*** are scarce natural, human, or manufactured inputs used to produce goods and services.

b. Economic resources are sometimes called ***factors of production*** and are classified into four categories:

(1) ***land,*** or natural resources.

(2) ***labor,*** or the contributed time and abilities of people who are producing goods and services.

(3) ***capital*** (or capital goods), or the machines, tools, and equipment used to make other goods and services; economists refer to the purchase of such capital goods as ***investment.***

(4) ***entrepreneurial ability,*** or the special human talents of individuals who combine the other factors of production.

7. A macroeconomic model of production possibilities illustrates the economizing problem for society. The four assumptions usually made when such a production possibilities model is used are: (1) there is full employment of available resources; (2) the quantity and quality of resources are fixed; (3) the state of technology does not change; and (4) there are two types of goods being produced (***consumer goods*** and ***capital goods***).

a. The ***production possibilities table*** indicates the alternative combinations of goods an economy is capable of producing when it has achieved full employment and optimal allocation. The table illustrates the fundamental choice every economy must make: what quantity of each product it must sacrifice to obtain more of another.

b. The data in the production possibilities table can be plotted on a graph to obtain a ***production possibilities curve.*** Each point on the curve shows some maximum output of the two goods.

c. The opportunity cost of producing an additional unit of one good is the amount of the other good that is sacrificed. The ***law of increasing opportunity costs*** states that the opportunity cost of producing one more unit of a good (the marginal opportunity cost) increases as more of the good is produced.

(1) The production possibilities curve is bowed out from the origin because of the law of increasing opportunity costs.

(2) The reason the opportunity cost of producing an additional unit of a good increases as more of it is produced is because resources are not completely adaptable to alternative uses.

d. Optimal allocation means that resources are devoted to the best mix of goods to maximize satisfaction in society. This optimal mix is determined by assessing marginal costs and benefits.

(1) The marginal-cost curve for a good increases because of the law of increasing opportunity costs; the marginal-benefit curve decreases because the consumption of a good yields less and less satisfaction.

(2) When the marginal benefit is greater than the marginal cost, there is an incentive to produce more of the good, but when the marginal cost is greater than the marginal benefit, there is an incentive to produce less of the good.

(3) Optimal or efficient allocation is achieved when the marginal cost of a product equals the marginal benefit of a product.

8. Different outcomes will occur when assumptions underlying the production possibilities model are relaxed.

a. Unemployment. When the economy is operating at a point inside the production possibilities curve it means that resources are not fully employed.

b. ***Economic growth.*** The production possibilities curve shifts outward from economic growth because resources are no longer fixed and technology improves.

(1) Expansion in the quantity and quality of resources contributes to economic growth and shifts the production possibilities curve outward.

(2) Advancement in technology contributes to economic growth and also shifts the production possibilities curve outward.

(3) The combination of capital goods and consumer goods an economy chooses to produce in the present can determine the position of the production possibilities curve in the future. Greater production of capital goods relative to consumer goods in the present shifts the production possibilities curve farther outward in the future because that economy is devoting more of its resources to investment than consumption.

c. Trade. When there is international specialization and trade, a nation can obtain more goods and services than is indicated by the production possibilities curve for a domestic economy. The effect on production possibilities is similar to an increase in economic growth.

9. (*Last Word*). Sound reasoning about economic issues requires the avoidance of five pitfalls.

a. *Bias* is a preconceived belief or opinion that is not warranted by the facts.

b. *Loaded terminology* is the use of terms in a way that appeals to emotion and leads to a nonobjective analysis of the issues.

c. The *fallacy of composition* is the assumption that what is true of the part is necessarily true of the whole.

d. The *post hoc fallacy* ("after this, therefore because of this") is the mistaken belief that when one event precedes another, the first event is the cause of the second.

e. *Confusing correlation with causation* means that two factors may be related, but that does not mean that one factor caused the other.

■ HINTS AND TIPS

1. The **economic perspective** presented in the first section of the chapter has three features related to decision making: scarcity and the necessity of choice, purposeful self-interest in decision making, and marginal analysis of the costs and benefits of decisions. Although these features may seem strange to you at first, they are central to the economic thinking used to examine decisions and problems throughout the book.

2. The chapter introduces two pairs of terms: **microeconomics** and **macroeconomics;** and **positive economics** and **normative economics.** Make sure you understand what each pair means and how they are related to each other.

3. The **budget line** shows the consumer what it is possible to purchase in the two-good world, given an income. Make sure that you understand what a budget line is. To test your understanding, practice with different income levels and prices. For example, assume you had an income of $100 to spend for two goods (A and B). Good A costs $10 and Good B costs $5. Draw a budget line to show the possible combinations of A and B that you could purchase.

4. The **production possibilities curve** is a simple and useful economic model for an economy. Practice your understanding of it by using it to explain the following economic concepts: scarcity, choice, opportunity cost, the law of increasing opportunity costs, full employment, optimal allocation, unemployment, and economic growth.

5. **Opportunity cost** is always measured in terms of a forgone alternative. From a production possibilities table, you can easily calculate how many units of one product you forgo when you get another unit of a product.

■ IMPORTANT TERMS

Note: See the Glossary in the back of the book for definitions of terms.

economics
economic perspective
opportunity cost
utility
marginal analysis
scientific method
economic principle
other-things-equal assumption (*ceteris paribus*)
microeconomics
macroeconomics
aggregate
positive economics
normative economics
economizing problem
budget line
economic resources
land
factors of production
labor
capital
investment
entrepreneurial ability
consumer goods
capital goods
production possibilities curve
law of increasing opportunity costs
economic growth

SELF-TEST

■ FILL-IN QUESTIONS

1. The economic perspective recognizes that (resources, scarcity) ____________ require(s) choice and that choice has an opportunity (benefit, cost) ____________. There is no such thing as a "free lunch" in economics because scarce resources have (unlimited, alternative) ____________ uses.

2. The economic perspective also assumes that people make choices based on their self-interest and that they are (random, purposeful) ____________. It also is based on comparisons of the (extreme, marginal) ____________ costs and benefits of an economic decision.

3. Economics relies on the (model, scientific) ____________ method. Statements about economic behavior that enable the prediction of the likely effects of certain actions are economic (facts, theories) ____________. The most well-tested of these that have strong predictive accuracy are called economic (hypotheses, principles) ____________, or sometimes they are called (laws, actions) ____________. Simplified representations of economic behavior or how an economy works are called (policies, models) ____________.

4. Economic principles are often expressed as tendencies, or what is typical, and are (fallacies, generalizations) ____________ about people's economic behavior. When studying a relationship between two economic variables, economists assume that other variables or factors (do, do not) ____________ change, or in other words they are using the (utility, other-things-equal) ____________ assumption.

5. The study of output in a particular industry or of a particular product is the subject of (microeconomics, macroeconomics) ____________, and the study of the total output of the economy or the general level of prices is the subject of ____________.

6. The collection of specific units that are being added and treated as if they were one unit is an (assumption, aggregate) ____________.

7. Two different types of statements can be made about economic topics. A (positive, normative) ____________ statement explains what is by offering a scientific proposition about economic behavior that is based on economic theory and facts, but a ____________ statement includes a value judgment about an economic policy or the economy that suggests what ought to be. Many of the reported disagreements among economists usually involve (positive, normative) ____________ statements.

8. The economizing problem arises because individuals' and society's economic wants for more goods and services or higher-quality goods and services are (limited, unlimited) ____________ and the economic means or resources to satisfy those wants are ____________.

9. A schedule or curve that shows the various combinations of two products a consumer can (buy, sell) ____________ with a money income is called a (budget, marginal cost) ____________ line.

10. All combinations of goods inside a budget line are (attainable, unattainable) ____________, and all combinations of goods outside the budget line are ____________.

11. When a consumer's income increases, the budget line shifts to the (left, right) ____________, while a decrease in income shifts the budget line to the ____________.

12. The four types of economic resources are

a. ____________

b. ____________

c. ____________

d. ____________

13. When a production possibilities table or curve is constructed, four assumptions are made:

a. ____________

b. ____________

c. ____________

d. ____________

14. Goods that satisfy economic wants directly are (consumer, capital goods) ________, and goods that do so indirectly by helping produce other goods are ________ goods. Assume an economy can produce two basic types of goods, consumer and capital goods. If the economy wants to produce more consumer goods, then the capital goods the economy must give up are the opportunity (benefit, cost) ________ of producing those additional consumer goods.

15. The law of increasing opportunity costs explains why the production possibilities curve is (convex, concave) ________ from the origin. The economic rationale for the law is that economic resources (are, are not) ________ completely adaptable to alternative uses.

16. Optimal allocation of resources to production occurs when the marginal costs of the productive output are (greater than, less than, equal to) ________ the marginal benefits.

17. Following is a production possibilities curve for capital goods and consumer goods.

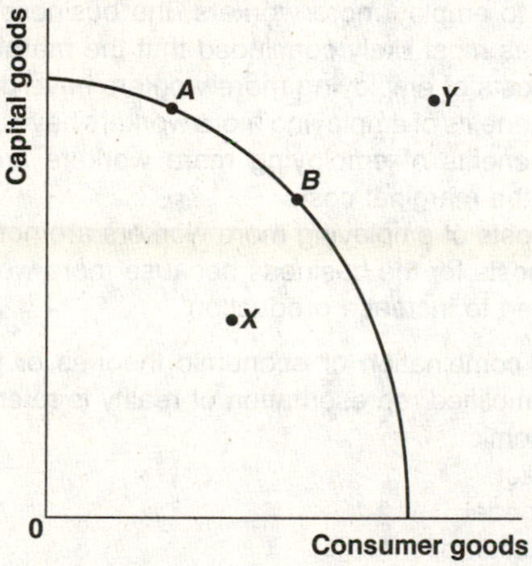

Capital goods

A

Y

B

X

0

Consumer goods

a. If the economy moves from point ***A*** to point ***B***, it will produce (more, fewer) ________ capital goods and (more, fewer) ________ consumer goods.

b. If the economy is producing at point ***X***, some resources in the economy are either (not available, unemployed) ________ or (underemployed, overemployed) ________.

c. If the economy moves from point ***X*** to point ***B*** (more, fewer) ________ capital goods and (more, fewer) ________ consumer goods will be produced.

d. If the economy is to produce at point ***Y***, there must be (unemployment, economic growth) ________.

18. Economic growth will shift a nation's production possibilities curve (inward, outward) ________, and it occurs because of a resource supply (decrease, increase) ________ or because of a technological (decline, advance) ________.

19. An economy can produce goods for the present such as (consumer, capital) ________ goods and goods for the future such as ________ goods. If an economy produces more goods for the future, then this is likely to lead to a (greater, smaller) ________ shift outward in the production possibilities curve over time compared to the case where the economy produces more goods for the present.

20. International specialization and trade enable a nation to obtain (more, less) ________ of output than is possible with the output limits imposed by domestic production possibilities. The gains in output for an economy from greater international specialization and trade are similar to those that occur because of resource (increases, decreases) ________ or a technological (decline, advance) ________.

■ TRUE–FALSE QUESTIONS

Circle T if the statement is true, F if it is false.

1. Economics is the social science that studies how individuals, institutions, and society make choices under conditions of scarcity. **T F**

2. From the economic perspective, "there is no such thing as a free lunch." **T F**

3. The economic perspective views individuals or institutions as making purposeful choices based on the marginal analysis of the costs and benefits of decisions. **T F**

4. The scientific method involves the observation of real world data, the formulation of hypotheses based on the data, and the testing of those hypotheses to develop theories. **T F**

5. A well-tested or widely accepted economic theory is often called an economic principle or law. **T F**

6. The other-things-equal assumption (*ceteris paribus*) is made to simplify the economic analysis. **T F**

7. Microeconomic analysis is concerned with the performance of the economy as a whole or its major aggregates. **T F**

8. Macroeconomic analysis is concerned with the economic activity of specific firms or industries. **T F**

9. The statement that "the legal minimum wage should be raised to give working people a decent income" is an example of a normative statement. **T F**

10. A person is using positive economics when the person makes value judgments about how the economy should work. **T F**

11. The conflict between the unlimited economic wants of individuals or societies and limited economic means and resources of individuals or societies gives rise to the economizing problem. **T F**

12. The budget line shows all combinations of two products that the consumer can purchase, given money income and the prices of the products. **T F**

13. A consumer is unable to purchase any of the combinations of two products which lie below (or to the left) of the consumer's budget line. **T F**

14. An increase in the money income of a consumer shifts the budget line to the right. **T F**

15. The factors of production are land, labor, capital, and entrepreneurial ability. **T F**

16. From the economist's perspective, investment refers to money income. **T F**

17. Given full employment and optimal allocation, it is not possible for an economy capable of producing just two goods to increase its production of both at any one point in time. **T F**

18. The opportunity cost of producing more consumer goods is the other goods and services the economy is unable to produce because it has decided to produce these additional consumer goods. **T F**

19. The opportunity cost of producing a good tends to increase as more of it is produced because resources less suitable to its production must be employed. **T F**

20. Drawing a production possibilities curve bowed out from the origin is a graphical way of showing the law of increasing opportunity costs. **T F**

21. The economic rationale for the law of increasing opportunity costs is that economic resources are fully adaptable to alternative uses. **T F**

22. Optimal allocation is determined by assessing the marginal costs and benefits of the output from the allocation of resources to production. **T F**

23. Economic growth means an increase in the production of goods and services and is shown by a movement of the production possibilities curve outward and to the right. **T F**

24. The more capital goods an economy produces today, the greater will be the total output of all goods it can produce in the future, other things being equal. **T F**

25. International specialization and trade permit an economy to overcome the limits imposed by domestic production possibilities and have the same effect on the economy as having more and better resources. **T F**

■ MULTIPLE-CHOICE QUESTIONS

Circle the letter that corresponds to the best answer.

1. What statement would best complete a short definition of economics? Economics studies

(a) how businesses produce goods and services
(b) the equitable distribution of society's income and wealth
(c) the printing and circulation of money throughout the economy
(d) how individuals, institutions, and society make optimal choices under conditions of scarcity

2. The idea in economics that "there is no such thing as a free lunch" means that

(a) the marginal benefit of such a lunch is greater than its marginal cost
(b) businesses cannot increase their market share by offering free lunches
(c) scarce resources have alternative uses or opportunity costs
(d) consumers are irrational when they ask for a free lunch

3. The opportunity cost of a new public stadium is the

(a) money cost of hiring guards and staff for the new stadium
(b) cost of constructing the new stadium in a future year
(c) change in the real estate tax rate to pay off the new stadium
(d) other goods and services that must be sacrificed to construct the new stadium

4. From the economic perspective, when a business decides to employ more workers, the business decision maker has most likely concluded that the marginal

(a) costs of employing more workers have decreased
(b) benefits of employing more workers have increased
(c) benefits of employing more workers are greater than the marginal costs
(d) costs of employing more workers are not opportunity costs for the business because more workers are needed to increase production

5. The combination of economic theories or principles into a simplified representation of reality is referred to as an economic

(a) fact
(b) model
(c) assumption
(d) hypothesis

6. Which would be studied in microeconomics?

(a) the output of the entire U.S. economy
(b) the general level of prices in the U.S. economy
(c) the output and price of wheat in the United States
(d) the total number of workers employed in the United States

7. When we look at the whole economy or its major aggregates, our analysis would be at the level of

(a) microeconomics
(b) macroeconomics
(c) positive economics
(d) normative economics

8. Which is a normative economic statement?

(a) The consumer price index rose 1.2 percent last month.
(b) The unemployment rate of 6.8 percent is too high.
(c) The average rate of interest on loans is 4.6 percent.
(d) The economy grew at an annual rate of 3.6 percent.

9. Sandra states that "there is a high correlation between consumption and income." Arthur replies that the correlation occurs because "people consume too much of their income and don't save enough."

(a) Both Sandra's and Arthur's statements are positive.
(b) Both Sandra's and Arthur's statements are normative.
(c) Sandra's statement is positive and Arthur's statement is normative.
(d) Sandra's statement is normative and Arthur's statement is positive.

10. Assume that a consumer can buy only two goods, ***A*** and ***B***, and has an income of $100. The price of ***A*** is $10 and the price of ***B*** is $20. The maximum amount of ***A*** the consumer is able to purchase is

(a) 5
(b) 10
(c) 20
(d) 30

11. Assume that a consumer can buy only two goods, ***A*** and ***B***, and has an income of $100. The price of ***A*** is $10 and the price of B is $20. What is the slope of the budget line if ***A*** is measured horizontally and ***B*** is measured vertically?

(a) −0.5
(b) −1.0
(c) −2.0
(d) −4.0

12. Tools, machinery, or equipment used to produce other goods would be examples of

(a) public goods
(b) capital goods
(c) social goods
(d) consumer goods

13. An entrepreneur innovates by

(a) making basic policy decisions in a business firm
(b) following government regulations to make a product
(c) coming up with a business idea or a concept
(d) commercializing a new product for a market

14. When a production possibilities schedule is written (or a production possibilities curve is drawn) in this chapter, four assumptions are made. Which is one of those assumptions?

(a) The state of technology changes.
(b) More than two products are produced.
(c) The economy has full employment of available resources.
(d) The quantities of all resources available to the economy are variable, not fixed.

Answer Questions 15, 16, and 17 on the basis of the data given in the following production possibilities table.

	Production possibilities (alternatives)					
	A	**B**	**C**	**D**	**E**	**F**
Capital goods	100	95	85	70	50	0
Consumer goods	0	100	180	240	280	300

15. If the economy is producing at production alternative **D**, the opportunity cost of 40 more units of consumer goods is

(a) 5 units of capital goods
(b) 10 units of capital goods
(c) 15 units of capital goods
(d) 20 units of capital goods

16. In the table above, the law of increasing opportunity costs is suggested by the fact that

(a) capital goods are relatively more scarce than consumer goods
(b) greater and greater quantities of consumer goods must be given up to get more capital goods
(c) smaller and smaller quantities of consumer goods must be given up to get more capital goods
(d) the production possibilities curve will eventually shift outward as the economy expands

17. The present choice of alternative **B** compared with alternative **D** would tend to promote

(a) increased consumption in the present
(b) decreased consumption in the future
(c) a greater increase in economic growth in the future
(d) a smaller increase in economic growth in the future

18. What is the economic rationale for the law of increasing opportunity costs?

(a) Optimal allocation and full employment of resources have not been achieved.
(b) Economic resources are not completely adaptable to alternative uses.
(c) Economic growth is being limited by the pace of technological advancement.
(d) An economy's present choice of output is determined by fixed technology and fixed resources.

19. The underallocation of resources by society to the production of a product means that the

(a) marginal benefit is greater than the marginal cost
(b) marginal benefit is less than the marginal cost
(c) opportunity cost of production is rising
(d) consumption of the product is falling

Answer Questions 20, 21, and 22 based on the following graph for an economy.

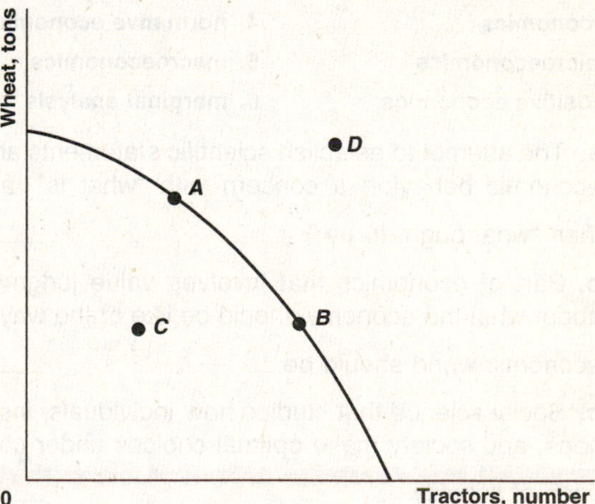

20. Unemployment and productive inefficiency would best be represented in the graph by point

(a) ***A***
(b) ***B***
(c) ***C***
(d) ***D***

21. The choice of point ***B*** over point ***A*** as the optimal product mix for society would be based on
(a) the state of technology
(b) full employment of resources
(c) the law of increasing opportunity costs
(d) a comparison of marginal costs and benefits

22. Economic growth could be represented by
(a) a movement from point ***A*** to point ***B***
(b) a movement from point ***B*** to point ***A***
(c) a shift in the production possibilities curve out to point ***C***
(d) a shift in the production possibilities curve out to point ***D***

23. If there is an increase in the resources available within the economy,
(a) the economy will be capable of producing fewer goods
(b) the economy will be capable of producing more goods
(c) the standard of living in the economy will decline
(d) the state of technology will deteriorate

24. Which situation would most likely shift the production possibilities curve for a nation in an outward direction?
(a) deterioration in product quality
(b) reductions in the supply of resources
(c) increases in technological advance
(d) rising levels of unemployment

25. You observe that more education is associated with more income and conclude that more income leads to more education. This would be an example of
(a) the post hoc fallacy
(b) the fallacy of composition
(c) confusing correlation and causation
(d) using the other-things-equal assumption

■ PROBLEMS

1. Use the appropriate number to match the terms with the phrases below.

1. economics	**4. normative economics**
2. microeconomics	**5. macroeconomics**
3. positive economics	**6. marginal analysis**

a. The attempt to establish scientific statements about economic behavior; a concern with "what is" rather than "what ought to be." ______

b. Part of economics that involves value judgments about what the economy should be like or the way the economic world should be. ______

c. Social science that studies how individuals, institutions, and society make optimal choices under conditions of scarcity. ______

d. Part of economics concerned with the economic behavior of individual units such as households, firms, and industries (particular markets). ______

e. The comparison of additional benefits and additional costs. ______

f. Part of economics concerned with the whole economy or its major sectors. ______

2. News report: "The worldwide demand for wheat from the United States increased and caused the price of wheat in the United States to rise." This is a *specific* instance of a more *general* economic principle. Of which economic *generalization* is this a particular example?

____

____

3. Following is a list of economic statements. Indicate in the space to the right of each statement whether it is positive (**P**) or normative (**N**). Then, in the last four lines below, write two of your own examples of positive economic statements and two examples of normative economic statements.

a. New York City should control the rental price of apartments. ______

b. Consumer prices rose at an annual rate of 4% last year. ______

c. Most people who are unemployed are just too lazy to work. ______

d. Generally, if you lower the price of a product, people will buy more of that product. ______

e. The profits of oil companies are too large and ought to be used to conduct research on alternative energy sources. ______

f. Government should do more to help the poor. ______

g. ______________________ P

h. ______________________ P

i. ______________________ N

j. ______________________ N

4. Following is a list of resources. Indicate in the space to the right of each whether the resource is land (**LD**), labor (**LR**), capital (**C**), entrepreneurial ability (**EA**), or some combinations of these resources.

a. Fishing grounds in the North Atlantic ______
b. A computer in a retail store ______
c. Oil shale deposits in Canada ______
d. An irrigation ditch in Nebraska ______
e. Bill Gates in his work in starting Microsoft ______
f. The oxygen breathed by human beings ______
g. A McDonald's restaurant in Rochester, Minnesota ______
h. The shelves of a grocery store ______
i. A machine in an auto plant ______

j. A person who creates a new Web site and uses it to start a successful business ______

k. A carpenter working for a construction company that is building a house ______

5. Following is a production possibilities table for two products, corn and cars. The table is constructed using the usual assumptions. Corn is measured in units of 100,000 bushels and cars in units of 100,000.

Combination	Corn	Cars
A	0	7
B	7	6
C	13	5
D	18	4
E	22	3
F	25	2
G	27	1
H	28	0

a. Follow the general rules for making graphs (see the appendix to Chapter 1); plot the data from the table on the graph below to obtain a production possibilities curve. Place corn on the vertical axis and cars on the horizontal axis.

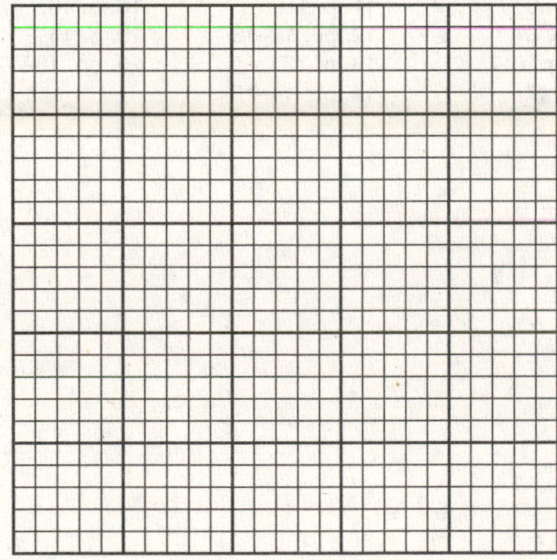

b. Fill in the following table showing the opportunity cost per unit of producing the 1st through the 7th car unit in terms of corn units.

Cars	Cost of production
1st	______
2nd	______
3rd	______
4th	______
5th	______
6th	______
7th	______

c. What is the *marginal* opportunity cost of the 3rd car unit in terms of units of corn? ______

d. What is the *total* opportunity cost of producing 6 car units in terms of units of corn? ______

■ SHORT ANSWER AND ESSAY QUESTIONS

1. What are the three interrelated features of the economic perspective?

2. What is the economic meaning of the statement "there is no such thing as a free lunch"?

3. What are the differences and similarities among the terms *hypothesis, theory, principle, law,* and *model*?

4. Why do economists use the "other things equal" assumption?

5. Why are economic principles necessarily generalized and abstract?

6. Explain the difference between microeconomics and macroeconomics.

7. What are some current examples of positive economic statements and normative economic statements?

8. Explain what the term "economizing problem" means for an individual and for society.

9. What is a budget line for an individual? How can it be used to illustrate trade-offs and opportunity costs?

10. What are the four economic resources? How is each resource defined?

11. What four assumptions are made in drawing a production possibilities curve or schedule?

12. What is the law of increasing opportunity costs? Why do opportunity costs increase?

13. What determines the optimal product mix for society's production possibilities?

14. How can unemployment be illustrated with the production possibilities curve?

15. What will be the effect of increasing resource supplies on production possibilities?

16. Describe how technological advances will affect the production possibilities curve.

17. Explain the trade-off between goods for the present and goods for the future and the effect of this trade-off on economic growth.

18. What qualification do international specialization and trade make for the interpretation of production possibilities?

19. Use the production possibilities curve to explain the economics of war.

20. Explain each of the five pitfalls to sound economic reasoning.

ANSWERS

Chapter 1 Limits, Alternatives, and Choices

FILL-IN QUESTIONS

1. scarcity, cost, alternative
2. purposeful, marginal
3. scientific, theories, principles, laws, models
4. generalizations, do not, other-things-equal (or *ceteris paribus*)
5. microeconomics, macroeconomics
6. aggregate
7. positive, normative, normative
8. unlimited, limited
9. buy, budget
10. attainable, unattainable
11. right, left
12. *a.* land or natural resources; *b.* labor; *c.* capital; *d.* entrepreneurial ability
13. *a.* there is full employment and optimal allocation; *b.* the available supplies of the factors of production are fixed; *c.* technology does not change during the course of the analysis; *d.* the economy produces only two products (any order for *a–d*)
14. consumer, capital, cost
15. concave, are not
16. equal to
17. *a.* fewer, more; *b.* unemployed, underemployed; *c.* more, more; *d.* economic growth
18. outward, increase, advance
19. consumer, capital, greater
20. more, increases, advance

TRUE–FALSE QUESTIONS

1. T, p. 4	**10.** F, p. 7	**19.** T, p. 13
2. T, p. 4	**11.** T, pp. 7, 10	**20.** T, pp. 12–13
3. T, pp. 4–5	**12.** T, pp. 8–9	**21.** F, p. 13
4. T, pp. 5–6	**13.** F, p. 9	**22.** T, p. 13
5. T, p. 6	**14.** T, p. 10	**23.** T, p. 15
6. T, p. 6	**15.** T, pp. 10–11	**24.** T, pp. 17–18
7. F, p. 6	**16.** F, p. 10	**25.** T, p. 18
8. F, p. 6–7	**17.** T, pp. 11–13	
9. T, p. 7	**18.** T, pp. 12–13	

MULTIPLE-CHOICE QUESTIONS

1. d, p. 4	**10.** b, p. 8	**19.** a, pp. 13–14
2. c, p. 4	**11.** a, pp. 8–9	**20.** c, pp. 14–15
3. d, p. 4	**12.** b, p. 10	**21.** d, pp. 13–14
4. c, p. 5	**13.** d, pp. 10–11	**22.** d, pp. 15–16
5. b, pp. 5–6	**14.** c, p. 11	**23.** b, p. 15
6. c, p. 6	**15.** d, p. 11	**24.** c, pp. 15–16
7. b, pp. 6–7	**16.** b, pp. 11–12	**25.** c, pp. 16–17
8. b, p. 7	**17.** c, p. 15	
9. c, p. 7	**18.** b, p. 13	

PROBLEMS

1. *a.* 3; *b.* 4; *c.* 1; *d.* 2; *e.* 6; *f.* 5
2. An increase in the demand for an economic good will cause the price of that good to rise.
3. *a.* N; *b.* P; *c.* N; *d.* P; *e.* N; *f.* N
4. *a.* LD; *b.* C; *c.* LD; *d.* C; *e.* EA; *f.* LD; *g.* C; *h.* C; *i.* C; *j.* EA; *k.* LR
5. *b.* 1, 2, 3, 4, 5, 6, 7 units of corn; *c.* 3; *d.* 21

SHORT ANSWER AND ESSAY QUESTIONS

1. pp. 4–5	**8.** pp. 7,10	**15.** pp. 15–16
2. p. 4	**9.** pp. 8–10	**16.** p. 16
3. pp. 5–6	**10.** pp. 10–11	**17.** pp. 17–18
4. p. 6	**11.** p. 11	**18.** p. 18
5. p. 6	**12.** pp. 12–13	**19.** p. 14
6. pp. 6–7	**13.** p. 13	**20.** pp. 16–17
7. p.7	**14.** pp. 14–15	

APPENDIX TO CHAPTER 1

Graphs and Their Meaning

This appendix introduces graphing in economics. Graphs help illustrate and simplify the economic theories and models presented throughout this book. The old saying that "a picture is worth 1000 words" applies to economics; graphs are the way that economists "picture" relationships between economic variables.

You must master the basics of graphing if these "pictures" are to be of any help to you. This appendix explains how to achieve that mastery. It shows you how to construct a graph from a table with data of two variables, such as income and consumption.

Economists usually, but not always, place the **independent variable** (income) on the horizontal axis and the **dependent variable** (consumption) on the vertical axis of the graph. Once the data points are plotted and a line is drawn to connect the plotted points, you can determine whether there is a **direct** or an **inverse relationship** between the variables. Identifying direct and inverse relationships between variables is an essential skill used repeatedly in this book.

Information from data in graphs and tables can be written in an equation. This work involves determining the **slope** and **intercept** from a straight line in a graph or data in a table. Using values for the slope and intercept, you can write a **linear equation** that will enable you to calculate what the dependent variable would be for a given level of the independent variable.

Some graphs used in the book are *nonlinear*. With **nonlinear curves,** the slope of the line is no longer constant throughout but varies as one moves along the curve. This slope can be estimated at a point by determining the slope of a straight line that is drawn tangent to the curve at that point. Similar calculations can be made for other points to see how the slope changes along the curve.

■ APPENDIX CHECKLIST

When you have studied this appendix you should be able to

☐ Explain why economists use graphs.
☐ Construct a graph of two variables using the numerical data from a table.
☐ Make a table with two variables from data on a graph.
☐ Distinguish between a direct and an inverse relationship when given data on two variables.
☐ Identify dependent and independent variables in economic examples and graphs.
☐ Describe how economists use the other-things-equal assumption (*ceteris paribus*) in graphing two variables.
☐ Calculate the slope of a straight line between two points when given the tabular data, and indicate whether the slope is positive or negative.
☐ Describe how slopes are affected by the choice of the units of measurement for either variable.
☐ Explain how slopes are related to marginal analysis.
☐ Graph infinite or zero slopes and explain their meaning.
☐ Determine the vertical intercept for a straight line in a graph with two variables.
☐ Write a linear equation using the slope of a line and the vertical intercept; when given a value for the independent variable, determine a value for the dependent variable.
☐ Estimate the slope of a nonlinear curve at a point using a straight line that is tangent to the curve at that point.

■ APPENDIX OUTLINE

1. Graphs illustrate the relationship between variables and give economists and students another way, in addition to verbal explanation, of understanding economic phenomena. Graphs are aids in describing economic theories and models.

2. The construction of a simple graph involves plotting the numerical data of two variables from a table.

a. Each graph has a ***horizontal axis*** and a ***vertical axis*** that can be labeled for each variable and then scaled for the range of the data point that will be measured on the axis.

b. Data points are plotted on the graph by drawing straight lines from the scaled points on the two axes to the place on the graph where the straight lines intersect.

c. A line or curve can then be drawn to connect the points plotted on the graph. If the graph is a straight line, it is *linear*. (It is acceptable and typical to call these straight lines "curves.")

3. A graph provides information about relationships between variables.

a. An upward-sloping line to the right on a graph indicates that there is a positive or ***direct relationship*** between two variables: an increase in one is associated with an increase in the other; a decrease in one is associated with a decrease in the other.

b. A downward-sloping line to the right means that there is a negative or ***inverse relationship*** between the two variables: an increase in one is associated with a decrease in the other; a decrease in one is associated with an increase in the other.

4. Economists are often concerned with determining cause and effect in economic events.

a. A ***dependent variable*** changes (increases or decreases) because of a change in another variable.

b. An ***independent variable*** produces or "causes" the change in the dependent variable.

c. In a graph, mathematicians place an independent variable on the horizontal axis and a dependent variable on the vertical axis; economists are more arbitrary in the placement of the dependent or independent variable on an axis.

5. Economic graphs are simplifications of economic relationships. When graphs are plotted, usually an implicit assumption is made that all other factors are being held constant. This "other-things-equal" or *ceteris paribus* assumption is used to simplify the analysis so the study can focus on the two variables of interest.

6. The ***slope of a straight line*** in a two-variable graph is the ratio of the vertical change to the horizontal change between two points.

a. A *positive* slope indicates that the relationship between the two variables is *direct.*

b. A *negative* slope indicates that there is an *inverse* relationship between the two variables.

c. Slopes are affected by the *measurement units* for either variable.

d. Slopes measure *marginal* changes.

e. Slopes can be *infinite* (line parallel to vertical axis) or zero (line parallel to horizontal axis).

7. The ***vertical intercept*** of a straight line in a two-variable graph is the point where the line intersects the vertical axis of the graph.

8. The slope and intercept of a straight line can be expressed in the form of a ***linear equation,*** which is written as $y = a + bx$. Once the values for the intercept (a) and the slope (b) are calculated, then given any value of the independent variable (x), the value of the dependent variable (y) can be determined.

9. The slope of a straight line is constant, but the slope of a nonlinear curve changes throughout. To estimate the slope of a ***nonlinear curve*** at a point, the slope of a straight line ***tangent*** to the curve at that point is calculated.

■ HINTS AND TIPS

1. This appendix will help you understand the graphs and problems presented throughout the book. Do not skip reading the appendix or working on the self-test questions and problems in this *Study Guide*. The time you invest now will pay off in improved understanding in later chapters. Graphing is a basic skill for economic analysis.

2. Positive and negative relationships in graphs often confuse students. To overcome this confusion, draw a two-variable graph with a positive slope and another two-variable graph with a negative slope. In each graph, show what happens to the value of one variable when there is a change in the value of the other variable.

3. A straight line in a two-variable graph can be expressed in an equation. Make sure you know how to interpret each part of the linear equation.

■ IMPORTANT TERMS

vertical axis	**independent variable**
horizontal axis	**slope of a straight line**
direct (positive) relationship	**vertical intercept**
inverse (negative) relationship	**linear equation**
dependent variable	**nonlinear curve**
	tangent

SELF-TEST

■ FILL-IN QUESTIONS

1. The relationship between two economic variables can be visualized with the aid of a two-dimensional (graph, matrix) ______________, which has (a horizontal, an inverse) ______________ axis and a (vertical, direct) ______________ axis.

2. Customarily, the (dependent, independent) ______________ variable is placed on the horizontal axis and the ______________ is placed on the vertical axis. The ______________ variable is said to change because of a change in the ______________ variable.

3. The vertical and horizontal (scales, ranges) ______________ of the graph are calibrated to reflect the ______________ of values in the table of data points on which the graph is based.

4. The graph of a straight line that slopes downward to the right indicates that there is (a direct, an inverse) ______________ relationship between the two variables. A graph of a straight line that slopes upward to the right tells us that the relationship is (direct, inverse) ______________. When the value of one variable increases and the value of the other variable increases, then the relationship is ______________; when the value of one increases, while the other decreases, the relationship is ______________.

5. When interpreting an economic graph, the "cause" or the "source" is the (dependent, independent) ______________ variable and the "effect" or "outcome" is the ______________ variable.

6. Other variables, beyond the two in a two-dimensional graph, that might affect the economic relationship are assumed to be (changing, held constant) ______________. This assumption is also referred to as the other-things-equal assumption or as (*post hoc, ceteris paribus*) ________________.

7. The slope of a straight line between two points is defined as the ratio of the (vertical, horizontal) ________________ change to the ________________ change.

8. When two variables move in the same direction, the slope will be (negative, positive) ________________; when the variables move in opposite directions, the slope will be ________________.

9. The slope of a line will be affected by the (units of measurement, vertical intercept) ________________.

10. The concept of a slope is important to economists because it reflects the influence of a (marginal, total) ________________ change in one variable on another variable.

11. A graph of a line with an infinite slope is (horizontal, vertical) ________________, while a graph of a line with a zero slope is ________________.

12. The point at which the slope of the line meets the vertical axis is called the vertical (tangent, intercept) ________________.

13. We can express the graph of a straight line with a linear equation that can be written as $y = a + bx$.

a. a is the (slope, intercept) ________________ and b is the ________________

b. y is the (dependent, independent) ________________ variable and x is the ________________ variable.

c. If a were 2, b were 4, and x were 5, then y would be ________________. If the value of x changed to 7, then y would be ________________. If the value of x changed to 3, then y would be ________________.

14. The slope of a (straight line, nonlinear curve) ________________ is constant throughout; the slope of a ________________ varies from point to point.

15. An estimate of the slope of a nonlinear curve at a certain point can be made by calculating the slope of a straight line that is (tangent, perpendicular) ________________ to the point on the curve.

■ TRUE–FALSE QUESTIONS

Circle T if the statement is true, F if it is false.

1. Economists design graphs to confuse people. **T F**

2. If the straight line on a two-variable graph slopes downward to the right, then there is a positive relationship between the two variables. **T F**

3. A variable that changes as a consequence of a change in another variable is considered a dependent variable. **T F**

4. Economists always put the independent variable on the horizontal axis and the dependent variable on the vertical axis of a two-variable graph. **T F**

5. *Ceteris paribus* means that other variables are changing at the same time. **T F**

6. In the ratio for the calculation of the slope of a straight line, the vertical change is in the numerator and the horizontal change is in the denominator. **T F**

7. If the slope of the linear relationship between consumption and income was .90, then it tells us that for every $1 increase in income there will be a $.90 increase in consumption. **T F**

8. The slope of a straight line in a two-variable graph will *not* be affected by the choice of the units for either variable. **T F**

9. The slopes of lines measure marginal changes. **T F**

10. Assume in a graph that price is on the vertical axis and quantity is on the horizontal axis. The absence of a relationship between price and quantity would be a straight line parallel to the vertical axis. **T F**

11. A line with an infinite slope in a two-variable graph is parallel to the horizontal axis. **T F**

12. In a two-variable graph, income is graphed on the vertical axis and the quantity of snow is graphed on the horizontal axis. If income was independent of the quantity of snow, then this independence would be represented by a line parallel to the horizontal axis. **T F**

13. If a linear equation is $y = 10 + 5x$, the vertical intercept is 5. **T F**

14. When a straight line is tangent to a nonlinear curve, then it intersects the curve at a particular point. **T F**

15. If the slope of the straight line on a two-variable (x, y) graph were .5 and the vertical intercept were 5, then a value of 10 for x would mean that y is also 10. **T F**

16. A slope of -4 for a straight line in a two-variable graph indicates that there is an inverse relationship between the two variables. **T F**

17. If x is an independent variable and y is a dependent variable, then a change in y results in a change in x. **T F**

18. An upward slope for a straight line that is tangent to a nonlinear curve indicates that the slope of the nonlinear curve at that point is positive. **T F**

19. If one pair of x, y points was (13, 10) and the other pair was (8, 20), then the slope of the straight line between the two sets of points in the two-variable graph, with **x** on the horizontal axis and **y** on the vertical axis, would be 2. **T F**

20. When the value of **x** is 2, a value of 10 for **y** would be calculated from a linear equation of $y = -2 + 6x$. **T F**

■ MULTIPLE-CHOICE QUESTIONS

Circle the letter that corresponds to the best answer.

1. If an increase in one variable is associated with a decrease in another variable, then we can conclude that the variables are
- **(a)** nonlinear
- **(b)** directly related
- **(c)** inversely related
- **(d)** positively related

2. The ratio of the vertical change to the horizontal change between two points of a straight line is the
- **(a)** slope
- **(b)** vertical intercept
- **(c)** horizontal intercept
- **(d)** point of tangency

3. There are two sets of **x**, **y** points on a straight line in a two-variable graph, with **y** on the vertical axis and **x** on the horizontal axis. If one set of points was (0, 5) and the other set (5, 20), the linear equation for the line would be
- **(a)** $y = 5x$
- **(b)** $y = 5 + 3x$
- **(c)** $y = 5 + 15x$
- **(d)** $y = 5 + .33x$

4. In a two-variable graph of data on the price and quantity of a product, economists place
- **(a)** price on the horizontal axis because it is the independent variable and quantity on the vertical axis because it is the dependent variable
- **(b)** price on the vertical axis because it is the dependent variable and quantity on the horizontal axis because it is the independent variable
- **(c)** price on the vertical axis even though it is the independent variable and quantity on the horizontal axis even though it is the dependent variable
- **(d)** price on the horizontal axis even though it is the dependent variable and quantity on the vertical axis even though it is the independent variable

5. In a two-dimensional graph of the relationship between two economic variables, an assumption is usually made that
- **(a)** both variables are linear
- **(b)** both variables are nonlinear
- **(c)** other variables are held constant
- **(d)** other variables are permitted to change

6. If the slope of a straight line is zero, then the straight line is
- **(a)** vertical
- **(b)** horizontal
- **(c)** upsloping
- **(d)** downsloping

Questions 7, 8, 9, and 10 are based on the following four data sets. In each set, the independent variable is in the left column and the dependent variable is in the right column.

(1)		*(2)*		*(3)*		*(4)*	
A	**B**	**C**	**D**	**E**	**F**	**G**	**H**
0	1	0	12	4	5	0	4
3	2	5	8	6	10	1	3
6	3	10	4	8	15	2	2
9	4	15	0	10	20	3	1

7. There is an inverse relationship between the independent and dependent variables in data sets
- **(a)** 1 and 4
- **(b)** 2 and 3
- **(c)** 1 and 3
- **(d)** 2 and 4

8. The vertical intercept is 4 in data set
- **(a)** 1
- **(b)** 2
- **(c)** 3
- **(d)** 4

9. The linear equation for data set 1 is
- **(a)** $B = 3A$
- **(b)** $B = 1 + 3A$
- **(c)** $B = 1 + .33A$
- **(d)** $A = 1 + .33B$

10. The linear equation for data set 2 is
- **(a)** $C = 12 - 1.25D$
- **(b)** $D = 12 + 1.25C$
- **(c)** $D = 12 - .80C$
- **(d)** $C = 12 - .80D$

Answer Questions 11, 12, 13, and 14 on the basis of the following diagram.

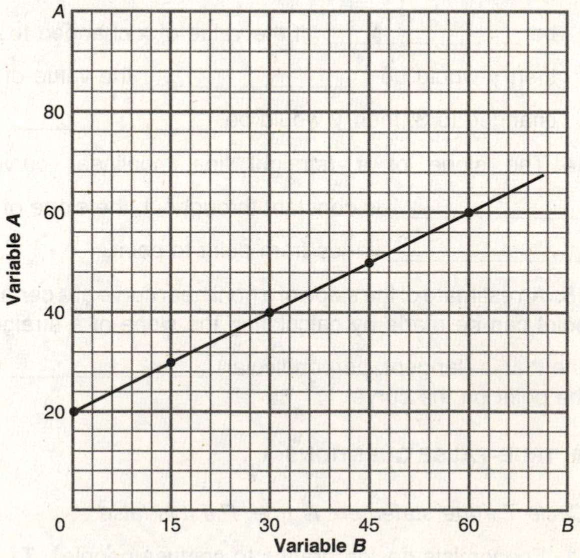

11. The variables **A** and **B** are
- **(a)** positively related
- **(b)** negatively related

(c) indirectly related
(d) nonlinear

12. The slope of the line is
(a) .33
(b) .67
(c) 1.50
(d) 3.00

13. The vertical intercept is
(a) 80
(b) 60
(c) 40
(d) 20

14. The linear equation for the slope of the line is
(a) $A = 20 + .33B$
(b) $B = 20 + .33A$
(c) $A = 20 + .67B$
(d) $B = 20 + .67A$

Answer Questions 15, 16, and 17 on the basis of the following diagram.

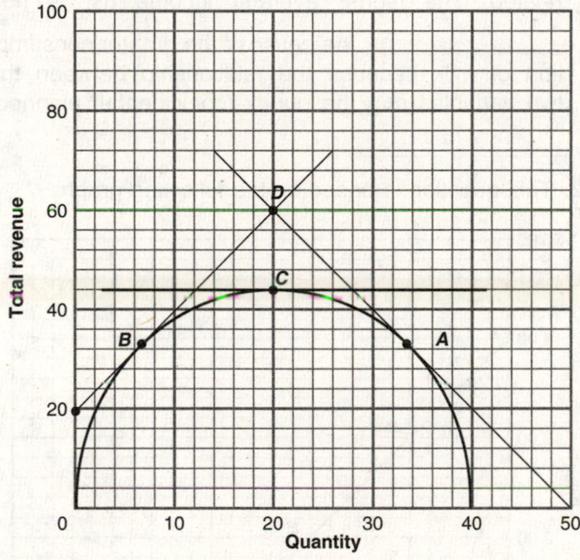

15. The slope of the straight line tangent to the curve at point ***A*** is
(a) 2
(b) −2
(c) −1.5
(d) −0.5

16. The slope of the straight line tangent to the curve at point ***B*** is
(a) −2
(b) 2
(c) 3
(d) 0.5

17. The slope of the straight line tangent to the curve at point ***C*** is
(a) −1
(b) 1
(c) 0
(d) undefined

18. Assume that the relationship between concert ticket prices and attendance is expressed in the equation $P = 25 - 1.25Q$, where ***P*** equals ticket price and ***Q*** equals concert attendance in thousands of people. On the basis of this equation, it can be said that
(a) more people will attend the concert when the price is high compared to when the price is low
(b) if 12,000 people attended the concert, then the ticket price was $10
(c) if 18,000 people attend the concert, then entry into the concert was free
(d) an increase in ticket price by $5 reduces concert attendance by 1000 people

19. If you know that the equation relating consumption (***C***) to income (***Y***) is $C = \$7,500 + .2Y$, then
(a) consumption is inversely related to income
(b) consumption is the independent variable and income is the dependent variable
(c) if income is $15,000, then consumption is $10,500
(d) if consumption is $30,000, then income is $10,000

20. If the dependent variable (vertical axis) changes by 22 units when the independent variable (horizontal axis) changes by 12 units, then the slope of the line is
(a) 0.56
(b) 1.83
(c) 2.00
(d) 3.27

■ PROBLEMS

1. Following are three tables for making graphs. On the graphs, plot the economic relationships contained in each table. Be sure to label each axis of the graph and indicate the unit measurement and scale used on each axis.

a. Use the table below to graph national income on the horizontal axis and consumption expenditures on the vertical axis in the graph below; connect the seven points and label the curve "Consumption." The relationship between income and consumption is (a direct, an inverse) ________________ one and the consumption curve is (an up-, a down-) ________________ sloping curve.

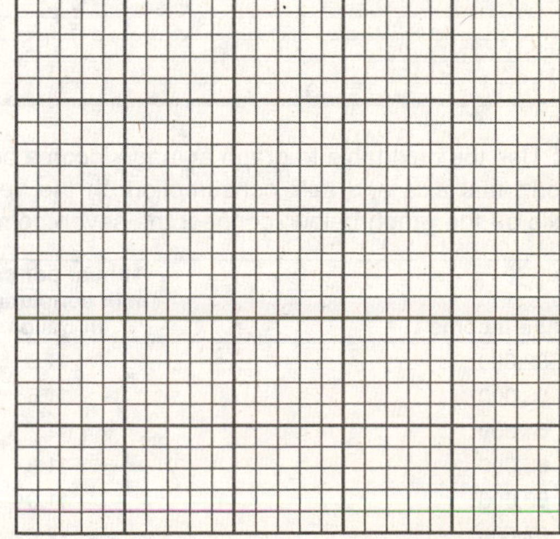

National income, billions of dollars	Consumption expenditures, billions of dollars
$ 600	$ 600
700	640
800	780
900	870
1000	960
1100	1050
1200	1140

b. Use the next table to graph investment expenditures on the horizontal axis and the rate of interest on the vertical axis on the graph below; connect the seven points and label the curve "Investment." The relationship between the rate of interest and investment expenditures is (a direct, an inverse) __________ one and the investment curve is (an up-, a down-) __________ sloping curve.

Rate of interest, %	Investment expenditures, billions of dollars
8	$ 220
7	280
6	330
5	370
4	400
3	420
2	430

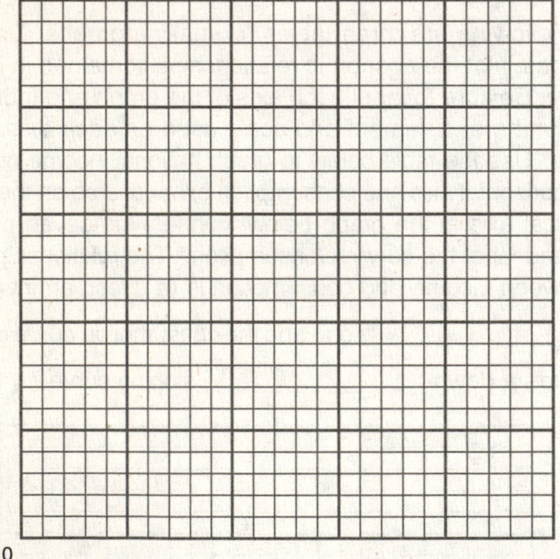

c. Use the next table to graph average income on the horizontal axis and milk consumption on the vertical axis on the graph below; connect the seven points.

Average income	Annual per capita milk consumption in gallons
$62,000	11.5
63,000	11.6
64,000	11.7
65,000	11.8
66,000	11.9
67,000	12.0
68,000	12.1

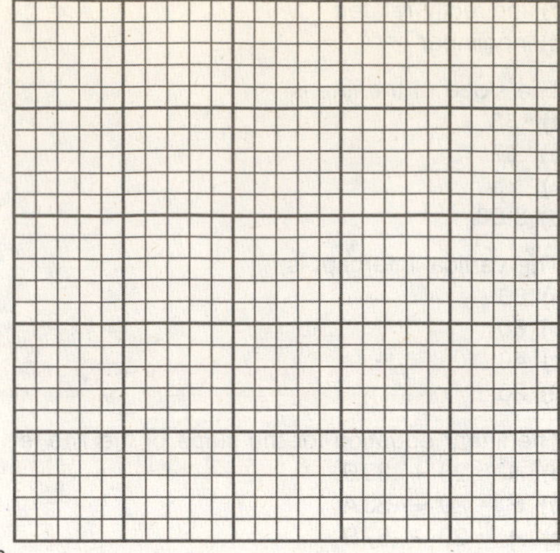

Based on the data, the average income and milk consumption (are, are not) __________ *correlated.* The higher average income (is, is not) __________ the *cause* of the greater consumption of milk because the relationship between the two variables may be purely (coincidental, planned) __________.

2. This question is based on the following graph.

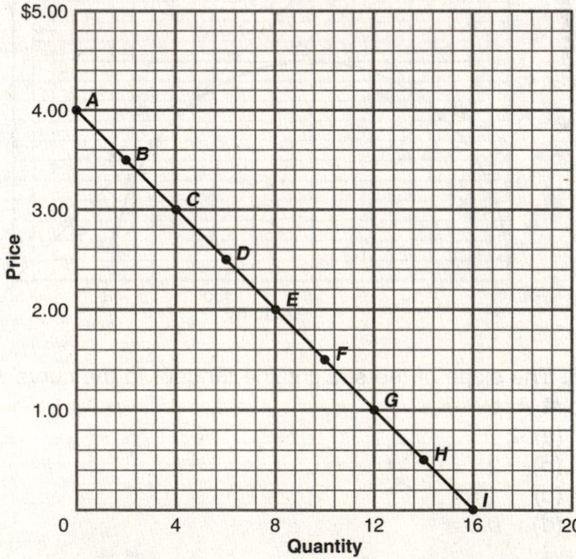

a. Construct a table for points ***A–I*** from the data shown in the graph.

b. According to economists, price is the (independent, dependent) __________ variable and quantity is the __________ variable.

c. Write a linear equation that summarizes the data.

3. The following three sets of data each show the relationship between an independent variable and a dependent variable. For each set, the independent variable is in the left column and the dependent variable is in the right column.

(1)		(2)		(3)	
A	*B*	*C*	*D*	*E*	*F*
0	10	0	100	0	20
10	30	10	75	50	40
20	50	20	50	100	60
30	70	30	25	150	80
40	90	40	0	200	100

a. Write an equation that summarizes the data for each of the sets (1), (2), and (3).
b. State whether each data set shows a positive or an inverse relationship between the two variables.
c. Plot data sets 1 and 2 on the following graph. Use the same horizontal scale for both sets of independent variables and the same vertical scale for both sets of dependent variables.

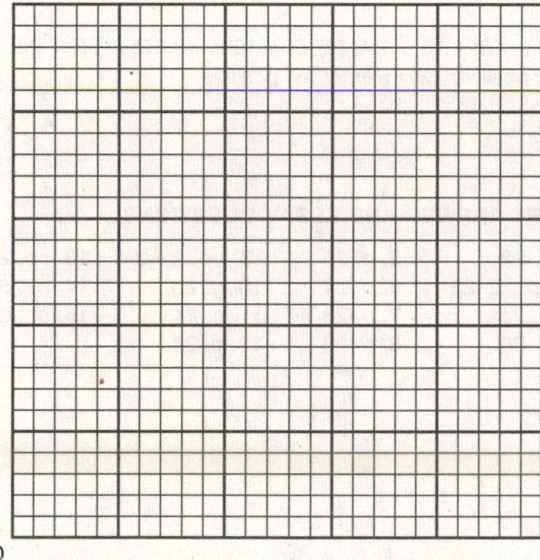

4. This problem is based on the following graph.

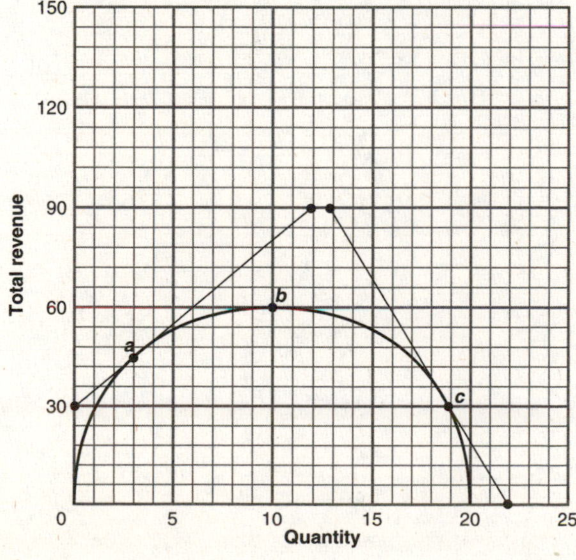

a. The slope of the straight line through point ***a*** is?
b. The slope of the straight line through point ***b*** is?
c. The slope of the straight line through point ***c*** is?

■ SHORT ANSWER AND ESSAY QUESTIONS

1. Why do economists use graphs in their work?

2. Give two examples of a graph that illustrates the relationship between two economic variables.

3. What does the slope tell you about a straight line? How would you interpret a slope of 4? A slope of −2? A slope of .5? A slope of −.25?

4. If the vertical intercept increases in value but the slope of a straight line stays the same, what happens to the graph of the line? If the vertical intercept decreases in value, what will happen to the line?

5. How do you interpret a vertical line on a two-variable graph? How do you interpret a horizontal line?

6. When you know that the price and quantity of a product are inversely related, what does this tell you about the slope of a line where price is on the vertical axis and quantity is on the horizontal axis? What do you know about the slope when the two variables are positively related?

7. Which variable is the dependent and which is the independent in the following economic statement: "A decrease in business taxes had a positive effect on investment spending."

8. How do you tell the difference between a dependent and an independent variable when examining economic relationships?

9. Why is an assumption made that all other variables are held constant when we construct a two-variable graph of the price and quantity of a product?

10. How do mathematicians and economists differ at times in how they construct two-dimensional graphs? Give an example.

11. How is the slope of a straight line in a two-variable graph affected by the choice of the units for either variable? Explain and give an example.

12. What is the relationship between the slopes of lines and marginal analysis?

13. Describe a case in which a straight line in a two-variable graph would have an infinite slope and a case in which the slope of a line would be zero.

14. If you know that the equation relating consumption (*C*) to income (*Y*) is $C = 10{,}000 + 5Y$, then what would consumption be when income is $5000? Construct an income-consumption table for five different levels of income.

15. How do the slopes of a straight line and a nonlinear curve differ? How do you estimate the slope of a nonlinear curve?

ANSWERS

Appendix to Chapter 1 Graphs and Their Meaning

FILL-IN QUESTIONS

1. graph, a horizontal, vertical
2. independent, dependent, dependent, independent
3. scales, ranges

4. an inverse, direct, direct, inverse
5. independent, dependent
6. held constant, *ceteris paribus*
7. vertical, horizontal
8. positive, negative
9. units of measurement
10. marginal
11. vertical, horizontal
12. intercept
13. *a.* intercept, slope; *b.* dependent, independent; *c.* 22, 30, 14
14. straight line, nonlinear curve
15. tangent

TRUE–FALSE QUESTIONS

1. F, p. 22	**8.** F, p. 24	**15.** T, p. 25
2. F, p. 23	**9.** T, p. 24	**16.** T, p. 24
3. T, p. 23	**10.** T, pp. 24–25	**17.** F, p. 23
4. F, p. 23	**11.** F, pp. 24–25	**18.** T, pp. 25–26
5. F, pp. 23–24	**12.** T, pp. 24–25	**19.** F, p. 25
6. T, p. 24	**13.** F, p. 25	**20.** T, p. 25
7. T, p. 24	**14.** F, pp. 25–26	

MULTIPLE-CHOICE QUESTIONS

1. c, p. 23	**8.** d, p. 25	**15.** b, pp. 25–26
2. a, p. 24	**9.** c, p. 25	**16.** b, pp. 25–26
3. b, p. 25	**10.** c, p. 25	**17.** c, pp. 25–26
4. c, p. 23	**11.** a, p. 23	**18.** b, p. 25
5. c, pp. 23–24	**12.** b, p. 24	**19.** c, p. 25
6. b, pp. 24–25	**13.** d, p. 25	**20.** b, p. 24
7. d, p. 23	**14.** c, p. 25	

PROBLEMS

1. *a.* a direct, an up-; *b.* an inverse, a down-; *c.* are, is not, coincidental

2. *a. table below*; *b.* independent, dependent; *c.* $P = 4.00 - .25Q$

Point	Price	Quantity
A	$4.00	0
B	3.50	2
C	3.00	4
D	2.50	6
E	2.00	8
F	1.50	10
G	1.00	12
H	.50	14
I	.00	16

3. *a.* (1) $B = 10 + 2A$; (2) $D = 100 - 2.5C$; (3) $F = 20 + .4E$; *b.* (1) positive; (2) inverse; (3) positive

4. *a.* 5; *b.* 0; *c.* −10

SHORT ANSWER AND ESSAY QUESTIONS

1. p. 22	**5.** p. 25	**9.** pp. 23–24	**13.** pp. 24–25
2. pp. 22–23	**6.** p. 24	**10.** p. 23	**14.** p. 25
3. p. 24	**7.** p. 23	**11.** p. 24	**15.** pp. 25–26
4. p. 25	**8.** p. 23	**12.** p. 24	

CHAPTER 2

The Market System and the Circular Flow

Every economy needs to develop an **economic system** to respond to the economizing problem of limited resources and unlimited wants. The two basic types of systems are the **command system** and the **market system.** In the command system, there is extensive public ownership of resources and the use of central planning for most economic decision making in the economy. In the market system there is extensive private ownership of resources and the use of markets and prices to coordinate and direct economic activity.

A major purpose of Chapter 2 is to explain the major characteristics of the market system because it is the one used in most nations. The first part of this section describes the **ideological** and **institutional** characteristics of the market system. In this system, most of the resources are owned as private property by citizens, who are free to use them as they wish in their own self-interest. Prices and markets express the self-interests of resource owners, consumers, and business firms. Competition regulates self-interest—to prevent the self-interest of any person or any group from working to the disadvantage of the economy and to make self-interests work for the benefit of the entire economy. Government plays an active, but limited, role in a market economy.

Three other characteristics are also found in a market economy. They are the employment of large amounts of **capital goods,** the development of **specialization,** and the **use of money.** Economies use capital goods and engage in specialization because this is a more efficient use of their resources; it results in larger total output and the greater satisfaction of wants. When workers, business firms, and regions within an economy specialize, they become dependent on each other for the goods and services they do not produce for themselves and must engage in trade. Trade is made more convenient by using money as a medium of exchange.

The chapter also explains in detail how the market system works. There are **Five Fundamental Questions** that any economic system must answer in its attempt to use its scarce resources to satisfy its material wants. The five questions or problems are: (1) What goods and services will be produced? (2) How will the goods and services be produced? (3) Who will get the goods and services? (4) How will the system accommodate change? (5) How will the system promote progress?

The explanation of how the market system finds answers to the Five Fundamental Questions is only an approximation—a simplified explanation—of the methods actually employed by the U.S. economy and other market economies. Yet this explanation contains enough realism to be truthful and is general enough to be understandable. If the aims of this chapter are accomplished, you can begin to understand the market system and methods our economy uses to solve the economizing problem presented in Chapter 1.

Although central planning served as a powerful form of economic decision making in command systems such as the Soviet Union and China (before its market reform), it had two serious problems. The first problem was one of **coordination,** which resulted in production bottlenecks and managers and bureaucrats missing production targets. Central planning also created an **incentive problem** because it sent out incorrect and inadequate signals for directing the efficient allocation of an economy's resources and gave workers little reason to work hard. The lack of incentives killed entrepreneurship and stifled innovation and technological advance.

The chapter ends with a description of the **circular flow diagram.** In a market economy, there is a resource market and product market that connect households and businesses. In the diagram, there is a monetary flow of money income, consumption expenditures, revenue, and costs. There also is a flow of resources and goods and services. The model shows that households and businesses have dual roles as buyers and sellers depending on whether they are operating in the product market or resource market.

■ CHECKLIST

When you have studied this chapter you should be able to

☐ Compare and contrast the command system with the market system.
☐ Identify the nine important characteristics of the market system.
☐ Describe the role of private property rights in the market system.
☐ Distinguish between freedom of enterprise and freedom of choice.
☐ Explain why self-interest is a driving force of the market system.
☐ Identify two features of competition in the market system.
☐ Explain the roles of markets and prices in the market system.
☐ Describe how the market system relies on technology and capital.
☐ Discuss how two types of specialization improve efficiency in the market system.

□ Describe the advantages of money over barter for the exchange of goods and services in the market system.
□ Describe the size and role of government in the market system.
□ List the Five Fundamental Questions to answer about the operation of a market economy.
□ Explain how a market system determines what goods and services will be produced and the role of consumer sovereignty and dollar votes.
□ Explain how goods and services will be produced in a market system.
□ Find the least costly combination of resources needed for production when given the technological data and the prices of the resources.
□ Explain how a market system determines who will get the goods and services it produces.
□ Describe the guiding function of prices to accommodate change in the market system.
□ Explain how the market system promotes progress by fostering technological advances and capital accumulation.
□ State how the "invisible hand" in the market system tends to promote public or social interests.
□ List three virtues of the market system.
□ Compare how a command economy coordinates economic activity with how a market economy coordinates economic activity.
□ Explain the problems with incentives in a command economy.
□ Draw the circular flow diagram, correctly labeling the two markets and the flows between the two markets.
□ Define the three main categories of businesses: sole proprietorship, partnership, and corporation.
□ Describe the role private property plays in helping a market economy find the most productive combination of resources (*Last Word*).

■ CHAPTER OUTLINE

1. An ***economic system*** is a set of institutions and a coordinating mechanism to respond to the economizing problem for an economy.

a. The ***command system*** (also called *socialism* or *communism*) is based primarily on extensive public ownership of resources and the use of central planning for most economic decision making. There used to be many examples of command economies (Soviet Union), but today there are few (North Korea, Cuba). Most former socialistic nations have been or are being transformed into capitalistic and market-oriented economies.

b. The ***market system*** (*capitalism*) has extensive private ownership of resources and uses markets and prices to coordinate and direct economic activity. In pure (*laissez-faire*) capitalism there is a limited government role in the economy. In a capitalist economy such as the United States, government plays a large role, but the two characteristics of the market system—private property and markets—dominate.

2. The market system has the following nine characteristics.

a. Private individuals and organizations own and control their property resources by means of the institution of ***private property.***

b. These individuals and organizations possess both the ***freedom of enterprise*** and the ***freedom of choice.***

c. These economic units are motivated largely by ***self-interest.***

d. ***Competition*** is based on the independent actions of buyers and sellers. They have the freedom to enter or leave markets. This competition spreads economic power and limits its potential abuse.

e. A ***market*** is a place, institution, or process where buyers and sellers interact with each other. Markets and prices are used to communicate and coordinate the decisions of buyers and sellers.

f. The market system employs complicated and advanced methods of production, new technology, and large amounts of capital equipment to produce goods and services efficiently.

g. It is a highly specialized economy. Human and geographic ***specialization*** increase the productive efficiency of the economy. Human specialization is also called ***division of labor.*** It increases productivity because it allows people to split up work into separate tasks and lets people do the task which they are best at doing. Geographic specialization lets nations produce what they do best and then trade with other nations for what else they want.

h. It uses ***money*** exclusively to facilitate trade and specialization. Money functions as a ***medium of exchange*** that is more efficient to use than ***barter*** for trading goods.

i. Government has an active but limited role.

3. The system of prices and markets and households' and business firms' choices furnish the market economy with answers to ***Five Fundamental Questions.***

a. *What goods and services will be produced?* In a market economy, there is ***consumer sovereignty*** because consumers are in command and express their wishes for the goods and services through ***dollar votes.*** The demands of consumers for products and the desires of business firms to maximize their profits determine what and how much of each product is produced and its price.

b. *How will the goods and services be produced?* The desires of business firms to maximize profits by keeping their costs of production as low as possible guide them to use the most efficient techniques of production and determine their demands for various resources; competition forces them to use the most efficient techniques and ensures that only the most efficient will be able to stay in business.

c. *Who will get the goods and services?* With resource prices determined, the money income of each household is determined; and with product prices determined, the quantity of goods and services these money incomes will buy is determined.

d. *How will the system accommodate change?* The market system is able to accommodate itself to changes in consumer tastes, technology, and resource supplies. The desires of business firms for maximum profits and competition lead the economy to make the appropriate adjustments in the way it uses its resources.

e. *How will the system promote progress?* Competition and the desire to increase profits promote better techniques of production and capital accumulation.

(1) The market system encourages technological advance because it can help increase revenue or decrease costs for businesses, thus increasing profits. The use of new technology spreads rapidly because firms must stay innovative or fail. There can also be ***creative destruction*** where new technology creates market positions of firms adopting the new technology and destroys the market position of firms using the old technology.

(2) Business owners will take their profit income and use it to make more capital goods that improve production and increase profits.

4. Competition in the economy compels firms seeking to promote their own interests to promote (as though led by an ***"invisible hand"***) the best interests of society as a whole.

a. Competition results in an allocation of resources appropriate to consumer wants, production by the most efficient means, and the lowest possible prices.

b. Three noteworthy merits of the market system are

(1) The *efficient* use of resources

(2) The *incentive* the system provides for productive activity

(3) The personal *freedom* allowed participants as consumers, producers, workers, or investors

5. The demise of command systems occurred largely because of two basic problems with a centrally planned economy.

a. The *coordination problem* involved the difficulty of coordinating the economy's many interdependent segments and avoiding the chain reaction that would result from a bottleneck in any one of the segments. This coordination problem became even more difficult as the economy grew larger and more complex, and more economic decisions had to be made in the production process. There were also inadequate measures of economic performance to determine the degree of success or failure of enterprises or to give clear signals to the economy.

b. The *incentive problem* arose because in a command economy incentives are ineffective for encouraging economic initiatives and work and for directing the most efficient use of productive resources. In a market economy, profits and losses signal what firms should produce, how they should produce, and how productive resources should be allocated to best meet the wants of a nation. Central planning in the two economies also lacked entrepreneurship and stifled innovation, both of which are important forces for achieving long-term economic growth. Individual workers lacked much motivation to work hard because pay was limited and there were either few consumer goods to buy or they were of low quality.

6. The ***circular flow diagram*** (or model) is a device used to clarify the relationships between households and businesses in the product and resource markets. It has two types of flows. The monetary flow of money income, consumption expenditures, business revenue, and business costs runs clockwise. The real flow of resources and goods and services runs counterclockwise.

a. ***Households*** are defined as one or more persons occupying a housing unit.

b. ***Businesses*** are of three types. A ***sole proprietorship*** is a business owned and operated by a single person. A ***partnership*** is a business owned and operated by two or more persons. A ***corporation*** is a legal entity or structure that operates as a business, so the corporation and not the individual owners are financially responsible for the business's debts and obligations.

c. In the ***resource market,*** households sell resources (labor, land, capital, and entrepreneurial ability), and in return, they receive money income. Businesses buy these resources, and their resource costs become the money income for households.

d. In the ***product market,*** businesses sell finished goods and services to households, and in return they receive revenue. Households make consumption expenditures to purchase these goods and services, and they use the money income they obtain from selling their resources to make these consumption expenditures.

7. (*Last Word*). There are tens of billions of ways that resources could be arranged in a market economy, but most combinations would be useless. The reason that a market economy produces the few combinations from the total possible that are productive and serve human goals is because of private property. With it, people have an incentive to make the best use of their resources and find the most rewarding combination.

■ HINTS AND TIPS

1. This chapter describes nine characteristics and institutions of a market system. After reading the section, check your understanding by listing the nine points and writing a short explanation of each one.

2. The section on the *Five Fundamental Questions* is both the most important and the most difficult part of the chapter. Detailed answers to the five questions are given in this section of the chapter. If you examine each one individually and in the order in which it is presented, you will more easily understand how the market system works. (Actually, the market system finds the answers simultaneously, but make your learning easier for now by considering them one by one.)

3. Be sure to understand the *importance* and *role* of each of the following in the operation of the market system: (1) the guiding function of prices, (2) the profit motive of business firms, (3) the entry into and exodus of firms from industries, (4) the meaning of competition, and (5) consumer sovereignty.

■ IMPORTANT TERMS

economic system
command system
market system
private property
freedom of enterprise
freedom of choice
self-interest
competition

market	**"invisible hand"**
specialization	**circular flow diagram**
division of labor	**households**
medium of exchange	**businesses**
barter	**sole proprietorship**
money	**partnership**
consumer sovereignty	**corporation**
dollar votes	**resource market**
creative destruction	**product market**

SELF-TEST

■ FILL-IN QUESTIONS

1. The institutional arrangements and coordinating mechanisms used to respond to the economic problem are called (*laissez-faire*, an economic system) ______.

2. In a command economy, property resources are primarily (publicly, privately) ______ owned. The coordinating device(s) in this economic system (is central planning, are markets and prices) ______.

3. In capitalism, property resources are primarily (publicly, privately) ______ owned. The means used to direct and coordinate economic activity (is central planning, are markets and prices) ______.

4. The ownership of property resources by private individuals and organizations is the institution of private (resources, property) ______. The freedom of private businesses to obtain resources and use them to produce goods and services is the freedom of (choice, enterprise) ______, while the freedom to dispose of property or money as a person sees fit is the freedom of ______.

5. Self-interest means that each economic unit attempts to do what is best for itself, but this might lead to an abuse of power in a market economy if it were not directed and constrained by (government, competition) ______. Self-interest and selfishness (are, are not) ______ the same thing in a market economy.

6. Broadly defined, competition is present if two conditions prevail; these two conditions are

a. ______

b. ______

7. In a capitalist economy, individual buyers communicate their demands and individual sellers communicate their supplies in the system of (markets, prices) ______, and the outcomes from economic decisions are a set of product and resource ______ that are determined by demand and supply.

8. In market economies, money functions chiefly as a medium of (commerce, exchange) ______. Barter between two individuals will take place only if there is a coincidence of (resources, wants) ______.

9. In a market system, government is active, but is assigned (a limited, an extensive) ______ role.

10. List the Five Fundamental Questions every economy must answer.

a. ______

b. ______

c. ______

d. ______

e. ______

11. Consumers vote with their dollars for the production of a good or service when they (sell, buy) ______ it, and because of this, consumers are said to be (dependent, sovereign) ______ in a market economy. The buying decisions of consumers (restrain, expand) ______ the possible choices of firms over what they produce so they make what is profitable.

12. Firms are interested in obtaining the largest economic profits possible, so they try to produce a product in the (most, least) ______ costly way. The most efficient production techniques depend on the available (income, technology) ______ and the (prices, quotas) ______ of needed resources.

13. The market system determines how the total output of the economy will be distributed among its households by determining the (incomes, expenditures) ______ of each household and by determining the (prices, quality) ______ for each good and service produced.

14. In market economies, change is almost continuous in consumer (preferences, resources) ______, in the supplies of ______, and in technology. To make the appropriate adjustments to these changes, a market economy allows price to perform its (monopoly, guiding) ______ function.

15. The market system fosters technological change. The incentive for a firm to be the first to use a new and improved technique of production or to produce a new and better product is a greater economic (profit, loss) ______, and the incentive for other firms to follow its lead is the avoidance of a ______.

16. Technological advance will require additional (capital, consumer) ______ goods, so the entrepreneur uses profit obtained from the sale of ______ goods to acquire (capital, consumer) ______ goods.

17. A market system promotes (unity, disunity) ______ between private and public interests. Firms and resource suppliers seem to be guided by (a visible, an invisible) ______ hand to allocate the economy's resources efficiently. The two *economic* arguments for a market system are that it promotes (public, efficient) ______ use of resources and that it uses (incentives, government) ______ for directing economic activity. The major *noneconomic* argument for the market system is that it allows for personal (wealth, freedom) ______.

18. Coordination and decision making in a market economy are (centralized, decentralized) ______, but in a command economy they are ______. The market system tends to produce a reasonably (efficient, inefficient) ______ allocation of resources, but in command economies it is ______ and results in production bottlenecks. As a command economy grows over time, the coordination problem becomes (more, less) ______ complex and indicators of economic performance are (adequate, inadequate) ______ for determining the success or failure of economic activities.

19. Another problem with the command economies is that economic incentives are (effective, ineffective) ______ for encouraging work or for giving signals to planners for efficient allocation of resources in the economy. Command economies do not have (production targets, entrepreneurship) ______ that is (are) important for technological advance, and because there was no business competition innovation (fostered, lagged) ______.

20. In the circular flow diagram or model,

a. Households are buyers and businesses are sellers in (product, resource) ______ markets, and businesses are buyers and households are sellers in ______ markets.

b. Resources flow from (households, businesses) ______ to be used by ______ to make goods and services.

c. Consumption expenditures flow as revenue to (households, businesses) ______ for the goods and services purchased by ______.

■ TRUE–FALSE QUESTIONS

Circle T if the statement is true, F if it is false.

1. A command economy is characterized by the private ownership of resources and the use of markets and prices to coordinate and direct economic activity. **T F**

2. In a market system, the government owns most of the property resources (land and capital). **T F**

3. Pure capitalism is also called *laissez-faire* capitalism. **T F**

4. Property rights encourage investment, innovation, exchange, maintenance of property, and economic growth. **T F**

5. The freedom of business firms to produce a particular consumer good is always limited by the desires of consumers for that good. **T F**

6. The pursuit of economic self-interest is the same thing as selfishness. **T F**

7. When a market is competitive, the individual sellers of a product are unable to reduce the supply of the product and control its prices. **T F**

8. The market system is an organizing mechanism and also a communication network. **T F**

9. Increasing the amount of specialization in an economy generally leads to the more efficient use of its resources. **T F**

10. One way human specialization can be achieved is through a division of labor in productive activity. **T F**

11. Money is a device for facilitating the exchange of goods and services. **T F**

12. "Coincidence of wants" means that two persons want to acquire the same good or service. **T F**

13. Shells may serve as money if sellers are generally willing to accept them as money. **T F**

14. One of the Five Fundamental Questions is who will control the output. **T F**

15. Industries in which economic profits are earned by the firms in the industry will attract the entry of new firms. **T F**

16. The consumers are sovereign in a market economy and register their economic wants with "dollar votes." **T F**

17. Economic efficiency requires that a given output of a good or service be produced in the least costly way. **T F**

18. If the market price of resource A decreases, firms will tend to employ smaller quantities of resource A. **T F**

19. The incentive that the market system provides to induce technological improvement is the opportunity for economic profits. **T F**

20. Creative destruction is the hypothesis that the creation of new products and production methods simultaneously destroys the market power of existing monopolies and businesses. **T F**

21. The tendency for individuals pursuing their own self-interests to bring about results that are in the best interest of society as a whole is often called the "invisible hand." **T F**

22. A basic economic argument for the market system is that it promotes an efficient use of resources. **T F**

23. A command economy is significantly affected by missed production targets. **T F**

24. Profit is the key indicator of success and failure in a command economy. **T F**

25. In the circular flow model, businesses sell goods and services and buy resources whereas households sell resources and buy goods and services. **T F**

■ MULTIPLE-CHOICE QUESTIONS

Circle the letter that corresponds to the best answer.

1. The private ownership of property resources and use of markets and prices to direct and coordinate economic activity is characteristic of
(a) socialism
(b) communism
(c) a market economy
(d) a command economy

2. Which is one of the main characteristics of the market system?
(a) central economic planning
(b) limits on freedom of choice
(c) the right to own private property
(d) an expanded role for government in the economy

3. In the market system, freedom of enterprise means that
(a) government is free to direct the actions of businesses
(b) businesses are free to produce products that consumers want
(c) consumers are free to buy goods and services that they want
(d) resources are distributed freely to businesses that want them

4. The maximization of profit tends to be the driving force in the economic decision making of
(a) workers
(b) consumers
(c) legislators
(d) entrepreneurs

5. How do consumers typically express self-interest?
(a) by minimizing their economic losses
(b) by maximizing their economic profits
(c) by seeking the lowest price for a product
(d) by seeking jobs with the highest wages and benefits

6. Which is a characteristic of competition as economists see it?
(a) a few sellers of all products
(b) the widespread diffusion of economic power
(c) a small number of buyers in product markets
(d) the relatively difficult entry into and exit from industries by producers

7. To decide how to use its scarce resources to satisfy economic wants, a market economy primarily relies on
(a) prices
(b) planning
(c) monopoly power
(d) production targets

8. The market system is a method of
(a) making economic decisions by central planning
(b) communicating and coordinating economic decisions
(c) promoting specialization, but not division of labor
(d) allocating money, but not economic profits or losses

9. When workers specialize in various tasks to produce a commodity, the situation is referred to as
(a) division of labor
(b) freedom of choice
(c) capital accumulation
(d) a coincidence of wants

10. In what way does human specialization contribute to an economy's output?
(a) It is a process of creative destruction.
(b) It serves as consumer sovereignty.
(c) It acts like an "invisible hand."
(d) It fosters learning by doing.

11. Which is a prerequisite of specialization?
(a) market restraints on freedom
(b) having a convenient means of exchanging goods
(c) letting government create a plan for the economy
(d) deciding who will get the goods and services in an economy

12. In the market system, the role of government is best described as
(a) limited
(b) extensive
(c) significant
(d) nonexistent

13. Which would necessarily result, sooner or later, from a decrease in consumer demand for a product?
(a) a decrease in the profits of firms in the industry
(b) an increase in the output of the industry
(c) an increase in the supply of the product
(d) an increase in the prices of resources employed by the firms in the industry

14. The demand for resources is
(a) increased when the price of resources falls
(b) most influenced by the size of government in a capitalist economy
(c) derived from the demand for the products made with the resources
(d) decreased when the product that the resources produce becomes popular

Answer Questions 15, 16, and 17 on the basis of the following information.

Suppose 50 units of product X can be produced by employing just labor and capital according to the four techniques (A, B, C, and D) shown below. Assume the prices of labor and capital are $5 and $4, respectively.

	A	B	C	D
Labor	1	2	3	4
Capital	5	3	2	1

15. Which technique is economically most efficient in producing product X?
(a) A
(b) B
(c) C
(d) D

16. If the price of product X is $1, the firm will realize
(a) an economic profit of $28
(b) an economic profit of $27
(c) an economic profit of $26
(d) an economic profit of $25

17. Now assume that the price of labor falls to $3 and the price of capital rises to $5. Which technique is economically most efficient in producing product X?
(a) A
(b) B
(c) C
(d) D

18. Which is the primary factor determining the share of the total output of the economy received by a household?
(a) the tastes of the household
(b) the medium of exchange used by the household
(c) the prices at which the household sells its resources
(d) ethical considerations in the operation of a market economy

19. If an increase in the demand for a product and a rise in its price cause an increase in the quantity supplied, price is successfully performing its
(a) guiding function
(b) circular flow role
(c) division-of-labor role
(d) medium-of-exchange function

20. In the market system, if one firm introduces a new and better method of production that enhances the firm's economic profits, other firms will be forced to adopt the new method to
(a) increase circular flow
(b) follow rules for capital accumulation
(c) avoid economic losses or bankruptcy
(d) specialize and divide the labor in an efficient way

21. The advent of personal computers and word processing software that eliminated the market for electric typewriters would be an example of
(a) specialization
(b) derived demand
(c) the "invisible hand"
(d) creative destruction

22. The chief economic virtue of the competitive market system is that it
(a) allows extensive personal freedom
(b) promotes the efficient use of resources
(c) provides an equitable distribution of income
(d) eliminates the need for decision making

23. In the system of central planning, the outputs of some industries became the inputs for other industries, but a failure of one industry to meet its production target would cause
(a) widespread unemployment
(b) inflation in wholesale and retail prices
(c) profit declines and potential bankruptcy of firms
(d) a chain reaction of production problems and bottlenecks

24. The two kinds of markets found in the circular flow model are
(a) real and money markets
(b) real and socialist markets
(c) money and command markets
(d) product and resource markets

25. In the circular flow model, businesses
(a) buy products and resources
(b) sell products and resources
(c) buy products and sell resources
(d) sell products and buy resources

■ PROBLEMS

1. Use the appropriate number to match the terms with the phrases below.

1. invisible hand	**4. consumer sovereignty**
2. coincidence of wants	**5. creative destruction**
3. division of labor	**6. specialization**

a. Using the resources of an individual, a firm, a region, or a nation to produce one (or a few) goods and services. ____________

b. The tendency of firms and resource suppliers seeking to further their own self-interest while also promoting the interests of society in a market economy. ____________

c. The situation where new products and production methods eliminate the market position of firms doing business using existing products or older production methods. ____________

d. Splitting the work required to produce a product into a number of different tasks that are performed by different workers. ____________

e. A situation in which the product the first trader wants to sell is the same as the product the second trader wants to buy, and the product the second trader wants to sell is the same as the product the first trader wants to buy. ____________

f. Determination by consumers of the types and quantities of goods and services that will be produced in a market economy. ____________

2. Assume that a firm can produce product A, product B, *or* product C with the resources it currently employs. These resources cost the firm a total of $50 per week. Assume, for the purposes of the problem, that the firm's employment of resources cannot be changed. Their market prices, and the quantities of A, B, and C these resources will produce per week, are given in the table below. Compute the firm's profit when it produces A, B, or C, and enter these profits in the table.

Product	Market Price	Output	Economic Profit
A	$7.00	8	$____
B	4.50	10	____
C	.25	240	____

a. Which product will the firm produce?

____

b. If the price of A rose to $8, the firm would

____

(Hint: You will have to recompute the firm's profit from the production of A.)

c. If the firm were producing A and selling it at a price of $8, what would tend to happen to the number of firms producing A?

____

3. Suppose that a firm can produce 100 units of product X by combining labor, land, capital, and entrepreneurial ability using three different methods. If it can hire labor at $2 per unit, land at $3 per unit, capital at $5 per unit, and entrepreneurship at $10 per unit, and if the amounts of the resources required by the three methods of producing 100 units of product X are as indicated in the table, answer the following questions.

	Method		
Resource	**1**	**2**	**3**
Labor	8	13	10
Land	4	3	3
Capital	4	2	4
Entrepreneurship	1	1	1

a. Which method is the least expensive way of producing 100 units of X? ________

b. If X sells for 70 cents per unit, what is the economic profit of the firm? $ ________

c. If the price of labor should rise from $2 to $3 per unit and if the price of X is 70 cents,

(1) the firm's use of

labor would change from ________ to ________

land would change from ________ to ________

capital would change from ________ to ________

entrepreneurship would not change

(2) The firm's economic profit would change from

$ ________ to $ ________

4. In the circular flow diagram below, the upper pair of flows (***a*** and ***b***) represents the resource market and the lower pair (***c*** and ***d***) the product market.

a
b
Resource market
Businesses
Households
Product market
c
d

Supply labels or explanations for each of the four flows:

a. ____________________

b. ____________________

c. ____________________

d. ____________________

■ SHORT ANSWER AND ESSAY QUESTIONS

1. The command system and the market system differ in two important ways. Compare and contrast the two economic systems.

2. Explain the major characteristics—institutions and assumptions—embodied in a market system.

3. What do each of the following seek if they pursue their own self-interest: consumers, resource owners, and business firms?

4. Explain what economists mean by competition. For a market to be competitive, why is it important that there be buyers and sellers and easy entry and exit?

5. How does an economy benefit from specialization and the division of labor?

6. Give an example of how specialization can benefit two separate and diversely endowed geographic regions.

7. What is money? What important function does it perform? Explain how money performs this function and how it overcomes the disadvantages associated with barter.

8. In what way do the desires of entrepreneurs to obtain economic profits and avoid losses make consumer sovereignty effective?

9. Why is the ability of firms to enter industries that are prosperous important to the effective functioning of competition?

10. Explain how an increase in the consumer demand for a product will result in more of the product being produced and more resources being allocated to its production.

11. Describe the production factor for businesses that determines what combinations of resources and technologies will be used to produce goods and services.

12. Who will get the output from a market economy? Explain.

13. How can the market system adapt to change? How is it done?

14. How do prices communicate information and guide and direct production in a market economy?

15. Explain how the market system provides a strong incentive for technological advance and creative destruction.

16. Describe how capital accumulation works. Who "votes" for the production of capital goods? Why do they "vote" for capital goods production? Where do they obtain the dollars needed to cast these "votes"?

17. "An invisible hand operates to identify private and public interests." What are private interests and what is the public interest? What is it that leads the economy to operate as if it were directed by an invisible hand?

18. Describe three virtues of the market system.

19. Explain the two major economic problems with command economies and why market economies avoid such problems.

20. In the circular flow model, what are the two markets? Define households and describe the three basic forms of businesses. What roles do households play and what roles do businesses play in each market?

ANSWERS

Chapter 2 The Market System and the Circular Flow

FILL-IN QUESTIONS

1. an economic system
2. publicly, is central planning
3. privately, are markets and prices
4. property, enterprise, choice
5. competition, are not
6. *a.* independently acting buyers and sellers operating in markets; *b.* freedom of buyers and sellers to enter or leave these markets
7. markets, prices
8. exchange, wants
9. a limited
10. *a.* What goods and services will be produced? *b.* How will the goods and services be produced? *c.* Who will get the goods and services? *d.* How will the system accommodate change? *e.* How will the system promote progress?
11. buy, sovereign, restrain
12. least, technology, prices
13. incomes, prices
14. preferences, resources, guiding
15. profit, loss
16. capital, consumer, capital
17. unity, an invisible, efficient, incentives, freedom
18. decentralized, centralized, efficient, inefficient, more, inadequate
19. ineffective, entrepreneurship, lagged
20. *a.* product, resource; *b.* households, businesses; *c.* businesses, households

TRUE–FALSE QUESTIONS

1. F, p. 30
2. F, p. 30
3. T, p. 30
4. T, pp. 30–31
5. T, p. 31
6. F, pp. 31–32
7. T, p. 32
8. T, p. 32
9. T, p. 33
10. T, p. 33
11. T, pp. 33–34
12. F, p. 33
13. T, p. 33
14. F, p. 34
15. T, pp. 34–35
16. T, p. 35
17. T, pp. 35–36
18. F, p. 36
19. T, p. 37
20. T, p. 37
21. T, p. 38
22. T, p. 38
23. T, pp. 38–39
24. F, pp. 38–39
25. T, pp. 40–41

MULTIPLE-CHOICE QUESTIONS

1. c, pp. 30–32
2. c, pp. 30–31
3. b, p. 31
4. d, pp. 31–32
5. c, p. 31
6. b, p. 32
7. a, p. 32
8. b, p. 32
9. a, p. 33
10. d, p. 33
11. b, p. 33
12. a, p. 34
13. a, p. 35
14. c, p. 35
15. b, p. 36
16. a, p. 36
17. d, p. 36
18. c, pp. 36–37
19. a, p. 37
20. c, p. 37
21. d, p. 37
22. b, p. 38
23. d, pp. 38–39
24. d, pp. 40–41
25. d, pp. 40–41

PROBLEMS

1. *a.* 6; *b.* 1; *c.* 5; *d.* 3; *e.* 2; *f.* 4
2. \$6, −\$5, \$10; *a.* C; *b.* produce A and have an economic profit of \$14; *c.* it would increase
3. *a.* method 2; *b.* 15; *c.* (1) 13, 8; 3, 4; 2, 4; (2) 15, 4
4. *a.* money income payments (wages, rent, interest, and profit); *b.* services or resources (land, labor, capital, and entrepreneurial ability); *c.* goods and services; d. expenditures for goods and services

SHORT ANSWER AND ESSAY QUESTIONS

1. p. 30
2. pp. 30–34
3. pp. 31–32
4. p. 32
5. p. 33
6. p. 33
7. pp. 33–34
8. p. 35
9. p. 35
10. pp. 35–36
11. p. 36
12. pp. 36–37
13. p. 37
14. p. 37
15. p. 37
16. pp. 37–38
17. p. 38
18. p. 38
19. pp. 38–40
20. pp. 40–41

CHAPTER 3

Demand, Supply, and Market Equilibrium

Chapter 3 introduces you to the most fundamental tools of economic analysis: demand and supply. Demand and supply are simply "boxes" or categories into which all the forces and factors that affect the price and the quantity of a good bought and sold in a competitive market are placed. Demand and supply determine price and quantity exchanged. It is necessary to understand *why* and *how* they do this.

Many students never learn to define demand and supply. They never learn (1) what an increase or decrease in demand or supply means, (2) the important distinctions between "demand" and "quantity demanded" and between "supply" and "quantity supplied," and (3) the equally important distinctions between a change in demand and a change in quantity demanded and between a change in supply and a change in quantity supplied.

Having learned these, however, it is no great trick to comprehend the so-called laws of demand and supply. The equilibrium price—that is, the price that will tend to prevail in the market as long as demand and supply do not change—is simply the price at which **quantity demanded** and **quantity supplied** are equal. The quantity bought and sold in the market (the equilibrium quantity) is the quantity demanded and supplied at the equilibrium price. If you can determine the equilibrium price and quantity under one set of demand and supply conditions, you can determine them under any other set.

This chapter includes a brief examination of the factors that determine demand and supply and the ways in which changes in these determinants will affect and cause changes in demand and supply. A graphic method is used in this analysis to illustrate demand and supply, equilibrium price and quantity, changes in demand and supply, and the resulting changes in equilibrium price and quantity. The **demand curve** and the **supply curve** are graphic representations of the same data contained in the schedules of demand and supply. The application section at the end of the chapter explains government-set prices. When the government sets a legal price in a competitive market, it creates a **price ceiling** or **price floor.** This prevents supply and demand from determining the equilibrium price and quantity of a product that will be provided by a competitive market. As you will learn, the economic consequence of a price ceiling is that it will result in a persistent shortage of the product. An example of a price ceiling would be price controls on apartment rents. A price floor will result in a persistent surplus of a product, and the example given is price supports for an agricultural product. You will use demand and supply over and over. It will turn out to be as important to you in economics as jet propulsion is to the pilot of an airplane: You can't get off the ground without it.

■ CHECKLIST

When you have studied this chapter you should be able to

☐ Explain the economic meaning of markets.

☐ Define demand and state the law of demand.

☐ Give three explanations for the inverse relationship between price and quantity demanded.

☐ Graph the demand curve when you are given a demand schedule.

☐ Explain the difference between individual demand and market demand.

☐ List the five major determinants of demand and explain how each one shifts the demand curve.

☐ Explain how changes in income affect the demand for normal goods and inferior goods.

☐ Explain how changes in the prices of a substitute good or a complementary good affect the demand for a product.

☐ Distinguish between change in demand and change in the quantity demanded.

☐ Define supply and state the law of supply.

☐ Graph the supply curve when given a supply schedule.

☐ Explain the difference between individual supply and market supply.

☐ List the major determinants of supply and explain how each shifts the supply curve.

☐ Distinguish between changes in supply and changes in the quantity supplied.

☐ Describe how the equilibrium price and quantity are determined in a competitive market.

☐ Define surplus and shortage.

☐ Determine when you are given the demand for and the supply of a good, the equilibrium price and the equilibrium quantity.

☐ Explain the meaning of the rationing function of prices.

☐ Distinguish between productive efficiency and allocative efficiency.

☐ Predict the effects of changes in demand on equilibrium price and quantity.

☐ Predict the effects of changes in supply on equilibrium price and quantity.

☐ Predict the effects of changes in both demand and supply on equilibrium price and quantity.

☐ Explain the economic effects of a government-set price ceiling on product price and quantity in a competitive market.

☐ Describe the economic consequences of a government-set price floor on product price and quantity.

■ CHAPTER OUTLINE

1. A market is any institution or mechanism that brings together buyers ("demanders") and sellers ("suppliers") of a particular good or service. This chapter assumes that markets are highly competitive.

2. ***Demand*** is a schedule of prices and the quantities that buyers would purchase at each of these prices during a selected period of time.

a. The ***law of demand*** states that there is an inverse or negative relationship between price and quantity demanded. Other things equal, as price increases, buyers will purchase fewer quantities, and as price decreases they will purchase more quantities. There are three explanations for the law of demand:

(1) ***Diminishing marginal utility:*** After a point, consumers get less satisfaction or benefit from consuming more and more units.

(2) ***Income effect:*** A higher price for a good decreases the purchasing power of consumers' incomes so they can't buy as much of the good.

(3) ***Substitution effect:*** A higher price for a good encourages consumers to search for cheaper substitutes and thus buy less of it.

b. The ***demand curve*** has a downward slope and is a graphic representation of the law of demand.

c. Market demand for a good is a sum of all the demands of all consumers of that good at each price. Although price has the most important influence on quantity demanded, other factors can influence demand. The factors, called ***determinants of demand,*** are consumer tastes (preferences), the number of buyers in the market, consumers' income, the prices of related goods, and consumer expectations.

d. An increase or decrease in the entire demand schedule and the demand curve (a change in demand) results from a change in one or more of the determinants of demand. For a particular good,

(1) an increase in *consumer tastes or preferences* increases its demand;

(2) an increase in *the number of buyers* increases its demand;

(3) *consumers' income* increases its demand if it is a ***normal good*** (one where income and demand are positively related), but an increase in consumers' income decreases its demand if it is an ***inferior good*** (one where income and demand are negatively related);

(4) an increase in *the price of a related good* will increase its demand if the related good is a ***substitute good*** (one that can be used in place of another) but an increase in the price of a related good will decrease its demand if the related good is a ***complementary good*** (one that is used with another good).

(5) an increase in *consumer expectations* of a future price increase or a future rise in income increases its current demand.

e. A ***change in demand*** means that the entire demand curve or schedule has changed because of a change in one of the above determinants of demand, but a ***change in the quantity demanded*** means that there has been a movement along an existing demand curve or schedule because of a change in price.

3. ***Supply*** is a schedule of prices and the quantities that sellers will sell at each of these prices during some period of time.

a. The ***law of supply*** shows a positive relationship between price and quantity supplied. Other things equal, as the price of the good increases, more quantities will be offered for sale, and as the price of the good decreases, fewer quantities will be offered for sale.

b. The ***supply curve*** is a graphic representation of supply and the law of supply; it has an upward slope indicating the positive relationship between price and quantity supplied.

c. The market supply of a good is the sum of the supplies of all sellers or producers of the good at each price.

d. Although price has the most important influence on the quantity supplied, other factors can also influence supply. The factors, called ***determinants of supply,*** are changes in (1) resource prices; (2) technology; (3) taxes and subsidies; (4) prices of other good; (5) price expectation; and (6) the number of sellers in a market.

e. A ***change in supply*** is an increase or decrease in the entire supply schedule and the supply curve. It is the result of a change in one or more of the determinants of supply that affect the cost of production. For a particular product,

(1) a decrease in *resource prices* increases its supply;

(2) an improvement in technology increases its supply;

(3) a decrease in *taxes* or an increase in *subsidies* increases its supply;

(4) a decrease in *the price of another good* that could be produced leads to an increase in its supply;

(5) an increase in *producer expectations* of higher prices for the good may increase or decrease its supply.

(6) an increase in the number of sellers or suppliers is likely to increase its supply.

f. A ***change in supply*** means that the entire supply curve or schedule has changed because of a change in one of the above determinants of supply, but a ***change in the quantity supplied*** means that there has been a movement along an existing supply curve or schedule because of a change in price.

4. The ***equilibrium price*** (or *market-clearing price*) of a product is that price at which quantity demanded and quantity supplied are equal. The quantity exchanged in the market (the ***equilibrium quantity***) is equal to the quantity demanded and supplied at the equilibrium price.

a. If the price of a product is above the market equilibrium price, there will be a ***surplus*** or *excess supply.* In this case, the quantity demanded is less than the quantity supplied at that price.

b. If the price of a product is below the market equilibrium price, there will be a ***shortage*** or *excess demand.* In this case, the quantity demanded is greater than the quantity supplied at that price.

c. The rationing function of prices is the elimination of surpluses and shortages of a product.

d. Competitive markets produce ***productive efficiency,*** in which the goods and services society desires are being produced in the least costly way. They also create ***allocative efficiency,*** in which resources are devoted to the production of goods and services society most highly values.

e. Changes in supply and demand result in changes in the equilibrium price and quantity. The simplest cases are ones where demand changes and supply remains constant, or where supply changes and demand remains constant. More complex cases involve simultaneous changes in supply and demand.

(1) *Demand changes.* An increase in demand, with supply remaining the same, will increase the equilibrium price and quantity; a decrease in demand with supply remaining the same will decrease the equilibrium price and quantity.

(2) *Supply changes.* An increase in supply, with demand staying the same, will decrease the equilibrium price and increase the equilibrium quantity; a decrease in supply, with demand staying the same, will increase the equilibrium price and decrease the equilibrium quantity.

(3) *Complex cases.* These four cases involve changes in demand *and* supply: both increase; both decrease; one increases and one decreases; and, one decreases and one increases. For the possible effects on the equilibrium price and quantity in the four complex cases, see #4 in the "Hints and Tips" section.

5. Supply and demand analysis has many important applications to government-set prices.

a. A ***price ceiling*** set by government prevents price from performing its rationing function in a market system. It creates a shortage (quantity demanded is greater than the quantity supplied) at the government-set price.

(1) Another rationing method must be found, so government often steps in and establishes one. But all rationing systems have problems because they exclude someone.

(2) A government-set price creates an illegal *black market* for those who want to buy and sell above the government-set price.

(3) One example of a legal price ceiling that creates a shortage would be rent control established in some cities to restrain the rental price of apartments.

b. A ***price floor*** is a minimum price set by government for the sale of a product or resource. It creates a surplus (quantity supplied is greater than the quantity demanded) at the fixed price. The surplus may induce the government to increase demand or decrease supply to eliminate the surplus. The use of price floors has often been applied to agricultural products such as wheat.

6. (*Last Word*). The supply and demand analysis can be used to understand the shortage of organ transplants. The demand curve for such organs is down-sloping and the supply is fixed (vertical) and left of the zero price on the demand curve. Transplanted organs have a zero price. At that price the quantity demanded is much greater than the quantity supplied, creating a shortage that is rationed with a waiting list. A competitive market for organs would increase the price of organs and then make them more available for transplant (make the supply curve up-sloping), but there are moral and cost objections to this change.

■ HINTS AND TIPS

1. This chapter is the most important one in the book. Make sure you spend extra time on it and master the material. If you do, your long-term payoff will be a much easier understanding of the applications in later chapters.

2. One mistake students often make is to confuse **change in demand** with **change in quantity demanded.** A change in demand causes the entire demand curve to *shift,* whereas a change in quantity demanded is simply a *movement* along an existing demand curve.

3. It is strongly recommended that you draw supply and demand graphs as you work on supply and demand problems so you can see a picture of what happens when demand shifts, supply shifts, or both demand and supply shift.

4. Make a chart and related graphs that show the eight possible outcomes from changes in demand and supply. Figure 3.7 in the text illustrates the *four single shift* outcomes:

(1) ***D increase: P*** ↑, ***Q*** ↑ (3) ***S increase: P*** ↓, ***Q*** ↑
(2) ***D decrease: P*** ↓, ***Q*** ↓ (4) ***S decrease: P*** ↑, ***Q*** ↓

Four shift combinations are described in Table 3.3 of the text. Make a figure to illustrate each combination.

(1) ***S*** ↑, ***D*** ↓: ***P*** ↓, ***Q*** ? (3) ***S*** ↑, ***D*** ↑: ***P*** ?, ***Q*** ↓
(2) ***S*** ↓, ***D*** ↑: ***P*** ↑, ***Q*** ? (4) ***S*** ↓, ***D*** ↓: ***P*** ?, ***Q*** ↓

5. Make sure you understand the "other-things-equal" assumption described in the Consider This box on salsa and coffee beans (p. 61). It will help you understand why the law of demand is not violated even if the price and quantity of a product increase over time.

6. Practice always helps in understanding graphs. Without looking at the textbook, draw a supply and demand graph with a **price ceiling** below the equilibrium price and show the resulting shortage in the market for a product. Then, draw a supply and demand graph with a **price floor** above the equilibrium price and show the resulting surplus. Explain to yourself what the graphs show. Check your graphs and your explanations by referring to textbook Figures 3.8 and 3.9 and the related explanations.

■ IMPORTANT TERMS

demand
demand schedule
law of demand
diminishing marginal utility
income effect
substitution effect
demand curve
determinants of demand

normal goods
inferior goods
substitute good
complementary good
change in demand
change in quantity demanded
supply
supply schedule
law of supply
supply curve
determinants of supply
change in supply
change in quantity supplied
equilibrium price
equilibrium quantity
surplus
shortage
productive efficiency
allocative efficiency
price ceiling
price floor

SELF-TEST

■ FILL-IN QUESTIONS

1. A market is the institution or mechanism that brings together buyers or (demanders, suppliers) __________ and sellers or __________ of a particular good or service.

2. The relationship between price and quantity in the demand schedule is (a direct, an inverse) __________ relationship; in the supply schedule the relationship is __________ one.

3. The added satisfaction or pleasure a consumer obtains from additional units of a product decreases as the consumer's consumption of the product increases. This phenomenon is called diminishing marginal (equilibrium, utility) __________.

4. A consumer tends to buy more of a product as its price falls because

a. The purchasing power of the consumer is increased and the consumer tends to buy more of this product (and of other products); this is called the (income, substitution) __________ effect.

b. The product becomes less expensive relative to similar products and the consumer tends to buy more of the original product and less of the similar products, which is called the __________ effect.

5. When demand or supply is graphed, price is placed on the (horizontal, vertical) __________ axis and quantity on the __________ axis.

6. The change from an individual to a market demand schedule involves (adding, multiplying) __________ the quantities demanded by each consumer at the various possible (incomes, prices) __________.

7. When the price of one product and the demand for another product are directly related, the two products are called (substitutes, complements) __________; however, when the price of one product and the demand for another product are inversely related, the two products are called __________.

8. When a consumer demand schedule or curve is drawn up, it is assumed that five factors that determine demand are fixed and constant. These five determinants of consumer demand are

a. __________

b. __________

c. __________

d. __________

e. __________

9. A decrease in demand means that consumers will buy (larger, smaller) __________ quantities at every price, or will pay (more, less) __________ for the same quantities.

10. A change in income or in the price of another product will result in a change in the (demand for, quantity demanded of) __________ the given product, while a change in the price of the given product will result in a change in the __________ the given product.

11. An increase in supply means that producers will make and be willing to sell (larger, smaller) __________ quantities at every price, or will accept (more, less) __________ for the same quantities.

12. A change in resource prices or the prices of other goods that could be produced will result in a change in the (supply, quantity supplied) __________ of the given product, but a change in the price of the given product will result in a change in the __________.

13. The fundamental factors that determine the supply of any commodity in the product market are

a. __________

b. __________

c. __________

d. __________

e. __________

f. __________

14. The equilibrium price of a product is the price at which quantity demanded is (greater than, equal to) __________ quantity supplied, and there (is, is not) __________ a surplus or a shortage at that price.

15. If quantity demanded is greater than quantity supplied, price is (above, below) __________ the equilibrium price; and the (shortage, surplus) __________ will cause the price to (rise, fall) __________. If quantity demanded is less than the quantity supplied, price is (above, below) ____________ the equilibrium price, and the (shortage, surplus) ____________ will cause the price to (rise, fall) ____________.

16. In the spaces next to **a–h,** indicate the effect [*increase* (+), *decrease* (−), or *indeterminate* (?)] on equilibrium price (***P***) and equilibrium quantity (***Q***) of each of these changes in demand and/or supply.

	P	*Q*
a. Increase in demand, supply constant	____	____
b. Increase in supply, demand constant	____	____
c. Decrease in demand, supply constant	____	____
d. Decrease in supply, demand constant	____	____
e. Increase in demand, increase in supply	____	____
f. Increase in demand, decrease in supply	____	____
g. Decrease in demand, decrease in supply	____	____
h. Decrease in demand, increase in supply	____	____

17. If supply and demand establish a price for a good so that there is no shortage or surplus of the product, then price is successfully performing its (utility, rationing) ____________ function. The price that is set is a market-(changing, clearing) ____________ price.

18. A competitive market produces two types of efficiency: goods and services will be produced in the least costly way, so there will be (allocative, productive) ____________ efficiency; and resources are devoted to the production of the mix of goods and services society most wants, or there is ____________ efficiency.

19. A price ceiling is the (minimum, maximum) ____________ legal price a seller may charge for a product or service, whereas a price floor is the ____________ legal price set by government.

20. If a price ceiling is below the market equilibrium price, a (surplus, shortage) ____________ will arise in a competitive market, and if a price floor is above the market equilibrium price, a (surplus, shortage) ____________ will arise in a competitive market.

■ TRUE–FALSE QUESTIONS

Circle T if the statement is true, F if it is false.

1. A market is any arrangement that brings together the buyers and sellers of a particular good or service. **T F**

2. Demand is the amount of a good or service that a buyer will purchase at a particular price. **T F**

3. The law of demand states that as price increases, other things being equal, the quantity of the product demanded increases. **T F**

4. The law of diminishing marginal utility is one explanation of why there is an inverse relationship between price and quantity demanded. **T F**

5. The substitution effect suggests that, at a lower price, you have the incentive to substitute the more expensive product for similar products which are relatively less expensive. **T F**

6. There is no difference between individual demand schedules and the market demand schedule for a product. **T F**

7. In graphing supply and demand schedules, supply is put on the horizontal axis and demand on the vertical axis. **T F**

8. If price falls, there will be an increase in demand. **T F**

9. If consumer tastes or preferences for a product decrease, the demand for the product will tend to decrease. **T F**

10. An increase in income will tend to increase the demand for a product. **T F**

11. When two products are substitute goods, the price of one and the demand for the other will tend to move in the same direction. **T F**

12. If two goods are complementary, an increase in the price of one will tend to increase the demand for the other. **T F**

13. A change in the quantity demanded means that there has been a change in demand. **T F**

14. Supply is a schedule that shows the amounts of a product a producer can make in a limited time period. **T F**

15. An increase in resource prices will tend to decrease supply. **T F**

16. A government subsidy for the production of a product will tend to decrease supply. **T F**

17. An increase in the prices of other goods that could be made by producers will tend to decrease the supply of the current good that the producer is making. **T F**

18. A change in supply means that there is a movement along an existing supply curve. **T F**

19. A surplus indicates that the quantity demanded is less than the quantity supplied at that price. **T F**

20. If the market price of a product is below its equilibrium price, the market price will tend to rise because demand will decrease and supply will increase. **T F**

21. The rationing function of prices is the elimination of shortages and surpluses. **T F**

22. Allocative efficiency means that goods and services are being produced by society in the least costly way. **T F**

23. If the supply of a product increases and demand decreases, the equilibrium price and quantity will increase. **T F**

24. If the demand for a product increases and the supply of the product decreases, the equilibrium price will increase and equilibrium quantity will be indeterminate. **T F**

25. A price ceiling set by government below the competitive market price of a product will result in a surplus. **T F**

■ MULTIPLE-CHOICE QUESTIONS

Circle the letter that corresponds to the best answer.

1. A schedule that shows the various amounts of a product consumers are willing and able to purchase at each price in a series of possible prices during a specified period of time is called
(a) supply
(b) demand
(c) quantity supplied
(d) quantity demanded

2. The reason for the law of demand can best be explained in terms of
(a) supply
(b) complementary goods
(c) the rationing function of prices
(d) diminishing marginal utility

3. Assume that the price of video game players falls. What will most likely happen to the equilibrium price and quantity of video games, assuming this market is competitive?
(a) Price will increase; quantity will decrease.
(b) Price will decrease; quantity will increase.
(c) Price will decrease; quantity will decrease.
(d) Price will increase; quantity will increase.

4. Given the following individuals' demand schedules for product X, and assuming these are the only three consumers of X, which set of prices and output levels below will be on the market demand curve for this product?

	Consumer 1	Consumer 2	Consumer 3
Price X	Q_{dx}	Q_{dx}	Q_{dx}
$5	1	2	0
4	2	4	0
3	3	6	1
2	4	8	2
1	5	10	3

(a) ($5, 2); ($1, 10)
(b) ($5, 3); ($1, 18)
(c) ($4, 6); ($2, 12)
(d) ($4, 0); ($1, 3)

5. Which change will decrease the demand for a product?
(a) a favorable change in consumer tastes
(b) an increase in the price of a substitute good
(c) a decrease in the price of a complementary good
(d) a decrease in the number of buyers

6. The income of a consumer decreases and the consumer's demand for a particular good increases. It can be concluded that the good is
(a) normal
(b) inferior
(c) a substitute
(d) a complement

7. Which of the following could cause a decrease in consumer demand for product X?
(a) a decrease in consumer income
(b) an increase in the prices of goods that are good substitutes for product X
(c) an increase in the price that consumers expect will prevail for product X in the future
(d) a decrease in the supply of product X

8. If two goods are substitutes for each other, an increase in the price of one will necessarily
(a) decrease the demand for the other
(b) increase the demand for the other
(c) decrease the quantity demanded of the other
(d) increase the quantity demanded of the other

9. If two products, A and B, are complements, then
(a) an increase in the price of A will decrease the demand for B
(b) an increase in the price of A will increase the demand for B
(c) an increase in the price of A will have no significant effect on the price of B
(d) a decrease in the price of A will decrease the demand for B

10. If two products, X and Y, are independent goods, then
(a) an increase in the price of X will significantly increase the demand for Y
(b) an increase in the price of Y will significantly increase the demand for X
(c) an increase in the price of Y will have no significant effect on the demand for X
(d) a decrease in the price of X will significantly increase the demand for Y

11. The law of supply states that, other things being constant, as price increases
(a) supply increases
(b) supply decreases
(c) quantity supplied increases
(d) quantity supplied decreases

12. If the supply curve moves from S_1 to S_2 on the graph below, there has been

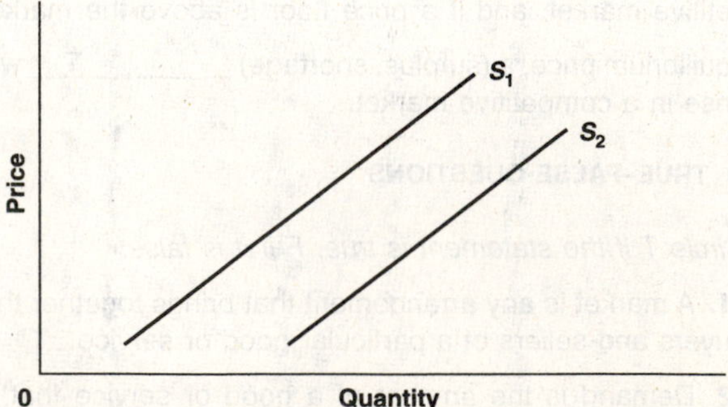

(a) an increase in supply
(b) a decrease in supply
(c) an increase in quantity supplied
(d) a decrease in quantity supplied

13. A decrease in the supply of a product would most likely be caused by
(a) an increase in business taxes
(b) an increase in consumer incomes
(c) a decrease in resource costs for production
(d) a decrease in the price of a complementary good

14. If the quantity supplied of a product is greater than the quantity demanded for a product, then
(a) there is a shortage of the product
(b) there is a surplus of the product
(c) the product is a normal good
(d) the product is an inferior good

15. If the price of a product is below the equilibrium price, the result will be
(a) a surplus of the good
(b) a shortage of the good
(c) a decrease in the supply of the good
(d) an increase in the demand for the good

16. Which would be the best example of allocative efficiency? When society devoted resources to the production of
(a) slide rules instead of handheld calculators
(b) horse-drawn carriages instead of automobiles
(c) computers with word processors instead of typewriters
(d) long-playing records instead of compact discs

Answer Questions 17, 18, and 19 on the basis of the data in the following table. Consider the following supply and demand schedules for bushels of corn.

Price	Quantity demanded	Quantity supplied
$20	395	200
22	375	250
24	350	290
26	320	320
28	280	345
30	235	365

17. The equilibrium price in this market is
(a) $22
(b) $24
(c) $26
(d) $28

18. An increase in the cost of labor lowers the quantity supplied by 65 bushels at each price. The new equilibrium price would be
(a) $22
(b) $24
(c) $26
(d) $28

19. If the quantity demanded at each price increases by 130 bushels, then the new equilibrium quantity will be
(a) 290
(b) 320
(c) 345
(d) 365

20. A decrease in supply and a decrease in demand will
(a) increase price and decrease the quantity exchanged
(b) decrease price and increase the quantity exchanged
(c) increase price and affect the quantity exchanged in an indeterminate way
(d) affect price in an indeterminate way and decrease the quantity exchanged

21. An increase in demand and a decrease in supply will
(a) increase price and increase the quantity exchanged
(b) decrease price and decrease the quantity exchanged
(c) increase price and the effect upon quantity exchanged will be indeterminate
(d) decrease price and the effect upon quantity exchanged will be indeterminate

22. An increase in supply and an increase in demand will
(a) increase price and increase the quantity exchanged
(b) decrease price and increase the quantity exchanged
(c) affect price in an indeterminate way and decrease the quantity exchanged
(d) affect price in an indeterminate way and increase the quantity exchanged

23. A cold spell in Florida devastates the orange crop. As a result, California oranges command a higher price. Which of the following statements best explains the situation?
(a) The supply of Florida oranges decreases, causing the supply of California oranges to increase and their price to increase.
(b) The supply of Florida oranges decreases, causing their price to increase and the demand for California oranges to increase.
(c) The supply of Florida oranges decreases, causing the supply of California oranges to decrease and their price to increase.
(d) The demand for Florida oranges decreases, causing a greater demand for California oranges and an increase in their price.

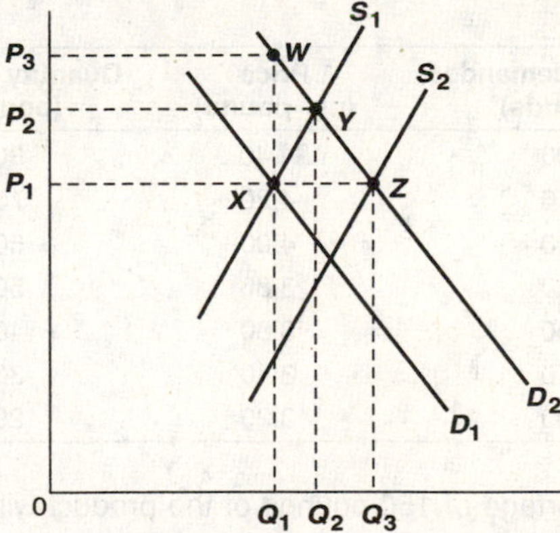

Answer Questions 24, 25, 26, and 27 based on the following graph showing the market supply and demand for a product.

24. Assume that the market is initially in equilibrium where D_1 and S_1 intersect. If there is an increase in the number of buyers, then the new equilibrium would most likely be at point
(a) *W*
(b) *X*

(c) Y
(d) Z

25. Assume that the equilibrium price and quantity in the market are P_2 and Q_2. Which factor would cause the equilibrium price and quantity to shift to P_1 and Q_3?
(a) an increase in product price
(b) an increase in demand
(c) an increase in supply
(d) a decrease in quantity

26. What would cause a shift in the equilibrium price and quantity from point Z to point X?
(a) a decrease in production costs and more favorable consumer tastes for the product
(b) an increase in the number of suppliers and an increase in consumer incomes
(c) an increase in production costs and a decrease in consumer incomes
(d) an improvement in production technology and a decrease in the price of a substitute good

27. Assume that the market is initially in equilibrium where D_1 and S_1 intersect. If consumer incomes increased and the technology for making the product improved, then new equilibrium would most likely be at
(a) P_1 and Q_1
(b) P_2 and Q_2
(c) P_1 and Q_3
(d) P_3 and Q_1

28. A maximum price set by the government that is designed to help consumers is a
(a) price ceiling
(b) price floor
(c) shortage
(d) surplus

Questions 29 and 30 relate to the following table that shows a hypothetical supply and demand schedule for a product.

Quantity demanded (pounds)	Price (per pound)	Quantity supplied (pounds)
200	$4.40	800
250	4.20	700
300	4.00	600
350	3.80	500
400	3.60	400
450	3.40	300
500	3.20	200

29. A shortage of 150 pounds of the product will occur if a government-set price is established at
(a) $3.20
(b) $3.40
(c) $3.80
(d) $4.00

30. If a price floor set by the government is established at $4.20, there will be a
(a) surplus of 300 pounds
(b) shortage of 300 pounds
(c) surplus of 450 pounds
(d) shortage of 450 pounds

■ PROBLEMS

1. Using the demand schedule below, plot the demand curve on the graph below the schedule. Label the axes and indicate for each axis the units being used to measure price and quantity.

Price	Quantity demanded 1000 bushels of soybeans
$7.20	10
7.00	15
6.80	20
6.60	25
6.40	30
6.20	35

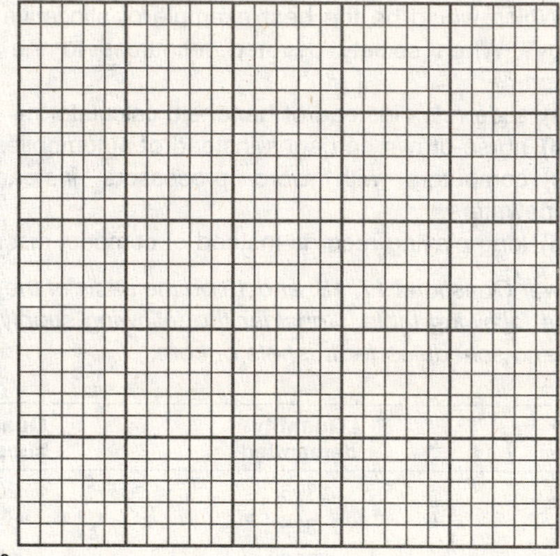

a. Plot the following supply schedule on the same graph.

Price	Quantity demanded 1000 bushels of soybeans
$7.20	40
7.00	35
6.80	30
6.60	25
6.40	20
6.20	15

b. The equilibrium price of soybeans will be $_____.
c. How many thousand bushels of soybeans will be exchanged at this price? ________
d. Indicate clearly on the graph the equilibrium price and quantity by drawing lines from the intersection of the supply and demand curves to the price and quantity axes.
e. If the federal government supported a price of $7.00 per bushel there would be a (shortage, surplus) ________ of ________ bushels of soybeans.

2. The demand schedules of three individuals (Ellie, Sam, and Lynn) for loaves of bread are shown in the following table. Assuming there are only three buyers of bread, determine and graph the total or market demand schedule for bread.

	Quantity demanded, loaves of bread			
Price	**Ellie**	**Sam**	**Lynn**	**Total**
$1.50	1	4	0	_____
1.40	3	5	1	_____
1.30	6	6	5	_____
1.20	10	7	10	_____
1.10	15	8	16	_____

3. Following is a demand schedule for bushels of apples. In columns 3 and 4 insert any new figures for quantity that represent in column 3 an increase in demand and in column 4 a decrease in demand.

(1) Price	(2) Quantity demanded	(3) Demand increases	(4) Demand decreases
$6.00	400	_____	_____
5.90	500	_____	_____
5.80	600	_____	_____
5.70	700	_____	_____
5.60	800	_____	_____
5.50	900	_____	_____

4. Assume that O'Rourke has, when his income is $100 per week, the demand schedule for good A shown in columns 1 and 2 of the following table and the demand schedule for good B shown in columns 4 and 5. Assume that the prices of A and B are $.80 and $5, respectively.

Demand for A (per week)			*Demand for B (per week)*		
(1) Price	**(2) Quantity demanded**	**(3) Quantity demanded**	**(4) Price**	**(5) Quantity demanded**	**(6) Quantity demanded**
$.90	10	0	$5.00	4	7
.85	20	10	4.50	5	8
.80	30	20	4.00	6	9
.75	40	30	3.50	7	10
.70	50	40	3.00	8	11
.65	60	50	2.50	9	12
.60	70	60	2.00	10	13

a. How much A will O'Rourke buy? _____

How much B? _____

b. Suppose that as a consequence of a $10 increase in O'Rourke's weekly income, the quantities demanded of A become those shown in column 3 and the quantities demanded of B become those shown in column 6.

(1) How much A will he now buy? _____

How much B? _____

(2) Good A is (normal, inferior) _____.

(3) Good B is _____.

5. The market demand for good X is shown in columns 1 and 2 of the following table. Assume the price of X to be $2 and constant.

(1) Price	(2) Quantity demanded	(3) Quantity demanded	(4) Quantity demanded
$2.40	1600	1500	1700
2.30	1650	1550	1750
2.20	1750	1650	1850
2.10	1900	1800	2000
2.00	2100	2000	2200
1.90	2350	2250	2450
1.80	2650	2550	2750

a. If, as the price of good Y rises from $1.25 to $1.35, the quantities demanded of good X become those shown in column 3, it can be concluded that X and Y are (substitute, complementary) _____ goods.

b. If, as the price of good Y rises from $1.25 to $1.35, the quantities of good X become those shown in column 4, it can be concluded that X and Y are _____ goods.

6. The existing demand and supply schedules are given in columns 1, 2, and 3 of the following table.

Demand and Supply Schedules			*New Demand and Supply Schedules*		
(1) Price	**(2) Quantity demanded**	**(3) Quantity supplied**	**(4) Price**	**(5) Quantity demanded**	**(6) Quantity supplied**
$5.00	10	50	$5.00	_____	_____
4.00	20	40	4.00	_____	_____
3.00	30	30	3.00	_____	_____
2.00	40	20	2.00	_____	_____
1.00	50	10	1.00	_____	_____

a. Now the demand *increases* by 10 units at each price and supply *decreases* by 10 units. Enter the new amounts for quantity demanded and quantity supplied in columns 5 and 6.

b. What was the old equilibrium price? _____

What will be the new equilibrium price? _____

c. What was the old equilibrium quantity? _____

What will be the new equilibrium quantity? _____

7. In a local market for hamburger on a given date, each of 300 identical sellers of hamburger has the following supply schedule.

(1) Price	(2) Quantity supplied—one seller, lbs	(3) Quantity supplied—all sellers, lbs
$2.05	150	_____
2.00	110	_____
1.95	75	_____
1.90	45	_____
1.85	20	_____
1.80	0	_____

a. In column 3 construct the market supply schedule for hamburger.

b. Following is the market demand schedule for hamburger on the same date and in the same local market as that given above.

Price	Quantity demanded, lbs
$2.05	28,000
2.00	31,000
1.95	36,000
1.90	42,000
1.85	49,000
1.80	57,000

If the federal government sets a price on hamburger of $1.90 a pound, the result would be a (shortage, surplus) ________ of ________ pounds of hamburger in this market.

8. Each of the following events would tend to increase or decrease either the demand for or the supply of electronic games and, as a result, will increase or decrease the price of these games. In the first blank indicate the effect on demand or supply (increase, decrease); in the second blank, indicate the effect on price (increase, decrease). Assume that the market for electronic games is a competitive one.

a. It becomes known by consumers that there is going to be a major sale on these games one month from now. ________; ________

b. The workers in the electronic games industry receive a $3 an hour wage increase. ________; ________

c. It is announced by a respected research institute that children who play electronic games also improve their grades in school. ________; ________

d. Because of an increase in productivity, the amount of labor necessary to produce a game decreases. ________; ________

e. The consumers who play these games believe that a shortage of the games is developing in the economy. ________; ________

f. The federal government imposes a $5 tax per game on the manufacturers of the electronic games. ________; ________

■ SHORT ANSWER AND ESSAY QUESTIONS

1. Define demand and the law of demand.

2. Use the diminishing marginal utility concept to explain why the quantity demanded of a product will tend to rise when the price of the product falls.

3. In past decades, the price of coffee in the United States rose significantly as a result of bad weather in coffee-producing regions. Use the income effect and the substitution effect concepts to explain why the quantity of coffee demanded in the United States significantly decreased.

4. What is the difference between individual demand and market demand? What is the relationship between these two types of demand?

5. Explain the difference between an increase in demand and an increase in the quantity demanded.

6. What are the factors that cause a change in demand? Use supply and demand graphs to illustrate what happens to price and quantity when demand increases.

7. How are inferior and normal (or superior) goods defined? What is the relationship between these goods and changes in income?

8. Why does the effect of a change in the price of related goods depend on whether a good is a substitute or complement? What are substitutes and complements?

9. A newspaper reports that "blue jeans have become even more popular and are now the standard clothing that people wear for both play and work." How will this change affect the demand for blue jeans? What will happen to the price and quantity of blue jeans sold in the market? Explain and use a supply and demand graph to illustrate your answer.

10. Compare and contrast the supply schedule with the demand schedule.

11. Supply does not remain constant for long because the factors that determine supply change. What are these factors? How do changes in them affect supply?

12. Explain the difference between an increase in supply and an increase in the quantity supplied.

13. Describe and illustrate with a supply and demand graph the effect of an increase in supply on price and quantity. Do the same for a decrease in supply.

14. The U.S. Congress passes a law that raises the excise tax on gasoline by $1 per gallon. What effect will this change have on the demand and supply of gasoline? What will happen to gasoline prices and quantity? Explain and use a supply and demand graph to illustrate your answer.

15. Given the demand for and the supply of a commodity, what price will be the equilibrium price of this commodity? Explain why this price will tend to prevail in the market and why higher (lower) prices, if they do exist temporarily, will tend to fall (rise).

16. What is the relationship between the price of a product and a shortage of the product? What is the relationship between the price of a product and a surplus of the product?

17. Explain why competition implies both productive efficiency and allocative efficiency.

18. Analyze the following quotation and explain the fallacies contained in it: "An increase in demand will cause price to rise; with a rise in price, supply will increase and the increase in supply will push price down. Therefore, an increase in demand results in little change in price because supply will increase also."

19. What are the consequences of a price ceiling for a product if it is set below the equilibrium price? Illustrate your answer with a graph.

20. What are the economic problems with price floors? How have they been used by government?

ANSWERS

Chapter 3 Demand, Supply, and Market Equilibrium

FILL-IN QUESTIONS

1. demanders, suppliers
2. an inverse, a direct
3. utility
4. *a.* income; *b.* substitution
5. vertical, horizontal
6. adding, prices
7. substitutes, complements
8. *a.* the tastes or preferences of consumers; *b.* the number of consumers in the market; *c.* the money income of consumers; *d.* the prices of related goods; *e.* consumer expectations with respect to future prices and income (any order for *a–e*)
9. smaller, less
10. demand for, quantity demanded of
11. larger, less
12. supply, quantity supplied
13. *a.* the technology of production; *b.* resource prices; *c.* taxes and subsidies; *d.* prices of other goods; *e.* producer expectations of price; *f.* the number of sellers in the market (any order for *a–f*)
14. equal to, is not
15. below, shortage, rise, above, surplus, fall
16. *a.* +, +; *b.* −, +; *c.* −, −; *d.* +, −; *e.* ?, +; *f.* +, ?; *g.* ?, −; *h.* −, ?
17. rationing, clearing
18. productive, allocative
19. maximum, minimum
20. shortage, surplus

TRUE–FALSE QUESTIONS

1. T, p. 48
2. F, p. 48
3. F, p. 49
4. T, p. 49
5. F, p. 49
6. F, pp. 49–50
7. F, pp. 48–49
8. F, pp. 50–51
9. T, p. 51
10. T, pp. 51–52
11. T, p. 52
12. F, p. 52
13. F, p. 53
14. F, p. 53
15. T, pp. 54–55
16. F, p. 55
17. T, p. 55
18. F, pp. 54–56
19. T, pp. 56–57
20. F, pp. 57–58
21. T, p. 58
22. F, pp. 58–59
23. F, pp. 59–60
24. T, pp. 59–60
25. F, p. 61

MULTIPLE-CHOICE QUESTIONS

1. b, p. 48
2. d, p. 49
3. d, pp. 56–58
4. b, p. 50
5. d, pp. 51–52
6. b, pp. 51–52
7. a, pp. 51–52
8. b, p. 52
9. a, p. 52
10. c, p. 52
11. c, p. 53
12. a, pp. 53–55
13. a, pp. 54–55
14. b, pp. 56–57
15. b, pp. 56–57
16. c, pp. 58–59
17. c, pp. 56–57
18. d, pp. 54–57
19. d, pp. 56–57
20. d, pp. 59–60
21. c, pp. 59–60
22. d, pp. 59–60
23. b, pp. 59–60
24. c, pp. 59–60
25. c, pp. 59–60
26. c, pp. 59–60
27. c, pp. 59–60
28. a, p. 61
29. b, p. 61
30. c, pp. 63–64

PROBLEMS

1. *a.* graph; *b.* 6.60; *c.* 25,000; *d.* graph; *e.* surplus, 20,000
2. Total: 5, 9, 17, 27, 39
3. Each quantity in column 3 is greater than in column 2, and each quantity in column 4 is less than in column 2.
4. *a.* 30, 4; *b.* (1) 20, 7; (2) inferior; (3) normal (superior)
5. *a.* complementary; *b.* substitute
6. *a.* column 5 (quantity demanded): 20, 30, 40, 50, 60; column 6 (quantity supplied): 40, 30, 20, 10, 0; *b.* $3.00, $4.00; *c.* 30, 30
7. *a.* 45,000; 33,000; 22,500; 13,500; 6,000; 0; *b.* shortage, 28,500
8. *a.* decrease demand, decrease price; *b.* decrease supply, increase price; *c.* increase demand, increase price; *d.* increase supply, decrease price; *e.* increase demand, increase price; *f.* decrease supply, increase price

SHORT ANSWER AND ESSAY QUESTIONS

1. pp. 48–49
2. p. 49
3. p. 49
4. p. 50
5. p. 53
6. p. 52
7. pp. 51–52
8. p. 52
9. pp. 50–51
10. pp. 48–49, 53
11. pp. 54–56
12. pp. 54–56
13. pp. 59–60
14. pp. 59–60
15. pp. 56–59
16. pp. 56–586
17. pp. 58–59
18. pp. 59–60
19. pp. 61–63
20. pp. 63–64

APPENDIX TO CHAPTER 3

Additional Examples of Supply and Demand

The first section of the appendix gives more examples of the effects of **changes in supply and demand** on price and quantity. You first will read about simple changes in which either the demand curve changes or the supply curve changes, but not both. These simple changes result in predictable effects on the price and quantity of a product, such as lettuce or a foreign currency such as the euro. Then you are given examples of complex changes, using pink salmon, gasoline, and sushi. In these cases, there is a simultaneous shift in supply and demand. Here the effect of changes in supply and demand on price and quantity will be less certain and will depend on the direction and extent of the changes.

The appendix then extends your understanding of what happens in markets if **pre-set prices** are above or below the equilibrium price. You have already learned that when the government intervenes in a competitive market and sets the price below equilibrium (a price ceiling), it creates a shortage of a product. Similarly, when government sets a price above the equilibrium price (a price floor), it will result in a surplus. As you will learn, shortages and surpluses can also occur in competitive markets when sellers set the price in advance of sales and that pre-set price turns out to be below or above the equilibrium or actual price. The examples given in the text are ticket prices for sporting events that are priced too low or too high by the sellers, resulting in shortages and surpluses.

Supply and demand analysis is one of the most important means for improving your understanding of the economic world. If you master its use, it will help you explain many events and outcomes in everyday life. This appendix helps you achieve that mastery and understanding.

■ APPENDIX CHECKLIST

When you have studied this appendix you should be able to

☐ Explain and graph the effect of a decrease in the supply of a product (lettuce) on its equilibrium price and quantity.
☐ Define the main characteristics of the foreign exchange market.
☐ Describe and graph the effect of an increase in the demand for a foreign currency (the euro) on its equilibrium price and quantity.
☐ Distinguish between the appreciation and depreciation of a currency.
☐ Discuss and graph the effects of an increase in the supply of and a decrease in demand for a product (pink salmon) on its equilibrium price and quantity.
☐ Predict and graph the effects of a decrease in the supply of and an increase in the demand for a product (gasoline) on its equilibrium price and quantity.
☐ Explain and graph the effects of an equal increase in the supply of and demand for a product (sushi) on its equilibrium price and quantity.
☐ Discuss and graph how a seller price for a service (Olympic figure skating finals) that is set below the equilibrium price will result in a shortage.
☐ Describe and graph how a seller price for a service (Olympic curling preliminaries) that is set above the equilibrium price will result in a surplus.

■ APPENDIX OUTLINE

1. ***Changes in supply and demand*** result in changes in the equilibrium price and quantity. The simplest cases are ones where demand changes and supply remain constant, or where supply changes and demand remain constant. More complex cases involve simultaneous changes in supply and demand.

a. *Supply increase.* In a competitive market for lettuce, if a severe freeze destroys a portion of the lettuce crop, then the supply of lettuce will decrease. The decrease in the supply of lettuce, with demand remaining the same, will increase the equilibrium price and decrease the equilibrium quantity.

b. *Demand increase.* In a competitive market for euros, an increase in the demand for euros because of the rising popularity of European goods, with supply remaining the same, will increase the equilibrium price and quantity of euros.

(1) The ***foreign exchange market*** is where foreign currencies, such as the European euro and U.S. dollar, are traded for each other. The equilibrium prices for foreign currencies are called ***exchange rates*** and represent how much of each currency can be exchanged for another currency. In the dollar–euro market, the dollar price of a euro would be on the vertical axis and the quantity of euro would be on the horizontal axis. The intersection of the up-sloping supply of euro curve and down-sloping demand for euro curve would determine the dollar price of a euro.

(2) If U.S. demand for European goods increased, then more euros will be needed to pay for these imported goods, and so the demand for euros would increase. This change increases the dollar price of euros, which

means that the U.S. dollar has ***depreciated*** relative to the euro and that the euro has ***appreciated*** relative to the dollar.

c. *Supply increase and demand decrease.* Over the years, improved fishing techniques and technology contributed to an increase in the supply of pink salmon. Also, an increase in consumer incomes and a lowering of the price of substitute fish contributed to reducing the demand for pink salmon. As a result the price of pink salmon fell. The equilibrium quantity could have increased, decreased, or stayed the same. In this case, the increase in supply was greater than the decrease in demand, so the equilibrium quantity increased.

d. *Demand increase and supply decrease.* An increase in the price of oil, a resource used to produce gasoline, resulted in a decrease in the supply of gasoline. At the same time, rising incomes and a stronger economy created a greater demand for gasoline. This decrease in supply and increase in demand increased the equilibrium price. The equilibrium quantity could have increased, decreased, or stayed the same. In this case, the decrease in supply was less than the increase in demand, so the equilibrium quantity increased.

e. *Demand increase and supply increase.* An increase in the taste for sushi among U.S. consumers resulted in an increase in the demand for this product. At the same time, there was an increase in the number of sushi bars and other food outlets that provide sushi, thus increasing its supply. This increase in both demand and supply increased the equilibrium quantity of sushi. The equilibrium price could have increased, decreased, or stayed the same. In this case, the increase in demand was the same as the increase in supply, so the equilibrium price remained the same.

2. ***Pre-set prices*** that the seller establishes below or above the equilibrium price can produce shortages and surpluses. If a price is set below the equilibrium price by a seller, then at that pre-set price the quantity demanded is greater than the quantity supplied, resulting in a ***shortage.*** If a price is set above the equilibrium price by a seller, then at that pre-set price the quantity demanded is less than the quantity supplied, resulting in a ***surplus.***

a. The shortage is typical of the market for tickets to more popular sporting events such as Olympic figure skating finals. The shortage of tickets at the pre-set price creates a secondary market (*black market*) for tickets in which buyers bid for tickets held by the initial purchaser. The ticket scalping drives up the price of tickets.

b. The surplus is typical of the market for tickets to less popular sporting events such as Olympic curling preliminaries at which there are many empty seats.

■ HINTS AND TIPS

1. This appendix offers applications and extensions of Chapter 3 in the textbook, so check your understanding of the corresponding text and appendix sections: (a) Review the Chapter 3 section on "Changes in Supply, Demand, and Equilibrium" before reading the Web appendix section on "Changes in Supply and Demand"; and (b) review the text Chapter 3 section on "Application: Government-Set Prices" before reading the appendix section on "Pre-Set Prices."

2. Correct terminology is important for mastering supply and demand analysis. You must remember the distinction between a change in demand and a change in quantity demanded or a change in supply and a change in quantity supplied. Consider the case of a single shift in demand with supply staying the same. As the demand curve increases along the existing supply curve, it increases the quantity supplied, but it does not increase supply (which would be a shift in the entire supply curve).

SELF-TEST

■ FILL-IN QUESTIONS

1. A decrease in the supply of lettuce will result in an equilibrium price that (increases, decreases) ______________ and an equilibrium quantity that ______________.

2. In the foreign exchange market for euros that are priced in U.S. dollars, an increase in the demand for euros (increases, decreases) ______________ the U.S. dollar price of a euro and ______________ the equilibrium quantity of euros. This change means that the value of the euro (appreciates, depreciates) ______________ relative to the U.S. dollar and that the value of the U.S. dollar ______________ relative to the euro.

3. An increase in the price of corn resulted in an increase in the (demand for, supply of) ______________ farmland in the corn belt and a decrease in the ______________ corn-fed beef.

4. An increase in the supply of pink salmon that is greater than the decrease in the demand for pink salmon will result in an equilibrium price that (increases, decreases, stays the same) ______________ and an equilibrium quantity that ______________.

5. An increase in the demand for gasoline that is greater than the decrease in the supply of gasoline will result in an equilibrium price that (increases, decreases, stays the same) ______________ and an equilibrium quantity that ______________.

6. A large increase in the price of gasoline is most likely to (increase, decrease) ______________ the demand for low-gas-mileage SUVs and trucks and ______________ the demand for high-gas-mileage hybrid cars.

7. An increase in the demand for sushi that is equal to the increase in the supply of sushi will result in an equilibrium price that (increases, decreases, stays the same) ______________ and an equilibrium quantity that ______________.

8. If government sets a legal price for a product, a shortage would arise from a price (ceiling, floor) ______________ and a surplus would arise from a price ______________.

9. If a pre-set price is set by the seller below the equilibrium price it will create a (surplus, shortage) ______________, but if a pre-set price is set by the seller above the equilibrium price it will create a ______________.

10. A market for tickets to popular sporting events in which buyers bid for tickets held by initial purchasers is referred to as a (primary, secondary) ______________ market. In these markets, ticket (destruction, scalping) ______________ occurs.

■ TRUE–FALSE QUESTIONS

Circle T if the statement is true, F if it is false.

1. An increase in the supply of lettuce decreases its equilibrium price and increases its equilibrium quantity. **T F**

2. A decrease in the demand for tomatoes increases the equilibrium price and decreases the equilibrium quantity. **T F**

3. When demand for euros increases because the United States imports more European goods, then the U.S. dollar price of the euro will increase and the euro has appreciated in value. **T F**

4. In the market for pink salmon, the reason that the equilibrium quantity increased was that the increase in supply was greater than the decrease in demand. **T F**

5. In a market for beef, the equilibrium price will increase when the increase in supply is greater than the increase in demand. **T F**

6. In the market for sushi, an equal increase in supply and demand will increase the equilibrium price, but have no effect on the equilibrium quantity. **T F**

7. In a market for flat-screen TVs, an increase in supply that is greater than the increase in demand will result in a lower equilibrium price. **T F**

8. If a seller pre-sets a price that turns out to be below the actual equilibrium price, a shortage will develop in the market. **T F**

9. Ticket scalping often occurs in markets where there is a surplus of tickets. **T F**

10. If a sporting event is not sold out, this indicates that the ticket prices for the event were pre-set above the actual equilibrium price. **T F**

■ MULTIPLE-CHOICE QUESTIONS

Circle the letter that corresponds to the best answer.

1. Bad weather in coffee-producing regions of the world devastated the coffee crop. As a result, coffee prices increased worldwide. Which of the following statements best explains the situation?

(a) The demand for coffee increased.
(b) The supply of coffee decreased.
(c) The demand for coffee increased and the supply of coffee increased.
(d) The demand for coffee decreased and the supply of coffee decreased.

2. Assume that the supply of tomatoes in a competitive market increases. What will most likely happen to the equilibrium price and quantity of tomatoes?

(a) Price will increase; quantity will decrease
(b) Price will decrease; quantity will increase
(c) Price will decrease; quantity will decrease
(d) Price will increase; quantity will increase

3. Assume that the demand for security services increases in a competitive market. What will most likely happen to the equilibrium price and quantity of security services?

(a) price will increase; quantity will decrease
(b) price will decrease; quantity will increase
(c) price will decrease; quantity will decrease
(d) price will increase; quantity will increase

4. A decrease in the demand for beef is more than offset by an increase in its supply. As a result the equilibrium price will

(a) increase and the equilibrium quantity will decrease
(b) increase and the equilibrium quantity will increase
(c) decrease and the equilibrium quantity will decrease
(d) decrease and the equilibrium quantity will increase

5. A decrease in the supply of oil is more than offset by an increase in its demand. As a result, the equilibrium price will

(a) increase and the equilibrium quantity will decrease
(b) increase and the equilibrium quantity will increase
(c) decrease and the equilibrium quantity will decrease
(d) decrease and the equilibrium quantity will increase

6. An increase in the demand for lumber that is less than the increase in the supply of lumber will

(a) increase the equilibrium price and quantity of lumber
(b) decrease the equilibrium price and quantity of lumber
(c) increase the equilibrium price and decrease the equilibrium quantity of lumber
(d) decrease the equilibrium price and increase the equilibrium quantity of lumber

7. What will happen to the equilibrium quantity and price of a product in a competitive market when there is an equal increase in demand and supply?

(a) equilibrium quantity and price will both increase
(b) equilibrium quantity and price will both decrease
(c) equilibrium quantity will increase and equilibrium price will stay the same
(d) equilibrium quantity will stay the same and equilibrium price will increase

8. What will happen to the equilibrium quantity and price of a product in a competitive market when the decrease in demand exactly offsets the increase in supply?
(a) equilibrium quantity will increase and equilibrium price will decrease
(b) equilibrium quantity will decrease and equilibrium price will increase
(c) equilibrium quantity will increase and equilibrium price will stay the same
(d) equilibrium quantity will stay the same and equilibrium price will decrease

9. Which of the following is a correct statement?
(a) price ceilings increase supply
(b) price ceilings create shortages
(c) price floors create shortages
(d) price floors increase demand

10. If a seller sets a price for a product that turns out to be below the equilibrium price, then there will be a
(a) shortage of the product
(b) surplus of the product
(c) price floor for a product
(d) zero price for the product

11. A surplus means that
(a) demand for a product is greater than the supply
(b) supply of the product is greater than the demand
(c) quantity demanded is less than the quantity supplied at that price
(d) quantity demanded is greater than the quantity supplied at that price

Answer Questions 12, 13, and 14 based on the following graph showing the market supply and demand for a product.

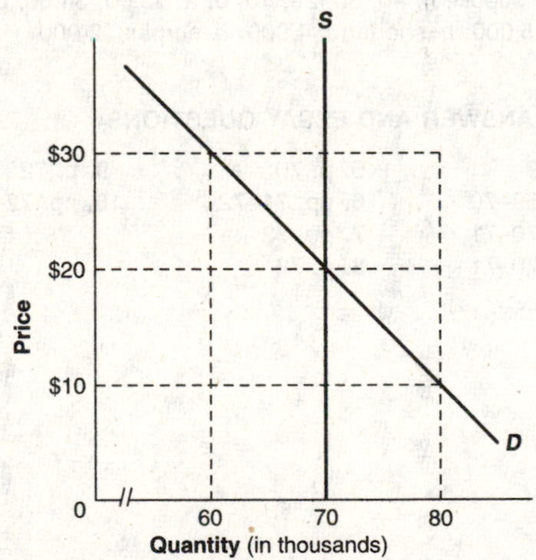

12. Given this market, if a seller pre-sets the price at $10, then this action results in a
(a) surplus of 10,000 units
(b) surplus of 80,000 units
(c) shortage of 10,000 units
(d) shortage of 80,000 units

13. Given this market, if a seller pre-sets the price at $30, then this action results in a
(a) surplus of 10,000 units
(b) surplus of 60,000 units
(c) surplus of 70,000 units
(d) shortage of 10,000 units

14. What price will eliminate a surplus or shortage in this market?
(a) $0
(b) $10
(c) $20
(d) $30

15. A market for tickets in which buyers bid for tickets held by initial purchasers rather than the original seller is a
(a) primary market
(b) secondary market
(c) pre-set market
(d) surplus market

■ PROBLEMS

1. The existing demand and supply schedules are given in columns 1, 2, and 3 of the following table.

Demand and Supply Schedules			*New Demand and Supply Schedules*		
(1) Price	(2) Quantity demanded	(3) Quantity supplied	(4) Price	(5) Quantity demanded	(6) Quantity supplied
$5.00	10	50	$5.00	____	____
4.00	20	40	4.00	____	____
3.00	30	30	3.00	____	____
2.00	40	20	2.00	____	____
1.00	50	10	1.00	____	____

Now the demand *increases* by 10 units at each price and supply *decreases* by 10 units. Enter the new amounts for quantity demanded and quantity supplied in columns 5 and 6.

a. What was the old equilibrium price? ____________
What will be the new equilibrium price? ____________
b. What was the old equilibrium quantity? ____________
What will be the new equilibrium quantity? ____________

2. The demand and supply schedules for a certain product are those given in the following table. Answer the related questions.

Quantity demanded	Price	Quantity supplied
12,000	$10	18,000
13,000	9	17,000
14,000	8	16,000
15,000	7	15,000
16,000	6	14,000
17,000	5	13,000
18,000	4	12,000

The equilibrium price of the product is $ ____________
and the equilibrium quantity is ____________.
a. If a seller established a pre-set price of $5 on this product, there would be a (shortage, surplus) ____________ of ____________ units.

b. If a seller established a pre-set price of $8, there would be a (shortage, surplus) ____________ of ____________ units.

■ SHORT ANSWER AND ESSAY QUESTIONS

1. Explain, using a supply and demand graph, how a freeze in a vegetable crop will affect the equilibrium price and quantity.

2. Use the foreign exchange market for euros to explain how an increase in the demand for euros affects its value relative to the U.S. dollar and the equilibrium quantity of euros exchanged in this market. In this case, which currency, the euro or the U.S. dollar, has appreciated or depreciated?

3. When there are single shifts in the supply or demand curve, you can predict the effects on both equilibrium price and quantity. When there are simultaneous shifts in demand and supply, you can make only one prediction of the effects with any certainty. Why?

4. You observe that the equilibrium price has decreased and the equilibrium quantity has increased. What supply and demand conditions would best explain this outcome?

5. If increase in the demand for gasoline outweighs the decrease in the supply of gasoline, what is the most likely effect on the equilibrium price and quantity? Explain and show your answer with a graph.

6. You observe that the equilibrium quantity has increased but the equilibrium price has stayed the same. What supply and demand conditions would best explain this outcome?

7. What are price ceilings and price floors and how are they related to pre-set prices?

8. What are the consequences if a seller sets a price below the actual equilibrium price?

9. Why do secondary markets arise? Give examples of such markets.

10. Explain, using a supply and demand graph, the situation that arises when there are many unsold tickets to a sporting event. Why does this occur?

ANSWERS

Appendix to Chapter 3 Additional Examples of Supply and Demand

FILL-IN QUESTIONS

1. increases, decreases
2. increases, increases, appreciates, depreciates
3. demand for, supply of
4. decreases, increases
5. increases, increases
6. decrease, increase
7. stays the same, increases
8. ceiling, floor
9. shortage, surplus
10. secondary, scalping

TRUE–FALSE QUESTIONS

1. T, p. 69
2. F, p. 69
3. T, pp. 69–70
4. T, p. 70
5. F, p. 70
6. F, pp. 71–72
7. T, pp. 71–72
8. T, p. 72
9. F, p. 72
10. T, pp. 72–73

MULTIPLE-CHOICE QUESTIONS

1. b, p. 69
2. b, p. 69
3. d, pp. 69–70
4. d, p. 70
5. b, p. 71
6. d, p. 71
7. c, pp. 71–72
8. d, pp. 71–72
9. b, pp.72–73
10. a, p. 72
11. c, p. 72
12. c, pp. 72–73
13. a, pp. 72–73
14. c, pp. 72–73
15. b, p. 72

PROBLEMS

1. column 5 (quantity demanded): 20, 30, 40, 50, 60; column 6 (quantity supplied): 40, 30, 20, 10, 0; *a.* $3.00, $4.00; *b.* 30, 30
2. $7, 15,000; *a.* shortage, 4,000; *b.* surplus, 2,000

SHORT ANSWER AND ESSAY QUESTIONS

1. p. 69
2. pp. 69–70
3. pp. 70–71
4. pp. 70–71
5. p. 70
6. pp. 71–72
7. pp. 72
8. p. 72
9. p. 72
10. pp. 72–73

CHAPTER 4

Elasticity

Chapter 4 is basically a continuation of Chapter 3. The previous chapter provided a basic understanding of supply and demand. Now the economic principles, problems, and policies to be studied require a more detailed discussion of **elasticity** and how it relates to supply and demand.

The concept of **price elasticity of demand** is of great importance for studying the material found in the remainder of the text. You must understand (1) what price elasticity measures; (2) how the price-elasticity formula is applied to measure the price elasticity of demand; (3) the difference between price elastic, price inelastic, and unit elastic; (4) how total revenue varies by the type of price elasticity of demand; (5) the meaning of perfect price elasticity and of perfect price inelasticity of demand; (6) the four major determinants of price elasticity of demand; and (7) the practical application of the concept to many economic issues.

When you have become thoroughly acquainted with the concept of price elasticity of demand, you will find that you have very little trouble understanding the **price elasticity of supply.** The transition requires no more than the substitution of the words "quantity supplied" for the words "quantity demanded." You should concentrate your attention on the meaning of price elasticity of supply and how it is affected by time. Several examples are provided to show how it affects the prices of many products.

The chapter also introduces you to two other elasticity concepts. The **cross elasticity of demand** measures the sensitivity of a change in the quantity demanded for one product due to a change in the price of another product. This concept is especially important in identifying whether two goods are substitutes to each other, complements to each other, or independent of each other. The **income elasticity of demand** assesses the change in the quantity demanded of a product resulting from a change in consumer incomes. It is useful for categorizing goods as normal or inferior. For normal goods, as income increases, the demand for them increases, whereas for inferior goods as income increases, the demand for them decreases.

So elasticity as presented in this chapter is all about the responsiveness of changes in quantity to a change in price or income. Understanding this concept will be useful for answering many questions about demand and supply.

■ CHECKLIST

When you have studied this chapter you should be able to

☐ Describe the concept of the price elasticity of demand.
☐ Compute the coefficient for the price when given the demand data.
☐ State the midpoint formula for price elasticity of demand and explain how it refines the original formula for price elasticity.
☐ State two reasons why the formula for price elasticity of demand uses percentages rather than absolute amounts in measuring consumer responsiveness.
☐ Explain the meaning of elastic, inelastic, and unit elastic as they relate to demand.
☐ Describe the concepts of perfectly elastic demand and perfectly inelastic demand and illustrate them with graphs.
☐ Apply the total-revenue test to determine whether demand is elastic, inelastic, or unit-elastic.
☐ Describe the relationship between price elasticity of demand and the price range for most demand curves.
☐ Explain why the slope of the demand curve is not a sound basis for judging price elasticity.
☐ Illustrate graphically the relationship between price elasticity of demand and total revenue.
☐ List the four major determinants of the price elasticity of demand, and explain how each determinant affects price elasticity.
☐ Describe several applications of the concept of price elasticity of demand.
☐ Describe the concept of the price elasticity of supply.
☐ Compute the coefficient for the price elasticity of supply when given the relevant data.
☐ Explain the effect of three time periods (market period, short run, and long run) on price elasticity of supply.
☐ Describe several applications of price elasticity of supply.
☐ Describe the concept of the cross elasticity of demand.
☐ Compute the coefficient for the cross elasticity of demand when given relevant data.
☐ Use the cross elasticity of demand to categorize substitute goods, complementary goods, and independent goods.
☐ Give applications of cross elasticity of demand.
☐ Describe the concepts of the income elasticity of demand.
☐ Compute the coefficient for the income elasticity of demand when given relevant data.
☐ Use the income elasticity of demand to categorize goods as normal or inferior.
☐ Provide some insights using the concept of income elasticity.
☐ Use the concept of elasticity of demand to explain why different consumers pay different prices (*Last Word*).

■ CHAPTER OUTLINE

1. ***Price elasticity of demand*** is a measure of the responsiveness or sensitivity of quantity demanded to changes in the price of a product. When quantity demanded is relatively responsive to a price change, demand is said to be ***elastic.*** When quantity demanded is relatively unresponsive to a price change, demand is said to be ***inelastic.***

a. The degree of elasticity can be measured by using a formula to compute the elasticity coefficient. E_d = percentage change in quantity demanded of product X *divided by* the percentage change in the price of product X.

(1) A ***midpoint formula*** calculates price elasticity across a price and quantity range to overcome the problem of selecting the reference points for the price range and the quantity range. In this formula, the *average* of the two quantities and the *average* of the two prices are used as reference points. This formula can be done in three steps: (a) calculate the change in quantity divided by the average of the two quantities; (b) calculate the change in price divided by the average of the two prices; (c) divide the quantity result from (a) by the price result from (b). For example, if the price falls from $5 to $4 while the quantity demanded rises from 10 units to 20 units, then using the midpoint formula, the price elasticity of demand is: (a) [10 − 20] divided by [(10 + 20)/2] = .67; (b) [(5 − 4) divided by [(5 + 4)/2] = .22; (c) thus .67 divided by .22 means that E_d is approximately equal to 3.

(2) Economists use percentages rather than absolute amounts in measuring responsiveness because with absolute amounts the choice of units or scale can arbitrarily affect the perception of responsiveness.

(3) The price elasticity of demand coefficient is a negative number (has a minus sign) because price and quantity demanded are inversely related. Economists ignore the minus sign in front of the coefficient and focus their attention on its absolute value.

b. The coefficient of price elasticity has several interpretations.

(1) ***Elastic demand*** occurs when the percentage change in quantity demanded is greater than the percentage change in price. The elasticity coefficient is greater than 1.

(2) ***Inelastic demand*** occurs when the percentage change in quantity demanded is less than the percentage change in price. The elasticity coefficient is less than 1.

(3) ***Unit elasticity*** occurs when the percentage change in quantity demanded is equal to the percentage change in price. The elasticity coefficient is equal to 1.

(4) ***Perfectly inelastic demand*** means that a change in price results in no change in quantity demanded of a product, whereas ***perfectly elastic demand*** means that a small change in price causes buyers to purchase all they desire of a product.

c. ***Total revenue (TR)*** changes when price changes. The ***total-revenue test*** shows that when demand is

(1) *elastic,* a decrease in price will increase total revenue and an increase in price will decrease total revenue.

(2) *inelastic,* a decrease in price will decrease total revenue and an increase in price will increase total revenue.

(3) *unit-elastic,* an increase or decrease in price will not affect total revenue.

d. Note several points about the graph of a linear demand curve and price elasticity of demand.

(1) It is not the same at all prices. Demand is typically elastic at higher prices and inelastic at lower prices.

(2) It cannot be judged from the slope of the demand curve.

e. The relationship between price elasticity of demand and total revenue can be shown by graphing the demand curve and the total-revenue curve, one above the other. In this case, the horizontal axis for each graph uses the same quantity scale. The vertical axis for demand represents price. The vertical axis for the total-revenue graph measures total revenue.

(1) When demand is price elastic, as price declines and quantity increases along the demand curve, total revenue increases in the total-revenue graph.

(2) Conversely, when demand is price inelastic, as price declines and quantity increases along the demand curve, total revenue decreases.

(3) When demand is unit-elastic, as price and quantity change along the demand curve, total revenue remains the same.

f. The price elasticity of demand for a product depends on four determinants.

(1) The number of good substitutes for the product. The more substitute products that are available for a product, the greater the price elasticity of demand for the product.

(2) Its relative importance in the consumer's budget. The higher the price of product relative to consumers' incomes, the greater the price elasticity of demand.

(3) Whether it is a necessity or a luxury. Luxuries typically have a greater price elasticity of demand than necessities.

(4) The period of time under consideration. The longer the time period, the greater the elasticity of demand for a product.

g. Price elasticity of demand has practical applications to public policy and business decisions. The concept is relevant to bumper crops in agriculture, excise taxes, and the decriminalization of illegal drugs.

2. ***Price elasticity of supply*** is a measure of the sensitivity of quantity supplied to changes in the price of a product. Both the general formula and the midpoint formula for price elasticity of supply are similar to those for the price elasticity of demand, but "quantity supplied" replaces "quantity demanded." This means that the price elasticity of supply is the percentage change in quantity supplied of a product divided by its percentage change in the price of the product. There is a midpoint formula that is an average of quantities and prices and is used for calculating the elasticity of supply across quantity or price ranges. The price elasticity of supply depends primarily on the amount of time sellers have to adjust to a price change. The easier and faster suppliers can respond to changes in price, the greater the price elasticity of supply.

a. In the ***market period,*** there is too little time for producers to change output in response to a change in price. As a consequence supply is perfectly inelastic. Graphically, this means that the supply curve is vertical at that market level of output.

b. In the ***short run,*** producers have less flexibility to change output in response to a change in price because they have fixed inputs that they cannot change. They have only a limited control over the range in which they can vary their output. As a consequence, supply is *price inelastic* in the short run.

c. In the ***long run,*** producers can make adjustments to all inputs to vary production. As a consequence, supply is *price elastic* in the long run. There is no total-revenue test for price elasticity of supply because price and total revenue move in the same direction regardless of the degree of price elasticity of supply.

d. Price elasticity of supply has many practical applications for explaining price volatility. The concept is relevant to the pricing of antiques and gold, for which the supply is perfectly inelastic.

3. Two other elasticity concepts are important.

a. The ***cross elasticity of demand*** measures the degree to which the quantity demanded of one product is affected by a change in the price of another product. Cross elasticities of demand are

(1) positive for products that are substitutes;

(2) negative for products that are complements; and

(3) zero or near zero for products that are unrelated or independent.

b. The ***income elasticity of demand*** measures the effect of a change in income on the quantity demanded of a product. Income elasticities of demand are

(1) positive for normal or superior products, which means that more of them are demanded as income rises; and

(2) negative for inferior products, which means that less of them are demanded as income rises.

4. (*Last Word*). There are many examples of dual or multiple pricing of products. The main reason for the differences is differences in the price elasticity of demand among groups. Business travelers have a more inelastic demand for travel than leisure travelers and thus can be charged more for an airline ticket. Prices for children are often lower than prices for adults for the same service (for example, movie tickets or restaurant meals) because children have more elastic demand for the service. Low-income groups have a more elastic demand for higher education than high-income groups, so high-income groups are charged the full tuition price and lower-income groups get more financial aid to offset the tuition price.

■ HINTS AND TIPS

1. This chapter is an extension of the material presented in Chapter 3. Be sure you thoroughly read and study Chapter 3 again before you read and do the self-test exercises for this chapter.

2. You should **not judge** the price elasticity of demand based on the slope of the demand curve unless it is horizontal (*perfectly elastic*) or vertical (*perfectly inelastic*). Remember that elasticity varies from elastic to inelastic along a down-sloping, linear demand curve. The price elasticity equals 1 at the midpoint of a down-sloping linear demand curve.

3. Master the **total-revenue test** for assessing the price elasticity of demand (review Table 4.2). For many problems, the total-revenue test is easier to use than the midpoint formula for identifying the type of elasticity (elastic, inelastic, unit), and the test has many practical applications.

4. Do not just memorize the elasticity formulas in this chapter. Instead, work on understanding what they mean and how they are used for economic decisions. The elasticity formulas simply measure the *responsiveness* of a percentage change in *quantity* to a percentage change in some other characteristic (price or income). The elasticity formulas each have a similar structure: A percentage change in some type of *quantity* (demanded, supplied) is divided by a percentage change in the other variable. The price elasticity of demand measures the responsiveness of a percentage change in *quantity demanded* for a product to a percentage change in its *price.* The cross elasticity of demand measures the percentage change in the *quantity demanded of product X* to a percentage change in the *price of product Y.* The income elasticity of demand is the percentage change in *quantity demanded* for a product to a percentage change in *income.* The price elasticity of supply is the percentage change in the *quantity supplied* of a product to a percentage change in its price.

■ IMPORTANT TERMS

price elasticity of demand	**total-revenue test**
midpoint formula	**price elasticity of supply**
elastic demand	**market period**
inelastic demand	**short run**
unit elasticity	**long run**
perfectly inelastic demand	**cross elasticity of demand**
perfectly elastic demand	**income elasticity of demand**
total revenue	

SELF-TEST

■ FILL-IN QUESTIONS

1. If a relatively large change in price results in a relatively small change in quantity demanded, demand is (elastic, inelastic) _______________. If a relatively small change in price results in a relatively large change in quantity demanded, demand is (elastic, inelastic) _______________.

2. The midpoint formula for the price elasticity of demand uses the (total, average) ________________ of the two quantities as a reference point in calculating the percentage change in quantity and the (total, average) ________________ of the two prices as a reference point in calculating the percentage change in price.

3. The price elasticity formula is based on (absolute amounts, percentages) ________________ because it avoids the problems caused by the arbitrary choice of units and permits meaningful comparisons of consumer (responsiveness, incomes) ________________ to changes in the prices of different products.

4. If a change in price causes no change in quantity demanded, demand is perfectly (elastic, inelastic) ________________ and the demand curve is (horizontal, vertical) ________________. If an extremely small change in price causes an extremely large change in quantity demanded, demand is perfectly (elastic, inelastic) ________________ and the demand curve is (horizontal, vertical) ________________.

5. Two characteristics of the price elasticity of a linear demand curve are that elasticity (is constant, varies) ________________ over the different price ranges, and that the slope is (a sound, an unsound) ________________ basis for judging its elasticity.

6. Assume that the price of a product declines in cases a, b, and c.

a. When demand is inelastic, the loss of revenue due to the lower price is (less, greater) ________________ than the gain in revenue due to the greater quantity demanded.

b. When demand is elastic, the loss of revenue due to the lower price is (less, greater) ________________ than the gain in revenue due to the greater quantity demanded.

c. When demand is unit-elastic, the loss of revenue due to the lower price (exceeds, is equal to) ________________ the gain in revenue due to the greater quantity demanded.

7. Complete the following summary table.

If demand is	The elasticity coefficient is	If price rises, total revenue will	If price falls, total revenue will
Elastic	_____	_____	_____
Inelastic	_____	_____	_____
Unit-elastic	_____	_____	_____

8. What are the four most important determinants of the price elasticity of demand?

a. ________________

b. ________________

c. ________________

d. ________________

9. The price elasticity of demand will tend to be greater when the number of substitute goods that are available for the product is (larger, smaller) ________________.

10. The price elasticity of demand will tend to be greater when the price of the product relative to consumers' income is (lower, higher) ________________.

11. The price elasticity of demand will tend to be greater when a product is considered to be a (necessity, luxury) ________________.

12. The price elasticity of demand will tend to be greater when the time period under consideration for a change in quantity is (shorter, longer) ________________.

13. The demand for most farm products is highly (elastic, inelastic) ________________, which means that large crop yields will most likely (increase, decrease) ________________ the total revenue of farmers. Governments often tax products such as liquor, gasoline, and cigarettes because the price elasticity of the demand is (elastic, inelastic) ________________. A higher tax on such products will (increase, decrease) ________________ tax revenue.

14. The price elasticity of supply measures the percentage change in (price, quantity supplied) ________________ divided by the percentage change in ________________. The most important factor affecting the price elasticity of supply is (revenue, time) ________________. It is easier to shift resources to alternative uses when there is (more, less) ________________ time.

15. In the market period, the price elasticity of supply will be perfectly (elastic, inelastic) ________________ and the supply curve will be (horizontal, vertical) ________________. Typically, in the short run the price elasticity of supply is (more, less) ________________ elastic but in the long run the price elasticity of supply is ________________ elastic.

16. There is a total-revenue test for the elasticity of (demand, supply) ________________. There is no total-revenue test for the elasticity of (demand, supply) ________________ because regardless of the degree of elasticity, price and total revenue are (directly, indirectly) ________________ related.

17. The measure of the sensitivity of the consumption of one product given a change in the price of another product is the (cross, income) ________________ elasticity of demand, while the measure of the responsiveness of consumer purchases to changes in income is the ______________ elasticity of demand.

18. When the cross elasticity of demand is positive, two products are (complements, substitutes) ______________, but when the cross elasticity of demand is negative, they are ______________.

19. When a percentage change in the price of one product has no effect on another product, then the cross elasticity of demand will be (zero, one) ______________ and the two products would be classified as being (dependent, independent) ______________.

20. If consumers increase purchases of a product as consumer incomes increase, then a good is classified as (inferior, normal) ______________, but if consumers decrease purchases of a product as consumer incomes increase, then a good is classified as ______________.

■ TRUE–FALSE QUESTIONS

Circle T if the statement is true, F if it is false.

1. If the percentage change in price is greater than the percentage change in quantity demanded, the price elasticity coefficient is greater than 1. **T F**

2. If the quantity demanded for a product increases from 100 to 150 units when the price decreases from $14 to $10, using the midpoint formula, the price elasticity of demand for this product in this price range is 1.2. **T F**

3. A product with a price elasticity of demand equal to 1.5 is described as price inelastic. **T F**

4. If the price of a product increases from $5 to $6 and the quantity demanded decreases from 45 to 25, then according to the total-revenue test, the product is price inelastic in this price range. **T F**

5. Total revenue will not change when price changes if the price elasticity of demand is unitary. **T F**

6. When the absolute value of the price elasticity coefficient is greater than 1 and the price of the product decreases, then the total revenue will increase. **T F**

7. The flatness or steepness of a demand curve is based on absolute changes in price and quantity, while elasticity is based on relative or percentage changes in price and quantity. **T F**

8. Demand tends to be inelastic at higher prices and elastic at lower prices along a down-sloping linear demand curve. **T F**

9. Price elasticity of demand and the slope of the demand curve are two different things. **T F**

10. In general, the larger the number of substitute goods that are available, the less the price elasticity of demand. **T F**

11. Other things equal, the higher the price of a good relative to consumers' incomes, the greater the price elasticity of demand. **T F**

12. Other things equal, the higher the price of a good relative to the longer the time period the purchase is considered, the greater the price elasticity of demand. **T F**

13. The more that a good is considered to be a "luxury" rather than a "necessity," the less is the price elasticity of demand. **T F**

14. The demand for most agricultural products is price inelastic. Consequently, an increase in supply will reduce the total income of producers of agricultural products. **T F**

15. A state government seeking to increase its excise-tax revenues is more likely to increase the tax rate on restaurant meals than on gasoline. **T F**

16. The degree of price elasticity of supply depends on how easily and quickly producers can shift resources between alternative uses. **T F**

17. If an increase in product price results in no change in the quantity supplied, supply is perfectly elastic. **T F**

18. The market period is a time so short that producers cannot respond to a change in demand and price. **T F**

19. The price elasticity of supply will tend to be more elastic in the long run. **T F**

20. There is a total revenue test for the elasticity of supply. **T F**

21. Cross elasticity of demand is measured by the percentage change in quantity demanded over the percentage change in income. **T F**

22. For a substitute product, the coefficient of the cross elasticity of demand is positive. **T F**

23. Two products are considered to be independent or unrelated when the cross elasticity of demand is zero. **T F**

24. The degree to which consumers respond to a change in their incomes by buying more or less of a particular product is measured by the income elasticity of demand. **T F**

25. Inferior goods have a positive income elasticity of demand. **T F**

■ MULTIPLE-CHOICE QUESTIONS

Circle the letter that corresponds to the best answer.

1. If, when the price of a product rises from $1.50 to $2, the quantity demanded of the product decreases from 1000 to 900, the price elasticity of demand coefficient, using the midpoint formula, is

(a) 3.00
(b) 2.71
(c) 0.37
(d) 0.33

2. If a 1% fall in the price of a product causes the quantity demanded of the product to increase by 2%, demand is
(a) inelastic
(b) elastic
(c) unit-elastic
(d) perfectly elastic

3. In the following diagram, D_1 is a

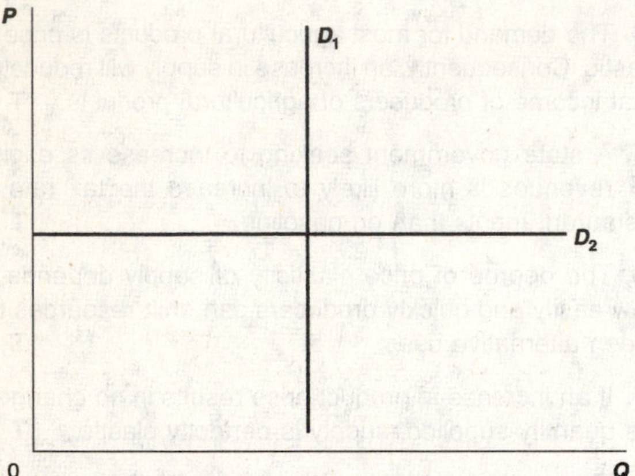

(a) perfectly elastic demand curve
(b) perfectly inelastic demand curve
(c) unit-elastic demand curve
(d) a long-run demand curve

4. Compared to the lower-right portion, the upper-left portion of most demand curves tends to be
(a) more inelastic
(b) more elastic
(c) unit-elastic
(d) perfectly inelastic

5. In which range of the demand schedule is demand price inelastic?

Price	Quantity demanded
$11	50
9	100
7	200
5	300
3	400

(a) $11 – $9
(b) $9 – $7
(c) $7 – $5
(d) $5 – $3

6. If a business increased the price of its product from $7 to $8 when the price elasticity of demand was inelastic, then
(a) total revenues decreased
(b) total revenues increased
(c) total revenues remained unchanged
(d) total revenues were perfectly inelastic

7. You are the sales manager for a pizza company and have been informed that the price elasticity of demand for your most popular pizza is greater than 1. To increase total revenues, you should.
(a) increase the price of the pizza
(b) decrease the price of the pizza
(c) hold pizza prices constant
(d) decrease demand for your pizza

8. Assume Amanda Herman finds that her total spending on compact discs remains the same after the price of compact discs falls, other things equal. Which of the following is true about Amanda's demand for compact discs with this price change?.
(a) It is unit price elastic.
(b) It is perfectly price elastic.
(c) It is perfectly price inelastic.
(d) It increased in response to the price change.

Questions 9, 10, and 11 are based on the following graph.

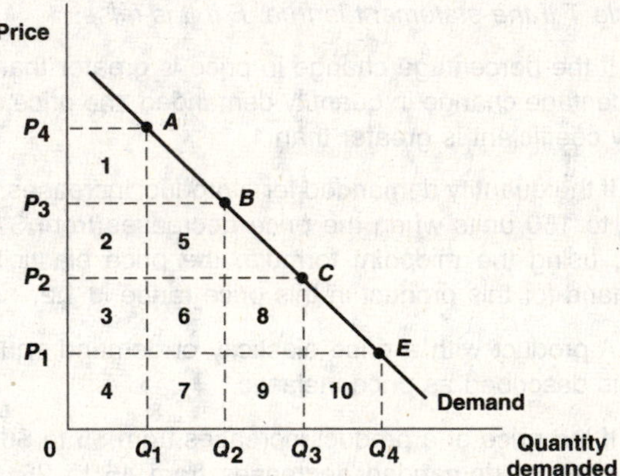

9. If price is P_3, then total revenue is measured by the area
(a) $0P_3CQ_3$
(b) $0P_3BQ_2$
(c) $0P_3BQ_3$
(d) $0P_3CQ_2$

10. If price falls from P_2 to P_1, then in this price range demand is
(a) relatively inelastic because the loss in total revenue (areas 3 + 6 + 8) is greater than the gain in total revenue (area 10)
(b) relatively elastic because the loss in total revenue (areas 3 + 6 + 8) is greater than the gain in total revenue (area 10)
(c) relatively inelastic because the loss in total revenue (area 10) is less than the gain in total revenue (areas 3 + 6 + 8)
(d) relatively inelastic because the loss in total revenue (areas 4 + 7 + 9 + 10) is greater than the gain in total revenue (areas 3 + 6 + 8)

11. As price falls from P_4 to P_3, you know that demand is
(a) elastic because total revenue decreased from $0P_4AQ_1$ to $0P_3BQ_2$
(b) inelastic because total revenue decreased from $0P_3BQ_2$ to $0P_4AQ_1$
(c) elastic because total revenue increased from $0P_4AQ_1$ to $0P_3BQ_2$
(d) inelastic because total revenue decreased from $0P_4AQ_1$ to $0P_3BQ_2$

12. Which is characteristic of a product whose demand is elastic?
(a) The price elasticity coefficient is less than 1.
(b) Total revenue decreases if price decreases.
(c) Buyers are relatively insensitive to price changes.
(d) The percentage change in quantity is greater than the percentage change in price.

13. The demand for Nike basketball shoes is more price elastic than the demand for basketball shoes as a whole. This is best explained by the fact that
(a) Nike basketball shoes are a luxury good, not a necessity
(b) Nike basketball shoes are the best made and widely advertised
(c) there are more complements for Nike basketball shoes than for basketball shoes as a whole
(d) there are more substitutes for Nike basketball shoes than for basketball shoes as a whole

14. Which is characteristic of a good whose demand is inelastic?
(a) There are a large number of good substitutes for the good for consumers.
(b) The buyer spends a small percentage of total income on the good.
(c) The good is regarded by consumers as a luxury.
(d) The period of time for which demand is given is relatively long.

15. From a time perspective, the demand for most products is
(a) less elastic in the short run and unit-elastic in the long run
(b) less elastic in the long run and unit-elastic in the short run
(c) more elastic in the short run than in the long run
(d) more elastic in the long run than in the short run

16. If a 5% fall in the price of a commodity causes quantity supplied to decrease by 8%, supply is
(a) inelastic
(b) unit-elastic
(c) elastic
(d) perfectly inelastic

17. In the following diagram, what is the price elasticity of supply between points *A* and *C* (using the midpoint formula)?.

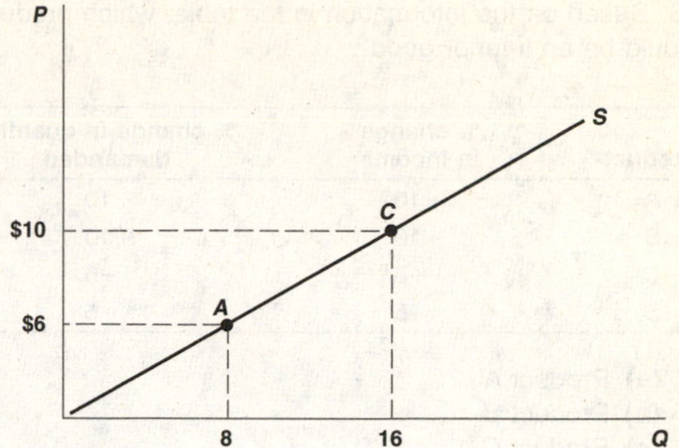

(a) 1.33
(b) 1.67
(c) 1.85
(d) 2.46

18. If supply is inelastic and demand decreases, the total revenue of sellers will
(a) increase
(b) decrease
(c) decrease only if demand is elastic
(d) increase only if demand is inelastic

19. The chief determinant of the price elasticity of supply of a product is
(a) the number of good substitutes the product has
(b) the length of time sellers have to adjust to a change in price
(c) whether the product is a luxury or a necessity
(d) whether the product is a durable or a nondurable good

20. A study shows that the coefficient of the cross elasticity of Coke and Sprite is negative. This information indicates that Coke and Sprite are
(a) normal goods
(b) complementary goods
(c) substitute goods
(d) independent goods

21. If a 5% increase in the price of one good results in a decrease of 2% in the quantity demanded of another good, then it can be concluded that the two goods are
(a) complements
(b) substitutes
(c) independent
(d) normal

22. Most goods can be classified as *normal* goods rather than inferior goods. The definition of a normal good means that
(a) the percentage change in consumer income is greater than the percentage change in price of the normal good
(b) the percentage change in quantity demanded of the normal good is greater than the percentage change in consumer income
(c) as consumer income increases, consumer purchases of a normal good increase
(d) the income elasticity of demand is negative

23. Based on the information in the table, which product would be an inferior good?

Product	% change in income	% change in quantity demanded
A	−10	+10
B	+10	+10
C	+5	+5
D	−5	−5

(a) Product A
(b) Product B
(c) Product C
(d) Product D

24. For which product is the income elasticity of demand most likely to be negative?
(a) automobiles
(b) bus tickets
(c) computers
(d) tennis rackets

25. During a recession, the quantity demanded for which product is likely to be most affected by the decline in consumer incomes?
(a) the buying of ketchup
(b) purchases of toothpaste
(c) the sales of toilet paper
(d) meals bought at restaurants

■ PROBLEMS

1. Complete the following table, using the demand data given, by computing total revenue at each of the seven prices and the six price elasticity coefficients between each of the seven prices, and indicate whether demand is elastic, inelastic, or unit-elastic between each of the seven prices.

Price	Quantity demanded	Total revenue	Elasticity coefficient	Character of demand
$1.00	300	_____		
.90	400	_____	_____	_____
.80	500	_____	_____	_____
.70	600	_____	_____	_____
.60	700	_____	_____	_____
.50	800	_____	_____	_____
.40	900	_____	_____	_____

2. Use the data from the table for this problem. On the *first* of the two following graphs, plot the demand curve (price and quantity demanded) and indicate the elastic, inelastic, and unit-elastic portions of the demand curve. On the *second* graph, plot the total revenue on the vertical axis and the quantity demanded on the horizontal axis. (*Note:* The scale for quantity demanded that you plot on the horizontal axis of each graph should be the same.)

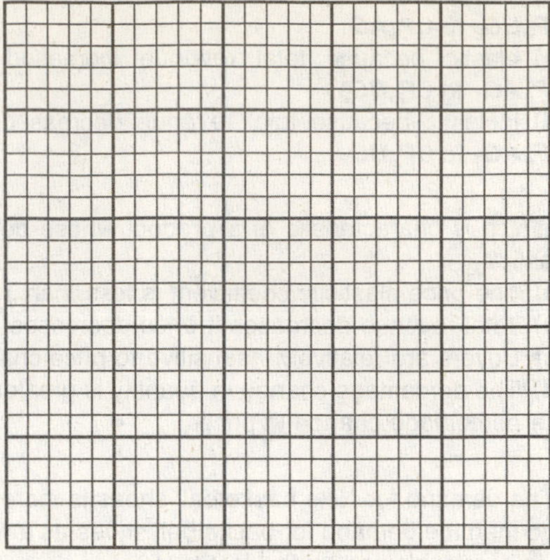

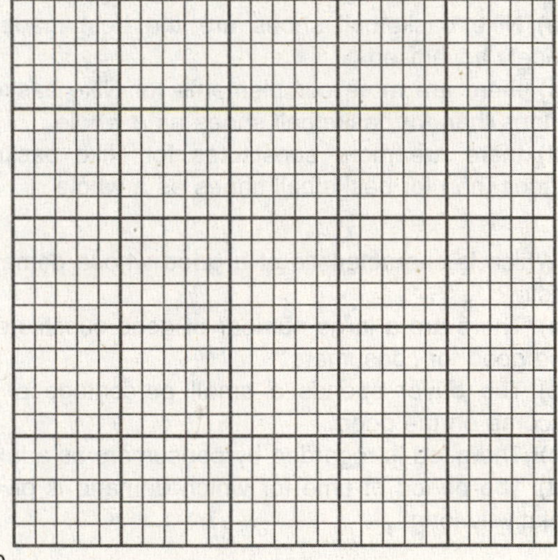

a. As price decreases from $1.00 to $0.70, demand is (elastic, inelastic, unit-elastic) ____________ and total revenue (increases, decreases, remains the same) ____________.

b. As price decreases from $0.70 to $0.60, demand is (elastic, inelastic, unit-elastic) ____________ and total revenue (increases, decreases, remains the same) ____________.

c. As price decreases from $0.60 to $0.40, demand is (elastic, inelastic, unit-elastic) ____________ and total revenue (increases, decreases, remains the same) ____________.

3. Using the supply data in the following schedule, complete the table by computing the six price elasticity of supply coefficients between each of the seven prices, and indicate whether supply is elastic, inelastic, or unit-elastic.

Price	Quantity demanded	Elasticity coefficient	Character of supply
$1.00	800		
.90	700	____	____
.80	600	____	____
.70	500	____	____
.60	400	____	____
.50	300	____	____
.40	200	____	____

4. The following graph shows three different supply curves (S_1, S_2, and S_3) for a product bought and sold in a competitive market.

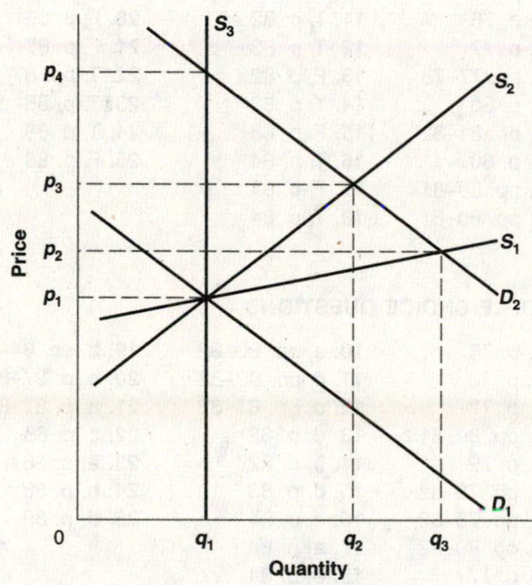

a. The supply curve for the

(1) market period is the one labeled ____________.

(2) short run is the one labeled ____________.

(3) long run is the one labeled ____________.

b. No matter what the period of time under consideration, if the demand for the product were D_1, the equilibrium price of the product would be ____________ and the equilibrium quantity would be ____________.

(1) If demand were to increase to D_2 in the market period the equilibrium price would increase to ____________ and the equilibrium quantity would be ____________.

(2) In the short run the price of the product would increase to ____________ and the quantity would increase to ____________.

(3) In the long run the price of the product would be ____________ and the quantity would be ____________.

c. The longer the period of time allowed to sellers to adjust their outputs the (more, less) ____________ elastic is the supply of the product.

d. The more elastic the supply of a product, the (greater, less) ____________ the effect on equilibrium price and the ____________ the effect on equilibrium quantity of an increase in demand.

5. For the following three cases, use a midpoint formula to calculate the coefficient for the cross elasticity of demand and identify the relationship between the two goods (complement, substitute, or independent).

a. The quantity demanded for good A increases from 300 to 400 as the price of good B increases from $1 to $2.

Coefficient: ________ Relationship: ________

b. The quantity demanded for good J decreases from 2000 to 1500 as the price of good K increases from $10 to $15.

Coefficient: ________ Relationship: ________

c. The quantity demanded for good X increases from 100 to 101 units as the price of good Y increases from $8 to $15.

Coefficient: ________ Relationship: ________

6. Use the information in the following table to identify the income characteristic of each product A–E using the following labels: **N** = normal (or superior), **I** = inferior.

Product	% change in income	% change in quantity demanded	Income type (N or I)
A	10	10	____
B	1	15	____
C	5	−12	____
D	5	−2	____
E	10	1	____

■ SHORT ANSWER AND ESSAY QUESTIONS

1. Define and explain the price elasticity of demand in terms of the relationship between the relative (percentage) change in quantity demanded and the relative (percentage) change in price. Use the elasticity coefficient in your explanation.

2. What is meant by perfectly elastic demand? By perfectly inelastic demand? What does the demand curve look like when demand is perfectly elastic and when it is perfectly inelastic?.

3. Demand seldom has the same elasticity at all prices. What is the relationship between the price of most products and the price elasticity of demand for them?

4. What is the relationship—if there is one—between the price elasticity of demand and the slope of the demand curve?

5. When the price of a product declines, the quantity demanded of it increases. When demand is elastic, total revenue is greater at the lower price, but when demand is inelastic, total revenue is smaller. Explain why total revenue will sometimes increase and why it will sometimes decrease.

6. Explain the effect of the number of substitutes on the price elasticity of demand.

7. Why does the price elasticity of demand differ based on the price of a good as a proportion of household income? Give examples.

8. Is the quantity demanded for necessities more or less responsive to a change in price? Explain using examples.

9. What role does time play in affecting the elasticity of demand?

10. How do opponents of the decriminalization of illegal drugs use elasticity to make their arguments?

11. Explain what determines the price elasticity of supply of an economic good or service.

12. Why is there no total-revenue test for the elasticity of supply?

13. Discuss the supply and demand conditions for antiques. Why are antique prices so high?

14. Use the concepts of the elasticity of supply to explain the volatility of gold prices.

15. How can goods be classified as complementary, substitute, or independent? On what basis is this judgment made?

16. Explain why knowledge of the cross elasticity of demand is important to business.

17. Give an example showing how the government implicitly uses the idea of cross elasticity of demand in its policy-making.

18. Discuss the relationship between the quantity demand for a product and how that quantity responds to a change in income.

19. Supply definitions of a normal good and an inferior good. Illustrate each definition with an example.

20. What is an example of insights that income elasticity of demand coefficients provide about recessions?

ANSWERS

Chapter 4 Elasticity

FILL-IN QUESTIONS

1. inelastic, elastic
2. average, average
3. percentages, responsiveness
4. inelastic, vertical, elastic, horizontal
5. varies, an unsound
6. *a.* greater; *b.* less; *c.* is equal to
7. Elastic: greater than 1, decrease, increase; Inelastic: less than 1, increase, decrease; Unit-elastic: equal to 1, remain constant, remain constant
8. *a.* The number of good substitute products; *b.* The relative importance of the product in the total budget of the buyer; *c.* Whether the good is a necessity or a luxury; *d.* The period of time in which demand is being considered (any order *a–d*)
9. larger
10. higher
11. luxury
12. longer
13. inelastic, decrease, inelastic, increase
14. quantity supplied, price, time, more
15. inelastic, vertical, less, more
16. demand, supply, directly
17. cross, income
18. substitutes, complements
19. zero, independent
20. normal, inferior

TRUE-FALSE QUESTIONS

1. F, p. 76
2. T, p. 76
3. F, p. 77
4. F, pp. 77–78
5. T, p. 80
6. T, pp. 81–82
7. T, p. 80
8. F, pp. 80–81
9. T, pp. 80–81
10. F, pp. 81–82
11. T, p. 82
12. T, p. 83
13. F, p. 82
14. T, p. 83
15. F, p. 83
16. T, p. 84
17. F, p. 84
18. T, p. 84
19. T, p. 85
20. F, p. 85
21. F, p. 87
22. T, pp. 87–88
23. T, p. 88
24. T, p. 88
25. F, p. 88

MULTIPLE-CHOICE QUESTIONS

1. c, p. 76
2. b, p. 76
3. b, p. 77
4. b, pp. 80–81
5. d, p. 79
6. b, pp. 78–82
7. b, pp. 78–82
8. a, pp. 80–82
9. b, p. 77
10. a, pp. 80–82
11. c, pp. 80–82
12. d, pp. 81–82
13. d, p. 82
14. b, p. 82
15. d, p. 83
16. c, p. 84
17. a, p. 84
18. b, p. 84
19. b, pp. 84–85
20. b, p. 87–88
21. a, p. 87–88
22. c, p. 88
23. a, p. 88
24. b, p. 88
25. d, p. 89

PROBLEMS

1. Total revenue: $300, 360, 400, 420, 420, 400, 360; Elasticity coefficient: 2.71, 1.89, 1.36, 1, 0.73, 0.53; Character of demand: elastic, elastic, elastic, unit-elastic, inelastic, inelastic.
2. *a.* elastic, increases; *b.* unit-elastic, remains the same; *c.* inelastic, decreases.
3. Elasticity coefficient: 1.27, 1.31, 1.36, 1.44, 1.57, 1.8; Character of supply: elastic, elastic, elastic, elastic, elastic, elastic
4. *a.* (1) S_3; (2) S_2; (3) S_1; *b.* p_1, q_1, (1) p_4, q_1; (2) p_3, q_2; (3) p_2, q_3; *c.* more; *d.* less, greater
5. *a.* .43, substitute; *b.* –.71, complement; *c.* .02, independent
6. N, N, I, I, N

SHORT ANSWER AND ESSAY QUESTIONS

1. p. 76
2. pp. 77–78
3. pp. 77–78
4. pp. 78–82
5. pp. 78–82
6. pp. 81–82
7. p. 82
8. p. 82
9. p. 83
10. p. 83
11. p. 84
12. p. 85
13. pp. 85–86
14. pp. 86–87
15. pp. 87–88
16. p. 88
17. p. 88
18. p. 88
19. p. 88
20. p. 89

CHAPTER 5

Market Failures: Public Goods and Externalities

This chapter is another extension of supply and demand analysis that you learned about in Chapter 3. In that chapter, the assumption was made that competitive markets were highly efficient and allocated scare resources to their most valued use from society's perspective. Sometimes, however, competitive markets are inefficient with the allocation of society's scarce resources, and therefore competitive markets can end up overproducing, underproducing, or not producing some products. These market inefficiencies are referred to as **market failures,** which are presented as two types in the first major section of the chapter. **Demand-side market failures** arise when demand curves do not take into account the full willingness of consumers to pay for a product. **Supply-side market failures** occur when supply curves do not incorporate the full cost of producing a product.

To better understand these failures, this first major section of the chapter also presents some new concepts that should enhance your understanding of **economic efficiency** because of the focus on the efficient allocation of resources. This extension requires an explanation of **consumer surplus** and **producer surplus.** Consumer surplus is the difference between the maximum price consumers are willing to pay for a product and the actual price. Producer surplus is the difference between the minimum price producers are willing to accept for a product and the actual price. The chapter also revisits the concept of **allocative efficiency** and explains that it is achieved when the combination of consumer and producer surplus is at a maximum.

Government often intervenes in the private economy to correct the market inefficiencies and provide **public goods,** as you will learn in the second major section of the chapter. A private good is characterized by rivalry and excludability, but a public good is characterized by nonrivalry and nonexcludability. These differences mean that the demand curve and supply curve for a public good will differ from those of a private good. You are shown how the demand curve for a public good is constructed and how the optimal allocation of a public good is determined. The demand and supply curves for a public good are related to the collective marginal benefit and cost of providing the good. Governments sometimes use **cost-benefit analysis** to determine if they should undertake some specific action or project. This analysis requires the government to estimate the marginal costs and the marginal benefits of the project, and it can be used to decide when such projects should be expanded, contracted, or eliminated.

The third major topic of the chapter is **externalities,** situations in market transactions that create negative or positive spillovers to third parties that are not involved in the buying or selling transactions. Government may intervene in the market economy to reduce inefficiencies associated with negative externalities or engage in activities that capture more of the benefits from positive externalities. Government often uses direct controls (legislation) and taxes to limit or correct negative externalities. It uses subsidies for consumers or producers to realize more of the benefits from positive externalities. In some cases, where the positive externalities are large, the government may provide the product to people without charge or at a minimal fee. This discussion of government intervention, however, needs to be modified by the Coase theorem, which shows that individual bargaining can be used to settle some externality problems.

To correct for the negative externalities associated with pollution, government can create a market for externality rights that results in an **optimal reduction of an externality,** and this cost-benefit approach will be more effective and efficient than simply banning pollution emissions through legislation. All of this analysis has direct application to the problem of CO_2 emissions and government policies as discussed in the Last Word.

The final brief section of the chapter places government's role in the economy in context. While in theory there may be justification for government intervention in some cases to correct for externalities, in practice finding policies or solutions is subject to a political process that can result in inefficient outcomes.

■ CHECKLIST

When you have studied this chapter you should be able to

☐ Describe the concept of market failure in competitive markets.
☐ Distinguish between a demand-side market failure and a supply-side market failure.
☐ Define consumer surplus and give a graphical example.
☐ Define producer surplus and give a graphical example.
☐ Use consumer surplus and producer surplus to explain how efficiency is achieved in a competitive market.
☐ List the three conditions for achieving allocative efficiency at a quantity level in a competitive market.
☐ Use a supply and demand graph to illustrate efficiency losses (or deadweight losses).

☐ Use the two concepts of rivalry and excludability to describe a private good.
☐ Use the two concepts of nonrivalry and nonexcludability to describe a public good.
☐ Calculate the demand for a public good when given tabular data.
☐ Explain how marginal benefit is reflected in the demand for a public good.
☐ Describe the relationship between marginal cost and the supply of a public good.
☐ Identify on a graph where there is an overallocation, an underallocation, and an optimal quantity of a public good.
☐ Use cost-benefit analysis to determine how many resources a government should allocate to a project.
☐ Discuss the concept of quasi-public goods and why government often provides them.
☐ Describe negative externalities and give an example.
☐ Describe positive externalities and give an example.
☐ Use supply and demand graphs to illustrate how negative externalities and positive externalities affect the allocation of resources.
☐ Discuss two means government uses to achieve economic efficiency when there are negative externalities.
☐ Describe how some externality problems can be solved through individual bargaining based on the Coase theorem.
☐ Describe three government options to correct for the underallocation of resources when positive externalities are large and diffuse.
☐ Explain and illustrate with a graph a rule for determining society's optimal reduction of a negative externality.
☐ Determine the price a government agency should charge in a market for externality rights (e.g., cap-and-trade program for air pollution), when given the data for analysis.
☐ Compare the advantages of a market for externality rights with the policy of direct government controls.
☐ Explain the qualifications to government's role in the economy and the potential for government failure.
☐ Discuss the economics issues involved in the use of a carbon tax and cap-and-trade program (*Last Word*).

■ CHAPTER OUTLINE

1. ***Market failures*** can occur when competitive markets do not allocate the scarce resources to their most valued or best use. These market failures can be of two types.

a. ***Demand-side market failures*** arise when the consumers' full willingness to pay for a good or service is not fully captured in the demand for the good or service. For example, people will not have much incentive to pay to view outdoor fireworks because they can usually still view the fireworks without paying.

b. ***Supply-side market failures*** often result from a situation where a business firm does not have to pay the full cost of producing a product. For example, a power plant that uses coal may not have to pay completely for the emissions it discharges into the atmosphere as part of the cost of producing electricity.

c. When markets are economically efficient, the demand curve in the market must include the full willingness of consumers to pay for the product and the supply curve must capture the full cost of producing the product.

d. ***Consumer surplus*** is the difference between the maximum price consumers are willing to pay for a product and the actual (equilibrium) price paid. Graphically, it is the triangular area bounded by the portion of the vertical axis between the equilibrium price and the demand curve intersection, the portion of the demand curve above the equilibrium price, and the horizontal line at the equilibrium price from the vertical axis to the demand curve. Price and consumer surplus are inversely (negatively) related: Higher prices reduce it and lower prices increase it.

e. ***Producer surplus*** is the difference between the minimum price producers are willing to accept for a product and the actual (equilibrium) price received. Graphically, it is the triangular area bounded by the portion of the vertical axis between the equilibrium price and the supply curve intersection, the portion of the supply curve below the equilibrium price, and the horizontal line at the equilibrium price from the vertical axis to the supply curve. Price and producer surplus are directly (positively) related: Higher prices increase it and lower prices decrease it.

f. The equilibrium quantity shown by the intersection of demand and supply curves reflects *economic efficiency.*

(1) ***Productive efficiency*** is achieved because production costs are minimized at each quantity level of output.

(2) ***Allocative efficiency*** is achieved at the equilibrium quantity of output because three conditions are satisfied: (a) marginal benefit equals marginal cost; (b) maximum willingness to pay equals minimum acceptable price; and, (c) the combination of the consumer and producer surplus is at a maximum.

g. If quantity is less than or greater than the equilibrium quantity or most efficient level, there are ***efficiency losses*** (or ***deadweight losses***) to buyers and sellers. The efficiency losses reduce the maximum possible size of the combined consumer and producer surplus.

2. When market failures arise because a demand curve for a product fails to reflect consumers' willingness to pay, then a public good that has net benefits for society fails to be produced.

a. A ***private good,*** such as a soft drink, is characterized by rivalry and excludability. ***Rivalry*** means that consumption of the product by a buyer eliminates the possibility of consumption of that product by another person. If, for example, one person buys and drinks a soft drink, it is not possible for another person to drink or consume it. ***Excludability*** refers to the ability of the seller to exclude a person from consuming the product if the person does not pay for it. In our example, if a person does not pay for the soft drink, the seller can prevent or exclude the person from obtaining or consuming the soft drink.

b. A ***public good,*** such as national defense or street lighting, is characterized by nonrivalry and nonexcludability. ***Nonrivalry*** means that once a public good is consumed by one person, it is still available for consumption by another person. In the case of street lighting, even if one person enjoys the benefits from having streets illuminated (consumes it), that situation does not diminish or reduce the benefit of the lighting for another person. ***Nonexcludability*** means that those individuals who do not pay for the public good can still obtain the benefits from the public good. For street lighting, once it is provided to one person, other persons will benefit from having it available even if they do not pay for it. These two characteristics create a ***free-rider problem*** where once a producer provides a public good everyone including nonpayers can receive the benefits.

c. The ***optimal quantity of a public good*** can be evaluated using demand and supply analysis.

(1) The ***demand for a public good*** is determined by summing the prices that people are willing to pay collectively for the last unit of the public good at each possible quantity demanded, whereas the demand for a private good is determined by summing the quantities demanded at each possible price. The demand curve for a public good is down-sloping because of the law of diminishing marginal utility.

(2) The ***supply curve of a public good*** is up-sloping because of the law of diminishing returns. The provision of additional units of the public good reflects increasing marginal costs.

(3) The optimal allocation of a public good is determined by the intersection of the supply and demand curves. If the marginal benefit (MB) is greater than the marginal cost (MC) of the public good, there is an underallocation of a public good. If MB is less than MC, there is an overallocation of the public good. Only when the MB = MC is there an optimal allocation of the public good.

d. Government uses ***cost-benefit analysis*** to decide if it should use resources for a project and to determine the total quantity of resources it should devote to a project. The ***marginal cost = marginal benefit rule*** is used to make the decision. Additional resources should be devoted to a project only so long as the marginal benefits to society from the project exceed society's marginal costs. In this case, the total benefits minus the total costs (net benefits) are at a maximum amount.

e. Government also provides ***quasi-public goods*** that have large external benefits. Although these goods (such as education or highways) can be provided by the private market because people can be excluded from obtaining them if they do not pay for them, if left to be provided by the private market, these goods will be underproduced or underconsumed. Government provides access to these quasi-public goods at a reduced cost to encourage their production or consumption and increase the external benefits for society.

f. Government reallocates resources from the private economy (consumption and investment) to produce public and quasi-public goods. This reallocation is achieved by levying taxes on the private economy and using the tax revenues to produce these public and quasi-public goods, thereby changing the composition of the economy's total output.

3. An ***externality*** is a spillover from a market transaction to a third party that did not purchase the product. The spillover to the third party can be either positive or negative depending on the conditions.

a. ***Negative externalities*** occur when the cost for the product does not reflect the full cost of producing it from society's perspective, and therefore a third party who is not part of the private transaction winds up bearing some of the production cost. For example, if a corporation pollutes the environment while making a product and neither the corporation nor the consumer of the product pays for the cost of that pollution, then the pollution cost is an external cost that is borne by third parties, who are the other members of society adversely affected by the pollution. Negative externalities cause supply-side market failures. All the costs associated with the product are not reflected in the supply curve, and therefore, the producer's supply curve lies to the right of the full-cost supply curve. This situation results in an *overallocation* of resources to the production of a product and an efficiency loss.

b. ***Positive externalities*** are outcomes that benefit third parties without these parties paying for the benefits. Health immunizations and education are examples of services that have external benefits to others who do not pay for the services. Positive externalities cause demand-side market failures. All the benefits from the production of the product are not fully reflected in the demand curve, and therefore, the demand curve lies to the left of the full-benefits demand curve. This situation results in an *underallocation* of resources to the production of a product and an efficiency loss.

c. Government can intervene in the private market to increase economic efficiency when there are substantial external costs or benefits from the production of a product.

(1) *Direct controls* use legislation to ban or limit the activities that produce a negative externality. In the ideal case, these direct controls raise the cost of production so that it reflects the full cost, thus shifting the original supply curve to the left and reducing equilibrium output. Examples of such direct controls include federal legislation for clean air or clean water.

(2) *Taxes* can be imposed as another way to reduce or limit negative externalities. Such taxes raise the cost of production, thereby shifting the original supply curve leftward and reducing equilibrium output. Some negative externalities get resolved through private bargaining if the externalities are not widespread and the negotiating costs can be kept low.

(3) *Subsides and government provision* are options that can be used when there are positive externalities from a product. External benefits can be encouraged by subsidizing consumers to purchase a product or by subsidizing producers to make them, such as is done with certain types of health immunizations. When the positive externalities are large, it may make sense from an economic efficiency perspective for the government to provide the product at no cost to the consumer.

d. (Consider This). As shown by Ronald Coase in the ***Coase Theorem,*** some negative or positive externality situations can be addressed through individual or private bargaining and without government intervention.
e. In most cases, the ***optimal reduction of an externality*** is not zero from society's perspective and there is a price to be paid. This condition means that society must consider the marginal benefit and marginal cost of reducing a negative externality.
(1) The equilibrium occurs where the marginal cost to society from reducing the negative externality is just equal to the marginal benefit from reducing the negative externality (MB = MC).
(2) Over time, shifts in the marginal-cost and marginal-benefit curves change the optimal level of externality reduction.
(3) When positive externalities are extremely large, government may decide to provide the good or service.

4. Market failures can be used to justify government interventions in the private economy to encourage or discourage the production and consumption of particular products and increase economic efficiency. However, the expanded economic role of government to correct market failure is conducted in the context of politics. This political process can lead to imperfect and inefficient outcomes.

5. (*Last Word*). There are market-based approaches to externality problems that establish property rights where none existed before. A cap-and-trade program creates a market for property rights to a negative externality. In this program, the government sets a limit for the amount of CO_2 emissions permitted in a region (a cap) and allocates pollution permits to firms in the region based on their typical amount of output and emissions. Then if a firm wanted to expand its output and emissions, it would have to purchase pollution permits from other firms (trade) that wanted to reduce their output and emissions or did not use their limit. A firm would only expand production if the marginal benefit of the additional output was greater than the marginal cost of buying the additional pollution permits. One major problem, however, with this system is the difficulty of monitoring CO_2 emissions by firms and ensuring compliance with permits. As an alternative, many economists have proposed a tax on the use of carbon-based resources such as coal or oil. This alternative would raise the cost of using carbon resources that contribute to pollution and reduce the enforcement costs.

■ HINTS AND TIPS

1. The term "surplus" in this chapter should not be confused with its previous use related to pre-set prices and price floors. What the consumer surplus refers to is the extra utility or satisfaction that consumers get when they do not have to pay the price they were willing to pay and actually pay the lower equilibrium price. The producer surplus arises when producers receive an equilibrium price that is above the minimum price that they consider acceptable to selling the product.

2. Make sure you understand the difference between the demand for public and private goods. The **demand for a private good** is determined by adding the quantities demanded at each possible price. The **demand for a public good** is determined by adding the prices people collectively are willing to pay for the last unit of the public good at each possible quantity demanded.

3. Table 5.5 is important because it summarizes the private actions and government policies taken to correct for negative or positive externalities. The government can influence the allocation of resources in a private market by taking actions that increase or decrease demand or supply.

■ IMPORTANT TERMS

market failures
demand-side market failures
supply-side market failures
consumer surplus
producer surplus
efficiency losses (or deadweight losses)
private goods
rivalry
excludability
public goods
nonrivalry
nonexcludability
free-rider problem
cost-benefit analysis
quasi-public goods
externality
Coase theorem
optimal reduction of an externality

SELF-TEST

■ FILL-IN QUESTIONS

1. When it is impossible to charge consumers what they are willing to pay for a product, the situation that arises is a market failure on the (supply side, demand side) ______________, but when a firm does not have to pay the full cost of producing its output, it often leads to a market failure on the ______________.

2. A consumer surplus is the difference between the actual price and the (minimum, maximum) ______________ price a consumer is (or consumers are) willing to pay for a product. In most markets, consumers individually or collectively gain more total utility or satisfaction when the actual or equilibrium price they have to pay for a product is (less, more) ______________ than what they would have been willing to pay to obtain the product. Consumer surplus and price are (positively, negatively) ______________ related. This means that higher prices (increase, decrease) ______________ consumer surplus and lower prices ______________ it.

3. A producer surplus is the difference between the actual or equilibrium price and the (minimum, maximum)

_________ acceptable price a producer is (or producers are) willing to accept in exchange for a product. In most markets, sellers individually or collectively benefit when they sell their product at an actual or equilibrium price that is (less, more) _________ than what they would have been willing to receive in exchange for the product. Producer surplus and price are (positively, negatively) _________ related. This means that higher prices (increase, decrease) _________ producer surplus and lower prices _________ it.

4. When competition forces producers to use the best techniques and combinations of resources to make a product, then (allocative, productive) _________ efficiency is being achieved. When the correct or optimal quantity of output of a product is being produced relative to the other goods and services, then _________ efficiency is being achieved.

5. Allocative efficiency occurs at quantity levels where marginal benefit is (greater than, less than, equal to) _________ marginal cost, maximum willingness to pay by consumers is _________ the minimum acceptable price for producers, and the combined consumer and producer surplus is at a (minimum, maximum) _________.

6. When there is overproduction of a product, there are efficiency (gains, losses) _________ and when there is underproduction there are efficiency _________. In both cases, the combined consumer and producer surplus is (greater than, less than) _________ the maximum that would occur at the efficient quantity of output.

7. Rivalry means that when one person buys and consumes a product, it (is, is not) _________ available for purchase and consumption by another person. Excludability means that the seller (can, cannot) _________ keep people who do not pay for the product from obtaining its benefits. Rivalry and excludability apply to (private, public) _________ goods.

8. One characteristic of a public good is (rivalry, nonrivalry) _________ and the other characteristic of a public good is (excludability, nonexcludability) _________. A private firm will not find it profitable to produce a public good because there is a (free-rider, principal–agent) _________ problem because once the good is provided, everyone, including those who do not pay for it, can obtain the benefits.

9. With a private good, to compute the market demand you add together the (prices people are willing to pay, quantities demanded) _________ at each possible (price, quantity demanded) _________. With a public good, to compute the collective demand you add together the (prices people are willing to pay, quantities demanded) _________ for the last unit of the public good at each possible (price, quantity demanded) _________.

10. The demand curve slopes downward for a public good because of the law of diminishing marginal (returns, utility) _________; the supply curve for a public good is upsloping because of the law of diminishing _________. The demand curve for a public good is, in essence, a marginal-(benefit, cost) _________ curve; the supply curve for a public good reflects rising marginal _________. The optimal quantity of a public good will be shown by the intersection of the collective demand and supply curves, which means that marginal (benefit, cost) _________ of the last unit equals that unit's marginal _________.

11. In applying cost-benefit analysis, government should use more resources in the production of public goods if the marginal (cost, benefit) _________ from the additional public goods exceeds the marginal _________ that results from having fewer private goods. This rule will determine which plan from a cost-benefit analysis will result in the (maximum, minimum) _________ net benefit to society.

12. To reallocate resources from the production of private goods to the production of public and quasi-public goods, government reduces the demand for private goods by (taxing, subsidizing) _________ consumers and then uses the (profits, tax revenue) _________ to buy public or quasi-public goods.

13. There is a negative externality whenever some of the costs of producing a product spill over to people other than the immediate (seller, buyer) _________ and there is a positive externality when some of the benefits from consuming a product spill over to people other than the immediate _________.

14. When there is a negative externality firms do not pay the full cost of production and therefore their supply curves will increase or shift more to the (left, right) _________ than would be the case if firms paid the full cost of production. When there is a positive externality, consumers do not capture the full benefits of the product and therefore the demand curves will decrease or shift more to the (right, left) _________ than would be the case if all the benefits were captured by the buyers of the product.

15. When there are negative externalities in competitive markets, the result is an (over, under) _________ allocation of resources to the production of the good or service. When there are positive externalities, the result is an (over, under) _________ allocation of resources to the production of the good or service.

16. Government may use direct controls to reduce negative externalities by passing legislation that restricts business activity. When direct controls are imposed, the cost of production will (increase, decrease) ______________, the supply curve will (increase, decrease) ______, and output will ____________.

17. Government also can place taxes on specific products to reduce negative externalities. With these excise taxes, the costs of production will (increase, decrease) ____________, the supply curve will __________, and output will __________.

18. The government may correct for the underallocation of resources where (negative, positive) ________ externalities are large and diffuse. This objective can be achieved by (taxing, subsidizing) __________ buyers or producers and through government (provision, consumption) ________ of a good or service.

19. In the case of positive externalities, the government can give a subsidy to consumers that will increase the (supply, demand) __________ for a product or it can give a subsidy to businesses that will increase the ____________ for the product. In either case, the output of the product will (increase, decrease) __________.

20. Reducing negative externalities comes at a "price" to society, and therefore society must decide how much of a decrease it wants to (buy, sell) "________." Further abatement of a negative externality increases economic efficiency if the marginal cost is (greater than, equal to, less than) ________ the marginal benefit, but it is economically inefficient if the marginal benefit is ________ the marginal cost. The optimal reduction of a negative externality occurs where the society's marginal benefit is (greater than, equal to, less than) ________ society's marginal cost.

■ TRUE–FALSE QUESTIONS

Circle T if the statement is true, F if it is false.

1. Demand-side market failures arise when demand curves do not reflect consumers' full willingness to pay for a product. **T F**

2. If demand and supply reflected all the benefits and costs of producing a product, there would be economic efficiency in the production of the product. **T F**

3. Consumer surplus is the difference between the minimum and maximum price a consumer is willing to pay for a good. **T F**

4. Consumer surplus is a utility surplus that reflects a gain in total utility or satisfaction. **T F**

5. Consumer surplus and price are directly or positively related. **T F**

6. Producer surplus is the difference between the actual price a producer receives for a product and the minimum price the producer would have been willing to accept for the product. **T F**

7. The higher the actual price, the less the amount of producer surplus. **T F**

8. Efficiency losses are increases in the combined consumer and producer surplus. **T F**

9. Private goods are characterized by rivalry and excludability and public goods are characterized by nonrivalry and nonexcludability. **T F**

10. When determining the collective demand for a public good, you add the prices people are willing to pay for the last unit of the public good at each possible quantity demanded. **T F**

11. When the marginal benefit of a public good exceeds the marginal cost, there will be an overallocation of resources to that public good use. **T F**

12. The optimal allocation of a public good is determined by the rule that marginal cost (MC) equals marginal revenue (MR). **T F**

13. An externality is a cost or benefit accruing to an individual or group—a third party—which is external to the market transaction. **T F**

14. In a competitive product market and in the absence of negative externalities, the supply curve reflects the costs of producing the product. **T F**

15. If demand and supply reflected all the benefits and costs of a product, the equilibrium output of a competitive market would be identical with its optimal output. **T F**

16. There is an underallocation of resources to the production of a commodity when negative externalities are present. **T F**

17. One way for government to correct for a negative externality from the production of a product is to increase the demand for the product. **T F**

18. When negative externalities are involved in the production of a product, more resources are allocated to the production of that product and more of the product is produced than is optimal or most efficient. **T F**

19. The Coase theorem suggests that government intervention is required whenever there are negative or positive externalities. **T F**

20. Taxes that are imposed on businesses that create an externality will lower the marginal cost of production and increase supply. **T F**

21. Subsidizing the firms producing goods that provide positive externalities will usually result in a better allocation of resources. **T F**

22. If a society has marginal costs of $10 for pollution abatement and the marginal benefit of pollution abatement is $8, to achieve an optimal amount of the pollution the society should increase the amount of pollution abatement. **T F**

23. Changes in technology or changes in society's attitudes toward pollution can affect the optimal amount of pollution abatement. **T F**

24. One solution to the negative externalities caused by pollution is to create a market for pollution rights in which the negative externalities from pollution are turned into private costs. **T F**

25. Political pressure can make it difficult to find and implement an economically efficient solution to an externality problem. **T F**

■ MULTIPLE-CHOICE QUESTIONS

Circle the letter that corresponds to the best answer.

1. Katie is willing to pay $50 for a product and Tom is willing to pay $40. The actual price that they have to pay is $30. What is the amount of the consumer surplus for Katie and Tom combined?

(a) $30
(b) $40
(c) $50
(d) $60

2. Given the demand curve, the consumer surplus is

(a) increased by higher prices and decreased by lower prices
(b) decreased by higher prices and increased by lower prices
(c) increased by higher prices, but not affected by lower prices
(d) decreased by lower prices, but not affected by higher prices

3. The difference between the actual price that a producer receives (or producers receive) and the minimum acceptable price is producer

(a) cost
(b) wealth
(c) surplus
(d) investment

4. The minimum acceptable price for a product that Juan is willing to receive is $20. It is $15 for Carlos. The actual price they receive is $25. What is the amount of the producer surplus for Juan and Carlos combined?

(a) $10
(b) $15
(c) $20
(d) $25

5. When the combined consumer and producer surplus is at a maximum for a product,

(a) the quantity supplied is greater than the quantity demanded
(b) the market finds alternative ways to ration the product
(c) the market is allocatively efficient
(d) the product is a nonpriced good

6. When the output is greater than the optimal level of output for a product there are efficiency

(a) gains from the underproduction of the product
(b) losses from the underproduction of the product
(c) gains from the overproduction of the product
(d) losses from the overproduction of the product

7. How do public goods differ from private goods? Public goods are characterized by

(a) rivalry and excludability
(b) rivalry and nonexcludability
(c) nonrivalry and excludability
(d) nonrivalry and nonexcludability

8. There is a free-rider problem when people

(a) are willing to pay for what they want
(b) are not willing to pay for what they want
(c) benefit from a good without paying for its cost
(d) want to buy more than is available for purchase in the market

Answer Questions 9, 10, 11, and 12 on the basis of the following information for a public good. $\boldsymbol{P_1}$ *and* $\boldsymbol{P_2}$ *represent the prices individuals 1 and 2, the only two people in the society, are willing to pay for the last unit of a public good.* $\boldsymbol{P_c}$ *represents the price (or collective willingness to pay) for a public good, and* $\boldsymbol{Q_s}$ *represents the quantity supplied of the public good at those prices.*

Q_d	P_1	P_2	P_c	Q_s
1	$4	$5	$9	5
2	3	4	7	4
3	2	3	5	3
4	1	2	3	2
5	0	1	1	1

9. What amount is this society willing to pay for the first unit of the public good?

(a) $10
(b) $9
(c) $8
(d) $7

10. What amount is this society willing to pay for the third unit of the public good?

(a) $5
(b) $6
(c) $7
(d) $8

11. Given the supply curve Q_s, the optimal price and quantity of the public good in this society will be

(a) $9 and 5 units
(b) $5 and 3 units
(c) $5 and 4 units
(d) $3 and 2 units

12. If this good were a private good instead of a public good, the total quantity demanded at the $4 price would be

(a) 3 units
(b) 4 units
(c) 5 units
(d) 6 units

Answer Questions 13, 14, and 15 for a public good on the basis of the following graph.

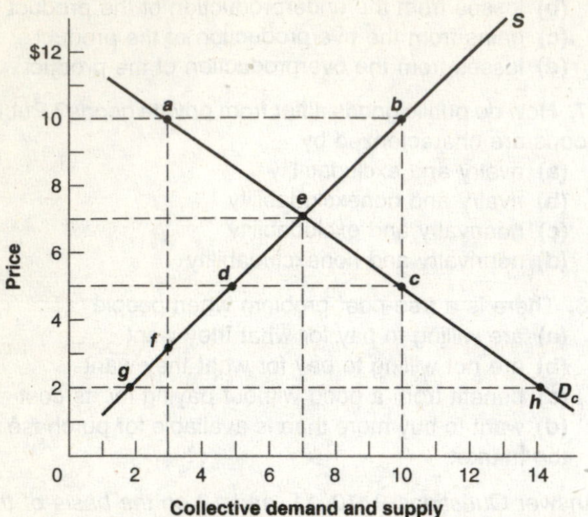

13. Where the marginal benefits equal the collective marginal costs is represented by point

(a) ***b***
(b) ***c***
(c) ***d***
(d) ***e***

14. Which line segment would indicate the amount by which the marginal benefit of this public good is less than the marginal cost?

(a) ***ab***
(b) ***bc***
(c) ***fa***
(d) ***gh***

15. If 3 units of this public good are produced, the marginal

(a) cost of $10 is greater than the marginal benefit of $3
(b) cost of $10 is greater than the marginal benefit of $5
(c) benefit of $10 is greater than the marginal cost of $5
(d) benefit of $10 is greater than the marginal cost of $3

16. Assume that a government is considering a new antipollution program and may choose to include in this program any number of four different projects. The marginal cost and the marginal benefits of each of the four projects are given in the table below.

Project	Marginal cost	Marginal benefit
#1	$ 2 million	$ 5 million
#2	5 million	7 million
#3	10 million	9 million
#4	20 million	15 million

What total amount should this government spend on the antipollution program?

(a) $2 million
(b) $7 million
(c) $17 million
(d) $37 million

17. When the production and consumption of a product entail negative externalities, a competitive product market results in a(n)

(a) underallocation of resources to the product
(b) overallocation of resources to the product
(c) optimal allocation of resources to the product
(d) higher price for the product

18. A positive externality in the production of some product will result in

(a) overproduction
(b) underproduction
(c) the optimal level of production if consumers are price takers
(d) the optimal level of production if consumers are utility maximizers

Use the following graph which shows the supply and demand for a product to answer Questions 19, 20, and 21.

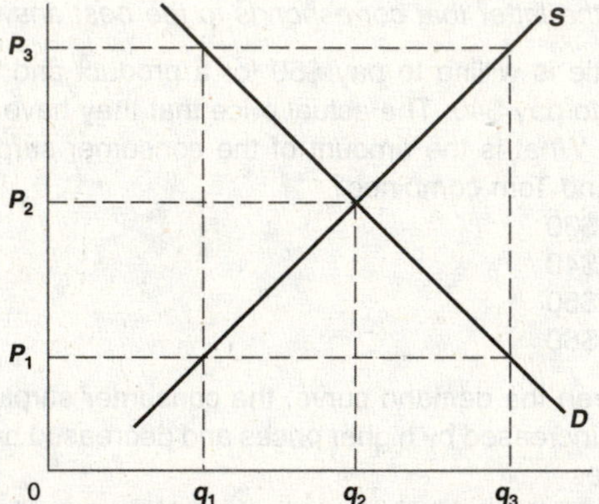

19. If there are neither negative nor positive externalities, the output that results in the optimal allocation of resources to the production of this product is

(a) q_1
(b) q_2
(c) q_3
(d) 0

20. If the market for a product was in equilibrium at output level q_2 but the optimal level of output for society was at q_1, the government could correct for this

(a) negative externality with a subsidy to consumers
(b) negative externality with a subsidy to producers
(c) positive externality with a subsidy to producers
(d) negative externality with a tax on producers

21. If the market for a product was in equilibrium at output level q_2 but the optimal level of output for society was at q_3, the government could correct for this

(a) overallocation of resources by direct controls on consumers
(b) underallocation of resources through taxes on producers
(c) overallocation of resources through a market for externality rights
(d) underallocation of resources through subsidies to producers

22. How does government try to capture more of the benefits for society when there is a positive externality?

(a) by taxing consumers
(b) by taxing producers
(c) by subsidizing producers
(d) by ignoring the free-rider problem

Use the following table to answer Questions 23, 24, and 25. The data in the table show the marginal costs and marginal benefits to a city for five different levels of pollution abatement.

Quantity of pollution abatement	Marginal cost	Marginal benefit
500 tons	$500,000	$100,000
400 tons	300,000	150,000
300 tons	200,000	200,000
200 tons	100,000	300,000
100 tons	50,000	400,000

23. If the city seeks an optimal reduction of the externality, it will select how many tons of pollution abatement?
(a) 100
(b) 300
(c) 400
(d) 500

24. If the marginal benefit of pollution abatement increased by $150,000 at each level because of the community's desire to attract more firms, the optimal level of pollution abatement in tons would be
(a) 200
(b) 300
(c) 400
(d) 500

25. What would cause the optimal level of pollution abatement to be 200 tons?
(a) technological improvement in production that decreases marginal costs by $150,000 at each level
(b) an increase in the health risk from this pollution that increases marginal benefits by $200,000 at each level
(c) the need to replace old pollution monitoring equipment with new equipment that increases marginal costs by $200,000 at each level
(d) reduction in the public demand for pollution control that decreases marginal benefits by $100,000 at each level

■ PROBLEMS

1. Given the following information, calculate the consumer surplus for each individual A to F.

(1) Person	(2) Maximum price willing to pay	(3) Actual price (equilibrium price)	(4) Consumer surplus
A	$25	$12	____
B	23	12	____
C	18	12	____
D	16	12	____
E	13	12	____
F	12	12	____

2. Given the following information, calculate the producer surplus for each producer A to F.

(1) Producers	(2) Minimum acceptable price	(3) Actual price (equilibrium price)	(4) Producer surplus
A	$4	$12	____
B	5	12	____
C	7	12	____
D	9	12	____
E	10	12	____
F	12	12	____

3. Answer this question based on the following graph showing the market supply and demand for a product. Assume that the output level is Q_1.

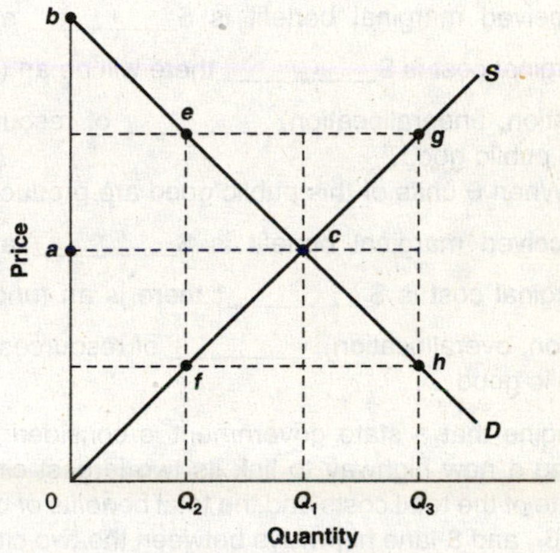

a. The area of consumer surplus would be shown by the area ____________.
b. The area of producer surplus would be shown by the area ____________.
c. The area that maximizes the combined consumer and producer surplus is ____________.
d. If the output level is now Q_2, then there are efficiency losses shown by area ____________.
e. If the output level is now Q_3, then there are efficiency losses shown by area ____________.

4. Data on two individuals' preferences for a public good are reflected in the following table. P_1 and P_2 represent the prices individuals 1 and 2, the only two people in the society, are willing to pay for the last unit of the public good.

Quantity	P_1	P_2
1	$6	$6
2	5	5
3	4	4
4	3	3
5	2	2
6	1	1

a. Complete the table below showing the collective demand for the public good in this society.

Q_d	Price	Q_s
1	____	7
2	____	6
3	____	6
4	____	4
5	____	3
6	____	2

b. Given the supply schedule for this public good as shown by the Q_s column, the optimal quantity of this public good is ________ units and the optimal price is $________.

c. When 3 units of this public good are produced, the perceived marginal benefit is $________ and the marginal cost is $________; there will be an (overallocation, underallocation) ________ of resources to this public good.

d. When 6 units of this public good are produced, the perceived marginal benefit is $________ and the marginal cost is $________; there is an (underallocation, overallocation) ________ of resources to this public good.

5. Imagine that a state government is considering constructing a new highway to link its two largest cities. Its estimate of the total costs and the total benefits of building 2-, 4-, 6-, and 8-lane highways between the two cities are shown in the table below. (All figures are in millions of dollars.)

Project	Total cost	Marginal cost	Total benefit	Marginal benefit
No highway	$ 0		$ 0	
2-lane highway	500	$____	650	$____
4-lane highway	680	____	750	____
6-lane highway	760	____	800	____
8-lane highway	860	____	825	____

a. Compute the marginal cost and the marginal benefit of the 2-, 4-, 6-, and 8-lane highways.

b. Will it benefit the state to allocate resources to construct a highway? ________

c. If the state builds a highway,

(1) it should be a ________-lane highway.

(2) the total cost will be $ ________ million.

(3) the total benefit will be $ ________ million.

(4) the *net* benefit will be $ ________ million.

6. The following graph shows the demand and supply curves for a product bought and sold in a competitive market.

a. Assume that there are no negative or positive externalities associated with the production of this product. The optimal level of output would be (Q_1, Q_2, Q_3) ________.

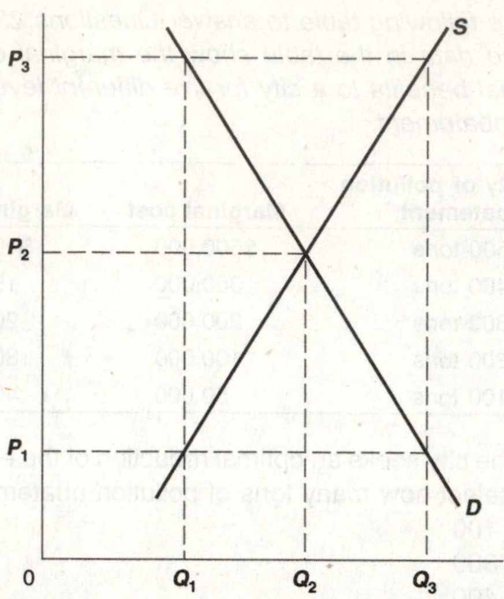

b. Assume that there are negative externalities associated with the cost of production of this product that are not reflected in the optimal output. In this case, the supply curve will shift to the (right, left) ________ and equilibrium level of output would most likely be (Q_1, Q_2, Q_3) ________. There would be an (under, over) ________ allocation of resources to the production of this product. To return to the optimal level of output, government would most likely (tax, subsidize) ________ the producers, which would (decrease, increase) ________ the supply of the product and return the supply curve to its original position at the optimal level of output.

c. Assume that there are positive externalities associated with the production of this product. In this case, the demand curve will shift to the (right, left) ________ and the new equilibrium level of output would most likely be (Q_1, Q_2, Q_3) ________. There would be an (under, over) ________ allocation of resources to the production of this product. To bring about the production of the optimal output for this product, government might (tax, subsidize) ________ the consumers of this product, which would (increase, decrease) ________ the demand of the product and return the demand curve to its original position at the optimal level of output.

7. Assume the atmosphere of a large metropolitan area is able to reabsorb 1500 tons of pollutants per year. The following schedule shows the price polluters would be willing to pay for the right to dispose of 1 ton of pollutants per year and the total quantity of pollutants they would wish to dispose of at each price.

Price (per ton of pollutant) rights	Total quantity of pollutant rights demanded (tons)
$ 0	4000
1000	3500
2000	3000
3000	2500
4000	2000
5000	1500
6000	1000
7000	500

a. If there were no emission fee, polluters would put _______________ tons of pollutants in the air each year, and this quantity of pollutants would exceed the ability of nature to reabsorb them by _______________ tons.

b. To reduce pollution to the capacity of the atmosphere to recycle pollutants, an emission fee of $_______________ per ton should be set.

c. Were this emission fee set, the total emission fees set would be $_______________.

d. Were the quantity of pollution rights demanded at each price to increase by 500 tons, the emission fee could be increased by $_______________ and total emission fees collected would increase by $_______________.

■ SHORT ANSWER AND ESSAY QUESTIONS

1. Explain the difference between demand-side market failures and supply-side market failures. Give several examples of each one.

2. How is the consumer surplus related to utility or satisfaction? Explain, using a supply and demand graph.

3. Define, using a supply and demand graph, the meaning of producer surplus.

4. Use consumer and producer surplus to describe efficiency losses in a competitive market. Provide a supply and demand graph to show such losses.

5. Distinguish between a private and a public good. Include in your answer an explanation of rivalry, excludability, and the free-rider problem.

6. Contrast how you construct the demand curve for a public good with the procedure for constructing the demand curve for a private good using individual demand schedules.

7. Explain the relationship between the marginal cost and benefit of a public good when there is an underallocation, an overallocation, and an optimal allocation of resources for the provision of the public good.

8. Describe benefit–cost analysis, and state the rules used to make decisions from marginal and total perspectives.

9. Why are quasi-public goods provided by government even if they could be produce by the private sector?

10. How are resources reallocated from the private economy to produce public or quasi-public goods?

11. What are externalities? Give examples of positive externalities and negative externalities.

12. How does the existence of negative externalities affect the allocation of resources and the prices of products?

13. Describe what happens in a market in terms of demand, supply, output, and price when there are positive externalities associated with a product.

14. What two basic actions can government take to correct for negative externalities in a market?

15. How can government respond to situations in which there are positive externalities associated with a product and it wants to increase output?

16. Explain why the "Fable of the Bee" is a good reminder that it is a fallacy to assume that government must always get involved to remedy externalities.

17. What rule can society use to determine the optimal level of pollution abatement?

18. How does time change answers about the optimal level of pollution abatement?

19. Discuss the economic issues involved in the use of a cap-and-trade program and the use of a carbon tax to reduce or mitigate the adverse effects from carbon dioxide emissions.

20. Why is it difficult for government to correct for externalities through the political process?

ANSWERS

Chapter 5 Market Failures: Public Goods and Externalities

FILL-IN QUESTIONS

1. demand side, supply side
2. maximum, less, negatively, decrease, increase
3. minimum, more, positively, increase, decrease
4. productive, allocative
5. equal to, equal to, maximum
6. losses, losses, less than
7. is not, can, private
8. nonrivalry, nonexcludability, free-rider
9. quantities demanded, price, prices, quantity demanded
10. utility, returns, benefit, cost, benefit, cost (*either order for last two*)
11. benefit, cost, maximum
12. taxing, tax revenue
13. seller, buyer
14. right, left
15. over, under
16. increase, decrease, decrease
17. increase, decrease, decrease
18. positive, subsidizing, provision
19. demand, supply increase
20. buy, less than, less than, equal to

TRUE-FALSE QUESTIONS

1. T, p. 93
2. T, p. 93
3. F, pp. 93–94
4. T, p. 94
5. F, p. 94
6. T, p. 95
7. F, pp. 95–96
8. F, pp. 98–99
9. T, pp. 99–100
10. T, pp. 101–102
11. F, p. 102
12. F, pp. 103–104
13. T, pp. 104–105
14. T, p.105
15. T, pp. 105–106
16. F, pp. 105–106
17. F, pp. 106–107
18. T, pp. 105–106
19. F, p. 106
20. F, p. 107
21. T, pp. 107–108
22. F, pp. 108–109
23. T, p. 109
24. T, p. 110
25. T, p. 112

MULTIPLE-CHOICE QUESTIONS

1. a, pp. 95–96
2. b, pp. 94–95
3. c, p. 95
4. b, pp. 94–95
5. c, pp. 96–97
6. d, pp. 98–99
7. d, pp. 99–100
8. c, p. 100
9. b, pp. 101–102
10. a, pp. 101–102
11. b, pp. 101–102
12. a, pp. 101–102
13. d, p. 102
14. b, p. 102
15. d, p. 102
16. b, pp. 102–103
17. b, p. 105
18. b, p. 105
19. b, pp. 104–105
20. d, pp. 105–107
21. d, pp. 105–107
22. c, p.107
23. b, pp. 108–109
24. c, pp. 108–109
25. c, pp. 108–109

PROBLEMS

1. 13, 11, 6, 4, 1, 0
2. 8, 7, 5, 3, 2, 0
3. *a.* abc; *b.* 0ac; *c.* 0bc; *d.* efc; *e.* ghc
4. *a.* $12, 10, 8, 6, 4, 2; *b.* 4, 6; *c.* 8, 4, underallocation; *d.* 2, 10, overallocation
5. *a.* Marginal cost: $500, $180, $80, $100; Marginal benefit: $650, $100, $50, $25; *b.* yes; *c.* (1) 2, (2) $500, (3) $650, (4) $150
6. *a.* Q_2; *b.* right, Q_3, over, tax, decrease; *c.* left, Q_1, under, subsidize, increase
7. *a.* 4000, 2500; *b.* 5000; *c.* 7,500,000; *d.* 1000, 1,500,000

SHORT ANSWER AND ESSAY QUESTIONS

1. p. 93
2. pp. 94–95
3. pp. 95–96
4. pp. 96–99
5. pp. 99–100.
6. pp. 101–102
7. pp. 101–102
8. pp. 102–103
9. p. 104
10. p. 104
11. pp. 104–105
12. p. 105
13. pp. 105–106
14. pp. 106–107
15. pp. 107–108
16. p. 106
17. pp. 108–109
18. p. 109
19. p. 110
20. pp. 109, 111

CHAPTER 6

Introduction to Macroeconomics

The purpose of this chapter is to introduce you to **macroeconomics,** which studies the entire economy or its major aspects such as consumption and investment. Macroeconomics is concerned with both short-run fluctuations that create conditions giving rise to an up-and-down **business cycle** and also long-run trends for economic growth that bring rising living standards.

The monitoring of the macro economy requires measures of performance. Three such measures are briefly described in this chapter; more will be explained about them in later chapters. Real gross domestic product or **real GDP** provides an overall indicator of output or production in the economy. **Unemployment** measures the degree to which labor resources are being fully used in the economy. **Inflation** tracks the overall increase in the level of prices in the economy. Each measure is important for tracking the short-run and long-run health of the economy and for creating macroeconomic models to address important policy questions.

Since the late 1770s we have witnessed the miracle of **modern economic growth.** Before that time economic output per person had remained relatively constant, but since that time economic output per person has risen substantially and along with it the standard of living in those nations that have experienced such growth. In fact, much of the difference between rich and poor nations today can be attributed to their historical participation in this modern economic growth, as you will learn in a later chapter in this section of the textbook. To achieve such economic growth requires saving and investment and a banking and financial system to allocate resources to economic investment in newly created capital goods.

The **expectations** that people hold are important for macroeconomics because they influence economic behavior. When business firms expect economic conditions to be bad, they are less likely to invest in new plant and equipment and not taking these actions can reduce future economic growth. And when expectations go unmet, they can be experienced as **economic shocks** to the economy that can change economic decisions. Although there are both demand shocks and supply shocks in a macro economy, the focus of the attention in the chapter is on *demand* shocks because they result in the short-run fluctuations that can significantly change output and employment.

To understand what happens when there is a demand shock to the economy the chapter makes a distinction between situations in which there are flexible prices and those in which there are inflexible prices (or "sticky prices"). If prices are perfectly flexible in an economy, then a change or shock from demand results in a change in the overall level of prices. If, however, prices are inflexible or sticky as they often are in the short run, then a change in demand results in a change in output and employment in the economy. As you will learn from this introductory chapter, the macroeconomic models that will be presented in more detail in later chapters can be categorized based on whether prices are considered to be flexible or inflexible and whether there is a short-run or long-run time horizon.

■ CHECKLIST

When you have studied this chapter you should be able to

☐ Explain what macroeconomics studies are.
☐ Define real gross domestic product or real GDP.
☐ Distinguish between real GDP and nominal GDP.
☐ Explain why unemployment is a loss to the economy.
☐ Describe the problem that inflation presents to the economy.
☐ Give examples of the types of policy questions that are investigated with the use of macroeconomic models.
☐ Compare economic growth in ancient and preindustrial times with modern economic growth.
☐ Explain how participating or not participating in modern economic growth accounts for differences in the standards of living of nations.
☐ Offer some comparisons of GDP per person across rich and poor nations.
☐ Define saving and investment.
☐ Distinguish between economic investment and financial investment.
☐ Explain why saving and investment are so important for economic growth.
☐ Discuss the role of banks and other financial institutions as related to saving and investment in the economy.
☐ Explain why macroeconomics must take into account expectations and shocks.
☐ Distinguish between demand shocks and supply shocks.
☐ Discuss why demand shocks present a major problem for the macro economy.
☐ Illustrate graphically what happens for a firm when there is a demand shock and prices are flexible.
☐ Illustrate graphically what happens for a firm when there is a demand shocks and prices are inflexible or sticky.
☐ Explain how firms use inventories to adjust to demand shocks.

☐ Describe the effects of demand shocks on output, employment, and inventories in an economy when prices are inflexible.
☐ Cite economic evidence on the stickiness of prices.
☐ Present two reasons why prices are often inflexible in the short run.
☐ Categorize macroeconomic models on the basis of price flexibility and time perspective.
☐ Explain the possible relationship between the use of computerized inventory tracking systems and recessions (*Last Word*).

■ CHAPTER OUTLINE

1. This chapter is an introduction to ***macroeconomics,*** which studies the behavior of the whole economy, or its major aggregates such as consumption and investment. It focuses on two topics: long-run economic growth and short-run changes in output and employment (the ***business cycle***). The long-term growth trend leads to higher output and standards of living for an economy, but along the way there can be short-run variability that produces a decline in output (***recession***). The purpose of the chapter is to give an overview of the major performance measures for the economy and then preview the short-run and long-run macro models that will be described in more detail in later chapters.

2. Several performance measures are used for tracking the macro economy and to develop policies to address short-run or long-run conditions or problems.

a. ***Real gross domestic product,*** or ***real GDP,*** is a measure of the value of final goods and services produced by the domestic economy during a time period, typically a year. The term *real* refers to the fact that in comparing the value of GDP (prices times quantities) from one year to the next, prices are held constant so only quantities of goods and services produced by the economy (or real output) changes. Output also can be measured by ***nominal GDP.*** There is a problem with this measure for measuring output changes because both prices and quantities change from one year to the next.

b. ***Unemployment*** is a condition that arises when a person who is willing to work seeks a job but does not find one. High rates of unemployment mean that an economy is not fully employing its labor resources, which reduces potential production and leads to other social problems.

c. ***Inflation*** is an increase in the general level of prices. Prices for individual products can rise or fall, but if there is a rise in prices overall, then an economy is experiencing inflation. Inflation erodes the purchasing power of incomes and reduces the value of savings.

d. Policymakers seek to maximize economic growth and at the same time minimize the adverse effects of unemployment and inflation. To do so, they construct macroeconomic models to assess the short-run and long-run performance of the economy. Such models can be useful for addressing important macroeconomic questions such as what can be done by government policies to control information or foster long-run economic growth.

3. In ancient times and in the preindustrial periods of human history, the characteristic of economic growth was that output would increase, but so would the population. As a consequence, output per person remained fairly constant and living standards stayed about the same. With the Industrial Revolution of the late 1700s, however, economies experienced ***modern economic growth*** in which output per person and standards of living increased. Such growth explains the large differences in living standards today among nations. Richer nations have a longer history of modern economic growth than poorer nations.

a. Economic growth depends on devoting some current output to increase future output. This process involves the use of ***saving*** (when current spending is less than current income) and ***investment*** (when resources are devoted to the production of future output). The amount of economic investment is limited by the amount of saving available for such investment.

(1) There often is confusion about the term *investment.* ***Economic investment*** refers to the purchase of newly created capital goods such as new tools, new machinery, or new buildings that are bought with the purpose of expanding a business.

(2) ***Financial investment*** refers to the purchase of an asset such as a stock, bond, or real estate that is made for the purpose of financial gain. Financial investment simply transfers ownership of an asset from one party to another.

b. The primary source of savings is households and the primary economic investors are businesses. Savings get transferred to economic investors through banks and other financial institutions such as insurance companies and mutual funds. For these reasons, the condition of the banking and financial sector is important for economic growth and macroeconomic policy.

4. Uncertainty, expectations, and shocks all affect macroeconomic behavior.

a. The future is uncertain, so the consumer and business participants in the economy have to act from ***expectations*** of what will happen. Their expectations about the future will shape their economic decisions.

(1) When expectations differ significantly from reality, that is, the unexpected happens, then the participants in the economy experience ***economic shocks. Demand shocks*** occur with unexpected changes in the demand for products. ***Supply shocks*** occur with unexpected changes in the supply of products. Such shocks can be positive or negative depending on whether the surprising changes are beneficial or costly for a person or group. In the view of many economists, most short-run fluctuations in the economy come from demand shocks, so demand shocks will be given the primary focus in this chapter and subsequent chapters.

b. For an individual firm, if the price for the product is flexible, a change in the demand for the product will result in a change in price to achieve equilibrium at the set quantity of output (vertical supply curve). Such a change in demand would not change the output for a firm, but only the price of a product. Similarly, for the entire economy, if prices of products are completely flexible, then output would remain the same both in the short run or the long run and only the level of prices for products would change.

c. Demand shocks, however, present a major macroeconomic problem for the economy because the prices of most products are inflexible or slow to change in the short run ("sticky").

(1) For an individual firm, when a price is inflexible, then the response to a demand shock is a change in output and employment. Similarly, for the entire economy, if most prices are fixed or "sticky," a demand shock will cause short-term fluctuations in output and employment. For example, if the demand for most products falls, firms will cut production, causing output and economic growth to decrease and unemployment to increase.

(2) Firms attempt to address the problem of fluctuating demand by maintaining an ***inventory,*** which is a store of output that has been produced but not sold. When demand is low, the inventory stock would rise as unsold products are added. When demand is high, the inventory would fall as previously produced products are sold from the inventory stock. But such a practice of using inventories to meet unexpected changes in demand only helps for a short period of time. If inventories become large and remain so for a long period of time, they are costly to maintain and end up hurting business profits. As a result, firms will cut production and employment to reduce the inventory buildup. These changes in turn will reduce GDP and increase unemployment.

d. The economic data indicate that there are many ***inflexible prices*** or ***"sticky prices"*** for goods and services in the economy. In fact, for many final goods and services there is a 4.3-month time lag before prices change. There are several reasons for sticky prices. First, consumers prefer stable and predictable prices, so there is pressure on businesses to keep prices stable and not upset consumers. Second, businesses may not want to cut prices because that may result in a price war with competing firms.

5. Macroeconomic models can be categorized based on price stickiness. In the very short run, prices are almost totally inflexible, so that any change in demand will result in a change in output and employment. As time passes, however, prices become more flexible and a change in demand produces little change in output or employment. The price flexibility/inflexibility distinction is important for categorizing macroeconomic models. Short-run macroeconomic models assume that prices are inflexible or sticky, and thus demand shocks change output and employment. Long-run macroeconomic models assume ***flexible prices,*** and thus demand shocks only have an effect on prices and not on output or employment.

6. (*Last Word*). Computerized inventory tracking has increased how quickly firms can respond to unexpected changes in demand. This changed helped moderate business cycle fluctuations of the past 25 years.

■ HINTS AND TIPS

1. Read this chapter for a conceptual understanding of what is to come in later chapters. A key idea is that *the flexibility of prices determines the degree to which demand shocks influence output and employment in an economy.* The distinction between flexible and inflexible prices is useful for categorizing the macroeconomic models and for understanding economic growth as discussed in later chapters.

2. One important definitional distinction the chapter makes is between *economic* investment and *financial* investment. Economic investment involves the purchase of *newly created* capital goods to be used for production of goods or services by a business. Financial investment typically means purchasing ownership of a paper asset such as a stock or bond, or in other cases a used asset, such as an antique car, in the expectation that the price will appreciate and there will be financial gain when the asset is sold.

■ IMPORTANT TERMS

the business cycle	**economic investment**
recession	**financial investment**
real GDP (gross domestic product)	**expectations**
nominal GDP	**economic shocks**
unemployment	**demand shocks**
inflation	**supply shocks**
modern economic growth	**inventory**
saving	**inflexible prices ("sticky prices")**
investment	**flexible prices**

SELF-TEST

■ FILL-IN QUESTIONS

1. Macroeconomics studies the business cycle or (short-run, long-run) ______________ fluctuations in output and employment and ______________ economic growth that leads to higher standards of living over time.

2. To tell if an economy is growing from one year to the next year, economists compare (nominal, real) ______________ GDP from one year to the next because it shows if there is a change in output rather than prices.

3. An increase in the overall level of prices is called (sticky prices, inflation) ______________. The condition where a person is willing to work but cannot get a job is (recession, unemployment) ______________.

4. The basic difference between modern economic growth and economic growth in ancient or preindustrial times is that with modern economic growth output per person (increases, stays about the same) ______________ whereas with growth in ancient or preindustrial times, output per person.

5. Richer nations have experienced modern economic growth for (shorter, longer) ______________ time periods than have poorer nations and as a consequence their standards of living are significantly (lower, higher) ______________.

6. When current consumption is less than current output, it creates (investment, saving) ______________, and when economic resources are devoted to increasing future output, such activity is considered to be ______________.

7. The purchase of newly created capital goods for the purpose of expanding or growing a business would be considered by economists to be an example of (financial, economic) ______________ investment whereas the purchase of an asset such as a share of stock in a corporation in the expectation that its price would appreciate would be an example of ______________ investment.

8. The amount of economic investment is ultimately limited by the amount of (saving, inventory) ______________, and for there to be more investment then ______________ must increase. Such an increase, however, means that there will be a(n) (increase, decrease) ______________ in current consumption.

9. The principal source of savings is (businesses, households) ______________ and the main economic investors are ______________. The transfer of savings to investors is done primarily through (government, banks) ______________ and other financial institutions.

10. Expectations are important in macroeconomics because people will save and invest more if they hold (positive, negative) ______________ expectations about the future, but they will save and invest less if they hold ______________ expectations about the future.

11. Uncertainty about the future means that expectations may not be met, which creates a(n) (investment, shock) ______________, and there can be a demand ______________ or a supply ______________.

12. A situation where demand turns out to be higher than expected would be a (positive, negative) ______________ demand shock, but a situation in which demand turns out to be lower than expected would be a ______________ demand shock.

13. Many economists think that most short-run fluctuations are the result of (supply, demand) ______________ shocks, although it is also possible for there to be ______________ shocks; but the textbook will focus primarily on ______________ shocks.

14. In the short run, real world prices are often (flexible, inflexible) ______________, but in the long run, prices are more ______________. When prices are inflexible, they are referred to as being ("sticky," "stuck") ______________.

15. In the short run, the only way for the economy to adjust to demand shocks when prices are inflexible or sticky is through changes in (prices, output) ______________ and employment, but in the long run, the adjustments are made through changes in ______________.

16. A store of output that has been produced but not sold is a(n) (financial investment, inventory) ______________, and they help businesses adjust to short-run changes in demand.

17. If demand for a product increases, then business firms can respond by (increasing, decreasing) ______________ their inventories of the product, and if the demand for the product decreases, then business firms can respond by ______________ their inventories of the product.

18. If prices are fixed and there is a negative demand shock, it will cause sales to (increase, decrease) ______________ and inventories to ______________, and if they become too high, then firms will have to ______________ output and ______________ employment.

19. One reason that prices are sticky is that consumers prefer (stable, fluctuating) ______________ prices, and businesses do not want to annoy consumers. Another reason is that cutting prices may result in a price (shock, war) ______________ with competing firms that will be counterproductive for business.

20. In short-run macroeconomic models, prices tend to be (inflexible, flexible) ______________ and output and employment change with changes in demand, but in macroeconomic models with a longer time horizon, prices tend to be ______________ and output and employment remain relatively constant.

■ TRUE–FALSE QUESTIONS

Circle T if the statement is true, F if it is false.

1. Macroeconomics studies long-run economic growth and short-run economic fluctuations. **T F**

2. Real GDP totals the dollar value of all goods and services within the borders of a given country using their current prices during the year they were produced. **T F**

3. Unemployment is a waste of resources because the economy gives up the goods and services that unemployed workers could have produced if they had been working. **T F**

4. If a household's income does not rise as fast as the prices of goods and services that it consumes, its standard of living will rise. **T F**

5. An example of a macroeconomic policy question would be "Can governments promote long-run economic growth?" **T F**

6. Modern economic growth means that output rises at about the same rate as the population. **T F**

7. The vast differences in living standards between rich and poor nations today are largely the result of only some nations having experienced modern economic growth. **T F**

8. To raise living standards over time, an economy must devote at least some fraction of its current output to increasing future output. **T F**

9. An example of economic investment, as economists use the term, would be the purchase of a corporate stock or bond. **T F**

10. The only way that an economy can pay for more investment to achieve higher consumption in the future is to increase saving in the present. **T F**

11. Banks and other financial institutions collect the savings of households after paying interest, dividends, or capital gains and then lend those funds to businesses. **T F**

12. Expectations about the future are important because if people expect a good future, households will increase their savings and businesses will reduce their investments. **T F**

13. Economies are exposed to both demand shock and supply shocks. **T F**

14. A positive demand shock refers to a situation where demand turns out to be lower than expected. **T F**

15. Economists believe that most short-run fluctuations in the economy are the result of demand shocks. **T F**

16. In the short run, the prices of most goods and services change very quickly. **T F**

17. Fluctuations in the business cycle arise because the actual demand for goods and services is either higher or lower than what people expected. **T F**

18. If prices are flexible for an economy, an increase in demand will result in a significant change in output and employment. **T F**

19. An inventory is a store of output that has been produced and sold. **T F**

20. Given fixed prices, a negative demand shock for businesses will reduce sales, increase inventories, and eventually reduce output and employment. **T F**

21. The prices for most goods and services that people consume are sticky in the short run. **T F**

22. One reason that prices are sticky is that business firms try to please consumers by giving them predictable and stable prices for planning. **T F**

23. Another reason prices are sticky is that business firms want to engage in a price war with rival firms to gain market share. **T F**

24. Only in the short run are prices totally inflexible. **T F**

25. A macroeconomic model that allows for flexible prices would be more useful for understanding how the economy behaves over time. **T F**

■ MULTIPLE-CHOICE QUESTIONS

Circle the letter that corresponds to the best answer.

1. Short-run fluctuations in output and employment are often referred to as
(a) recession
(b) inflation
(c) the business cycle
(d) modern economic growth

2. Economic growth in an economy is best measured from one year to the next by comparing the change in
(a) the rate of inflation
(b) the rate of unemployment
(c) nominal GDP
(d) real GDP

3. Unemployment is undesirable because it
(a) increases inflation
(b) wastes labor resources
(c) contributes to sticky prices
(d) raises interest rates in the economy

4. A major problem with inflation is that it
(a) lowers housing prices
(b) increases the rate of saving
(c) reduces purchasing power
(d) decreases government spending

5. Which one of the following is a question that a macroeconomic model would help to clarify?
(a) Can governments promote long-run economic growth?
(b) Is the purchase of General Electric stock a worthwhile financial investment?
(c) Should the sales tax in a city be raised from 7 percent to 9 percent?
(d) Does a large rise in the price of gasoline significantly reduce consumer spending on gasoline?

6. What was the average percentage increase in the output of the United States from 1995 to the start of the 2007–2009 recession?
(a) 1.1 percent
(b) 2.7 percent
(c) 3.6 percent
(d) 4.1 percent

7. Before the Industrial Revolution began in England in the late 1700s, standards of living showed
(a) significant growth
(b) significant decline
(c) virtually no growth
(d) wide swings from growth to decline

8. Modern economic growth is characterized as a situation in which
(a) inflation is almost zero
(b) output per person is rising
(c) unemployment is minimal
(d) the prices of products are flexible

9. An annual growth rate of 2 percent implies that the standard of living in an economy will double in
(a) 10 years
(b) 20 years
(c) 35 years
(d) 70 years

10. What accounts for the vast differences in the living standards today between rich and poor countries?
(a) purchasing power parity
(b) rising rates of inflation
(c) increases in nominal GDP
(d) modern economic growth

11. About how many times greater, on average, are the material standards of living of citizens in the richest nations compared with the material living standards of citizens in the poorest nations?
(a) 5 times
(b) 10 times
(c) 50 times
(d) 100 times

12. When current spending is less than current income, it generates
(a) saving
(b) investment
(c) demand shocks
(d) supply shocks

13. Which of the following *purchases* would be an example of an economic investment by a business?
(a) shares of stock in another business
(b) a used factory from another business
(c) new computers to improve data analysis
(d) a certificate of deposit with a high interest rate

14. The reason that economic investment is important is that it
(a) enables higher levels of consumption in the future
(b) enables higher levels of consumption in the present
(c) increases the rate of saving in the present
(d) decreases the rate of saving in the future

15. A well-functioning banking and financial system helps to promote economic growth and stability by
(a) paying high interest rates on deposits
(b) offering dividends on corporate stocks
(c) directing savings to the most productive investments
(d) increasing current consumption and future consumption

16. If people and businesses hold positive attitudes about the future they are more likely to
(a) save less and invest less
(b) save more and invest more
(c) save more and invest less
(d) save less and invest more

17. Macroeconomic behavior is most significantly influenced by
(a) purchasing power parity
(b) expectations about the future
(c) the price of agricultural land
(d) employment in the construction industry

18. Economic forecasters had expected consumer spending to increase by 5 percent this year, but instead it increases by 0.5 percent. This situation would be an example of a
(a) positive supply shock
(b) negative supply shock
(c) positive demand shock
(d) negative demand shock

19. The primary reason that economists think most short-run fluctuations in the economy are the result of demand shocks is that the prices of many goods and services are
(a) flexible in the short run
(b) inflexible in the short run
(c) flexible in the long run
(d) inflexible in the long run

20. Alpha Dog Foods is a business firm which produces 10,000 units of dog food a week, which is the optimal output for the firm. If prices for this product are flexible and Alpha Dog Foods experiences an unexpected decrease in demand, it is most likely to
(a) increase the product price
(b) decrease the product price
(c) increase the production of the product
(d) decrease the production of the product

21. Swirlpool typically sells 5,000 energy-efficient dishwashers at the fixed price of $1,000 a month, which is a price it has used for a long time. If there is an unexpected decrease in the demand for this product, then Swirlpool is most likely to
(a) increase the product price
(b) decrease the product price
(c) increase production of the product
(d) decrease production of the product

22. If demand falls for many goods and services across the entire economy for an extended period of time and prices are sticky, most firms that produce those goods and services will be forced to
(a) increase production and increase employment
(b) decrease production and decrease employment
(c) decrease production, but increase employment
(d) increase production, but decrease employment

23. Reliable economic reports indicate that consumers are spending more on goods and services this year. This trend is highly likely to continue for the next few years because of a growing economy. If prices for these goods and services are sticky, then the businesses producing these goods and services are most likely to
(a) lower prices and hire more workers
(b) raise prices and hire more workers
(c) increase output and hire more workers
(d) decrease output and hire fewer workers

24. Which of the following good or service is most inflexible, or sticky, in price?
(a) milk
(b) gasoline
(c) newspapers
(d) airline tickets

25. Macroeconomic models of the economy over the long term are more likely to assume that the economy has
(a) stuck prices
(b) sticky prices
(c) flexible prices
(d) inflexible prices

■ PROBLEMS

1. Assume that in Year 1 an economy produces 100 units of output that sell for $50 a unit, on average. In Year 2, the economy produces the same 100 units of output, but sells them for $55 a unit, on average.

a. What is nominal GDP in Year 1? ________. What is nominal GDP in Year 2? ________. Nominal GDP increased from Year 1 to Year 2 because (prices, output) ________ increased.

b. Use Year 1 prices to calculate real GDP in Year 1 and Year 2. What is real GDP in Year 1? ________. What is real GDP in Year 2? ________. Real GDP did not increase from Year 1 to Year 2 because (prices, output) ________ did not change.

2. The following is a demand and supply model for a business firm producing a product. Assume that 100 units of output is the optimal and most profitable level of production for the firm. Assume that the price for the product is flexible.

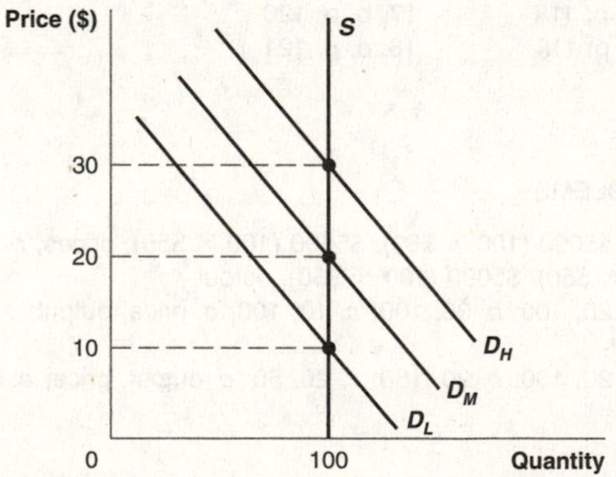

a. At the medium level of demand (D_M), the equilibrium price will be $________ and the equilibrium quantity will be ________ units.

b. If there is a demand shock that unexpectedly lifts demand higher (D_H), the equilibrium price will be $________ and the equilibrium quantity will be ________ units.

c. If there is a demand shock that unexpectedly lowers demand (D_L), the equilibrium price will be $________ and the equilibrium quantity will be ________ units.

d. Generalizing for the individual firm, if there are demand shocks, they get accommodated by a change in (price, output) ________, but not a change in ________.

e. And applying this logic to the economy as a whole, if prices are flexible in the economy and there are demand shocks, the economy would adjust through a change in (price, output) ________, but not a change in ________.

3. The following is a different demand and supply model for the same business firm producing a product as in problem 2. Assume that 100 units of output is the optimal and most profitable level of production for the firm. Now assume that the price for the product is inflexible.

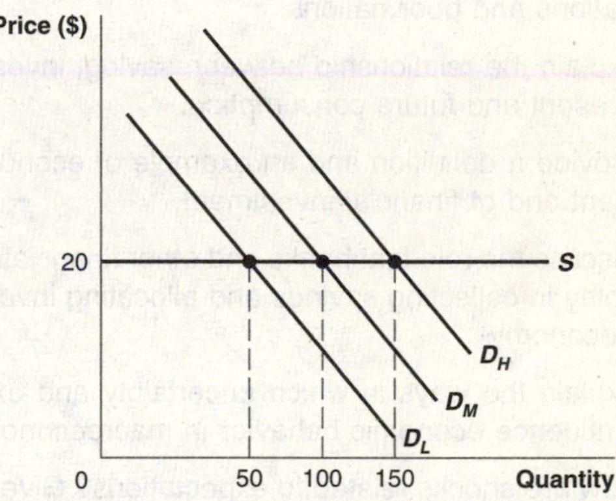

a. At the medium level of demand (D_M), the equilibrium price will be $________ and the equilibrium quantity will be ________ units.

b. If there is a demand shock that unexpectedly lifts demand higher (D_H), the equilibrium price will be $________ and the equilibrium quantity will be ________ units.

c. If there is a demand shock that unexpectedly lowers demand (D_L), the equilibrium price will be $________ and the equilibrium quantity will be ________ units.

d. Generalizing for the individual firm, if there are demand shocks, they get accommodated by a change in (price, output) ________, but not a change in ________.

e. And applying this logic to the economy as a whole, if prices are inflexible in the economy and there are demand shocks, the economy would adjust through a change in (price, output) ________, but not a change in ________.

■ SHORT ANSWER AND ESSAY QUESTIONS

1. Explain how business cycles can be thought of as short-term fluctuations or variability in the rate of economic growth.

2. Describe the basic difference between real GDP and nominal GDP. Which concept is more useful for measuring change in the economy over time? Why?

3. What is the opportunity cost of unemployment for the economy?

4. How does inflation affect people's standard of living and saving?

5. What types of policy questions can macroeconomic models help answer? Give two examples.

6. Compare and contrast the characteristics of economic growth in ancient or preindustrial times with modern economic growth today.

7. What accounts for differences in living standards between rich and poor countries today?

8. Describe differences in purchasing power parity of rich nations and poor nations.

9. Explain the relationship between saving, investment, and present and future consumption.

10. Provide a definition and an example of economic investment and of financial investment.

11. Discuss the role that banks and other financial institutions play in collecting savings and allocating investment in an economy.

12. Explain the ways in which uncertainty and expectations influence economic behavior in macroeconomics.

13. How are shocks related to expectations? Give an example of a positive and a negative demand shock.

14. Discuss the relationship between demand shocks and business cycle fluctuations.

15. How does an economy adjust to a demand shock when prices are flexible?

16. How does an economy adjust to a demand shock when prices are sticky?

17. Explain what happens to inventories when prices are sticky and there is a demand shock.

18. Describe and give examples of the stickiness of prices based on the average number of months between price changes for selected goods and services.

19. Describe two reasons why businesses hesitate to change prices.

20. How can price stickiness be used to categorize macroeconomic models?

ANSWERS

Chapter 6 Introduction to Macroeconomics

FILL-IN QUESTIONS

1. short-run, long-run
2. real
3. inflation, unemployment
4. increases, stays about the same
5. longer, higher
6. saving, investment
7. economic, financial
8. saving, saving, decrease
9. households, businesses, banks
10. positive, negative
11. shock, shock, shock
12. positive, negative
13. demand, supply, demand
14. inflexible, flexible, sticky
15. output, prices
16. inventory
17. decreasing, increasing
18. decrease, increase, decrease, decrease
19. stable, war
20. inflexible, flexible

TRUE–FALSE QUESTIONS

1. T, p. 116	**10.** T, p. 119	**19.** F, p. 123
2. F, p. 117	**11.** T, p. 120	**20.** T, pp. 122–123
3. T, p. 117	**12.** F, p. 120	**21.** T, pp. 124–125
4. F, p. 117	**13.** T, p. 121	**22.** T, pp. 124–125
5. T, p. 118	**14.** F, p. 121	**23.** F, p. 126
6. F, p. 118	**15.** T, p. 121	**24.** T, p. 126
7. T, p. 118	**16.** F, p. 121	**25.** T, p. 126
8. T, p. 119	**17.** T, p. 122	
9. F, p. 120	**18.** F, p. 122	

MULTIPLE-CHOICE QUESTIONS

1. c, p. 116	**10.** d, p. 118	**19.** b, p. 121
2. d, p. 117	**11.** c, p. 119	**20.** b, p. 122
3. b, p. 117	**12.** a, p. 119	**21.** d, p. 122
4. c, p. 117	**13.** c, p. 120	**22.** b, pp. 122–123
5. a, p. 118	**14.** a, pp. 119–120	**23.** c, p. 124
6. b, p. 118	**15.** c, p. 120	**24.** c, pp. 124–125
7. c, p. 118	**16.** b, p. 120	**25.** c, p. 126
8. b, p. 118	**17.** b, p. 120	
9. c, p. 118	**18.** d, p. 121	

PROBLEMS

1. *a.* \$5000 (100 × \$50), \$5500 (100 × \$55), prices; *b.* \$5000 (100 × \$50), \$5000 (100 × \$50), output

2. *a.* 20, 100; *b.* 30, 100; *c.* 10, 100; *d.* price, output; *e.* price, output

3. *a.* 20, 100; *b.* 20, 150; *c.* 20, 50; *d.* output, price; *e.* output, price

SHORT ANSWER AND ESSAY QUESTIONS

1. p. 116	**8.** p. 119	**15.** p. 122
2. p. 117	**9.** p. 119	**16.** pp. 122–123
3. p. 117	**10.** p. 120	**17.** p. 123
4. p. 117	**11.** p. 120	**18.** pp. 124–125
5. p. 118	**12.** p. 120	**19.** pp. 125–126
6. pp. 118–119	**13.** pp. 120–121	**20.** p. 126
7. pp. 118–119	**14.** p. 121	

CHAPTER 7

Measuring Domestic Output and National Income

The subject of Chapter 7 is **national income accounting.** The first measure that you will learn about in the chapter is the **gross domestic product (GDP).** The GDP is an important economic statistic because it provides the best estimate of the total market value of all final goods and services produced by our economy in one year. You will also discover why GDP is a monetary measure that counts only the value of final goods and services and excludes nonproductive transactions such as secondhand sales.

National income accounting involves estimating output, or income, for the nation's society as a whole, rather than for an individual business firm or family. Note that the terms **output** and **income** are interchangeable because the nation's domestic output and its income are identical. The value of the nation's output equals the total expenditures for this output, and these expenditures become the income of those who have produced this output. Consequently, there are two equally acceptable methods—expenditures or income—for determining GDP.

From an **expenditure** perspective, GDP is composed of four expenditure categories: personal consumption expenditures **(C),** gross private domestic investment **(I_g)**, government purchases **(G),** and net exports **(X_n).** These expenditures become income for people or the government when they are paid out in the form of employee compensation, rents, interest, proprietors' income, corporate profits, and taxes on production and imports. GDP can be calculated from national income by making adjustments to account for net foreign factor income, a statistical discrepancy, and depreciation. In national income accounting, the amount spent to purchase this year's total output is equal to money income derived from production of this year's output.

This chapter also explains the relationship of GDP to other **national income** accounts. These accounts include *net domestic product* (NDP), *national income* (NI) as derived from NDP, *personal income* (PI), and *disposable income* (DI). The relationship between GDP, NDP, NI, PI, and DI is shown in Table 7.4 of the text. The circular flow using the expenditures and income approaches to GDP are illustrated in Figure 7.3 of the text.

The next to the last section of the chapter shows you how to calculate **real GDP** from **nominal GDP.** This adjustment is important because nominal GDP is measured in monetary units, so if accurate comparisons are to be made for GDP over time, these monetary measures must be adjusted to take account of changes in the price level. A simple example is presented to show how a GDP price index is constructed. The index is then used to adjust *nominal GDP* to obtain *real GDP* and make correct GDP comparisons from one year to the next. The text also provides data for the U.S. economy so you can see why the calculation of real GDP is necessary and how it is used.

The last section of the chapter looks at the **shortcomings of GDP** as a measure of total output and economic well-being. You will learn about economic factors that are excluded from GDP measurement—nonmarket or illegal transactions, changes in leisure and product quality, differences in the composition and distribution of output, and the environmental effects of GDP production—and how their exclusion can lead to an under- or overstatement of economic well-being. Although national income accounts are not perfect measures of all economic conditions, they are still reasonably accurate and useful indicators of the performance of the national economy.

■ CHECKLIST

When you have studied this chapter you should be able to

- ☐ Identify three ways national income accounting can be used for economic decision making.
- ☐ Give a definition of the gross domestic product (GDP).
- ☐ Explain why GDP is a monetary measure.
- ☐ Describe how GDP measures value added and avoids multiple counting.
- ☐ Give examples of two types of nonproduction transactions that are excluded from GDP.
- ☐ Describe the relationship between the expenditures and income approaches to GDP accounting.
- ☐ List the three types of expenditures included in personal consumption expenditures (*C*).
- ☐ Identify three items included in gross private domestic investment (I_g).
- ☐ Explain how positive or negative changes in inventories affect investment.
- ☐ Distinguish between gross and net investment.
- ☐ Discuss how differences in the amount of net investment affect the production capacity of the economy.
- ☐ List the two components included in government purchases (*G*).
- ☐ Describe the meaning and calculation of net exports (X_n).
- ☐ Compute GDP using the expenditures approach when given national income accounting data.
- ☐ Identify the six income items that make up U.S. national income.
- ☐ List three things that can happen to corporate profits.

□ Explain why taxes on production and imports are included as part of national income.
□ Describe the effect of net foreign factor income on national income accounts.
□ Define consumption of fixed capital and discuss how it affects national income accounts.
□ Compute GDP using the income approach when given national income accounting data.
□ Define net domestic product (NDP).
□ Show how to derive U.S. national income (NI) from net domestic product (NDP).
□ Define personal income (PI) in national income accounts.
□ Explain how to obtain disposable income (DI) from personal income (PI).
□ Use Figure 7.3 in the text to describe the circular flow model for GDP.
□ Distinguish between nominal and real GDP.
□ Construct a price index when given price and quantity data.
□ Obtain a price index when given data on nominal and real GDP.
□ Discuss some real-world factors that affect the GDP price index.
□ List seven shortcomings of GDP as a measure of total output and economic well-being.
□ Identify some of the sources of data the Bureau of Economic Analysis uses to estimate consumption, investment, government purchases, and net exports (*Last Word*).

■ CHAPTER OUTLINE

1. ***National income accounting*** consists of concepts that enable those who use them to measure the economy's output, to compare it with past outputs, to explain its size and the reasons for changes in its size, and to formulate policies designed to increase it.

2. The market value of all final goods and services produced in the domestic economy during the year is measured by the ***gross domestic product (GDP).***

a. GDP is a *monetary measure* that is calculated in dollar terms rather than in terms of physical units of output.

b. GDP includes in its calculation only the value of ***final goods*** (consumption goods, capital goods, and services purchased by final users and that will not be resold or processed further during the *current* year).

(1) GDP excludes the value of ***intermediate goods*** (ones that are purchased for resale or further processing) because including both final goods and intermediate goods would result in ***multiple counting*** of the goods and overstate GDP.

(2) Another way to avoid multiple counting is to measure and add only the ***value added*** at each stage of the production process. Value added is the market value of a firm's output minus the value of the inputs the firm bought from others to produce the output.

c. Nonproduction transactions are not included in GDP.

(1) Purely financial transactions such as public transfer payments, private transfer payments, and stock market transactions are simply exchanges of money or paper assets and do not create output.

(2) Sales of secondhand or used goods are excluded because they were counted in past production and do not contribute to current production.

d. Measurement of GDP can be accomplished by either the expenditures approach or the income approach, but the same result is obtained by the two methods.

3. Computation of the GDP by the ***expenditures approach*** requires the summation of the total amounts of the four types of spending for final goods and services.

a. ***Personal consumption expenditures (C)*** are the expenditures of households for ***durable goods*** and ***nondurable goods*** and for ***services.***

b. ***Gross private domestic investment*** (***I_g***) is the sum of the spending by business firms for machinery, equipment, and tools; spending by firms and households for new construction (buildings); and the changes in the inventories of business firms.

(1) An increase in inventories in a given year increases investment that year because it is part of the output of the economy that was produced but not sold that year; a decrease in inventories in a given year decreases investment that year because it was included as part of the output from a prior year.

(2) Investment does not include expenditures for stocks or bonds (a transfer of paper assets) or for used or secondhand capital goods (because they were counted as part of investment in the year they were new capital goods).

(3) Gross investment exceeds net investment by the value of the capital goods worn out during the year. An economy in which net investment is positive is one with an expanding production capacity.

c. ***Government purchases (G)*** are the expenditures made by all levels of governments (federal, state, and local) for final goods from businesses, and for the direct purchases of resources, including labor.

(1) The government purchases are made to provide public goods and services, and for spending on publicly owned capital (public goods with a long lifetime such as highways or schools).

(2) It should be noted that transfer payments made by the government to individuals, such as Social Security payments, are not included in government purchases because they simply transfer income to individuals and do not generate production.

d. ***Net exports (X_n)*** in an economy is calculated as the difference between exports (X) and imports (M). It is equal to the expenditures made by foreigners for goods and services produced in the economy minus the expenditures made by the consumers, governments, and investors of the economy for goods and services produced in foreign nations.

e. In equation form, $C + I_g + G + X_n = GDP$.

4. Computation of GDP by the ***income approach*** requires adding the income derived from the production and sales of final goods and services. The six income items are:

a. *Compensation of employees* (the sum of wages and salaries *and* wage and salary supplements, such as social insurance and private pension or health funds for workers).

b. *Rents* (the income received by property owners). This rent is a net measure of the difference between gross rent and property depreciation.

c. *Interest* (only the interest payments made by financial institutions or business firms are included; interest payments made by government are excluded).

d. *Proprietors' income* (the profits or net income of sole proprietors or unincorporated business firms).

e. *Corporate profits* (the earnings of corporations). They are allocated in the following three ways: as corporate income taxes, dividends paid to stockholders, and undistributed corporate profits retained by corporations.

f. ***Taxes on production and imports*** are added because they are initially income for households that later gets paid to government in the form of taxes. This category includes general sales taxes, excise taxes, business property taxes, license fees, and custom duties.

g. The sum of all of the above six categories equals national income (employee compensation, rents, interest, proprietors' income, corporate profits, and taxes on production and imports). To obtain GDP from national income, three adjustments must be made.

(1) Net foreign factor income is subtracted from national income because it reflects income earned from production outside the United States. Net foreign factor income is income earned by American-owned resources abroad minus income earned by foreign-owned resources in the United States.

(2) A statistical discrepancy is added to national income to make the income approach match the expenditures approach.

(3) The ***consumption of fixed capital*** is added to national income to get to GDP because it is a cost of production that does not add to anyone's income. It covers depreciation of private capital goods and publicly owned capital goods such as roads or bridges.

5. Four other national accounts are important in evaluating the performance of the economy. Each has a distinct definition and can be computed by making additions to or deductions from another measure.

a. ***Net domestic product (NDP)*** is the annual output of final goods and services over and above the privately and publicly owned capital goods worn out during the year. It is equal to the GDP minus depreciation (consumption of fixed capital).

b. ***National income (NI)*** is the total income *earned* by U.S. owners of land and capital and by the U.S. suppliers of labor and entrepreneurial ability during the year *plus* taxes on production and imports. It equals NDP *minus* a statistical discrepancy and plus net foreign factor income.

c. ***Personal income (PI)*** is the total income *received*—whether it is earned or unearned—by the households of the economy before the payment of personal taxes. It is found by taking national income and *adding* transfer payments, and then *subtracting* taxes on production and imports, Social Security contributions, corporate income taxes, and undistributed corporate profits.

d. ***Disposable income (DI)*** is the total income available to households after the payment of personal taxes. It is calculated by taking personal income and then *subtracting* personal taxes. It is also equal to personal consumption expenditures plus personal saving.

e. The relationships among the five income–output measures are summarized in Table 7.4.

f. Figure 7.3 is a more realistic and complex circular flow diagram that shows the flows of expenditures and incomes among the households, business firms, and governments in the economy.

6. ***Nominal GDP*** is the total output of final goods and services produced by an economy in 1 year multiplied by the market prices when they were produced. Prices, however, change each year. To compare total output over time, nominal GDP is converted to ***real GDP*** to account for these price changes.

a. There are two methods for deriving *real GDP* from *nominal GDP*. The first method involves computing a ***price index.***

(1) This price index is a ratio of the price of a market basket in a given year to the price of the same market basket in a base year, with the ratio multiplied by 100. If the market basket of goods in the base year was $10 and the market basket of the same goods in the next year was $15, then the price index would be 150 [$15/10 × 100].

(2) To obtain real GDP, divide nominal GDP by the price index expressed in hundredths. If nominal GDP was $14,000 billion and the price index was 120, then real GDP would be $11,666.6 billion [$14,000 billion/1.20].

b. In the second method, nominal GDP is broken down into prices and quantities for each year. Real GDP is found by using base-year prices and multiplying them by each year's physical quantities. The GDP price index for a particular year is the ratio of nominal GDP to real GDP for that year. If nominal GDP was $14,000 billion and real GDP was $11,666.6 billion, then the GDP index would be 1.20 [$14,000 billon/$11,666.6 billion].

c. In the real world, complex methods are used to calculate the GDP price index. The price index is useful for calculating real GDP. The price index number for a reference period is arbitrarily set at 100.

(1) For years when the price index is below 100, dividing nominal GDP by the price index (in hundredths) inflates nominal GDP to obtain real GDP.

(2) For years when the price index is greater than 100, dividing nominal GDP by the price index (in hundredths) deflates nominal GDP to obtain real GDP.

7. GDP has shortcomings as a measure of total output and economic well-being.

a. It excludes the value of nonmarket final goods and services that are not bought and sold in the markets, such as the unpaid work done by people on their houses.

b. It excludes the amount of increased leisure enjoyed by the participants in the economy.

c. It does not fully account for the value of improvements in the quality of products that occur over the years.

d. It does not measure the market value of the final goods and services produced in the underground sector of the economy because that income and activity is not reported.

e. It does not record the pollution or environmental costs of producing final goods and services.

f. It does not measure changes in the composition and the distribution of the domestic output.

g. It does not measure noneconomic sources of well-being such as a reduction in crime, drug or alcohol abuse, or better relationships among people and nations.

8. (*Last Word*). The Bureau of Economic Analysis (BEA) is a unit of the Department of Commerce that is responsible for compiling the National Income and Product Accounts. It obtains data from multiple sources to estimate consumption, investment, government purchases, and net exports for the calculation of GDP.

■ HINTS AND TIPS

1. Read through the chapter several times. A careful reading will enable you to avoid the necessity of memorizing. Begin by making sure you know precisely what GDP means and what is included in and excluded from its measurement.

2. Accounting is essentially an adding-up process. This chapter explains in detail and lists the items that must be added to obtain GDP by the *expenditures approach* or *income approach*. It is up to you to learn what to add on the expenditure side and what to add on the income side. Figure 7.1 is an important accounting reference for this task.

3. Changes in the price level have a significant effect on the measurement of GDP. Practice converting nominal GDP to real GDP using a price index. Problems 4 and 5 in this *Study Guide* should help you understand nominal and real GDP and the conversion process.

4. GDP is a good measure of the market value of the output of final goods and services that are produced in an economy in 1 year; however, the measure is not perfect, so you should be aware of its limitations, which are noted at the end of the chapter.

■ IMPORTANT TERMS

national income accounting
gross domestic product (GDP)
intermediate goods
final goods
multiple counting
value added
expenditures approach
income approach
personal consumption expenditures (C)
durable goods
nondurable goods
services
gross private domestic investment (I_g)
net private domestic investment
government purchases (G)
net exports (X_n)
taxes on production and imports
national income (NI)
consumption of fixed capital (depreciation)
net domestic product (NDP)
personal income (PI)
disposable income (DI)
nominal GDP
real GDP
price index

SELF-TEST

■ FILL-IN QUESTIONS

1. National income accounting is valuable because it provides a means of keeping track of the level of (unemployment, production) ______ in the economy and the course it has followed over the long run and the information needed to make public (policies, payments) ______ that will improve the performance of the economy.

2. Gross domestic product (GDP) measures the total (market, nonmarket) ______ value of all (intermediate, final) ______ goods and services produced in a country (in 1 year, over 2 years) ______.

3. GDP for a nation includes goods and services produced (within, outside) ______ its geographic boundaries. This condition means that the production of cars at a Toyota plant located in the United States would be (included, excluded) ______ in the calculation of U.S. GDP.

4. GDP is a (monetary, nonmonetary) ______ measure that permits comparison of the (relative, absolute) ______ worth of goods and services.

5. In measuring GDP, only (intermediate, final) ______ goods and services are included; if ______ goods and services were included, the accountant would be (over-, under-) ______ stating GDP, or (single, multiple) ______ counting.

6. GDP accounting excludes (production, nonproduction) ______ transactions. These include (financial, nonfinancial) ______ transactions such as public or private transfer payments or the sale of securities, and (first-, second-) ______ hand sales.

7. Personal consumption expenditures are the expenditures of households for goods such as automobiles, which are (durable, nondurable) ______, and goods such as food, which are ______, plus expenditures for (housing, services) ______.

8. Gross private domestic investment basically includes the final purchases of (capital, consumer) ______ goods by businesses, all (construction of new, sales of existing) ______ buildings and houses, and changes in (services, inventories) ______.

9. The difference between gross and net private domestic investment is equal to (depreciation, net exports) ______. If gross private domestic investment is greater than depreciation, net private domestic investment is (positive, negative) ____________ and the production capacity of the economy is (declining, expanding) ____________.

10. An economy's *net* exports equal its exports (minus, plus) ____________ its imports. If exports are less than imports, net exports are (positive, negative) ____________, but if exports are greater than imports, net exports are ____________.

11. Using the expenditure approach, the GDP equation equals ($NDP + NI + PI$, $C + I_g + G + X_n$) ____________.

12. The compensation of employees in the system of national income accounting consists of actual wages and salaries (plus, minus) ____________ wage and salary supplements. Salary supplements are the payments employers make to Social Security or (public, private) ____________ insurance programs and to ____________ pension, health, and welfare funds.

13. Corporate profits are disposed of in three ways: corporate income (taxes, interest) ____________, (depreciation, dividends) ____________, and undistributed corporate (taxes, profits) ____________.

14. Three adjustments are made to national income to obtain (GDP, DI) ____________. Net foreign factor income is (added, subtracted) ____________, a statistical discrepancy is ____________, and the consumption of fixed capital is ____________.

15. Gross domestic product overstates the economy's production because it fails to make allowance for (multiple counting, depreciation) ____________ or the need to replace (consumer, capital) ____________ goods. When the adjustment is made, the calculations produce (net domestic product, national income) ____________.

16. National income is equal to net domestic product (plus, minus) ____________ net foreign factor income ____________, a statistical discrepancy. Personal income equals national income (plus, minus) ____________ transfer payments ____________ the sum of taxes on production and imports, Social Security contributions, corporate income taxes, and undistributed corporate profits. Disposable income equals personal income (plus, minus) ____________ personal taxes.

17. A GDP that reflects the prices prevailing when the output is produced is called unadjusted, or (nominal, real) ____________ GDP, but a GDP figure that is deflated or inflated for price level changes is called adjusted or ____________ GDP.

18. To calculate a price index in a given year, the combined price of a market basket of goods and services in that year is (divided, multiplied) ____________ by the combined price of the market basket in the base year. The result is then ____________ by 100.

19. Real GDP is calculated by dividing (the price index, nominal GDP) ____________ by ____________. The price index expressed in hundredths is calculated by dividing (real, nominal) ____________ GDP by ____________ GDP.

20. For several reasons, GDP has shortcomings as a measure of total output or economic well-being.

a. It does not include the (market, nonmarket) ____________ transactions that result in the production of goods and services or the amount of (work, leisure) ____________ of participants in the economy.

b. It fails to record improvements in the (quantity, quality) ____________ of the products produced, or the changes in the (level, composition) ____________, and distribution of the economy's total output.

c. It does not take into account the undesirable effects of GDP production on the (government, environment) ____________ or the goods and services produced in the (market, underground) ____________ economy.

■ TRUE–FALSE QUESTIONS

Circle T if the statement is true, F if it is false.

1. National income accounting allows us to assess the performance of the economy and make policies to improve that performance. **T F**

2. Gross domestic product measures at their market values the total output of all goods and services produced in the economy during a year. **T F**

3. GDP is a count of the physical quantity of output and is not a monetary measure. **T F**

4. Final goods are consumption goods, capital goods, and services that are purchased by their end users rather than being ones used for further processing or manufacturing. **T F**

5. GDP includes the sale of intermediate goods and excludes the sale of final goods. **T F**

6. The total value added to a product and the value of the final product are equal. **T F**

7. Social Security payments and other public transfer payments are counted as part of GDP. **T F**

8. The sale of stocks and bonds is excluded from GDP. **T F**

9. In computing gross domestic product, private transfer payments are excluded because they do not represent payments for currently produced goods and services. **T F**

10. The two approaches to the measurement of the gross domestic product yield identical results because one approach measures the total amount spent on the products produced by business firms during a year while the second approach measures the total income of business firms during the year. **T F**

11. Personal consumption expenditures only include expenditures for durable and nondurable goods. **T F**

12. The expenditure made by a household to have a new home built is a personal consumption expenditure. **T F**

13. In national income accounting, any increase in the inventories of business firms is included in gross private domestic investment. **T F**

14. If gross private domestic investment is greater than depreciation during a given year, the economy's production capacity has declined during that year. **T F**

15. Government purchases include spending by all units of government on the finished products of business, but exclude all direct purchases of resources such as labor. **T F**

16. The net exports of an economy equal its exports of goods and services less its imports of goods and services. **T F**

17. The income approach to GDP includes compensation of employees, rents, interest income, proprietors' income, corporate profits, and taxes on production and imports. **T F**

18. Taxes on production and imports are the difference between gross private domestic investment and net private domestic investment. **T F**

19. Net foreign factor income is the difference between the earnings of foreign-owned resources in the United States and the earnings from U.S.-supplied resources abroad. **T F**

20. A GDP that has been deflated or inflated to reflect changes in the price level is called real GDP. **T F**

21. To adjust nominal GDP for a given year to obtain real GDP, it is necessary to multiply nominal GDP by the price index (expressed in hundredths) for that year. **T F**

22. If nominal GDP for an economy is $11,000 billion and the price index is 110, then real GDP is $10,000 billion. **T F**

23. GDP is a precise measure of the economic well-being of society. **T F**

24. The productive services of a homemaker are included in GDP. **T F**

25. The external costs from pollution and other activities associated with the production of the GDP are deducted from total output. **T F**

■ MULTIPLE-CHOICE QUESTIONS

Circle the letter that corresponds to the best answer.

1. Which is a primary use for national income accounting?
(a) It provides a basis for assessing the performance of the economy.
(b) It measures economic efficiency in specific industries.
(c) It estimates expenditures on nonproduction transactions.
(d) It analyzes the cost of pollution to the economy.

2. Gross domestic product (GDP) is defined as
(a) personal consumption expenditures and gross private domestic investment
(b) the sum of wage and salary compensation of employees, corporate profits, and interest income
(c) the market value of final goods and services produced within a country in 1 year
(d) the market value of all final and intermediate goods and services produced by the economy in 1 year

3. GDP provides an indication of society's valuation of the relative worth of goods and services because it
(a) provides an estimate of the value of secondhand sales
(b) gives increased weight to security transactions
(c) is an estimate of income received
(d) is a monetary measure

4. To include the value of the parts used in producing the automobiles turned out during a year in gross domestic product for that year would be an example of
(a) including a nonmarket transaction
(b) including a nonproduction transaction
(c) including a noninvestment transaction
(d) multiple counting

5. Which of the following is a public transfer payment?
(a) the Social Security benefits sent to a retired worker
(b) the sale of shares of stock in Microsoft Corporation
(c) the sale of a used (secondhand) toy house at a garage sale
(d) the birthday gift of a check for $50 sent by a grandmother to her grandchild

6. The sale in year 2 of an automobile produced in year 1 would not be included in the gross domestic product for year 2; doing so would involve
(a) including a nonmarket transaction
(b) including a nonproduction transaction
(c) including a noninvestment transaction
(d) public transfer payments

7. The service a babysitter performs when she stays at home with her baby brother while her parents are out and for which she receives no payment is not included in the gross domestic product because
(a) this is a nonmarket transaction
(b) this is a nonproduction transaction
(c) this is a noninvestment transaction
(d) multiple counting would be involved

8. According to national income accounting, money income derived from the production of this year's output is equal to
(a) corporate profits and the consumption of fixed capital
(b) the amount spent to purchase this year's total output
(c) the sum of interest income and the compensation of employees
(d) gross private domestic investment less the consumption of fixed capital

9. Which would be considered an investment according to economists?
(a) the purchase of newly issued shares of stock in Microsoft
(b) the construction of a new computer chip factory by Intel
(c) the resale of stock originally issued by the General Electric corporation
(d) the sale of a retail department store building by Sears to JCPenney

10. A refrigerator was produced by its manufacturer in year 1, sold to a retailer in year 1, and sold by the retailer to a final consumer in year 2. The refrigerator was
(a) counted as consumption in year 1
(b) counted as savings in year 1
(c) counted as investment in year 1
(d) not included in the gross domestic product of year 1

11. The annual charge that estimates the amount of private capital equipment used up in each year's production is called
(a) investment
(b) depreciation
(c) value added
(d) multiple counting

12. If gross private domestic investment is greater than depreciation, the economy will most likely be
(a) static
(b) declining
(c) expanding
(d) inflationary

13. GDP in an economy is $3452 billion. Consumer expenditures are $2343 billion, government purchases are $865 billion, and gross investment is $379 billion. Net exports are
(a) +$93 billion
(b) +$123 billion
(c) −$45 billion
(d) −$135 billion

14. What can happen to the allocation of corporate profits?
(a) It is paid to proprietors as income.
(b) It is paid to stockholders as dividends.
(c) It is paid to the government as interest income.
(d) It is retained by the corporation as rents.

15. The allowance for the private and publicly owned capital that has been used up or consumed in producing the year's GDP is
(a) net domestic product
(b) consumption of fixed capital
(c) undistributed corporate profits
(d) taxes on production and imports

Questions 16 through 22 use the national income accounting data given in the following table.

	Billions of dollars
Net private domestic investment	$ 32
Personal taxes	39
Transfer payments	19
Taxes on production and imports	8
Corporate income taxes	11
Personal consumption expenditures	217
Consumption of fixed capital	7
U.S. exports	15
Dividends	15
Government purchases	51
Net foreign factor income	0
Undistributed corporate profits	10
Social Security contributions	4
U.S. imports	17
Statistical discrepancy	0

16. Gross private domestic investment is equal to
(a) $32 billion
(b) $39 billion
(c) $45 billion
(d) $56 billion

17. Net exports are equal to
(a) −$2 billion
(b) $2 billion
(c) −$32 billion
(d) $32 billion

18. The gross domestic product is equal to
(a) $298 billion
(b) $302 billion
(c) $317 billion
(d) $305 billion

19. The net domestic product is equal to
(a) $298 billion
(b) $302 billion
(c) $317 billion
(d) $321 billion

20. National income is equal to
(a) $245 billion
(b) $278 billion
(c) $298 billion
(d) $310 billion

21. Personal income is equal to
(a) $266 billion
(b) $284 billion
(c) $290 billion
(d) $315 billion

22. Disposable income is equal to
(a) $245 billion
(b) $284 billion

(c) $305 billion
(d) $321 billion

23. If both nominal gross domestic product and the level of prices are rising, it is evident that
(a) real GDP is constant
(b) real GDP is declining
(c) real GDP is rising but not so rapidly as prices
(d) no conclusion can be drawn concerning the real GDP of the economy on the basis of this information

24. Suppose nominal GDP rose from $500 billion to $600 billion while the GDP price index increased from 125 to 150. Real GDP
(a) was constant
(b) increased
(c) decreased
(d) cannot be calculated from these figures

25. In an economy, the total expenditure for a market basket of goods in year 1 (the base year) was $4000 billion. In year 2, the total expenditure for the same market basket of goods was $4500 billion. What was the GDP price index for the economy in year 2?
(a) .88
(b) 1.13
(c) 188
(d) 113

26. Nominal GDP is less than real GDP in an economy in year 1. In year 2, nominal GDP is equal to real GDP. In year 3, nominal GDP is slightly greater than real GDP. In year 4, nominal GDP is significantly greater than real GDP. Which year is most likely to be the base year that is being used to calculate the price index for this economy?
(a) 1
(b) 2
(c) 3
(d) 4

27. Nominal GDP was $3774 billion in year 1 and the GDP deflator was 108 and nominal GDP was $3989 in year 2 and the GDP deflator that year was 112. What was real GDP in years 1 and 2, respectively?
(a) $3494 billion and $3562 billion
(b) $3339 billion and $3695 billion
(c) $3595 billion and $3725 billion
(d) $3643 billion and $3854 billion

28. A price index one year was 145, and the next year it was 167. What is the approximate percentage change in the price level from one year to the next as measured by that index?
(a) 12%
(b) 13%
(c) 14%
(d) 15%

29. GDP accounting includes
(a) the goods and services produced in the underground economy
(b) expenditures for equipment to reduce the pollution of the environment
(c) the value of the leisure enjoyed by citizens
(d) the goods and services produced but not bought and sold in the markets of the economy

30. Which is a major reason why GDP is *not* an accurate index of society's economic well-being?
(a) It includes changes in the value of leisure.
(b) It excludes many improvements in product quality.
(c) It includes transactions from the underground economy.
(d) It excludes transactions from the buying and selling of stocks.

■ PROBLEMS

1. Following are national income accounting figures for the United States.

	Billions of dollars
Exports	$ 367
Dividends	60
Consumption of fixed capital	307
Corporate profits	203
Compensation of employees	1722
Government purchases	577
Rents	33
Taxes on production and imports	255
Gross private domestic investment	437
Corporate income taxes	88
Transfer payments	320
Interest	201
Proprietors' income	132
Personal consumption expenditures	1810
Imports	338
Social Security contributions	148
Undistributed corporate profits	55
Personal taxes	372
Net foreign factor income	0
Statistical discrepancy	0

a. In the following table, use any of these figures to prepare an income statement for the economy similar to the one found in Table of the text.

Receipts: Expenditures approach		*Allocations: Income approach*	
Item	**Amount**	**Item**	**Amount**
______	$______	______	$______
______	$______	______	$______
______	$______	______	$______
______	$______	______	$______
		______	$______
		______	$______
		National income	$______
		______	$______
		______	$______
		______	$______
Gross domestic product	$______	Gross domestic product	$______

b. Use the other national accounts to find

(1) Net domestic product is $________

(2) National income is $________

(3) Personal income is $________

(4) Disposable income is $________

2. A farmer owns a plot of ground and sells the right to pump crude oil from his land to a crude oil producer. The crude oil producer agrees to pay the farmer $50 a barrel for every barrel pumped from the farmer's land.

a. During one year 10,000 barrels are pumped.

(1) The farmer receives a payment of $________ from the crude oil producer.

(2) The value added by the farmer is $________.

b. The crude oil producer sells the 10000 barrels pumped to a petroleum refiner at a price of $110 a barrel.

(1) The crude oil producer receives a payment of $________ from the refiner.

(2) The value added by the crude oil producer is $________.

c. The refiner employs a pipeline company to transport the crude oil from the farmer's land to the refinery and pays the pipeline company a fee of $5 a barrel for the oil transported.

(1) The pipeline company receives a payment of $________ from the refiner.

(2) The value added by the pipeline company is $________.

d. From the 10,000 barrels of crude oil, the refiner produces 400,000 gallons of gasoline which is sold to distributors and gasoline service stations at an average price of $3.50 per gallon.

(1) The total payment received by the refiner from its customers is $________.

(2) The value added by the refiner is $________.

e. The distributors and service stations sell the 400,000 gallons of gasoline to consumers at an average price of $3.75 a gallon.

(1) The total payment received by distributors and service stations is $________.

(2) The value added by them is $________.

(3) The total of the value added by the farmer, crude oil producer, pipeline company, refiner, and distributors and service stations is $________, and the market value of the gasoline sold to customers (the final good) is $________.

3. Following is a list of items which may or may not be included in the five income-output measures of the national income accounts **(GDP, NDP, NI, PI, DI).** Indicate in the space to the right of each which of the income-output measures includes this item; it is possible for the item to be included in none, one, two, three, four, or all of the measures. If the item is included in none of the measures, indicate why it is not included.

a. Interest on the national debt ________

b. The sale of a used computer ________

c. The production of shoes that are not sold by the manufacturer ________

d. The income of a dealer in illegal drugs ________

e. The purchase of a share of common stock on the New York Stock Exchange ________

f. The interest paid on the bonds of the General Electric, a corporation ________

g. The labor performed by a homemaker ________

h. The labor performed by a paid babysitter ________

i. The monthly check received by a college student from her parents ________

j. The purchase of a new tractor by a farmer ________

k. The labor performed by an assembly line worker in repapering his own kitchen ________

l. The services of a lawyer ________

m. The purchase of shoes from the manufacturer by a shoe retailer ________

n. The monthly check received from the Social Security Administration by a college student whose parents have died ________

o. The rent a homeowner would receive if she did not live in her own home ________

4. Following is hypothetical data for a market basket of goods in year 1 and year 2 for an economy.

a. Compute the expenditures for year 1.

MARKET BASKET FOR YEAR 1 (BASE YEAR)

Products	Quantity	Price	Expenditures
Toys	3	$10	$____
Pencils	5	2	$____
Books	7	5	$____
Total			$____

b. Compute the expenditures for year 2.

MARKET BASKET FOR YEAR 2

Products	Quantity	Price	Expenditures
Toys	3	$11	$____
Pencils	5	3	$____
Books	7	6	$____
Total			$____

c. In the space below, show how you computed the GDP price index for year 2. ________

5. The following table shows nominal GDP figures for 3 years and the price indices for each of the 3 years. (The GDP figures are in billions.)

Year	Nominal GDP	Price Index	Real GDP
1929	$104	121	$____
1933	56	91	$____
1939	91	100	$____

a. Use the price indices to compute the real GDP in each year. (You may round your answers to the nearest billion dollars.) Write answers in the table.

b. Which of the 3 years appears to be the base year? ________

c. Between

(1) 1929 and 1933 the economy experienced (inflation, deflation) ________.

(2) 1933 and 1939 it experienced ________.

d. The nominal GDP figure

(1) for 1929 was (deflated, inflated, neither) ________.

(2) for 1933 was ________.

(3) for 1939 was ________.

e. The price level

(1) fell by ________% from 1929 to 1933.

(2) rose by ________% from 1933 to 1939.

■ SHORT ANSWER AND ESSAY QUESTIONS

1. Of what use is national income accounting to economists and policymakers?

2. What is the definition of GDP? How are the values of output produced at a U.S.-owned factory in the United States and a foreign-owned factory in the United States treated in GDP accounting?

3. Why is GDP a monetary measure?

4. How does GDP accounting avoid multiple counting and exaggeration of the value of GDP?

5. Why does GDP accounting exclude nonproduction transactions?

6. What are the two principal types of nonproduction transactions? List examples of each type.

7. What are the two sides to GDP accounting? What are the meaning and relationship between the two sides?

8. What would be included in personal consumption expenditures by households?

9. How is gross private domestic investment defined?

10. Is residential construction counted as investment or consumption? Explain.

11. Why is a change in inventories an investment?

12. How do you define an expanding production capacity using the concepts of gross private domestic investment and depreciation?

13. What do government purchases include and what do they exclude?

14. How are imports and exports handled in GDP accounting?

15. What are six income components of GDP that add up to national income? Define and explain the characteristics of each component.

16. What are the three adjustments made to the national income to get it to equal GDP? Define and explain the characteristics of each one.

17. Explain how to calculate net domestic product (NDP), national income (NI), personal income (PI), and disposable income (DI).

18. What is the difference between real and nominal GDP? Describe two methods economists use to determine real GDP. Illustrate each method with an example.

19. Describe the real world relationship between nominal and real GDP in the United States. Explain why nominal GDP may be greater or less than real GDP depending on the year or period selected.

20. Why might GDP not be considered an accurate measure of total output and the economic well-being of society? Identify seven shortcomings of GDP.

ANSWERS

Chapter 7 Measuring Domestic Output and National Income

FILL-IN QUESTIONS

1. production, policies
2. market, final, in 1 year
3. within, included
4. monetary, relative
5. final, intermediate, over, multiple
6. nonproduction, financial, second
7. durable, nondurable, services
8. capital, construction of new, inventories
9. depreciation, positive, expanding
10. minus, negative, positive
11. $C + I_g + G + X_n$
12. plus, public, private
13. taxes, dividends, profits
14. GDP, subtracted, added, added
15. depreciation, capital, net domestic product
16. plus, minus, plus, minus, minus
17. nominal, real
18. divided, multiplied
19. nominal GDP, the price index, nominal, real
20. *a.* nonmarket, leisure; *b.* quality, composition; *c.* environment, underground

TRUE–FALSE QUESTIONS

1. T, p. 130	**6.** T, pp. 131	**11.** F, p. 133
2. F, p. 130	**7.** F, p. 131	**12.** F, p. 133
3. F, p. 130	**8.** T, p. 132	**13.** T, pp. 133–134
4. T, pp. 130–131	**9.** T, p. 132	**14.** F, p. 134
5. F, pp. 130–131	**10.** F, p. 132	**15.** F, p. 134

16. T, p. 135
17. T, p. 136
18. F, pp. 136–137
19. T, p. 137
20. T, p. 141
21. F, p. 142
22. T, p. 142
23. F, p. 143
24. F, p. 143
25. F, p. 144

MULTIPLE-CHOICE QUESTIONS

1. a, p. 130
2. c, p. 130
3. d, p. 130
4. d, pp. 130–131
5. a, p. 131
6. b, p. 132
7. a, pp. 131, 143
8. b, p. 132
9. b, p. 133
10. c, p. 133–134
11. b, p. 134
12. c, p. 134
13. d, p. 135
14. b, p. 136
15. b, p. 137
16. b, pp. 133–134
17. a, p. 135
18. d, p. 135
19. a, pp. 138
20. c, pp. 138
21. b, pp. 138
22. a, pp. 139
23. d, p. 141
24. a, p. 142
25. d, p. 142
26. b, pp. 142–143
27. a, pp. 142–143
28. d, pp. 142–143
29. b, p. 144
30. b, pp. 143–144

PROBLEMS

1. *a.* See the following table; *b.* (1) 2546, (2) 2546, (3) 2320, (4) 1948

Receipts: Expenditures approach Item	Amount	*Allocations: Income approach* Item	Amount
Personal consumption expenditures	$1810	Compensation of employees	$1722
		Rents	33
Gross private domestic investment	437	Interest	201
		Proprietors' income	132
		Corporate profits	203
Government purchases	577	Taxes on production and imports	255
Net exports	29	National income	$2546
		Net foreign factor Income	0
		Consumption of fixed capital	307
Gross domestic product	$2853	Gross domestic product	$2853

2. *a.* 500,000, (2) 500,000; *b.* (1) 1,100,000, (2) 600,000; *c.* (1) 50,000, (2) 50,000; *d.* (1) 1,400,000, (2) 250,000; *e.* (1) 1,500,000, (2) 100,000; *f.* 1,500,000, 1,500,000

3. *a.* personal income and disposable income, a public transfer payment; *b.* none, a secondhand sale; *c.* all, represents investment (additions to inventories); *d.* none, illegal production and incomes are not included if not reported; *e.* none, a purely financial transaction; *f.* all; *g.* none, a nonmarket transaction; *h.* all if reported as income, none if not reported; *i.* none, a private transfer payment; *j.* all; *k.* none, a nonmarket transaction; *l.* all; *m.* all, represents additions to the inventory of the retailer; *n.* personal income and disposable income, a public transfer payment; *o.* all, estimate of rental value of owner-occupied homes is included in rents as if it were income and in personal consumption expenditures as if it were payment for a service

4. *a.* 30, 10, 35, 75; *b.* 33, 15, 42, 90; *c.* ($90/75) × 100 = 120

5. *a.* 86, 62, 91; *b.* 1939; *c.* (1) deflation, (2) inflation; *d.* (1) deflated, (2) inflated, (3) neither; *e.* (1) 24.8 (2) 9.9.

SHORT ANSWER AND ESSAY QUESTIONS

1. p. 130
2. p. 130
3. p. 130
4. pp. 130–131
5. pp. 131–132
6. pp. 131–132
7. p. 132
8. p. 133
9. p. 133
10. p. 133
11. p. 133
12. p. 133–134
13. p. 134
14. p. 135
15. p. 136
16. pp. 137–138
17. pp. 138–139
18. p. 141
19. pp. 142–143
20. pp. 143–144

CHAPTER 8

Economic Growth

The economic health of a nation relies on economic growth because it reduces the burden of scarcity. Small differences in real growth rates result in large differences in the standards of living in nations. The first short section of the chapter describes how economists measure economic growth, explains why economic growth is important, and presents some basic facts about the U.S. growth rates.

What is especially fascinating about this topic is that continuous and sustained increases in economic growth and the resulting significant improvements in living standards within a lifetime are a relatively new development from a historical perspective. As described in the second section of the chapter, the era of **modern economic growth** began with the invention of the steam engine in 1776 and the industrial revolution that followed it. Not all nations, however, experienced such modern growth at the same time or period, which explains why some nations have a higher standard of living than other nations. As you will learn, it is possible for the poorer nations to catch up with the richer nations if they can sustain a higher level of growth.

The third section of the chapter describes the institutional structures that also promote and sustain modern economic growth in the richer, **leader countries.** These structures involve establishing strong property rights, protecting patents and copyrights, maintaining efficient financial institutions, providing widespread education, advocating free trade among nations, and using a system of markets and prices to allocate scarce resources. The poorer, **follower countries** are often missing one or more of these institutional features.

A major purpose of the chapter is to explain the factors that contribute to this economic growth. The fourth section presents the six main determinants of economic growth. The four **supply factors** increase the output potential of the economy. Whether the economy actually produces its full potential—that is, whether the economy has both full employment and full production—depends upon two other factors: the level of aggregate demand (the **demand factor**) and the efficiency with which the economy allocates resources (the **efficiency factor**).

The fifth section of the chapter places the factors contributing to economic growth in graphical perspective with the use of the production possibilities model that was originally presented in Chapter 1. It is now used to discuss how the two major supply factors—labor input and labor productivity—shift the production possibilities curve outward.

Growth accounting is discussed in the sixth section of the chapter. Economic growth in the United States depends on the increase in the size of its labor force and on the increase in labor productivity. This latter element has been especially important in recent years and is attributed to five factors: technological advances, the expansion of the stock of capital goods, the improved education and training of its labor force, economies of scale, and the reallocation of resources.

The seventh section of the chapter evaluates the recent rise in the average rate of **productivity growth.** A major development in recent years was the almost doubling of the rate of labor productivity from 1995–2009 compared with that in the 1973–1995 period. This change heralded to some observers that the United States had achieved a recent rise in the average rate of productivity growth that is characterized by advances in technology, more entrepreneurship, increasing returns from resource inputs, and greater global competition. Whether this higher rate of growth is a long-lasting trend remains to be seen because the trend may simply be a short-run rather than a long-run change.

The eighth and last section of the chapter raises an important question: Is more **economic growth desirable and sustainable?** This controversy has two sides. The antigrowth view is based on the environmental problems it creates, its effects on human values, and doubts about whether growth can be sustained. The defense of growth is based in part on its contribution to higher standards of living, improvements in worker safety and the environment, and history of sustainability.

■ CHECKLIST

When you have studied this chapter you should be able to

- ☐ Define economic growth in two different ways.
- ☐ Explain why economic growth is an important goal.
- ☐ Use the rule of 70 to show how different growth rates affect real domestic output over time.
- ☐ Describe the growth record of the U.S. economy since 1950.
- ☐ Explain how modern economic growth changed work, living standards, and societies.
- ☐ Discuss reasons for the uneven distribution of economic growth in modern times.
- ☐ Describe the differences in economic growth for leader countries and follower countries.
- ☐ Explain how substantial differences in living standards can be caused by differences in labor supply.
- ☐ List and describe six institutional structures that promote economic growth.

☐ Identify four supply factors that are determinants of economic growth.
☐ Explain the demand factor as a determinant of economic growth.
☐ Describe the efficiency factor as a determinant of economic growth.
☐ Show graphically how economic growth shifts the production possibilities curve.
☐ Explain the rationale for an equation for real GDP that is based on labor inputs and labor productivity.
☐ Compare the relative importance of the two major means of increasing the real GDP in the United States.
☐ Describe the main sources of growth in the productivity of labor in the United States and state their relative importance.
☐ Describe the rise in the average rate of productivity growth in the United States since 1973.
☐ Explain the relationship between productivity growth and the standard of living and state why it is important.
☐ Discuss how the microchip and information technology contributed to the recent rise in the average rate of productivity growth.
☐ Describe the sources of increasing returns and economies of scale within the recent rise in the average rate of productivity growth.
☐ Explain how the rise in the average rate of productivity growth increases global competition.
☐ Discuss the implications from the rise in the average rate of productivity growth for long-term economic growth.
☐ Offer a skeptical perspective on the longevity of the rise in the average rate of productivity growth.
☐ Present several arguments against more economic growth.
☐ Make a case for more economic growth.
☐ Explain the factors that have contributed to China's high rate of economic growth over the past 25 years and the challenges for that economy (*Last Word*).

■ CHAPTER OUTLINE

1. ***Economic growth*** can be defined in two ways: as an increase in real GDP over some time period or as an increase in ***real GDP per capita*** over some time period. This second definition takes into account the size of the population. With either definition economic growth is calculated as a percentage rate of growth per year.

a. Economic growth is important because it lessens the burden of scarcity; it provides the means of satisfying economic wants more fully and fulfilling new wants.

b. One or two percentage point differences in the rate of growth result in substantial differences in annual increases in the economy's output. The approximate number of years required to double GDP can be calculated by the ***rule of 70*** which involves dividing 70 by the annual percentage rate of growth.

c. In the United States, the rate of growth in real GDP has been about 3.2 percent annually since 1950. The growth rate for real per capita GDP in the United States has been about 2.3 percent annually since 1950.

(1) The growth record, however, may be understated because it does not take into account improvements in product quality or increases in leisure time. The effects of growth on the environment or quality of life could be negative *or* positive.

(2) U.S. growth rates vary quarterly and annually depending on a variety of factors; sustained growth is both a historically new occurrence and also one that is not shared equally by all countries.

2. ***Modern economic growth*** can be described as an improvement in living standards that is continual and sustained over time. The result is a substantial improvement in the standard of living in less than a human lifetime. Such modern economic growth began in England around 1776 with the invention and use of the steam engine, the mass production of goods, and expanded trade among nations. Subsequent developments include the use of electric or other sources of power, more technological development, and new products and services. This modern economic growth contributed to the transformation of the culture, society, and politics of nations.

a. There has been an uneven distribution of this modern economic growth among nations, and such a distribution accounts for the large differences in per capita GDP among nations. The United States and nations of western Europe experienced modern economic growth many years earlier than did other nations, and as a result have standards of living that are much higher than most other nations.

b. It is possible for poorer countries with a lower per capita income ***(follower countries)*** to catch up with richer nations that have a higher per capita income ***(leader countries).*** Leader countries must invent and implement new technology to grow their economies, but such a process means the growth rates in leader nations will be slow. Follower countries can have a faster growth rate because they simply adopt the existing technologies and apply them to the country, thereby skipping the lengthy process of technological development of the leader countries.

(1) Small differences in growth rates can lead to the eventual convergence and similarity in real GDP per capita of leader countries and follower countries over time (see Table 8.2).

(2) The real GDP per capita of the United States is higher than other leader countries (e. g., France) because of differences in labor supply: a larger fraction of the U.S. population is employed and U.S. employees work more hours per week.

3. Institutional structures are important for starting and sustaining modern economic growth because they increase saving and investment, develop new technologies, and promote more efficient allocation of resources. Such institutional structures include strong support for property rights, the use of patents and copyrights, efficient financial institutions, widespread education and literacy, free trade, and a competitive market system. There are other factors that also contribute, such as a stable political system and positive social or cultural attitudes toward work and risk taking.

4. The ***determinants of growth*** depend on supply, demand, and efficiency factors.

a. The ***supply factor*** includes the quantity and quality of resources (natural, human, and capital) and technology.

b. The ***demand factor*** influences the level of aggregate demand in the economy that is important for sustaining full employment of resources.

c. The ***efficiency factor*** affects the efficient use of resources to obtain maximum production of goods and services (productive efficiency) and to allocate them to their highest and best use by society (allocative efficiency).

5. A familiar ***economic model*** can be used for the analysis of economic growth.

a. In the ***production possibilities model,*** economic growth shifts the production possibilities curve outward because of improvement in supply factors. Whether the economy operates on the frontier of the curve or inside the curve depends on the demand factor and efficiency factors.

b. Discussions of growth, however, focus primarily on supply factors. From this perspective, economic growth is obtained by increasing the *labor inputs* and by increasing the labor productivity. This relationship can be expressed in equation terms: Real GDP = Worker-hours × Labor productivity.

(1) The hours of work are determined by the size of the working-age population and the ***labor-force participation rate*** (the percentage of the working age population in the labor force).

(2) ***Labor productivity*** (real output per work hour) is determined by many factors such as technological advance, the quantity of capital goods, the quality of labor, and the efficiency in the use of inputs.

6. Several factors are important in ***growth accounting.***

a. The two main factors are increases in quantity of labor (hours of work) and increases in labor productivity. In recent years the most important factor has been increased labor productivity, so it is worthwhile identifying the main *five factors* to help increase labor productivity.

b. ***Technological advance*** is combining given amounts of resources in new and innovative ways that result in a larger output. It involves the use of new managerial methods and business organizations that improve production. Technological advance is also embodied in new capital investment that adds to the productive capacity of the economy. It accounted for about 40 percent of the recent increase in productivity growth.

c. The ***quantity of capital*** has expanded with the increase in saving and investment spending in capital goods. This private investment has increased the quantity of each worker's tools, equipment, and machinery. There is also public investment in ***infrastructure*** in the United States. The increase in the quantity of capital goods explains about 30 percent of productivity growth.

d. Increased investment in ***human capital*** (the training and education of workers) has expanded the productivity of workers, and has accounted for about 15 percent of productivity growth.

e. Two other factors, taken together, account for about 15 percent of productivity growth.

(1) ***Economies of scale*** means that there are reductions in the per-unit cost for firms as output expands. These economies occur as the market for products expands and firms have the opportunity to increase output to meet this greater demand.

(2) ***Improved allocation of resources*** occurs when workers are shifted from lower-productivity employment to higher-productivity employment in an economy. Included in this category would be reductions in discrimination in labor markets and reduced barriers to trade, both of which increase the efficient use of labor resources.

7. Increases in ***productivity growth,*** even small ones, can have a substantial effect on average real hourly wages and the standard of living in an economy. From 1973–1995, labor productivity grew by an average of 1.5 percent yearly, but from 1995–2009 it grew by 2.8 percent yearly. Clearly, productivity has accelerated since 1995. The recent rise in the average rate of productivity growth means there can be a faster rate of economic growth and improvement in standards of living.

a. The reasons for the rise in the average rate of productivity growth are based on several factors.

(1) There has been a dramatic rise in entrepreneurship and innovation based on the microchip and ***information technology.***

(2) The new ***start-up firms*** often experience ***increasing returns,*** which means a firm's output increases by a larger percentage than the increase in its resource inputs. These increasing returns have been achieved by more specialized inputs, the spreading of development costs, simultaneous consumption, ***network effects,*** and ***learning by doing.***

(3) The new technology and improvements in communication have increased global competition, thus lowering production costs, restraining price increases, and stimulating innovation to remain competitive.

b. The recent rise in the average rate of productivity growth means there can be a faster rate of economic growth and improvement in standards of living. This development does not mean that the business cycle is dead, but rather that the trend line for productivity growth and economic growth has become steeper.

c. Questions remain about whether there is a new trend of higher productivity rates or just a short upturn in the business cycle. Skeptics wonder whether the increase in productivity growth can be sustained over a longer period of time or whether the economy will return to its long-term trend in productivity.

d. The conclusion is that the prospects for productivity growth to continue are good because of the wider use of information technology, yet in the past few years productivity growth has slowed, which raises questions about whether the rise in the average rate of productivity growth is a long-run trend and sustainable.

8. There is an ongoing debate about whether economic growth is ***desirable and sustainable.***

a. The antigrowth view sees several problems: Growth pollutes the environment; may produce more goods and services, but does not create a better life; and may not be sustainable at the current rate of resource depletion.

b. The defense of economic growth is based on several considerations: Growth produces a higher standard of living and reduces the burden of scarcity; the technology it creates improves people's lives and can reduce pollution; and it is sustainable because market incentives encourage the use of substitute resources.

9. (*Last Word*). China has experienced annual rates of economic growth of nearly 9 percent over the past 25 years. Real income per capita has also increased by about 8 percent annually since 1980. The increased output and rising incomes have fueled increases in saving and investment that in turn contribute to an increase in the stock of capital goods and technological advance. This economic growth is not without economic problems such as rising inflation, government inefficiencies, the unemployment of rural workers, trade disputes, and uneven economic development within the nation.

■ HINTS AND TIPS

1. Chapter 8 contains very little economics that should be new to you. Chapter 1 introduced you to the production possibilities model that is now discussed in more detail. Chapter 6 introduced you to GDP and modern economic growth.

2. Table 8.3 is important if you want to understand the factors that influence economic growth in the United States. The figures in the table indicate the relative importance of each major factor in different periods. In recent years, almost all of U.S. economic growth arose from increases in labor productivity. Five factors affecting the growth of labor productivity include technological advance, quantity of capital, education and training, economies of scale, and resource allocation.

3. The last two sections of the chapter focus on major economic issues about which there is some debate. You will want to evaluate the evidence for and against the idea that there is a lasting increase in productivity growth. You will want to understand the advantages and disadvantages of economic growth.

■ IMPORTANT TERMS

economic growth	**labor productivity**
real GDP per capita	**growth accounting**
rule of 70	**infrastructure**
modern economic growth	**human capital**
follower countries	**economies of scale**
leader countries	**information technology**
supply factor	**start-up firms**
demand factor	**increasing returns**
efficiency factor	**network effects**
labor-force participation rate	**learning by doing**

SELF-TEST

■ FILL-IN QUESTIONS

1. Economic growth is best measured either by an increase in (nominal, real) ____________ GDP over a time period or by an increase in ____________ GDP per capita over a time period. A rise in real GDP per capita (increases, decreases) ____________ the standard of living and ____________ the burden of scarcity in the economy.

2. Assume an economy has a real GDP of $3600 billion. If the growth rate is 5 percent, real GDP will increase by ($360, $180) ____________ billion next year; but if the rate of growth is only 3 percent, the annual increase in real GDP will be ($54, $108) ____________ billion. A two percentage point difference in the growth rate results in a ($72, $254) ____________ billion difference in the annual increase in real GDP.

3. Since 1950, real GDP in the United States increased at an annual rate of about (2.0, 3.2) ____________ percent and real GDP per capita increased at an annual rate of about ____________ percent.

4. Modern economic growth is uneven across countries because leader countries have experienced such growth for a (shorter, longer) ____________ time period and follower countries have experienced such growth for a ____________ time period. It is possible for a follower country to catch up with the standard of living of a leader country if the economic growth rate for the follower country is significantly (smaller, larger) ____________ than the growth rate for the leader country, and the difference is sustained over time.

5. Among the institutional structures that contribute to modern economic growth in leader countries are established property (lines, rights) ____________, protection for copyrights and (movies, patents) ____________, the efficient channeling of savings and investment, (financial, government) ____________ institutions, widespread programs for (immigration, education) ____________, specialization in production by nations that comes from (free, restricted) ____________ trade, and the use of the competitive market system.

6. The four supply factors in economic growth are

a. ____________

b. ____________

c. ____________

d. ____________

7. To realize its growing production potential, a nation must fully employ its expanding supplies of resources, which is the (efficiency, demand) ______________ factor in economic growth, and it must also achieve productive and allocative ______________, the other factor contributing to economic growth.

8. In the production possibilities model, economic growth increases primarily because of (demand, supply) ______________ factors that shift the production possibilities curve to the (left, right) ______________; but if there is less than full employment and production, the economy (may, may not) ______________ realize its potential.

9. Real GDP of any economy in any year is equal to the quantity of labor employed (divided, multiplied) ______________ by the productivity of labor. The quantity of labor is measured by the number of (businesses, hours of labor) ______________. Productivity is equal to real GDP per (capita, worker-hour) ______________.

10. The quantity of labor employed in the economy in any year depends on the size of the (unemployed, employed) ______________ labor force and the length of the average workweek. The size element depends on the size of the working-age population and the labor-force (unemployment, participation) ______________ rate.

11. The recent record of economic growth in the United States shows that the increase in the quantity of labor is (more, less) ______________ important than increases in labor productivity in accounting for economic growth.

12. Factors contributing to labor productivity include

a. technological ______________

b. increases in the quantity of ______________ and in the quantity available per ______________

c. the improved ______________ and ______________ of workers

d. economies of ______________

e. the improved ______________ of resources.

13. An increase in the quantity of the capital stock of a nation is the result of saving and (consumption, investment) ______________. A key determinant of labor productivity is the amount of capital goods available per (consumer, worker) ______________.

14. Infrastructure, such as highways and bridges, is a form of (private, public) ______________ investment that complements ______________ capital goods.

15. The knowledge and skills that make a productive worker are a form of (physical, human) ______________ capital. This type of capital is often obtained through (consumption, education) ______________.

16. Reductions in per-unit costs that result from the increase in the size of markets and firms are called (improved resource allocation, economies of scale) ______________, but the movement of a worker from a job with lower productivity to one with higher productivity would be an example of ______________.

17. A sustained increase in labor productivity over time will (increase, decrease) ______________ real output, ______________ real income, and ______________ real wages.

18. The characteristics of the recent rise in the average rate of productivity growth are (advances, declines) ______________ in information technology, business firms that experience returns to scale that are (decreasing, increasing) ______________, and global competition that is ______________.

19. Skeptics contend that the increase in the rate of productivity growth may be a (short-run, long-run) ______________ trend that is not sustainable over a ______________ period.

20. Critics of economic growth contend that it (cleans up, pollutes) ______________ the environment, it (does, does not) ______________ solve problems such as poverty and homelessness, and (is, is not) ______________ sustainable. Defenders of economic growth say that it creates (less, greater) ______________ material abundance, results in a (higher, lower) ______________ standard of living, and an efficient and sustainable allocation of resources based on price (discounts, incentives) ______________.

■ TRUE–FALSE QUESTIONS

Circle T if the statement is true, F if it is false.

1. Economic growth is measured as either an increase in real GDP or an increase in real GDP per capita. **T F**

2. Real GDP is the best measure of economic growth for comparing standards of living among nations. **T F**

3. Suppose two economies both have GDPs of $500 billion. If the GDPs grow at annual rates of 3 percent in the first economy and 5 percent in the second economy, the difference in their amounts of growth in one year is $10 billion. **T F**

4. Since 1950, the U.S. data show that the average annual rate of growth was greater for real GDP per capita than for real GDP. **T F**

5. Growth rate estimates generally attempt to take into account changes in the quality of goods produced and changes in the amount of leisure members of the economy enjoy. **T F**

6. Before the advent of modern economic growth starting in England in the later 1700s, living standards showed no sustained increases over time. **T F**

7. Poorer follower countries can never catch up with and or surpass the living standards of rich leader countries. **T F**

8. An institutional structure that promotes economic growth is a competitive market system. **T F**

9. Changes in the physical and technical agents of production are supply factors for economic growth that enable an economy to expand its potential GDP. **T F**

10. The demand factor in economic growth refers to the ability of the economy to expand its production as the demand for products grows. **T F**

11. An increase in the quantity and quality of natural resources is an efficiency factor for economic growth. **T F**

12. A shift outward in the production possibilities curve is the direct result of improvements in supply factors for economic growth. **T F**

13. The real GDP of an economy in any year is equal to its input of labor divided by the productivity of labor. **T F**

14. The hours of labor input depend on the size of the employed labor force and the length of the average workweek. **T F**

15. Increased labor productivity has been more important than increased labor inputs in the growth of the U.S. economy since 1995. **T F**

16. The largest factor increasing labor productivity in the U.S. economy has been technological advance. **T F**

17. One determinant of labor productivity is the quantity of capital goods available to workers. **T F**

18. Public investment in the form of new infrastructure often complements private capital investment. **T F**

19. Education and training contribute to a worker's stock of human capital. **T F**

20. Economies of scale are reductions in per-unit cost that result in a decrease in the size of markets and firms. **T F**

21. Moving workers from sectors of the economy with lower productivity to sectors of the economy with higher productivity improves the allocation of resources in the economy. **T F**

22. Productivity growth is the basic source of improvements in real wage rates and the standard of living. **T F**

23. More specialized inputs and network effects are two sources of increasing returns and economies of scale in the recent rise in the average rate of productivity growth. **T F**

24. Critics of economic growth say that it adds to environmental problems, increases human stress, and exhausts natural resources. **T F**

25. Defenders of economic growth say it is sustainable in the short run, but not in the long run. **T F**

■ MULTIPLE-CHOICE QUESTIONS

Circle the letter that corresponds to the best answer.

1. Which of the following is the best measure of economic growth?
(a) the supply factor
(b) the demand factor
(c) real GDP per capita
(d) nominal GDP per capita

2. If the real output of an economy were to increase from \$2000 billion to \$2100 billion in 1 year, the rate of growth of real output during that year would be
(a) 1%
(b) 5%
(c) 10%
(d) 50%

3. Which is a benefit of real economic growth to a society?
(a) The society is less able to satisfy new wants.
(b) Everyone enjoys a greater nominal income.
(c) The burden of scarcity increases.
(d) The standard of living increases.

4. Which concept would be associated with sustained and ongoing increases in living standards that can cause dramatic increases in the standard of living within less than a single human lifetime?
(a) increasing returns
(b) economies of scale
(c) growth accounting
(d) modern economic growth

5. Which one of the following is true?
(a) Poor follower countries can catch up and even surpass the living standards of rich leader countries.
(b) As a result of modern economic growth, there are no sustained increases in growth over time.
(c) Differences in labor supply make a minimal contribution to differences in living standards.
(d) There is a relatively even distribution of economic growth across nations.

6. Which is an institutional structure that most promotes economic growth?
(a) enforcing property rights
(b) moving to a command economy
(c) eliminating patents and copyrights
(d) placing restrictions on international trade

7. A supply factor in economic growth would be
(a) an increase in the efficient use of resources
(b) a decline in the rate of resource depletion
(c) an improvement in the quality of labor
(d) an increase in consumption spending

8. Which is a demand factor in economic growth?
(a) an increase in the purchasing power of the economy
(b) an increase in the economy's stock of capital goods
(c) more natural resources
(d) technological progress

Use the following graph to answer Questions 9 and 10.

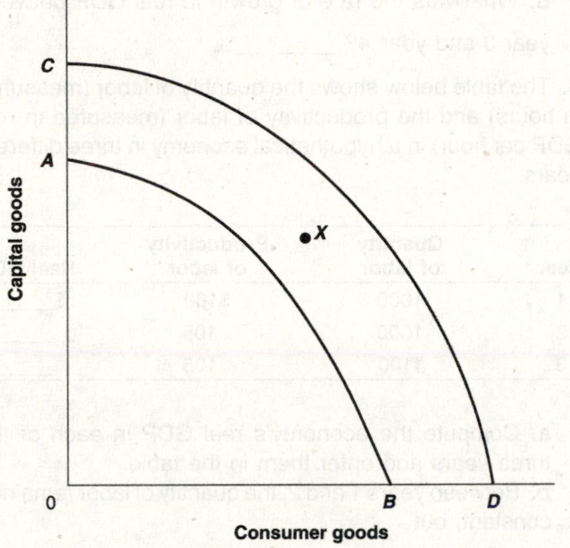

9. If the production possibilities curve of an economy shifts from ***AB*** to ***CD,*** it is most likely the result of what factor affecting economic growth?
(a) a supply factor
(b) a demand factor
(c) an efficiency factor
(d) an allocation factor

10. If the production possibilities curve for an economy is at ***CD*** but the economy is operating at point ***X,*** the reasons are most likely
(a) supply and environmental factors
(b) demand and efficiency factors
(c) labor inputs and labor productivity
(d) technological progress

11. Total output or real GDP in any year is equal to
(a) labor inputs divided by resource outputs
(b) labor productivity multiplied by real output
(c) worker-hours multiplied by labor productivity
(d) worker-hours divided by labor productivity

12. Assume that an economy has 1000 workers, each working 2000 hours per year. If the average real output per worker-hour is $9, then total output or real GDP will be
(a) $2 million
(b) $9 million
(c) $18 million
(d) $24 million

13. What is the other major factor that, when combined with the growth of labor productivity, accounts for long-term economic growth in the United States?
(a) an increase in government spending
(b) an increase in the quantity of labor
(c) a decrease in the interest rate
(d) a decrease in personal taxes

14. The factor accounting for the largest increase in the productivity of labor in the United States has been
(a) economies of scale
(b) technological advance
(c) the quantity of capital
(d) the education and training of workers

15. How does a nation typically acquire more capital goods?
(a) by reducing the workweek and increasing leisure
(b) by saving income and using it for capital investment
(c) by increasing government regulation on the capital stock
(d) by reducing the amount of capital goods available per worker

16. An example of U.S. public investment in infrastructure would be
(a) an airline company
(b) a natural gas pipeline
(c) an auto and truck plant
(d) an interstate highway

17. Economists call the knowledge and skills that make a productive worker
(a) the labor-force participation rate
(b) learning by doing
(c) human capital
(d) infrastructure

18. What economic concept would be most closely associated with a situation where a large manufacturer of food products uses extensive assembly lines with computerization and robotics that serve to reduce per-unit costs of production?
(a) economies of scale
(b) sustainability of growth
(c) network effects
(d) simultaneous consumption

19. The decline of discrimination in education and labor markets increased the overall rate of labor productivity in the economy by giving groups freedom to move from jobs with lower productivity to ones with higher productivity. This development would be an example of a(n)
(a) fall in the labor-force participation rate
(b) rise in the natural rate of unemployment
(c) improvement in resource allocation
(d) technological advance

20. From 1995 to 2009, the average rate of productivity growth was approximately
(a) 0.7%
(b) 1.4%
(c) 2.8%
(d) 5.6%

21. A core element of the productivity speedup in recent years is an increase in entrepreneurship and innovation based on
(a) more government spending
(b) higher rates of price inflation

(c) the use of less specialized inputs
(d) advances in information technology

22. Increasing returns would be a situation where a firm
(a) triples its workforce and other inputs, and its output doubles
(b) doubles its workforce and other inputs, and its output triples
(c) doubles its workforce and other inputs, and its output doubles
(d) quadruples its workforce and other inputs, and its output triples

23. Which would be a source of increasing returns and economies of scale within the recent rise in the average rate of productivity growth?
(a) social environment
(b) noninflationary growth
(c) simultaneous consumption
(d) less specialized inputs

24. A skeptic of the longevity of the increase in productivity growth would argue that it
(a) is based on learning by doing instead of infrastructure
(b) raises tax revenues collected by government
(c) lowers the natural rate of unemployment
(d) is based on a short-run trend

25. Defenders of rapid economic growth say that it
(a) produces an equitable distribution of income
(b) creates common property resources
(c) leads to higher living standards
(d) spreads costs of development

■ PROBLEMS

1. Given the hypothetical data in the table below, calculate the annual rates of growth in real GDP and real per capita GDP over the period given. The numbers for real GDP are in billions.

Year	Real GDP	Annual growth in %	Real GDP per capita	Annual growth in %
1	$2,416		$11,785	
2	2,472	____	11,950	____
3	2,563	____	12,213	____
4	2,632	____	12,421	____
5	2,724	____	12,719	____
6	2,850	____	12,948	____

2. Suppose the real GDP and the population of an economy in seven different years were those shown in the following table.

Year	Population, million	Real GDP, billions of dollars	Per capita real GDP
1	30	$ 9	$300
2	60	24	____
3	90	45	____
4	120	66	____
5	150	90	____
6	180	99	____
7	210	105	____

a. How large would the real per capita GDP of the economy be in each of the other six years? Put your figures in the table.
b. What would have been the size of the optimum population of this economy? ________
c. What was the *amount* of growth in real GDP between year 1 and year 2? $ ________
d. What was the rate of growth in real GDP between year 3 and year 4? ________%

3. The table below shows the quantity of labor (measured in hours) and the productivity of labor (measured in real GDP per hour) in a hypothetical economy in three different years.

Year	Quantity of labor	Productivity of labor	Real GDP
1	1000	$100	$____
2	1000	105	____
3	1100	105	____

a. Compute the economy's real GDP in each of the three years and enter them in the table.
b. Between years 1 and 2, the quantity of labor remained constant, but
(1) the productivity of labor increased by ________%, and
(2) as a consequence, real GDP increased by ________%.
c. Between years 2 and 3, the productivity of labor remained constant, but
(1) the quantity of labor increased by ________%, and
(2) as a consequence, real GDP increased by ________%.
d. Between years 1 and 3
(1) real GDP increased by ________%, and
(2) this rate of increase is approximately equal to the sum of the rates of increase in the (quantity, productivity) ________ and the ________ of labor.

4. Use the rule of 70 to calculate how many years it will take to double the standard of living in an economy given different average annual rates of growth in labor productivity and enter the answers in the table.

Productivity	Years
1.0%	____
1.4	____
1.8	____
2.2	____
2.6	____
3.0	____

What can you conclude about the effect of small changes in the average annual rate of productivity growth on the standard of living? ________

■ SHORT ANSWER AND ESSAY QUESTIONS

1. What two ways are used to measure economic growth? Why does the size of the population matter when considering growth rates?

2. Why is economic growth a widely held and desired economic goal? Explain the reasons.

3. Describe the growth rate for the United States since 1950. What three qualifications should be made about the rate?

4. Explain how modern economic growth occurred and how it has affected nations and societies.

5. Why is there an uneven distribution of economic growth?

6. Explain how it is possible for the standards of living in poorer nations to catch up with the standards of living in richer nations. What role does technology play in the catch-up process?

7. Why is the GDP per capita in the United States so much higher than that of other rich leader nations?

8. Describe six institutional structures that promote economic growth in a nation. What other factors also influence a nation's capacity for economic growth?

9. What are the six basic determinants of economic growth? What are the essential differences between the supply, demand, and efficiency factors?

10. How does economic growth affect production possibilities? What demand and efficiency assumptions are necessary to achieve maximum productive potential?

11. What is the relationship between the real GDP produced in any year and the quantity of labor employed and labor productivity? What factor appears to be more important for growth?

12. What is technological advance, and why are technological advance and capital formation closely related processes?

13. What is the relationship between investment and the stock of capital? What is the connection between increases in the capital stock and the rate of economic growth?

14. What increases the "quality" or human capital of labor? How is this quality usually measured? What are some of the problems with this path to improving the quality of the labor force?

15. Explain how economies of scale and resource allocation contribute to labor productivity.

16. Explain the relationship between the average rate of productivity growth and real output, real income, and real wages.

17. Discuss how the microchip and information technology contributed to the recent rise in the average rate of productivity growth.

18. Describe five sources of increasing returns and economies of scale within the recent rise in the average rate of productivity growth.

19. Identify and explain implications from the recent rise in the average rate of productivity growth for long-term economic growth. Is the recent rise in the average rate of productivity growth a long-lasting trend?

20. What arguments are made for and against economic growth in the United States?

ANSWERS

Chapter 8 Economic Growth

FILL-IN QUESTIONS

1. real, real, increases, decreases
2. $180, $108, $72
3. 3.2, 2.0
4. longer, shorter, larger
5. rights, patents, financial, education, free
6. *a.* quantity and quality of natural resources; *b.* quantity and quality of human resources; *c.* the supply or stock of capital goods; *d.* technology (any order for *a–d*)
7. demand, efficiency
8. supply, right, may not
9. multiplied, hours of labor, worker-hour
10. employed, participation
11. less
12. *a.* advance; *b.* capital, worker; *c.* education, training (either order); *d.* scale; *e.* allocation
13. investment, worker
14. public, private
15. human, education
16. economies of scale, improved resource allocation
17. increase, increase, increase
18. advances, increasing, increasing
19. short-run, long-run
20. pollutes, does not, is not, greater, higher, incentives

TRUE–FALSE QUESTIONS

1. T, p. 150
2. F, p. 150
3. T, p. 150
4. F, p. 151
5. F, p. 151
6. T, p. 152
7. F, pp. 153–155
8. T, p. 156
9. T, p. 156
10. F, p. 157
11. F, p. 157
12. T, p. 157
13. F, p. 158
14. T, p. 158
15. T, pp. 158–159
16. T, p. 159
17. T, pp. 159–160
18. T, p. 160
19. T, p. 160
20. F, p. 161
21. F, p. 161
22. T, p. 162
23. T, p. 163
24. T, p. 165
25. F, p. 165, 167

MULTIPLE-CHOICE QUESTIONS

1. c, p. 150
2. b, p. 150
3. d, p. 150
4. d, p. 152
5. a, pp. 153–154
6. a, p. 155
7. c, p. 156
8. a, p. 157
9. a, p. 157
10. b, p. 157
11. c, p. 158
12. c, p. 158
13. b, p. 158
14. b, p. 159
15. b, pp. 159–160
16. d, p. 160
17. c, p. 160
18. a, p. 161
19. c, p. 161
20. c, p. 162
21. d, p. 162
22. b, p. 163
23. c, p. 163
24. d, p. 164
25. c, p. 165, 167

PROBLEMS

1. *real GDP:* years 1–2 (2.3%); years 2–3 (3.7%); years 3–4 (2.7%); years 4–5 (3.5%); years 5–6 (4.6%); *real GDP per capita:* years 1–2 (1.4%); years 2–3 (2.2%); years 3–4 (1.7%); years 4–5 (2.4%); years 5–6 (1.8%)

2. *a.* 400, 500, 550, 600, 550, 500; *b.* 150 million; *c.* $15 billion; *d.* 46.7%

3. *a.* 100,000, 105,000, 115,500; *b.* (1) 5, (2) 5; *c.* (1) 10, (2) 10; *d.* (1) 15.5, (2) quantity, productivity

4. 70, 50, 39, 31, 27, 23. Small changes make a large difference in the number of years it takes for the standard of living to double in an economy, especially at very low average rates of productivity growth.

SHORT ANSWER AND ESSAY QUESTIONS

1. p. 150	**8.** pp. 155–156	**15.** p. 161
2. p. 150	**9.** pp. 156–157	**16.** p. 162
3. p. 151	**10.** pp. 157–158	**17.** p. 163
4. p. 152	**11.** p. 158	**18.** pp. 163–164
5. pp. 152–153	**12.** p. 159	**19.** p. 164
6. pp. 153–154	**13.** pp. 159–160	**20.** p. 165, 167
7. pp. 154–155	**14.** pp. 160–161	

CHAPTER 9

Business Cycles, Unemployment, and Inflation

This chapter begins with an explanation of **business cycles:** the ups and downs in real output of the economy that occur over several years. What may not be immediately evident to you, but will become clear as you read this chapter, is that these alternating periods of prosperity and hard times have taken place over a long period in which the trends in real output, employment, and the standard of living have been upward. During this long history booms and busts have occurred quite irregularly; their duration and intensity have been so varied that it is better to think of them as economic instability rather than regular business cycles.

Two principal problems result from the instability of the economy. The first problem is described in the second section of the chapter. Here you will find an examination of the **unemployment** that accompanies a downturn in the level of economic activity in the economy. You will first learn how economists measure the unemployment rate in the economy and the problems they encounter. You will also discover that there are three different kinds of unemployment and that full employment means that less than 100 percent of the labor force is employed. You will also find out how unemployment imposes an economic cost on the economy and that this cost is unequally distributed among different groups in our society.

The second major problem that results from economic instability is **inflation.** It is examined in the third section of the chapter, and also in the following two sections. Inflation is an increase in the general (or average) level of prices in an economy. It does not have a unique cause: it may result from increases in demand, from increases in costs, or from both sources.

Regardless of its cause, inflation may impose a real hardship on different groups in our society as you will learn in the fourth section of the chapter. Inflation arbitrarily redistributes real income and wealth in the economy. Unanticipated inflation hurts those on fixed incomes, those who save money, and those who lend money. If inflation is anticipated, some of its burden can be reduced, but that depends on whether a group can protect their income with cost-of-living or interest rate adjustments.

Finally, inflation has redistribution effects on the real output of the economy as described in the last section of the chapter. **Cost-push inflation** and **demand-pull inflation** have different effects on output and employment that vary with the severity of the inflation. In the extreme, an economy can experience very high rates of inflation—**hyperinflation**—that can result in its breakdown.

Understanding the business cycle and the twin problems of unemployment and inflation are important because it prepares you for later chapters and the explanations of how the macro economy works.

■ CHECKLIST

When you have finished this chapter you should be able to

- ☐ Explain what is meant by the business cycle.
- ☐ Describe the four phases of a generalized business cycle.
- ☐ Explain the relationship between business cycles and economic shocks to the economy.
- ☐ Describe the immediate cause of the cyclical changes in the levels of real output and employment.
- ☐ Identify differences in the way cyclical fluctuations affect industries producing capital and consumer durable goods, and how they affect industries producing consumer nondurable goods and services.
- ☐ Describe how the Bureau of Labor Statistics (BLS) measures the rate of unemployment, and list the two criticisms of their survey data.
- ☐ Distinguish among frictional, structural, and cyclical types of unemployment, and explain the causes of these three kinds of unemployment.
- ☐ Define full employment and the full-employment unemployment rate (or the natural rate of unemployment).
- ☐ Use actual and potential GDP to define a GDP gap.
- ☐ State Okun's law on the economic cost of unemployment.
- ☐ Discuss the unequal burdens of unemployment.
- ☐ Describe the noneconomic costs of unemployment.
- ☐ Offer international comparisons of unemployment.
- ☐ Define the meaning of inflation.
- ☐ Calculate the rate of inflation using the Consumer Price Index.
- ☐ Make international comparisons of inflation rates.
- ☐ Define demand-pull inflation.
- ☐ Define cost-push inflation and per-unit production costs.
- ☐ Describe the complexities involved in distinguishing between demand-pull and cost-push inflation.
- ☐ Distinguish between real and nominal income.
- ☐ Calculate real income using data on nominal income and the price level.
- ☐ Explain how fixed-income receivers, savers, and creditors are hurt by unanticipated inflation.
- ☐ Explain how flexible-income receivers or debtors are not harmed and may be helped by unanticipated inflation.

☐ Discuss why the redistributive effects of inflation are less severe when it is anticipated.
☐ Explain the difference between the real and the nominal interest rates.
☐ Make three final points about the redistribution effects of inflation.
☐ Describe the effect of cost-push inflation on real output.
☐ Compare and contrast the views of economists about the effects of mild demand-pull inflation on real output.
☐ Describe hyperinflation and its effects on prices and real output.
☐ Explain the relationship, or lack of it, between the stock market and the macro economy (*Last Word*).

■ CHAPTER OUTLINE

1. Although the long-term trend for the U.S. economy is one of economic growth and expansion, the growth pattern has been interrupted by periods of economic instability, or ***business cycles.***

a. The business cycle means alternating periods of prosperity and recession even if the long-term trends show economic growth.

(1) The typical cyclical pattern, however, is peak, recession, trough, and expansion to another peak. ***Peak*** is the maximum level of real output at the start of the cycle. It is followed by a ***recession,*** which is a period of decline in real output that lasts six months or longer. When real output is no longer declining, it has hit its ***trough.*** This low point is followed by ***expansion*** or recovery in which the economy experiences an increase in real output.

(2) These recurrent periods of ups and downs in real output (and associated income and employment) are irregular in their duration and intensity.

b. Economists think that changes in the levels of output and employment are largely the result of economic shocks. They require difficult adjustments to be made by households and businesses in the economy and such adjustments are not easily or quickly made because prices tend to be sticky. For example, if total spending unexpectedly falls and prices are relatively fixed, business firms will not be able to sell all their output and have to cut back on production. As a consequence, GDP falls, income falls, unemployment rises, and the economy moves into recession. The possible economic shocks to the economy that cause unexpected changes include irregular periods of innovation; changes in productivity; monetary factors; political events or shifts; and financial instability. Although economic shocks come from different sources, the immediate cause of most cyclical changes in output and employment is unexpected changes in the level of total spending in the economy.

c. The business cycle affects almost the entire economy, but it does not affect all parts in the same way and to the same degree: The production of capital and consumer durable goods fluctuates more than the production of consumer nondurable goods and services during the cycle, because the purchase of capital and consumer durable goods can be postponed.

2. One of the twin problems arising from the economic instability of the business cycle is ***unemployment.***

a. The ***unemployment rate*** is calculated by dividing the number of persons in the ***labor force*** who are unemployed by the total number of persons in the labor force. Unemployment data have been criticized for at least two reasons:

(1) Part-time workers are considered fully employed.

(2) ***Discouraged workers*** who have left the labor force are not counted as unemployed.

b. Full employment does not mean that all workers in the labor force are employed and there is no unemployment; some unemployment is normal. There are at least three types of unemployment.

(1) ***Frictional unemployment*** is due to workers with marketable skills searching for new jobs or waiting to take new jobs. This type of unemployment is short-term, inevitable, and also generally desirable because it allows people to find more optimal employment.

(2) ***Structural unemployment*** is due to the changes in technology and in the types of goods and services consumers wish to buy. These changes affect the total demand for labor in particular industries or regions. Such unemployed workers have few desired marketable skills so they often need retraining, more education, or have to move if they are to be employed.

(3) ***Cyclical unemployment*** arises from a decline in total spending in the economy that pushes an economy into an economic downturn or recession. With the onset of recession, businesses cut production, real GDP falls, and unemployment eventually rises.

c. "Full employment" is less than 100 percent because some frictional and structural unemployment is unavoidable. The ***full-employment unemployment rate*** or the ***natural rate of unemployment (NRU)*** is the sum of frictional and structural unemployment and is achieved when cyclical unemployment is zero (the real output of the economy is equal to its ***potential output***). NRU is the unemployment rate that is consistent with full employment. It is not, however, automatically achieved and changes over time. Currently it is about 4 to 5 percent of the labor force.

d. Unemployment has an economic cost.

(1) The ***GDP gap*** is a measure of that cost. It is the difference between actual and potential GDP. When the difference is negative, it means that the economy is underperforming relative to its potential.

(2) ***Okun's law*** predicts that for every 1 percent the actual unemployment rate exceeds the natural rate of unemployment, there is a negative GDP gap of about 2 percent.

(3) This cost of unemployment is unequally distributed among different groups of workers in the labor force. Workers in lower-skilled occupations have higher unemployment than workers in higher-skilled occupations. Teenagers have higher unemployment rates than do adults. The unemployment rate for African Americans and Hispanics is higher than it is for whites. Less educated workers have higher unemployment rates than more educated workers.

e. Unemployment also has noneconomic costs in the form of social, psychological, and health problems for individuals and families. High unemployment rates in nations also can contribute to political unrest and violence.

f. Unemployment rates differ across nations because of differences in phases of the business cycle and natural rates of unemployment.

3. Over its history, the U.S. economy has experienced not only periods of unemployment but periods of ***inflation.***

a. Inflation is an increase in the general level of prices in the economy. During any period, the prices of products can rise, fall, or stay the same. Inflation occurs when there is an overall rise in the prices of products.

b. The primary measure of inflation in the United States is the ***Consumer Price Index (CPI).***

(1) The index is calculated by comparing the prices of a "market basket" of consumer goods in a particular year to the prices for that same market basket in a base period, and then multiplying it by 100 to get a percentage change.

(2) The rate of inflation from one year to the next is equal to the percentage change in the CPI between the current year and the preceding year. The CPI was 207.3 in 2007 and 201.6 in 2006. The rate of inflation was 2.8 percent. The calculation is $[(207.3 - 201.6)/201.6] \times 100 = 2.8\%$. The CPI was 215.3 in 2008 and 214.5 in 2009. The rate of inflation from 2008 to 2009 was −0.4 percent. This decline in the price level means that economy experienced ***deflation*** over that year period.

(3) ***The rule of 70*** can be used to calculate the number of years it will take for the price level to double at any given rate of inflation. For example, if the rate of inflation is 3 percent a year, it will take about 23 years for the price level to double [70/3 = 23].

c. The United States has experienced both inflation and deflation, but the past half-century has been a period of inflation. Other industrial nations have also experienced inflation.

d. There are at least two types of inflation. They may operate separately or simultaneously to raise the price level.

(1) ***Demand-pull inflation*** is the result of excess total spending in the economy, or "too much spending chasing too few goods." With this inflation, increasing demand is pulling up the price level.

(2) ***Cost-push inflation*** is the result of factors that raise ***per-unit production costs.*** This average cost is found by dividing the total cost of the resource inputs by the amount of output produced. As these costs rise, profits get squeezed and firms cut back on production. The rising costs push the price level higher, and output also declines. The major source of this inflation has been supply shocks from an increase in the prices of resource inputs.

e. It is difficult to distinguish between demand-pull and cost-push inflation in the real world. Demand-pull inflation can continue as long as there is excess spending. Cost-push inflation is self-limiting because as the price level rises, it reduces output and employment, and these recession effects constrain additional price increases.

f. Measures of inflation can vary considerably from month to month because of volatility in the prices of certain items in the CPI such as the cost of food or energy. Economists and policy-makers often use a measure of ***core inflation*** that removes from the inflation rate calculation the often temporary and volatility swings in food and energy prices.

4. Inflation arbitrarily redistributes real income and wealth. It benefits some groups and hurts other groups in the economy.

a. Whether someone benefits or is hurt by inflation is measured by what happens to real income. Inflation injures those whose real income falls and benefits those whose real income rises.

(1) ***Real income*** is determined by dividing ***nominal income*** by the price level expressed in hundredths.

(2) The percentage change in real income can be approximated by subtracting the percentage change in the price level from the percentage change in nominal income.

(3) The redistribution effects of inflation depend on whether it is anticipated or unanticipated.

b. ***Unanticipated inflation*** hurts *fixed-income receivers, savers,* and *creditors* because it lowers the real value of their assets.

c. Unanticipated inflation may not affect or may help *flexible-income receivers.* For example, some union workers get automatic ***cost-of-living adjustments (COLAs)*** in their pay when the CPI rises. It helps *debtors* because it lowers the real value of debts to be repaid.

d. When there is ***anticipated inflation*** people can adjust their nominal incomes to reflect the expected rise in the price level, and the redistribution of income and wealth is lessened. To reduce the effects of inflation on a ***nominal interest rate,*** an inflation premium (the expected rate of inflation) is added to the ***real interest rate.***

e. There are three other redistribution issues associated with inflation. There can be a decline in the price level, or ***deflation,*** and if unanticipated, it has the reverse effects that inflation has on various groups. Inflation can have mixed effects (positive or negative), depending on the composition of a household's assets. The effects of inflation are arbitrary and not directed at any one group or type.

5. Inflation also has an effect on real output that varies by the type of inflation and its severity.

a. Cost-push inflation reduces real output, employment, and income.

b. Views of mild demand-pull inflation vary. It may reduce real output, or it may be a necessary by-product of economic growth.

c. ***Hyperinflation***—extremely high rates of inflation—can lead to a breakdown of the economy by redistributing income and reducing real output and employment.

6. (*Last Word*). Do changes in the stock market affect the economy? The evidence indicates that changes in stock prices have only a weak effect on consumption and investment and the macro economy. Stock market bubbles where there is a large increase in stock prices that then decline rapidly can adversely affect the macro economy. Stock prices are a relatively good indicator of future business conditions because they are related to business profits.

■ HINTS AND TIPS

1. Some students get confused by the seemingly contradictory term **full-employment unemployment rate** and related unemployment concepts. Full employment does not mean that everyone who wants to work has a job; it means that the economy is achieving its potential output and has a natural rate of unemployment. Remember that there are three types of unemployment: frictional, structural, and cyclical. There will always be some unemployment arising from frictional reasons (e.g., people searching for jobs) or structural reasons (e.g., changes in industry demand), and these two types of unemployment are "natural" for an economy. When there is cyclical unemployment because of a downturn in the business cycle, the economy is not producing its potential output. Thus, full-employment unemployment rate means that there are no cyclical reasons causing unemployment, only frictional or structural reasons.

2. To verify your understanding of how to calculate the unemployment rate, GDP gap, or inflation rate, do problems 1, 2, and 3 in this *Study Guide* chapter.

3. Inflation is a rise in the *general* level of prices, not just a rise in the prices of a few products. An increase in product price is caused by supply or demand factors. You now know why the prices for many products rise in an economy. The macroeconomic reasons given in Chapter 9 for the increase in the general level of prices are different from the microeconomic reasons for a price increase that you learned about in Chapter 3.

■ IMPORTANT TERMS

business cycle	**Okun's law**
peak	**inflation**
recession	**Consumer Price Index (CPI)**
trough	**deflation**
expansion	**demand-pull inflation**
unemployment rate	**cost-push inflation**
labor force	**per-unit production costs**
discouraged workers	**core inflation**
frictional unemployment	**real income**
structural unemployment	**nominal income**
cyclical unemployment	**unanticipated inflation**
full-employment rate of unemployment	**cost-of-living adjustments (COLAs)**
natural rate of unemployment (NRU)	**anticipated inflation**
	nominal interest rate
potential output	**real interest rate**
GDP gap	**hyperinflation**

SELF-TEST

■ FILL-IN QUESTIONS

1. The business cycle is a term that encompasses the recurrent ups, or (decreases, increases) ____________, and downs, or ____________, in the level of business activity in the economy. The order of the four phases of a typical business cycle are peak, (expansion, trough, recession) ____________, ____________, and ____________.

2. Business cycle fluctuations arise because of economic (shocks, deflation) ____________ that the economy has difficulty adjusting to quickly or easily because in the short run, prices are (flexible, sticky) ____________. Such economic shocks cause unexpected changes in the level of total (money, spending) ____________.

3. Expansion and contraction of the economy affect to a greater extent the production and employment in the consumer (durables, nondurables) ____________ and (capital, consumer) ____________ goods industries than they do (durable, nondurable) ____________ goods and service industries.

4. The unemployment rate is found by dividing the number of (employed, unemployed) ____________ persons by the (population, labor force) ____________ and (multiplying, dividing) ____________ by 100.

5. In calculating the unemployment rate, the U.S. Bureau of Labor Statistics treats part-time workers as (unemployed, employed, not in the labor force) ____________ and discouraged workers who are not actively seeking work as ____________. Critics of the official BLS calculation contend that such designations mean that unemployment is (overstated, understated) ____________.

6. When workers are searching for new jobs or waiting to start new jobs, this type of unemployment is called (structural, frictional, cyclical) ____________, but when workers are laid off because of changes in the consumer demand and technology in industries or regions, this unemployment is called ____________; when workers are unemployed because of insufficient total spending in the economy, this type of unemployment is called ____________.

7. The full-employment unemployment rate is called the (Okun, natural) ____________ rate of unemployment. It is equal to the total of (frictional and structural, cyclical and frictional) ____________ unemployment in the economy. It is realized when the (frictional, cyclical)

_____________ unemployment in the economy is equal to zero and when the actual output of the economy is (less than, equal to) _____________ its potential output.

8. The GDP gap is equal to the actual GDP (minus, plus) _____________ the potential GDP. For every percentage point the unemployment rate rises above the natural rate, there will be a GDP gap of (2, 5) _____________ percent.

9. The burdens of unemployment are borne more heavily by (black, white) _____________, (adult, teenage) _____________, and (white-collar, blue-collar) workers, and the percentage of the labor force unemployed for 15 or more weeks is much (higher, lower) _____________ than the overall unemployment rate.

10. Inflation means (an increase, a decrease) _____________ in the general level of (unemployment, prices) _____________ in the economy.

11. To calculate the rate of inflation from year 1 to year 2, subtract the price index for year 1 from year 2, then (multiply, divide) _____________ the result by the price index for year 1, and _____________ by 100.

12. To find the approximate number of years it takes the price level to double, (multiply, divide) _____________ 70 by the percentage annual increase in the rate of inflation. This approximation is called (Okun's law, rule of 70) _____________.

13. The basic cause of demand-pull inflation is (an increase, a decrease) _____________ in total spending beyond the economy's capacity to produce. This type of inflation is characterized as "too (little, much) _____________ spending chasing too (few, many) _____________ goods."

14. Cost-push inflation is explained in terms of factors that raise per-unit (inflation, production) _____________ costs. When these costs rise, they (increase, decrease) _____________ profits and _____________ the amount of output firms are willing to supply, which causes the price level for the economy as a whole to _____________.

15. The amount of goods and services one's nominal income can buy is called (variable, real) _____________ income. If one's nominal income rises by 10 percent and the price level by 7 percent, the percentage of increase in (variable, real) _____________ income would be (1, 2, 3) _____________. If nominal income was $60,000 and the price index, expressed in hundredths, was 1.06, then (variable, real) _____________ income would be ($56,604, $63,600) _____________.

16. Unanticipated inflation hurts those whose nominal incomes are relatively (fixed, flexible) _____________, penalizes (savers, borrowers) _____________, and hurts (creditors, debtors) _____________.

17. The redistributive effects of inflation are less severe when it is (anticipated, unanticipated) _____________. Clauses in labor contracts that call for automatic adjustments of workers' incomes from the effects of inflation are called (unemployment benefits, cost-of-living) _____________ adjustments.

18. The percentage increase in purchasing power that the lender receives from the borrower is the (real, nominal) _____________ rate of interest; the percentage increase in money that the lender receives is the _____________ rate of interest. If the nominal rate of interest is 8 percent and the real interest rate is 5 percent, then the inflation premium is (8, 5, 3) _____________ percent.

19. Cost-push inflation (increases, decreases) _____________ real output. The output effects of demand-pull inflation are (more, less) _____________ certain. Some economists argue that mild demand-pull inflation (increases, decreases) _____________ real output while others argue that it _____________ real output.

20. An extraordinary rapid rise in the general price level is (deflation, hyperinflation) _____________. Economists generally agree that there may be an economic collapse, and often political chaos, from _____________.

■ TRUE–FALSE QUESTIONS

Circle T if the statement is true, F if it is false.

1. The business cycle is best defined as alternating periods of increases and decreases in the rate of inflation in the economy. **T F**

2. Business cycles tend to be of roughly equal duration and intensity. **T F**

3. Fluctuations in real output in the economy are caused by economic shocks, and because prices are sticky, it is difficult for the economy to quickly adjust to such shocks. **T F**

4. During a recession, industries that produce capital goods and consumer durables typically suffer smaller output and employment declines than do industries providing service and nondurable consumer goods. **T F**

5. The unemployment rate is equal to the number of people in the labor force divided by the number of people who are unemployed. **T F**

6. Discouraged workers, those people who are able to work but quit looking for work because they cannot find a job, are counted as unemployed by the U.S. Bureau of Labor Statistics. **T F**

7. Frictional unemployment is not only inevitable but also partly desirable so that people can voluntarily move to better jobs. **T F**

8. The essential difference between frictionally and structurally unemployed workers is that the former *do not have* and the latter *do have* marketable skills. **T F**

9. Most frictionally unemployed workers stay in the unemployment pool for a long time. **T F**

10. Cyclical unemployment is caused by a decline in total spending **T F**

11. If unemployment in the economy is at its natural rate, the actual and potential outputs of the economy are equal. **T F**

12. An economy cannot produce an actual real GDP that exceeds its potential real GDP. **T F**

13. The economy's GDP gap is measured by subtracting its potential GDP from its actual GDP. **T F**

14. The economic cost of cyclical unemployment is the goods and services that are not produced. **T F**

15. Unemployment imposes equal burdens on different groups in the economy. **T F**

16. Inflation is defined as an increase in the total output of an economy. **T F**

17. From one year to the next, the Consumer Price Index rose from 154.5 to 160.5. The rate of inflation was therefore 6.6 percent. **T F**

18. If the price level increases by 10 percent each year, the price level will double every 10 years. **T F**

19. The essence of demand-pull inflation is "too much spending chasing too few goods." **T F**

20. Cost-push inflation explains rising prices in terms of factors that increase per-unit production cost. **T F**

21. A person's real income is the amount of goods and services that the person's nominal (or money) income will enable him or her to purchase. **T F**

22. Whether inflation is anticipated or unanticipated, the effects of inflation on the distribution of income are the same. **T F**

23. Borrowers are hurt by unanticipated inflation. **T F**

24. Cost-push inflation reduces real output. **T F**

25. Hyperinflation is caused by reckless expansion of the money supply and causes severe declines in real output **T F**

■ MULTIPLE-CHOICE QUESTIONS

1. Which is one of the four phases of a business cycle?
(a) inflation
(b) recession
(c) unemployment
(d) hyperinflation

2. Most economists believe that the immediate determinant of the levels of domestic output and employment is
(a) the price level
(b) the level of total spending
(c) the size of the civilian labor force
(d) the nation's stock of capital goods

3. Production and employment would be *least* affected by a severe recession in which type of industry?
(a) nondurable consumer goods
(b) durable consumer goods
(c) capital goods
(d) labor goods

4. The unemployment rate in an economy is 8 percent. The total population of the economy is 250 million, and the size of the civilian labor force is 150 million. The number of employed workers in this economy is
(a) 12 million
(b) 20 million
(c) 138 million
(d) 140 million

5. The labor force includes those who are
(a) less than 16 years of age
(b) in mental institutions
(c) not seeking work
(d) employed

6. The unemployment data collected by the Bureau of Labor Statistics have been criticized because
(a) part-time workers are not counted in the number of workers employed
(b) discouraged workers are not considered a part of the labor force
(c) it covers frictional unemployment, but not cyclical unemployment, which inflates unemployment figures
(d) the underground economy may understate unemployment

7. A worker who loses a job at a petroleum refinery because consumers and business firms switch from the use of oil to the burning of coal is an example of
(a) frictional unemployment
(b) structural unemployment
(c) cyclical unemployment
(d) disguised unemployment

8. A worker who has quit one job and is taking 2 weeks off before reporting to a new job is an example of
(a) frictional unemployment
(b) structural unemployment
(c) cyclical unemployment
(d) disguised unemployment

9. Insufficient total spending in the economy results in
(a) frictional unemployment
(b) structural unemployment
(c) cyclical unemployment
(d) disguised unemployment

10. The full-employment unemployment rate in the economy has been achieved when
(a) frictional unemployment is zero
(b) structural unemployment is zero
(c) cyclical unemployment is zero
(d) the natural rate of unemployment is zero

11. At the natural rate of unemployment (NRU) the economy is said to
(a) be at the trough of the business cycle
(b) be producing its potential output
(c) have a declining GDP gap
(d) have low rate of inflation

12. Okun's law predicts that when the actual unemployment rate exceeds the natural rate of unemployment by two percentage points, there will be a negative GDP gap of about
(a) 2% of the potential GDP
(b) 3% of the potential GDP
(c) 4% of the potential GDP
(d) 5% of the potential GDP

13. If the negative GDP gap were equal to 6% of the potential GDP, the actual unemployment rate would exceed the natural rate of unemployment by
(a) two percentage points
(b) three percentage points
(c) four percentage points
(d) five percentage points

14. The burden of unemployment is *least* felt by
(a) white-collar workers
(b) African-Americans
(c) teenagers
(d) males

15. If the Consumer Price Index was 110 in one year and 117 in the next year, then the rate of inflation from one year to the next was
(a) 3.5%
(b) 4.7%
(c) 6.4%
(d) 7.1%

16. The price of a good has doubled in about 14 years. The approximate annual percentage rate of increase in the price level over this period has been
(a) 2%
(b) 3%
(c) 4%
(d) 5%

17. Which contributes to cost-push inflation?
(a) an increase in employment and output
(b) an increase in per-unit production costs
(c) a decrease in resource prices
(d) an increase in unemployment

18. Only two resources, capital and labor, are used in an economy to produce an output of 300 million units. If the total cost of capital resources is $150 million and the total cost of labor resources is $50 million, then the per-unit production costs in this economy are
(a) $0.67 million
(b) $1.50 million
(c) $2.00 million
(d) $3.00 million

19. If a person's nominal income increases by 8% while the price level increases by 10%, the person's real income
(a) increases by 2%
(b) increases by 18%
(c) decreases by 18%
(d) decreases by 2%

20. If the average level of nominal income in a nation is $21,000 and the price level index is 154, the average real income would be about
(a) $12,546
(b) $13,636
(c) $15,299
(d) $17,823

21. Who would be hurt by *unanticipated* inflation?
(a) those living on incomes with cost-of-living adjustments
(b) those who find prices rising less rapidly than their nominal incomes
(c) those who lent money at a fixed interest rate
(d) those who became debtors when prices were lower

22. With no inflation, a bank would be willing to lend a business firm $10 million at an annual interest rate of 8%. But if the rate of inflation was anticipated to be 6%, the bank would charge the firm an annual interest rate of
(a) 2%
(b) 6%
(c) 8%
(d) 14%

23. Cost-push inflation
(a) lowers interest rates
(b) lowers the price level
(c) deceases real output
(d) increases real output

24. What do economists think about the effects of mild demand-pull inflation on real output?
(a) They are positive because businesses must change prices.
(b) They are negative because economic growth depends on total spending.
(c) They are mixed, and could be positive or negative.
(d) They are zero and it indicates that there are no effects.

25. If an economy has experienced an inflation rate of over 1000% per year for several years, this economic condition would best be described as
(a) a cost-of-living adjustment
(b) cost-push inflation
(c) hyperinflation
(d) GDP gap

■ PROBLEMS

1. The following table gives statistics on the labor force and total employment during year 1 and year 5. Make the computations necessary to complete the table. (Numbers of persons are in thousands.)

	Year 1	Year 5
Labor force	84,889	95,453
Employed	80,796	87,524
Unemployed	____	____
Unemployment rate	____	____

a. How is it possible that *both* employment and unemployment increased? ____

____

b. In relative terms, if unemployment increases, employment will decrease. Why? ____

____

c. Would you say that year 5 was a year of full employment? ____

d. Why is the task of maintaining full employment over the years more than just a problem of finding jobs for those who happen to be unemployed at any given time? ____

____

2. Suppose that in year 1 an economy is at full employment, has a potential and actual real GDP of $3000 billion, and has an unemployment rate of 5.5%.

a. Compute the GDP gap in year 1 and enter it in the table below.

Year	Actual GDP	Potential GDP	GDP gap
1	$3000.0	$3000	$____
2	3724.0	3800	____
3	3712.5	4125	____

b. The actual and potential real GDPs in years 2 and 3 are also shown in the table. Compute and enter into the table the GDP gaps in these 2 years.

c. In year 2, the actual real GDP is ____% of the potential real GDP. (Hint: Divide the actual real GDP by the potential real GDP and multiply by 100.)

(1) The actual real GDP is ____% less than the potential real GDP.

(2) Using Okun's law, the unemployment rate will rise from 5.5% in year 1 and be ____% in year 2.

d. In year 3 the actual real GDP is ____% of the potential real GDP.

(1) The actual real GDP is ____% less than the potential real GDP.

(2) The unemployment rate, according to Okun's law, will be ____%.

3. The following table shows the price index in the economy at the end of four different years.

Year	Price index	Rate of inflation
1	100.00	
2	112.00	____%
3	123.20	____
4	129.36	____

a. Compute and enter in the table the rates of inflation in years 2, 3, and 4.

b. Employing the rule of 70, how many years would it take for the price level to double at each of these three inflation rates? ____

c. If nominal income increased by 15% from year 1 to year 2, what was the approximate percentage change in real income? ____

d. If nominal income increased by 7% from year 2 to year 3, what was the approximate percentage change in real income? ____

e. If nominal income was $25,000 in year 2, what was real income that year? ____

f. If nominal income was $25,000 in year 3, what was real income that year? ____

g. If the nominal interest rate was 14% to borrow money from year 1 to year 2, what was the approximate real rate of interest over that period? ____

h. If the nominal interest rate was 8% to borrow money from year 3 to year 4, what was the approximate real rate of interest over that period? ____

4. Indicate the most likely effect—beneficial **(B)**, detrimental **(D)**, or indeterminate **(I)**—of unanticipated inflation on each of these persons:

a. A retired business executive who now lives each month by spending a part of the amount that was saved and deposited in a fixed-rate savings account for a long term. ____

b. A retired private-school teacher who lives on the dividends received from shares of stock owned. ____

c. A farmer who borrowed $500,000 from a bank at a fixed rate; the loan must be repaid in the next 10 years. ____

d. A retired couple whose sole source of income is the pension they receive from a former employer. ____

e. A widow whose income consists entirely of interest received from the corporate bonds she owns. ____

f. A public school teacher. ____

g. A member of a union who works for a firm that produces computers. ____

■ SHORT ANSWER AND ESSAY QUESTIONS

1. Define the business cycle. Describe the four phases of a business cycle.

2. In the opinion of most economists, what is the cause of the fluctuations in the levels of output in the economy?

3. Compare the manner in which the business cycle affects output and employment in the industries producing capital and durable goods with the way it affects industries producing nondurable goods and services. What causes these differences?

4. How is the unemployment rate measured in the United States?

5. What two criticisms have been made of the method the Bureau of Labor Statistics uses to determine the unemployment rate?

6. Distinguish among frictional, structural, and cyclical unemployment.

7. Do frictionally unemployed workers remain unemployed for a long period of time? Explain your answer.

8. When is there full employment in the U.S. economy? (Answer in terms of the unemployment rate, the actual and potential output of the economy, and the markets for labor.)

9. What is the natural rate of unemployment? Will the economy always operate at the natural rate?

10. What is the economic cost of unemployment, and how is this cost measured? What is the quantitative relationship (called Okun's law) between the unemployment rate and the cost of unemployment?

11. What groups in the economy tend to bear the burdens of unemployment?

12. How does the unemployment rate in the United States compare with the rates for other industrialized nations in recent years?

13. What is inflation, and how is the rate of inflation measured?

14. What has been the experience of the United States with inflation since the 1960s? How does the inflation rate in the United States compare with those of other industrialized nations in recent years?

15. Compare and contrast demand-pull and cost-push types of inflation.

16. Why do economists and policy-makers use core inflation for evaluating inflation?

17. What is the difference between the effects of unanticipated inflation and the effects of anticipated inflation on the redistribution of real incomes in the economy?

18. What are the effects of cost-push inflation on real output?

19. What are the effects of demand-pull inflation on real output? Are economists in agreement about these effects? Discuss.

20. Why does hyperinflation have a devastating impact on real output and employment? Explain what happens during hyperinflation.

ANSWERS

Chapter 9 Business Cycles, Unemployment, and Inflation

FILL-IN QUESTIONS

1. increases, decreases, recession, trough, expansion
2. shocks, sticky, spending
3. durables, capital, nondurable
4. unemployed, labor force, multiplying
5. employed, not in the labor force, understated
6. frictional, structural, cyclical
7. natural, frictional and structural, cyclical, equal to
8. minus, 2
9. black, teenage, blue-collar, lower
10. an increase, prices
11. divide, multiply
12. divide, rule of 70
13. an increase, much, few
14. production, decrease, decrease, increase
15. real, real, 3, real, $56,604
16. fixed, savers, creditors
17. anticipated, cost-of-living
18. real, nominal, 3
19. decreases, less, increases, decreases
20. hyperinflation, hyperinflation

TRUE–FALSE QUESTIONS

1. F, p. 171
2. F, p. 171
3. T, p. 172
4. F, p. 173
5. F, pp. 173–174
6. F, p. 174
7. T, p. 174
8. F, pp. 174–175
9. F, pp. 174–175
10. T, p. 175
11. T, p. 175
12. F, pp. 175–176
13. T, pp. 175–176
14. T, p. 176
15. F, p. 176, 178
16. F, p. 179
17. F, p. 179
18. F, p. 179
19. T, p. 180
20. T, pp. 180–181
21. T, p. 182
22. F, p. 182–184
23. F, p. 183
24. T, p. 185
25. T, pp. 185, 187

MULTIPLE-CHOICE QUESTIONS

1. b, p. 171
2. b, p. 172
3. a, p. 173
4. c, pp. 173–174
5. d, pp. 173–174
6. b, p. 174
7. b, pp. 174–175
8. a, p. 175
9. c, p. 175
10. c, p. 175
11. b, p. 175
12. c, p. 176
13. b, p. 176
14. a, p. 176, 178
15. c, p. 179
16. d, p. 179
17. b, pp. 180–181
18. a, pp. 180–181
19. d, p. 182
20. b, p. 182
21. c, pp. 182–183
22. d, p. 184
23. c, p. 185
24. c, p. 185
25. c, p. 185, 187

PROBLEMS

1. year 1; 4,093, 4.8; year 5: 7,929, 8.3; *a.* the labor force increased more than employment increased; *b.* because unemployment and employment in relative terms are percentages of the labor force and *always* add to 100%, and if one increases the other must decrease; *c.* no economist would argue that the full-employment unemployment rate is as high as 8.3% and year 5 was not a year of full employment; *d.* the number of people looking for work expands

2. *a.* 0; *b.* 76, 412.5; *c.* 98, (1) 2, (2) 6.5; *d.* 90, (1) 10, (2) 10.5
3. *a.* 12, 10, 5; *b.* 5.8, 7, 14; *c.* 3; *d.* –3; *e.* $22,321; *f.* $20,292; *g.* 2; *h.* 3
4. *a.* D; *b.* I; *c.* B; *d.* D; *e.* D; *f.* I; *g.* I

SHORT ANSWER AND ESSAY QUESTIONS

1. p. 171	**8.** p. 175	**15.** pp. 180–181
2. p. 172	**9.** p. 175	**16.** pp. 181–182
3. p. 173	**10.** pp. 175–176	**17.** pp. 182–184
4. pp. 173–174	**11.** pp. 176, 178	**18.** p. 185
5. p. 174	**12.** p. 178	**19.** p. 185
6. pp. 174–175	**13.** p. 179	**20.** pp. 185, 187
7. p. 174	**14.** pp. 179–180	

CHAPTER 10

Basic Macroeconomic Relationships

This chapter introduces you to three basic relationships in the economy: income and consumption, the interest rate and investment, and changes in spending and changes in output. The relationships between these economic "aggregates" are essential building blocks for understanding the macro models that will be presented in the next two chapters.

The first section of Chapter 10 describes the largest aggregate in the economy—**consumption.** An explanation of consumption, however, also entails a study of saving because saving is simply the part of disposable income that is not consumed. This section develops the consumption and saving schedules and describes their main characteristics. Other key concepts are also presented: average propensities to consume (APC) and save (APS), marginal propensities to consume (MPC) and save (MPS), and the nonincome determinants of consumption and saving.

Investment is the subject of the next section of the chapter. The purchase of capital goods depends on the rate of return that business firms expect to earn from an investment and on the real rate of interest they have to pay for the use of money. Because firms are anxious to make profitable investments and to avoid unprofitable ones, they undertake all investments that have an expected rate of return greater than (or equal to) the real rate of interest and do not undertake an investment when the expected rate of return is less than the real interest rate. This relationship between the real interest rate and the level of investment spending is an inverse one: the lower the interest rate, the greater the investment spending. It is illustrated by a down-sloping **investment demand curve.** As you will learn, this curve can be shifted by six factors that can change the expected rate of return on investment. You will also learn that investment, unlike consumption, is quite volatile and is the most unstable component of total spending in the economy.

The third section of the chapter introduces you to the concept of the **multiplier.** It shows how an initial change in spending for consumption or investment changes real GDP by an amount that is larger than the initial stimulus. You also will learn about the rationale for the multiplier and how to interpret it. The multiplier can be derived from the marginal propensity to consume and the marginal propensity to save. You will have learned about these marginal propensities at the beginning of the chapter and now they are put to further use as you end the chapter.

■ CHECKLIST

When you have studied this chapter you should be able to

□ Explain how consumption and saving are related to disposable income.
□ Draw a graph to illustrate the relationships among consumption, saving, and disposable income.
□ Construct a hypothetical consumption schedule.
□ Construct a hypothetical saving schedule, and identify the level of break-even income.
□ Compute the four propensities (APC, APS, MPC, and MPS) when given the necessary data.
□ State the relationship between the APC and the APS as income increases.
□ Demonstrate that the MPC is the slope of the consumption schedule and the MPS is the slope of the saving schedule.
□ Explain the four nonincome determinants of consumption and saving (wealth, borrowing, expectations, and real interest rates).
□ Use a graph with real GDP on the horizontal axis to show shifts in consumption and saving schedules.
□ Explain the difference between a change in the amount consumed and a change in the consumption schedule.
□ Describe how a change in taxes shifts consumption and saving schedules.
□ Explain how the expected rate of return affects investment decisions.
□ Describe the influence of the real interest rate on an investment decision.
□ Draw a graph of an investment demand curve for the business sector and explain what it shows.
□ Explain how each of the six noninterest determinants of investment (costs, business taxes, technological change, stock of capital goods, inventory change, and expectations) will shift the investment demand curve.
□ Give four reasons why investment spending tends to be unstable.
□ Define the multiplier effect in words, with a ratio, and using an equation.
□ Make three clarifying points about the multiplier.
□ Explain the rationale for the multiplier using two facts.
□ Discuss the relationship between the multiplier and the marginal propensities.
□ Find the value of the multiplier when you are given the necessary data.

☐ Discuss the reasons why the size of the multiplier varies from textbook example to the real world.

☐ Give a humorous example of the multiplier effect (*Last Word*).

■ CHAPTER OUTLINE

1. There is a positive or direct relationship between consumption and disposable income (after-tax income) because as disposable income increases so does consumption. Saving is disposable income not spent for consumer goods. Disposable income is the most important determinant of both consumption and saving. The relationship among disposable income, consumption, and saving can be shown by a graph with consumption on the vertical axis and disposable income on the horizontal axis. The ***45-degree line*** on the graph would show where consumption would equal disposable income. If consumption is less than disposable income, the difference is saving.

a. The ***consumption schedule*** shows the amounts that households plan to spend for consumer goods at various levels of income, given a price level. ***Break-even income*** is where consumption is equal to disposable income.

b. The ***saving schedule*** indicates the amounts households plan to save at different income levels, given a price level.

c. The average propensity to consume (APC) and the average propensity to save (APS) and the marginal propensity to consume (MPC) and the marginal propensity to save (MPS) can be computed from the consumption and saving schedules.

(1) The ***average propensity to consume (APC)*** and the ***average propensity to save (APS)*** are, respectively, the percentages of income spent for consumption and saved, and they sum to 1.

(2) The ***marginal propensity to consume (MPC)*** and the ***marginal propensity to save (MPS)*** are, respectively, the percentages of additional income spent for consumption and saved, and sum to 1.

(3) The MPC is the slope of the consumption schedule, and the MPS is the slope of the saving schedule when the two schedules are graphed.

d. In addition to income, there are several other important nonincome determinants of consumption and saving. Changes in *these nonincome determinants* will cause the consumption and saving schedules to change. An increase in spending will shift the consumption schedule upward and a decrease in spending will shift it downward. Similarly, an increase in saving will shift the saving schedule upward and a decrease in saving will shift it downward.

(1) The amount of wealth affects the amount that households spend and save. Wealth is the difference between the values of a household's assets and its liabilities. If household wealth increases, people will spend more because they think they have more assets from which to support current consumption possibilities (the ***wealth effect***), and they will save less. During a recession there is typically a "reverse wealth effect" as wealth declines, and consequently people spend less and save more. Such a situation creates a ***paradox of thrift*** in which more saving helps household budgets and at the same time the decline in spending from more saving worsens the recession.

(2) The level of household *borrowing* influences consumption. Increased borrowing will increase current consumption possibilities, which shift the consumption schedule upward. But borrowing reduces wealth by increasing debt, which in turn reduces future consumption possibilities because the borrowed money must be repaid.

(3) *Expectations* about the future affect spending and saving decisions. If prices are expected to rise in the future, people will spend more today and save less.

(4) *Real interest rates* change spending and saving decisions. When real interest rates fall, households tend to consume more, borrow more, and save less.

e. Several other considerations need to be noted:

(1) Macroeconomists are more concerned with the effects of changes in consumption and saving on *real GDP,* so it replaces disposable income on the horizontal axis of the consumption or saving schedules.

(2) A change in the amount consumed (or saved) is a movement along the consumption (or saving) schedule, but a change in consumption (or saving) due to a change in one of the nonincome determinants is a shift in the entire consumption (or saving) schedule.

(3) Changes in wealth, borrowing, expectations, and real interest rates shift consumption and saving schedules in opposite directions. For example, an increase in wealth will increase consumption and will decrease saving as people consume more out of current income. If households borrow they can expand current consumption, but that will decrease current saving. Expectations of rising future prices will increase current consumption and decrease current saving. A fall in real interest rates increases current consumption and provides less incentive for current saving.

(4) Changes in taxes shift the consumption and saving schedules in the same direction. An increase in taxes will reduce both consumption and saving; a decrease in taxes will increase both consumption and saving.

(5) Both consumption and saving schedules tend to be stable over time unless changed by major tax increases or decreases. The stability arises from long-term planning and because some nonincome determinants cause shifts that offset each other.

2. The investment decision is a marginal benefit and marginal cost decision that depends on the expected rate of return (r) from the purchase of additional capital goods and the real rate of interest (i) that must be paid for borrowed funds.

a. The ***expected rate of return*** is directly related to the net profits (revenues less operating costs) that are expected to result from an investment. It is the marginal benefit of investment for a business.

b. The *real rate of interest* is the price paid for the use of money. It is the marginal cost of investment for a business. When the expected real rate of return is greater (less) than the real rate of interest, a business will (will not) invest because the investment will be profitable (unprofitable).

c. For this reason, the lower (higher) the real rate of interest, the greater (smaller) will be the level of investment spending in the economy; the ***investment demand curve*** shows this inverse relationship between the real rate of interest and the level of spending for capital goods. The amount of investment by the business sector is determined at the point where the marginal benefit of investment (*r*) equals the marginal cost (*i*).

d. There are at least six noninterest determinants of investment demand, and a change in any of these determinants will shift the investment demand curve.

(1) If the *acquisition, maintenance, and operating costs* for capital goods change, then this change in costs will change investment demand. Rising costs decrease investment demand and declining costs increase it.

(2) Changes in *business taxes* are like a change in costs so they have a similar effect on investment demand as the previous item.

(3) *An increase in technological progress* will stimulate investment and increase investment demand.

(4) *The stock of existing capital goods* will influence investment decisions. If the economy is overstocked, there will be a decrease in investment demand, and if the economy is understocked, there will be an increase in investment demand.

(5) *Planned changes in inventories* affect investment demand. If there is a planned increase in inventories, then investment demand will increase; a planned decrease in inventories will decrease investment demand.

(6) *Expectations* of the future are important. If expectations are positive because of more expected sales or profits, there is likely to be an increase in investment demand. Negative expectations will have an opposite effect on investment demand.

e. Unlike consumption and saving, investment is inherently unstable. This volatility creates occasional and substantial unexpected shifts in the investment demand curve and thus leads to significant changes in investment spending. Four factors explain this instability in investment that shifts the investment demand curve.

(1) *Variability of expectations* concerning such factors as exchange rates, the state of the economy, and the stock market can create positive or negative expectations that change investment spending.

(2) *Durability of capital goods* causes an indefinite useful lifespan, so when they get replaced may depend on the optimism or pessimism of business owners. If owners are more optimistic about the future they will likely spend more to obtain new capital goods.

(3) *Irregularity of innovation* means that technological progress is highly variable and contributes to instability in investment spending decisions.

(4) *Variability of profits* influences the investment spending of businesses; current high profits encourage investment, current low profits discourage investment.

3. There is a direct relationship between a change in spending and a change in real GDP, assuming that prices are sticky. An initial change in spending, however, results in a change in real GDP that is greater than the initial change in spending. This outcome is called the *multiplier effect.* The ***multiplier*** is the ratio of the change in the real GDP to the initial change in spending. The initial change in spending typically comes from investment spending, but changes in consumption, net exports, or government spending can also have multiplier effects.

a. The multiplier effect occurs because a change in the dollars spent by one person alters the income of another person in the same direction, and because any change in the income of one person will change the person's consumption and saving in the same direction by a fraction of the change in income. For example, assuming a marginal propensity to consume (MPC) of .75, a change in investment spending of $5.00 will cause a change in consumption of $3.75. The change in consumption ($3.75) will become someone else's income in the second round. The process will continue through successive rounds, but the amount of income in each round will diminish by 25 percent because that is the amount saved from each change in income. After all rounds are completed, the initial change of $5 in investment spending produces a total of $20 change because the multiplier was 4 (see the table in Figure 10.8 in the text).

b. There is a formula for calculating the multiplier. The multiplier is directly related to the marginal propensity to consume (MPC) and inversely related to the marginal propensity to save (MPS). The multiplier is equal to [1/(1 − MPC)]. It is also equal to [1/MPS]. The significance of the multiplier is that relatively small changes in the spending plans of business firms or households bring about large changes in the equilibrium real GDP.

c. The simple multiplier that has been described differs from the actual multiplier for the economy. In the simple case the only factor that reduced income in successive rounds was the fraction that went to savings. For the domestic economy, there are other leakages from consumption besides saving, such as spending on imports, payment of taxes, or inflation. These factors reduce the value of the multiplier. For the U.S. economy, the multiplier is estimated to be a high of 2.5 to a low of zero depending on the assumptions made and analysis conducted.

4. (*Last Word*). Art Buchwald once wrote a humorous story about the multiplier that illustrates the spiral effect on consumer spending from a reduction in income. A car salesman reserved a new car for a regular customer, but the customer can't buy the car because he is getting a divorce. The car salesman then tells his painter he can't afford to have his house painted. The house painter then decides to return a new television he bought from the store. And so the story continues from one person to another.

■ HINTS AND TIPS

1. An important graph in the chapter is the **consumption schedule** (see Figure 10.2 of the text). Know how to interpret it. There are two lines on the graph. The 45-degree reference line shows all points where disposable income equals consumption (there is no saving). The consumption schedule line shows the total amount of disposable income spent on consumption at each and every income level. Where the two lines *intersect,* all disposable income is spent (consumed). At all income levels to the right of the intersection, the consumption line lies below the 45-degree line, and not all disposable income is spent (there is saving). To the left of the intersection, the consumption line lies above the 45-degree line and consumption exceeds disposable income (there is dissaving).

2. Always remember that **marginal propensities** sum to 1 (MPC + MPS = 1). The same is true for average propensities (APC + APS = 1). Thus, if you know the value of one marginal propensity (e.g., MPC), you can always figure out the other (e.g., 1 − MPC = MPS).

3. The **multiplier** effect is a key concept in this chapter and in the ones that follow, so make sure you understand how it works.

a. The multiplier is simply the ratio of the change in real GDP to the *initial* changes in spending. Multiplying the *initial* change in spending by the *multiplier* gives you the amount of change in real GDP.

b. The multiplier effect works in both positive and negative directions. An *initial* decrease in spending will result in a larger decrease in real GDP, or an *initial* increase in spending will create a larger increase in real GDP.

c. The multiplier is directly related to the marginal propensities. The multiplier equals 1/MPS. The multiplier also equals 1/(1 − MPC).

d. The main reason for the multiplier effect is that the *initial* change in income (spending) induces additional rounds of income (spending) that add progressively less in each round as some of the income (spending) gets saved because of the marginal propensity to save (see the table in Figure 10.8 of the text).

■ IMPORTANT TERMS

45° (degree) line
consumption schedule
break-even income
saving schedule
average propensity to consume (APC)
average propensity to save (APS)
marginal propensity to consume (MPC)
marginal propensity to save (MPS)
wealth effect
paradox of thrift
expected rate of return
investment demand curve
multiplier

SELF-TEST

■ FILL-IN QUESTIONS

1. The consumption schedule shows the various amounts that households plan to (save, consume) ____________ at various levels of disposable income, while the saving schedule shows the various amounts that households plan to ____________.

2. Both consumption and saving are (directly, indirectly) ____________ related to the level of disposable income. At lower levels of disposable income, households tend to spend a (smaller, larger) ____________ proportion of this income and save a ____________ proportion, but at higher levels of disposable income, they tend to spend a (smaller, larger) ____________ proportion of this income and save a ____________ proportion. At the break-even income, consumption is (greater than, less than, equal to) ____________ disposable income.

3. As disposable income falls, the average propensity to consume (APC) will (rise, fall) ____________ and the average propensity to save (APS) will ____________.

4. The sum of APC and APS is equal to (0, 1) ____________. If the APC is .90, then the APS is (.10, 1) ____________.

5. The marginal propensity to consume (MPC) is the change in (consumption, income) ____________ divided by the change in ____________.

6. The marginal propensity to save (MPS) is the change in (saving, income) ____________ divided by the change in ____________.

7. The sum of MPC and MPS is equal to (0, 1) ____________. If the MPC is .75, then the MPS is (0, .25) ____________.

8. The MPC is the numerical value of the slope of the (consumption, saving) ____________ schedule, and the MPS is the numerical value of the slope of the ____________ schedule.

9. The most important determinants of consumption spending, other than the level of income, are

a. ____________
b. ____________
c. ____________
d. ____________

10. An increase in the consumption schedule means that the consumption schedule shifts (upward, downward) ____________ and a decrease in the consumption schedule means that it will shift ____________, and these shifts occur because of a change in one of the nonincome determinants. An increase in the amount consumed occurs because of an increase in (income, stability) ____________.

11. The investment spending decision depends on the expected rate of (interest, return) ______ and the real rate of ______.

12. The expected rate of return is the marginal (cost, benefit) ______ of investment and the real rate of return is the marginal ______ of investment.

13. If the expected rate of return on an investment is greater than the real rate of interest for the use of money, a business firm will (increase, decrease) ______ its investment spending, but if the expected rate of return is less than the real rate of interest, the firm will ______ its investment spending.

14. The relationship between the real rate of interest and the total amount of investment in the economy is (direct, inverse) ______ and is shown in the investment (supply, demand) ______ curve. This curve shows that if the real rate of interest rises, the quantity of investment will (increase, decrease) ______, but if the real rate of interest falls, the quantity of investment will ______.

15. Six noninterest determinants of investment demand are

a. ______

b. ______

c. ______

d. ______

e. ______

f. ______

16. The demand for new capital goods tends to be unstable because of the (durability, nondurability) ______ of capital goods, the (regularity, irregularity) ______ of innovation, the (stability, variability) ______ of current and expected profits, and the ______ of expectations.

17. The multiplier is the change in real GDP (multiplied, divided) ______ by an initial change in spending. When the initial change in spending is ______ by the multiplier, the result equals the change in real GDP.

18. The multiplier means that an increase in initial spending may create a multiple (increase, decrease) ______ in real GDP, and also that a decrease in initial spending may create a multiple ______ in real GDP.

19. The multiplier has a value equal to 1 divided by the marginal propensity to (consume, save) ______, which is the same thing as 1 divided by the quantity of 1 minus the marginal propensity to ______.

20. The higher the value of the marginal propensity to consume, the (larger, smaller) ______ the value of the multiplier, but the larger the value of the marginal propensity to save, the ______ the value of the multiplier.

■ TRUE–FALSE QUESTIONS

Circle T if the statement is true, F if it is false.

1. Consumption equals disposable income plus saving. **T F**

2. The most significant determinant of the level of consumer spending is disposable income. **T F**

3. Historical data suggest that the level of consumption expenditures is directly related to the level of disposable income. **T F**

4. Consumption rises and saving falls when disposable income increases. **T F**

5. Empirical data suggest that households tend to spend a similar proportion of a small disposable income as they do of a larger disposable income. **T F**

6. The break-even income is the income level at which business begins to make a profit. **T F**

7. The average propensity to save is equal to the level of saving divided by the level of consumption. **T F**

8. The marginal propensity to consume is the change in consumption divided by the change in income. **T F**

9. The slope of the saving schedule is equal to the average propensity to save. **T F**

10. An increase in wealth will increase the consumption schedule (shift the consumption curve upward). **T F**

11. An increase in the taxes paid by consumers will decrease both the amount they spend for consumption and the amount they save. **T F**

12. Both the consumption schedule and the saving schedule tend to be relatively stable over time. **T F**

13. The real interest rate is the nominal interest rate minus the rate of inflation. **T F**

14. A business firm will purchase additional capital goods if the real rate of interest it must pay exceeds the expected rate of return from the investment. **T F**

15. An increase in the stock of capital goods on hand will decrease the investment demand. **T F**

16. An increase in planned inventories will decrease the investment demand. **T F**

17. Investment tends to be relatively stable over time. **T F**

18. The irregularity of innovations and the variability of business profits contribute to the instability of investment expenditures. **T F**

19. The multiplier is equal to the change in real GDP multiplied by the initial change in spending. **T F**

20. The initial change in spending for the multiplier is usually associated with investment spending because of investment's volatility. T F

21. The multiplier effect works only in a positive direction in changing GDP. T F

22. The multiplier is based on the idea that any change in income will cause both consumption and saving to vary in the same direction as a change in income and by a fraction of that change in income. T F

23. The higher the marginal propensity to consume, the larger the size of the multiplier. T F

24. When it is computed as 1/MPS, the multiplier reflects only the leakage of income into saving. T F

25. The value of the actual multiplier for the economy will usually be greater than the value of a textbook multiplier because the actual multiplier is based only on the marginal propensity to save. T F

■ MULTIPLE-CHOICE QUESTIONS

Circle the letter that corresponds to the best answer.

1. Saving equals
   (a) investment plus consumption
   (b) investment minus consumption
   (c) disposable income minus consumption
   (d) disposable income plus consumption

2. As disposable income decreases, *ceteris paribus,*
   (a) both consumption and saving increase
   (b) consumption increases and saving decreases
   (c) consumption decreases and saving increases
   (d) both consumption and saving decrease

3. Households tend to spend a larger portion of
   (a) a small disposable income than a large disposable income
   (b) a large disposable income than a small disposable income
   (c) their disposable income on saving when the rate of return is high
   (d) their saving than their disposable income when the rate of return is low

4. If consumption spending increases from $358 to $367 billion when disposable income increases from $412 to $427 billion, it can be concluded that the marginal propensity to consume is
   (a) 0.4
   (b) 0.6
   (c) 0.8
   (d) 0.9

5. If disposable income is $375 billion when the average propensity to consume is 0.8, it can be concluded that
   (a) the marginal propensity to consume is also 0.8
   (b) the marginal propensity to save is 0.2
   (c) consumption is $325 billion
   (d) saving is $75 billion

6. As the disposable income of the economy increases,
   (a) both the APC and the APS rise
   (b) the APC rises and the APS falls
   (c) the APC falls and the APS rises
   (d) both the APC and the APS fall

7. The slope of the consumption schedule or line for a given economy is the
   (a) marginal propensity to consume
   (b) average propensity to consume
   (c) marginal propensity to save
   (d) average propensity to save

Answer Questions 8 and 9 on the basis of the following graph.

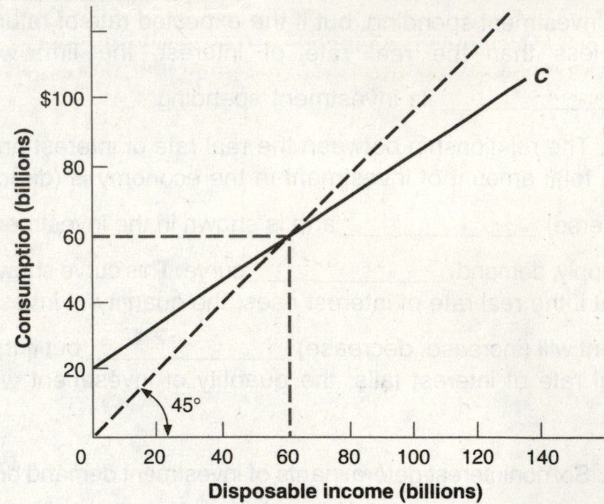

8. This graph indicates that
   (a) consumption decreases after the $60 billion level of disposable income
   (b) the marginal propensity to consume decreases after the $60 billion level of disposable income
   (c) consumption decreases as a percentage of disposable income as disposable income increases
   (d) consumption increases as disposable income decreases

9. If the relevant saving schedule were constructed, one would find that
   (a) the marginal propensity to save is negative up to the $60 billion level of disposable income
   (b) the marginal propensity to save increases after the $60 billion level of disposable income
   (c) saving is zero at the $60 billion level of disposable income
   (d) saving is $20 billion at the $0 level of disposable income

*Answer Questions 10, 11, and 12 on the basis of the following disposable income **(DI)** and consumption **(C)** schedules for a private, closed economy. All figures are in billions of dollars.*

DI	*C*
$ 0	$ 4
40	40
80	76
120	112
160	148
200	184

10. If plotted on a graph, the slope of the consumption schedule would be
(a) 0.6
(b) 0.7
(c) 0.8
(d) 0.9

11. At the $160 billion level of disposable income, the average propensity to save is
(a) 0.015
(b) 0.075
(c) 0.335
(d) 0.925

12. If consumption increases by $5 billion at each level of disposable income, then the marginal propensity to consume will
(a) change, but the average propensity to consume will not change
(b) change, and the average propensity to consume will change
(c) not change, but the average propensity to consume will change
(d) not change, and the average propensity to consume will not change

13. If the slope of a linear saving schedule decreases, then it can be concluded that the
(a) MPS has decreased
(b) MPC has decreased
(c) income has decreased
(d) income has increased

14. An increase in wealth shifts the consumption schedule
(a) downward and the saving schedule upward
(b) upward and the saving schedule downward
(c) downward and the saving schedule downward
(d) upward and the saving schedule upward

15. Expectations of a recession are likely to lead households to
(a) increase consumption and saving
(b) decrease consumption and saving
(c) decrease consumption and increase saving
(d) increase consumption and decrease saving

16. Higher real interest rates are likely to
(a) increase consumption and saving
(b) decrease consumption and saving
(c) decrease consumption and increase saving
(d) increase consumption and decrease saving

17. An increase in taxes shifts the consumption schedule
(a) downward and the saving schedule upward
(b) upward and the saving schedule downward
(c) downward and the saving schedule downward
(d) upward and the saving schedule upward

18. Which relationship is an inverse one?
(a) consumption and disposable income
(b) investment spending and the rate of interest
(c) saving and disposable income
(d) investment spending and GDP

19. A decrease in investment demand would be a consequence of a decline in
(a) the rate of interest
(b) the level of wages paid
(c) business taxes
(d) expected future sales

20. Which would increase investment demand?
(a) an increase in business taxes
(b) an increase in planned inventories
(c) a decrease in the rate of technological change
(d) an increase in the cost of acquiring capital goods

21. Which best explains the variability of investment?
(a) the predictable useful life of capital goods
(b) constancy or regularities in business innovations
(c) instabilities in the level of profits
(d) business pessimism about the future

22. If there was a change in investment spending of $10 and the marginal propensity to save was .25, then real GDP would increase by
(a) $10
(b) $20
(c) $25
(d) $40

23. If the marginal propensity to consume is 0.6 and real GDP falls by $25, this is caused by a decrease in initial spending of
(a) $10.00
(b) $15.00
(c) $16.67
(d) $20.00

24. If the marginal propensity to consume is 0.67 and initial spending increases by $25, real GDP will
(a) increase by $75
(b) decrease by $75
(c) increase by $25
(d) decrease by $25

25. If in an economy a $150 billion increase in investment spending creates $150 billion of new income in the first round of the multiplier process and $105 billion in the second round, the multiplier and the marginal propensity to consume will be, respectively,
(a) 5.00 and 0.80
(b) 4.00 and 0.75
(c) 3.33 and 0.70
(d) 2.50 and 0.40

■ PROBLEMS

1. The following table is a consumption schedule. Assume that taxes and transfer payments are zero and that all saving is personal saving.

(GDP = DI)	C	S	APC	APS
1500	$1540	$____	1.027	−.027
1600	1620	____	1.013	−.013
1700	1700	____	____	____
1800	1780	____	.989	.011
1900	1860	____	.979	.021
2000	1940	____	____	____
2100	2020	____	.962	.038
2200	2100	____	____	____

a. Compute saving at each of the eight levels of disposable income and the missing average propensities to consume and to save.
b. The break-even level of disposable income is $________.
c. As disposable income rises, the marginal propensity to consume remains constant. Between each two GDPs the MPC can be found by dividing $________ by $________, and is equal to ________.
d. The marginal propensity to save also remains constant when the GDP rises. Between each two GDPs the MPS is equal to $________ divided by $________, or to ________.
e. Plot the consumption schedule, the saving schedule, and the 45-degree line on the graph below.
(1) The numerical value of the slope of the consumption schedule is ________, and the term that is used to describe it is the ________.
(2) If the relevant saving schedule were constructed, the numerical value of the slope of the saving schedule would be ________, and the term that is used to describe it would be the ________.

2. Indicate in the space to the right of each of the following events whether the event will tend to increase (1) or decrease (2) the saving schedule.
a. Development of consumer expectations that prices will be higher in the future ________
b. Gradual shrinkage in the quantity of real assets owned by consumers ________
c. Increase in household borrowing ________
d. Growing belief that disposable income will be lower in the future ________
e. Expectations that there will be a current shortage of consumer goods ________
f. Rise in the actual level of disposable income ________
g. An increase in household wealth ________
h. Development of a belief by consumers that the Federal government can and will prevent recessions in the future ________

3. The following schedule has eight different expected rates of return and the dollar amounts of the investment projects expected to have each of these return rates.

Expected rate of return	Investment projects (billions)
18%	$ 0
16	10
14	20
12	30
10	40
8	50
6	60
4	70

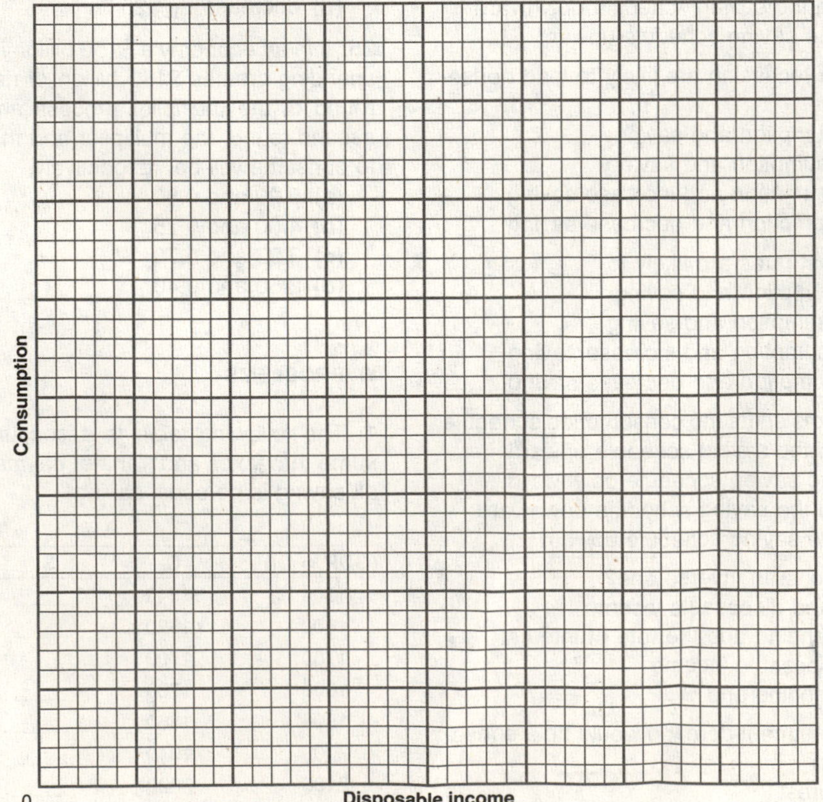

a. If the real rate of interest in the economy were 18%, business firms would plan to spend $_______ billion for investment, but if the real interest rate were 16%, they would plan to spend $_______ for investment.
b. Should the real interest rate be 14%, and they would still wish to make the investments they were willing to make at real interest rates of 18% and 16%, they would plan to spend an additional $_______ billion for investment, and their total investment would be $_______ billion.
c. If the real rate of interest were 12%, they would make all the investments they had planned to make at higher real interest rates plus an additional $_______ billion, and their total investment spending would be $_______ billion.
d. Complete the following table by computing the amount of planned investment at the four remaining real interest rates.

Real rate of interest	Amount of investment (billions)
18%	$ 0
16	10
14	30
12	60
10	_____
8	_____
6	_____
4	_____

e. Graph the schedule you completed on the graph below. Plot the real rate of interest on the vertical axis and the amount of investment planned at each real rate of interest on the horizontal axis.
f. Both the graph and the table show that the relationship between the real rate of interest and the amount of investment spending in the economy is _______. This means that when the real rate of interest

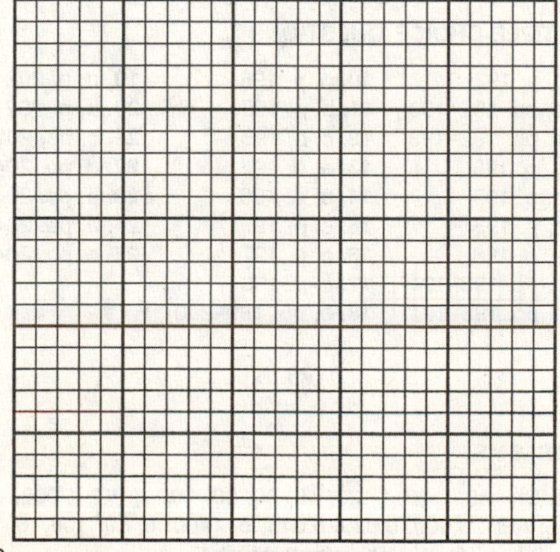

(1) increases, investment will (increase, decrease) _______.
(2) decreases, investment will _______.
g. It also means that should we wish to
(1) increase investment, we would need to _______ the real rate of interest.
(2) decrease investment, we would have to _______ the real rate of interest.
h. This graph (or table) is the _______ curve.

4. Indicate in the spaces to the right of the following events whether the event would tend to increase (+) or decrease (−) investment spending.
a. Rising stock market prices _______
b. Development of expectations by business executives that business taxes will be higher in the future _______
c. Step-up in the rates at which new products and new production processes are being introduced _______
d. Business beliefs that wage rates may be lower in the future and labor and capital are complementary resources _______
e. An expectation of a recession _______
f. A belief that business is "too good" and the economy is due for a period of "slow" consumer demand _______
g. Rising costs in the construction industry _______
h. A rapid increase in the size of the economy's population _______
i. A recent period of a high level of investment spending, which has resulted in productive capacity in excess of the current demand for goods and services _______

5. Assume the marginal propensity to consume is 0.8 and the change in investment is $10. Complete the following table modeled after the table in Figure 10.8 in the textbook.

	Change in income	Change in consumption	Change in saving
Increase in gross investment of $10	$ + 10	$_____	$_____
Second round	_____	_____	_____
Third round	_____	_____	_____
Fourth round	_____	_____	_____
Fifth round	_____	_____	_____
All other rounds	16.38	13.10	3.28
Totals	_____	_____	_____

■ SHORT ANSWER AND ESSAY QUESTIONS

1. What is the most important determinant of consumer spending and personal saving? What is the relationship between consumer spending and personal saving?

2. Use a graph to illustrate the historical relationship between consumption and disposable income in the U.S. economy. Explain why the slope of the consumption line will be less than the 45-degree reference line.

3. Describe the relationship between consumption and disposable income, called the consumption schedule. Draw a graph of this schedule.

4. Describe the relationship between saving and disposable income, called the saving schedule. Draw a graph of this schedule.

5. Define the two average propensities and the two marginal propensities.

6. Explain briefly how the average propensity to consume and the average propensity to save vary as disposable income varies. Why do APC and APS behave this way? What happens to consumption and saving as disposable income varies?

7. Why do the sum of the APC and the APS and the sum of the MPC and the MPS always equal exactly 1?

8. What is the relationship between MPC and MPS and the slopes of the consumption schedule and saving schedule?

9. Explain briefly and explicitly *how* changes in the four nonincome determinants will affect the consumption schedule and the saving schedule and *why* such changes will affect consumption and saving in the way you have indicated.

10. Why does taxation shift both the consumption and saving schedules in the same direction?

11. What is the difference between a change in the amount consumed and a change in the consumption schedule? Explain your answer using a graph.

12. Are consumption and saving schedules relatively stable? Explain.

13. Discuss the marginal cost and marginal benefit of an investment decision. How are the marginal cost and the marginal benefit of investment measured?

14. Draw an investment demand curve. Use it to explain why investment spending tends to rise when the real rate of interest falls, and vice versa.

15. Identify and explain how six noninterest determinants of investment spending can increase or decrease the amount of investment. Illustrate the changes with a graph.

16. Why does the level of investment spending tend to be highly unstable? State four reasons.

17. What is the multiplier effect? Give an equation and example to show how it works.

18. State the rationale for the multiplier effect.

19. How is the multiplier effect related to the marginal propensities? Explain in words and equations.

20. How large is the actual multiplier effect? Explain the reasons for the difference between the textbook example of the multiplier and actual multiplier for the economy.

ANSWERS

Chapter 10 Basic Macroeconomic Relationships

FILL-IN QUESTIONS

1. consume, save
2. directly, larger, smaller, smaller, larger, equal to
3. rise, fall
4. 1, .10
5. consumption, income
6. saving, income
7. 1, .25
8. consumption, saving
9. *a.* wealth; *b.* borrowing; *c.* expectations; *d.* real interest rate; (any order for *a–d*)
10. upward, downward, income
11. return, interest
12. benefit, cost
13. increase, decrease
14. inverse, demand, decrease, increase
15. *a.* the cost of acquiring, maintaining, and operating capital goods; *b.* business taxes; *c.* technological change; *d.* the stock of capital goods on hand; *e.* planned changes in inventories; *f.* expectations
16. durability, irregularity, variability, variability
17. divided, multiplied
18. increase, decrease
19. save, consume
20. larger, smaller

TRUE–FALSE QUESTIONS

1. F, p. 192
2. T, p. 192
3. T, p. 192
4. F, pp. 193–194
5. F, pp. 193–194
6. F, pp. 193–194
7. F, p. 195
8. T, p. 195
9. F, p. 196
10. T, p. 196
11. T, p. 198
12. T, p. 198
13. T, p. 199
14. F, pp. 199–201
15. T, p. 202
16. F, p. 202
17. F, pp. 202–203
18. T, p. 203
19. F, p. 204
20. T, p. 204
21. F, p. 204
22. T, pp. 204–205
23. T, p. 206
24. T, p. 206
25. F, pp. 207–208

MULTIPLE-CHOICE QUESTIONS

1. c, p. 192
2. d, pp. 192–193
3. a, pp. 192–193
4. b, p. 195
5. d, p. 195
6. c, p. 195
7. a, p. 196
8. c, pp. 193–194
9. c, pp. 193–194
10. d, p. 196
11. b, p. 195
12. c, p. 195
13. a, p. 196
14. b, p. 196
15. c, p. 197
16. c, p. 197
17. c, p. 198
18. b, pp. 199–200
19. d, p. 202
20. b, p. 202
21. c, pp. 202–203
22. d, pp. 204–206
23. a, pp. 204–206
24. a, pp. 204–206
25. c, pp. 204–206

PROBLEMS

1. *a.* S: −40, −20, 0, 20, 40, 60, 80, 100; APC: 1.000, 0.970, 0.955; APS: 0.000, 0.030, 0.045; *b.* 1700; *c.* 80, 100, .8; *d.* 20, 100, .20; *e.* (1) .8, MPC, (2) .2, MPS

2. *a.* −; *b.* +; *c.* −; *d.* +; *e.* −; *f.* none; *g.* −; *h.* −

3. *a.* 0, 10; *b.* 20, 30; *c.* 30, 60; *d.* 100, 150, 210, 280; *f.* inverse, (1) decrease, (2) increase; *g.* (1) lower, (2) raise; *h.* investment-demand

4. *a.* +; *b.* −; *c.* +; *d.* +; *e.* −; *f.* −; *g.* −; *h.* +; *i.* −

5. Change in income: 8.00, 6.40, 5.12, 4.10, 50; Change in consumption: 8.00, 6.40, 5.12, 4.10, 3.28, 40.00; Change in saving: 2.00, 1.60, 1.28, 1.02, 0.82, 10.00

SHORT ANSWER AND ESSAY QUESTIONS

1. p. 192
2. pp. 192–193
3. pp. 193–194
4. pp. 193–195
5. p. 195
6. p. 195
7. pp. 195–196
8. p. 196
9. pp. 196–197
10. p. 198
11. p. 197
12. p. 198
13. pp. 199–200
14. pp. 199–200
15. pp. 201–202
16. pp. 202–203
17. p. 204
18. pp. 204–205
19. p. 206
20. pp. 207–208

CHAPTER 11

The Aggregate Expenditures Model

This chapter develops the first macroeconomic model of the economy presented in the textbook—the **aggregate expenditures model.** You will find out what determines the demand for real domestic output (real GDP) and how an economy achieves an equilibrium level of output. The chapter begins with some history and simplifying assumptions for the model. As you will learn, one of the main assumptions is that the prices are fixed.

The chapter then explains how the investment decisions of individual firms can be used to construct an **investment schedule.** The investment schedule is then combined with the consumption schedule to form an aggregate expenditures schedule that shows the various amounts that will be spent in a private closed economy at each possible output or income level. These aggregate expenditures in tabular or graphical form can be used to find **equilibrium GDP** for this economy. It will be important for you to understand how equilibrium GDP is determined and why this level of output will be produced when you are given information about consumption and investment schedules.

Two other features of this simplified aggregate expenditures model are worth noting. Saving and *actual* investment are always equal because they are defined in exactly the same way: the output of the economy minus its consumption. **Saving and planned investment,** however, are equal only when real GDP is at its equilibrium level. When real GDP is *not* at its equilibrium level, saving and planned investment are *not* equal and there are **unplanned changes in inventories.** Equilibrium real GDP is achieved when saving and *planned* investment are equal and there are no unplanned changes in inventories.

From Chapter 11 you will also learn **what causes real GDP to rise and fall** based on changes or additions to aggregate expenditures. The first change that will be discussed is the effect of a change in investment spending on equilibrium real GDP in a private closed economy. The initial change in investment will increase equilibrium real GDP by more than the initial investment stimulus because of the multiplier effect.

The methods used to find the equilibrium real GDP in a private open economy (one that exports and imports) is the same one as for a private closed economy. The economy will tend to produce a real GDP that is equal to aggregate expenditures. The only difference is that now the aggregate expenditures include not only consumption and investment but also the **net exports** (exports minus imports). An increase in net exports, like an increase in investment, will increase the equilibrium real GDP. A change in net exports also has a multiplier effect on real GDP just like a change in investment.

The section "Adding the Public Sector" introduces **government taxing and spending** into the analysis of equilibrium real GDP. Government purchases of goods and services add to aggregate expenditures, and taxation reduces the disposable income of consumers, thereby reducing both the amount of consumption and the amount of saving that will take place at any level of real GDP. You will need to know the level of real GDP that will be produced and why.

It is important to be aware that the equilibrium real GDP is not necessarily the real GDP at which full employment is achieved. Aggregate expenditures may be greater or less than the full-employment real GDP. If they are greater, there is an **inflationary expenditure gap.** If they are less, there exists a **recessionary expenditure gap.** The chapter explains how to measure the size of each expenditure gap: the amount by which the aggregate expenditures schedule must change to bring the economy to its full-employment real GDP. The chapter ends with a direct application of the recessionary gap to the recession of 2007–2009.

The aggregate expenditures model is a valuable tool for explaining such economic events as recession, inflation, and economic growth.

■ CHECKLIST

When you have studied this chapter you should be able to

☐ Describe the history, assumptions, and simplifications underpinning the aggregate expenditures model.

☐ Construct an investment schedule showing the relationship between planned investment and GDP.

☐ Combine the consumption and investment schedule to form an aggregate expenditures schedule to explain the equilibrium levels of output, income, and employment in a private closed economy.

☐ Explain why the economy will tend to produce its equilibrium GDP rather than some smaller or larger level of real GDP.

☐ Illustrate graphically equilibrium in an aggregate expenditures model with consumption and investment components.

☐ Explain the relationship between saving and planned investment at equilibrium GDP.

☐ State the conditions for changes in inventories at equilibrium GDP.

☐ Discuss why equilibrium real GDP changes when the aggregate expenditure schedule shifts upward due to an increase in investment spending.
☐ Use the concept of net exports to define aggregate expenditures in a private open economy.
☐ Describe the net export schedule and its relationship to real GDP.
☐ Explain what the equilibrium real GDP in a private open economy will be when net exports are positive and when net exports are negative.
☐ Find the equilibrium real GDP in a private open economy when given the tabular or graphical data.
☐ Give three examples of how circumstances or policies abroad can affect domestic GDP.
☐ List three simplifying assumptions used to add the public sector to the aggregate expenditures model.
☐ Find the equilibrium real GDP in an economy in which the government purchases goods and services when given the tabular or graphical data.
☐ Determine the effect on the equilibrium real GDP when lump-sum taxes are included in the aggregate expenditures model.
☐ Describe the conditions for leakages and injections and unplanned changes in inventories at the equilibrium level of GDP.
☐ Distinguish between the equilibrium real GDP and the full-employment real GDP.
☐ Explain the meaning of a recessionary gap and calculate one when you are provided with the relevant data.
☐ Present Keynes's solution to a recessionary expenditure gap.
☐ Define inflationary expenditure gap and calculate one when you are provided with the relevant data.
☐ Apply the concepts of a recessionary expenditure gap to the recession of 2007–2009.
☐ Describe Say's law and Keynes's critique of it (*Last Word*).

■ CHAPTER OUTLINE

1. The development of the ***aggregate expenditures model*** occurred during the Great Depression when there was high unemployment and underutilized capital. Prices in such an economy were fixed or stuck (an extreme version of the sticky price model already discussed in Chapter 6) because the oversupply of productive resources kept prices low. As a result, business had to make output and employment decisions based on unplanned changes in inventories arising from economic shocks.

a. The aggregate expenditures model with its constant price assumption is valuable for analysis of our modern economy because in many cases prices are sticky or stuck in the short run. The model can be useful for understanding how economic shocks affect output and employment when prices are fixed or sticky.

b. Two simplifications are made to begin the model construction. First, it is assumed that the economy is private and closed, which means there is no international trade or government spending (or taxes). Second, it is assumed that output or income measures are equal (real GDP = disposable income, DI). These simplifications are relaxed later in the chapter.

2. The investment decisions of businesses in an economy can be aggregated to form an ***investment schedule*** that shows the amounts business firms collectively intend to invest (their ***planned investment***) at each possible level of GDP. An assumption is made that investment is independent of disposable income or real GDP.

3. In the aggregate expenditures model, the ***equilibrium GDP*** is the real GDP at which

a. aggregate expenditures (consumption plus planned investment) equal real GDP, or $C + Ig = GDP$;

b. in graphical terms, the aggregate expenditures schedule crosses the 45-degree line. The slope of this curve is equal to the marginal propensity to consume.

4. There are two other features of equilibrium GDP.

a. The investment schedule indicates what investors plan to do. Actual investment consists of both planned and unplanned investment (unplanned changes in inventories). At above equilibrium levels of GDP, saving is greater than planned investment, and there will be unintended or unplanned investment through increases in inventories. At below equilibrium levels of GDP, planned investment is greater than saving, and there will be unintended or unplanned disinvestment through a decrease in inventories.

b. Equilibrium is achieved when planned investment equals saving and there are no ***unplanned changes in inventories.***

5. Changes in investment (or consumption) will cause the equilibrium real GDP to change in the same direction by an amount greater than the initial change in investment (or consumption). The reason for this greater change is the ***multiplier effect.***

6. In a private ***open economy*** there are ***net exports*** (X_n), which are defined as exports (X) minus imports (M).

a. The equilibrium real GDP in a private open economy means real GDP is equal to consumption plus investment plus net exports.

b. The net export schedule will be positive or negative. The schedule is positive when exports are greater than imports; it is negative when imports are greater than exports.

c. Any increase in X_n will increase the equilibrium real GDP with a multiplier effect. A decrease in X_n will do just the opposite.

d. In a private open economy model, circumstances and policies abroad can affect the real GDP in the United States.

(1) If there is an increase in real output and incomes in other nations that trade with the United States, then because of this prosperity abroad the United States can sell more goods abroad, which increases net exports, and thus increases real GDP in the United States. A decline in the real output or incomes of other trading nations has the opposite effects.

(2) A depreciation in the value of the U.S. dollar will increase the purchasing power of foreign currency and

this change will increase U.S. exports. The result is an increase in net exports and real GDP. An appreciation in the value of the U.S. dollar has the opposite effect.

(3) During recessions, nations often look for ways to increase exports and decrease imports, thus increasing net exports and giving a boost to real GDP. Although it is tempting for governments to pursue a policy of raising tariffs or devaluing a currency as a means to increase net exports, such government intervention is short-sighted because other nations are likely to retaliate and take the same actions. When that happens there is a negative effect on net exports and a reduction in GDP as happened during the Great Depression.

7. Changes in ***government spending*** and ***tax rates*** can affect equilibrium real GDP. This simplified analysis assumes that government purchases do not affect investment or consumption, that taxes are purely personal taxes, and that a fixed amount of tax revenue is collected regardless of the level of GDP (a ***lump-sum tax***).

a. ***Government purchases*** of goods and services add to the aggregate expenditures schedule and increase equilibrium real GDP; an increase in these purchases has a multiplier effect on equilibrium real GDP.

b. ***Taxes*** decrease consumption and the aggregate expenditures schedule by the amount of the tax times the **MPC.** They decrease saving by the amount of the tax times the **MPS.** An increase in taxes has a negative multiplier effect on the equilibrium real GDP.

(1) When government both taxes and purchases goods and services, the equilibrium GDP is the real GDP at which aggregate expenditures (*consumption* + *investment* + *net exports* + *government purchases of goods and services*) equals real GDP.

(2) From a ***leakages*** and ***injections*** perspective, the equilibrium GDP is the real GDP at which leakages (*saving* + *imports* + *taxes*) equals injections (*investment* + *exports* + *government purchases*).

(3) At equilibrium real GDP, there are no unplanned changes in inventories.

8. The ***equilibrium level of real GDP*** may turn out to be an equilibrium that is at less than full employment, at full employment, or at full employment with inflation.

a. If the equilibrium real GDP is less than the real GDP consistent with full-employment real GDP, there exists a ***recessionary expenditure gap.*** Aggregate expenditures are less than what is needed to achieve full-employment real GDP. The size of the recessionary expenditure gap equals the amount by which the aggregate expenditures schedule must increase (shift upward) to increase real GDP to its full-employment level.

(1) Keynes's solution to close a recessionary expenditure gap and achieve full-employment GDP was either to increase government spending or decrease taxes. An increase in government expenditures or a cut in taxes would work through the multiplier to lift aggregate expenditures. One caution about the price assumption, however, is worth noting. As an economy moves to its full-employment or potential GDP, prices should not be assumed to be stuck or sticky, and thus will rise because there is no longer a large supply of unemployed resources to restrain price increases. Such a flexible-prices condition will be analyzed in the aggregate demand–aggregate supply model of the next chapter.

b. If aggregate expenditures are *greater* than those consistent with full-employment real GDP, then there is an ***inflationary expenditure gap.*** This expenditure gap results from excess spending and will increase the price level, creating demand-pull inflation. The size of the inflationary expenditure gap equals the amount by which the aggregate expenditures schedule must decrease (shift downward) if the economy is to achieve full-employment real GDP.

c. The U.S. recession of 2007–2009 is an example of a recessionary expenditure gap as investment spending declined, thus reducing aggregate expenditures. Aggregate expenditures were insufficient to achieve a full-employment level of GDP and produced one of the largest negative GDP gaps since the Great Depression. In response, the federal government tried to lift aggregate expenditures by providing tax rebates and increasing government spending.

9. (*Last Word*). Classical economists held the view that when there were deviations from full employment in the economy, it would eventually adjust and achieve equilibrium. This view was based on *Say's law,* which says that supply creates its own demand. It implies that the production of goods will create the income needed to purchase the produced goods. The events of the Great Depression led to doubts about this law and it was challenged by John Maynard Keynes in his 1936 book *General Theory of Employment, Interest, and Money.* Keynes showed that supply may not create its own demand because not all income need be spent in the period it was earned, thus creating conditions for high levels of unemployment and economic decline.

■ HINTS AND TIPS

1. Do not confuse the **investment demand curve** for the business sector with the **investment schedule** for an economy. The former shows the inverse relationship between the real interest rate and the amount of total investment by the business sector, whereas the latter shows the collective investment intentions of business firms at each possible level of disposable income or real GDP.

2. The distinction between **actual investment, planned investment,** and **unplanned investment** is important for determining the equilibrium level of real GDP. Actual investment includes both planned and unplanned investment. At any level of real GDP, saving and actual investment will always be equal by definition, but saving and planned investment may not equal real GDP because there may be unplanned investment (unplanned changes in inventories). Only at the equilibrium level of real GDP will saving and planned investment be equal (there is no unplanned investment).

3. There is an important difference between **equilibrium** and **full-employment real GDP** in the aggregate expenditures model. Equilibrium means no tendency for the economy to change its output (or employment) level. Thus, an economy can experience a low level of output and high unemployment and still be at equilibrium. The *recessionary expenditure gap* shows how much aggregate expenditures need to increase, so that when this increase is multiplied by the multiplier, it will shift the economy to a higher equilibrium and to the full-employment level of real GDP. Remember that you multiply the needed increase in aggregate expenditures (the recessionary expenditure gap) by the multiplier to calculate the change in real GDP that moves the economy from below to full-employment equilibrium.

■ IMPORTANT TERMS

planned investment
investment schedule
aggregate expenditures schedule
equilibrium GDP
leakage
injection
unplanned changes in inventories
net exports
lump-sum tax
recessionary expenditure gap
inflationary expenditure gap

SELF-TEST

■ FILL-IN QUESTIONS

1. In the aggregate expenditures model, when total spending falls, then total output and employment (increase, decrease) ____________, and when total spending rises, then total output and employment ____________.

2. Some simplifying assumptions used in the first part of the chapter are that the economy is (an open, a closed) ____________ economy, that the economy is (private, public) ____________, that real GDP equals disposable (consumption, income) ____________, and that an increase in aggregate expenditures will (increase, decrease) ____________ real output and employment, but not raise the price level.

3. A schedule showing the amounts business firms collectively intend to invest at each possible level of GDP is the (consumption, investment) ____________ schedule. For this schedule, it is assumed that planned (saving, investment) ____________ is independent of the level of current disposable income or real output.

4. Assuming a private and closed economy, the equilibrium level of real GDP is determined where aggregate expenditures are (greater than, less than, equal to) ____________ real domestic output, consumption plus investment is ____________ real domestic output, and the aggregate expenditures schedule or curve intersects the (90-degree, 45-degree) ____________ line.

5. A leakage is (an addition to, a withdrawal from) ____________ the income expenditure stream, whereas an injection is ____________ the income expenditure stream. In this chapter, an example of a leakage is (investment, saving) ____________, and an example of an injection is ____________.

6. If aggregate expenditures are greater than the real domestic output, saving is (greater than, less than) ____________ planned investment, there are unplanned (increases, decreases) ____________ in inventories, and real GDP will (rise, fall) ____________.

7. If aggregate expenditures are less than the real domestic output, saving is (greater than, less than) ____________ planned investment, there are unplanned (increases, decreases) ____________ in inventories, and real GDP will (rise, fall) ____________.

8. If aggregate expenditures are equal to the real domestic output, saving is (greater than, less than, equal to) ____________ planned investment, unplanned changes in inventories are (negative, positive, zero) ____________, and real GDP will neither rise nor fall.

9. An upshift in the aggregate expenditures schedule will (increase, decrease) ____________ the equilibrium GDP. The upshift in the aggregate expenditures schedule can result from (an increase, a decrease) ____________ in the consumption schedule or ____________ in the investment schedule.

10. When investment spending increases, the equilibrium real GDP (increases, decreases) ____________, and when investment spending decreases, the equilibrium real GDP ____________. The changes in the equilibrium real GDP are (greater, less) ____________ than the initial changes in investment spending because of the (lump-sum tax, multiplier) ____________.

11. In a private open economy, a nation's net exports are equal to its exports (plus, minus) ____________ its imports. In the private open economy, aggregate expenditures are equal to consumption (plus, minus) ____________ investment (plus, minus) ____________ net exports.

12. What would be the effect, an increase (+) or a decrease (−), of each of the following on a private open economy's equilibrium real GDP?

a. an increase in imports ________
b. an increase in exports ________
c. a decrease in imports ________
d. a decrease in exports ________
e. an increasing level of national income among trading partners ________

f. an increase in trade barriers imposed by trading partners ______

g. a depreciation in the value of the economy's currency ______

13. Increases in public spending will (decrease, increase) ______ the aggregate expenditures schedule and equilibrium real GDP, but decreases in public spending will ______ the aggregate expenditures schedule and equilibrium real GDP.

14. A tax yielding the same amount of tax revenue at each level of GDP is a (lump-sum, constant) ______ tax.

15. Taxes tend to reduce consumption at each level of real GDP by an amount equal to the taxes multiplied by the marginal propensity to (consume, save) ______; saving will decrease by an amount equal to the taxes multiplied by the marginal propensity to ______.

16. In an economy in which government both taxes and purchases goods and services, the equilibrium level of real GDP is the real GDP at which aggregate (output, expenditures) ______ equal(s) real domestic ______, and at which real GDP is equal to consumption (plus, minus) ______ investment (plus, minus) ______ net exports (plus, minus) ______ purchases of goods and services by government.

17. When the public sector is added to the model, the equation for the leakages and injections shows (consumption, investment) ______ plus (imports, exports) ______, plus purchases of goods and services by government equals (consumption, saving) ______ plus (exports, imports) ______ plus taxes.

18. A recessionary expenditure gap exists when equilibrium real GDP is (greater, less) ______ than the full-employment real GDP. To bring real GDP to the full-employment level, the aggregate expenditures schedule must (increase, decrease) ______ by an amount equal to the difference between the equilibrium and the full-employment real GDP (multiplied, divided) ______ by the multiplier.

19. Keynes believed that prices during the Great Depression were (flexible, fixed) ______ because large amounts of productive resources in the economy were unemployed. In such conditions, he thought the government could increase real GDP to achieve full-employment without a rise in the price level by (increasing, decreasing) ______ government spending or ______ taxes.

20. The amount by which aggregate spending at the full-employment GDP exceeds the full-employment level of real GDP is (a recessionary, an inflationary) ______ expenditure gap. To eliminate this expenditure gap, the aggregate expenditures schedule must (increase, decrease) ______.

■ TRUE–FALSE QUESTIONS

Circle T if the statement is true, F if it is false.

1. The basic premise of the aggregate expenditures model is that the amount of goods and services produced and the level of employment depend directly on the level of total spending. **T F**

2. In the aggregate expenditures model of the economy, the price level is assumed to be fixed or stuck. **T F**

3. The investment schedule is a schedule of planned investment rather than a schedule of actual investment. **T F**

4. The equilibrium level of GDP is that GDP level corresponding to the intersection of the aggregate expenditures schedule with the 45-degree line. **T F**

5. At levels of GDP below equilibrium, the economy wants to spend at higher levels than the levels of GDP the economy is producing. **T F**

6. At levels of GDP below equilibrium, aggregate expenditures are less than GDP, which causes inventories to rise and production to fall. **T F**

7. Saving is an injection into and investment is a leakage from the income expenditures stream. **T F**

8. Saving and actual investment are always equal. **T F**

9. Saving at any level of real GDP equals planned investment plus unplanned changes in inventories. **T F**

10. The equilibrium level of GDP will change in response to changes in the investment schedule or the consumption schedule. **T F**

11. If there is a decrease in the investment schedule, there will be an upshift in the aggregate expenditures schedule. **T F**

12. Through the multiplier effect, an initial change in investment spending can cause a magnified change in domestic output and income. **T F**

13. The net exports of an economy equal the sum of its exports and imports of goods and services. **T F**

14. An increase in the volume of a nation's exports, other things being equal, will expand the nation's real GDP. **T F**

15. An increase in the imports of a nation will increase the exports of other nations. **T F**

16. A falling level of real output and income among U.S. trading partners enables the United States to sell more goods abroad. **T F**

17. An appreciation of the dollar will increase net exports. **T F**

18. If the MPS were 0.3 and taxes were levied by the government so that consumers paid $20 in taxes at each level of real GDP, consumption expenditures at each level of real GDP would be $14 less. **T F**

19. Equal changes in government spending and taxes do not have equivalent effects on real GDP. **T F**

20. At equilibrium, the sum of leakages equals the sum of injections. **T F**

21. The equilibrium real GDP is the real GDP at which there is full employment in the economy. **T F**

22. The existence of a recessionary expenditure gap in the economy is characterized by the full employment of labor. **T F**

23. Keynes's solution to the recessionary expenditure gap of the Great Depression was to increase government spending and cut taxes. **T F**

24. The closer an economy is to its full-employment level of output, the less likely it is that any increase in aggregate expenditures will lead to inflation rather than an increase in real GDP. **T F**

25. An inflationary expenditure gap is the amount by which the economy's aggregate expenditures schedule must shift downward to eliminate demand-pull inflation and still achieve the full-employment GDP. **T F**

■ MULTIPLE-CHOICE QUESTIONS

Circle the letter that corresponds to the best answer.

1. The premise of the model in this chapter is that the amount of goods and services produced, and therefore the level of employment, depends
- **(a)** directly on the rate of interest
- **(b)** directly on the level of total expenditures
- **(c)** inversely on the level of disposable income
- **(d)** inversely on the quantity of resources available

2. If the economy is private, closed to international trade, and government neither taxes nor spends, then real GDP equals
- **(a)** saving
- **(b)** consumption
- **(c)** disposable income
- **(d)** investment spending

Question 3 is based on the following consumption schedule.

Real GDP	C
$200	$200
240	228
280	256
320	284
360	312
400	340
440	368
480	396

3. If the investment schedule is $60 at each level of output, the equilibrium level of real GDP will be
- **(a)** $320
- **(b)** $360
- **(c)** $400
- **(d)** $440

4. If real GDP is $275 billion, consumption is $250 billion, and investment is $30 billion, real GDP
- **(a)** will tend to decrease
- **(b)** will tend to increase
- **(c)** will tend to remain constant
- **(d)** equals aggregate expenditures

5. On a graph, the equilibrium real GDP is found at the intersection of the 45-degree line and the
- **(a)** saving curve
- **(b)** consumption curve
- **(c)** investment demand curve
- **(d)** aggregate expenditures curve

6. Which is an injection of spending into the income expenditures stream?
- **(a)** investment
- **(b)** imports
- **(c)** saving
- **(d)** taxes

7. When the economy's real GDP exceeds its equilibrium real GDP,
- **(a)** leakages equal injections
- **(b)** planned investment exceeds saving
- **(c)** there is unplanned investment in the economy
- **(d)** aggregate expenditures exceed the real domestic output

8. If saving is greater than planned investment
- **(a)** saving will tend to increase
- **(b)** businesses will be motivated to increase their investments
- **(c)** real GDP will be greater than planned investment plus consumption
- **(d)** aggregate expenditures will be greater than the real domestic output

9. At the equilibrium level of GDP,
- **(a)** actual investment is zero
- **(b)** unplanned changes in inventories are zero
- **(c)** saving is greater than planned investment
- **(d)** saving is less than planned investment

Answer Questions 10 and 11 on the basis of the following table for a private closed economy. All figures are in billions of dollars.

Real rate of return	Investment	Consumption	GDP
10%	$ 0	$200	$200
8	50	250	300
6	100	300	400
4	150	350	500
2	200	400	600
0	250	450	700

10. If the real rate of interest is 4%, then the equilibrium level of GDP will be
(a) $300 billion
(b) $400 billion
(c) $500 billion
(d) $600 billion

11. An *increase* in the real interest rate by 4% will
(a) increase the equilibrium level of GDP by $200 billion
(b) decrease the equilibrium level of GDP by $200 billion
(c) decrease the equilibrium level of GDP by $100 billion
(d) increase the equilibrium level of GDP by $100 billion

12. Compared with a private closed economy, aggregate expenditures and GDP will
(a) increase when net exports are positive
(b) decrease when net exports are positive
(c) increase when net exports are negative
(d) decrease when net exports are zero

Use the data in the following table to answer Questions 13 and 14.

Real GDP	$C + I_g$	Net exports
900	$ 913	$3
920	929	3
940	945	3
960	961	3
980	977	3
1000	993	3
1020	1009	3

13. The equilibrium real GDP in this private open economy is
(a) $960
(b) $980
(c) $1000
(d) $1020

14. If net exports are increased by $4 billion at each level of GDP, the equilibrium real GDP would be
(a) $960
(b) $980
(c) $1000
(d) $1020

15. An increase in the real GDP of an economy will, other things remaining constant,
(a) increase its imports and the real GDPs in other economies
(b) decrease its imports and the real GDPs in other economies
(c) increase its imports and decrease the real GDPs in other economies
(d) decrease its imports and increase the real GDPs in other economies

16. Other things remaining constant, which would increase an economy's real GDP and employment?
(a) an increase in the exchange rate for foreign currencies
(b) the imposition of tariffs on goods imported from abroad
(c) an appreciation of the dollar relative to foreign currencies
(d) an increase in the level of national income among the trading partners for this economy

17. The economy is operating at the full-employment level of output. A depreciation of the dollar will most likely result in
(a) a decrease in exports
(b) an increase in imports
(c) a decrease in real GDP
(d) an increase in the price level

Answer Questions 18 and 19 on the basis of the following diagram.

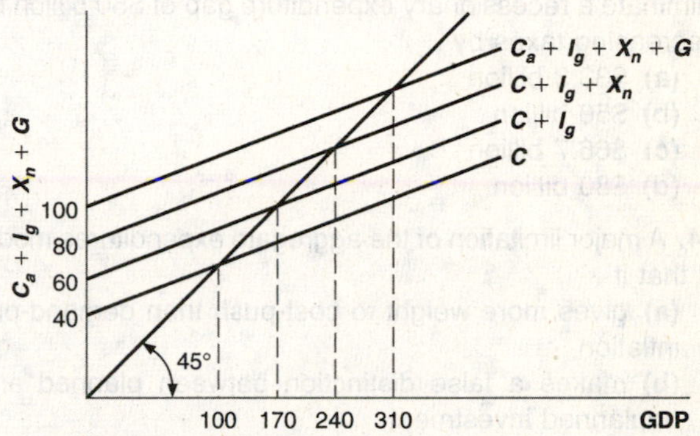

18. If this were a private open economy without a government sector, the level of GDP would be
(a) $100
(b) $170
(c) $240
(d) $310

19. In this graph it is assumed that investment, net exports, and government expenditures
(a) vary directly with GDP
(b) vary inversely with GDP
(c) are independent of GDP
(d) are all negative

Questions 20 and 21 are based on the following consumption schedule.

Real GDP	*C*
$300	$290
310	298
320	306
330	314
340	322
350	330
360	338

20. If taxes were zero, government purchases of goods and services $10, planned investment $6, and net exports zero, equilibrium real GDP would be
(a) $310
(b) $320
(c) $330
(d) $340

21. If taxes were $5, government purchases of goods and services $10, planned investment $6, and net exports zero, equilibrium real GDP would be
(a) $300
(b) $310
(c) $320
(d) $330

22. The amount by which an economy's aggregate expenditures must shift upward to achieve full-employment GDP is
(a) an injection
(b) a lump-sum tax
(c) a recessionary expenditure gap
(d) an unplanned change in inventories

23. If the MPC in an economy is 0.75, government could eliminate a recessionary expenditure gap of $50 billion by decreasing taxes by
(a) $33.3 billion
(b) $50 billion
(c) $66.7 billion
(d) $80 billion

24. A major limitation of the aggregate expenditures model is that it
(a) gives more weight to cost-push than demand-pull inflation
(b) makes a false distinction between planned and unplanned investment
(c) assumes that prices are stuck or inflexible even as the economy moves near potential GDP
(d) explains recessionary expenditure gaps but not inflationary expenditure gaps

25. Assume that the marginal propensity to save is 0.1 in an economy. To reduce the level of real GDP by $50 billion in that economy to achieve a full employment level of output, it will be necessary to
(a) decrease the aggregate expenditures schedule by $50 billion
(b) decrease the aggregate expenditures schedule by $5 billion
(c) increase the aggregate expenditures schedule by $50 billion
(d) increase the aggregate expenditures schedule by $5 billion

■ PROBLEMS

1. Following are two schedules showing several GDPs and the level of investment spending (I) at each GDP. (All figures are in billions of dollars.)

Schedule number 1		*Schedule number 2*	
GDP	***I***	***GDP***	***I***
$1850	$90	$1850	$75
1900	90	1900	80
1950	90	1950	85
2000	90	2000	90
2050	90	2050	95
2100	90	2100	100
2150	95	2150	105

a. Each schedule is a(n) _______ schedule.
b. When such a schedule is drawn up, it is assumed that the real rate of interest is _______.
c. In schedule
(1) number 1, GDP and I are (unrelated, directly related) _______.
(2) number 2, GDP and I are _______.
d. Should the real rate of interest rise, investment spending at each GDP would (increase, decrease) _______ and the curve relating GDP and investment spending would shift (upward, downward) _______.

2. The following table shows consumption and saving at various levels of real GDP. Assume the price level is constant, the economy is closed to international trade, and there is no government, no business savings, no depreciation, and no net foreign factor income earned in the United States.

Real GDP	***C***	***S***	I_g	$C + I_g$	***UI***
$1300	$1290	$10	$22	1312	−12
1310	1298	12	22	1320	−10
1320	1306	14	___	___	___
1330	1314	16	___	___	___
1340	1322	18	___	___	___
1350	1330	20	___	___	___
1360	1338	22	___	___	___
1370	1346	24	___	___	___
1380	1354	26	___	___	___
1390	1362	28	22	1384	+6
1400	1370	30	22	1392	+8

a. The next table is an investment demand schedule that shows the amounts investors plan to invest at different rates of interest. Assume the rate of interest is 6%. In the previous table, complete the gross investment, the consumption-plus-investment, and unplanned investment (***UI***) columns, showing unplanned increase in inventories with a + and unplanned decrease in inventories with a −.

Interest rate	I_g
$10%	$ 0
9	7
8	13
7	18
6	22
5	25

b. The equilibrium real GDP will be $ _______.
c. The value of the marginal propensity to consume in this problem is _______, and the value of the marginal propensity to save is _______.
d. The value of the simple multiplier is _______.

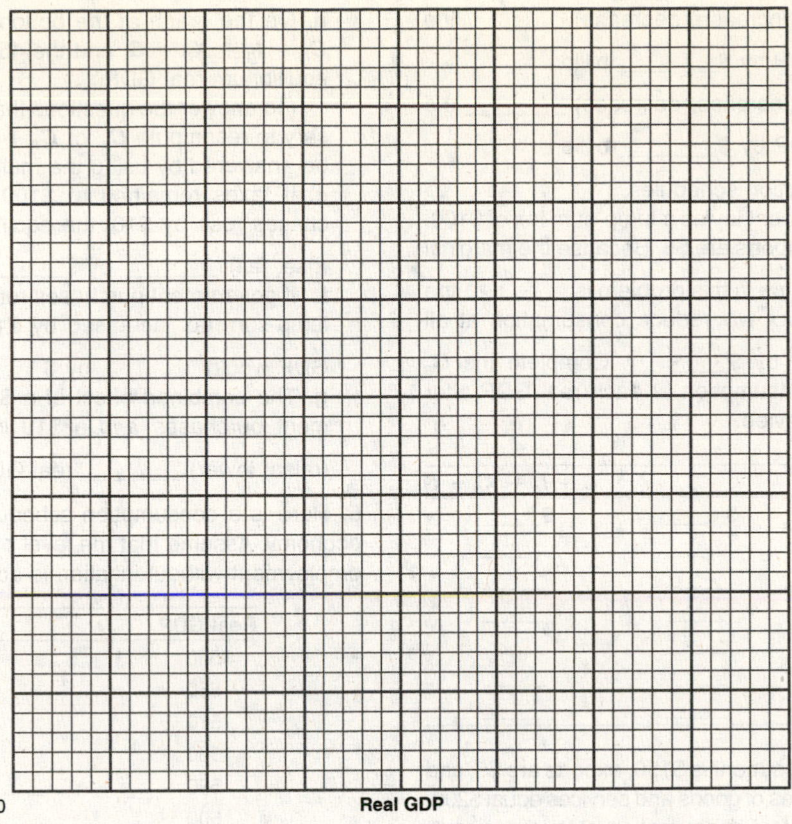

e. If the rate of interest should fall from 6% to 5%, investment would (increase, decrease) _______ by $_______; and the equilibrium real GDP would, as a result, (increase, decrease) _______ by $_______.

f. Suppose the rate of interest were to rise from 6% to 7%. Investment would (increase, decrease) _______ by $_______ and the equilibrium real GDP would _______ by $_______.

g. Assuming the rate of interest is 6%, on the graph at the top of this page, plot ***C, C + I_g,*** and the 45-degree line, and indicate the equilibrium real GDP.

3. The second column of the schedule below shows what aggregate expenditures (consumption plus investment) would be at various levels of real domestic product in a private closed economy.

a. Were this economy to become a private open economy, the volume of exports would be a constant $90 billion (column 3), and the volume of imports would be a constant $86 billion (column 4). At each of the seven levels of real GDP (column 1), net exports would be $_______ billion (column 5).

b. Compute aggregate expenditures in this private open economy at the seven real GDP levels and enter them in the table (column 6).

c. The equilibrium real GDP in this private open economy would be _______ billion.

d. The value of the multiplier in this private open economy is equal to _______.

e. A $10 billion increase in

(1) Possible levels of, real GDP (billions)	(2) Aggregate expenditures private closed economy (billions)	(3) Exports (billions)	(4) Imports (billions)	(5) Net exports (billions)	(6) Aggregate expenditures, private open economy (billions)
$ 750	$ 776	$90	$86	$_____	$_____
800	816	90	86	_____	_____
850	856	90	86	_____	_____
900	896	90	86	_____	_____
950	936	90	86	_____	_____
1000	976	90	86	_____	_____
1050	1016	90	86	_____	_____

(1) exports would (increase, decrease) _______ the equilibrium real GDP by $_______ billion.

(2) imports would (increase, decrease) _______ the equilibrium real GDP by $_______ billion.

4. Below are consumption schedules.

a. Assume government levies a lump-sum tax of $100. Also assume that imports are $5. Because the marginal propensity to consume in this problem is _______, the imposition of this tax will reduce consumption at all levels of real GDP by $_______. Complete the C_a column to show consumption at each real GDP after this tax has been levied.

Real GDP	C	C_a	$C + I_g + X_n + G$
$1500	$1250	$_____	$_____
1600	1340	_____	_____
1700	1430	_____	_____
1800	1520	_____	_____
1900	1610	_____	_____
2000	1700	_____	_____
2100	1790	_____	_____

b. Suppose that investment is $150, exports are $5, and government purchases of goods and services equal $200. Complete the (after-tax) consumption-plus-investment-plus-net-exports-plus-government-purchases column ($C_a + I_g + X_n + G$).

c. The equilibrium real GDP is $_______.

d. On the graph at the bottom of the page, plot C_a, $C_a + I_g + X_n + G$, and the 45-degree line. Show the equilibrium real GDP.

(To answer the questions that follow, it is *not* necessary to recompute C_a, or $C_a + I_g + X_n + G$. They can be answered by using the multipliers.)

e. If taxes remained at $100 and government purchases rose by $10, the equilibrium real GDP would (rise, fall) _______ by $_______.

f. If government purchases remained at $200 and the lump-sum tax increased by $10, the equilibrium real GDP would _______ by $_______.

g. The combined effect of a $10 increase in government purchases *and* a $10 increase in taxes is to (raise, lower) _______ real GDP by $_______.

5. Here is a consumption schedule for a private closed economy. Assume that the level of real GDP at which full employment without inflation is achieved is $590.

Real GDP	C
$550	$520
560	526
570	532
580	538
590	544
600	550
610	556
620	562
630	568

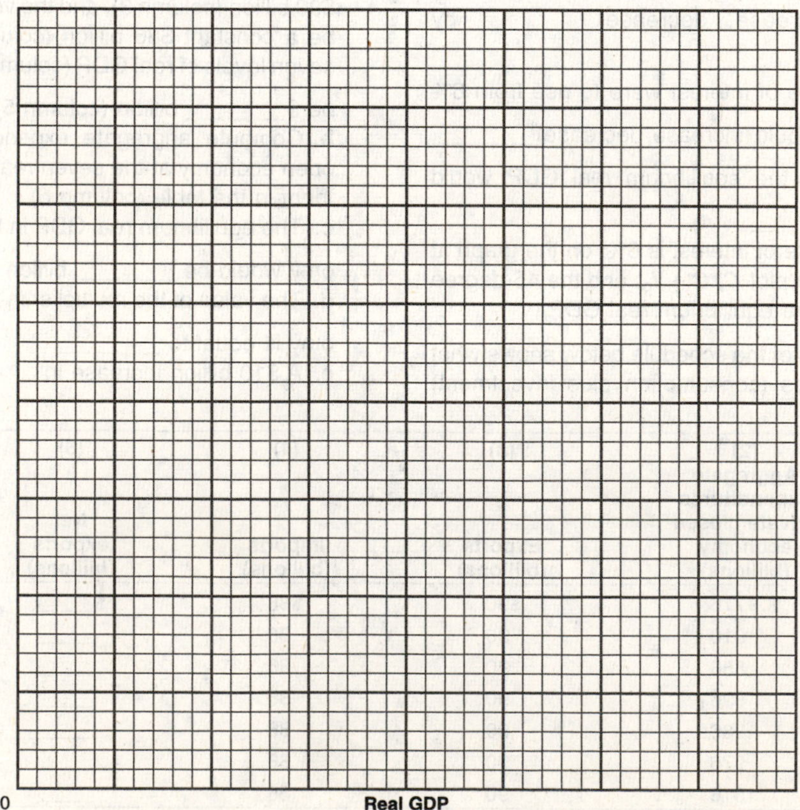

a. The value of the multiplier is _______.

b. If planned investment is $58, the equilibrium nominal GDP is $_____ and exceeds full-employment real GDP by $_______. There is a(n) _______ expenditure gap of $_______.

c. If planned investment is $38, the equilibrium real GDP is $_______ and is less than full-employment real GDP by $_______. There is a(n) _______ expenditure gap of $_______.

■ SHORT ANSWER AND ESSAY QUESTIONS

1. What does it mean that an economy is private and closed?

2. What assumptions are made in this chapter about production capacity, unemployment, and the price level?

3. What is the difference between an investment demand curve and an investment schedule?

4. Why is the equilibrium level of real GDP that level of real GDP at which domestic output equals aggregate expenditures? What will cause real GDP to rise if it is below this level, and what will cause it to fall if it is above this level?

5. Explain what is meant by a leakage and by an injection. Which leakage and which injection are considered in this chapter? Why is the equilibrium real GDP the real GDP at which the leakages equal the injections?

6. Why is it important to distinguish between planned and actual investment in explaining how a private closed economy achieves its equilibrium level of real GDP?

7. Why does the equilibrium level of real GDP change?

8. How do exports and imports get included in the aggregate expenditures model?

9. What happens to the aggregate expenditures schedule when net exports increase or decrease?

10. Give some examples of international economic linkages affecting the domestic level of GDP. What is the problem with using tariffs and devaluations to increase net exports?

11. Explain the simplifying assumptions used to include the public sector in the aggregate expenditures model.

12. Describe how government expenditures affect equilibrium GDP.

13. What effect will taxes have on the consumption schedule?

14. Explain why, with government taxing and spending, the equilibrium real GDP is the real GDP at which real GDP equals consumption plus investment plus net exports plus government purchases of goods and services.

15. Use leakages and injections to explain how changes in the different components of aggregate expenditures cause GDP to move to its equilibrium level.

16. Explain what is meant by a recessionary expenditure gap.

17. What was Keynes's solution to a recessionary gap? Explain one major limitation caution with the use of the aggregate expenditures model.

18. What is an inflationary expenditure gap? Could an economy actually achieve and maintain an equilibrium real GDP that is substantially above the full-employment level of output? Explain.

19. What economic conditions contributed to the recessionary expenditure gap in the U.S. economy from 2007 to 2009?

20. Explain how the aggregate expenditure theory emerged as a critique of classical economics and as a response to the Great Depression.

ANSWERS

Chapter 11 The Aggregate Expenditures Model

FILL-IN QUESTIONS

1. decrease, increase
2. a closed, private, income, increase
3. investment, investment
4. equal to, equal to, 45-degree
5. a withdrawal from, an addition to, saving, investment
6. less than, decreases, rise
7. greater than, increases, fall
8. equal to, zero
9. increase, an increase, an increase
10. increases, decreases, greater, multiplier
11. minus, plus, plus
12. *a.* –; *b.* +; *c.* +; *d.* –; *e.* +; *f.* –; *g.* +
13. increase, decrease
14. lump-sum
15. consume, save
16. expenditures, output, plus, plus, plus
17. investment, exports, saving, imports
18. less, increase, divided
19. fixed, increasing, decreasing
20. an inflationary, decrease

TRUE–FALSE QUESTIONS

1. T, p. 211	**10.** T, p. 217	**19.** T, p. 224
2. T, p. 212	**11.** F, p. 217	**20.** T, p. 225
3. T, p. 212	**12.** T, p. 217	**21.** F, p. 225
4. T, pp. 214–215	**13.** F, p. 218	**22.** F, p. 225
5. T, p. 214	**14.** T, p. 219	**23.** T, p. 226
6. F, p. 214	**15.** T, pp. 220–221	**24.** F, p. 227
7. F, p. 216	**16.** F, pp. 220–221	**25.** T, p. 227
8. T, pp. 216–217	**17.** F, p. 221	
9. T, pp. 216–217	**18.** T, pp. 222–223	

MULTIPLE-CHOICE QUESTIONS

1. b, p. 211	**10.** c, pp. 212–214	**19.** c, p. 220
2. c, p. 212	**11.** b, pp. 212–214	**20.** c, pp. 222–223
3. c, pp. 212–213	**12.** a, pp. 218–219	**21.** b, pp. 222–224
4. b, pp. 214–215	**13.** b, pp. 219–220	**22.** c, p. 225
5. d, p. 215	**14.** c, pp. 219–220	**23.** c, pp. 225–226
6. a, p. 216	**15.** a, pp. 219–220	**24.** c, p. 227
7. c, pp. 216–217	**16.** d, pp. 220–221	**25.** b, p. 227
8. c, pp. 216–217	**17.** d, p. 221	
9. b, pp. 216–217	**18.** c, p. 220	

PROBLEMS

1. *a.* investment; *b.* constant (given); *c.* (1) unrelated, (2) directly related; *d.* decrease, downward

2. *a.* I_g: 22, 22, 22, 22, 22, 22, 22; $C + I_g$: 1,328, 1,336, 1,344, 1,352, 1,360, 1,368, 1,376; ***UI***: −8, −6, −4, −2, 0, +2, +4; *b.* 1,360; *c.* 0.8, 0.2; *d.* 5; *e.* increase, 3, increase, 15; *f.* decrease, 4, decrease, 20; *g.* graph similar to Figure11.2 in text.

3. *a.* $4 (and put $4 in each of the seven net exports values in the table); *b.* $780, 820, 860, 900, 940, 980, 1,020; *c.* $900; *d.* 5; *e.* (1) increase, $50, (2) decrease, $50

4. 0.9, 90, C_a: 1,160, 1,250, 1,340, 1,430, 1,520, 1,610, 1,700; *b.* $C_a + I_g + X_n + G$: 1510, 1600, 1690, 1780, 1870, 1960, 2050; *c.* 1600; *d.* plot graph; *e.* rise, 100; *f.* fall, 90; *g.* raise, 10

5. 2.5; *b.* 620, 30, inflationary, 12; *c.* 570, 20, recessionary, 8

SHORT ANSWER AND ESSAY QUESTIONS

1. p. 212	**8.** pp. 218–220	**15.** p. 225
2. p. 212	**9.** pp. 219–220	**16.** p. 225
3. pp. 212–213	**10.** pp. 220–221	**17.** pp. 226–227
4. pp. 213–214	**11.** p. 222	**18.** p. 227
5. pp. 216–217	**12.** pp. 222–223	**19.** pp. 227, 229
6. pp. 216–217	**13.** pp. 222–224	**20.** p. 228
7. pp. 217–218	**14.** pp. 224–225	

CHAPTER 12

Aggregate Demand and Aggregate Supply

Chapter 12 introduces another macro model of the economy, one based on aggregate demand and aggregate supply. This model can be used to explain real domestic output and the level of prices at any point in time and to understand what causes output and the price level to change.

The **aggregate demand (AD) curve** is down-sloping because of the real balances, interest rate, and foreign purchases effects resulting from changes in the price level. With a down-sloping aggregate demand curve, changes in the price level have an inverse effect on the level of spending by domestic consumers, businesses, government, and foreign buyers, and thus on real domestic output, *assuming other things equal.* This change would be equivalent to a movement along an existing aggregate demand curve: A lower price level increases the quantity of real domestic output demanded, and a higher price level decreases the quantity of real domestic output demanded.

The aggregate demand curve can increase or decrease because of a change in one of the nonprice level **determinants of aggregate demand.** The determinants include changes affecting consumer, investment, government, and net export spending. You will learn that underlying each demand determinant are various factors that cause the determinant to change. The size of the change involves two components. For example, if one of these spending determinants increases, then aggregate demand will increase. The change in aggregate demand involves an increase in initial spending plus a multiplier effect that results in a greater change in aggregate demand than the initial change.

The **aggregate supply (AS) curve** shows the relationship between the output of producers and the price level, but it varies based on the time horizon and variability of input and output prices. In the immediate short run, the aggregate supply curve is horizontal at one price level because input prices and output prices are inflexible or fixed. In the short run, however, the up-sloping shape of the aggregate supply curve reflects what happens to per-unit production costs as real domestic output increases or decreases. In the long run, the aggregate supply curve is vertical because input and output prices are fully flexible, so a change in the price level does not change resource utilization at the full-employment level of output.

You should remember that an assumption has also been made that other things are equal when one moves along an aggregate supply curve. When other things change, the short-run aggregate supply curve can shift. The **determinants of aggregate supply** include changes in input prices, changes in productivity, and changes in the legal and institutional environment for production. As with aggregate demand, you will learn that there are underlying factors that cause these supply determinants to change.

The intersection of the aggregate demand and aggregate supply curves determines **equilibrium real output** and the **equilibrium price level.** Assuming that the determinants of aggregate demand and aggregate supply do not change, there are pressures that will tend to keep the economy at equilibrium. If a determinant changes, then aggregate demand, aggregate supply, or both can shift.

When aggregate demand increases, this will lead to changes in equilibrium real output and the price level. If the economy is operating at full employment, the increase in AD may not have its full multiplier effect on the real GDP of the economy, and it will result in **demand-pull inflation.** There can also be a decrease in aggregate demand, but it may reduce output and not the price level. In this case, there can be downward price inflexibility for several reasons, as you will learn in the chapter.

Aggregate supply may increase or decrease. An increase in aggregate supply gives a double bonus for the economy because the price level falls, and output and employment increase. Conversely, a decrease in aggregate supply doubly harms the economy because the price level increases, and output and employment fall, and thus the economy experiences **cost-push inflation.**

The aggregate demand–aggregate supply model is an important framework for determining the equilibrium level of real domestic output and prices in an economy. The model will be used extensively throughout the remaining macroeconomics content to analyze how different parts of the economy function.

■ CHECKLIST

When you have studied this chapter you should be able to

☐ Define aggregate demand.

☐ Describe the characteristics of the aggregate demand curve.

☐ Use the real-balances, interest-rate, and foreign purchases effects to explain why the aggregate demand curve slopes downward.

☐ Use a graph to distinguish between a movement along a fixed aggregate demand curve and a shift in aggregate demand.

☐ Give an example of the effect of the multiplier on an increase in aggregate demand.

☐ List the four major determinants of aggregate demand.
☐ Describe the four factors affecting the consumer spending determinant of aggregate demand.
☐ Explain the two factors affecting the investment spending determinant of aggregate demand.
☐ Discuss how changes in the government spending determinant change aggregate demand.
☐ Explain the two factors that affect the net export spending determinant of aggregate demand.
☐ Show with a graph how the four major spending determinants of aggregate demand (and their underlying factors) can increase or decrease aggregate demand.
☐ Define aggregate supply in the immediate short run, the short run, and the long run.
☐ Explain why the aggregate supply curve in the immediate short run is horizontal.
☐ Explain why the aggregate supply curve in the short run is up-sloping.
☐ Explain why the aggregate supply curve in the long run is vertical.
☐ Identify the three major determinants of aggregate supply.
☐ Describe two factors that change the input prices determinant of aggregate supply.
☐ Explain what changes the productivity determinant of aggregate supply.
☐ Identify two factors that change the legal-institutional environment determinant of aggregate supply.
☐ Show with a graph how the three major determinants of aggregate supply (and their underlying factors) can increase or decrease aggregate supply.
☐ Explain why in equilibrium the economy will produce a particular combination of real output and the price level rather than another combination.
☐ Show the effects of an increase in aggregate demand on the real output and the price level and relate the changes to demand-pull inflation.
☐ Illustrate the effects of a decrease in aggregate demand on real output and the price level in the economy and relate the changes to recession and unemployment.
☐ Explain the meaning of the terms *deflation* and *disinflation*.
☐ Give five reasons for downward inflexibility of changes in the price level when aggregate demand decreases.
☐ Explain the effects of a decrease in aggregate supply on real output and the price level and relate the changes to cost-push inflation.
☐ Describe the effects of an increase in aggregate supply on real output and the price level.
☐ Explain how increases in productivity reduce inflationary pressures using an aggregate demand–aggregate supply graph.
☐ Explain why increases in oil prices have lost their strong effect on core inflation and the U.S. economy (*Last Word*).

■ CHAPTER OUTLINE

1. This chapter introduces the ***aggregate demand–aggregate supply model*** (AD–AD model). It explains why real domestic output *and* the price level fluctuate in the economy. The chapter begins by explaining the meaning and characteristics of aggregate demand.

a. ***Aggregate demand*** is a curve that shows the total quantity of goods and services (real output) that will be purchased (demanded) at different price levels. With aggregate demand there is an inverse or negative relationship between the amount of real output demanded and the price level, so the curve slopes downward.

b. Three reasons account for the inverse relationship between real output and the price level, and the downward slope of the aggregate demand curve.

(1) ***Real-balances effect:*** An increase in the price level decreases the purchasing power of financial assets with a fixed money value, and because those who own such assets are now poorer, they spend less for goods and services. A decrease in the price level has the opposite effect.

(2) ***Interest-rate effect:*** With the supply of money fixed, an increase in the price level increases the demand for money, increases interest rates, and as a result reduces those expenditures (by consumers and business firms) that are sensitive to increased interest rates. A decrease in the price level has the opposite effects.

(3) ***Foreign purchases effect:*** An increase in the price level (relative to foreign price levels) will reduce U.S. exports, because U.S. products are now more expensive for foreigners, and expand U.S. imports, because foreign products are less expensive for U.S. consumers. As a consequence, net exports will decrease, which means there will be a decrease in the quantity of goods and services demanded in the U.S. economy as the price level rises. A decrease in the price level (relative to foreign price levels) will have opposite effects.

2. Spending by domestic consumers, businesses, government, and foreign buyers that is independent of changes in the price level are ***determinants of aggregate demand.*** The amount of changes in aggregate demand involves two components: the amount of the initial change in one of the determinants and a multiplier effect that multiplies the initial change. These determinants are also called aggregate demand shifts because a change in one of them, other things equal, will shift the entire aggregate demand curve. Figure 12.2 shows the shifts. What follows is a description of each of the four major determinants and underlying factors.

a. ***Consumer spending*** can increase or decrease AD. If the price level is constant, and consumers decide to spend more, then AD will increase; if consumers decide to spend less, then AD will decrease. Four factors increase or decrease consumer spending.

(1) *Consumer wealth:* If the real value of financial assets such as stocks, bond, or real estate increases (minus any liabilities for these assets), then consumers will feel wealthier, spend more, and AD increases. If the real value of financial assets falls, a "reverse wealth effect" sets in, so consumers will spend less and AD will decrease.

(2) *Household borrowing:* If consumers borrow more money, they can increase their consumption spending, thus increasing AD. Conversely, if consumers cut back on their borrowing for consumption spending, AD

decreases. Also, if consumers increase their savings rate to pay off their debt, AD decreases.

(3) *Consumer expectations:* If consumers become more optimistic about the future, they will likely spend more and AD will increase. If consumers expect the future to be worse, they will decrease their spending and AD will decrease.

(4) *Personal taxes:* Cuts in personal taxes increase disposable income and the capacity for consumer spending, thus increasing AD. A rise in personal taxes decreases disposable income, consumer spending, and AD.

b. *Investment spending* can increase or decrease AD. If the price level is constant, and businesses decide to spend more on investment, then AD will increase. If businesses decide to spend less on investment, then AD will decrease. Three factors increase or decrease investment spending.

(1) *Real interest rates:* A decrease in real interest rates will increase the quantity of investment spending, thus increasing AD. An increase in real interest rates will decrease the quantity of investment spending, thus decreasing AD.

(2) *Expected returns:* If businesses expect higher returns on investments in the future, they will likely increase their investment spending today, so AD will increase. If businesses expect lower returns on investments in the future, they will decrease their investment spending today, and AD will decrease. These expected returns are influenced by expectations about future business conditions, the state of technology, the degree of excess capacity (the amount of unused capital goods), and business taxes.

(a) More positive future expectations, more technological progress, less excess capacity, and lower taxes will increase investment spending and thus increase AD.

(b) Less positive future expectations, less technological progress, more excess capacity, and higher taxes will decrease investment spending and thus decrease AD.

c. *Government spending* has a direct effect on AD, assuming that tax collections and interest rates do not change as a result of the spending. More government spending tends to increase AD and less government spending will decrease AD.

d. *Net export spending* can increase or decrease AD. If the price level is constant and net exports (exports minus imports) should increase, then AD will increase. If net exports are negative, then AD will decrease. Two factors explain the increase or decrease in net export spending.

(1) *National income abroad:* An increase in the national income of other nations will increase the demand for all goods and services, including U.S. exports. If U.S. exports increase relative to U.S. imports, then net exports will increase, and so will AD. A decline in national incomes abroad will tend to reduce U.S. net exports and thus reduces AD.

(2) *Exchange rates:* A depreciation in the value of the U.S. dollar means that U.S. imports should decline because domestic purchasers cannot buy as many imports as they used to buy. U.S. exports should increase because foreigners have more purchasing power to buy U.S. products. These events increase net exports, and thus increase AD. An appreciation in the value of the dollar will decrease net exports, and thus decrease AD.

3. *Aggregate supply* is a curve that shows the total quantity of goods and services that will be produced (supplied) at different price levels. The shape of the aggregate supply curve will differ depending on the time horizon and how quickly input prices and output prices can change.

a. In the ***immediate short run,*** the aggregate supply curve is horizontal because both input prices and output prices remain fixed. The horizontal shape implies that the total amount of output supplied in the economy depends directly on the amount of spending at the fixed price level.

b. In the ***short run,*** the aggregate supply curve is up-sloping because input prices are fixed or highly inflexible and output prices are flexible, and thus changes in the price level increase or decrease the real profits of firms. The curve is relatively flat below the full-employment level of output because there is excess capacity and unemployed resources so per-unit production costs stay relatively constant as output expands, but beyond the full-employment level of output, per-unit production costs rise rapidly as output increases because resources are fully employed and efficiency falls.

c. In the ***long run,*** the aggregate supply curve is vertical at the full-employment level of output for the economy because both input prices and output prices are flexible. Any change in output prices is matched by a change in input prices, so there is no profit incentive for firms to produce more than is possible at full-employment output.

4. The ***determinants of aggregate supply*** that shift the curve include changes in the prices of inputs for production, changes in productivity, and changes in the legal and institutional environment in the economy, as outlined in Figure 12.5.

a. A change in ***input prices*** for resources used for production will change aggregate supply in the short run. Lower input prices increase AS and higher input prices decrease AS. These input prices are both for domestic and imported resources.

(1) *Domestic resource prices* include the prices for labor, capital, and natural resources used for production. If any of these input prices decrease, then AS will increase because the per-unit cost of production will decrease. When the prices of these domestic factors of production increase, then AS will decrease.

(2) The *price of imported resources* is the cost of paying for resources imported from other nations. If the value of the dollar appreciates, then it will cost less to pay for imported resources used for production. As a result, per-unit production costs will decrease, and AS will increase. Conversely, if the value of the dollar depreciates, then it will cost more to import resources, so AS will decrease.

b. As ***productivity*** improves, per-unit production costs will fall and AS will increase. This outcome occurs because productivity (output divided by input) is the denominator for the formula for per-unit production costs (which is: total input cost divided by productivity). As productivity declines, per-unit production costs will increase, so AS will decrease.

c. Changes in the ***legal and institutional environment*** for business can affect per-unit production costs and thus AS.

(1) A decrease in *business taxes* is like a reduction in the per-unit cost of production, so it will increase AS. The same effect occurs when there is an increase in *business subsidies*. The raising of taxes or lowering of subsidies for business will increase per-unit production costs and decrease AS.

(2) A decrease in the amount of *government regulation* is similar to a decrease in the per-unit cost of production, so it will increase AS. An increase in government regulation will raise costs, and thus will decrease AS.

5. The ***equilibrium real output*** and the ***equilibrium price level*** are at the intersection of the aggregate demand and the aggregate supply curves. If the price level were below equilibrium, then producers would supply less real output than was demanded by purchasers. Competition among buyers would bid up the price level and producers would increase their output, until an equilibrium price level and quantity were reached. If the price level were above equilibrium, then producers would supply more real output than was demanded by purchasers. Competition among sellers would lower the price level and producers would reduce their output, until an equilibrium price level and quantity were reached. The aggregate demand and aggregate supply curves can also *shift to change equilibrium.*

a. An ***increase in aggregate demand*** would result in an increase in both real domestic output and the price level. An increase in the price level beyond the full-employment level of output is associated with *demand-pull inflation.* A classic example occurred during the late 1960s because of a sizable increase in government spending for domestic programs and the war in Vietnam.

b. A ***decrease in aggregate demand*** reduces real output and increases cyclical unemployment, but it may not decrease the price level. In 2008, there was a significant decline in investment spending that reduced aggregate demand and led to a fall in real output and a rise in cyclical unemployment. The rate of inflation fell (there was *disinflation*), but there was no decline in the price level (*deflation*). The reason why the economy experiences a "GDP gap with no deflation" is that the *price level is inflexible downward.* The price level is largely influenced by labor costs which account for most of the input prices for the production of many goods and services. There are at least five interrelated reasons for this downward inflexibility of the price level.

(1) The fear of a starting a *price war* in which firms compete with each other on lowering prices regardless of the cost of production. Such price wars hurt business profits and make firms reluctant to cut prices for fear of starting one.

(2) Firms are reluctant to change input prices if there are costs related to changing the prices or announcing the change. Such ***menu costs*** increase the waiting time before businesses make any price changes.

(3) If wages are determined largely by *long-term contracts,* it means that wages cannot be changed in the short run.

(4) *Morale, effort, and productivity* may be affected by changes in wage rates. If current wages are ***efficiency wages*** that maximize worker effort and morale, employers may be reluctant to lower wages because such changes reduce work effort and productivity.

(5) The *minimum wage* puts a legal floor on the wages for the least skilled workers in the economy.

c. A ***decrease in aggregate supply*** means there will be a decrease in real domestic output (economic growth) and employment along with a rise in the price level, or *cost-push inflation.* This situation occurred in the mid-1970s when the price of oil substantially increased and significantly increased the cost of production for many goods and services and reduced productivity.

d. An ***increase in aggregate supply*** arising from an increase in productivity has the beneficial effects of improving real domestic output and employment while maintaining a stable price level. Between 1996 and 2000, the economy experienced strong economic growth, full employment and very low inflation. These outcomes occurred because of an increase in aggregate demand in combination with an increase in aggregate supply from an increase in productivity due to technological change.

6. (*Last Word*). In the mid-1970s, sizable increases in the price of oil increased production costs and reduced productivity, thus decreasing aggregate supply. These changes led to cost-push inflation, higher unemployment, and a decline in real output. More recent increases in oil prices during 2005 and again in 2007 and 2008 did not have the adverse effects on the U.S. economy as was the case in past decades. Although there were many reasons for this switch, perhaps most important was that oil was not as significant a resource for production in the U.S. economy as it had been in the past. The U.S. economy was about 33 percent less sensitive to fluctuations in oil prices than in the early 1980s.

■ HINTS AND TIPS

1. Aggregate demand and supply are the tools used to explain what determines the economy's real output and price level. These tools, however, are **different from the demand and supply** used in Chapter 3 to explain what determines the output and price of a *particular* product. Instead of thinking about the quantity of a *particular* good or service demanded or supplied, it is necessary to think about the total or *aggregate* quantity of all final goods and services demanded (purchased) and supplied (produced). You will have no difficulty with the way demand and supply are used in this chapter once you switch from thinking about a *particular* good or service and its price to the *aggregate* of all final goods and services and their average price.

2. Make a chart showing each of the **determinants** of aggregate demand (see Figure 12.2) and aggregate supply (Figure 12.5). In the chart, state the direction of the change in each determinant, and then state the likely resulting change in AD or AS. For example, if consumer wealth *increases,* then AD *increases.* Or, if imported prices for resources *increase,* then AS *decreases.* This simple chart can help you see in one quick glance all the possible changes in determinants and their likely effects on AD or AS. Problem 2 in this *Study Guide* will give you an application for this chart.

3. Make sure you know the difference between a **movement** along an existing aggregate demand or supply curve and a **shift** in (increase or decrease in) an aggregate demand or supply curve. Figures 12.7 and 12.9 illustrate the distinction.

4. Unlike the aggregate demand curve, the shape of the aggregate supply curve actually varies based on time horizon and how quickly input prices and output prices change. In the immediate short run, input prices and output prices are fixed, so AS is horizontal at a particular price level (Figure 12.3). In the short run, input prices are fixed, but output prices can change, so the AS is up-sloping around the full-employment level of output (Figure 12.4). In the long run, input and output prices are flexible, but the economy can only produce at the full-employment level of output, so AS is vertical (Figure 12.5).

■ IMPORTANT TERMS

aggregate demand–aggregate supply (AD–AS) model
aggregate demand (AD)
real-balances effect
interest-rate effect
foreign purchases effect
determinants of aggregate demand
aggregate supply (AS)
immediate-short-run aggregate supply curve
short-run aggregate supply curve
long-run aggregate supply curve
determinants of aggregate supply
productivity
equilibrium real output
equilibrium price level
menu costs
efficiency wages

SELF-TEST

■ FILL-IN QUESTIONS

1. Aggregate demand and aggregate supply together determine the equilibrium real domestic (price, output) ____________ and the equilibrium ____________ level.

2. The aggregate demand curve shows the quantity of goods and services that will be (supplied, demanded) ____________ or purchased at various price levels. For aggregate demand, the relationship between real output and the price level is (positive, negative) ____________.

3. The aggregate demand curve slopes (upward, downward) ____________ because of the (real-balances, consumption) ____________ effect, the (profit, interest) ____________-rate effect, and the (domestic, foreign) ____________ purchases effect.

4. For the aggregate demand curve, an increase in the price level (increases, decreases) ____________ the quantity of real domestic output demanded, whereas a decrease in the price level ____________ the quantity of real domestic output demanded, assuming other things equal.

5. For the aggregate demand curve, when the price level changes, there is a (movement along, change in) ____________ the curve. When the entire aggregate demand curve shifts, there is a change in (the quantity of real output demanded, aggregate demand) ____________.

6. List the four factors that may change consumer spending, and thus shift aggregate demand:

a. ____________
b. ____________
c. ____________
d. ____________

7. List two major factors that may change investment spending, and thus shift aggregate demand:

a. ____________
b. ____________

8. If government spending increases, then aggregate demand is likely to (increase, decrease) ____________, but if government spending decreases, it is likely to ____________.

9. If there is an increase in national income abroad, then net export spending is most likely to (increase, decrease) ____________ and if there is a depreciation of the value of the U.S. dollar, then net exports are likely to ____________. When net exports increase, aggregate demand will (increase, decrease) ____________.

10. The aggregate supply curve shows the quantity of goods and services that will be (demanded, supplied) ____________ or produced at various price levels. The shape of the immediate-short-run aggregate supply curve is (vertical, horizontal, up-sloping) ____________, while the shape of the short-run aggregate supply curve is ____________, and the shape of the long-run aggregate supply curve is ____________.

11. For the short-run aggregate supply curve, as the price level increases, real domestic output (increases, decreases) ____________, and as the price level decreases, real domestic output ____________. The relationship between the price level and real domestic output supplied is (positive, negative) ____________.

12. Aggregate supply shifts may result from:

a. a change in input prices caused by a change in

(1) ________________

(2) ________________

b. a change in (consumption, productivity) ________

c. a change in the legal and institutional environment caused by a change in

(1) ________________

(2) ________________

13. The equilibrium real domestic output and price level are found at the (zero values, intersection) ________ of the aggregate demand and the aggregate supply curves. At this price level, the aggregate quantity of goods and services demanded is (greater than, less than, equal to) ________ the aggregate quantity of goods and services supplied. And at this real domestic output, the prices producers are willing to (pay, accept) ________ are equal to the prices buyers are willing to ________.

14. If the price level were below equilibrium, the quantity of real domestic output supplied would be (greater than, less than) ________ the quantity of real domestic output demanded. As a result competition among buyers eliminates the (surplus, shortage) ________ and bids up the price level.

15. If the price level were above equilibrium, the quantity of real domestic output supplied would be (greater than, less than) ________ the quantity of real domestic output demanded. As a result competition among producers eliminates the (surplus, shortage) ________ and lowers the price level.

16. An increase in aggregate demand will (increase, decrease) ________ real domestic output and will ________ the price level. If the economy is initially operating at its full-employment level of output, and aggregate demand increases, it will produce (demand-pull, cost-push) ________ inflation.

17. If aggregate demand decreases, then real domestic output will (increase, decrease) ________. Such a change often produces economic conditions called (inflation, recession) ________ and unemployment (rises, falls) ________.

18. When aggregate demand decreases, the price level is often inflexible (upward, downward) ________. This inflexibility occurs because of wage (contracts, flexibility) ________, workers are paid (efficiency, inefficiency) ________ wages, there is a (maximum, minimum) ________ wage, businesses experience menu (benefits, costs) ________, and there is fear of (price, wage) ________ wars.

19. A decrease in aggregate supply will (increase, decrease) ________ real output and ________ the price level. Such a change in aggregate supply contributes to (demand-pull, cost-push) ________ inflation.

20. An increase in aggregate supply will (increase, decrease) ________ real domestic output and ________ the price level. If aggregate demand increased, the price level would (increase, decrease) ________, but a simultaneous increase in aggregate supply (reinforces, offsets) ________ this change and helps keep the price level stable.

■ TRUE–FALSE QUESTIONS

Circle T if the statement is true, F if it is false.

1. Aggregate demand reflects a positive relationship between the price level and the amount of real output demanded. **T F**

2. The explanation as to why the aggregate demand curve slopes downward is the same as the explanation as to why the demand curve for a single product slopes downward. **T F**

3. A fall in the price level increases the real value of financial assets with fixed money values and, as a result, increases spending by the holders of these assets. **T F**

4. Given a fixed supply of money, a rise in the price level increases the demand for money in the economy and drives interest rates downward. **T F**

5. A rise in the price level of an economy (relative to foreign price levels) tends to increase that economy's exports and to reduce its imports of goods and services. **T F**

6. A movement along a fixed aggregate demand curve is the same as a shift in aggregate demand. **T F**

7. Changes in aggregate demand involve a change in initial spending from one of the determinants and a multiplier effect on spending. **T F**

8. A change in aggregate demand is caused by a change in the price level, *other things equal.* **T F**

9. The real-balances effect is one of the determinants of aggregate demand. **T F**

10. A large decline in household borrowing will increase consumption spending and aggregate demand. **T F**

11. A rise in excess capacity, or unused existing capital goods, will reduce the demand for new capital goods and therefore reduce aggregate demand. **T F**

12. Appreciation of the dollar relative to foreign currencies will tend to increase net exports and aggregate demand. **T F**

13. The immediate short-run aggregate supply curve is horizontal and the short-run aggregate supply curve is upsloping. **T F**

14. The aggregate supply curve is vertical in the long run at the full-employment level of output. **T F**

15. When the determinants of short-run aggregate supply change, they alter the per-unit production cost at each price level and thereby aggregate supply. **T F**

16. Productivity is a measure of real output per unit of input. **T F**

17. Per-unit production cost is determined by dividing total input cost by units of output. **T F**

18. At the equilibrium price level, the real domestic output purchased is equal to the real domestic output produced. **T F**

19. In the short run, an increase in aggregate demand will increase both the price level and the real domestic output. **T F**

20. An increase in aggregate demand is associated with cost-push inflation. **T F**

21. The greater the increase in the price level that results from an increase in aggregate demand, the greater will be the increase in the equilibrium real GDP. **T F**

22. A significant decrease in aggregate demand can result in recession and cyclical unemployment. **T F**

23. Fear of price wars tends to make the price level more flexible rather than less flexible. **T F**

24. A decrease in aggregate supply decreases the equilibrium real domestic output and increases the price level, resulting in cost-push inflation. **T F**

25. An increase in aggregate supply driven by productivity increases can offset the inflationary pressures from an increase in aggregate demand. **T F**

■ MULTIPLE-CHOICE QUESTIONS

Circle the letter that corresponds to the best answer.

1. The aggregate demand curve is the relationship between the
(a) price level and what producers will supply
(b) price level and the real domestic output purchased
(c) price level and the real domestic output produced
(d) real domestic output purchased and the real domestic output produced

2. When the price level rises,
(a) the demand for money and interest rates rises
(b) spending that is sensitive to interest-rate changes increases
(c) holders of financial assets with fixed money values increase their spending
(d) holders of financial assets with fixed money values have more purchasing power

3. One explanation for the downward slope of the aggregate demand curve is that a change in the price level results in
(a) a multiplier effect
(b) an income effect
(c) a substitution effect
(d) a foreign purchases effect

4. A sharp decline in the real value of stock prices, which is independent of a change in the price level, would best be an example of
(a) the interest-rate effect
(b) the foreign purchases effect
(c) a change in household borrowing
(d) a change in real value of consumer wealth

5. The aggregate demand curve will be increased by
(a) a decrease in the price level
(b) an increase in the price level
(c) a depreciation in the value of the U.S. dollar
(d) an increase in the excess capacity of factories

6. The aggregate supply curve is the relationship between the
(a) price level and the real domestic output purchased
(b) price level and the real domestic output produced
(c) price level that producers are willing to accept and the price level purchasers are willing to pay
(d) real domestic output purchased and the real domestic output produced

7. The short-run aggregate supply curve assumes that
(a) nominal wages respond to changes in the price level
(b) nominal wages do not respond to changes in the price level
(c) the economy is operating at full-employment output
(d) the economy is operating at less than full-employment output

8. In the long run, the aggregate supply curve is
(a) up-sloping
(b) down-sloping
(c) vertical
(d) horizontal

9. If the prices of imported resources increase, then this event would most likely
(a) decrease aggregate supply
(b) increase aggregate supply
(c) increase aggregate demand
(d) decrease aggregate demand

Suppose that real domestic output in an economy is 50 units, the quantity of inputs is 10, and the price of each input is $2. Answer Questions 10, 11, 12, and 13 on the basis of this information.

10. The level of productivity in this economy is
(a) 5
(b) 4
(c) 3
(d) 2

11. The per-unit cost of production is
(a) $0.40
(b) $0.50
(c) $2.50
(d) $3.50

12. If productivity increased such that 60 units are now produced with the quantity of inputs still equal to 10, then per-unit production costs would

(a) remain unchanged and aggregate supply would remain unchanged
(b) increase and aggregate supply would decrease
(c) decrease and aggregate supply would increase
(d) decrease and aggregate supply would decrease

13. All else equal, if the price of each input increases from $2 to $4, productivity would

(a) decrease from $4 to $2 and aggregate supply would decrease
(b) decrease from $5 to $3 and aggregate supply would decrease
(c) decrease from $4 to $2 and aggregate supply would increase
(d) remain unchanged and aggregate supply would decrease

14. If Congress passed much stricter laws to control the air pollution from businesses, this action would tend to

(a) increase per-unit production costs and shift the aggregate supply curve to the right
(b) increase per-unit production costs and shift the aggregate supply curve to the left
(c) increase per-unit production costs and shift the aggregate demand curve to the left
(d) decrease per-unit production costs and shift the aggregate supply curve to the left

15. An increase in business taxes will tend to

(a) decrease aggregate demand but not change aggregate supply
(b) decrease aggregate supply but not change aggregate demand
(c) decrease aggregate demand and decrease aggregate supply
(d) decrease aggregate supply and increase aggregate demand

16. If at a particular price level, real domestic output from producers is less than real domestic output desired by buyers, there will be a

(a) surplus and the price level will rise
(b) surplus and the price level will fall
(c) shortage and the price level will rise
(d) shortage and the price level will fall

Answer Questions 17, 18, and 19 on the basis of the following aggregate demand–aggregate supply schedule for a hypothetical economy.

Real domestic output demanded (in billions)	Price level	Real domestic output supplied (in billions)
$1500	175	$4500
$2000	150	$4000
$2500	125	$3500
$3000	100	$3000
$3500	75	$2500
$4000	50	$2000

17. The equilibrium price level and quantity of real domestic output will be

(a) 100 and $2500
(b) 100 and $3000
(c) 125 and $3500
(d) 150 and $4000

18. If the quantity of real domestic output demanded increased by $2000 at each price level, the new equilibrium price level and quantity of real domestic output would be

(a) 175 and $4000
(b) 150 and $4000
(c) 125 and $3500
(d) 100 and $3000

19. Using the original data from the table, if the quantity of real domestic output demanded *increased* by $1500 and the quantity of real domestic output supplied *increased* by $500 at each price level, the new equilibrium price level and quantity of real domestic output would be

(a) 175 and $4000
(b) 150 and $4500
(c) 125 and $4000
(d) 100 and $3500

20. An increase in aggregate demand with a short-run aggregate supply curve will increase

(a) the price level and have no effect on real domestic output
(b) the real domestic output and have no effect on the price level
(c) the price level and decrease the real domestic output
(d) both real output and the price level

21. In the aggregate demand–aggregate supply model, an increase in the price level will

(a) increase the real value of wealth
(b) increase the strength of the multiplier
(c) decrease the strength of the multiplier
(d) have no effect on the strength of the multiplier

22. Aggregate demand decreases and real output falls but the price level remains the same. Which factor most likely contributes to downward price inflexibility?

(a) an increase in aggregate supply
(b) the foreign purchases effect
(c) lower interest rates
(d) efficiency wages

23. Fear of price wars, menu costs, and wage contracts are associated with

(a) a price level that is inflexible upward
(b) a price level that is inflexible downward
(c) a domestic output that cannot be increased
(d) a domestic output that cannot be decreased

24. If there were cost-push inflation,

(a) both the real domestic output and the price level would decrease
(b) the real domestic output would increase and rises in the price level would become smaller
(c) the real domestic output would decrease and the price level would rise
(d) both the real domestic output and rises in the price level would become greater

25. An increase in aggregate supply will
(a) increase the price level and real domestic output
(b) decrease the price level and real domestic output
(c) decrease the price level and increase the real domestic output
(d) decrease the price level and have no effect on real domestic output

■ PROBLEMS

1. Following is an aggregate supply schedule.

Price level	Real domestic output supplied
250	2100
225	2000
200	1900
175	1700
150	1400
125	1000
100	900

a. Plot this aggregate supply schedule on the graph below.
b. The following table has three aggregate demand schedules.

Price level	*Real domestic output demanded*		
(1)	(2)	(3)	(4)
250	1400	1900	500
225	1500	2000	600
200	1600	2100	700
175	1700	2200	800
150	1800	2300	900
125	1900	2400	1000
100	2000	2500	1100

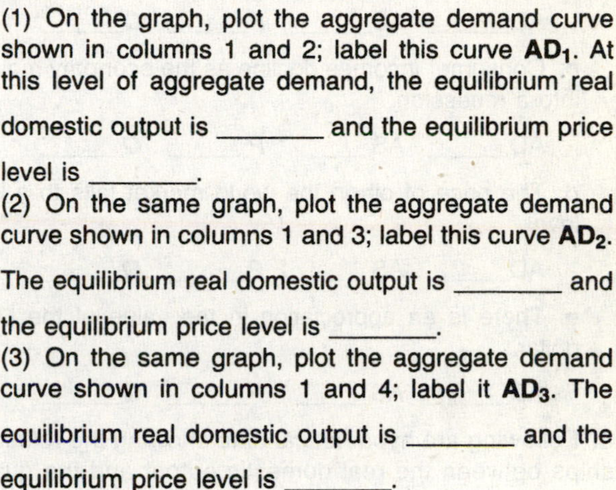

(1) On the graph, plot the aggregate demand curve shown in columns 1 and 2; label this curve **AD_1**. At this level of aggregate demand, the equilibrium real domestic output is ______ and the equilibrium price level is ______.
(2) On the same graph, plot the aggregate demand curve shown in columns 1 and 3; label this curve **AD_2**. The equilibrium real domestic output is ______ and the equilibrium price level is ______.
(3) On the same graph, plot the aggregate demand curve shown in columns 1 and 4; label it **AD_3**. The equilibrium real domestic output is ______ and the equilibrium price level is ______.

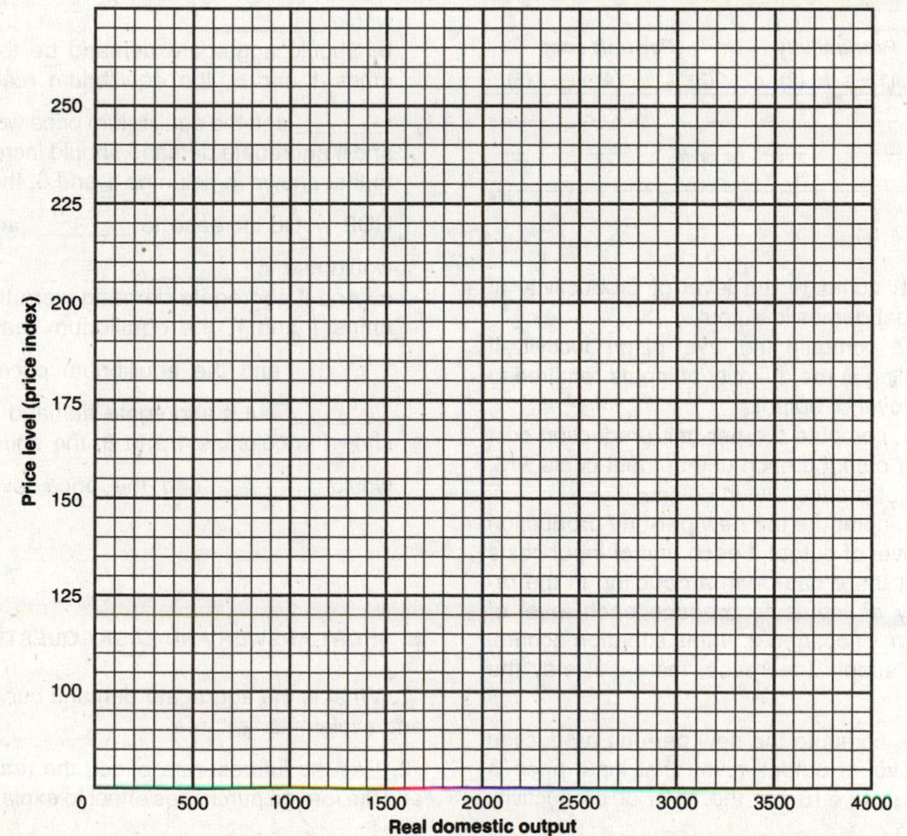

2. In the following list, what will most likely happen as a result of each event to (1) aggregate demand (AD); (2) aggregate supply (AS); (3) the equilibrium price level (***P***); and (4) equilibrium real domestic output (***Q***)? Assume that all other things remain constant when the event occurs and that the aggregate supply curve is a short-run one. Use the following symbols to indicate the expected effects: ***I*** = increase, ***D*** = decrease, ***S*** = remains the same, and ***U*** = uncertain.

a. A decrease in labor productivity.

AD_____ AS_____ ***P*****_____** ***Q*****_____**

b. A fall in the interest rate for business loans.

AD_____ AS_____ ***P*****_____** ***Q*****_____**

c. Consumer incomes decline as the economy moves into a recession.

AD_____ AS_____ ***P*****_____** ***Q*****_____**

d. The price of oil on the world market falls to a low level.

AD_____ AS_____ ***P*****_____** ***Q*****_____**

e. There is an appreciation in the value of the U.S. dollar.

AD_____ AS_____ ***P*****_____** ***Q*****_____**

3. Following are hypothetical data showing the relationships between the real domestic output and the quantity of input resources needed to produce each level of output.

Output	Input	*Productivity* (1)	(2)	*Per unit cost* (3)	(4)	(5)
2500	500	____	____	____	____	____
2000	400	____	____	____	____	____
1500	300	____	____	____	____	____

a. In column 1, compute the level of productivity at each level of real domestic output.

b. In column 2, compute the level of productivity if there is a doubling in the quantity of inputs required to produce each level of output.

c. In column 3, compute the per-unit production cost at each level of output if each unit of input costs $15, given the level of productivity in column 1.

d. In column 4, compute the new per-unit production cost at each level of output if each unit of input costs $15, given that there has been a doubling in the required quantity of inputs to produce each level of output as shown in column 2. If this situation occurs, will aggregate supply (decrease, increase, stay the same)? ________

e. In column 5, compute the new per-unit production cost at each level of output, given that input price is now $10 instead of $15 but the level of productivity stays as it was originally shown in column 1. What will happen to the aggregate supply curve if this situation occurs? ________

4. Columns 1 and 2 in the table that follows are the aggregate supply schedule of an economy.

(1) Price level	(2) Real GDP	(3) AD_1	(4) AD_2	(5) AD_3	(6) AD_4	(7) AD_5	(8) AD_6
260	2540	940	1140	1900	2000	2090	2390
240	2490	1040	1240	2000	2100	2190	2490
220	2430	1140	1340	2100	2200	2290	2590
200	2390	1240	1440	2200	2300	2390	2690
190	2350	1390	1590	2250	2350	2540	2740
180	2300	1440	1640	2300	2400	2590	2890
160	2200	1540	1740	2400	2500	2690	2990
140	2090	1640	1840	2500	2600	2790	3090
120	1940	1740	1940	2600	2700	2890	3190
100	1840	1840	2040	2700	2800	2990	3290

a. If the aggregate demand in the economy were columns 1 and 3, the equilibrium real GDP would be ________ and the equilibrium price level would be ________, and if aggregate demand should increase to that shown in columns 1 and 4, the equilibrium real GDP would increase to ________ and the price level would ________.

b. Should aggregate demand be that shown in columns 1 and 5, the equilibrium real GDP would be ________ and the equilibrium price would be ________, and if aggregate demand should increase by 100 units to that shown in columns 1 and 6, the equilibrium real GDP would increase to ________ and the price level would rise to ________.

c. And if aggregate demand were that shown in columns 1 and 7, the equilibrium real GDP would be ________ and the equilibrium price level would be ________, but if aggregate demand increased to that shown in columns 1 and 8, the equilibrium real GDP would ________ and the price level would rise to ________.

■ SHORT ANSWER AND ESSAY QUESTIONS

1. What is the aggregate demand curve? Draw a graph and explain its features.

2. Use the interest-rate effect, the real-balances effect, and the foreign purchases effect to explain the relationship between the price level and the real domestic output demanded.

3. Explain the wealth effect and its impact on purchasing power. Give an example.

4. What roles do the expectations of consumers and businesses play in influencing aggregate demand?

5. How is aggregate demand changed by changes in net export spending? What factors cause changes in net export spending?

6. Explain the shape of the immediate-short-run aggregate supply curve. How do time and prices affect its shape?

7. Why does the short-run aggregate supply curve slope upward? Why is it relatively flat at outputs below the full-employment output level and relatively steep at outputs above it?

8. Why is the aggregate supply curve in the long run a vertical curve? Why is output not affected by the price level in the long run?

9. Describe how changes in the international economy influence aggregate demand or aggregate supply.

10. How does an increase or decrease in per-unit production costs change aggregate supply? Give examples.

11. How does the legal and institutional environment affect aggregate supply? Give examples.

12. Explain how a change in business taxes affects aggregate demand and aggregate supply.

13. What real domestic output is the equilibrium real domestic output? What will happen to real output if the price level is below equilibrium?

14. What are the effects on the real domestic output and the price level when aggregate demand increases along the short-run aggregate supply curve?

15. What is the relationship between the effect of an increase in aggregate demand on real GDP and the rise in the price level that accompanies it? Discuss it in terms of the multiplier effect.

16. If prices were as flexible downward as they are upward, what would be the effects on real domestic output and the price level of a decrease in aggregate demand?

17. Discuss five reasons why prices in the economy tend to be inflexible in a downward direction.

18. What are the effects on the real domestic output and the price level of a decrease in aggregate supply?

19. Describe and graph an increase in aggregate supply and its effects on the price level and real output.

20. Explain why changes in oil prices have less of an effect on the U.S. economy than in past decades.

ANSWERS

Chapter 12 Aggregate Demand and Aggregate Supply

FILL-IN QUESTIONS

1. output, price
2. demanded, negative
3. downward, real-balances, interest, foreign
4. decreases, increases
5. movement along, aggregate demand
6. *a.* consumer wealth; *b.* consumer expectations; *c.* household borrowing; *d.* personal taxes (any order for *a–d*)
7. *a.* interest rates; *b.* expected returns on investment (either order for *a–b*)
8. increase, decrease
9. increase, increase, increase
10. supplied, horizontal, up-sloping, vertical
11. increases, decreases, positive
12. *a.* (1) domestic resource availability, (2) prices of imported resources (any order for 1–2); *b.* productivity; *c.* (1) business taxes and subsidies, (2) government regulation (any order for 1–2)
13. intersection, equal to, accept, pay
14. less than, shortage
15. greater than, surplus
16. increase, increase, demand-pull
17. decrease, recession, rises
18. downward, contracts, efficiency, minimum, costs, price
19. decrease, increase, cost-push
20. increase, decrease, increase, offsets

TRUE–FALSE QUESTIONS

1. F, p. 234	**10.** F, pp. 235–236	**19.** T, pp. 244–246
2. F, p. 234	**11.** T, p. 237	**20.** F, pp. 244–246
3. T, pp. 234–235	**12.** F, pp. 237–238	**21.** F, p. 246
4. F, p. 235	**13.** T, pp. 238–239	**22.** T, pp. 246–247
5. F, p. 235	**14.** T, pp. 240–241	**23.** F, p. 247
6. F, p. 235	**15.** T, p. 241	**24.** T, p. 248
7. T, p. 235	**16.** T, p. 243	**25.** T, pp. 248, 250
8. F, p. 235	**17.** T, p. 243	
9. F, p. 236	**18.** T, p. 244	

MULTIPLE-CHOICE QUESTIONS

1. b, p. 234	**10.** a, p. 243	**19.** c, p. 248
2. a, p. 235	**11.** a, p. 243	**20.** d, pp. 244–246
3. d, p. 235	**12.** c, p. 243	**21.** c, p. 246
4. d, p. 236	**13.** d, p. 243	**22.** d, p. 247
5. c, pp. 236–237	**14.** b, pp. 243–244	**23.** b, p. 247
6. b, p. 238	**15.** c, p. 243	**24.** c, p. 248
7. b, p. 239	**16.** c, pp. 244–245	**25.** c, pp. 248, 250
8. c, p. 240	**17.** b, pp. 244–245	
9. a, p. 242	**18.** b, pp. 245–246	

PROBLEMS

1. *b.* (1) 1700, 175, (2) 2000, 225, (3) 1000, 125
2. *a. S, D, I, D*; *b. I, S, I, I*; *c. D, S, D, D*; *d. I, I, U, I*; *e. D, I, D, U*
3. *a.* 5, 5, 5; *b.* 2.5, 2.5, 2.5; *c.* $3, $3, $3; *d.* $6, $6, $6, decrease; *e.* $2, $2, $2, it will increase
4. *a.* 1840, 100, 1940, 120; *b.* 2300, 180, 2350, 190; *c.* 2390, 200, 2490, 240

SHORT ANSWER AND ESSAY QUESTIONS

1. p. 234	**8.** pp. 241–242	**15.** pp. 245–246
2. pp. 234–235	**9.** pp. 237, 242	**16.** pp. 246–247
3. p. 236	**10.** pp. 241–243	**17.** p. 247
4. pp. 236–237	**11.** p. 243	**18.** p. 248
5. p. 237	**12.** pp. 243–244	**19.** pp. 248, 250
6. pp. 238–239	**13.** pp. 244–245	**20.** p. 249
7. pp. 239–240	**14.** pp. 244–245	

APPENDIX TO CHAPTER 12

The Relationship of the Aggregate Demand Curve to the Aggregate Expenditure Model

This appendix explains how the aggregate expenditures (AE) model that you learned about in Chapter 11 is related to the aggregate demand (AD) curve that was presented in Chapter 12. There are two short sections to this appendix. The first one focuses on the derivation of the aggregate demand curve from the AE model. The second one explains how shifts in aggregate demand are related to shifts in aggregate expenditures.

Although the aggregate expenditures model is a fixed-price-level model and the aggregate demand–aggregate supply model is a variable-price-level model, there is a close relationship between the two models. The important thing to understand is that prices can be fixed or constant at different levels. The AD curve can be derived from the aggregate expenditures model by letting the price level be constant at different levels. For example, the lower (the higher) the level at which prices are constant in the aggregate expenditures model, the larger (the smaller) will be the equilibrium real GDP in that model of the economy. Various output-price-level combinations can be traced to derive an AD curve that slopes downward, as shown in Figure 1 in the text.

The aggregate demand curve can shift (increase or decrease) because of a change in the nonprice level **determinants of aggregate demand.** The determinants include changes in factors affecting consumer, investment, government, and net export spending. These determinants are similar to the components of the aggregate expenditures model. It is easy to show the relationship between the shifts in the two models. A change in spending will cause a shift (upward or downward) in the aggregate expenditures schedule as shown in Figure 2 in the text. The initial change in spending when multiplied times the multiplier would be equal to the size of the horizontal shift in AD, assuming a constant price level.

■ APPENDIX CHECKLIST

When you have studied this appendix you should be able to

☐ Contrast the aggregate expenditures and the aggregate demand–aggregate supply models by comparing the variability of the price level and real GDP.

☐ Use a graph to derive the aggregate demand curve from the aggregate expenditures model.

☐ Explain the effect of a change in a determinant of aggregate demand on aggregate expenditures.

☐ Use a graph to show the relationship between a shift in aggregate expenditures and a shift in aggregate demand.

☐ Discuss how the initial change in spending and the multiplier effect influence the size of the shift in aggregate demand.

■ APPENDIX OUTLINE

1. This appendix introduces the ***aggregate demand–aggregate supply model*** of the economy to explain why real domestic output *and* the price level fluctuate. This model has an advantage over the aggregate expenditures model because it allows the price level to vary (rise and fall) rather than be constant or fixed as in the aggregate expenditures model.

2. The ***aggregate demand curve*** can be derived from the intersections of the aggregate expenditures curves and the 45-degree curve. As the price level falls, the aggregate expenditures curve shifts upward and the equilibrium real GDP increases, but as the price level rises, the aggregate expenditures curve shifts downward and the equilibrium real GDP decreases. The inverse relationship between the price level and equilibrium real GDP is the aggregate demand curve. Note that for the ***aggregate expenditures model,***

- **a.** changes in real balances (wealth) increase or decrease the consumption schedule;
- **b.** changes in the interest rate increase or decrease the investment schedule; and
- **c.** changes in imports or exports affect net exports, which can increase or decrease the net export schedule.

3. If the price level is constant, any change in nonprice-level determinants of consumption and planned investment that shifts the aggregate expenditures curve upward will increase the equilibrium real GDP and shift the AD curve to the right by an amount equal to the initial increase in aggregate expenditures times the ***multiplier***. Conversely, any change in nonprice-level determinants of consumption and planned investment that shifts the aggregate expenditures curve downward will decrease the equilibrium real GDP and shift the AD curve to the left by an amount equal to the initial decrease in aggregate expenditures times the multiplier.

■ HINTS AND TIPS

1. Figure 1 is worth extra study to see the relationship between the quantity (real domestic output) and the price level in both models. The upper panel shows the aggregate expenditures model with aggregate expenditures on the vertical axis and quantity on the horizontal axis. The lower panel shows the aggregate demand model with the price level on the vertical axis and quantity on the horizontal axis. Thus the horizontal axes in both graphs are the same and directly related. The connection between the price levels in each graph is more indirect but they are related nevertheless as shown in Figure 1.

2. Figure 2 shows how shifts are accounted for in each model. A shift upward in aggregate expenditures is the same as a shift outward in aggregate demand. The magnitude of the change in quantity will depend on the multiplier effect, but in both models quantity increases by the same amount.

■ IMPORTANT TERMS

aggregate demand–aggregate supply model
aggregate demand curve
aggregate expenditures model
multiplier

SELF-TEST

■ FILL-IN QUESTIONS

1. In the aggregate demand–aggregate supply model, the price level is (fixed, variable) ____________, but in the aggregate expenditures model, the price level is ____________.

2. In the aggregate expenditures model, a lower price level would (raise, lower) ____________ the consumption, investment, and aggregate expenditures curves, and the equilibrium level of real GDP would (rise, fall) ____________.

3. In the aggregate expenditures model, a higher price level would (raise, lower) ____________ the consumption, investment, and aggregate expenditures curves, and the equilibrium level of real GDP would (rise, fall) ____________.

4. This relationship between the price level and equilibrium real GDP in the aggregate expenditures model is (direct, inverse) ____________ and can be used to derive the aggregate (demand, supply) ____________ curve.

5. If the price level were constant, an increase in the aggregate expenditures curve would shift the aggregate demand curve to the (right, left) ____________ by an amount equal to the upward shift in aggregate expenditures times the (interest rate, multiplier) ____________. A decrease in the aggregate expenditures curve would shift the aggregate demand curve to the (right, left) ____________ by an amount equal to the (upward, downward) ____________ shift in aggregate expenditures times the (interest rate, multiplier) ____________.

■ TRUE–FALSE QUESTIONS

Circle T if the statement is true, F if it is false.

1. Both the graph of the aggregate demand curve and the aggregate expenditures model show the price level on the vertical axis. **T F**

2. The higher the price level, the smaller the real balances of consumers and the lower the aggregate expenditures schedule. **T F**

3. An increase in the price level will shift the aggregate expenditures schedule upward. **T F**

4. An increase in investment spending will shift the aggregate expenditures curve upward and the aggregate demand curve leftward. **T F**

5. A shift in the aggregate demand curve is equal to the initial change in spending times the multiplier. **T F**

■ MULTIPLE-CHOICE QUESTIONS

Circle the letter that corresponds to the best answer.

1. If the price level in the aggregate expenditures model were lower, the consumption and aggregate expenditures curves would be
(a) lower, and the equilibrium real GDP would be smaller
(b) lower, and the equilibrium real GDP would be larger
(c) higher, and the equilibrium real GDP would be larger
(d) higher, and the equilibrium real GDP would be smaller

2. In the aggregate expenditures model, a decrease in the price level, other things held constant, will shift the
(a) consumption, investment, and net exports curves downward
(b) consumption, investment, and net exports curves upward
(c) consumption and investment curves upward, but the net exports curve downward
(d) consumption and net export curves upward, but the investment curve downward

3. An increase in investment spending will
(a) increase aggregate expenditures and increase aggregate demand
(b) decrease aggregate expenditures and decrease aggregate demand
(c) increase aggregate expenditures and decrease aggregate demand
(d) decrease aggregate expenditures and increase aggregate demand

4. A decrease in net export spending will shift the
(a) aggregate expenditures schedule upward and the aggregate demand curve rightward
(b) aggregate expenditures schedule upward and the aggregate demand curve leftward
(c) aggregate expenditures schedule downward and the aggregate demand curve rightward
(d) aggregate expenditures schedule downward and the aggregate demand curve leftward

5. An increase in aggregate expenditures shifts the aggregate demand curve to the
   (a) right by the amount of the increase in aggregate expenditures
   (b) right by the amount of the increase in aggregate expenditures times the multiplier
   (c) left by the amount of the increase in aggregate expenditures
   (d) left by the amount of the increase in aggregate expenditures times the multiplier

■ PROBLEMS

1. Column 1 of the following table shows the real GDP an economy might produce.

(1) Real GDP	(2) $AE_{1.20}$	(3) $AE_{1.00}$	(4) $AE_{0.80}$
$2100	$2110	$2130	$2150
2200	2200	2220	2240
2300	2290	2310	2330
2400	2380	2400	2420
2500	2470	2490	2510
2600	2560	2580	2600

a. If the price level in this economy were $1.20, the aggregate expenditures (AE) at each real GDP would be those shown in column 2 and the equilibrium real GDP would be $_______.
b. If the price level were $1.00, the aggregate expenditures at each real GDP would be those shown in column 3 and the equilibrium real GDP would be $_______.
c. If the price level were $0.80, the aggregate expenditures at each real GDP would be those shown in column 4 and the equilibrium real GDP would be $_______.
d. Show in the following schedule the equilibrium real GDP at each of the three price levels.

Price level	Equilibrium real GDP
$1.20	$ _____
1.00	_____
0.80	_____

(1) This schedule is the aggregate (demand, supply) _______ schedule.
(2) The equilibrium real GDP is (directly, inversely) _______ related to the price level.

■ SHORT ANSWER AND ESSAY QUESTIONS

1. What do the horizontal axes measure in a graph of the aggregate expenditures model and the aggregate demand curve?

2. Why is there an inverse relationship between aggregate expenditures and the price level? Explain, using real balance, the interest rate, and foreign purchases.

3. Describe how the aggregate demand curve can be derived from the aggregate expenditures model.

4. What is the effect of an increase in aggregate expenditures on the aggregate demand curve? Explain in words and with a graph.

5. What role does the multiplier play in shifting aggregate expenditures and aggregate demand?

ANSWERS

Appendix to Chapter 12 The Relationship of the Aggregate Demand Curve to the Aggregate Expenditures Model

FILL-IN QUESTIONS

1. variable, fixed
2. raise, rise
3. lower, fall
4. inverse, demand
5. right, multiplier, left, downward, multiplier

TRUE–FALSE QUESTIONS

1. F, p. 254 **2.** T, p. 254 **3.** F, p. 255 **4.** F, p. 255 **5.** T, p. 255

MULTIPLE-CHOICE QUESTIONS

1. c, p. 254 **2.** b, p. 254 **3.** a, pp. 254–255 **4.** d, p. 255 **5.** b, p. 255

PROBLEMS

1. *a.* 2200; *b.* 2400; *c.* 2600; *d.* 2200, 2400, 2600, (1) aggregate demand, (2) inversely

SHORT ANSWER AND ESSAY QUESTIONS

1. p. 254 **2.** p. 255 **3.** pp. 254–255 **4.** p. 255 **5.** p. 255

CHAPTER 13

Fiscal Policy, Deficits, and Debt

Over the years, the most serious macroeconomic problems have been those resulting from the swings of the business cycle. Learning what determines the equilibrium level of real output and prices in an economy and what causes them to fluctuate makes it possible to find ways to achieve maximum output, full employment, and stable prices. In short, macroeconomic principles can suggest policies to control both recession and inflation in an economy.

As you will discover in Chapter 13, the Federal government may use **fiscal policy,** changes in government spending, or taxation to influence the economy's output, employment, and price level. The chapter first discusses discretionary fiscal policy to show how it affects aggregate demand. **Expansionary fiscal policy** is used to stimulate the economy and pull it out of a slump or recession by increasing government spending, decreasing taxes, or some combination of the two. **Contractionary fiscal policy** is enacted to counter inflationary pressure in the economy by cutting government spending, raising taxes, or a combination of the two.

Discretionary fiscal policy requires that Congress take action to change tax rates, modify transfer payment programs, or purchase goods and services. **Nondiscretionary fiscal policy** does not require Congress to take any action and is a **built-in stabilizer** for the economy. The economy has a progressive tax system that provides such automatic or built-in stability. When GDP increases, net tax revenues will increase to reduce inflationary pressure and when GDP declines, net tax revenues will fall to stimulate the economy.

To evaluate the direction of fiscal policy requires understanding of the **cyclically adjusted budget** and the distinction between a **cyclical deficit** and a cyclically adjusted deficit. This budget analysis enables economists to determine whether Federal fiscal policy is expansionary, contractionary, or neutral, and to determine what policy should be enacted to improve the economy's economic performance. From this budget analysis you will gain insights into the course of U.S. fiscal policy in recent years.

Fiscal policy is not without its problems, criticisms, or complications. There are timing problems in getting it implemented. There are political considerations in getting it accepted by politicians and voters. If the fiscal policy is temporary rather than permanent it is thought to be less effective. Some economists criticize the borrowing of money by the Federal government for expansionary fiscal policy because they think it will raise interest rates and crowd out investment spending, thus reducing the policy effects. The debate over the value of fiscal policy is an ongoing one as you will learn from the chapter.

Any budget surplus or deficit from a change in fiscal policy affects the size of the **public debt** (often called the national debt). Over the years the United States accumulated a public debt that now totals slightly more than $9 trillion. This debt increased because budget deficits accumulate over time and are not offset by budget surpluses. The size of the public debt is placed into perspective by (1) describing who owns the debt; (2) comparing it (and interest payments on the debt) to the size of the economy (GDP); and (3) looking at the sizes of the public debt in other industrial nations.

The last sections of the chapter examine the economic implications or **consequences of the public debt.** These economic problems do not include bankrupting the Federal government because the government can meet its obligations by refinancing and taxation. Nor does the public debt simply shift the economic burden to future generations because the public debt is a public credit for the many people who hold that debt in the form of U.S. securities. Rather, the public debt and payment of interest on the debt contribute to important problems: increased inequality in income, reduced incentives for work and production, decreased standard of living when part of the debt is paid to foreigners, and the possible crowding out of private investment.

■ CHECKLIST

When you have studied this chapter you should be able to

☐ Distinguish between discretionary and nondiscretionary fiscal policy.

☐ Explain expansionary fiscal policy on aggregate demand when the price level is inflexible downward.

☐ Compare and contrast an expansionary fiscal policy through increased government spending or decreased taxation.

☐ Describe contractionary fiscal policy on aggregate demand when the price level is inflexible downward.

☐ Compare and contrast a contractionary fiscal policy through decreased government spending or increased taxation.

☐ Assess whether it is preferable to use government spending or taxes to counter recession and reduce inflation.

☐ Explain the relationship between net tax revenues and GDP.

☐ Describe automatic or built-in stabilizers and their economic importance.

☐ Indicate how the built-in stabilizers help to counter recession and inflation.
☐ Describe how automatic stabilizers are affected by different tax systems (progressive, proportional, and regressive).
☐ Distinguish between the actual budget and the cyclically adjusted budget for evaluating discretionary fiscal policy.
☐ Describe recent U.S. fiscal policy using the cyclically adjusted budget.
☐ Describe projections for U.S. budget deficits and surpluses.
☐ Use the cyclically adjusted budget to evaluate discretionary fiscal policy.
☐ Outline three timing problems that may arise with fiscal policy.
☐ Discuss the political considerations affecting fiscal policy.
☐ Explain how expectations of policy reversals in the future change the effectiveness of fiscal policy.
☐ Describe how changes in state and local finances may offset fiscal policy at the federal level.
☐ Explain the crowding-out effect of fiscal policy.
☐ Discuss current thinking on fiscal policy.
☐ Explain the relationship of budget deficits and surpluses to the public debt.
☐ List the major types of owners of the public debt.
☐ Compare the size of the public debt to GDP.
☐ Compare the U.S. public debt with the debt of other advanced industrial nations.
☐ Compare interest payments on the public debt to GDP.
☐ State two reasons why a large public debt will not bankrupt the federal government.
☐ Discuss whether the public debt imposes a burden on future generations.
☐ State the effect of the public debt on income distribution.
☐ Explain how the public debt affects incentives.
☐ Evaluate the differences between foreign and domestic ownership of the public debt.
☐ Describe the crowding-out effect from a public debt.
☐ State two factors that offset the crowding-out effect of a public debt.
☐ Describe the shortfall affecting Social Security and Medicare and the policy options (*Last Word*).

■ CHAPTER OUTLINE

1. ***Fiscal policy*** consists of the changes made by the Federal government in its budget expenditures and tax revenues to expand or contract the economy. In making these changes, the Federal government may seek to increase the economy's real output and employment, or control its rate of inflation.

2. Fiscal policy is *discretionary* when changes in government spending or taxation are designed to change the level of real GDP, employment, incomes, or the price level. The ***Council of Economic Advisers (CEA)*** advises the U.S. President on such policies. Specific action then needs to be taken by Congress to initiate this discretionary policy, in contrast to *nondiscretionary* fiscal policy that occurs automatically (see item 3).

a. ***Expansionary fiscal policy*** is generally used to counteract the negative economic effects of a recession or cyclical downturn in the economy (a decline in real GDP and rising unemployment). The purpose of the policy is to stimulate the economy by increasing aggregate demand. The policy will create a ***budget deficit*** (government spending greater than tax revenues) if the budget was in balance before the policy was enacted. Assume the price level is fixed. There are three options for increasing aggregate demand
(1) The government can increase its discretionary spending. The initial increase from this spending will be increased by the multiplier effect. Since the price level is fixed, real output will rise by the full extent of the multiplier effect.
(2) Another option would be for the government to reduce taxes. Some of the tax cut would be saved, but some of it would be spent. The spent portion would provide an initial stimulus to the economy that would be magnified by the full extent of the multiplier effect since the price level is fixed.
(3) The government may decide to use some combination of increased government spending and tax reductions to increase aggregate demand.

b. ***Contractionary fiscal policy*** is a restrictive form of fiscal policy generally used to correct an inflation gap. Assume that the economy is at a full-employment level of output. If aggregate demand increases (shifts rightward), it will increase output and at the same time pull up output prices, creating demand-pull inflation. If government does nothing, input prices will rise in the long run to match the increase in output prices, creating more inflation. The purpose of contractionary fiscal policy is to reduce aggregate demand pressures that increase the price level. If the government budget is balanced before the policy is enacted, it will create a ***budget surplus*** (tax revenues are greater than government spending). The contractionary effect on the economy from the initial reduction in spending from the policy will be reinforced by the multiplier effect. Three policy options are used, but account should be taken of the ratchet effect (the price level is inflexible downward).
(1) The government can decrease spending. If the price level is fixed because of the ratchet effect, the multiplier will have a full effect in decreasing output, but there will be no change the price level. Government policy will have to take into account this ratchet effect to calibrate the decline in aggregate demand so it does not cause a recession.
(2) The government can increase taxes. The amount of the tax increase will need to be greater than a decrease in government spending because some of the tax increase will reduce saving, and not just consumption.
(3) The government can use some combination of decreased government spending and increased taxes to reduce aggregate demand.

c. Whether government purchases or taxes should be altered to reduce recession and control inflation depends on whether an expansion or a contraction of the public sector is desired.

3. In the U.S. economy there are automatic or ***built-in stabilizers*** that serve as nondiscretionary or passive fiscal policy. Such stabilizers work through net tax revenues (tax revenues minus government transfer payments and subsidies). These net tax revenues automatically or

passively increase as the GDP rises and automatically or passively decrease as the GDP falls.

a. The economic importance of this net tax system is that it serves as a built-in stabilizer of the economy. On the one hand, it reduces purchasing power during periods of prosperity to counteract increases in aggregate demand that can contribute to demand-pull inflation. On the other hand, it expands purchasing power (after tax income) during periods of declining output and high employment.

b. The degree of built-in stability in the economy depends on the responsiveness of net tax revenues to changes in GDP. As GDP increases, the average tax rates will increase in a ***progressive tax system,*** remain constant in a ***proportional tax system,*** and decrease in a ***regressive tax system.*** Thus, there is more built-in stability or net tax responsiveness for the economy in progressive tax systems. Built-in stabilizers, however, can only reduce and cannot eliminate economic fluctuations, so discretionary fiscal policy or monetary policy may be needed to moderate large fluctuations in the business cycle.

4. To evaluate the direction of discretionary fiscal policy, adjustments need to be made to the actual budget deficits or surpluses.

a. The ***cyclically adjusted budget*** is a better index than the actual budget of the direction of government fiscal policy because it indicates what the Federal budget deficit or surplus would be if the economy were to operate at its full-employment level of GDP (its potential output). In the case of a budget deficit, the cyclically adjusted budget removes the ***cyclical deficit*** that is produced by a decline in real GDP because of a downturn in the business cycle, and reveals the size of the *cyclically adjusted deficit,* indicating how expansionary the fiscal policy was that year if the economy had achieved its potential level of GDP.

b. Recent data on *cyclically adjusted budget deficits or surpluses* show the years that fiscal policy was expansionary or contractionary. From 2000–2004 surpluses decreased and deficits increased, so fiscal policy was expansionary. From 2004–2007 deficits declined, so fiscal policy was contractionary.

c. Fiscal policy during the Great Recession was expansionary. In 2008 the U.S. Congress passed an economic stimulus package and provided some tax breaks. A substantially larger economic stimulus package was passed in 2009. These actions changed the cyclically adjusted deficits from 1.2 percent of GDP in 2007 to −2.8 percent in 2008 and to −7.3 percent in 2009. Fiscal policy clearly became significantly more expansionary during this period.

d. Figure 13.5 in the text shows past changes in U.S. budget deficits and surpluses. It also shows projections, but these can change with changes in fiscal policy and economic growth.

5. Certain ***problems, criticisms, and complications*** arise in enacting and applying fiscal policy.

a. There will be problems of *timing.* First, it takes time to recognize the need for fiscal policy because it takes time for data to be collected that provide strong evidence of downturns or upturns in the business cycles. Second, it takes time for the U.S. President and U.S. Congress to take the appropriate administrative and legislative actions to respond to a recognized problem. Third, there is the need for time for the policy to become operational and take the desired effect on output or inflation.

b. There may be *political considerations* with fiscal policy that counter the economic effects. Elected officials may cause a ***political business cycle*** if they lower taxes and increase spending before an election to stimulate the economy and then do the opposite after an election.

c. Fiscal policy may be less effective if people expect it to be reversed in the future, thus making the policy temporary rather than permanent.

d. The fiscal policies of state and local governments can run counter to Federal fiscal policy and offset it (for example, state and local fiscal policy can be contractionary while Federal fiscal policy is expansionary).

e. An expansionary fiscal policy may, by raising the level of interest rates in the economy, reduce investment spending and weaken the effect of the policy on real GDP. The extent of this ***crowding-out effect*** depends on the condition of the economy. The crowding-out effect is likely to be relatively small when the economy is in a recession and experiences slack investment demand. It is likely to be more serious when the economy is near full-employment because the public demand for money to finance government competes with the private demand for money to fund economic investments.

f. Current thinking about discretionary fiscal policy shows differing perspectives. Some economists think that fiscal policy is ineffective because of all the potential problems and complications. They recommend the use of monetary policy to guide the economy. Other economists think that fiscal policy can be useful for directing the economy and that it can reinforce or support monetary policy. There is general agreement, however, that fiscal policy should be designed so that its incentives and investments strengthen long-term productivity and economic growth.

6. The ***public debt*** at any time is the sum of the Federal government's previous annual deficits, minus any annual surpluses. In 2009 the total public debt was $11.9 trillion.

a. The pubic debt is owned by various holders of ***U.S. securities*** (financial instruments issued by the U.S. government to borrow money such as U.S. Treasury bills, notes, and bonds). Over 40 percent (43%) of the public debt is held by Federal government agencies (36%) and the Federal Reserve (7%). Almost 60 percent (57%) is owned by a "public" that includes U.S. individuals (10%), U.S. banks and financial institutions (11%), foreigners (29%), and others such as state and local governments (7%).

b. It is better to consider the size of the debt as a percentage of the economy's GDP than the absolute amount because the percentage shows the capacity of the economy to handle the debt. In 2009, the percentage of the public debt held by the public (47%) was much higher than in previous years of the decade.

c. Many industrial nations have public debts as a percentage of GDP that are greater than that of the United States.

d. Interest payments as a percentage of the economy's GDP reflect the level of taxation (average tax rate) required to pay interest on the public debt. The percentage in 2009 (1.3%) is down from previous years.

7. The ***false contentions*** about a large debt are that it will eventually bankrupt the government and that borrowing to finance expenditures passes the cost on to future generations.

a. The debt *cannot bankrupt* the government because the government can refinance it by selling new bonds and using the proceeds to pay existing bondholders. It also has the constitutional authority to levy taxes to pay the debt.

b. The burden of the debt *cannot be shifted to future generations* because U.S. citizens and institutions hold most of the debt. Repayment of any portion of the principal and the payment of interest on it does not reduce the wealth or purchasing power in the United States because it would be paid to U.S. citizens and institutions. The only exception is the payment of the part of debt that would go to foreign owners of the debt.

8. The public debt does create ***real and potential problems*** in the economy.

a. The payment of interest on the debt probably increases *income inequality* because this payment typically goes to wealthier individuals.

b. The payment of taxes to finance these interest payments may *reduce incentives* to bear risks, to innovate, to invest, and to save, and therefore slow economic growth in the economy.

c. The portion of the debt held by foreign citizens and institutions (the ***external public debt***) requires the repayment of principal and the payment of interest to foreign citizens and institutions. This repayment would *transfer to foreigners* a part of the real output of the U.S. economy.

d. An increase in government spending may impose a burden on future generations by *crowding out* private investment spending, and thus reducing the future stock of capital goods.

(1) If government spending is financed by increased public debt, the increased borrowing of the Federal government will raise interest rates and reduce private investment spending. Future generations will inherit a smaller stock of capital goods.

(2) The burden imposed on future generations is lessened if the increase in government expenditures is for worthwhile ***public investments*** that increase the productive capacity of the economy. This public investment also can complement and stimulate private investment spending that increases the future capital stock.

9. (*Last Word*). *Social Security* is a U.S. retirement program that taxes payroll income and uses the money to pay for mandated benefits to retirees and others. *Medicare* is a U.S. health care program for people 65 years of age and older that also taxes payroll income to pay for the health care benefits. The problem for both Social Security and Medicare is that the funds paid into the trust fund for each program are likely to be depleted in the coming years or decades. Each program, therefore, faces a number of unpleasant options such as reducing program benefits or increasing taxes to provide sufficient funding to keep each program solvent.

■ HINTS AND TIPS

1. Fiscal policy is a broad concept that covers several kinds of policies. The main difference is between discretionary and nondiscretionary fiscal policies. Discretionary fiscal policy is active and means that Congress has taken specific actions to change taxes or government spending to influence the economy. It can be expansionary or contractionary. Nondiscretionary fiscal policy is passive, or automatic, because changes in net tax revenues will occur without specific actions by Congress.

2. An increase in government spending that is equal to a cut in taxes will not have an equal effect on real GDP. To understand this point, assume that the MPC is .75, the increase in government spending is $8 billion, and the decrease in taxes is $8 billion. The multiplier would be 4 because it equals 1/(1 − .75). The increase in government spending will increase real GDP by $32 billion ($8 billion × 4). Of the $8 billion decrease in taxes, however, one-quarter of it will be saved ($8 billion × .25 = $2 billion) and just three-quarters will be spent ($8 billion × .75 = $6 billion). Thus, the tax cut results in an increase in *initial* spending in the economy of $6 billion, not $8 billion as was the case with the increase in government spending. The tax cut effect on real GDP is $24 billion ($6 billion × 4), not $32 billion.

3. Make sure you know the difference between a **budget deficit** (government spending greater than tax revenue for a year) and the **public debt** (the accumulation over time of budget deficits that are offset by any budget surpluses). These two terms are often confused.

4. The best way to gauge the size of budget deficits, the public debt, or interest on the public debt is to calculate each one as a *percentage of real GDP*. The absolute size of these three items is *not* a good indicator of whether it causes problems for the economy.

5. Try to understand the real rather than the imagined problems caused by the public debt. The debt will not cause the country to go bankrupt, nor will it be a burden on future generations.

■ IMPORTANT TERMS

fiscal policy
Council of Economic Advisers (CEA)
expansionary fiscal policy
budget deficit
contractionary fiscal policy
budget surplus
built-in stabilizer
cyclically adjusted budget
cyclical deficit
political business cycle
crowding-out effect
public debt
U.S. securities
external public debt
public investments

SELF-TEST

FILL-IN QUESTIONS

1. Policy actions taken by Congress designed to change government spending or taxation are (discretionary, nondiscretionary) ______________ fiscal policy, but when the policy takes effect automatically or independently of Congress, then it is ______________ fiscal policy.

2. Expansionary fiscal policy is generally designed to (increase, decrease) ______________ aggregate demand and thus ______________ real GDP and employment in the economy. Contractionary fiscal policy is generally used to (increase, decrease) ______________ aggregate demand and thus ______________ real GDP to halt demand-pull inflation.

3. Expansionary fiscal policy can be achieved with an increase in (government spending, taxes) ______________, a decrease in ______________, or a combination of the two; contractionary fiscal policy can be achieved by a decrease in (government spending, taxes) ______________, an increase in ______________, or a combination of the two.

4. An increase of government spending of $5 billion from an expansionary fiscal policy for an economy might ultimately produce an increase in real GDP of $20 billion. This magnified effect occurs because of the (multiplier, crowding-out) ______________ effect.

5. Net taxes equal taxes (plus, minus) ______________ transfer payments and subsidies. (They are called "taxes" in this chapter.) In the United States, as GDP increases, tax revenues will (increase, decrease) ______________, and as the GDP decreases, tax revenues will ______________.

6. Because tax revenues are (directly, indirectly) ______________ related to the GDP, the economy has some (artificial, built-in) ______________ stability. If the GDP increases, then tax revenue will increase, and the budget surplus will (increase, decrease) ______________, thus (stimulating, restraining) ______________ the economy when it is needed. When GDP decreases, tax revenues decrease, and the budget deficit (increases, decreases) ______________, thus (stimulating, restraining) ______________ the economy when it is needed.

7. As GDP increases, the average tax rates will increase with a (progressive, proportional, regressive) ______________ tax system, remain constant with a ______________ tax system, and decrease with a ______________ tax system. With a progressive tax system, there is (more, less) ______________ built-in stability for the economy.

8. A deficit produced by swings in the business cycle is (actual, cyclical) ______________. When there is a large cyclical deficit, the cyclically adjusted budget deficit will be (greater, less) ______________ than the actual budget deficit.

9. If there are growing deficits in the cyclically adjusted budget, then the direction of fiscal policy is (contractionary, expansionary) ______________ and if there are growing surpluses in the cyclically adjusted budget, then fiscal policy is ______________.

10. There is a problem of timing in the use of discretionary fiscal policy because of the time between the beginning of a recession or inflation and awareness of it, or (an administrative, an operational, a recognition) ______________ lag; the time needed for Congress to adjust fiscal policy, or ______________ lag; and the time needed for fiscal policy to take effect, or ______________ lag.

11. Political problems arise in the application of discretionary fiscal policy to stabilize the economy because government has (one, several) ______________ economic goals, state and local fiscal policies may (reinforce, counter) ______________ Federal fiscal policy, and politicians may use fiscal policies in a way that creates (an international, a political) ______________ business cycle.

12. Expectations among households and businesses that fiscal policy will be reversed in the future make fiscal policy (more, less) ______________ effective. For example, if taxpayers expect a tax cut to be temporary, they may save (more, less) ______________ now to pay for a future increase in the tax rate and spend ______________ now. As a result, consumption and aggregate demand (increase, decrease) ______________.

13. When the Federal government employs an expansionary fiscal policy to increase real GDP and employment in the economy, it usually has a budget (surplus, deficit) ______________ and (lends, borrows) ______________ in the money market. These actions may (raise, lower) ______________ interest rates in the economy and (stimulate, crowd out) ______________ private investment spending.

14. Current thinking on the advisability and effectiveness of discretionary fiscal policy shows general (agreement, disagreement) ______________ about the value of fiscal policy in the short run, and general ______________ about evaluating fiscal policy for its contribution to long-run productivity growth.

15. The public debt is equal to the sum of the Federal government's past budget (deficits, surpluses) __________ minus its budget __________. The most meaningful way to measure the public debt is relative to (interest rates, GDP) __________. Of the public debt, Federal government agencies and the Federal Reserve hold about (43, 57) __________ percent and commercial banks, financial institutions, state and local governments, and individuals and institutions here and abroad hold about __________ percent. Most of the public debt is (internal, external) __________ because foreigners hold only about (9, 29) __________ percent.

16. The possibility that the Federal government will go bankrupt is a false issue. It does not need to reduce its debt; it can retire maturing U.S. securities by (taxing, refinancing) __________ them. The government can also pay its debts by increasing (interest, tax) __________ rates.

17. If the public debt is held domestically, then for U.S. taxpayers it is (a liability, an asset) __________ and for U.S. citizens and institutions owning the U.S. debt securities, it is __________.

18. The public debt and the payment of interest on it may (increase, decrease) __________ income inequality in the economy and __________ the incentives to work, take risks, save, and invest in the economy. The public debt is a burden on an economy if it is held by (foreigners, U.S. citizens) __________.

19. A public debt imposes a burden on future generations if the borrowing done to finance an increase in government expenditures results in (an increase, a decrease) __________ in interest rates, __________ in investment spending, and __________ in the stock of capital goods for future generations.

20. The size of the burden from the crowding out of private investment is lessened if government expenditures are used to finance worthwhile (increases, decreases) __________ in physical and human capital that contribute to the productive capacity of the economy, or if they (encourage, discourage) __________ more private investment that complements the public investment.

■ TRUE–FALSE QUESTIONS

Circle T if the statement is true, F if it is false.

1. Discretionary fiscal policy is independent of Congress and left to the discretion of state and local governments. **T F**

2. Expansionary fiscal policy during a recession or depression will create a budget deficit or add to an existing budget deficit. **T F**

3. A decrease in taxes is one of the options that can be used to pursue a contractionary fiscal policy. **T F**

4. To increase initial consumption by a specific amount, government must reduce taxes by more than that amount because some of the tax cut will be saved by households. **T F**

5. A reduction in taxes and an increase in government spending would be characteristic of a contractionary fiscal policy. **T F**

6. Built-in stabilizers are not sufficiently strong to prevent recession or inflation, but they can reduce the severity of a recession or inflation. **T F**

7. The less progressive the tax system, the greater the economy's built-in stability. **T F**

8. The cyclically adjusted budget indicates how much government must spend and tax if there is to be full employment in the economy. **T F**

9. The key to assessing discretionary fiscal policy is to observe the change in the cyclically adjusted budget. **T F**

10. Fiscal policy during the Great Recession of 2007–2009 was contractionary. **T F**

11. Recognition, administrative, and operational lags in the timing of Federal fiscal policy make fiscal policies more effective in reducing the rate of inflation and decreasing unemployment in the economy. **T F**

12. Economists who see evidence of a political business cycle argue that members of Congress tend to increase taxes and reduce expenditures before elections and to reduce taxes and increase expenditures after elections. **T F**

13. If households expect that a tax cut will be temporary, they are likely to spend more and save less, thus reinforcing the intended effect of the tax cut on aggregate demand. **T F**

14. State and local governments' fiscal policies have tended to assist and reinforce the efforts of the Federal government to counter recession and inflation. **T F**

15. The crowding-out effect occurs when an expansionary fiscal policy decreases the interest rate, increases investment spending, and strengthens fiscal policy. **T F**

16. The public debt is the total accumulation of the deficits, minus any surpluses, that the Federal government has incurred over time. **T F**

17. The public debt as a percentage of GDP is higher in the United States than in most other industrial nations. **T F**

18. Interest payments as a percentage of GDP reflect the level of taxation (average tax rate) required to service the public debt. **T F**

19. A large public debt will bankrupt the Federal government because the Federal government cannot refinance the debt or increase taxes to pay it. **T F**

20. The public debt is also a public credit. **T F**

21. The payment of interest on the public debt probably increases income inequality. **T F**

22. The additional taxes needed to pay the interest on the public debt increase incentives to work, save, invest, and bear risks. **T F**

23. Selling U.S. securities to foreigners to finance increased expenditures by the Federal government imposes a burden on future generations. **T F**

24. The crowding-out effect increases the investment-demand curve and investment in private capital goods. **T F**

25. If government spending is for public investments that increase the capital stock, then this spending can increase the future production capacity of the economy. **T F**

■ MULTIPLE-CHOICE QUESTIONS

Circle the letter that corresponds to the best answer.

1. Which combination of policies would be the most expansionary?
(a) an increase in government spending and taxes
(b) a decrease in government spending and taxes
(c) an increase in government spending and a decrease in taxes
(d) a decrease in government spending and an increase in taxes

2. An economy is in a recession and the government decides to increase spending by $4 billion. The MPC is .8. What would be the full increase in real GDP from the change in government spending?
(a) $3.2 billion
(b) $4 billion
(c) $16 billion
(d) $20 billion

3. Which combination of fiscal policies would be the most contractionary?
(a) an increase in government spending and taxes
(b) a decrease in government spending and taxes
(c) an increase in government spending and a decrease in taxes
(d) a decrease in government spending and an increase in taxes

4. When government tax revenues change automatically and in a countercyclical direction over the course of the business cycle, this is an example of
(a) the political business cycle
(b) nondiscretionary fiscal policy
(c) the cyclically adjusted budget
(d) crowding out

5. If the economy is to have built-in stability, when real GDP falls,
(a) tax revenues and government transfer payments both should fall
(b) tax revenues and government transfer payments both should rise
(c) tax revenues should fall and government transfer payments should rise
(d) tax revenues should rise and government transfer payments should fall

Answer Questions 6, 7, and 8 on the basis of the following diagram.

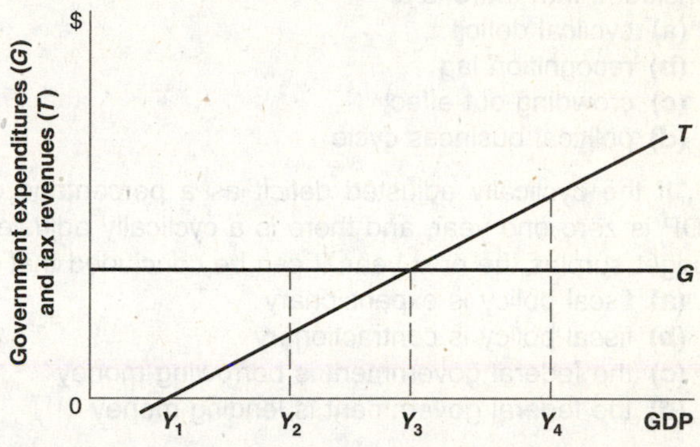

6. If the slope of the line ***T*** were steeper, there would be
(a) more built-in stability for the economy
(b) less built-in stability for the economy
(c) no change in the built-in stability for the economy
(d) the need for more emphasis on discretionary fiscal policy

7. If the slope of the line ***T*** were flatter, there would be
(a) larger cyclical deficits produced as GDP moved from Y_3 to Y_2
(b) smaller cyclical deficits produced as GDP moved from Y_3 to Y_2
(c) larger cyclically adjusted deficits produced as GDP moved from Y_3 to Y_2
(d) smaller cyclically adjusted deficits produced as GDP moved from Y_3 to Y_2

8. Actions by the Federal government to increase the progressivity of the tax system
(a) flatten the slope of line ***T*** and increase built-in stability
(b) flatten the slope of line ***T*** and decrease built-in stability
(c) steepen the slope of line ***T*** and increase built-in stability
(d) steepen the slope of line ***T*** and decrease built-in stability

Use the following table to answer question 9. The table shows the cyclically adjusted budget deficit or surplus as a percentage of GDP over a five-year period.

Year	Deficit (−) or Surplus (+)
1	−2.1%
2	−3.0
3	−1.5
4	+0.5
5	+1.0

9. In which year did fiscal policy become more expansionary?
(a) Year 2
(b) Year 3
(c) Year 4
(d) Year 5

10. If the cyclically adjusted budget shows a deficit of about $200 billion and the actual budget shows a deficit of about $250 billion over a several-year period, it can be concluded that there is a
(a) cyclical deficit
(b) recognition lag
(c) crowding-out effect
(d) political business cycle

11. If the cyclically adjusted deficit as a percentage of GDP is zero one year, and there is a cyclically adjusted budget surplus the next year, it can be concluded that
(a) fiscal policy is expansionary
(b) fiscal policy is contractionary
(c) the federal government is borrowing money
(d) the federal government is lending money

12. During the Great Recession of 2007–2009 the federal government
(a) decreased spending and increased taxes
(b) increased spending and decreased taxes
(c) decreased spending and decreased taxes
(d) increased spending and increased taxes

13. The length of time involved for the fiscal action taken by Congress to affect output, employment, or the price level is referred to as the
(a) administrative lag
(b) operational lag
(c) recognition lag
(d) fiscal lag

14. The crowding-out effect of an expansionary (deficit) fiscal policy is the result of government borrowing in the money market which
(a) increases interest rates and net investment spending in the economy
(b) increases interest rates and decreases net investment spending
(c) decreases interest rates and increases net investment spending
(d) decreases interest rates and net investment spending

15. Current thinking about discretionary fiscal policy among mainstream economists is that it should be designed to
(a) counteract the effects of monetary policy
(b) contribute to long-run economic growth
(c) "fine-tune" the economy in the short run, but not in the long run
(d) control inflationary pressure, but not be used to fight recession

16. The public debt is the sum of all previous
(a) expenditures of the Federal government
(b) budget deficits of the Federal government
(c) budget deficits minus any budget surpluses of the Federal government
(d) budget surpluses less the current budget deficit of the Federal government

17. To place the public debt in perspective based on the wealth and productive capacity of the economy, it is more meaningful to
(a) examine its absolute size
(b) calculate the interest payments on the debt
(c) measure it relative to the gross domestic product
(d) compare it to imports, exports, and the trade deficit

18. According to many economists, the primary burden of the debt is the
(a) absolute size of the debt for the economy
(b) annual interest charges from bonds sold to finance the public debt
(c) deficit arising from a decline in exports and increase in imports
(d) government spending that the public debt finances for the economy

19. A major reason that a public debt cannot bankrupt the Federal government is because the Federal government has
(a) an annually balanced budget
(b) the Social Security trust fund
(c) the power to levy taxes
(d) a strong military defense

20. Incurring an internal debt to finance a war does not pass the cost of the war on to future generations because
(a) the opportunity cost of the war was borne by the generation that fought it
(b) the government need not pay interest on internally held debts
(c) there is never a need for government to refinance the debt
(d) wartime inflation reduces the relative size of the debt

21. Which would be a consequence of the retirement of the internally held (U.S.-owned) portion of the public debt?
(a) a reduction in the nation's productive capacity
(b) a reduction in the nation's standard of living
(c) a redistribution of the nation's wealth among its citizens
(d) a decrease in aggregate demand in the economy

22. Which is an important consequence of the public debt of the United States?
(a) It decreases the need for U.S. securities.
(b) It transfers a portion of the U.S. output to foreign nations.
(c) It reduces the income inequality in the United States.
(d) It leads to greater saving at every level of disposable income.

23. Greater interest charges on the public debt can lead to
(a) fewer purchases of U.S. securities by foreigners
(b) more private investment spending in the economy

(c) lower taxes, and thus greater incentives to work and invest
(d) higher taxes, and thus reduced incentives to work and invest

24. The crowding-out effect of borrowing to finance an increase in government expenditures
(a) reduces current spending for private investment
(b) increases the privately owned stock of real capital
(c) reduces the economic burden on future generations
(d) increases incentives to innovate

25. The crowding-out effect from government borrowing is reduced when
(a) interest rates are rising
(b) the economy is operating at full employment
(c) government spending improves human capital in the economy
(d) private investment spending can substitute for government spending

■ PROBLEMS

1. Columns 1 and 2 in the following table are an aggregate supply schedule. Columns 1 and 3 are aggregate demand schedules.

(1) Price level	(2) Real GDP_1	(3) AD_1	(4) AD_2
220	$2390	$2100	$2200
200	2390	2200	2340
190	2350	2250	2350
180	2300	2300	2400
160	2200	2400	2500

a. The equilibrium real GDP is $________ and the price level is ________.

b. Suppose that an expansionary fiscal policy increases aggregate demand from that shown in columns 1 and 3 to that shown in columns 1 and 4. The price level will increase to ________, and this rise in the price level will result in real GDP increasing to $________.

2. The following table shows seven real GDPs and the net tax revenues of government at each real GDP.

Real GDP	Net tax revenues	Government purchases	Government deficit/surplus
$ 850	$170	$_____	$_____
900	180	_____	_____
950	190	_____	_____
1000	200	_____	_____
1050	210	_____	_____
1100	220	_____	_____
1150	230	_____	_____

a. Looking at the two columns on the left side of the table, it can be seen that
(1) when real GDP increases by $50, net tax revenues (increase, decrease) ________ by $________.
(2) when real GDP decreases by $100, net tax revenues (increase, decrease) ________ by $________.
(3) the relationship between real GDP and net tax revenues is (direct, inverse) ________.

b. Assume the simple multiplier has a value of 10 and that investment spending in the economy decreases by $10.
(1) *If* net tax revenues remained constant, the equilibrium real GDP would decrease by $________.
(2) But when real GDP decreases, net tax revenues also decrease; and this decrease in net tax revenues will tend to (increase, decrease) ________ the equilibrium real GDP.
(3) And, therefore, the decrease in real GDP brought about by the $10 decrease in investment spending will be (more, less) ________ than $100.
(4) The direct relationship between net tax revenues and real GDP has (lessened, expanded) ________ the impact of the $10 decrease in investment spending on real GDP.

c. Suppose the simple multiplier is also 10 and government wishes to increase the equilibrium real GDP by $50.
(1) *If* net tax revenues remained constant, government would have to increase its purchases of goods and services by $________.
(2) But when real GDP rises, net tax revenues also rise, and this rise in net tax revenues will tend to (increase, decrease) ________ the equilibrium real GDP.
(3) The effect, therefore, of the $5 increase in government purchases will also be to increase the equilibrium real GDP by (more, less) ________ than $50.
(4) The direct relationship between net tax revenues and real GDP has (lessened, expanded) ________ the effect of the $5 increase in government purchases, and to raise the equilibrium real GDP by $50, the government will have to increase its purchases by (more, less) ________ than $5.

d. Imagine that the full-employment real GDP of the economy is $1150 and that government purchases of goods and services are $200.
(1) Complete the previous table by entering the government purchases and computing the budget deficit or surplus at each of the real GDPs. (Show a government deficit by placing a minus sign in front of the amount by which expenditures exceed net tax revenues.)
(2) The cyclically adjusted surplus equals $________.
(3) If the economy were in a recession and producing a real GDP of $900, the budget would show a (surplus, deficit) ________ of $________.

(4) This budget deficit or surplus makes it appear that government is pursuing (an expansionary, a contractionary) ________ fiscal policy, but this deficit or surplus is not the result of a countercyclical fiscal policy but the result of the ________.

(5) If government did not change its net tax *rates,* it could increase the equilibrium real GDP from $900 to the full-employment real GDP of $1150 by increasing its purchases by (approximately) $70. At the full-employment real GDP the budget would show a (surplus, deficit) ________ of $________.

(6) If government did not change its purchases, it would increase the equilibrium real GDP from $900 to the full-employment real GDP of $1150 by decreasing net tax revenues at all real GDPs by a lump sum of (approximately) $80. The cyclically adjusted budget would have a (surplus, deficit) ________ of $________.

3. a. Complete the table below by computing the average tax rates, given the net tax revenue data in columns 2, 4, and 6. Calculate the average tax rates in percentages to one decimal place (for example, 5.4%).

b. As real GDP increases in column 1, the average tax rate (increases, decreases, remains the same) ________ in column 3, ________ in column 5, and ________ in column 7. The tax system is (progressive, proportional, regressive) ________ in column 2, ________ in column 4, and ________ in column 6.

c. On the graph below plot the real GDP, net tax revenue, and government spending data given in columns 1, 2, 4, 6, and 8. The tax revenue system with the steepest slope is found in column ________, and it is (progressive, proportional, regressive) ________ while the one with the flattest slope is found in column ________, and it is ________.

(1) Real GDP	(2) Net tax revenue	(3) Average tax rate	(4) Net tax revenue	(5) Average tax rate	(6) Net tax revenue	(7) Average tax rate	(8) Government spending
$1000	$100	____%	$100	____%	$100	____%	$120
1100	120	____	110	____	108	____	120
1200	145	____	120	____	115	____	120
1300	175	____	130	____	120	____	120
1400	210	____	140	____	123	____	120

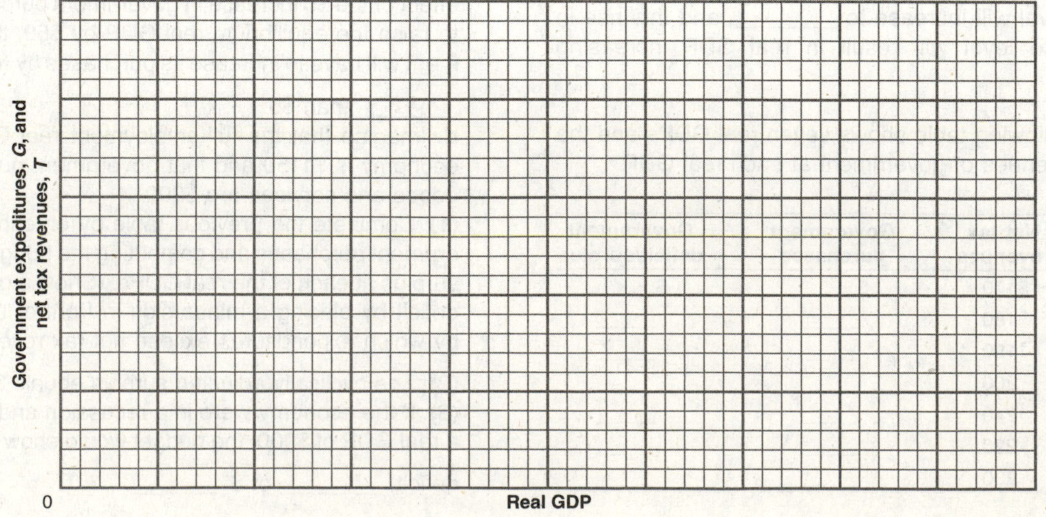

4. a. Complete the table below by stating whether the direction of discretionary fiscal policy was contractionary (**C**), expansionary (**E**), or neither (**N**), given the hypothetical budget data for an economy.

(1) Year	(2) Actual budget deficit (−) or surplus (+)	(3) Standardized budget deficit (−) or surplus (+)	(4) Direction of fiscal policy
1	− $170 billion	− $130 billion	____
2	− 120 billion	− 90 billion	____
3	+ 40 billion	+ 20 billion	____
4	− 60 billion	− 50 billion	____
5	− 120 billion	− 100 billion	____

b. The best gauge of the direction of fiscal policy is the (actual, cyclically adjusted) ________ budget deficit or surplus because it removes the (cyclical, actual) ________ component from the discussion of the budget situation.

c. (1) In what years were there cyclical deficits, and what was the amount of the cyclical deficit in each of those years? ________

(2) In what year was the actual budget surplus greater than the cyclically adjusted budget surplus, and by what amount greater? ________

5. The following table gives data on interest rates and investment demand (in billions of dollars) in a hypothetical economy.

Interest rate	I_{d1}	I_{d2}
10%	$250	$300
8	300	350
6	350	400
4	400	450
2	450	500

a. Use the I_{d1} schedule. Assume that the government needs to finance a budget deficit and this public borrowing increases the interest rate from 4% to 6%. How much crowding out of private investment will occur? ________

b. Now assume that the deficit is used to improve the capital stock of the economy and that, as a consequence, the investment-demand schedule changes from I_{d1} to I_{d2}. At the same time, the interest rate rises from 4% to 6% as the government borrows money to finance the deficit. How much crowding out of private investment will occur in this case? ________

c. Graph the two investment-demand schedules on the next graph and show the difference between the two events. Put the interest rate on the vertical axis and the quantity of investment demanded on the horizontal axis.

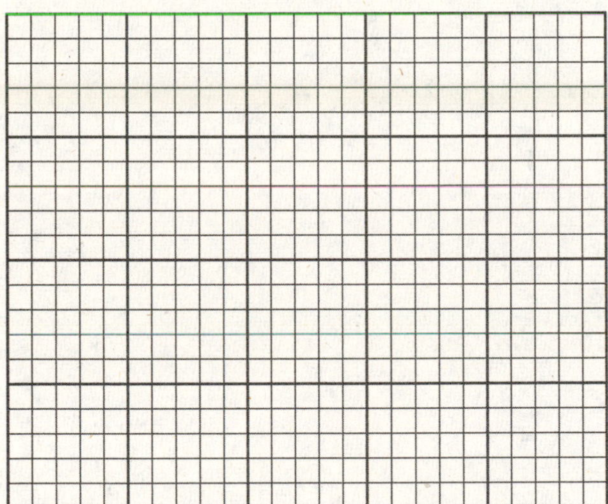

■ SHORT ANSWER AND ESSAY QUESTIONS

1. What are the Federal government's three options for conducting either an expansionary fiscal policy or a contractionary fiscal policy?

2. Compare and contrast the effect of expansionary fiscal policy and of contractionary fiscal policy on aggregate demand, output, and the price level. Draw a graph to illustrate the likely effects of each. Assume that there is a ratchet effect.

3. What is the effect of the multiplier on the initial change in spending from fiscal policy? When the government wants to increase initial consumption by a specific amount, why must the government reduce taxes by more than that amount?

4. Explain the fiscal policies that would be advocated during a recession and during a period of inflation by those who (*a*) wish to expand the public sector and (*b*) wish to contract the size of government.

5. What is a built-in stabilizer? How do built-in stabilizers work to reduce rises and falls in the level of nominal GDP?

6. Supply definitions of progressive, proportional, and regressive tax systems. What are the implications of each type of tax system for the built-in stability of the economy?

7. Explain the distinction between a cyclical deficit and a cyclically adjusted deficit. Which type of deficit provides the best indication of the direction of fiscal policy? Why?

8. Discuss the history of recent U.S. fiscal policy based on changes in the cyclically adjusted budget and the Great Recession of 2007–2009.

9. Explain the three kinds of time lags that make it difficult to use fiscal policy to stabilize the economy.

10. How might the direction of fiscal policy at the Federal level be countered by the actions of state and local governments?

11. Evaluate the strength of a crowding-out effect when the economy is in recession or experiencing a period of strong economic growth.

12. What is the current thinking about the advisability and effectiveness of discretionary fiscal policy?

13. How are budget deficits and surpluses related to the public debt?

14. Who owns the public debt? What percentage is held by the two major groups? What percentage of the public debt is held by foreigners?

15. Why can't the public debt result in the bankruptcy of the Federal government? What two actions can the government take to prevent bankruptcy?

16. If most of the public debt was owned by American citizens and institutions, and the government decided to pay off the debt, what would happen? Explain.

17. Was the increase in the cost of the public debt that resulted from World War II a burden borne by the wartime generation or future generations? Explain.

18. How does the public debt affect the distribution of income and incentives to work, to save, or to assume risk in the economy?

19. What are the economic implications of the portion of the public debt held by foreigners?

20. How does the public debt crowd out private investment and impose a burden on future generations? What two qualifications might lessen the crowding-out effect on the size of the economic burden that has shifted to future generations?

ANSWERS

Chapter 13 Fiscal Policy, Deficits, and Debt

FILL-IN QUESTIONS

1. discretionary, nondiscretionary
2. increase, increase, decrease, decrease
3. government spending, taxes, government spending, taxes
4. multiplier
5. minus, increase, decrease
6. directly, built-in, increase, restraining, increases, stimulating
7. progressive, proportional, regressive, more
8. cyclical, less
9. expansionary, contractionary
10. a recognition, an administrative, an operational
11. several, counter, a political
12. less, more, less, decrease
13. deficit, borrows, raise, crowd out
14. disagreement, agreement
15. deficits, surpluses, GDP, 57, 47, internal, 29
16. refinancing, tax
17. a liability, an asset
18. increase, decrease, foreigners
19. an increase, a decrease, a decrease
20. increases, encourage

TRUE–FALSE QUESTIONS

1. F, p. 258
2. T, p. 258–259
3. F, p. 259
4. T, p. 259
5. F, p. 259–260
6. T, p. 261–262
7. F, p. 262–263
8. F, p. 263
9. T, p. 263–264
10. F, p. 265
11. F, p. 267
12. F, p. 267
13. F, p. 267–268
14. F, p. 268
15. F, p. 268
16. T, p. 269
17. F, p. 270
18. T, p. 270–271
19. F, p. 271
20. T, p. 271–272
21. T, p. 272
22. F, p. 272
23. T, p. 272
24. F, p. 272–273
25. T, p. 273

MULTIPLE-CHOICE QUESTIONS

1. c, pp. 258–259
2. d, pp. 258–259
3. d, pp. 259–260
4. b, pp. 261–262
5. c, p. 262
6. a, pp. 262–263
7. b, pp. 262–263
8. c, pp. 262–263
9. a, pp. 263–264
10. a, pp. 263–264
11. b, pp. 263–264
12. b, p. 265
13. b, p. 267
14. b, p. 268
15. b, p. 269
16. c, p. 269
17. c, p. 270
18. b, pp. 270–271
19. c, p. 271
20. a, pp. 271–272
21. c, pp. 271–272
22. b, p. 272
23. d, p. 272
24. a, p. 272
25. c, p. 273

PROBLEMS

1. *a.* 2,300, 180; *b.* 190, 2,350
2. *a.* increase, $10, (2) decrease, $20, (3) direct; *b.* (1) $100, (2) increase, (3) less, (4) lessened; *c.* (1) $5, (2) decrease, (3) less, (4) lessened, more; *d.* (1) government purchases are $200 at all GDPs, government surplus or deficit: −30, −20, −10, 0, 10, 20, 30, (2) $30, (3) deficit, $20, (4) an expansionary, recession, (5) deficit, $40, (6) deficit, $50
3. *a.* column 3: 10.0, 10.9, 12.1, 13.5, 15.0; column 5: 10.0 at each GDP level; column 7: 10.0, 9.8, 9.6, 9.2, 8.8; *b.* increases, remains the same, decreases; progressive, proportional, regressive; *c.* 2, progressive, 6, regressive
4. *a.* (Year 1–2) contractionary, (Year 2–3) contractionary, (Year 3–4) expansionary, (Year 4–5) expansionary; *b.* cyclically adjusted, cyclical; *c.* (1) year 1 ($40 billion), year 2 ($30 billion), year 4 ($10 billion), year 5 ($20 billion), (2) year 3 ($20 billion)
5. *a.* $50 billion; *b.* none; *c.* graph

SHORT ANSWER AND ESSAY QUESTIONS

1. pp. 258–261
2. pp. 258–261
3. pp. 258–259
4. p. 261
5. pp. 261–262
6. pp. 262–263
7. p. 263
8. pp. 264–265
9. p. 267
10. p. 268
11. p. 268
12. p. 269
13. p. 269
14. pp. 269–270
15. p. 271
16. pp. 271–272
17. pp. 271–272
18. p. 272
19. p. 272
20. pp. 272–273

CHAPTER 14

Money, Banking, and Financial Institutions

Chapter 14 explains how the financial system affects the operation of the economy. The chapter is largely descriptive and factual. Pay particular attention to the following: (1) what the money supply is and the function money performs; (2) what gives value to or "backs" money in the United States; and (3) the principal institutions of the U.S. financial system and their functions.

Several points are worth repeating. First, money is whatever performs the three functions of money (***medium of exchange, unit of account, store of value***). People are willing to accept and trust the use of money for transactions because people are willing to exchange goods and services for it. So money is backed by trust or acceptability *and not by gold.* Money also helps people measure the value of goods and services they want to buy or sell. In addition, money stores value for people so they can use it in the future to make purchases.

Second, the central bank in the United States consists of the 12 **Federal Reserve Banks** and the **Board of Governors** of the **Federal Reserve System** which oversees their operation. These banks, while privately owned by the commercial banks, are operated more or less as public agencies of the federal government. They operate on a not-for-profit basis but are used primarily to regulate the nation's money supply in the best interests of the economy as a whole, and secondarily, to perform other services for the banks, the government, and the economy. They are able to perform their primary function because they are bankers' banks in which depository institutions (commercial banks and the thrifts) can deposit and borrow money. They do not deal directly with the public.

Third, these depository institutions accept deposits and make loans, but they also are able to create money by lending checkable deposits. Because they are able to do this, they have a strong influence on the size of the money supply and the purchasing power of money. The Federal Reserve Banks exist primarily to regulate the money supply and its value by influencing and controlling the amount of money depository institutions create.

A major section in the chapter discusses the **financial crisis of 2007 and 2008.** Here you will learn about mortgage-backed securities and how they contributed to the crisis. Defaults on these securities led to widespread losses for major banks and financial firms throughout the economy and the failure or near-failure of some firms. The U.S. government responded initially with a program of emergency loans (TARP) to save some of the major financial firms because they were considered "too big to fail." The Federal Reserve also established many innovative lending facilities to help extend money and credit to banks, thrifts, and other financial firms in its role as a lender of last resort. This crisis forced more consolidation and mergers in the **financial services industry** and led to new financial regulations and reform measures.

■ CHECKLIST

When you have studied this chapter you should be able to

☐ List and explain the three functions of money.

☐ Describe the liquidity of an asset and give examples of it.

☐ Give an ***M*1** definition of money.

☐ Describe the characteristics of the currency component of ***M*1**.

☐ Explain the role of checkable deposits as a component of ***M*1**.

☐ Describe the two major types of institutions offering checkable deposits.

☐ Offer two qualifications about what is excluded from the money supply.

☐ Give an ***M*2** definition of money and describe its components.

☐ Distinguish between credit cards and money.

☐ Explain why money is debt in the U.S. economy and who holds that debt.

☐ State three reasons why currency and checkable deposits are money and have value.

☐ Describe the relationship between the purchasing power of money and the price level.

☐ Discuss how inflation affects the acceptability of money.

☐ Explain what role government plays in maintaining or stabilizing the purchasing power of money.

☐ Describe the framework of the Federal Reserve.

☐ Explain the historical background of the Federal Reserve.

☐ Describe the purposes of the Board of Governors of the Federal Reserve.

☐ Explain why the Federal Reserve Banks are central banks, quasi-public banks, and bankers' banks.

☐ Discuss the functions of the FOMC of the Federal Reserve.

☐ Discuss the relationship between the Federal Reserve and commercial banks and thrifts.

☐ List and explain the seven major functions of the Federal Reserve System and indicate which one is most important.

☐ Explain the reason for the independence of the Federal Reserve.

☐ Discuss the main features of the financial crisis of 2007 and 2008.

☐ Describe the causes and consequences of the mortgage default crisis.

☐ Explain the process of securitization and its importance to the financial system.

☐ Describe why financial firms failed or almost failed during the financial crisis.

☐ Explain the purpose of the Troubled Asset Relief Program (TARP).

☐ Describe the seven programs the Fed uses to serve as the lender of last resort.

☐ Explain the major characteristics of the financial services industry after the financial crisis.

☐ Discuss how electronic payments have transformed banking (*Last Word*).

■ CHAPTER OUTLINE

1. Money is whatever performs the three ***basic functions of money:*** It is a ***medium of exchange*** for buying and selling goods and services. It serves as a ***unit of account*** for measuring the monetary cost of goods and services. It is a ***store of value*** so people can transfer purchasing power from the present to the future. A key advantage of money, especially in its cash form, is that is widely accepted and easy to use for transactions. Other assets, such as real estate, stocks, or bonds, must first be converted to money before they can be use to make purchases. Ease with which such assets can be converted to money without losing purchasing power is a measure of the ***liquidity*** of an asset.

2. Money is a stock of items rather than a flow such as income. Any item that is widely accepted as a medium of exchange can serve as money, and many types of such items have done so throughout history.

a. The narrowly defined money supply is called ***M*1** and has two principal components.

(1) One component is *currency:* It consists of coins that are ***token money,*** which means the value of the metal in the coin is less than the face value of the coin. It also consists of paper money in the form of ***Federal Reserve Notes.***

(2) The second component is ***checkable deposits.*** They allow a person to transfer ownership of deposits to others by the writing of checks; these checks are generally accepted as a medium of exchange.

(3) The two major types of financial institutions offering checkable deposits are ***commercial banks*** and ***thrift institutions.***

(4) There also is currency and checkable deposits owned by the federal government, commercial banks and thrift institutions, and the Federal Reserve Banks. They are excluded from the calculation of ***M*1** or in the other definitions of the money supply.

b. ***M*2** is a broader definition of money and includes not only the currency and checkable deposits in ***M*1** but also **near-monies** that do not function directly or fully as a medium of exchange, but which can be easily converted to currency or checkable deposits. ***M*2** includes;

(1) ***M*1** (currency and checkable deposits); plus

(2) savings deposits, which includes money in ***savings accounts*** and also ***money market deposit accounts (MMDAs)*** [an interest-bearing account with short-term securities]; plus

(3) ***small time deposits*** of less than $100,000, such as "certificates of deposit" (CDs); plus

(4) ***money market mutual funds (MMMFs)*** held by individuals.

3. The ***money supply gets its "backing"*** from the ability of the government to keep the purchasing power of money stable.

a. Money is debt or the promise of a commercial bank, a thrift institution, or a Federal Reserve Bank to pay, but these debts cannot be redeemed for anything tangible.

b. Money has value only because

(1) It is acceptable for the exchange of desirable goods and services;

(2) It is ***legal tender*** (legally acceptable for payment of debts); and

(3) It is relatively scarce because its value depends on supply and demand conditions.

c. The purchasing power of money is the amount of goods and services a unit of money will buy.

(1) The purchasing power of the U.S. dollar is inversely related to the price level: Value of the dollar ($\$V$) = 1 divided by price level (P) expressed as an index number (in hundredths), or $\$V = 1/P$.

(2) Rapid inflation can erode the purchasing power of money and public confidence in it. Such situations limit the functions of money as a medium of exchange, measure of value, or store of value.

d. Money is backed by the confidence the public has that the purchasing power of money will remain stable. U.S. monetary authorities (the Federal Reserve) are responsible for using monetary policy to maintain price-level stability and the purchasing power of money. The actions of the U.S. government are also important because sound fiscal policy supports price-level stability.

4. The monetary and financial sector of the economy is significantly influenced by the ***Federal Reserve System (the Fed)*** and the nation's banks and thrift institutions.

a. The banking system remains centralized and regulated by government because historical problems in the U.S. economy led to different kinds of money and the mismanagement of the money supply. The U.S. Congress passed the Federal Reserve Act of 1913 to establish the Fed as the nation's central bank to be responsible for issuing currency and controlling the nation's money supply.

b. The ***Board of Governors*** of the Fed exercises control over the supply of money and the banking system. The U.S. president appoints the seven members of the Board of Governors, who serve for 14 years. He also selects the board chair and vice-chair, who serve for 4-year terms.

c. The ***12 Federal Reserve Banks*** of the Fed have three main functions.

(1) They serve as the nation's *central bank* to implement the policies set by the Board of Governors.

(2) They are *quasi-public banks* that blend private ownership of each Federal Reserve Bank with public control of each bank through the Board of Governors.

(3) They are "bankers' banks" that perform banking services for the member banks in their regions.

d. The ***Federal Open Market Committee (FOMC)*** is responsible for acting on the monetary policy set by the Board of Governors. The FOMC includes the seven members of the Board of Governors, the president of the New York Federal Reserve Bank, plus 4 other presidents of Federal Reserve banks (who serve on a rotating basis). The FOMC conducts open market operations to buy and sell government securities to control the nation's money supply and influence interest rates.

e. The U.S. banking system contains about 6,800 commercial banks. Roughly three-fourths of these are banks charted by states and about one-fourth of these are banks chartered by the federal government. The banking system also includes about 8,700 thrift institutions, such as savings and loans and credit unions. Both banks and thrifts are directly affected by the Fed's decisions concerning the money supply and interest rates.

f. The Fed performs seven functions: issuing currency, setting reserve requirements and holding reserves for banks, lending money to banks and thrifts, collecting and processing checks, serving as the fiscal agent for the federal government, supervising banks, and controlling the money supply. The last function is the most important.

g. The Federal Reserve is an independent agency of government with control of the money supply and influence over interest rates. This independence helps insulate it from political pressure from the U.S. Congress or the U.S. President when the Fed decides to adopt a necessary, but possibly unpopular, monetary policy such as raising interest rates to combat inflation.

5. The financial crisis of 2007 and 2008 was the most serious one the U.S. economy experienced since the Great Depression of the 1930s.

a. Defaults on home mortgage loans caused losses for financial institutions that either directly or indirectly loaned these funds. Many loans were ***subprime mortgage loans,*** which were made to individuals with higher credit risk and at higher interest rates. As the economy declined and unemployment rose, the banks suffered reserve losses and had less capacity to extend loans or credit. Contributing to the problem was that some mortgages were bundled together to create ***mortgage-backed securities,*** which in essence are bonds backed by mortgage payments. Banks then lent money to investment firms to purchase such bonds. When defaults rose, banks lost more money on the loans made to the investment firms, thus further reducing bank reserves.

b. The process of bundling and segmenting financial contracts, such as loans, mortgages, or corporate bonds, into a financial instrument is called ***securitization.*** It was viewed favorably because it was designed to spread the risk of any default to a broader group of financial institutions and investors who held these securities. Insurance could be purchased on these securities with collateralized default swaps.

c. As mortgage default rates rose, these mortgage-backed securities spread losses throughout the economy to the financial institutions and investors who held them or insured them both in the United States and other nations. These losses led to the failure or near-failure of many large financial firms and less availability of money and credit for the economy.

d. The **Troubled Asset Relief Program (TARP)** was established by the federal government in late 2008 to make emergency loans to important U.S. financial institutions and businesses. A $700 billion "bailout" fund was used to support such firms as AIG, Citibank, and Bank of America, and also businesses such as General Motors and Chrysler. TARP, however, also created a ***moral hazard*** because it set a precedent for helping or rewarding some firms for taking larger risks than they otherwise would have without such government backing because the large firms were considered "too big to fail."

e. The Federal Reserve serves as the lender of last resort. During the financial crisis it established many innovative facilities that were designed to keep money and credit available and flowing to financial institutions and businesses. It did so by loaning more funds and purchasing hard-to-sell securities from banks and other institutions. It also paid banks interest on the deposits they were required to keep at the Federal Reserve or that they held in their bank vaults.

6. The U.S. ***financial services industry*** consists not only of banks and thrifts, but also of insurance companies, mutual fund companies, pension funds, and securities firms. Over the past few decades, there has been a significant convergence in the types of financial services (banking, insurance, mutual funds, and other investments) offered by different types of firms. The recent financial crisis further contributed to consolidation among banks and among other firms in the financial services industry. Also, in response to the financial crisis, regulations and legislation have been enacted or are being considered to provide better safeguards for the financial system and address the moral hazard of "too big to fail." For example, in mid-2010 the **Wall Street Reform and Consumer Protection Act** was passed by the Congress and signed by the president.

7. (*Last Word*) The character of money has changed with the shift to the widespread use of electronic payment systems. The extensive use of credit and debit cards, electronic transfer of funds, and electronic transactions accounts (such as PayPal) to make purchases and settle debts are just some of the innovations, but more are likely to be developed and used in the future as individuals and businesses make greater use of technology for handling electronic payments.

■ HINTS AND TIPS

1. The value of money is largely based on trust or acceptability. You are willing to accept money in exchange for a good or service because you are confident you will be able to use that money to purchase other goods and services or store its value for later use. If you lose trust in money, then it no longer functions as a medium of exchange, store of value, or measure of value for you and probably many other people.

2. Most students typically think of money as only currency: coins and paper money in circulation. A key component of the money supply, however, is the checkable deposits held at banks and thrift institutions on which checks can be drawn.

3. There are two definitions of the ***money supply*** that you must know about, from the narrow *M*1 to the broader *M*2. The essential relationship among them is that currency and checkable deposits are the main parts of each one.

4. A good portion of the chapter explains the framework of the Federal Reserve. The institutional features are important for understanding how the nation's central bank works, and the Fed will be a major focus of later chapters.

■ IMPORTANT TERMS

medium of exchange
unit of account
store of value
liquidity
***M*1**
token money
Federal Reserve Notes
checkable deposits
commercial banks
thrift institutions
***M*2**
near-monies
savings account
money market deposit account (MMDA)
time deposits
money market mutual fund (MMMF)
legal tender
Federal Reserve System
Board of Governors
Federal Reserve Banks
Federal Open Market Committee (FOMC)
subprime mortgage loans
mortgage-backed securities
securitization
moral hazard
Troubled Asset Relief Program (TARP)
financial services industry
Wall Street Reform and Consumer Protection Act

SELF-TEST

■ FILL-IN QUESTIONS

1. When money is usable for buying and selling goods and services, it functions as (a unit of account, a store of value, a medium of exchange) __________, but when money serves as a measure of relative worth, it functions as __________, and when money serves as a liquid asset it functions as __________.

2. The ease with which an asset can be converted into money such cash with little or no loss in purchasing power is its (credit, liquidity) __________. Assets that can be converted into cash more easily than other assets are (more, less) __________ liquid assets.

3. All coins in circulation in the United States are (paper, token) __________ money, which means that their intrinsic value is (less, greater) __________ than the face value of the coin.

4. Paper money and coins are considered (currency, checkable deposits) __________ and are one major component of *M*1; the other major component is (currency, checkable deposits) __________.

5. *M*2 is equal to *M*1 plus (checking, savings) __________ deposits that include money market (deposit accounts, mutual funds) __________, plus (small, large) __________ time deposits, and plus money market (deposit accounts, mutual funds) __________.

6. Credit cards (are, are not) __________ considered money but rather a form of (paper money, loan) __________ from the institution that issued the card.

7. Paper money is the circulating debt of (banks and thrifts, the Federal Reserve Banks) __________, while checkable deposits are the debts of __________. In the United States, currency and checkable deposits (are, are not) __________ backed by gold and silver.

8. Money has value because it is (unacceptable, acceptable) __________ in exchange for products and resources, because it is (legal, illegal) __________ tender, and because it is relatively (abundant, scarce) __________.

9. The purchasing power of money varies (directly, inversely) __________ with the price level. To find the value of $1 (multiply, divide) __________ 1 by the price level.

10. Runaway inflation may significantly (increase, decrease) __________ the purchasing power of money and __________ its acceptance as a medium of exchange.

11. Government's responsibility in stabilizing the purchasing power of money calls for effective control over the (demand for, supply of) __________ money and the application by the president and Congress of appropriate (monetary, fiscal) __________ policies.

12. The Federal Reserve System is composed of the Board of (Banks, Governors) ____________ and the 12 Federal Reserve ____________. These policies of the Federal Reserve are often carried out by the (Federal Deposit Insurance Corporation, Federal Open Market Committee) ____________.

13. The Federal Reserve Banks are (private, quasi-public) ____________ banks, serve as (consumers', bankers') ____________ banks, and are (local, central) ____________ banks whose policies are coordinated by the Board of Governors.

14. The Federal Open Market Committee meets regularly to buy and sell government (currency, securities) ____________ to control the nation's money supply and influence (productivity, interest rates) ____________.

15. The U.S. banking system is composed of about commercial banks, about three-fourths of which are (national, state) ____________ banks and about one-fourth of which are ____________ banks. The system also includes thrift institutions most of which are (credit unions, investment banks) ____________.

16. The seven major functions of the Fed are

a. ____________

b. ____________

c. ____________

d. ____________

e. ____________

f. ____________

g. ____________

Of these, the most important function is ____________ ____________.

17. The Congress established the Fed as a(n) (dependent, independent) ____________ agency of government. The objective was to protect it from political pressure so it could control (taxes, inflation) ____________.

18. The financial crisis of 2007 and 2008 largely started with a major wave of defaults on (corporate bonds, home mortgage loans) ____________ many of which were (prime, subprime) ____________. Many banks and financial institutions took losses on these securities that were backed by (corporate bonds, home mortgages) ____________, thus weakening the health of these institutions and reducing the availability of money and credit in the economy.

19. Securitization is the process of dividing and grouping bundles of loans, mortgages, corporate bonds or other financial (debt, credit) ____________ so it becomes new security that is bought and sold. In the case of mortgage-backed securities, they were designed to (increase, decrease) ____________ the financial return and ____________ risk to the buyer. Insurance could be bought on these securities in the form of collateralized default (paper, swaps) ____________. When the housing market declined in 2007 and 2008, the securities fell in value, and insurers had to make payment on them, thus exposing many investors and financial firms to large (profits, losses) ____________.

20. In response to the crisis, the U.S. Treasury was authorized to make emergency loans to major financial firms considered too (little, big) ____________ to fail under the Trouble Asset Relief Program, but these bailouts created a (principal-agent, moral hazard) ____________ problem because they wound up helping those firms that took on more risk than they would have without the expected government backing. The Federal Reserve also tried to improve the flow of money and credit in the financial system by serving as the (borrower, lender) ____________ of last resort and establishing various programs for this purpose.

■ TRUE–FALSE QUESTIONS

Circle T if the statement is true, F if it is false.

1. When the price of a product is stated in terms of dollars and cents, then money is functioning as a unit of account. **T F**

2. Real estate would be an example of a highly liquid asset. **T F**

3. The money supply designated *M*1 is the sum of currency and savings deposits. **T F**

4. The currency component of *M*1 includes both coins and paper money. **T F**

5. If a coin is token money, its face value is less than its intrinsic value. **T F**

6. Both commercial banks and thrift institutions accept checkable deposits. **T F**

7. The checkable deposits of the federal government at the Federal Reserve Banks are a component of *M*1. **T F**

8. *M*2 exceeds *M*1 by the amount of savings deposits (including money market deposit accounts), small time deposits, and the money market mutual funds of individuals. **T F**

9. A *small* time deposit is one that is less than $100,000. **T F**

10. The money supply in the United States essentially is "backed" by the government's ability to keep the value of money relatively stable. **T F**

11. The major components of the money supply are debts, or promises to pay. **T F**

12. Currency and checkable deposits are money because they are acceptable to sellers in exchange for goods and services. **T F**

13. If money is to have a fairly stable value, its supply must be limited relative to the demand for it. **T F**

14. The amount a dollar will buy varies directly with the price level. **T F**

15. Price-level stability requires effective management and regulation of the nation's money supply. **T F**

16. Members of the Board of Governors of the Federal Reserve System are appointed by the president of the United States and confirmed by the Senate. **T F**

17. The Federal Reserve Banks are owned and operated by the U.S. government. **T F**

18. Federal Reserve Banks are bankers' banks because they make loans to and accept deposits from depository institutions. **T F**

19. The Federal Open Market Committee (FOMC) is responsible for keeping the stock market open and regulated. **T F**

20. The Federal Reserve Banks are responsible for issuing currency. **T F**

21. At times, the Fed lends money to banks and thrifts, charging them an interest rate called the *bank and thrift rate.* **T F**

22. The Federal Reserve acts as the fiscal agent for the federal government. **T F**

23. Congress established the Fed as an independent agency to protect it from political pressure so that it can effectively control the money supply and maintain price stability. **T F**

24. The financial crisis of 2007 and 2008 resulted from the making of bad mortgage loans, a decline in real estate prices, and an unprecedented rise in mortgage loan defaults. **T F**

25. The main purpose of the establishment of new programs or facilities by the Federal Reserve during the financial crisis of 2007 and 2008 was to issue more corporate bonds. **T F**

■ MULTIPLE-CHOICE QUESTIONS

Circle the letter that corresponds to the best answer.

1. Which one is an economic function of money?
(a) a store of gold
(b) a unit of account
(c) a factor of production
(d) a medium of communications

2. Each month Marti puts a certain percentage of her income in a bank account that she plans to use in the future to purchase a car. For Marti, the money saved in the bank account is primarily functioning as
(a) legal tender
(b) token money
(c) store of value
(d) medium of exchange

3. Which one of the following items would be considered to be perfectly liquid from an economic perspective?
(a) cash
(b) stocks
(c) real estate
(d) certificate of deposits

4. Which one of the following is included in the *currency* component of ***M*1**?
(a) gold certificates
(b) silver certificates
(c) checkable deposits
(d) Federal Reserve Notes

5. Checkable deposits are money because they are
(a) legal tender
(b) fiat money
(c) token money
(d) a medium of exchange

6. What type of financial institution accepts deposits from and lends to "members," who are usually a group of people who work for the same company?
(a) credit unions
(b) commercial banks
(c) mutual savings banks
(d) savings and loan associations

7. Which of the following would be excluded from ***M*1** and other measures of the money supply?
(a) coins held by the public
(b) currency held by banks
(c) Federal Reserve Notes held by the public
(d) checkable deposits of individuals at commercial banks

8. Which constitutes the largest element in the ***M*2** money supply?
(a) savings deposits
(b) small time deposits
(c) checkable deposits
(d) money market mutual funds held by individuals

Use the following table to answer Questions 9 and 10 about the money supply, given the following hypothetical data for the economy.

Item	Billions of dollars
Savings deposits, including MMDAs	$3452
Small time deposits	997
Currency	721
Checkable deposits	604
Money market mutual funds of individuals	703
Money market mutual funds of businesses	1153

9. The size of the *M*1 money supply is
(a) $1307
(b) $1325
(c) $1719
(d) $1856

10. The size of the *M*2 money supply is
(a) $4777
(b) $5774
(c) $6477
(d) $7630

11. Are credit cards considered to be money?
(a) Yes, because their value is included in the calculation of *M*1.
(b) Yes, because their value is included in the calculation of *M*2.
(c) No, because they provide a short-term loan to cardholders from a financial institution that issued the card.
(d) No, because the card transactions are not insured either by the Federal Reserve banks or the U.S. Treasury.

12. The major components of the money supply—paper money and checkable deposits—are
(a) legal tender
(b) token money
(c) debts, or promises to pay
(d) assets of the Federal Reserve Banks

13. Which *best* describes the backing of money in the United States?
(a) the gold bullion that is stored in Fort Knox, Kentucky
(b) the belief of holders of money that it can be exchanged for desirable goods and services
(c) the willingness of banks and the government to surrender something of value in exchange for money
(d) the confidence of the public in the ability of government to pay off the national debt

14. If the price level increases 20%, the purchasing power of money decreases
(a) 14.14%
(b) 16.67%
(c) 20%
(d) 25%

15. High rates of inflation in an economy will
(a) increase the purchasing power of money
(b) decrease the conversion of money to gold
(c) increase the use of money as a measure of value
(d) decrease the use of money as a medium of exchange

16. To keep the purchasing power of money fairly stable, the Federal Reserve
(a) buys corporate stock
(b) employs fiscal policy
(c) controls the money supply
(d) uses price and wage controls

17. The members of the Board of Governors of the Federal Reserve System are appointed by
(a) member banks of the Federal Reserve System
(b) members of the Federal Open Market Committee
(c) the U.S. president and confirmed by the Senate
(d) the presidents of the 12 Federal Reserve Banks

18. The Board of Governors and 12 Federal Reserve Banks as a system serve as
(a) a central bank
(b) a regulator of the stock market
(c) the printer of U.S. paper money
(d) the issuer of the nation's gold certificates

19. The 12 Federal Reserve Banks are
(a) publicly owned and controlled
(b) privately owned and controlled
(c) privately owned, but publicly controlled
(d) publicly owned, but privately controlled

20. The Federal Reserve Banks perform essentially the same functions for
(a) the public as do commercial banks and thrifts
(b) federal government as does the U.S. Treasury
(c) commercial banks and thrifts as those institutions do for the public
(d) commercial banks and thrifts as does the Federal Deposit Insurance Corporation

21. The Federal Open Market Committee (FOMC) of the Federal Reserve System is primarily responsible for
(a) supervising the operation of banks to make sure they follow regulations and monitoring banks so they do not engage in fraud
(b) handling the Fed's collection of checks and adjusting legal reserves among banks
(c) setting the Fed's monetary policy and directing the buying and selling of government securities
(d) acting as the fiscal agent for the federal government and issuing currency

22. The Federal Reserve is responsible for
(a) supervising all banks and thrifts
(b) printing currency for banks and thrifts
(c) collecting federal taxes from banks and thrifts
(d) holding the required reserves of banks and thrifts

23. The most important function of the Federal Reserve is
(a) issuing currency
(b) controlling the money supply
(c) supervising banks and thrifts
(d) lending money to banks and thrifts

24. One of the contributing factors to the financial crisis of 2007 and 2008 was
(a) overstating the moral hazard problem
(b) understating the benefits of devaluing the U.S. dollar
(c) overestimating the expected profits made by oil companies
(d) underestimating the risk of losses on mortgage-backed securities

25. What did the U.S. Congress do in response to the financial crisis of 2007 and 2008?
(a) set up the primary dealer credit facility (PDCF)
(b) set up the Troubled Asset Relief Program (TARP)
(c) set up the commercial paper funding facility (CPFF)
(d) set up the money market investor funding facility (MMIFF)

■ PROBLEMS

1. From the figures in the following table it can be concluded that

Item	Billions of dollars
Small time deposits	$1014
MMMFs held by individuals	743
Checkable deposits	622
Savings deposits, including MMDAs	3649
Currency	730
MMMFs held by businesses	1190

a. *M*1 is equal to the sum of $________ and $________, so it totals $________ billion.

b. *M*2 is equal to *M*1 plus $________ and $________ and $________ and $________, so it totals $________ billion.

2. Complete the following table that shows the relationship between a percentage change in the price level and the percentage change in the purchasing power of money. Calculate the percentage change in the purchasing power of money to one decimal place.

Change in price level	Change in purchasing power of money
a. *rises* by:	
5%	− ____.____ %
10%	− ____.____
15%	− ____.____
20%	− ____.____
25%	− ____.____
b. *falls* by:	
5%	+ ____.____
10%	+ ____.____
15%	+ ____.____

■ SHORT ANSWER AND ESSAY QUESTIONS

1. How would you define money based on its three functions?

2. What is the definition of liquidity as it relates to money? Give examples of liquid and illiquid assets.

3. What are the two components of the *M*1 supply of money in the United States?

4. Why are coins token money?

5. What are checkable deposits?

6. Describe the different types of institutions that offer checkable deposits.

7. Are the checkable deposits of government, the Fed, commercial banks, and other financial institutions included in *M*1? Explain.

8. Define *M*2 and explain why it is used.

9. What is the purpose of having two definitions of the money supply? What is the relationship between the two definitions?

10. What backs the money used in the United States? What determines the purchasing power of money?

11. Explain the relationship between the purchasing power of money and the price level.

12. What must government do if it is to stabilize the purchasing power of money?

13. Describe the purpose and membership of the Board of Governors of the Federal Reserve System.

14. Explain the three major characteristics of the Federal Reserve Banks.

15. What is the Federal Open Market Committee and how does it operate?

16. Describe the differences in commercial banks and thrifts in terms of numbers, purpose, and regulation agencies.

17. What are the seven major functions of the Fed and which function is most important?

18. Explain how the mortgage default crisis and securitization contributed to the failure or near-failure of many financial firms from 2007 to 2009.

19. Discuss the measures taken by the U.S. government and Federal Reserve to counteract the financial crisis of 2007 and 2008.

20. Describe the postcrisis financial services industry and the key provisions of the Wall Street Reform and Consumer Protection Act.

ANSWERS

Chapter 14 Money, Banking, and Financial Institutions

FILL-IN QUESTIONS

1. a medium of exchange, a unit of account, a store of value
2. liquidity, more
3. token, less
4. currency, checkable deposits
5. savings, deposit accounts, small, mutual funds
6. are not, loan
7. the Federal Reserve Banks, banks and thrifts, are not
8. acceptable, legal, scarce
9. inversely, divide
10. decrease, decrease
11. supply of, fiscal
12. Governors, Banks, Federal Open Market Committee
13. quasi-public, bankers', central
14. securities, interest rates
15. state, national, credit unions
16. *a.* issuing currency; *b.* setting reserve requirements and holding reserves; *c.* lending money to banks and thrifts; *d.* collecting and processing checks; *e.* serving as fiscal agent for the federal government; *f.* bank supervision; *g.* controlling the money supply; controlling the money supply
17. independent, inflation

18. home mortgage loans, subprime, home mortgages
19. debt, increase, decrease, swaps, losses
20. big, moral hazard, lender

TRUE–FALSE QUESTIONS

1. T, p. 281
2. F, p. 281
3. F, p. 282
4. T, p. 282
5. F, p. 282
6. T, p. 283
7. F, p. 283
8. T, pp. 284–285
9. T, pp. 284–285
10. T, p. 285
11. T, p. 285
12. T, p. 285
13. T, p. 285
14. F, pp. 285–286
15. T, p. 286
16. T, p. 287
17. F, pp. 287–288
18. T; p. 288
19. F, p. 289
20. T, p. 289
21. F, p. 289
22. T, p. 290
23. T, p. 290
24. T, pp. 290–291
25. F, p. 293

MULTIPLE-CHOICE QUESTIONS

1. b, p. 281
2. c, p. 281
3. a, p. 281
4. d, p. 282
5. d, pp. 282–283
6. a, p. 283
7. b, p. 283
8. a, pp. 283–284
9. b, p. 283
10. c, pp. 283–284
11. c, p. 284
12. c, pp. 284–285
13. b, p. 285
14. b, pp. 285–286
15. d, p. 286
16. c, p. 286
17. c, p. 287
18. a, p. 287
19. c, p. 288
20. c, p. 288
21. c, p. 289
22. d, p. 289
23. b, p. 290
24. d, p. 292
25. b, p. 292

PROBLEMS

1. *a.* 733, 622 (either order), 1,352; *b.* 3649, 1014, 743 (any order), 6758
2. *a.* 4.8, 9.1, 13, 16.7, 20; *b.* 5.3, 11.1, 17.6

SHORT ANSWER AND ESSAY QUESTIONS

1. p. 281
2. p. 281
3. p. 282
4. p. 282
5. pp. 282–283
6. p. 283
7. p. 283
8. pp. 283–284
9. pp. 283–284
10. pp. 284–285
11. pp. 285–286
12. p. 287
13. p. 287
14. pp. 287–288
15. p. 289
16. p. 289
17. pp. 289–290
18. pp. 290–292
19. pp. 292–293
20. pp. 293–296

CHAPTER 15

Money Creation

Chapter 14 explained the institutional structure of banking in the United States today, the functions which banks and the other depository institutions and money perform, and the composition of the money supply. Chapter 15 explains how banks create money—**checkable-deposits**—and the factors that determine and limit the money-creating ability of commercial banks. The other depository institutions, such as thrift institutions, also create checkable deposits, but this chapter focuses on the commercial banks to simplify the discussion.

The convenient and simple device used to explain commercial banking operations and money creation is the **balance sheet.** Shown within it are the **assets, liabilities,** and **net worth** of commercial banks. All banking transactions affect this balance sheet. The first step to understanding how money is created is to understand how various simple and typical transactions affect the commercial bank balance sheet.

In reading this chapter you must analyze for yourself the effect of each and every banking transaction discussed on the balance sheet. The important items in the balance sheet are checkable deposits and reserves because **checkable deposits are money.** The ability of a bank to create new checkable deposits is determined by the amount of reserves the bank has. Expansion of the money supply depends on the possession by commercial banks of excess reserves. They do not appear explicitly in the balance sheet but do appear there implicitly because **excess reserves** are the difference between the **actual reserves** and the **required reserves** of commercial banks.

Two cases—the single commercial bank and the banking system—are presented to help you build an understanding of banking and money creation. It is important to understand that the money-creating potential of a single commercial bank differs from the money-creating potential of the entire banking system. It is equally important to understand how the money-creating ability of many single commercial banks is **multiplied** and influences the **money-creating ability** of the banking system as a whole.

■ CHECKLIST

When you have studied this chapter you should be able to

☐ Recount the story of how goldsmiths came to issue paper money and became bankers who created money and held fractional reserves.

☐ Cite two significant characteristics of the fractional reserve banking system today.

☐ Define the basic items in a bank's balance sheet.

☐ Describe what happens to a bank's balance sheet when the bank is created, it buys property and equipment, and it accepts deposits.

☐ Explain the effects of the deposit of currency in a checking account on the composition and size of the money supply.

☐ Define the reserve ratio.

☐ Compute a bank's required and excess reserves when you are given the needed balance-sheet figures.

☐ Explain why a commercial bank is required to maintain a reserve and why a required reserve is not sufficient to protect the depositors from losses.

☐ Indicate whether required reserves are assets or liabilities for commercial banks and the Federal Reserve.

☐ Describe how the deposit of a check drawn on one commercial bank and deposited into another will affect the reserves and excess reserves of the two banks.

☐ Show what happens to the money supply when a commercial bank makes a loan.

☐ Show what happens to the money supply when a commercial bank buys government securities.

☐ Describe what would happen to a commercial bank's reserves if it made loans (or bought government securities) in an amount greater than its excess reserves.

☐ State the money-creating potential of a commercial bank (the amount of money a commercial bank can safely create by lending or buying securities).

☐ Explain how a commercial bank's balance sheet reflects the banker's pursuit of the two conflicting goals of profit and liquidity.

☐ Explain how the federal funds market helps reconcile the goals of profits and liquidity for commercial banks.

☐ State the money-creating potential of the banking system.

☐ Explain how it is possible for the banking system to create an amount of money that is a multiple of its excess reserves when no individual commercial bank ever creates money in an amount greater than its excess reserve.

☐ Define the monetary multiplier.

☐ Use the monetary multiplier and the amount of excess reserves to compute the money-creating potential of the banking system.

☐ Illustrate with an example using the monetary multiplier how money can be destroyed in the banking system.

☐ Discuss how bank panics during the early 1930s led to a contraction of the nation's money supply and worsened economic conditions (*Last Word*).

■ CHAPTER OUTLINE

1. The United States has a ***fractional reserve banking system.*** This term means that banks only keep a part or a fraction of their checkable deposits backed by cash reserves.

a. The history of the early goldsmiths illustrates how paper money came into use in the economy and how banks create money. The goldsmiths accepted gold as deposits and began making loans and issuing money in excess of their gold holdings.

b. The goldsmiths' fractional reserve system is similar to today's fractional reserve banking system, which has two significant characteristics: banks can create money in such a system; and banks are subject to "panics" or "runs," and thus need government regulation.

2. The ***balance sheet*** of a single commercial bank is a statement of the *assets, liabilities,* and *net worth* (stock shares) of the bank at a specific time; and in the balance sheet, the bank's assets equal its liabilities plus its net worth. This balance sheet changes with various transactions.

a. *Transaction 1: Creating a bank.* A commercial bank is founded by selling shares of stock and obtaining cash in return. Stock is a liability and cash is an asset.

b. *Transaction 2: Acquiring property and equipment.* A commercial bank needs property and equipment to carry on the banking business. They are assets of the bank.

c. *Transaction 3: Accepting deposits.* When a bank accepts deposits of cash, the cash becomes an asset to the bank, and checkable deposit accounts that are created are a liability. The deposit of cash in the bank does not affect the total money supply. It only changes its composition by substituting checkable deposits for currency (cash) in circulation.

d. *Transaction 4: Depositing reserves in the Federal Reserve Bank.*

(1) Three reserve concepts are vital to an understanding of the money-creating potential of a commercial bank.

(a) The ***required reserves,*** which a bank *must* maintain at its Federal Reserve Bank (or as ***vault cash*** at the bank—which can be ignored in this textbook example), equal the reserve ratio multiplied by the checkable deposit liabilities of the commercial bank.

(b) The ***actual reserves*** of a commercial bank are its deposits at the Federal Reserve Bank (plus the vault cash which is ignored in this textbook example).

(c) The ***excess reserves*** are equal to the actual reserves less the required reserves.

(2) The ***reserve ratio*** is the ratio of required reserves to a bank's own checkable deposit liabilities. The Fed has the authority to establish and change the ratio within limits set by Congress.

e. *Transaction 5: Clearing a check drawn against the bank.* The writing of a check on the bank and its deposit in a second bank results in a loss of reserves (assets) and checkable deposits (liabilities) for the first bank and a gain in reserves and deposits for the second bank.

3. A ***single commercial bank*** in a multi-bank system can create money as the following two additional transactions show.

a. *Transaction 6: Granting a loan.* When a single commercial bank grants a loan to a borrower, its balance sheet changes. Checkable deposit liabilities are increased by the amount of the loan and the loan value is entered as an asset. In essence, the borrower gives an IOU (a promise to repay the loan) to the bank, and in return the bank creates money by giving the borrower checkable deposits. The bank has "monetized" the IOU and created money. When the borrower writes a check for the amount of the loan to pay for something and that check clears, then the checkable deposits are reduced by the amount of that check. A bank only lends its funds in an amount equal to its pre-loan excess reserves because it fears the loss of reserves to other commercial banks in the economy.

b. *Transaction 7: Buying government securities.* When a bank buys government securities, it increases its own checkable deposit liabilities and therefore the supply of money by the amount of the securities purchase. The bank assets increase by the amount of the securities it now holds. The bank only buys securities in an amount equal to its excess reserves because it fears the loss of reserves to other commercial banks in the economy.

c. An individual commercial bank balances its desire for profits (which result from the making of loans and the purchase of securities) with its desire for liquidity or safety (which it achieves by having excess reserves or vault cash). The federal funds market allows banks with excess reserves to lend funds overnight to banks that are short of required reserves. The interest rate paid on the overnight loans is the ***federal funds rate.***

4. The ability of a ***banking system*** composed of many individual commercial banks to lend and create money is a multiple (greater than 1) of its excess reserves and is equal to the excess reserves of the banking system multiplied by the checkable-deposit (or monetary) multiplier.

a. The banking system as a whole can do this even though no single commercial bank ever lends an amount greater than its excess reserves because the banking system, unlike a single commercial bank, does not lose reserves. If a bank receives a deposit of currency, it increases its checkable deposits. This change increases the amount of excess reserves the bank has available for loan. If a loan is made on these excess reserves, then it creates additional checkable deposits that, when spent, may be deposited in another bank. That other bank now has additional excess reserves and can increase its lending, and so the process continues.

b. The ***monetary multiplier*** is equal to the reciprocal of the required reserve ratio for checkable deposits. The maximum expansion of checkable deposits is equal to the initial excess reserves in the banking system times the monetary multiplier. To illustrate, if the required reserve ratio was 20 percent, then the monetary multiplier would be 5 (or 1 divided by .20). If excess reserves in the banking system were $80 million, then a maximum of $400 million in money could be created (or, 5 times $80 million).

c. The money-creating process of the banking system can also be reversed. When loans are paid off, money is destroyed.

5. (*Last Word*). During the early 1930s, more than 6,000 banks failed within three years. This resulted in a multiple contraction of the nation's money supply that totaled about 25 percent. The decline in the money supply contributed to the Great Depression. In 1933, banks were shut for a week for a bank holiday and a deposit insurance program was established to give confidence to bank depositors and to reduce the potential for panics, bank runs, and large withdrawals of deposits.

■ HINTS AND TIPS

1. Note that several terms are used interchangeably in this chapter: "commercial bank" (or "bank") is sometimes called "thrift institution" or "depository institution."

2. A bank's balance sheet must balance. The bank's assets are either claimed by owners (net worth) or by nonowners (liabilities). *Assets = Liabilities + Net worth.*

3. Make a running balance sheet in writing for yourself as you read about each of the eight transactions in the text for the Wahoo Bank. Then determine if you understand the material by telling yourself (or a friend) the story for each transaction without using the text.

4. The **maximum amount of checkable-deposit expansion** is determined by multiplying two factors: the excess reserves by the monetary multiplier. Each factor, however, is affected by the required reserve ratio. The monetary multiplier is calculated by dividing 1 by the required reserve ratio. Excess reserves are determined by multiplying the required reserve ratio by the amount of new deposits. Thus, a change in the required reserve ratio will change the monetary multiplier and the amount of excess reserves. For example, a required reserve ratio of 25% gives a monetary multiplier of 4. For $100 in new money deposited, required reserves are $25 and excess reserves are $75. The maximum checkable-deposit expansion is $300 (4 × $75). If the reserve ratio drops to 20%, the monetary multiplier is 5 and excess reserves are $80, so the maximum checkable-deposit expansion is $400. Both factors have changed.

5. Be aware that the monetary multiplier can result in *money destruction* as well as money creation in the banking system. You should know how the monetary multiplier reinforces effects in one direction or the other.

■ IMPORTANT TERMS

fractional reserve banking system	**actual reserves**
balance sheet	**excess reserves**
required reserves	**reserve ratio**
vault cash	**federal funds rate**
	monetary multiplier

SELF-TEST

■ FILL-IN QUESTIONS

1. The banking system used today is a (total, fractional) ______________ reserve system, which means that (100%, less than 100%) ______________ of the money deposited in a bank is kept on reserve.

2. There are two significant characteristics to the banking system of today. Banks can create (reserves, money) ______________ depending on the amount of ______________ they hold. Banks are susceptible to (panics, regulation) ______________ or "runs," and to prevent this situation from happening, banks are subject to government ______________.

3. The balance sheet of a commercial bank is a statement of the bank's (gold account, assets) ______________, the claims of the owners of the bank, called (net worth, liabilities) ______________, and claims of the nonowners, called ______________. This relationship would be written in equation form as ______________.

4. The coins and paper money that a bank has in its possession are (petty, vault) ______________ cash or (till, capital) ______________ money.

5. When a person deposits cash in a commercial bank and receives a checkable deposit in return, the size of the money supply has (increased, decreased, not changed) ______________.

6. The legal reserve of a commercial bank (ignoring vault cash) must be kept on deposit at (a branch of the U.S. Treasury, its district Federal Reserve Bank) ______________.

7. The reserve ratio is equal to the commercial bank's (required, gold) ______________ reserves divided by its checkable-deposit (assets, liabilities) ______________.

8. The authority to establish and vary the reserve ratio within limits legislated by Congress is given to the (U.S. Treasury, Fed) ______________.

9. If commercial banks are allowed to accept (or create) deposits in excess of their reserves, the banking system is operating under a system of (fractional, currency) ______________ reserves.

10. The excess reserves of a commercial bank equal its (actual, required) ______________ reserves minus its ______________ reserves.

11. The basic purpose for having member banks deposit a legal reserve in the Federal Reserve Bank in their district is to provide (liquidity for, control of) ___________ the banking system by the Fed.

12. When a commercial bank deposits a legal reserve in its district Federal Reserve Bank, the reserve is (a liability, an asset) ___________ to the commercial bank and ___________ to the Federal Reserve Bank.

13. When a check is drawn on Bank X, deposited in Bank Y, and cleared, the reserves of Bank X are (increased, decreased, not changed) ___________ and the reserves of Bank Y are ___________; deposits in Bank X are (increased, decreased, not changed) ___________ and deposits in Bank Y are ___________.

14. A single commercial bank in a multibank system can safely make loans or buy government securities equal in amount to the (required, excess) ___________ reserves of that commercial bank.

15. When a commercial bank makes a new loan of $10,000, the supply of money (increases, decreases) ___________ by $___________. When a commercial bank buys a $10,000 government bond from a securities dealer, the supply of money (increases, decreases) ___________ by $___________.

16. A bank ordinarily pursues two conflicting goals; one goal is the desire to make money, or (profits, liquidity) ___________, and the other goal is the need for safety, or ___________.

17. When a bank lends temporary excess reserves held at its Federal Reserve Bank to other commercial banks that are temporarily short of legal reserves, it is participating in the (government securities, federal funds) ___________ market. The interest rate paid on these overnight loans is called the (government securities, federal funds) ___________ rate.

18. The monetary multiplier is equal to 1 divided by the (excess, required) ___________ reserve ratio. The greater the reserve ratio, the (larger, smaller) ___________ the monetary multiplier.

19. The banking system can make loans (or buy government securities) and create money in an amount equal to its (required, excess) ___________ reserves multiplied by the (required reserve ratio, monetary multiplier) ___________.

20. Assume that the required reserve ratio is 16.67% and the banking system is $6 million short of required reserves. If the banking system is unable to increase its reserves, the banking system must (increase, decrease) ___________ the money supply by ($6, $36) ___________ million.

■ TRUE–FALSE QUESTIONS

Circle T if the statement is true, F if it is false.

1. Goldsmiths increased the money supply when they accepted deposits of gold and issued paper receipts to the depositors. **T F**

2. Modern banking systems use gold as the basis for the fractional reserve system. **T F**

3. The balance sheet of a commercial bank shows the transactions in which the bank has engaged during a given period of time. **T F**

4. A commercial bank's assets plus its net worth equal the bank's liabilities. **T F**

5. Cash held by a bank is sometimes called vault cash. **T F**

6. When a bank accepts deposits of cash and puts them into a checking account, there has been a change in the composition of the money supply. **T F**

7. A commercial bank may maintain its legal reserve either as a deposit in its Federal Reserve Bank or as government bonds in its own vault. **T F**

8. The required reserves that a commercial bank maintains must equal its own checkable-deposit liabilities multiplied by the required reserve ratio. **T F**

9. The actual reserves of a commercial bank equal excess reserves plus required reserves. **T F**

10. Required reserves are sufficient to meet demands for the return of all funds that are held as checkable deposits at commercial banks. **T F**

11. Required reserves help the Fed control the lending ability of commercial banks. **T F**

12. The reserve of a commercial bank in the Federal Reserve Bank is an asset of the Federal Reserve Bank. **T F**

13. A check for $1000 drawn on Bank X by a depositor and deposited in Bank Y will increase the reserves in Bank Y by $1000. **T F**

14. A bank that has a check drawn and collected against it will lose to the recipient both reserves and deposits equal to the value of the check. **T F**

15. When Manfred Iron and Coal Company borrows $30,000 from a bank, the money supply has increased by $30,000. **T F**

16. A single commercial bank can safely lend an amount equal to its excess reserves multiplied by the monetary multiplier ratio. **T F**

17. The granting of a $5000 loan and the purchase of a $5000 government bond from a securities dealer by a commercial bank have the same effect on the money supply. **T F**

18. The selling of a government bond by a commercial bank will increase the money supply. **T F**

19. A commercial bank seeks both profits and liquidity, but these are conflicting goals. **T F**

20. The federal funds rate is the interest rate at which the federal government lends funds to commercial banks. **T F**

21. The reason that the banking system can lend by a multiple of its excess reserves, but each individual bank can only lend "dollar for dollar" with its excess reserves, is that reserves lost by a single bank are not lost to the banking system as a whole. **T F**

22. The monetary multiplier is excess reserves divided by required reserves. **T F**

23. The maximum checkable-deposit expansion is equal to excess reserves divided by the monetary multiplier. **T F**

24. If the banking system has $10 million in excess reserves and if the reserve ratio is 25%, the system can increase its loans by $40 million. **T F**

25. When a borrower repays a loan of $500, either in cash or by check, the supply of money is reduced by $500. **T F**

■ MULTIPLE-CHOICE QUESTIONS

Circle the letter that corresponds to the best answer.

1. The fractional reserve system of banking started when goldsmiths began
(a) accepting deposits of gold for safe storage
(b) issuing receipts for the gold stored with them
(c) using deposited gold to produce products for sale to others
(d) issuing paper money in excess of the amount of gold stored with them

2. The claims of the owners of the bank against the bank's assets is the bank's
(a) net worth
(b) liabilities
(c) balance sheet
(d) fractional reserves

3. When cash is deposited in a checkable-deposit account in a commercial bank, there is
(a) a decrease in the money supply
(b) an increase in the money supply
(c) no change in the composition of the money supply
(d) a change in the composition of the money supply

4. A commercial bank has actual reserves of $9000 and liabilities of $30,000, and the required reserve ratio is 20%. The excess reserves of the bank are
(a) $3000
(b) $6000
(c) $7500
(d) $9000

5. The primary reason commercial banks must keep required reserves on deposit at Federal Reserve Banks is to
(a) protect the deposits in the commercial bank against losses
(b) provide the means by which checks drawn on the commercial bank and deposited in other commercial banks can be collected
(c) add to the liquidity of the commercial bank and protect it against a "run" on the bank
(d) provide the Fed with a means of controlling the lending ability of the commercial bank

6. Reserves that a commercial bank deposits at a Federal Reserve Bank are
(a) an asset to the Federal Reserve Bank and a liability of the commercial bank
(b) an asset of the commercial bank and a liability of the Federal Reserve Bank
(c) used as insurance funds for the Federal Deposit Insurance Corporation
(d) used as insurance for the National Credit Union Administration

7. A depositor places $750 in cash in a commercial bank, and the reserve ratio is 33.33%; the bank sends the $750 to the Federal Reserve Bank. As a result, the *actual reserves* and the *excess reserves* of the bank have been increased, respectively, by
(a) $750 and $250
(b) $750 and $500
(c) $750 and $750
(d) $500 and $500

8. A bank that has a check drawn and collected against it will
(a) lose to the recipient bank both reserves and deposits
(b) gain from the recipient bank both reserves and deposits
(c) lose to the recipient bank reserves, but gain deposits
(d) gain from the recipient bank reserves, but lose deposits

9. A commercial bank has no excess reserves until a depositor places $600 in cash in the bank. The bank then adds the $600 to its reserves by sending it to the Federal Reserve Bank. The commercial bank then lends $300 to a borrower. As a consequence of these transactions the size of the money supply has
(a) not been affected
(b) increased by $300
(c) increased by $600
(d) increased by $900

10. A commercial bank has excess reserves of $500 and a required reserve ratio of 20%; it grants a loan of $1000 to a borrower. If the borrower writes a check for $1000 that is deposited in another commercial bank, the first bank will be short of reserves, after the check has been cleared, in the amount of
(a) $200
(b) $500
(c) $700
(d) $1000

11. The buying of government securities by commercial banks is most similar to the
(a) making of loans by banks because both actions increase the money supply

(b) making of loans by banks because both actions decrease the money supply
(c) repayment of loans to banks because both actions decrease the money supply
(d) repayment of loans to banks because both actions increase the money supply

12. A commercial bank sells a $1000 government security to a securities dealer. The dealer pays for the bond in cash, which the bank adds to its vault cash. The money supply has
(a) not been affected
(b) decreased by $1000
(c) increased by $1000
(d) increased by $1000 multiplied by the reciprocal of the required reserve ratio

13. A commercial bank has deposit liabilities of $100,000, reserves of $37,000, and a required reserve ratio of 25%. The amount by which a *single commercial bank* and the amount by which the *banking system* can increase loans are, respectively,
(a) $12,000 and $48,000
(b) $17,000 and $68,000
(c) $12,000 and $60,000
(d) $17,000 and $85,000

14. If the required reserve ratio were 12.5%, the value of the monetary multiplier would be
(a) 5
(b) 6
(c) 7
(d) 8

15. The commercial banking system has excess reserves of $700, makes new loans of $2100, and is just meeting its reserve requirements. The required reserve ratio is
(a) 20%
(b) 25%
(c) 30%
(d) 33.33%

16. The commercial banking system, because of a recent change in the required reserve ratio from 20% to 30%, finds that it is $60 million short of reserves. If it is unable to obtain any additional reserves it must decrease the money supply by
(a) $60 million
(b) $180 million
(c) $200 million
(d) $300 million

17. Only one commercial bank in the banking system has an excess reserve, and its excess reserve is $100,000. This bank makes a new loan of $80,000 and keeps an excess reserve of $20,000. If the required reserve ratio for all banks is 20%, the potential expansion of the money supply from this $80,000 loan is
(a) $80,000
(b) $100,000
(c) $400,000
(d) $500,000

Use the following balance sheet for the First National Bank to answer Questions 18, 19, 20, 21, and 22. Assume the required reserve ratio is 20%.

Assets		Liabilities and Net Worth	
Reserves	$ 50,000	Checkable deposits	$150,000
Loans	70,000	Stock shares	100,000
Securities	30,000		
Property	100,000		

18. This commercial bank has excess reserves of
(a) $10,000
(b) $20,000
(c) $30,000
(d) $40,000

19. This bank can safely expand its loans by a maximum of
(a) $50,000
(b) $40,000
(c) $30,000
(d) $20,000

20. Using the original bank balance sheet, assume that the bank makes a loan of $10,000 and has a check cleared against it for the amount of the loan; its reserves and checkable deposits will now be
(a) $40,000 and $140,000
(b) $40,000 and $150,000
(c) $30,000 and $150,000
(d) $60,000 and $140,000

21. Using the original bank balance sheet, assume that the bank makes a loan of $15,000 and has a check cleared against it for the amount of the loan; it will then have excess reserves of
(a) $5,000
(b) $10,000
(c) $15,000
(d) $20,000

22. If the original bank balance sheet was for the commercial banking *system*, rather than a single bank, loans and deposits could have been expanded by a maximum of
(a) $50,000
(b) $100,000
(c) $150,000
(d) $200,000

Answer Questions 23 and 24 on the basis of the following consolidated balance sheet for the commercial banking system. All figures are in billions. Assume that the required reserve ratio is 12.5%.

Assets		Liabilities and Net Worth	
Reserves	$ 40	Checkable deposits	$200
Loans	80	Stock shares	120
Securities	100		
Property	200		

23. The maximum amount by which this commercial banking system can expand the supply of money by lending is
(a) $120 billion
(b) $240 billion
(c) $350 billion
(d) $440 billion

24. If there is a deposit of $20 billion of new currency into checking accounts in the banking system, excess reserves will increase by
(a) $16.5 billion
(b) $17.0 billion
(c) $17.5 billion
(d) $18.5 billion

25. If the dollar amount of loans made in some period is less than the dollar amount of loans paid off, checkable deposits will
(a) expand and the money supply will increase
(b) expand and the money supply will decrease
(c) contract and the money supply will decrease
(d) contract and the money supply will increase

■ PROBLEMS

1. The following table shows the simplified balance sheet of a commercial bank. Assume that the figures given show the bank's assets and checkable-deposit liabilities *prior to each of the following four transactions.* Draw up the balance sheet as it would appear after each of these transactions is completed and place the balance-sheet figures in the appropriate column. Do *not* use the figures you place in columns **a**, **b**, and **c** when you work the next part of the problem; start all parts of the problem with the printed figures.

		(a)	(b)	(c)	(d)
Assets:					
Cash	$100	$____	$____	$____	$____
Reserves	200	____	____	____	____
Loans	500	____	____	____	____
Securities	200	____	____	____	____
Liabilities and net worth:					
Checkable deposits	900	____	____	____	____
Stock shares	100	100	100	100	100

a. A check for $50 is drawn by one of the depositors of the bank, given to a person who deposits it in another bank, and cleared (column a).
b. A depositor withdraws $50 in cash from the bank, and the bank restores its vault cash by obtaining $50 in additional cash from its Federal Reserve Bank (column b).
c. A check for $60 drawn on another bank is deposited in this bank and cleared (column c).
d. The bank sells $100 in government bonds to the Federal Reserve Bank in its district (column d).

2. Following are five balance sheets for a single commercial bank (columns 1a–5a). The required reserve ratio is 20%.
a. Compute the required reserves (A), ignoring vault cash, the excess reserves (B) of the bank (if the bank is short of reserves and must reduce its loans or obtain additional reserves, show this by placing a minus sign in front of the amounts by which it is short of reserves), and the amount of new loans it can extend (C).

	(1a)	(2a)	(3a)	(4a)	(5a)
Assets:					
Cash	$ 10	$ 20	$ 20	$ 20	$ 15
Reserves	40	40	25	40	45
Loans	100	100	100	100	150
Securities	50	60	30	70	60
Liabilities and net worth:					
Checkable deposits	175	200	150	180	220
Stock shares	25	20	25	50	50
A. Required reserves	$____	$____	$____	$____	$____
B. Excess reserves	____	____	____	____	____
C. New loans	____	____	____	____	____

b. In the following table, draw up for the individual bank the five balance sheets as they appear after the bank has made the new *loans* that it is capable of making.

	(1b)	(2b)	(3b)	(4b)	(5b)
Assets:					
Cash	$____	$____	$____	$____	$____
Reserves	____	____	____	____	____
Loans	____	____	____	____	____
Securities	____	____	____	____	____
Liabilities and net worth:					
Checkable deposits	____	____	____	____	____
Stock shares	____	____	____	____	____

3. The following table shows several reserve ratios. Compute the monetary multiplier for each reserve ratio and enter the figures in column 2. In column 3 show the maximum amount by which a single commercial bank can increase its loans for each dollar's worth of excess reserves it possesses. In column 4 indicate the maximum amount by which the banking system can increase its loans for each dollar's worth of excess reserves in the system.

(1)	(2)	(3)	(4)
12.50%	$____	$____	$____
16.67	____	____	____
20	____	____	____
25	____	____	____
30	____	____	____
33.33	____	____	____

4. The following table is the simplified consolidated balance sheet for all commercial banks in the economy. Assume that the figures given show the banks' assets and liabilities *prior to each of the following three transactions* and that the reserve ratio is 20%. Do *not* use the figures you placed in columns 2 and 4 when you begin parts **b** and **c** of the problem; start parts **a**, **b**, and **c** of the problem with the printed figures.

		(1)	(2)	(3)	(4)	(5)	(6)
Assets:							
Cash	$ 50	$___	$___	$___	$___	$___	$___
Reserves	100	___	___	___	___	___	___
Loans	200	___	___	___	___	___	___
Securities	200	___	___	___	___	___	___
Liabilities and net worth:							
Checkable deposits	500	___	___	___	___	___	___
Stock shares	50	50	50	50	50	50	50
Loans for Federal Reserve	0	___	___	___	___	___	___
Excess reserves		___	___	___	___	___	___
Maximum possible expansion of the money supply		___	___	___	___	___	___

a. The public deposits $5 in cash in the banks and the banks send the $5 to the Federal Reserve, where it is added to their reserves. Fill in column 1. If the banking system extends the maximum amount of new loans that it is capable of extending, show in column 2 the balance sheet as it would then appear.

b. The banking system sells $8 worth of securities to the Federal Reserve. Complete column 3. Assuming the system extends the maximum amount of credit of which it is capable, fill in column 4.

c. The Federal Reserve lends $10 to the commercial banks; complete column 5. Complete column 6 showing the condition of the banks after the maximum amount of new loans that the banks are capable of making is granted.

■ SHORT ANSWER AND ESSAY QUESTIONS

1. How did the early goldsmiths come to issue paper money and then become bankers?

2. Explain the difference between a 100% and fractional reserve system of banking.

3. What are two significant characteristics of a fractional reserve system of banking?

4. Why does a bank's balance sheet balance?

5. Explain what happens to the money supply when a bank accepts deposits of cash.

6. What are legal reserves? How are they determined? How are legal reserves related to the reserve ratio?

7. Define the meaning of excess reserves. How are they calculated?

8. Explain why bank reserves can be an asset to the depositing commercial bank but a liability to the Federal Reserve Bank receiving them.

9. Do the reserves held by commercial banks satisfactorily protect the bank's depositors? Are the reserves of commercial banks needed? Explain your answers.

10. The owner of a sporting goods store writes a check on her account in a Kent, Ohio, bank and sends it to one of her suppliers, who deposits it in his bank in Cleveland, Ohio. How does the Cleveland bank obtain payment from the Kent bank? If the two banks were in Kent and New York City, how would one bank pay the other? How are the excess reserves of the two banks affected?

11. Explain why the granting of a loan by a commercial bank increases the supply of money.

12. Why is a single commercial bank able to lend safely only an amount equal to its excess reserves?

13. How does the buying or selling of government securities by commercial banks influence the money supply?

14. Commercial banks seek both profits and safety. Explain how the balance sheet of the commercial banks reflects the desires of bankers for profits and for liquidity.

15. What is the federal funds rate?

16. Discuss how the federal funds market helps banks reconcile the two goals of profits and liquidity.

17. No one commercial bank ever lends an amount greater than its excess reserves, but the banking system as a whole is able to extend loans and expand the money supply by an amount equal to the system's excess reserves multiplied by the reciprocal of the reserve ratio. Explain why this is possible and how the multiple expansion of deposits and money takes place.

18. What is the monetary multiplier? How does it work?

19. What would happen to the maximum checkable-deposit creation if the reserve ratio increased or if the reserve ratio decreased? Explain using numerical examples.

20. Why does the repayment of a loan decrease the supply of money?

ANSWERS

Chapter 15 Money Creation

FILL-IN QUESTIONS

1. fractional, less than 100%
2. money, reserves, panics, regulation
3. assets, net worth, liabilities, assets = liabilities + net worth
4. vault, till

5. not changed
6. its district Federal Reserve Bank
7. required, liabilities
8. Fed
9. fractional
10. actual, required
11. control of
12. an asset, a liability
13. decreased, increased, decreased, increased
14. excess
15. increases, 10,000, increases, 10,000
16. profits, liquidity
17. federal funds, federal funds
18. required, smaller
19. excess, monetary multiplier
20. decrease, $36

TRUE–FALSE QUESTIONS

1. F, p. 300
2. F, p. 300
3. F, p. 301
4. F, p. 301
5. T, p. 301
6. T, p. 302
7. F, pp. 302–303
8. T, p. 302
9. T, p. 303
10. F, p. 303
11. T, p. 303
12. F, p. 303
13. T, pp. 303–304
14. T, pp. 303–304
15. T, pp. 304–305
16. F, pp. 304–305
17. T, p. 306
18. F, p. 306
19. T, p. 306
20. F, p. 306
21. T, p. 307
22. F, p. 309
23. F, p. 309
24. T, p. 309
25. T, p. 311

MULTIPLE-CHOICE QUESTIONS

1. d, p. 300
2. a, p. 301
3. d, p. 302
4. a, p. 303
5. d, p. 303
6. b, p. 303
7. b, p. 303
8. a, pp. 303–304
9. b, pp. 304–305
10. b, pp. 304–305
11. a, p. 306
12. b, p. 306
13. a, pp. 307–308
14. d, p. 309
15. d, p. 309
16. c, p. 309
17. c, p. 309
18. b, p. 303
19. d, p. 303
20. b, pp. 303–305
21. a, pp. 303–305
22. b, pp. 307–309
23. a, p. 309
24. c, pp. 307–309
25. c, p. 311

PROBLEMS

1. Table

	(a)	(b)	(c)	(d)
Assets:				
Cash	$100	$100	$100	$100
Reserves	150	150	260	300
Loans	500	500	500	500
Securities	200	200	200	100
Liabilities and net worth:				
Checkable deposits	850	850	960	900
Stock shares	100	100	100	100

2. *a.* Table (and * below)

	(1a)	(2a)	(3a)	(4a)	(5a)
A. Required reserves	$35	$40	$30	$36	$44
B. Excess reserves	5	0	−5	4	1
C. New loans	5	0	*	4	1

b. Table (and * below)

	(1b)	(2b)	(3b)	(4b)	(5b)
Assets:					
Cash	$ 10	$ 20	$ 20	$ 20	$ 15
Reserves	40	40	25	40	45
Loans	105	100	*	104	151
Securities	50	60	30	70	60
Liabilities and net worth:					
Checkable deposits	180	200	*	184	221
Stock shares	25	20	25	50	50

*If an individual bank is $5 short of reserves it must either obtain additional reserves of $5 by selling loans, securities, or its own IOUs to the reserve bank or contract its loans by $25.

3. Table

(1)	(2)	(3)	(4)
12.50%	$8	$1	$8
16.67	$6	1	$6
20	$5	1	$5
25	$4	1	$4
30	$3.33	1	$3.33
33.33	$3	1	$3

4. Table

	(1)	(2)	(3)	(4)	(5)	(6)
Assets:						
Cash	$ 50	$ 50	$ 50	$ 50	$ 50	$ 50
Reserves	105	105	108	108	110	110
Loans	200	220	200	240	200	250
Securities	200	200	192	192	200	200
Liabilities and net worth:						
Checkable deposits	505	525	500	540	500	550
Stock shares	50	50	50	50	50	50
Loans from Federal Reserve	0	0	0	0	10	10
Excess reserves	4	0	8	0	10	0
Maximum possible expansion of the money supply	20	0	40	0	50	0

SHORT ANSWER AND ESSAY QUESTIONS

1. p. 300	**8.** p. 303	**15.** p. 307
2. p. 300	**9.** p. 303	**16.** p. 307
3. p. 300	**10.** pp. 303–304	**17.** pp. 307–309
4. p. 303	**11.** pp. 304–305	**18.** p. 309
5. pp. 301–302	**12.** p. 305	**19.** p. 309
6. p. 302	**13.** p. 306	**20.** p. 311
7. p. 303	**14.** p. 307	

CHAPTER 16

Interest Rates and Monetary Policy

Chapter 16 is the third chapter dealing with money and banking. It explains how the Federal Reserve affects output, income, employment, and the price level of the economy. Central bank policy designed to affect these variables is called **monetary policy,** the goal of which is price-level stability, full employment, and economic growth.

The work of the Fed focuses on the interest rate and supply and demand in the market for money. The total **demand for money** is made up of a **transactions demand** and an **asset demand for money.** Because money is used as a medium of exchange, consumers and business firms wish to hold money for transactions purposes. The quantity of money they demand for this purpose is directly related to the size of the economy's nominal GDP.

Money also is used as a store of value that creates an asset demand. Consumers and businesses who own assets may choose to have some of their assets in the form of money (rather than in stocks, bonds, goods, or property). Holding money, however, imposes a cost on those who hold it. This cost is the interest they lose when they own money rather than an interest-earning asset such as a bond. Consumers and businesses will demand less money for asset purposes when the rate of interest (the cost of holding money) is high and demand more money when the rate of interest is low; the quantity of money demanded as an asset is inversely related to the interest rate.

The total demand for money is the sum of the transactions demand and the asset demand. It is affected by both nominal GDP and the rate of interest. The total demand and the supply of money determine interest rates in the market for money. The inverse relationship between bond prices and interest rates helps this market adjust to shortages or surpluses of money.

The chapter explains how the Federal Reserve achieves its responsibility for **monetary policy.** In this discussion, attention should be paid to the following: (1) the important items on the balance sheet of the Federal Reserve Banks and (2) the four major tools available to the Federal Reserve to control monetary policy, and how the employment of these tools can affect the reserves, excess reserves, actual money supply, and money-creating potential of the banking system. The most important tool is the buying and selling of government securities in the open market.

The Federal Reserve targets the Federal funds rate because it is the interest rate it can best control. This rate is the interest rate that banks charge each other on overnight loans of temporary excess reserves. The Federal Reserve uses open-market operations to buy government securities and this increases the excess reserves of banks, thus lowering the Federal funds rate. In this case, the Federal Reserve is pursuing an expansionary monetary policy that increases the money supply and decreases interest rates. Conversely, the Federal Reserve can sell government securities and decrease excess reserves, and thus raise the Federal funds rate. In this case, the Federal Reserve is pursuing a restrictive monetary policy that decreases the money supply and increases interest rates.

The discussion of the Federal funds rate is followed with an explanation of how changes in the money supply ultimately affect the economy. They achieve this objective by describing how the demand for money and the supply of money determine the interest rate (in the market for money), and how the interest rate and the investment demand schedule determine the level of equilibrium GDP. The effects of an expansionary monetary policy or a restrictive monetary policy in this cause-effect chain are illustrated with examples and summarized in Table 16.3. Changes in monetary policy shift aggregate demand across the aggregate supply curve, thus changing real output and the price level.

One of the concluding sections of the chapter evaluates monetary policy. The major strengths are related to its speed and flexibility and isolation from political pressures. As you will learn, the Federal Reserve has been quite active in recent years in using monetary policy to counter recession by lowering the interest rate and using other innovations to expand the flow of money and credit in the economy.

Monetary policy, however, is not without its problems or complications. There can be lags between the time actions are taken and the time the monetary policy influences economic activity. Monetary policy also can suffer from cyclical asymmetry by being more influential in controlling inflation than in preventing recessions. In this respect, the Fed faces the problem of a liquidity trap. When the Fed uses its monetary policy tools to make liquidity available to banks, banks can still be reluctant to lend money because of ongoing concerns about the economic health of the economy.

The *Last Word* for this chapter is a figure that gives you the "big picture." It is important because it gives you an overview of the economic factors and government policies that affect aggregate demand and aggregate supply. It summarizes much of the economic theory and policy that have been discussed in this chapter and ones that preceded it.

■ CHECKLIST

When you have studied this chapter you should be able to

☐ Explain what interest is and why it is important.
☐ Give a definition of the transactions demand for money.

☐ Give a definition of the asset demand for money.
☐ Illustrate graphically how the transactions and asset demands for money combine to form the total demand for money.
☐ Describe the market for money and what determines the equilibrium rate of interest.
☐ Explain how changes in nominal GDP and in the money supply affect the interest rate.
☐ Illustrate with an example how disequilibrium in the market for money is corrected through changes in bond prices.
☐ List the important assets and liabilities of the Federal Reserve Banks.
☐ Identify the four tools of monetary policy.
☐ Explain how the Federal Reserve can expand the money supply by buying government securities from commercial banks and from the public.
☐ Explain how the Federal Reserve can contract the money supply by selling government securities to commercial banks and to the public.
☐ Describe how raising or lowering the reserve ratio can increase or decrease the money supply.
☐ Illustrate how raising or lowering the discount rate can increase or decrease the money supply.
☐ Explain how the Federal Reserve uses the term auction facility to alter bank reserves and bank lending.
☐ Discuss the relative importance of monetary policy tools.
☐ Explain how the Federal Reserve uses monetary policy to target the Federal funds rate.
☐ Describe the actions the Fed can take to pursue an expansionary monetary policy.
☐ Describe the relationship between the Federal funds rate and the prime interest rate.
☐ Describe the actions the Fed can take to pursue a restrictive monetary policy.
☐ Explain the Taylor rule and its implications for monetary policy.
☐ Draw the demand-for-money and the supply-of-money curves and use them to show how a change in the supply of money will affect the interest rate in the market for money.
☐ Draw an investment demand curve to explain the effects of changes in the interest rate on investment spending.
☐ Construct an aggregate supply and aggregate demand graph to show how aggregate demand and the equilibrium level of GDP are affected by changes in interest rates and investment spending.
☐ Use a cause-effect chain to explain the links between a change in the money supply and a change in the equilibrium level of GDP when there is an expansionary monetary policy and a restrictive monetary policy.
☐ List several advantages of monetary policy over fiscal policy.
☐ Evaluate recent monetary policy in the United States.
☐ Describe two problems or complications of monetary policy.
☐ Summarize the key factors and policies affecting aggregate supply and demand, and the level of output, employment, income, and prices in an economy (*Last Word*).

■ CHAPTER OUTLINE

1. The fundamental ***goal of monetary policy*** is to achieve and maintain price stability, full employment, and economic growth. The Federal Reserve can accomplish this goal by exercising control over the amount of excess reserves held by commercial banks, and thereby influencing the size of the money supply and the total level of spending in the economy.

2. ***Interest*** is the price paid for the use of money. Although there are many interest rates, the text uses the generic term "interest rate" for the purposes of this chapter. This interest rate is determined by demand and supply in the market for money.

a. Business firms and households wish to hold and, therefore, demand money for two reasons.

(1) Because they use money as a medium of exchange, they have a ***transactions demand for money*** that is directly related to the nominal gross domestic product (GDP) of the economy.

(2) Because they also use money as a store of value, they have an ***asset demand for money*** that is inversely related to the rate of interest.

(3) Their ***total demand for money*** is the sum of the transactions demand and asset demand for money.

b. In the ***market for money,*** the demand for money and the supply of money determine the equilibrium interest rate. Graphically, the demand for money is a downsloping line and the supply of money is a vertical line, and their intersection determines the equilibrium interest rate.

c. Disequilibrium in this market is corrected by changes in **bond prices** and their inverse relationship with interest rates.

(1) If there is a decrease in the money supply, there will be a shortage of money, so bonds will be sold to obtain money. The increase in supply of bonds will drive down bond prices, causing interest rates to rise until the shortage of money is eliminated.

(2) If there is an increase in the money supply, there will be a surplus of money, so bonds will be bought. The increased demand for bonds will drive up bond prices, causing interest rates to fall until the surplus of money is eliminated.

3. By examining the consolidated ***balance sheet*** and the principal assets and liabilities of the Federal Reserve Banks, an understanding of the ways the Federal Reserve can control and influence the reserves of commercial banks and the money supply can be obtained.

a. The principal ***assets*** of the Federal Reserve Banks are U.S. government securities and loans to commercial banks.

b. The principal ***liabilities*** are Federal Reserve Notes (outstanding), the reserve deposits of commercial banks, and U.S. Treasury deposits.

4. The Federal Reserve Banks use four principal tools (techniques or instruments) to control the reserves of banks and the size of the money supply.

a. The Federal Reserve can *buy or sell government securities* through its ***open-market operations*** to change the excess reserves of banks and thus the lending ability of the banking system.

(1) Buying government securities in the open market from either banks or the public increases the excess reserves of banks.

(2) Selling government securities in the open market to either banks or the public decreases the excess reserves of banks.

b. The Federal Reserve can *raise or lower* the ***reserve ratio.***

(1) Raising the reserve ratio decreases the excess reserves of banks and the size of the monetary (checkable-deposit) multiplier.

(2) Lowering the reserve ratio increases the excess reserves of banks and the size of the monetary multiplier.

c. The Federal Reserve can *raise or lower* the ***discount rate.*** Raising the discount rate discourages banks from borrowing reserves from the Fed. Lowering the discount rate encourages banks to borrow from the Fed.

d. The Federal Reserve can auction off to banks the right to borrow reserves for a set period of time (usually 28 days) through its ***term auction facility.*** Banks submit bids for the amount of desired reserves and the interest rate they would pay for them. The equilibrium interest rate is the lowest rate that brings the quantity demanded and quantity supplied of reserves into balance. The use of such auctions by the Federal Reserve increases the excess reserves of banks.

e. Of the four main monetary tools, open-market operations is the most important because it is the most flexible and direct.

5. The ***Federal funds rate,*** the interest rate that banks charge each other for overnight loans of excess reserves, is a focus of monetary policy. The Federal Reserve can influence the Federal funds rate by buying or selling government securities. When the Federal Reserve buys bonds, banks have more excess reserves to lend overnight so the Federal funds rate falls. Conversely, when the Federal Reserve sells bonds, banks have fewer excess reserves to lend overnight so the Federal funds rate rises. A graph of the market for Federal funds has the interest rate on the vertical axis and the quantity of reserves on the horizontal axis. The demand for reserves is a down-sloping demand curve. The supply of reserves is a horizontal line at the desired rate because the supply of reserves is set by the Federal Reserve.

a. An ***expansionary monetary policy*** can be implemented by actions of the Federal Reserve to buy government securities in open-market operations to lower the Federal funds rate. This policy expands the money supply, putting downward pressure on other interest rates, and helps to stimulate aggregate demand. The ***prime interest rate*** is the benchmark rate that banks use to decide on the interest rate for loans to businesses and individuals; it rises and falls with the Federal funds rate.

b. A ***restrictive monetary policy*** can be implemented by actions of the Federal Reserve to sell government securities in open-market operations that raises the Federal funds rate. This policy contracts the money supply, putting upward pressure on other interest rates, and helps to reduce aggregate demand to maintain a stable price level.

c. The Federal Reserve does not target inflation or follow a monetary rule, but it does appear to be guided by a rule of thumb called the ***Taylor rule.*** It specifies conditions for raising and lowering the Federal funds rate based on the current rate of inflation and the relationship between potential and real GDP. For example, when real GDP equals potential GDP and the inflation rate is at its Fed target rate of 2 percent, then the real Federal funds rate should be 2 percent (or a 4 percent nominal rate). If real GDP should rise by 1 percent above potential GDP, the *real* Federal funds rate should increase by half a percentage point. Conversely, if real GDP should fall by 1 percent below potential GDP, the real Federal funds rate should decrease by half a percentage point.

6. Monetary policy affects the ***equilibrium GDP*** in many ways.

a. The cause-effect chain goes from the money market to investment spending to equilibrium GDP (see text Figure 16.5).

(1) In the market for money, the demand curve for money and the supply curve of money determine the real interest rate.

(2) This rate of interest in turn determines investment spending.

(3) Investment spending then affects aggregate demand and the equilibrium levels of real output and prices.

b. If recession or slow economic growth is a major problem, the Federal Reserve can institute an expansionary monetary policy that increases the money supply, causing the interest rate to fall and investment spending to increase, thereby increasing aggregate demand and increasing real GDP by a multiple of the increase in investment.

c. If inflation is the problem, the Federal Reserve can adopt a restrictive monetary policy that decreases the money supply, causing the interest rate to rise and investment spending to decrease, thereby reducing aggregate demand and controlling inflation.

7. Monetary policy is considered more important and valuable for stabilizing the national economy because of its several advantages over fiscal policy: it is quicker and more flexible; and it is more protected from political pressure.

a. Recent U.S. monetary policy has been expansionary and restrictive in response to concerns about recession and inflation (see the Federal funds rate in Figure 16.4 in the textbook).

(1) In late 2000 to late 2002, the Federal Reserve reduced the Federal funds rate to counter an economic slowdown and recession during that period.

(2) From mid-2004 through mid-2006, the Federal funds rate was raised to contain expected inflation as the economy experienced robust economic growth and it stayed high until mid-2007.

(3) From mid-2007 the rate was cut in response to the mortgage debt crisis and a term auction facility was initiated in December 2007 to increase the reserves of

commercial banks. Further rate cuts in 2008 and 2009 reduced the rate to a range of 0 percent to 0.25 percent, where it stayed.

(4) The Fed took quick and innovative actions and responses to counter the adverse effects of the financial crisis of 2007 and 2008 for which it has been praised. It also has been criticized for leaving the Federal funds rate too low from 2002 to 2004, thus helping set the stage for the financial crisis.

b. There are limitations and real-world complications with monetary policy in spite of its successes over the years.

(1) It is subject to a recognition lag between the time the need for the policy is recognized and also an operations lag that occurs between the time the policy is implemented and it begins to influence economic activity.

(2) There is a ***cyclical asymmetry*** with monetary policy: A restrictive monetary policy works better than an expansionary monetary policy. A restrictive policy seems to work better because the Federal Reserve can easily withdraw and absorb excess reserves from banks and curtail economic activity. An expansionary policy may not work because even when the Federal Reserve makes more reserves available to banks, the economic conditions of recession or slow growth may make businesses hesitant to increase their borrowing and increase their investment spending. In addition, the Fed faces the problem of a ***liquidity trap*** in achieving its goal. Just adding liquidity in the form of excess reserves for the banking system may not be sufficient to get banks to increase their lending and add liquidity to the economy if the banks fear an uncertain economic future and are worried about whether their loans will be repaid.

8. (*Last Word*). The ***"big picture" of macroeconomics*** shows that the equilibrium levels of output, employment, income, and prices are determined by the interaction of aggregate supply and aggregate demand. There are three major components of aggregate supply: the prices of inputs or resources, factors affecting the productivity with which resources are used, and the legal and institutional environment. There are four major components of aggregate demand: consumption, investment, government spending, and net export spending. Fiscal, monetary, or other government policies may have an effect on the components of aggregate demand or supply, which in turn will affect the level of output, employment, income, and prices.

■ HINTS AND TIPS

1. Spend extra time learning how the **total demand for money** is determined (see Figure 16.1 in the text). The total demand for money is composed of the transactions and the asset demands for money. The **transactions demand for money** is influenced by the level of nominal GDP and is not affected by the interest rate, so it *is graphed as a vertical line.* The **asset demand for money** is affected by the interest rate, so it *is graphed as a down-sloping curve.* The total demand for money is also graphed as a *down-sloping curve* because of the influence of the asset demand, but the curve is shifted farther to the right than the asset demand curve because of the influence of the transactions demand.

2. One of the most difficult concepts to understand is the *inverse* relationship between bond prices and interest rates. The simple explanation is that interest yield from a bond is the ratio of the *fixed* annual interest payment to the bond price. The numerator is fixed, but the denominator (bond price) is variable. If the bond price falls, the interest yield on the bond rises because the fixed annual interest payment is being divided by a smaller denominator.

3. To acquire a thorough knowledge of how the Federal Reserve transactions affect required reserves, excess reserves, the actual money supply, and the potential money supply, carefully study the **balance sheets** that are used to explain these transactions. The items to watch are the reserves and checkable deposits. Be sure that you know why a change is made in each balance sheet, and be able to make the appropriate balance-sheet entries as you trace through the effects of each transaction. Problem 2 in this chapter provides additional practice.

4. You must understand and remember the **cause-effect chain of monetary policy.** The best way to learn it is to draw your own chain (graphs) that shows the links for an expansionary monetary policy and for a restrictive monetary policy as in Figure 16.5. Then check each step for how monetary policy can be used to counter recession or limit inflation using Table 16.3 in the text.

5. The single most important figure for a **"big picture" of the macroeconomics** is the *Last Word.* It presents the determinants of aggregate supply and aggregate demand and identifies the key policy variables that have been discussed in this chapter and previous chapters.

■ IMPORTANT TERMS

monetary policy	**Federal funds rate**
transactions demand for money	**expansionary monetary policy**
asset demand for money	**prime interest rate**
total demand for money	**restrictive monetary policy**
open-market operations	**Taylor rule**
reserve ratio	**cyclical asymmetry**
discount rate	**liquidity trap**
term auction facility	

SELF-TEST

■ FILL-IN QUESTIONS

1. The goal of monetary policy in the United States is to achieve and maintain stability in the (price level, tax level) _______________, a rate of (full, partial) _______________ employment in the economy, and economic growth.

2. The transactions demand varies (directly, inversely) ______________ with (the rate of interest, nominal GDP) ______________, and the asset demand varies (directly, inversely) ______________ with (the rate of interest, nominal GDP) ______________.

3. The sum of the transactions and asset demands for money is the total (demand, supply) ______________ of money, and the intersection of it with the ______________ of money determines the equilibrium (interest rate, price level) ______________.

4. When the quantity of money demanded exceeds the quantity of money supplied, bond prices (increase, decrease) ______________ and interest rates ______________. When the quantity of money demanded is less than the quantity of money supplied, bond prices (increase, decrease) ______________ and interest rates ______________.

5. The two important assets of the Federal Reserve Banks are (Treasury deposits, government securities) ______________ and (reserves of, loans to) ______________ commercial banks. The three major liabilities are (Treasury deposits, government securities) ______________, (reserves of, loans to) ______________ commercial banks, and (government securities, Federal Reserve Notes) ______________.

6. The four tools the monetary authority uses to control the money supply are (open, closed) ______________-market operations, changing the (loan, reserve) ______________ ratio, changing the (prime interest, discount) ______________ rate, and using a term (action, auction) ______________ facility to lend reserves to banks for a set term. The most effective and most often used tool of monetary policy is a change in (the reserve ratio, open-market operations) ______________.

7. When the Federal Reserve Banks buy government securities in the open market, the reserves of commercial banks will (increase, decrease) ______________ and when they sell government securities in the open market, the reserves of commercial banks will ______________.

8. If the Federal Reserve Banks were to sell $10 million in government bonds to the *public* and the reserve ratio were 25 percent, the supply of money would immediately be reduced by $______________, the reserves of commercial banks would be reduced by $______________, and the excess reserves of the banks would be reduced by $______________. But if these bonds were sold to the commercial banks, the supply of money would immediately be reduced by $______________, the reserves of the banks would be reduced by $______________, and the excess reserves of the banks would be reduced by $______________.

9. An increase in the reserve ratio will (increase, decrease) ______________ the size of the monetary multiplier and ______________ the excess reserves held by commercial banks, thus causing the money supply to (increase, decrease) ______________. A decrease in the reserve ratio will (increase, decrease) ______________ the size of the monetary multiplier and ______________ the excess reserves held by commercial banks, thus causing the money supply to (increase, decrease) ______________.

10. If the Federal Reserve Banks were to lower the discount rate, commercial banks would tend to borrow (more, less) ______________ from them, and this would (increase, decrease) ______________ their excess reserves.

11. A fourth tool the Federal Reserve can use for altering the excess reserves of banks is the (Taylor rule, term auction facility) ______________. With this tool, the Federal Reserve specifies the amount of reserves banks can (lend, borrow) ______________ for a specific period of time, and then banks submit bids stating the amount of reserves they want and the (exchange, interest) ______________ rate they will pay. The rate for all reserves is set at the (lowest, highest) ______________ rate bid by a bank that also ensures all available reserves will be taken by the banks.

12. The interest rate that banks charge one another for overnight loans is the (prime interest, Federal funds) ______________ rate, but the rate banks use as a benchmark for setting interest rates on loans is the ______________ rate. The (prime interest, Federal funds) ______________ rate is the focus of the monetary policy of the Federal Reserve.

13. An expansionary monetary policy would be characterized by actions of the Federal Reserve to (increase, decrease) ______________ the discount rate, ______________ reserve ratios, and (buy, sell) ______________ government bonds, whereas a restrictive monetary policy would include actions taken to (increase, decrease) ______________ the discount rate, ______________ reserve ratios, and (buy, sell) ______________ government bonds.

14. There is a cause-effect chain of monetary policy.

a. In the market for money, the demand for and the supply of money determine the equilibrium rate of (discount, interest) ______________.

b. This rate in turn determines the level of (government, investment) ______________ spending based on the ______________ demand curve.

c. This spending in turn affects aggregate (demand, supply) ______________, and the intersection of aggregate supply and demand determines the equilibrium level of real (interest, GDP) ______________ and the (discount, price) ______________ level.

15. This cause-effect chain can be illustrated with examples.

a. When there is an *increase* in the money supply curve, the real interest rate will (increase, decrease) ______________, investment spending will ______________, aggregate demand will (increase, decrease) ______________, and real GDP will ______________.

b. When there is a *decrease* in the money supply curve, the real interest rate will (increase, decrease) ______________, investment spending will ______________, aggregate demand will (increase, decrease) ______________, and real GDP will ______________.

16. To eliminate inflationary pressures in the economy, the traditional view holds that the monetary authority should seek to (increase, decrease) ______________ the reserves of commercial banks; this would tend to ______________ the money supply and to (increase, decrease) ______________ the rate of interest, and this in turn would cause investment spending, aggregate demand, and GDP to ______________. This action by monetary authorities would be considered (an easy, a tight) ______________ money policy.

17. If there were a serious problem with economic growth and unemployment in the economy, the Federal Reserve would typically pursue (an expansionary, a restrictive) ______________ monetary policy, in which case the Federal Reserve would (buy, sell) ______________ government bonds as a way of (increasing, decreasing) ______________ the money supply, and thereby ______________ interest rates; these events would have the effect of (increasing, decreasing) ______________ investment spending and thus ______________ real GDP.

18. An increase in the money supply will shift the aggregate (supply, demand) ______________ curve to the (right, left) ______________. A decrease in the money supply will shift the aggregate (supply, demand) ______________ curve to the (right, left) ______________. If the marginal propensity to consume is .75, then the multiplier will be (3, 4) ______________, and an initial increase in investment of $10 billion will (increase, decrease) ______________ aggregate demand by ($30, $40) ______________ billion.

19. Monetary policy has strengths. Compared to fiscal policy, monetary policy is speedier and (more, less) ______________ flexible, and ______________ isolated from political pressure. Since 1990, the Federal Reserve has been successful in countering recession by (raising, lowering) ______________ the Federal funds rate, and it has been successful in limiting inflation by ______________ the Federal funds rate.

20. Monetary policy has shortcomings and problems, too. It may be subject to timing (limits, lags) ______________ that occur between the time a need is recognized and the policy takes effect. It may be more effective in counteracting (recession, inflation) ______________ than ______________ because of cyclical asymmetry. When the Fed adds reserves to the banking system, banks may not increase their lending because of concerns about the economic health in the economy; thus the Fed may not be able to achieve its monetary policy goal because of this (moral hazard, liquidity trap) ______________.

■ TRUE–FALSE QUESTIONS

Circle T if the statement is true, F if it is false.

1. The goal of monetary policy is to lower interest rates. **T F**

2. There is a transactions demand for money because households and business firms use money as a store of value. **T F**

3. An increase in the price level would increase the transactions demand for money. **T F**

4. An increase in the nominal GDP, other things remaining the same, will increase both the total demand for money and the equilibrium rate of interest in the economy. **T F**

5. Bond prices and interest rates are inversely related. **T F**

6. The securities owned by the Federal Reserve Banks are almost entirely U.S. government bonds. **T F**

7. If the Federal Reserve Banks buy $15 in government securities from the public in the open market, the effect will be to increase the excess reserves of commercial banks by $15. **T F**

8. When the Federal Reserve sells securities in the open market, the price of these securities falls. **T F**

9. A change in the reserve ratio will affect the multiple by which the banking system can create money, but it will not affect the actual or excess reserves of member banks. **T F**

10. An increase in the required reserve ratio will increase the lending capacity of banks. **T F**

11. If the reserve ratio is lowered, some required reserves are turned into excess reserves. **T F**

12. When commercial banks borrow from the Federal Reserve Banks at the discount rate, they increase their excess reserves and their money-creating potential. **T F**

13. The Federal Reserve uses the term auction facility to increase the money supply by auctioning off a specific amount of reserves that banks can borrow for a short time period. **T F**

14. The least effective and least used tool of monetary policy is the open-market operations, in which government securities are bought and sold. **T F**

15. The Federal Reserve announces its changes in monetary policy by changing its targets for the Federal funds rate. **T F**

16. To increase the Federal funds interest rate, the Federal Reserve buys bonds in the open market to increase the excess reserves of banks. **T F**

17. The prime interest rate is the rate that banks charge other banks for overnight loans of excess reserves at Federal Reserve banks. **T F**

18. If the monetary authority wished to follow a restrictive monetary policy, it would sell government securities in the open market. **T F**

19. The Taylor rule provides a rule of thumb that is used for calculating the target that the Federal Reserve is likely to set for the Federal funds rate. **T F**

20. In the cause-effect chain, an expansionary monetary policy increases the money supply, decreases the interest rate, increases investment spending, and increases aggregate demand. **T F**

21. A restrictive monetary policy is designed to correct a problem of high unemployment and sluggish economic growth. **T F**

22. It is generally agreed that fiscal policy is more effective than monetary policy in controlling the business cycle because fiscal policy is more flexible. **T F**

23. Monetary policy is subject to more political pressure than fiscal policy. **T F**

24. Monetary policy is limited by a time lag that occurs from when the problem is recognized to when the policy becomes operational. **T F**

25. An expansionary monetary policy suffers from a "You can lead a horse to water, but you can't make the horse drink" problem. **T F**

■ MULTIPLE-CHOICE QUESTIONS

Circle the letter that corresponds to the best answer.

1. The organization directly responsible for monetary policy in the United States is the
- **(a)** U.S. Treasury
- **(b)** Federal Reserve
- **(c)** Internal Revenue Service
- **(d)** Congress of the United States

2. If the dollars held for transactions purposes are, on the average, spent five times a year for final goods and services, then the quantity of money people will wish to hold for transactions is equal to
- **(a)** five times the nominal GDP
- **(b)** 20% of the nominal GDP
- **(c)** five divided by the nominal GDP
- **(d)** 20% divided by the nominal GDP

3. There is an asset demand for money because money is
- **(a)** a store of value
- **(b)** a measure of value
- **(c)** a medium of exchange
- **(d)** a standard of deferred payment

4. An increase in the rate of interest would increase
- **(a)** the opportunity cost of holding money
- **(b)** the transactions demand for money
- **(c)** the asset demand for money
- **(d)** the prices of bonds

Use the table below to answer Questions 5 and 6. Assume the transactions demand for money is equal to 10% of the nominal GDP, the supply of money is $450 billion, and the asset demand for money is that shown in the table.

Interest Rate	Asset demand (billions)
14%	$100
13	150
12	200
11	250

5. If the nominal GDP is $3000 billion, the equilibrium interest rate is
- **(a)** 14%
- **(b)** 13%
- **(c)** 12%
- **(d)** 11%

6. If the nominal GDP is $3000 billion, an increase in the money supply from $450 billion to $500 billion would cause the equilibrium interest rate to
- **(a)** rise to 14%
- **(b)** fall to 11%
- **(c)** fall to 12%
- **(d)** remain unchanged

7. The total quantity of money demanded is
- **(a)** directly related to nominal GDP and the rate of interest
- **(b)** directly related to nominal GDP and inversely related to the rate of interest

(c) inversely related to nominal GDP and directly related to the rate of interest
(d) inversely related to nominal GDP and the rate of interest

8. The stock of money is determined by the Federal Reserve System and does not change when the interest rate changes; therefore, the
(a) supply of money curve is down-sloping
(b) demand for money curve is down-sloping
(c) supply of money curve is up-sloping
(d) supply of money curve is vertical

9. Which one of the following points would be true?
(a) Bond prices and the interest rate are directly related.
(b) A lower interest rate raises the opportunity cost of holding money.
(c) The supply of money is directly related to the interest rate.
(d) The total demand for money is inversely related to the interest rate.

Answer Questions 10 and 11 on the basis of the following information: Bond price = $10,000; bond fixed annual interest payment = $1000; bond annual rate of interest = 10%.

10. If the price of this bond decreases by $2500, the interest rate in effect will
(a) decrease by 1.1 percentage points
(b) decrease by 1.9 percentage points
(c) increase by 2.6 percentage points
(d) increase by 3.3 percentage points

11. If the price of this bond increases by $2000, the interest rate in effect will
(a) decrease by 1.7 percentage points
(b) decrease by 2.4 percentage points
(c) increase by 1.1 percentage points
(d) increase by 2.9 percentage points

12. The largest single asset in the Federal Reserve Banks' consolidated balance sheet is
(a) securities
(b) the reserves of commercial banks
(c) Federal Reserve Notes
(d) loans to commercial banks

13. The largest single liability of the Federal Reserve Banks is
(a) securities
(b) the reserves of commercial banks
(c) Federal Reserve Notes
(d) loans to commercial banks

14. Assume that there is a 20% reserve ratio and that the Federal Reserve buys $100 million worth of government securities. If the securities are purchased from the public, this action has the potential to increase bank lending by a maximum of
(a) $500 million, but only by $400 million if the securities are purchased directly from commercial banks
(b) $400 million, but by $500 million if the securities are purchased directly from commercial banks
(c) $500 million, and also by $500 million if the securities are purchased directly from commercial banks
(d) $400 million, and also by $400 million if the securities are purchased directly from commercial banks

15. Assuming that the Federal Reserve Banks sell $20 million in government securities to commercial banks and the reserve ratio is 20%, then the effect will be
(a) to reduce the actual supply of money by $20 million
(b) to reduce the actual supply of money by $4 million
(c) to reduce the potential money supply by $20 million
(d) to reduce the potential money supply by $100 million

16. Lowering the reserve ratio
(a) changes required reserves to excess reserves
(b) increases the amount of excess reserves banks must keep
(c) increases the discount rate
(d) decreases the discount rate

17. Commercial bank borrowing from the Federal Reserve
(a) is not permitted because of the Federal Reserve Act
(b) is permitted but only for banks that are bankrupt
(c) decreases the excess reserves of commercial banks and their ability to offer credit
(d) increases the excess reserves of commercial banks and their ability to offer credit

18. Which is the most important control used by the Federal Reserve to regulate the money supply?
(a) the reserve ratio
(b) open-market operations
(c) the discount rate
(d) term auction facility

19. The Federal funds rate is the rate that
(a) banks charge for overnight use of excess reserves held at the Federal Reserve banks
(b) banks charge for loans to the most creditworthy customers
(c) the Federal Reserve charges for short-term loans to commercial banks
(d) is charged for government bonds sold in the open-market operations of the Federal Reserve

20. When the Federal Reserve Banks decide to buy government bonds from banks and the public, the supply of reserves in the Federal funds market
(a) increases and the Federal funds rate decreases
(b) decreases and the Federal funds rate decreases
(c) increases and the Federal funds rate increases
(d) decreases and the Federal funds rate increases

21. When the Federal Reserve uses open-market operations to reduce the Federal funds rate several times over a year it is pursuing
(a) an expansionary monetary policy
(b) a restrictive monetary policy
(c) a prime interest rate policy
(d) a discretionary fiscal policy

22. The economy is experiencing high unemployment and a low rate of economic growth and the Fed decides to pursue an expansionary monetary policy. Which set of actions by the Fed would be most consistent with this policy?

(a) buying government securities and raising the reserve ratio
(b) selling government securities and raising the discount rate
(c) buying government securities and lowering the reserve ratio
(d) selling government securities and lowering the discount rate

23. The economy is experiencing inflation and the Federal Reserve decides to pursue a restrictive monetary policy. Which set of actions by the Fed would be most consistent with this policy?

(a) buying government securities and lowering the discount rate
(b) buying government securities and lowering the reserve ratio
(c) selling government securities and raising the discount rate
(d) selling government securities and lowering the discount rate

24. In the chain of cause and effect between changes in the excess reserves of commercial banks and the resulting changes in output and employment in the economy,

(a) an increase in excess reserves will decrease the money supply
(b) a decrease in the money supply will increase the rate of interest
(c) an increase in the rate of interest will increase aggregate demand
(d) an increase in aggregate demand will decrease output and employment

25. Which is most likely to be affected by changes in the rate of interest?

(a) tax rates
(b) investment spending
(c) government spending
(d) the imports of the economy

Use the following graph to answer Questions 26 and 27.

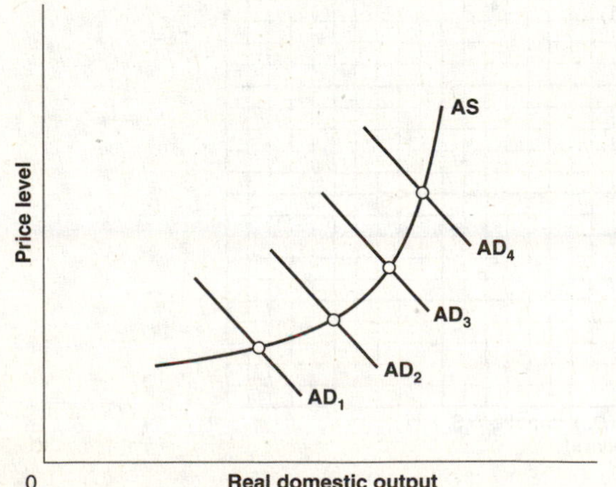

26. A shift from $\mathbf{AD_1}$ to $\mathbf{AD_2}$ would be most consistent with

(a) an increase in the reserve ratio by the Federal Reserve
(b) an increase in the discount rate by the Federal Reserve
(c) the buying of securities by the Federal Reserve
(d) the selling of securities by the Federal Reserve

27. Assume that the Federal Reserve lowers interest rates to increase investment spending. This monetary policy is most like to shift

(a) $\mathbf{AD_3}$ to $\mathbf{AD_2}$
(b) $\mathbf{AD_3}$ to $\mathbf{AD_4}$
(c) $\mathbf{AD_4}$ to $\mathbf{AD_3}$
(d) $\mathbf{AD_2}$ to $\mathbf{AD_1}$

28. A restrictive monetary policy would be most consistent with

(a) a decrease in the Federal funds rate and a decrease in the money supply
(b) a decrease in the Federal funds rate and an increase in the money supply
(c) an increase in the Federal funds rate and a decrease in the money supply
(d) an increase in the Federal funds rate and an increase in the money supply

29. Assume that monetary policy increases interest rates and results in a decrease in investment spending of $5 billion. If the marginal propensity to consume is .80, then aggregate demand is most likely to

(a) increase by $5 billion
(b) decrease by $5 billion
(c) increase by $25 billion
(d) decrease by $25 billion

30. Assume the Fed creates excess reserves that get added to the banking system, but banks decide not to increase their lending because they are worried about loans being paid back because of the poor economic health of the economy. This situation would best describe a

(a) moral hazard
(b) liquidity trap
(c) recognition lag
(d) transactions demand

■ PROBLEMS

1. The total demand for money is equal to the transactions demand plus the asset demand for money.

a. Assume each dollar held for transactions purposes is spent (on the average) four times per year to buy final goods and services.

(1) This means that transactions demand for money will be equal to (what fraction or percent) ________ of the nominal GDP, and,

(2) if the nominal GDP is $2000 billion, the transactions demand will be $________ billion.

b. The following table shows the number of dollars demanded for asset purposes at each rate of interest.

(1) Given the transactions demand for money in (*a*), complete the table.

Interest rate	Amount of money demanded (billions) For asset purposes	Total
16%	$ 20	$______
14	40	______
12	60	______
10	80	______
8	100	______
6	120	______
4	140	______

(2) On the following graph, plot the total demand for money (D_m) at each rate of interest.

c. Assume the money supply (S_m) is $580 billion.

(1) Plot this money supply on the graph.

(2) Using either the graph or the table, the equilibrium rate of interest is ______%.

d. Should the money supply

(1) increase to $600 billion, the equilibrium interest rate would (rise, fall) ______ to ______%.

(2) decrease to $540 billion, the equilibrium interest rate would ______ to ______%.

e. If the nominal GDP

(1) increased by $80 billion, the total demand for money would (increase, decrease) ______ by $______ billion at each rate of interest and the equilibrium rate of interest would (rise, fall) ______ by ______%.

(2) decreased by $120 billion, the total demand for money would ______ by $______ billion at each rate of interest and the equilibrium interest rate would ______ by ______%.

2. Suppose a bond with no expiration date pays a fixed $500 annually and sells for its face value of $5000.

a. Complete the following table and calculate the interest rate (to one decimal place) that would be obtained from the bond when the bond price is given or calculate the bond price when the interest rate is given.

Bond price	Interest rate
$4000	___.___%
$______	11.0
$5000	___.___
$5500	___.___
$______	8.0

b. Based on the results of the table, as the price increases on a bond with a fixed annual payment, the interest yield on the bond (decreases, increases)

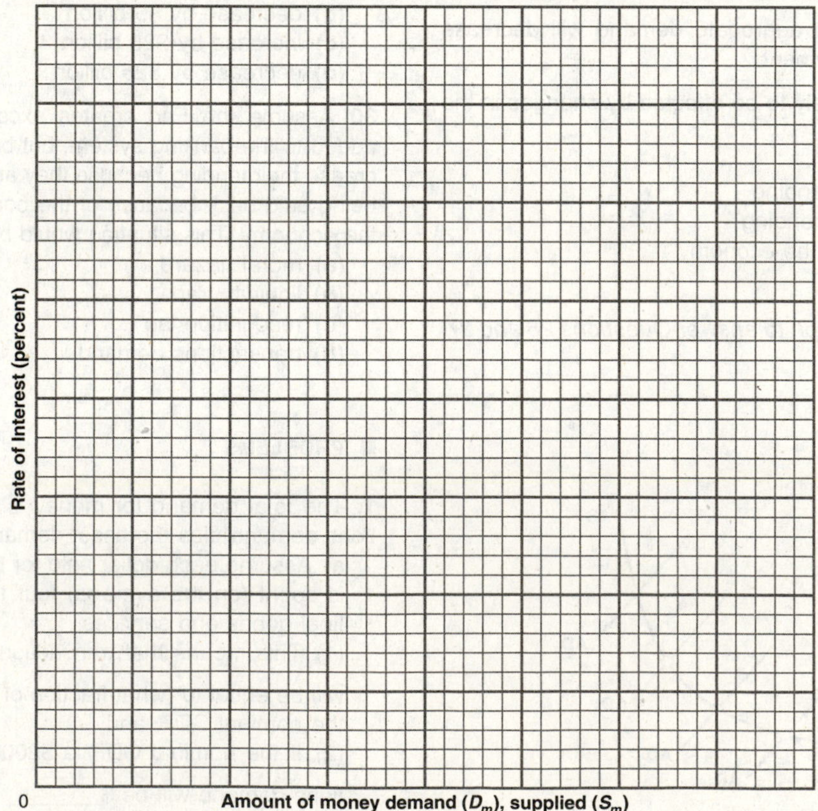

_______, but when the price of a bond decreases, the interest yield _______. Given this situation in an economy, you can conclude that a higher price for bonds (increases, decreases) _______ interest rates and that a lower price for bonds _______ interest rates.

3. Assume that the following consolidated balance sheet is for all commercial banks. Assume also that the required reserve ratio is 25% and that cash is *not* a part of the commercial banks' legal reserve.

Assets		Liabilities	
Cash	$ 50	Checkable deposits	$400
Reserves	100	Loans from Federal Reserve	25
Loans	150	Net worth	75
Securities	200		
	$ 500		$500

a. To *increase* the supply of money by $100, the Fed could (buy, sell) _______ securities worth $_______ in the open market.

b. To *decrease* the supply of money by $50, the Fed could (buy, sell) _______ securities worth $_______ in the open market.

4. At the bottom of this page are the consolidated balance sheets of the Federal Reserve and of the commercial banks. Assume that the reserve ratio for commercial banks is 25%, that cash is *not* a part of a bank's legal reserve, and that the figures in column 1 show the balance sheets of the Federal Reserve and the commercial banks *prior to each of the following five transactions.* Place the new balance sheet figures in the appropriate columns and complete A, B, C, D, and E in these columns. Do *not* use the figures you place in columns 2 through 5 when you work the next part of the problem; start all parts of the problem with the printed figures in column 1.

a. The Federal Reserve Banks sell $3 in securities to the public, which pays by check (column 2).

b. The Federal Reserve Banks buy $4 in securities from the commercial banks (column 3).

c. The Federal Reserve Banks lower the required reserve ratio for commercial banks to 20% (column 4).

d. The U.S. Treasury buys $5 worth of goods from U.S. manufacturers and pays the manufacturers by checks drawn on its accounts at the Federal Reserve Banks (column 5).

e. Because the Federal Reserve Banks have raised the discount rate, commercial banks repay $6 which they owe to the Federal Reserve (column 6).

5. On the graph on the next page is the demand-for-money curve that shows the amounts of money consumers and

	(1)	(2)	(3)	(4)	(5)	(6)
Federal Reserve Banks						
Assets:						
Gold certificates	$ 25	$_____	$_____	$_____	$_____	$_____
Securities	30	_____	_____	_____	_____	_____
Loans to commercial banks	10	_____	_____	_____	_____	_____
Liabilities:						
Reserves of commercial banks	50	_____	_____	_____	_____	_____
Treasury deposits	5	_____	_____	_____	_____	_____
Federal Reserve Notes	10	_____	_____	_____	_____	_____
Commercial Banks						
Assets:						
Reserves	$ 50	$_____	$_____	$_____	$_____	$_____
Securities	70	_____	_____	_____	_____	_____
Loans	90	_____	_____	_____	_____	_____
Liabilities:						
Checkable deposits	200	_____	_____	_____	_____	_____
Loans from Federal Reserve	10	_____	_____	_____	_____	_____
A. Required reserves		_____	_____	_____	_____	_____
B. Excess reserves		_____	_____	_____	_____	_____
C. How much has the money supply changed?		_____	_____	_____	_____	_____
D. How much more can the money supply change?		_____	_____	_____	_____	_____
E. What is the total of C and D?		_____	_____	_____	_____	_____

firms wish to hold at various rates of interest (when the nominal GDP in the economy is given).

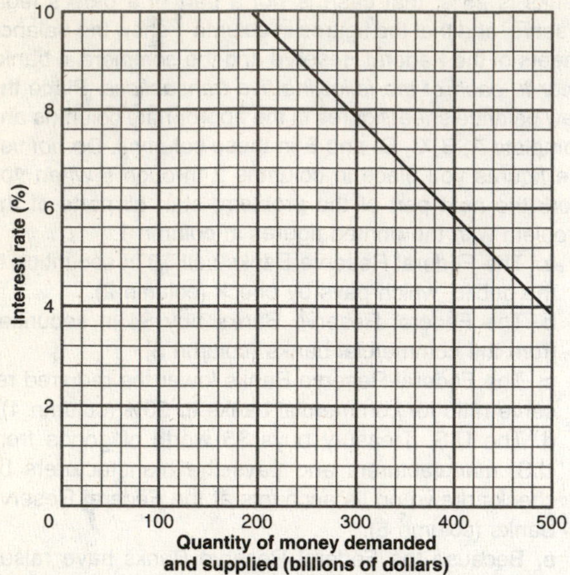

a. Suppose the supply of money is equal to $300 billion.
(1) Draw the supply-of-money curve on the above graph.
(2) The equilibrium rate of interest in the economy is

________%.

b. Below is a graph of an investment demand curve which shows the amounts of planned investment at various rates of interest. Given your answer to (2) above, how much will investors plan to spend for capital goods?

$________ billion.

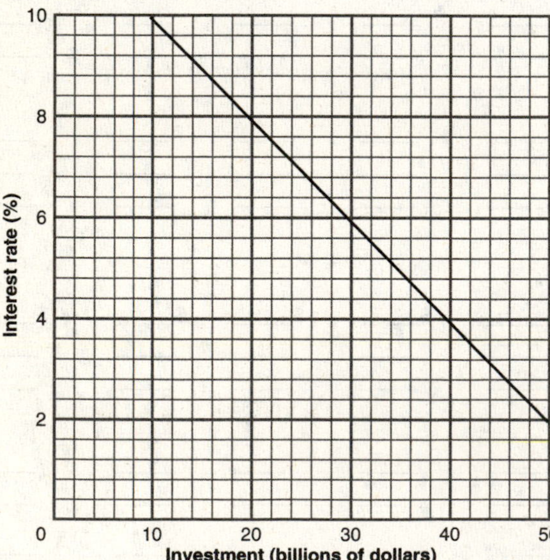

c. The following figure shows the aggregate supply (**AS**) curve in this economy. On the graph, draw an aggregate demand curve (**AD_1**) so that it crosses the **AS** in the middle of the curve. Label the price level (**P_1**) and output level (**Q_1**) associated with the intersection of **AD_1** and **AS**.

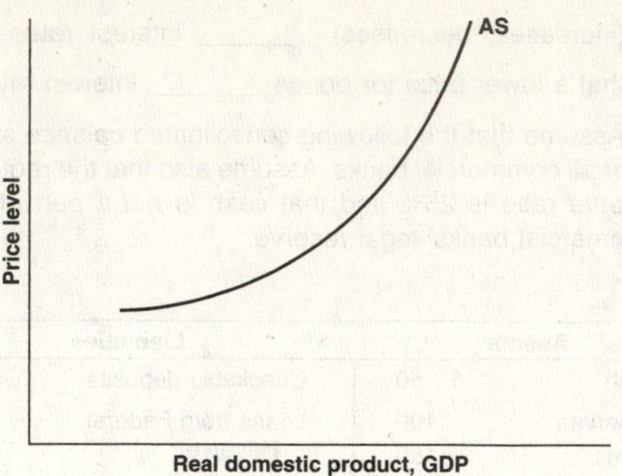

d. Now assume that monetary authorities increase the money supply to $400.
(1) On the market for money graph, plot the new money supply curve. The new equilibrium interest rate is ________%.
(2) On the investment graph, determine the level of investment spending that is associated with this new interest rate: $________ billion. By how much has investment spending increased as a result of the change in the interest rate? $________ billion.
(3) Assume that the marginal propensity to consume is .75. What is the multiplier? ________ By how much will the new investment spending increase aggregate demand? $________ billion.
(4) On the previous figure, indicate how the change in investment spending affects aggregate demand. Draw a new aggregate demand curve (**AD_2**) so that it crosses the **AS** curve. Also label the new price level (**P_2**) and output level (**Q_2**) associated with the intersection of **AD_2** and **AS**.

6. Columns 1 and 2 of the following table show the aggregate supply schedule. (The price level is a price index, and real domestic output is measured in billions of dollars.)

(1) Price level	(2) Real output	(3) AD_1	(4) AD_2
110	1600	1800	____
120	1700	1700	____
130	1790	1600	____
140	1800	1500	____
150	1940	1400	____
160	2000	1300	____

a. If the aggregate demand schedule were that shown in columns 1 and 3, the equilibrium real domestic output would be $________ billion and the price level would be ________.

b. Now assume that the Federal Reserve took actions to lower the Federal funds rate, and these actions increased investment spending in this economy by $60 billion. Also assume that the marginal propensity to consume in the economy was .8. How much would aggregate demand increase? $_______ billion

c. In column 4, enter this amount of increase in real domestic output at each price level to define the new **AD** schedule (**AD_2**).

d. What is the new equilibrium real domestic output? $_______ billion. And the new price level? _______.

■ SHORT ANSWER AND ESSAY QUESTIONS

1. What is the basic goal of monetary policy?

2. What are the two reasons people wish to hold money? How are these two reasons related to the functions of money?

3. Explain the determinant of each of the two demands for money and how a change in the size of these determinants will affect the amount of money people wish to hold.

4. The rate of interest is a price. Of what good or service is it the price? Explain how demand and supply determine this price.

5. Describe how changes in bond prices correct disequilibrium in the market for money. What is the relationship between bond prices and interest rates?

6. What are the important assets and liabilities of the Federal Reserve Banks?

7. Explain how the four monetary policy tools of the Federal Reserve Banks would be used to contract the supply of money. How would they be used to expand the supply of money?

8. What is the difference between the effects of the Federal Reserve's buying (selling) government securities in the open market from (to) commercial banks and from (to) the public?

9. Which of the monetary policy tools available to the Federal Reserve is most widely used? Why is it more important than other tools?

10. What happens to the Federal funds rate when the Federal Reserve expands or contracts the money supply through open-market operations?

11. What are the characteristics of an expansionary monetary policy? How does the Federal Reserve implement such policies?

12. What are the characteristics of a restrictive monetary policy? How does the Federal Reserve implement such policies?

13. What is the Taylor rule and how is it used?

14. Using four graphs, explain what determines (*a*) the equilibrium interest rate, (*b*) investment spending, and (*c*) the equilibrium GDP. Now use these four graphs to show the effects of a decrease in the money supply upon the equilibrium GDP.

15. Why are changes in the rate of interest more likely to affect investment spending than consumption and saving?

16. What policies will the Federal Reserve use to counter inflation, or unemployment and recession? Describe the effects on bank reserves, the money supply, interest rates, investment spending, aggregate demand, and real GDP from each policy.

17. What are the major strengths of monetary policy compared with fiscal policy?

18. Discuss how monetary policy has been used to counter recession and limit inflation since 2000.

19. What is meant by cyclical asymmetry and how does it apply to monetary policy?

20. Explain how a liquidity trap prevents the Fed from achieving its goals?

ANSWERS

Chapter 16 Interest Rates and Monetary Policy

FILL-IN QUESTIONS

1. price level, full
2. directly, nominal GDP, inversely, the rate of interest
3. demand, supply, interest rate
4. decrease, increase, increase, decrease
5. government securities, loans to, Treasury deposits, reserves of, Federal Reserve Notes
6. open, reserve, discount, auction, open-market operations
7. increase, decrease
8. 10 million, 10 million, 7.5 million, 0, 10 million, 10 million
9. decrease, decrease, decrease, increase, increase, increase
10. more, increase
11. term auction facility, borrow, interest, lowest
12. Federal funds, prime interest, Federal funds
13. decrease, decrease, buy, increase, increase, sell
14. *a.* interest; *b.* investment, investment; *c.* demand, GDP, price
15. *a.* decrease, increase, increase, increase; *b.* increase, decrease, decrease, decrease
16. decrease, decrease, increase, decrease, a tight
17. an expansionary, buy, increasing, decreasing, increasing, increasing
18. demand, right, demand, left, 4, increase, $40
19. more, more, lowering, raising
20. lags, inflation, recession, liquidity trap

TRUE–FALSE QUESTIONS

1. F, p. 314
2. F, p. 315
3. T, p. 315
4. T, pp. 315–317
5. T, p. 317
6. T, p. 318
7. F, p. 319
8. T, p. 321
9. F, pp. 321–322
10. F, pp. 321–322
11. T, p. 321
12. T, pp. 322–323
13. T, p. 323
14. F, p. 324
15. T, p. 324
16. F, pp. 324–325
17. F, pp. 325–326
18. T, p. 326
19. T, pp. 326–327
20. T, pp. 328–330
21. F, pp. 330–332
22. F, p. 332
23. F, p. 332
24. T, p. 333
25. T, p. 336

MULTIPLE-CHOICE QUESTIONS

1. b, p. 314
2. b, p. 315
3. a, p. 315
4. a, p. 315
5. b, pp. 315–317
6. c, pp. 315–317
7. b, pp. 315–317
8. d, p. 317
9. d, p. 317
10. d, p. 317
11. a, p. 317
12. a, p. 318
13. c, p. 318
14. b, pp. 319–320
15. d, pp. 320–321
16. a, p. 321
17. d, p. 322
18. b, p. 324
19. a, pp. 324–325
20. a, p. 325
21. a, pp. 325–386
22. c, pp. 325, 330–331
23. c, pp. 326, 331–332
24. b, pp. 328–330
25. b, pp. 329–330
26. c, pp. 329–331
27. b, pp. 330–331
28. c, p. 331
29. d, pp. 331–332
30. b, p. 336

PROBLEMS

1. *a.* (1) 1/4 (25%), (2) 500; *b.* (1) 520, 540, 560, 580, 600, 620, 640; *c.* (2) 10; *d.* (1) fall, 8, (2) rise, 14; *e.* (1) increase, 20, rise, 2, (2) decrease, 30, fall, 3

2. *a.* 12.5%, $4,545, 10.0%, 9.1%, $6,250; *b.* decreases, increases, decreases, increases

3. *a.* buy, 25; *b.* sell, 12 1/2

4. See below

5. *a.* (2) 8; *b.* 20; *c.* see Figure 16.5 in text; *d.* (1) 6, (2) 30, 10, (3) 4, 40, (4) see Figure 16.5 in text

6. *a.* 1700, 120; *b.* 300 (multiplier of 5 × $60 billion = $300 billion); *c.* 2100, 2000, 1900, 1800, 1700, 1600; *d.* 1800, 140

SHORT ANSWER AND ESSAY QUESTIONS

1. p. 314
2. p. 315
3. p. 315
4. pp. 316–317
5. p. 317
6. p. 318
7. pp. 320–323
8. pp. 319–321
9. pp. 323–324
10. pp. 324–325
11. pp. 325–326
12. p. 326
13. pp. 326–327
14. pp. 328–331
15. pp. 329–330
16. pp. 330–332
17. p. 332
18. pp. 332–333
19. p. 336
20. p. 336

	(2)	(3)	(4)	(5)	(6)
Federal Reserve Banks					
Assets:					
Gold certificates	$ 25	$ 25	$ 25	$ 25	$ 25
Securities	27	34	30	30	30
Loans to commercial banks	10	10	10	10	4
Liabilities:					
Reserves of commercial banks	47	54	50	55	44
Treasury deposits	5	5	5	0	5
Federal Reserve Notes	10	10	10	10	10
Commercial Banks					
Assets:					
Reserves	$ 47	$ 54	$ 50	$ 55	$ 44
Securities	70	66	70	70	70
Loans	90	90	90	90	90
Liabilities:					
Checkable deposits	197	200	200	205	200
Loans from Federal Reserve	10	10	10	10	4
A. Required reserves	49.25	50	40	51.25	50
B. Excess reserves	−2.25	4	10	3.75	−6
C. How much has the money supply changed?	−3	0	0	+5	0
D. How much more can the money supply change?	−9	+16	+50	+15	−24
E. What is the total of C and D?	−12	+16	+50	+20	−24

CHAPTER 17

Financial Economics

This chapter introduces you to financial economics—the study of investor preferences and how they affect the pricing and trading of financial assets such as stocks, bonds, and mutual funds. The chapter begins with a distinction between **financial investment,** which involves purchases of new or used assets for which there is an expected monetary return, and **economic investment,** which is spending for the production and accumulation of capital goods.

A central idea in financial economics is the concept of **present value.** This concept is important because it gives investors the ability to calculate the price to pay now for assets that will generate expected future payments. This concept is explained with the use of compound interest, a formula that shows how a given amount of money will grow over time if interest is paid on both the amount initially invested and on any interest payments. The compound interest formula is then rearranged to determine the present value that a person would have to invest in today's dollars to receive a certain dollar payment in the future. The present value formula has applications to decisions involving payouts from lotteries and how to structure deferred compensation or salary packages.

The chapter also discusses three popular financial assets—**stocks, bonds, and mutual funds.** It explains the key differences between these three assets in terms of ownership, risk, and return. A fundamental concept presented in this section is that the rate of return for an investment is inversely related to its price. As the price for a financial asset increases, its rate of return decreases, and vice versa.

One of the peculiar results of financial investments is that the rates of return for assets that are essentially identical will also be equal. The process that produces this result is **arbitrage.** If there are two identical assets and one has a higher rate of return than the other, then investors will purchase more of the asset with the higher rate of return, thus driving up its price and driving down its rate of return. Investors will sell the asset with the lower rate of return, thus driving down its price and increasing its rate of return. This process will continue until rates of return for the two assets are equal.

Risk is a major factor affecting financial assets. Some risk can be diversified by purchasing different types of assets with different returns that offset each other. Other risk is nondiversifiable and is measured with the use of beta, as you will learn in the chapter. A general relationship found with all types of financial assets is that the riskier the investment, the greater the compensation for bearing the risk that is demanded by investors, and thus the higher average return that is expected for such risky investments. One investment, however, is essentially risk-free and that would be the short-term U.S. government bonds. Such an investment is used to measure time preferences for consuming now or consuming in the future.

The last few sections of the chapter pull together all the previous material to present the **Security Market Line (SML)** and use it to discuss Federal Reserve policy. The SML shows that the average expected return for any investment is composed of two parts—one that compensates for time preference (as measured by a risk-free investment) and one that compensates for nondiversifiable risk (as measured by beta). It can be used to determine an investment's average expected rate of return based on its risk level—the higher the risk level, the higher the average rate of return. The Federal Reserve can shift the SML by changing the short-term interest rate. This action has the effect of changing the average expected return on all assets and changing the asset prices, thus influencing the direction of economic activity in the overall economy.

■ CHECKLIST

When you have studied this chapter you should be able to

☐ Distinguish between economic investment and financial investment.

☐ State the compound interest formula.

☐ Calculate the compound interest when you are given the interest rate, amount invested, and years of compounding.

☐ State the formula for calculating the present value of a future amount of money.

☐ Apply the present value formula to lottery and salary decisions.

☐ Describe the characteristics of stocks.

☐ Describe bonds and explain how they differ from stocks.

☐ Describe mutual funds and explain how they differ from stocks and bonds.

☐ Define the percentage rate of return for calculating investment returns.

☐ Explain why an investment's rate of return is inversely related to its price.

☐ Describe how the arbitrage process equalizes rates of return for investments with similar characteristics.

☐ Define diversification and its relationship to risk.

☐ Calculate the average expected rate of return when you are given investment data.
☐ Define beta as a measure of risk.
☐ Explain the relationship of risk and average expected returns.
☐ Describe what determines the risk-free rate of return.
☐ Define the two parts of the equation for the average expected rate of return.
☐ Use a graph to illustrate the features of the Security Market Line model.
☐ Explain how arbitrage affects average expected rates of return in the Security Market Line (SML).
☐ Use the SML to describe the effect of an increase in the risk-free interest rate by the Federal Reserve on the SML, financial assets, and the economy.
☐ Use the SML to explain how a decrease in the risk-free rate by the Federal Reserve during the Great Recession affected the SML, financial assets, and the economy.
☐ Explain why the rates of return on index mutual funds beat the rates of return on actively managed funds over time (*Last Word*).

■ CHAPTER OUTLINE

1. There is a difference between ***economic investment*** and ***financial investment.*** Economic investment refers to new additions to the nation's capital stock from building roads, factories, and houses. Financial investment refers to the purchase of an asset (new or used) with the expectation it will generate a monetary return. In this chapter, the general term "investment" will mean financial investment.

2. ***Present value*** states the current value or worth of returns or costs that are expected in the future. An investment's current price is equal to the present value of the investment's future returns.

a. The ***compound interest*** formula indicates how a given amount of money will increase if interest is paid on both the amount initially invested and also on any interest payments previously paid. The equation states that if X dollars are invested today at interest rate i and allowed to grow for t years, it will become $(1 + i)^t X$ dollars in t years.

b. The present value model uses the compound interest formula to calculate the present value that would have to be invested today to receive X dollars in t years. The equation states that an investment of $X/(1 + i)^t$ dollars today at interest rate i would increase to X dollars in t years.

c. Present value has applications to everyday experiences such as lottery payouts and deferred compensation. For example, the present value formula can be used to calculate how much a person who won the lottery would receive if that person took the winnings as a lump-sum payout instead of receiving equal payments spread over many years.

3. Many financial investments are available to people. Whatever the type, they share three characteristics. They require that investors pay a market price to obtain them; they give the asset owner the right to receive future payments; and the future payments are typically risky. The three most common and popular investments are stocks, bonds, and mutual funds.

a. ***Stocks*** are shares of ownership in corporations. Stocks have value because they give shareholders the right to receive any future profits produced by the corporations. Because of the ***limited liability rule,*** the risk of loss for investors is limited to the number of shares they own. Investors can gain from investing in profitable corporations because they can capture the ***capital gains*** (sell their shares at higher prices than they bought them) and they can often receive ***dividends,*** which are payouts of equal shares of the corporate profits. Stocks are risky because the future profits are unknown and it is possible for corporations to go ***bankrupt.***

b. ***Bonds*** are a type of debt or loan contract. Bonds give the holders the right to a fixed stream of future payments that serve to repay the loan or pay off the debt, so they are a more predictable investment than stocks. The risks from bonds involve possible ***default,*** or failure to make the promised payment by the corporations or government agencies that issued the bonds.

c. ***Mutual funds*** are a type of financial investment offered by companies that combine the money invested by many investors to buy a ***portfolio,*** which typically consists of a large number of stocks and/or bonds. The returns that are generated from these portfolios are owned by the individual investors and are paid to them. The risks from mutual funds are related to the risks of the stocks and bonds that they hold in their portfolios. Some funds are ***actively managed funds,*** with portfolio managers constantly trying to buy and sell stocks to maximize returns, while others are ***index funds*** that are ***passively managed funds*** that buy or sell assets to closely match a financial index.

d. The ***percentage rate of return*** for a financial asset is calculated by determining the change in value of the asset (gain or loss) and dividing it by the purchase price for the asset, and expressing the result as a percentage.

e. The rate of return for an investment is inversely related to its price. This means that the higher the price, the lower the rate of return.

4. ***Arbitrage*** is the process through the actions of investors which results in equalizing the average expected rates of return from assets that are very similar or identical. For example, if two identical assets have different rates of return, investors will buy the asset with the higher rate of return and sell the asset with the lower rate of return. As investors buy the asset with the higher rate of return, its price will increase and its average expected rate of return will decrease. As investors sell the asset with the lower rate of return, its price will decrease and its average expected rate of return will increase. The process continues until the average expected rates of return of the two assets converge and become equal.

5. ***Risk*** in financial investing means that future payments are uncertain, and many factors affect the degree of risk.

a. ***Diversification*** is a strategy designed to decrease investment risk in a portfolio by selecting a group of assets that have risks or returns that compensate each other, so that when returns on one investment are lower, they are offset by higher returns from another investment. Risk that can be eliminated by asset diversification is called ***diversifiable risk.*** Risk that cannot be eliminated by asset diversification is called ***nondiversifiable risk.*** An example of a nondiversifiable risk would be a general downturn in the economy that can simultaneously affect the returns of all investments in a similar way so that different assets do not have offsetting returns.

b. Investment decisions often involve comparing return and risk, especially nondiversifiable risk.

(1) Investors compare investments using ***average expected rates of return.*** This return is a ***probability-weighted average*** that gives higher weight to outcomes that are more likely to happen.

(2) ***Beta*** is a statistic measuring the nondiversifiable risk of an asset relative to the amount of nondiversifiable risk facing the ***market portfolio.*** This portfolio contains every asset trading in the financial markets, so it is diversified and consequently has eliminated all of its diversifiable risk and has only nondiversifiable risk.

c. There is a relationship between risk and average expected returns. Investors demand compensation for bearing risk. The riskier the asset, the higher its average expected rate of return will be. This relationship applies to all assets.

d. Rates of return compensate both for risk and time preference. Average expected rates of return must compensate for ***time preference*** because most people prefer to consume sooner rather than later. The rate of return that compensates *only* for time preference is assumed to be equal to the rate of interest from short-term U.S. government bonds. The return on these bonds is viewed as the ***risk-free interest rate*** because the U.S. government is almost 100% guaranteed to make its payments on time. The Federal Reserve has the power to set this interest rate and thereby influence the compensation for time preference across the economy.

6. An asset's average expected rate of return has two components. First there is the compensation for time preference which is the risk-free interest rate. Second, there is the compensation for nondiversifiable risk as measured by beta. This risk factor is often referred to by economists as the ***risk premium.*** The ***Security Market Line (SML)*** is a straight line that plots how the average expected rates of return on assets and portfolios in the economy must vary with their respective levels of nondiversifiable risk as measured by beta. The slope of the SML indicates how much investors dislike risk—a steeper slope shows that investors demand higher average expected rates of return for bearing increasingly large amounts of nondiversifiable risk and a flatter slope shows that investors require lower average expected rates of return to compensate them for risk bearing. Because of arbitrage, every asset in the economy should plot onto the SML.

a. The SML has several applications that are useful for understanding why investors follow the intentions and actions of the Federal Reserve.

(1) The ***Federal Reserve*** can raise the risk-free interest rate. The vertical intercept of the SML is determined by the risk-free interest rate and its slope is determined by the amount of compensation investors need for assuming nondiversifiable risk. The risk-free interest rate is controlled by the Federal Reserve through its control over the rate for short-term U.S. government bonds. The Federal Reserve can shift the SML upward by increasing this interest rate, which makes this risk-free asset more attractive. As investors sell other assets to buy this risk-free asset, the prices of other riskier assets fall, thus reducing investors' wealth. At the same time, the falling prices for assets raise the average expected rate of return of these assets.

(2) The SML can be used to explain what happened during the Great Recession. As the Federal Reserve drove down the risk-free interest rate, the SML moved downward as the vertical intercept fell. At the same time, the changed investor confidence caused the slope of the line to increase or become steeper. The Federal Reserve policy of lowering the risk-free interest rate should have increased the prices of other assets, but asset prices fell because investors became more fearful about investing in other assets and demanded a higher risk premium, thus increasing the slope of the line.

7. (*Last Word*). Actively managed mutual funds do much worse than passively managed index funds for several reasons. First, actively managed funds cannot select portfolios that do better than passively managed funds with similar levels of risk because of arbitrage. Second, actively managed funds charge higher fees than passively managed funds, thus increasing their cost and lowering their return.

■ HINTS AND TIPS

1. There are many new terms and concepts presented in this chapter, so take time to master each one in order to have the necessary knowledge to comprehend the chapter content. This content is not difficult once you master the basic terms and concepts.

2. The **Security Market Line** may seem more difficult than it is. It is simply a graph of the relationship between risk level (measured on the horizontal axis) and the average expected return (measured on the vertical axis). The line is up-sloping, reflecting the fact that a greater risk level is associated with a higher average expected return. The average expected return, however, is divided into two parts. One part is compensation for time preference and it is measured by the risk-free interest rate (the vertical intercept). The other part is a risk premium for a risk level associated with an asset's beta.

3. One purpose of the chapter is to show how the **Federal Reserve** can change the short-term interest rate and influence financial investments and thus the economy. The last section of the chapter makes that important connection and offers several applications.

■ IMPORTANT TERMS

economic investment	**percentage rate of return**
financial investment	**arbitrage**
present value	**risk**
compound interest	**diversification**
stocks	**diversifiable risk**
limited liability rule	**nondiversifiable risk**
capital gains	**average expected rate of return**
dividends	**probability-weighted average**
bankrupt	**beta**
bonds	**market portfolio**
default	**time preference**
mutual funds	**risk-free interest rate**
portfolio	**risk premium**
actively managed funds	**Security Market Line (SML)**
index funds	
passively managed funds	

SELF-TEST

■ FILL-IN QUESTIONS

1. Paying for new additions to the nation's capital stock would be (financial, economic) ____________ investment whereas buying an asset in the expectation that it will generate a monetary gain would be ____________ investment.

2. The compound interest formula defines the rate at which (present, future) ____________ amounts of money can be converted to ____________ amounts of money, and also the rate at which (present, future) ____________ amounts of money can be converted into ____________ amounts of money.

3. All financial investments share three features: They require that investors pay a (dividend, price) ____________ to acquire them; they give the owners the chance to receive (present, future) ____________ payments; and such payments are typically (riskless, risky) ____________.

4. An investment's proper current price is equal to the sum of the (present, future) ____________ values of each of the investment's expected ____________ payments.

5. Ownership shares in a corporation are (stocks, bonds) ____________ whereas debt contracts issued by corporations are ____________.

6. The primary risk for stocks is that future profits are (predictable, unpredictable) ____________ and the company may go bankrupt, whereas bonds are risky because of the possibility that the corporate or government issuers (may, may not) ____________ make the promised payments.

7. A mutual fund is a company that maintains a portfolio of (stocks or bonds, artworks and antiques) ____________. Portfolio managers who constantly buy and sell assets to generate high returns run (passively managed, actively managed) ____________ funds and portfolio managers who buy and sell assets to match whatever assets are contained in an underlying index run ____________ funds.

8. Average expected rates of return are (directly, inversely) ____________ related to an asset's current price, so when an asset's price rises, the average expected rate of return (rises, fall) ____________.

9. Assume that two assets are nearly identical, but one pays a higher rate of return than the other. As investors buy the asset with the higher rate of return, its price will (fall, rise) ____________ causing its average expected rate of return to ____________. At the same time, as investors sell the asset with the lower rate of return, its price will (fall, rise) ____________, causing its average expected rate of return to ____________. The process will continue until the two assets have (equal, unequal) ____________ average expected rates of return.

10. Risk means that investors are (certain, uncertain) ____________ what future payments from assets will be. Risks that can be canceled out by diversification are (diversifiable, nondiversifiable) ____________ risks, and risks that cannot be canceled out by diversification are ____________ risks.

11. Each investment's average expected rate of return is the probability (weighted, unweighted) ____________ average of the investment's possible future return. This probability weighting means that each of the possible future rates of return is (multiplied, divided) ____________ by its probability expressed as a decimal before being added together to obtain the average.

12. Beta is a relative measure of (diversifiable, nondiversifiable) ____________ risk and shows how the ____________ risk of a given asset or portfolio compares with that of the market portfolio.

13. Since the market portfolio contains every asset trading in the financial markets, it has eliminated all of its (diversifiable, nondiversifiable) _______________ risk and only has _______________ risk. The market portfolio is the perfect standard against which to measure levels of (diversifiable, nondiversifiable) _______________ risk.

14. The more risky an investment is, the (higher, lower) _______________ its average expected return will be to compensate the investor for taking a greater risk, and the less risky an investment is, the _______________ its average expected return will be because the investor needs less compensation for the risk taken. Investors' dislike of risk and uncertainty, however, causes them to pay higher prices for (more, less) _______________ risky assets even if the expected returns are lower, and lower prices for _______________ risky assets even if the expected returns are higher. This outcome means that asset prices and expected rates of return are (directly, inversely) _______________ related.

15. The compensation for time preference is the risk-free interest rate on (short-term, long-term) _______________ U.S. government bonds and the power to change this interest rate is held by the (U.S. Treasury, Federal Reserve) _______________.

16. The Security Market Line shows the relationship between average expected rates of (return, risk) _______________ and levels of _______________ that hold for every asset or portfolio trading in financial markets. The line's upward slope shows that investors must be compensated for higher levels of risk with (lower, higher) _______________ average expected rates of return.

17. If investors dislike risk, then the Security Market Line will be (flatter, steeper) _______________, but if investors are more comfortable with risk, then the line will be (flatter, steeper) _______________. When the line is steeper, it indicates that investors demand (more, less) _______________ compensation in terms of higher average expected rates of return for bearing increasingly large amounts of nondiversifiable risk, but when the line is flatter it indicates that investors demand _______________ compensation in terms of higher average expected rates of return for bearing higher levels of nondiversifiable risk.

18. Arbitrage will ensure that all investments having an identical level of risk will eventually also have an (equal, unequal) _______________ rate of return—the return given by the Security Market Line. If such an investment has a return that is greater than the average for a level of risk, investors will (sell, buy) _______________ it, thus (increasing, decreasing) _______________ the price and _______________ the average expected return. If such an investment has a return that is lower than the average for a level of risk, investors will (sell, buy) _______________ it, thus (increasing, decreasing) _______________ the price and _______________ the average expected return.

19. The Security Market Line's vertical intercept is the (prime, risk-free) _______________ interest rate set by the Federal Reserve and the slope determined by the amount of compensation that investors demand for bearing (diversifiable, nondiversifiable) _______________ risk. Assuming that the risk premium for investors does not change, when the Federal Reserve increases the risk-free interest rate, the SML line will shift (upward, downward) _______________ and the price of risky assets will (increase, decrease) _______________ and so will investor's wealth.

20. During the Great Recession, the Federal Reserve pursued a policy to (increase, decrease) _______________ the risk-free interest rate, the effect of which should have been to _______________ the prices of risky assets and investors' wealth, but the policy was overwhelmed by a change in the risk premium. During the Great Recession investors became significantly more fearful, causing their risk premium to (increase, decrease) _______________ and the prices of other assets and investors' wealth to _______________.

■ TRUE–FALSE QUESTIONS

Circle T if the statement is true, F if it is false.

1. The purchase of a share of corporate stock would be an example of a financial investment. **T F**

2. The compound interest formula states that if X dollars are invested today at interest rate i and allowed to grow for t years, they will become $(1 + i)^t X$ dollars in t years. **T F**

3. The present value formula states that a person would have to invest $X/(1 + i)^t$ dollars today at interest rate i for them to become X dollars in t years. **T F**

4. The current price of a financial investment should equal the total present value of all the asset's future payments. **T F**

5. Stocks are ownership shares in corporations and have value because they give shareholders the right to share in any future profits that the corporations may generate. **T F**

6. Bonds are risky because of the possibility that the corporations or government bodies that issued them may default on them, or not make the promised payments. **T F**

7. Mutual funds are investment companies that pool the money of many investors in order to buy a portfolio of assets. **T F**

8. Some mutual funds are actively managed while other mutual funds are passively managed index funds. **T F**

9. A financial investment's percentage rate of return is directly related to its price. **T F**

10. Arbitrage is the process whereby investors equalize the average expected rates of return generated by identical or nearly identical assets. **T F**

11. In finance, an asset is risky if its future payments are certain. **T F**

12. Diversification is an investment strategy that seeks to reduce the overall risk facing an investment portfolio by selecting a group of assets whose risks offset each other. **T F**

13. Nondiversifiable risks simultaneously affect all investments in the same direction so that it is not possible to select asset returns that offset each other. **T F**

14. Investors evaluate the possible future returns to risky projects using average expected rates of return, which give lower weight to outcomes that are more likely to happen. **T F**

15. Beta measures the nondiversifiable risk of an asset or portfolio relative to the amount of nondiversifiable risk facing the market portfolio. **T F**

16. By definition, the market portfolio has a beta of 1.0, so that if an asset has a beta of 0.67, it has a third more nondiversifiable risk than the market portfolio. **T F**

17. The riskier the asset, the higher its average expected rate of return will be. **T F**

18. The rate of return that compensates for time preference is assumed to be equal to the rate of interest generated by long-term U.S. government bonds. **T F**

19. The Federal Reserve has the power to set the short-term risk-free interest rate and thereby set the economy-wide compensation for time preference. **T F**

20. An asset's average expected rate of return will be the sum of the rate of return that compensates for time preference plus the rate of return that compensates for the asset's level of nondiversifiable risk as measured by beta. **T F**

21. The Security Market Line (SML) is a straight line that plots how the average expected rates of return on assets and portfolios in the economy must vary with their respective levels of nondiversifiable risk as measured by beta. **T F**

22. The slope of the Security Market Line indicates how much investors dislike risk. **T F**

23. Arbitrage ensures that every asset in the economy should plot onto the Security Market Line. **T F**

24. The Federal Reserve can shift the entire SML by changing risk-free interest rates and the compensation for time preference that must be paid to investors in all assets regardless of their risk level. **T F**

25. The power of the Federal Reserve to shift short-run interest rates gives it the ability to shift asset prices throughout the economy. **T F**

■ MULTIPLE-CHOICE QUESTIONS

Circle the letter that corresponds to the best answer.

1. Which would be an example of an economic investment?
- **(a)** the sale of a stock
- **(b)** the building a new factory
- **(c)** the buying of a mutual fund
- **(d)** the purchase of a corporate bond

2. A $100 deposit is placed in a savings account that pays an annual interest rate of 8 percent. What will be its value after two years?
- **(a)** $116.64
- **(b)** $125.97
- **(c)** $136.05
- **(d)** $146.93

3. The compound interest rate formula defines the rate at which
- **(a)** a future amount of money can be converted to a present amount of money
- **(b)** a present amount of money can be converted into present interest rates
- **(c)** a present amount of money can be divided by the interest rate
- **(d)** a present amount of money can be multiplied by the interest rate

4. Cecilia has the chance to buy an asset that is guaranteed to return a single payment of exactly $370 in 17 years. Assume that the interest rate is 8 percent, then the present value of that future payment is equal to:
- **(a)** ($370 − $70) = $300
- **(b)** ($370 − $29.6) = $340.4
- **(c)** $\$370/(1.08)^{17} = \$100$
- **(d)** ($370 × 1.08) + 17 = $416.60

5. Assume that Ricardo wins a $100 million lottery. Ricardo can be paid the $100 million in 20 payments of $5 million each over 20 years, or Ricardo can be paid a lump sum of the present values of each of the future payments. Assume that the interest rate is 5 percent a year, what is the lump sum?
- **(a)** $43.2 million
- **(b)** $50.4 million
- **(c)** $62.3 million
- **(d)** $110.5 million

6. Which of the following is NOT one of the common features of all investments?
- **(a)** The rate of return on the investments will be positive.
- **(b)** Investors are given the chance to receive future payments.
- **(c)** Investors are required to pay a market price to purchase them.
- **(d)** The future payments from the investments are typically risky.

7. Shares of ownership in a corporation are
- **(a)** bonds
- **(b)** stocks
- **(c)** dividends
- **(d)** mutual funds

8. Jamie buys 100 shares of General Electric stock for $35 a share one year and then sells the 100 shares for $40 a share the next year. After selling the shares, Jamie will realize a(n)
- **(a)** depreciation of $500
- **(b)** capital gain of $500
- **(c)** dividend increase of $500
- **(d)** interest payment of $500

9. Which type of investment is a loan contract?
- **(a)** bonds
- **(b)** stocks
- **(c)** actively managed mutual funds
- **(d)** passively managed mutual funds

10. Sang buys a house for $500,000 and rents it out for a monthly payment of $3,500. What is the percentage rate of return on this investment for the year?
- **(a)** 7.2 percent
- **(b)** 8.4 percent
- **(c)** 9.1 percent
- **(d)** 10.6 percent

11. Susie wants to buy a $10,000 bond that pays a fixed annual payment of $550. Before she is able to buy the bond, its price rises to $11,000. What happens to the rate of return on the bond because of the change in price?
- **(a)** It increased from 4.5% to 5.5%.
- **(b)** It decreased from 5.0% to 4.5%.
- **(c)** It increased from 5.0% to 5.5%.
- **(d)** It decreased from 5.5% to 5.0%.

12. The process whereby investors equalize the average expected rates of return generated by identical or nearly identical assets is
- **(a)** beta
- **(b)** arbitrage
- **(c)** diversifiable risk
- **(d)** nondiversifiable risk

13. In finance, an asset is risky if
- **(a)** it does not pay dividends
- **(b)** it does not have capital gains
- **(c)** its present value is positive
- **(d)** its future payments are uncertain

14. An investment strategy that seeks to reduce the overall risk facing an investment portfolio by selecting a group of assets whose risks offset each other is called
- **(a)** indexing
- **(b)** arbitrage
- **(c)** diversification
- **(d)** time preference

15. An investor wants to invest in the beverage industry, but does not know which of two major companies, Coca-Cola and Pepsi, will produce the greatest return, so the investor buys shares in both companies to lower the risk. In this case the investor is seeking to lower
- **(a)** systemic risk
- **(b)** diversifiable risk
- **(c)** nondiversifiable risk
- **(d)** the risk premium

16. The type of risk that pushes the returns from all investment in the same direction at the same time so there is no possibility of using good effects to offset bad effects is
- **(a)** constant
- **(b)** idiosyncratic
- **(c)** nondiversifiable
- **(d)** probability weighted

17. If an investment is 80 percent likely to return 10 percent per year and 20 percent likely to return 12 percent a year, then its probability weighted average is
- **(a)** 8.0%
- **(b)** 10.4%
- **(c)** 11.0%
- **(d)** 12.2%

18. Beta measures how the
- **(a)** risk premium compares with the time preference
- **(b)** risk-free interest rate compares with the diversifiable risk of a given asset
- **(c)** nondiversifiable risk of a given asset compares with that of a market portfolio
- **(d)** average expected rate of return compares with the probability weighted average

19. An asset with a beta of 2.0 has
- **(a)** 2% more risk than the risk-free interest rate
- **(b)** 100% more risk than the risk-free interest rate
- **(c)** half the nondiversifiable risk of that in a market portfolio of assets
- **(d)** twice the nondiversifiable risk of that in a market portfolio of assets

20. Asset prices and average expected returns are inversely related, so
- **(a)** more risky assets will have average expected rates of return similar to less risky assets
- **(b)** less risky assets will have higher average expected rates of return than more risky assets
- **(c)** more risky assets will have lower average expected rates of return than less risky assets
- **(d)** less risky assets will have lower average expected rates of return than more risky assets

21. The observation that people tend to be impatient and typically prefer to consume things in the present rather than the future is captured in the concept of
- **(a)** beta
- **(b)** risk premium
- **(c)** time preference
- **(d)** market portfolio

22. The best measure of the risk-free interest rate is the rate of return from
- **(a)** a portfolio of company stocks
- **(b)** bonds issued by U.S. corporations

(c) a passively managed mutual fund
(d) short-term U.S. government bonds

23. Each investment's average expected rate of return is
(a) the sum of the risk-free interest rate and the risk premium
(b) the risk-free interest rate multiplied times the risk premium
(c) the risk premium divided by the risk-free interest rate
(d) the risk premium minus the risk-free interest rate

24. The Security Market Line (SML) is a straight line that shows how the average expected rates of return on assets and portfolios in the economy must vary with their respective levels of
(a) diversifiable risk as measured by beta
(b) nondiversifiable risk as measured by beta
(c) the risk premium as measured by the risk-free interest rate
(d) time preference as measured by the risk-free interest rate

25. If the Federal Reserve decides to raise the interest rates on short-term U.S. government bonds, then the vertical intercept for the Security Market Line will shift
(a) upward and asset prices will fall
(b) upward and asset prices will rise
(c) downward and asset prices will fall
(d) downward and asset prices will rise

PROBLEMS

1. In the table below, enter the value at year's end of $100 compounded at 5 percent interest.

Years of compounding	Value at year's end
1	$____
2	____
3	____
4	____
5	____

2. In the table below, enter the *present value* of $10,000 that would be paid at the end of different years. Assume the interest rate is 5 percent. Round the answer to the nearest dollar.

Year period	Value at year's end
1	$____
2	____
3	____
4	____
5	____

3. Assume that the investment pays a monthly amount of $2000, but has a different price.
a. Calculate the percentage rate of return for an investment that a person might buy at different prices and enter it into the table.
b. Describe the relationship between the percentage rate of return and the asset price.

Purchase price	Percentage rate of return
$ 50,000	____
100,000	____
150,000	____
200,000	____

4. The table below shows different probabilities for the rate of return on an investment that might pay 10 percent a year or 12 percent a year. Calculate the probability weighted average for the return for this investment.

	10 percent return	12 percent return	Probability weight average
a.	50%	50%	____%
b.	60	40	____
c.	70	30	____
d.	80	20	____

SHORT ANSWER AND ESSAY QUESTIONS

1. Explain the difference between financial investment and economic investment and give examples.

2. Explain why the formula for compound interest defines not only the rate at which present amounts of money can be converted to future amounts of money, but also the rate at which future amounts of money can be converted to present amounts of money.

3. Assume you are given the choice between being paid $100 million in installments of $5 million per year over 20 years or having it all paid today. Assume the applicable interest rate for the installment payments is 5 percent. What would the present value be today and how did you calculate it?

4. Describe how present value can be used to analyze salary caps and deferred compensation issued.

5. What are the three common features of all financial investments?

6. Compare and contrast stocks, bonds, and mutual funds in terms of ownership, risk, and return.

7. What is the relationship between asset prices and rates of return? What is the cause of this relationship?

8. How does the arbitrage process work? Give an example.

9. Identify the two basic types of risk and explain the difference between them.

10. What is meant by the term probability weighted average as it applies to the average expected rate of return for investments? Give an example to illustrate the term.

11. Define beta and use it to explain risk. What is the beta for a market portfolio and why does it have this value?

12. Explain the relationship between risk and average expected return.

13. What is time preference? Give an example to illustrate its meaning.

14. Why are short-term U.S. government bonds considered to be risk-free investments?

15. How can the Federal Reserve influence the risk-free rate of return?

16. Define the components of the average expected rate of return.

17. What is the relationship between beta and the risk premium?

18. Use the Security Market Line to explain how arbitrage will ensure that all investments having an identical level of risk will also have an identical rate of return.

19. Explain what happens to the Security Market Line and the economy when the Federal Reserve changes policy and uses open market operations to raise the interest rates of short-term U.S. government bonds.

20. What happened to the Security Market Line during the Great Recession? Explain in terms of the risk-free interest rate and the risk premium. Why did asset prices fall?

ANSWERS

Chapter 17 Financial Economics

FILL-IN QUESTIONS

1. economic, financial
2. present, future, future, present
3. price, future, risky
4. present, future
5. stocks, bonds
6. unpredictable, may not
7. stocks and bond, actively managed, passively managed
8. inversely, falls
9. rise, fall, fall, rise, equal
10. uncertain, diversifiable, nondiversifiable
11. weighted, multiplied
12. nondiversifiable, nondiversifiable
13. diversifiable, nondiversifiable, nondiversifiable
14. higher, lower, less, more, inversely
15. short-term, Federal Reserve
16. return, risk, higher
17. steep, flatter, more, less
18. equal, buy, increasing, decreasing, sell, decreasing, increasing
19. risk-free, nondiversifiable, upward, decrease
20. decrease, increase, increase, decrease

TRUE–FALSE QUESTIONS

1. T, p. 342
2. T, p. 342
3. T, p. 343
4. T, p. 344
5. T, p. 345
6. T, p. 346
7. T, p. 346
8. T, p. 347
9. F, p. 347
10. T, pp. 347–348
11. F, p. 348
12. T, p. 349
13. T, p. 349
14. F, p. 350
15. T, p. 350
16. F, pp. 350–351
17. T, p. 351
18. F, p. 351
19. T, p. 352
20. T, p. 352
21. T, p. 352
22. T, p. 353
23. T, p. 353–354
24. T, pp. 354–355
25. T, p. 355

MULTIPLE-CHOICE QUESTIONS

1. b, p. 342
2. a, p. 342
3. a, p. 342
4. c, p. 343
5. c, p. 343
6. a, p. 345
7. b, p. 345
8. b, pp. 345–346
9. a, p. 346
10. b, p. 347
11. d, p. 347
12. b, p. 347
13. d, p. 348
14. c, p. 349
15. b, p. 349
16. c, p. 349
17. b, p. 350
18. c, p. 350
19. d, p. 350
20. d, p. 351
21. c, p. 351
22. d, pp. 351–352
23. a, p. 352
24. b, pp. 352
25. a, pp. 354–355

PROBLEMS

1. See table

Years of compounding	Value at year's end
1	$105.00
2	110.25
3	115.76
4	121.55
5	127.63

2. See table

Year period	Value at year's end
1	$9524
2	9070
3	8638
4	8227
5	7835

3. *a.* See table; *b.* As the asset or purchase price increases, the percentage rate of return decreases

Purchase price	Percentage rate of return
$ 50,000	48
100,000	24
150,000	16
200,000	12

4. See table

	10 percent return	12 percent return	Probability weighted average
a.	50%	50%	11.0%
b.	60	40	10.8
c.	70	30	10.6
d.	80	20	10.4

SHORT ANSWER AND ESSAY QUESTIONS

1. p. 342	**8.** pp. 347–348	**15.** p. 352
2. pp. 342–343	**9.** pp. 348–349	**16.** p. 352
3. p. 343	**10.** p. 350	**17.** p. 352
4. p. 345	**11.** p. 350	**18.** pp. 353–354
5. p. 345	**12.** p. 351	**19.** pp. 354–355
6. pp. 345–347	**13.** p. 351	**20.** p. 355
7. p. 347	**14.** pp. 351–352	

CHAPTER 18

Extending the Analysis of Aggregate Supply

Chapter 18 adds to the aggregate demand–aggregate supply (AD-AS) model first introduced in Chapter 12. This addition will give you the analytical tools to improve your understanding of the short-run and long-run relationships between unemployment and inflation.

The major extension to the AD-AS model is the explanation for the **short-run aggregate supply curve** and the **long-run aggregate supply curve.** In the **short run,** nominal wages and other input prices do not adjust fully as the price level changes, so an increase in the price level increases business profits and real output. In the **long run,** nominal wages and other input prices are fully responsive to previous changes in the price level, so business profits and employment return to their original levels. Thus, the long-run aggregate supply curve is vertical at the full-employment level of output.

The distinction between the short-run and long-run aggregate supply curves requires a reinterpretation of demand-pull inflation and cost-push inflation. Although **demand-pull inflation** will increase the price level and real output in the short run, once nominal wages increase, the temporary increase in output is gone, but the price level will be higher at the full-employment level of output. **Cost-push inflation** will increase the price level and decrease real output in the short run, but again, once nominal wages fall, output and the price level will return to their original positions. If government policymakers try to counter cost-push inflation by increasing aggregate demand, they may make matters worse by increasing the price level and causing the short-run aggregate supply curve to decrease, thereby setting off an inflationary spiral.

The extended AD-AS model also is useful for understanding recession and ongoing inflation in an economy. As for recession, it is the result of a decrease in aggregate demand. This decline eventually lowers nominal wages and other input prices. When this happens, aggregate supply increases to restore the previous equilibrium. As for ongoing inflation, it is the result of increases in aggregate demand over time that raise the price level and counter the downward pressure on the price level from economic growth and a long-run increase in aggregate supply.

The relationship between inflation and unemployment has been studied for many years. One influential observation, supported by data from the 1950s and 1960s, was embodied in the **Phillips Curve,** which suggested that there was a stable and predictable trade-off between the rate of inflation and the unemployment rate. During the 1960s, it was thought that this trade-off could be used for formulating sound monetary and fiscal policy to manage the economy.

The events of the 1970s and early 1980s, however, called into question the shape and stability of the Phillips Curve because the economy was experiencing both higher rates of inflation and unemployment—**stagflation.** The **aggregate supply shocks** of this period shifted the Phillips Curve rightward. When these shocks dissipated in the 1980s, the Phillips Curve began to shift back to its original position. From 1997 to 2008, points on the Phillips Curve were similar to those of the 1960s.

The conclusion to be drawn from studies of the Phillips Curve is that there is no long-run trade-off between inflation and unemployment. In the long run, the down-sloping Phillips Curve is actually a vertical line at the natural rate of unemployment. In the short run, if aggregate demand increases and reduces the unemployment rate below its natural rate, the result is only temporary. Eventually, the unemployment rate will return to its natural rate, but at a higher rate of inflation.

Aggregate supply can also be affected by taxation. **Supply-side economics** contends that aggregate supply is important for determining levels of inflation, unemployment, and economic growth. Tax cuts are proposed by supply-siders as a way to create more incentives to work, save, and invest, thus increasing productivity and aggregate supply. The relationship between marginal tax rates and tax revenues is expressed in the **Laffer Curve,** which suggests that cuts in tax rates can increase tax revenues if tax rates are too high for the economy. Critics contend, however, that the incentive effects are small, potentially inflationary, and can have positive or negative effects on tax revenues.

■ CHECKLIST

When you have studied this chapter you should be able to

☐ Give a definition of the short run and long run in macroeconomics based on the flexibility of input prices.

☐ Draw the short-run aggregate supply curve and describe its characteristics.

☐ Explain how the long-run aggregate supply curve is determined.

☐ Draw a graph that illustrates long-run equilibrium in the extended AD-AS model.

☐ Explain demand-pull inflation using the extended AD-AS model and identify its short-run and long-run outcomes.

☐ Describe cost-push inflation using the extended AD-AS model.
☐ Give two generalizations about the policy dilemma for government in dealing with cost-push inflation.
☐ Explain recession and the process of adjustment using the extended AD-AS model.
☐ Discuss the reasons for ongoing inflation in the extended AD-AS model.
☐ Show that a shift outward in the production possibilities curve is equivalent to a rightward shift in the economy's long-run aggregate supply curve.
☐ Illustrate graphically in the extended AD-AS model how economic growth shifts the short-run and long-run aggregate supply curves and what happens to aggregate demand over time.
☐ Explain how the deflationary effects of increases in aggregate supply from economic growth are typically offset by increases in aggregate demand from monetary policy, thus producing ongoing inflation.
☐ Make three significant generalizations about the inflation and unemployment relationship based on the extended AD-AS model.
☐ Draw a Phillips Curve and explain the basic trade-off it presents.
☐ Define stagflation.
☐ Explain why adverse aggregate supply shocks shifted the Phillips Curve over time.
☐ List events that contributed to the demise of stagflation.
☐ Use short-run and long-run Phillips Curves to explain inflation.
☐ Use short-run and long-run Phillips Curves to explain disinflation.
☐ Describe supply-siders' views of the effects of taxation on incentives to work, save, and invest.
☐ Use the Laffer Curve to explain the hypothesized relationship between marginal tax rates and tax revenues.
☐ State three criticisms of the Laffer Curve.
☐ Offer a rebuttal of the criticisms and an evaluation of supply-side economics.
☐ Discuss findings from recent research on whether tax increases reduce real GDP (*Last Word*).

■ CHAPTER OUTLINE

1. The aggregate supply curve has short-run and long-run characteristics. The ***short run*** is a period of time in which input prices are inflexible or fixed. In the short run, nominal wages (and other input prices) are unresponsive to changes in the price level. The ***long run*** is a period of time in which input prices are flexible. In the long run, nominal wages and other input prices are fully responsive to changes in the price level. The short-run and long-run characteristics of aggregate supply in combination with aggregate demand create the extended AD-AS model.

a. The ***short-run aggregate supply curve*** is upsloping: An increase in the price level increases real output, and also business revenues and profits, because nominal wages and other input prices do not change; in contrast, when the price level decreases, business revenue and profits decline, and so does real output, but nominal wages and other input prices do not change.

b. The ***long-run aggregate supply curve*** is vertical at the potential level of output. Increases in the price level will increase nominal wages and other input prices and cause a decrease (shift left) in the short-run aggregate supply curve. Conversely, declines in the price level will reduce nominal wages and other input prices and cause an increase (shift right) in the short-run aggregate supply curve. In either case, although the price level changes, output returns to its potential level, and the long-run aggregate supply curve is vertical at the full-employment level of output.

c. ***Equilibrium*** in the extended AD-AS model occurs at the price level and output where the aggregate demand crosses the long-run aggregate supply curve and also crosses the short-run aggregate supply curve.

2. The extended AD-AS model can be applied to explain conditions of inflation and recession in an economy.

a. ***Demand-pull inflation*** will increase (shift right) the aggregate demand curve, which increases the price level and causes a temporary increase in real output above the potential output of the economy. The greater demand for inputs will eventually lead to an increase in nominal wages and other input prices. The short-run aggregate supply curve, which was based on fixed nominal wages and other input prices, now decreases (shifts left), resulting in an even higher price level with real output returning to its prior level.

b. ***Cost-push inflation*** will decrease (shift left) the short-run aggregate supply curve. This situation will increase the price level and temporarily decrease real output, causing a recession. It creates a policy dilemma for government.

(1) If government takes actions to counter the cost-push inflation and recession by increasing aggregate demand, the price level will move to an even higher level, and the actions may set off an inflationary spiral.

(2) If government takes no action, the recession will eventually reduce nominal wages and other input prices, and eventually the short-run aggregate supply curve will shift back to its original position.

c. If aggregate demand decreases, it will result in a ***recession*** that decreases real output and increases unemployment. If an assumption is made that prices and wages are flexible downward, then the decline in aggregate demand pushes down nominal wages and other input prices. This decline in input prices will eventually increase short-run aggregate supply, thus increasing real output and restoring full employment to end the recession, but the process does not occur without a long period of high unemployment and lost output.

d. The AD-AS model also explains ongoing inflation in the economy. In the previous analysis inflation was finite, but the shifts in AD or AS were limited. But over time there are continuous shifts in AS and AD that give rise to ongoing inflation. Increases in AS because of economic growth would cause ongoing deflation. But such deflationary shifts from AS are more than offset by increases in AD, thus creating ongoing inflation.

(1) A shift outward in the production possibilities curve is equivalent to a shift rightward in the long-run aggregate supply curve for the economy.

(2) In either model, changes in the price level are not important because it does not shift either curve.

e. The extended AD-AS model takes into account economic growth with a rightward shift in the vertical long-run aggregate supply curve that increases an economy's potential output over time. But this shift is also accompanied by increases in aggregate demand over time. These increases in aggregate demand occur because central banks permit a certain amount of inflation in the economy to offset some of the deflationary effects of the increase in aggregate supply.

3. The short- and long-run relationships between inflation and unemployment are important and lead to three generalizations. First, in the short run there is a trade-off between the rate of inflation and the rate of unemployment. Second, shocks from aggregate supply can cause both higher rates of inflation and higher rates of unemployment. Third, in the long run there is no significant trade-off between inflation and unemployment.

a. If aggregate supply is constant and the economy is operating in the up-sloping range of aggregate supply, then the greater the rate of increase in aggregate demand, the higher the rate of inflation (and output) and the lower the rate of unemployment. This inverse relationship between the rate of inflation and unemployment is known as the ***Phillips Curve.*** In the 1960s, economists thought there was a predictable trade-off between unemployment and inflation. All society had to do was to choose the combination of inflation and unemployment on the Phillips Curve.

b. The ***aggregate supply shocks*** of the 1970s and early 1980s called into question the validity of the Phillips Curve. In that period, the economy experienced ***stagflation***—both higher rates of inflation and unemployment. The aggregate supply shocks came from an increase in resource prices (oil), shortages in agricultural production, higher wage demands, and declining productivity. These shocks decreased the short-run aggregate supply curve, which increased the price level and decreased output (and unemployment). These shocks shifted the Phillips Curve to the right or showed there was no dependable trade-off between inflation and unemployment.

c. The ***demise of stagflation*** came in the 1982–1989 period because of such factors as a severe recession in 1981–1982 that reduced wage demands, increased foreign competition that restrained price increases, and a decline in OPEC's monopoly power. The short-run aggregate supply curve increased, and the price level and unemployment rate fell. This meant that the Phillips Curve may have shifted back (left). Recent unemployment– inflation data are now similar to the Phillips Curve of the 1960s.

4. In the ***long run,*** there is no apparent trade-off between inflation and unemployment. Any rate of inflation is consistent with the natural rate of unemployment at that time. The long-run Phillips Curve is vertical at the natural rate of unemployment. In the ***short run,*** there can be a trade-off between inflation and unemployment.

a. An increase in aggregate demand may temporarily reduce unemployment as the price level increases and profits expand, but the actions also set other events into motion.

(1) The increase in the price level reduces the real wages of workers who demand and obtain higher nominal wages; these actions return unemployment to its original level.

(2) Back at the original level, there are now higher actual and expected rates of inflation for the economy, so the short-run Phillips Curve has shifted upward.

(3) The process is repeated if aggregate demand continues to increase. The price level rises as the short-run Phillips Curve shifts upward.

b. In the long run, the Phillips Curve is stable only as a vertical line at the natural rate of unemployment. After all adjustments in nominal wages to increases and decreases in the rate of inflation, the economy returns to its full-employment level of output and its natural rate of unemployment. There is no trade-off between unemployment and inflation in the long run.

c. ***Disinflation***—reductions in the inflation rate from year to year—is also explained by the distinction between the short-run and long-run Phillips Curves.

5. ***Supply-side economics*** views aggregate supply as active rather than passive in explaining changes in the price level and unemployment.

a. It argues that higher marginal tax rates reduce incentives to work and high taxes also reduce incentives to save and invest. These policies lead to a misallocation of resources, less productivity, and a decrease in aggregate supply. To counter these effects, supply-side economists call for a cut in marginal tax rates.

b. The ***Laffer Curve*** suggests that it is possible to lower tax rates and increase tax revenues, thus avoiding a budget deficit because the policies will result in less tax evasion and avoidance.

c. Critics of supply-side economics and the Laffer Curve suggest that the policy of cutting tax rates will not work because:

(1) It has only a small and uncertain effect on incentives to work (or on aggregate supply).

(2) It would increase aggregate demand relative to aggregate supply and thus reinforce inflation when there is full employment.

(3) The expected tax revenues from tax rate cuts depend on assumptions about the economy's position on the Laffer Curve. If tax cuts reduce tax revenues, it will create budget deficits.

d. Supply-siders argue that the tax cuts under the Reagan administration in the 1980s worked as would be expected: The cut in tax rates increased tax revenue. Critics contend that the reason was that aggregate demand increased as the economy came out of recession and not that aggregate supply increased. There is now general recognition that changes in marginal tax rates change people's behavior, although there is continuing debate about the size of the effect.

6. (*Last Word*). Economists Cristina Romer and David Romer developed a novel way to study the question of whether tax increases reduce real GDP. They identified four motivations for tax changes: to counteract other influences in the economy; to pay for more government spending; to correct budget deficits; and to promote long-term growth. The most reliable way to test for the effects of tax changes was to focus on one used to promote long-term growth or to correct budget deficits because they were uncomplicated by other factors. The results showed that tax changes affect output: a tax increase of 1 percent of GDP lowers real GDP by about 2 to 3 percent.

■ HINTS AND TIPS

1. Chapter 18 is a more difficult chapter because the AD-AS model is extended to include both short-run and long-run effects. Spend extra time mastering this material, but do not try to read everything at once. Break the chapter into its logical sections, and practice drawing each graph.

2. Be sure you understand the distinction between the **short-run** and **long-run aggregate supply curves.** Then use these ideas to explain demand-pull inflation, cost-push inflation, and recession. Doing problem 2 will be especially helpful.

3. Use Figure 18.9 in the text to help you understand why there is a difference in the short-run and long-run relationships between unemployment and inflation. Problem 4 will help your understanding of this complicated graph.

4. The rationales for tax cuts and tax increases have been at the forefront of fiscal policy since the 1980s. This chapter offers a detailed explanation of supply-side economics that has been used to justify the tax cut policies. The last section of the chapter will help you understand the arguments for and against such tax policies that have real-world applications.

■ IMPORTANT TERMS

short run	**Phillips Curve**
long run	**aggregate supply shocks**
short-run aggregate supply curve	**stagflation**
long-run aggregate supply curve	**disinflation**
	supply-side economics
	Laffer Curve

SELF-TEST

■ FILL-IN QUESTIONS

1. In an AD-AS model with a stable aggregate supply curve, when the economy is producing in the up-sloping portion of the aggregate supply curve, an increase in aggregate demand will (increase, decrease) ______________ real output and employment, but a decrease in aggregate supply will ______________ real output and employment.

2. In the short run, when the price level changes, nominal wages and other input prices are (responsive, unresponsive) ______________, but in the long run nominal wages and other input prices are ______________. In the short run, the aggregate supply curve is (up-sloping, vertical) ______________, but in the long run the curve is ______________.

3. Demand-pull inflation occurs with a shift in the aggregate demand curve to the (right, left) ______________, which will (decrease, increase) ______________ the price level and temporarily ______________ real output. As a consequence, the (short-run, long-run) ______________ aggregate supply curve will shift left because of a rise in (real, nominal) ______________ wages, producing a (lower, higher) ______________ price level at the original level of real output.

4. Cost-push inflation occurs with a shift in the short-run aggregate supply curve to the (right, left) ______________; thus the price level will (increase, decrease) ______________ and real output will temporarily ______________.

5. If government takes no actions to counter the cost-push inflation, the resulting recession will (increase, decrease) ______________ nominal wages and shift the short-run aggregate supply curve back to its original position, yet if the government tries to counter the recession with a(n) ______________ in aggregate demand, the price level will move even higher.

6. A recession will occur when there is (an increase, a decrease) ______________ in aggregate demand. If the controversial assumption is made that prices and wages are flexible downward, then the price level (rises, falls) ______________. Real wages will then (increase, decrease) ______________, but eventually nominal wages will ______________ and the aggregate supply curve will (increase, decrease) ______________ and end the recession.

7. In the extended aggregate demand–aggregate supply model, economic growth is illustrated by an (increase, decrease) ______________ in the long-run aggregate supply curve, which is (vertical, horizontal) ______________. When the price level also increases over time, it indicates that the aggregate demand curve has increased (more, less) ______________ rapidly than the long-run aggregate supply, and this results in ongoing inflation in an economy.

8. Along the up-sloping portion of the short-run aggregate supply curve, the greater the increase in aggregate demand, the (greater, smaller) ____________ the increase in the rate of inflation, the ____________ the increase in real output, and the (greater, smaller) ____________ the unemployment rate.

9. The original Phillips Curve indicates that there will be (a direct, an inverse) ____________ relationship between the rate of inflation and the unemployment rate. This means that high rates of inflation will be associated with a (high, low) ____________ unemployment rate, or that low rates of inflation will be associated with a ____________ unemployment rate.

10. The policy trade-off based on a stable Phillips Curve was that for the economy to reduce the unemployment rate, the rate of inflation must (increase, decrease) ____________, and to reduce the rate of inflation, the unemployment rate must ____________.

11. During the 1970s and early 1980s, aggregate (demand, supply) ____________ shocks made the Phillips Curve (stable, unstable) ____________. These shocks produced (demand-pull, cost-push) ____________ inflation that resulted in a simultaneous increase in the inflation rate and the unemployment rate, called (disinflation, stagflation) ____________.

12. The standard explanation for the Phillips Curve is that during the stagflation of the 1970s, the Phillips Curve shifted (right, left) ____________, and during the demise of stagflation from 1982–1989, the Phillips Curve shifted ____________. In this view, there is a trade-off between the unemployment rate and the rate of inflation, but changes in (short-run, long-run) ____________ aggregate supply can shift the Phillips Curve.

13. In the long run, the trade-off between the rate of inflation and the rate of unemployment (does, does not) ____________ exist, and the economy is stable at its natural rate of (unemployment, inflation) ____________.

14. The Phillips Curve may be down-sloping in the (short run, long run) ____________, but it is vertical in the ____________ at the natural rate of unemployment. A shift in aggregate demand that reduces the unemployment rate in the short run results in the long run in (an increase, a decrease) ____________ in the rate of inflation and a return to the natural rate of unemployment.

15. When the actual rate of inflation is higher than the expected rate, profits temporarily (fall, rise) ____________ and the unemployment rate temporarily (rises, falls) ____________. This case would occur during a period of (inflation, disinflation) ____________.

16. When the actual rate of inflation is lower than the expected rate, profits temporarily (fall, rise) ____________ and the unemployment rate temporarily (rises, falls) ____________. This case would occur during a period of (inflation, disinflation) ____________.

17. It is the view of supply-side economists that high marginal tax rates (increase, decrease) ____________ incentives to work, save, invest, and take risks. According to supply-side economists, a stimulus for the economy would be a substantial (increase, decrease) ____________ in marginal tax rates that would ____________ economic growth through (an increase, a decrease) ____________ in aggregate supply.

18. The Laffer Curve depicts the relationship between tax rates and (inflation, tax revenues) ____________. It is useful for showing how a (cut, rise) ____________ in marginal tax rates will increase aggregate supply.

19. In theory, the Laffer Curve shows that as the tax rates increase from 0%, tax revenues will (increase, decrease) ____________ to some maximum level, after which tax revenues will ____________ as the tax rates increase; or as tax rates are reduced from 100%, tax revenues will (increase, decrease) ____________ to some maximum level, after which tax revenues will ____________ as tax rates decrease.

20. Criticisms of the Laffer Curve are that the effects of a cut in tax rates on incentives to work, save, and invest are (large, small) ____________; that the tax cuts generate an increase in aggregate (demand, supply) ____________ that outweighs any increase in aggregate ____________ and may lead to inflation when at full employment; and that tax cuts can produce a (gain, loss) ____________ in tax revenues that will only add to a budget deficit.

■ TRUE-FALSE QUESTIONS

Circle T if the statement is true, F if it is false.

1. The short run in macroeconomics is a period in which nominal wages are fully responsive to changes in the price level. **T F**

2. The short-run aggregate supply curve has a negative slope. **T F**

3. The long-run aggregate supply curve is vertical because nominal wages and other input prices eventually change by the same amount as changes in the price level. T F

4. Demand-pull inflation will increase the price level and real output in the short run, but in the long run, only the price level will increase. T F

5. Cost-push inflation results in a simultaneous increase in the price level and real output. T F

6. When the economy is experiencing cost-push inflation, an inflationary spiral is likely to result when the government enacts policies to maintain full employment. T F

7. A recession is the result of an increase in the short-run aggregate supply curve. T F

8. If the economy is in a recession, prices and nominal wages and other input prices will presumably fall, and the short-run aggregate supply curve will increase, so that real output returns to its full-employment level. T F

9. Supply factors that shift the economy's production possibilities curve outward also cause a leftward shift in its long-run aggregate supply curve. T F

10. An increase in economic growth will increase the long-run aggregate supply curve and the short-run aggregate supply curve, but will decrease the aggregate demand curve. T F

11. The Phillips Curve shows an inverse relationship between the rate of inflation and the unemployment rate. T F

12. Stagflation refers to a situation in which both the price level and the unemployment rate are rising. T F

13. Aggregate supply shocks can cause both higher rates of inflation and higher rates of unemployment. T F

14. One explanation for the stagflation of the 1970s and early 1980s was an increase in aggregate demand. T F

15. Among the factors that contributed to the demise of stagflation during the 1980s was a recession in 1981 and 1982. T F

16. There is no apparent long-run trade-off between inflation and unemployment. T F

17. When the actual rate of inflation is higher than the expected rate, profits temporarily fall and the unemployment rate temporarily rises. T F

18. The long-run Phillips Curve is essentially a vertical line at the economy's natural rate of unemployment. T F

19. Disinflation is the same as mismeasurement of the inflation rate. T F

20. When the actual rate of inflation is lower than the expected rate of inflation, profits temporarily fall and the unemployment rate temporarily rises. T F

21. Most economists reject the idea of a short-run trade-off between the unemployment and inflation rates but accept the long-run trade-off. T F

22. Supply-side economists contend that aggregate demand is the only active factor in determining the price level and real output in an economy. T F

23. One proposition of supply-side economics is that the marginal tax rates on earned income should be reduced to increase the incentives to work. T F

24. Supply-side economists recommend a higher marginal tax rate on interest from saving because no productive work was performed to earn the interest. T F

25. The Laffer Curve suggests that lower tax rates will increase the rate of inflation. T F

■ MULTIPLE-CHOICE QUESTIONS

Circle the letter that corresponds to the best answer.

1. For macroeconomics, the short run is a period in which nominal wages and other input prices
(a) do not fully adjust as the price level stays constant
(b) change as the price level stays constant
(c) do not fully adjust as the price level changes
(d) change as the price level changes

2. Once sufficient time has elapsed for wage contracts to expire and nominal wage adjustments to occur, the economy enters
(a) the short run
(b) the long run
(c) a period of inflation
(d) a period of unemployment

3. A graph of the short-run aggregate supply curve is
(a) down-sloping, and a graph of the long-run aggregate supply curve is up-sloping
(b) up-sloping, and a graph of the long-run aggregate supply curve is vertical
(c) up-sloping, and a graph of the long-run aggregate supply curve is down-sloping
(d) vertical, and a graph of the long-run aggregate supply curve is up-sloping

4. In the extended AD-AS model, demand-pull inflation occurs because of an increase in aggregate demand that will eventually produce
(a) an increase in real wages, thus a decrease in the short-run aggregate supply curve
(b) an increase in nominal wages, thus an increase in the short-run aggregate supply curve
(c) a decrease in nominal wages, thus a decrease in the short-run aggregate supply curve
(d) an increase in nominal wages, thus a decrease in the short-run aggregate supply curve

5. In the short run, demand-pull inflation increases real
(a) output and decreases the price level
(b) wages and increases nominal wages
(c) output and increases the price level
(d) wages and decreases nominal wages

6. In the long run, demand-pull inflation
(a) decreases real wages
(b) increases the price level
(c) increases the unemployment rate
(d) decreases real output

7. A likely result of the government trying to reduce the unemployment associated with cost-push inflation through stimulative fiscal policy or monetary policy is
(a) an inflationary spiral
(b) stagflation
(c) a recession
(d) disinflation

8. What will occur in the short run if there is cost-push inflation and if the government adopts a hands-off approach to it?
(a) an increase in real output
(b) a fall in unemployment
(c) demand-pull inflation
(d) a recession

9. If prices and wages are flexible, a recession will increase real wages as the price level falls. Eventually, nominal wages will
(a) fall, and the short-run aggregate supply will increase
(b) rise, and the short-run aggregate supply will increase
(c) fall, and the short-run aggregate supply will decrease
(d) rise, and the short-run aggregate supply will decrease

10. A shift outward of the production possibilities curve would be equivalent to a shift
(a) upward in aggregate demand
(b) downward in aggregate demand
(c) rightward in long-run aggregate supply
(d) leftward in long-run aggregate supply

Use the following graph to answer Questions 11 and 12.

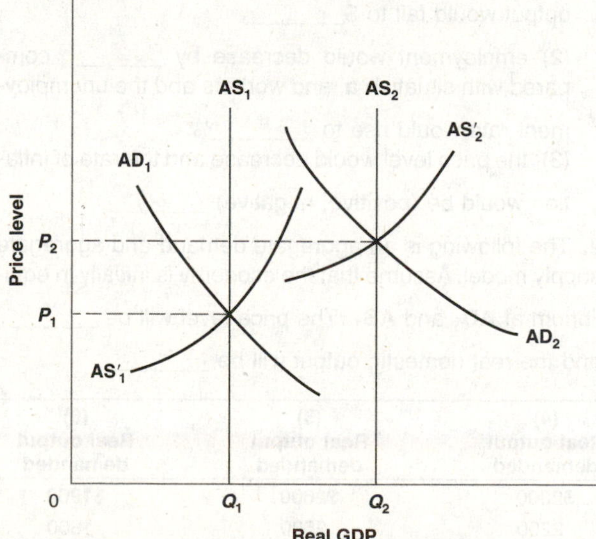

11. A shift from Q_1 to Q_2 is caused by a shift in the
(a) level of prices
(b) aggregate demand curve
(c) short-run aggregate supply curve
(d) long-run aggregate supply curve

12. Which combination would best explain a shift in the price level from P_1 to P_2 and an increase in real domestic output from Q_1 to Q_2?
(a) an increase in the long-run aggregate supply (AS_1 to AS_2) and in short-run aggregate supply (AS'_1 to AS'_2).
(b) an increase in aggregate demand (AD_1 to AD_2) and a decrease in long-run aggregate supply (AS_2 to AS_1).
(c) an increase in the long-run aggregate supply (AS_1 to AS_2), an increase in aggregate demand (AD_1 to AD_2), and an increase in short-run aggregate supply (AS'_1 to AS'_2).
(d) a decrease in the long-run aggregate supply (AS_2 to AS_1), a decrease in aggregate demand (AD_2 to AD_1), and a decrease in short-run aggregate supply (AS'_2 to AS'_1).

13. The traditional Phillips Curve is based on the idea that with a constant short-run aggregate supply curve, the greater the increase in aggregate demand
(a) the greater the unemployment rate
(b) the greater the rate of inflation
(c) the greater the increase in real output
(d) the smaller the increase in nominal wages

14. The traditional Phillips Curve shows the
(a) inverse relationship between the rate of inflation and the unemployment rate
(b) inverse relationship between the nominal wage and the real wage
(c) direct relationship between unemployment and demand-pull inflation
(d) trade-off between the short run and the long run

15. As the unemployment rate falls below its natural rate,
(a) excessive spending produces demand-pull inflation
(b) productivity rises and creates cost-push inflation
(c) the expected rate of inflation equals the actual rate
(d) there is an aggregate supply shock

16. If there are adverse aggregate supply shocks, with aggregate demand remaining constant, then there will be
(a) a decrease in the price level
(b) a decrease in the unemployment rate
(c) an increase in real output
(d) an increase in both the price level and the unemployment rate

17. A cause of both higher rates of inflation and higher rates of unemployment would be
(a) an increase in aggregate demand
(b) an increase in aggregate supply
(c) a decrease in aggregate demand
(d) a decrease in aggregate supply

18. Which would be a factor contributing to the demise of stagflation during the 1982–1989 period?
(a) a lessening of foreign competition
(b) a strengthening of the monopoly power of OPEC
(c) a recession brought on largely by a tight monetary policy
(d) an increase in regulation of airline and trucking industries

19. The economy is stable only in the
(a) short run at a high rate of profit
(b) short run at the natural rate of inflation
(c) long run at the natural rate of unemployment
(d) long run at the natural rate of inflation

20. When the actual inflation rate is higher than expected, profits temporarily
(a) fall and the unemployment rate temporarily falls
(b) rise and the unemployment rate temporarily falls
(c) rise and the unemployment rate temporarily rises
(d) fall and the unemployment rate temporarily rises

21. When the actual rate of inflation is lower than the expected rate, profits temporarily
(a) fall and the unemployment rate temporarily rises
(b) rise and the unemployment rate temporarily falls
(c) rise and the unemployment rate temporarily rises
(d) fall and the unemployment rate temporarily falls

22. In a disinflation situation, the
(a) actual rate of inflation is lower than the expected rate, so the unemployment rate will rise to bring the expected and actual rates into balance
(b) expected rate of inflation is lower than the actual rate, so the unemployment rate will rise to bring the expected and actual rates into balance
(c) actual rate of inflation is higher than the expected rate, so the unemployment rate will fall to bring the expected and actual rates into balance
(d) expected rate of inflation is higher than the actual rate, so the unemployment rate will fall to bring the expected and actual rates into balance

23. The long-run Phillips Curve is essentially
(a) horizontal at the natural rate of unemployment
(b) vertical at the natural rate of unemployment
(c) vertical at the natural rate of inflation
(d) horizontal at the natural rate of inflation

24. Supply-side economists contend that the U.S. system of taxation reduces
(a) unemployment but causes inflation
(b) incentives to work, save, and invest
(c) transfer payments to the poor
(d) the effects of cost-push inflation

25. Based on the Laffer Curve, a cut in the tax rate from 100% to a point before the maximum level of tax revenue will
(a) increase the price level
(b) increase tax revenues
(c) decrease real output
(d) decrease real wages

■ PROBLEMS

1. In columns 1 and 2 of the table at the bottom of this page is a portion of a short-run aggregate supply schedule. Column 3 shows the number of full-time workers (in millions) that would have to be employed to produce each of the seven real domestic outputs (in billions) in the short-run aggregate supply schedule. The labor force is 80 million workers and the full-employment output of the economy is $________.

a. If the aggregate demand schedule were that shown in columns 1 and 4,
(1) the price level would be ________ and the real output would be $________.
(2) the number of workers employed would be ________, the number of workers unemployed would be ________ million, and the unemployment rate would be ________%.

b. If aggregate demand were to increase to that shown in columns 1 and 5 and short-run aggregate supply remained constant,
(1) the price level would rise to ________ and the real output would rise to $________.
(2) employment would increase by ________ million workers and the unemployment rate would fall to ________%.
(3) the price level would increase by ________ and the rate of inflation would be ________%.

c. If aggregate demand were to decrease to that shown in columns 1 and 6 and short-run aggregate supply remained constant,
(1) the price level would fall to ________ and the real output would fall to $________.
(2) employment would decrease by ________ compared with situation **a**, and workers and the unemployment rate would rise to ________%.
(3) the price level would decrease and the rate of inflation would be (positive, negative) ________.

2. The following is an aggregate demand and aggregate supply model. Assume that the economy is initially in equilibrium at AD_1 and AS_1. The price level will be ________ and the real domestic output will be ________.

(1) Price level	(2) Real output supplied	(3) Employment (in millions)	(4) Real output demanded	(5) Real output demanded	(6) Real output demanded
130	$ 800	69	$2300	$2600	$1900
140	1300	70	2200	2500	1800
150	1700	72	2100	2400	1700
160	2000	75	2000	2300	1600
170	2200	78	1900	2200	1500
180	2300	80	1800	2100	1400
190	2300	80	1700	2000	1300

a. If there is demand-pull inflation, then
(1) in the short run, the new equilibrium is at point _______, with the price level at _______ and real output at _______;
(2) in the long run, nominal wages will rise so the aggregate supply curve will shift from _______ to _______. The equilibrium will be at point _______ with the price level at _______ and real output at _______, so the increase in aggregate demand has only moved the economy along its _______ curve.

b. Now assume that the economy is initially in equilibrium at point ***W***, where $\mathbf{AD_1}$ and $\mathbf{AS_1}$ intersect. If there is cost-push inflation, then
(1) in the short run, the new equilibrium is at point _______, with the price level at _______ and real output at _______.
(2) if the government tries to counter the cost-push inflation with expansionary monetary and fiscal policy, then aggregate demand will shift from _______ to _______, with the price level becoming _______ and real output _______, but this policy has a trap because the price level has shifted from _______ to _______ and the new level of inflation might shift _______ leftward.
(3) if government does not counter the cost-push inflation, the price level will eventually move to _______ and real output to _______ as the recession reduces nominal wages and shifts the aggregate supply curve from _______ to _______.

c. Now assume that the economy is initially in equilibrium at point ***Y***, where $\mathbf{AD_2}$ and $\mathbf{AS_2}$ intersect. If there is a recession that reduces investment spending, then
(1) aggregate demand decreases and real output shifts from _______ to _______, and, assuming that prices and wages are flexible downward, the price level shifts from _______ to _______.
(2) The recession causes nominal wages and other input prices to (rise, fall) _______ and when this happens, the short-run aggregate supply curve shifts from _______ to _______ to its new equilibrium at point _______. The equilibrium price level is _______ and the equilibrium level of output is _______ at the long-run aggregate supply curve _______.

3. The following is a traditional Phillips Curve.

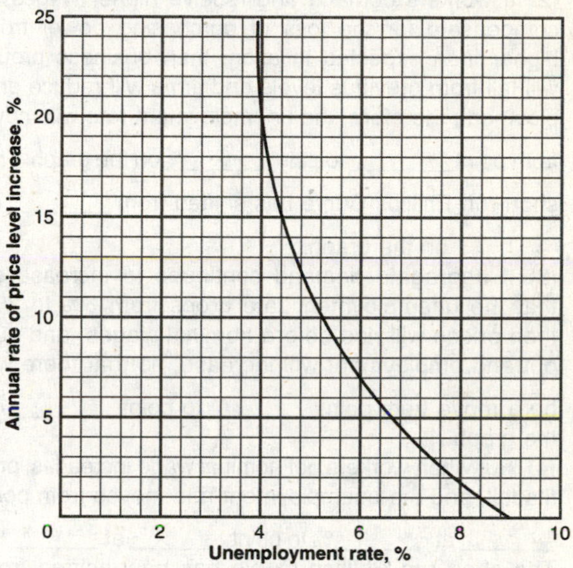

a. At full employment (a 4% unemployment rate) the price level would rise by _______% each year.
b. If the price level were stable (increasing by 0% a year), the unemployment rate would be _______%.
c. Which of the combinations along the Phillips Curve would you choose for the economy? _______
Why would you select this combination? _______

4. Following is a model of short- and long-run Phillips Curves.

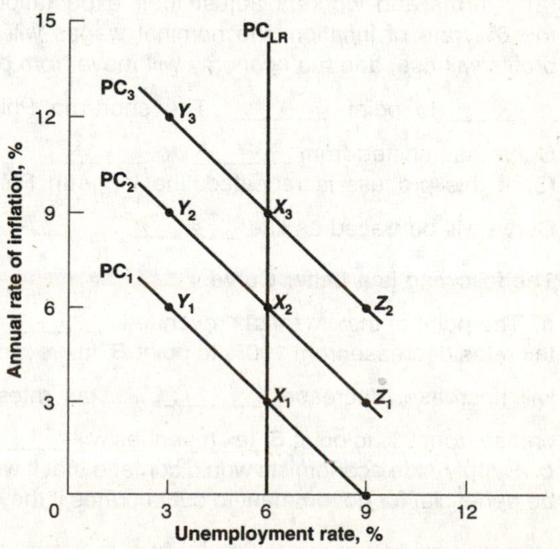

a. Suppose you begin at point X_1 and an assumption is made that nominal wages are set on the original expectation that a 3% rate of inflation will continue in the economy.

(1) If an increase in aggregate demand reduces the unemployment rate from 6% to 3%, then the actual rate of inflation will move to ________%. The higher product prices will lift profits of firms and they will hire more workers; thus in the short run the economy will temporarily move to point ________.

(2) If workers demand and receive higher wages to compensate for the loss of purchasing power from higher than expected inflation, then business profits will fall from previous levels and firms will reduce employment; therefore, the unemployment rate will move from point ________ to point ________ on the graph. The short-run Phillips Curve has shifted from ________ to ________ on the graph.

(3) If aggregate demand continues to increase so that the unemployment rate drops from 6% to 3%, then prices will rise before nominal wages, and output and employment will increase, so that there will be a move from point ________ to point ________ on the graph.

(4) But when workers get nominal wage increases, profits fall, and the unemployment rate moves from point ________ at ________% to point ________ at ________%. The short-run Phillips Curve has now shifted from ________ to ________ on the graph.

(5) The long-run Phillips Curve is the line ________.

b. Suppose you begin at point X_3, where the expected and actual rate of inflation is 9% and the unemployment rate is 6%.

(1) If there should be a decline in aggregate demand because of a recession and if the actual rate of inflation should fall to 6%, well below the expected rate of 9%, then business profits will fall and the unemployment rate will decrease to 9% as shown by the movement from point X_3 to point ________.

(2) If firms and workers adjust their expectation to the 6% rate of inflation, the nominal wages will fall, profits will rise, and the economy will move from point ________ to point ________. The short-run Phillips Curve has shifted from ________ to ________.

(3) If this process is repeated, the long-run Phillips Curve will be traced as line ________.

5. The following is a Laffer Curve.

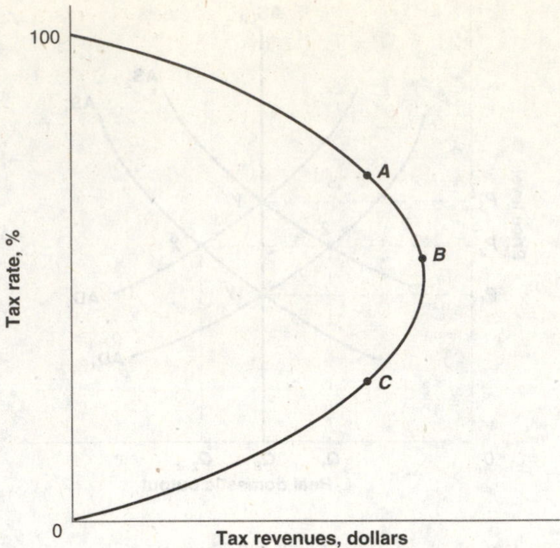

a. The point of maximum tax revenue is ________. As tax rates decrease from 100% to point *B*, tax revenues will (increase, decrease) ________. As tax rates increase from 0% to point *B*, tax revenues will ________.

b. Supply-side economists would contend that it would be beneficial for government to cut tax rates if they are (below, above) ________ point *B*, whereas critics of supply-side economics contend that it would be harmful for government to cut tax rates if they are ________ point *B*.

■ SHORT ANSWER AND ESSAY QUESTIONS

1. What distinguishes the short run from the long run in macroeconomics?

2. Identify the basic difference between a short-run and a long-run aggregate supply curve.

3. Explain what happens to aggregate supply when an increase in the price level results in an increase in nominal wages and other input prices.

4. Explain how to find equilibrium in the extended AD-AS model.

5. Describe the process of demand-pull inflation in the short run and in the long run.

6. How does demand-pull inflation influence the aggregate supply curve?

7. Describe cost-push inflation in the extended AD-AS model.

8. What two generalizations emerge from the analysis of cost-push inflation? Describe the two scenarios that provide the basis for the generalizations.

9. Describe recession in the extended AD-AS model.

10. Why do modern economies tend to experience positive rates of inflation? Explain using the extend AD-AS model.

11. What is a Phillips Curve? What two rates are related?

12. Explain how a Phillips Curve with a negative slope may be derived by holding aggregate supply constant and mentally increasing aggregate demand.

13. Were the rates of inflation and of unemployment consistent with the Phillips Curve in the 1960s? What do data on these two rates suggest about the curve since then?

14. What were the aggregate supply shocks to the U.S. economy during the 1970s and early 1980s? How did these shocks affect interpretation of the Phillips Curve?

15. How can there be a short-run trade-off between inflation and unemployment, but no long-run trade-off? Explain.

16. How can the Phillips Curve be used to explain both inflation and disinflation in the economy?

17. What are the characteristics of the long-run Phillips Curve? How is it related to the natural rate of unemployment?

18. Discuss why supply-side economists contend there are tax disincentives in the economy.

19. Draw and explain a Laffer Curve showing the relationship between tax rates and tax revenues.

20. Outline the three criticisms of the ideas expressed in the depiction of the Laffer Curve.

ANSWERS

Chapter 18 Extending the Analysis of Aggregate Supply

FILL-IN QUESTIONS

1. increase, decrease
2. unresponsive, responsive, up-sloping, vertical
3. right, increase, increase, short-run, nominal, higher
4. left, increase, decrease
5. decrease, increase
6. a decrease, falls, increase, decrease, increase
7. increase, vertical, more
8. greater, greater, smaller
9. an inverse, low, high
10. increase, increase
11. supply, unstable, cost-push, stagflation
12. right, left, short-run
13. does not, unemployment
14. short run, long run, an increase
15. rise, falls, inflation
16. fall, rises, disinflation
17. decrease, decrease, increase, an increase
18. tax revenues, cut
19. increase, decrease, increase, decrease
20. small, demand, supply, loss

TRUE–FALSE QUESTIONS

1. F, p. 362
2. F, pp. 362–363
3. T, pp. 362–363
4. T, pp. 364–365
5. F, pp. 365–366
6. T, pp. 365–366
7. F, p. 366
8. T, p. 366
9. F, p. 367
10. F, pp. 367–368
11. T, p. 369
12. T, p. 370
13. T, pp. 370–371
14. F, p. 370
15. T, pp. 371–372
16. T, p. 372
17. F, p. 373
18. T, p. 373
19. F, pp. 373–374
20. T, p. 374
21. F, pp. 373–374
22. F, p. 374
23. T, p. 374
24. F, p. 374
25. F, p. 375

MULTIPLE-CHOICE QUESTIONS

1. c, p. 362
2. b, p. 362
3. b, pp. 362–363
4. d, pp. 364–365
5. c, pp. 364–365
6. b, pp. 364–365
7. a, pp. 365–366
8. d, pp. 365–366
9. a, p. 366
10. c, p. 367
11. d, pp. 367–368
12. c, pp. 367–368
13. b, pp. 369–370
14. a, pp. 369–370
15. a, pp. 369–370
16. d, pp. 370–371
17. d, pp. 370–371
18. c, pp. 371–372
19. c, pp. 372–373
20. b, p. 373
21. a, p. 374
22. a, pp. 373–374
23. b, p. 374
24. b, p. 374
25. b, p. 375

PROBLEMS

1. 2300; *a.* (1) 160, 2,000, (2) 75, 5, 6.25; *b.* (1) 170, 2,200, (2) 3, 2.5, (3) 10, 6.25; *c.* (1) 150, 1,700, (2) 3, 10, (3) negative
2. P_1, Q_p; *a.* (1) X, P_2, Q_2 (2) AS_1, AS_2, Y, P_3, Q_p, AS_{LR}; *b.* (1) Z, P_2, Q_1, (2) AD_1, AD_2, P_3, Q_p, P_2, P_3, AS_2, (3) P_1, Q_p, AS_2, AS_1; *c.* (1) Q_p, Q_1, P_3, P_2, (2) fall, AS_2, AS_1, W, P_1, Q_p, AS_{LR}
3. *a.* 20; *b.* 9
4. *a.* (1) 6, Y_1, (2) Y_1, X_2, PC_1 PC_2, (3) X_2, Y_2, (4) Y_2, 3, X_3, 6, PC_2, PC_3, (5) PC_{LR}; *b.* (1) Z_2, (2) Z_2, X_2, PC_3, PC_2, (3) PC_{LR}
5. *a.* B, increase, decrease; *b.* above, below

SHORT ANSWER AND ESSAY QUESTIONS

1. p. 362
2. pp. 362–363
3. pp. 362–363
4. pp. 363–364
5. pp. 364–365
6. pp. 364–365
7. pp. 365–366
8. p. 366
9. p. 366
10. pp. 367–368
11. pp. 369–370
12. pp. 369–370
13. pp. 370–371
14. pp. 370–371
15. pp. 372–373
16. pp. 373–374
17. pp. 373–374
18. pp. 374–375
19. p. 375
20. pp. 375–376

CHAPTER 19

Current Issues in Macro Theory and Policy

Now that you understand the basic theory and models of the macro economy, you are ready to learn about different perspectives on how the economy functions and the current issues in macro theory and policy. The chapter achieves those purposes by breaking the discussion into three parts to address three important macro questions.

The first question is: **What causes macro instability in the economy?** Four different perspectives on the issues are given. First, from the *mainstream* view, this instability arises primarily from price stickiness that makes it difficult for the economy to adjust and achieve its potential output when there are aggregate demand or aggregate supply shocks to the economy. Second, *monetarists* focus on the money supply and assume that the competitive market economy has a high degree of stability, except when there is inappropriate monetary policy. The monetarist analysis is based on the equation of exchange and the assumption that the velocity of money is stable. Changes in the money supply, therefore, directly affect the level of nominal GDP. Third, *real-business-cycle* theorists see instability as coming from the aggregate supply side of the economy and from real factors that affect the long-term growth rather than monetary factors that affect aggregate demand. Fourth, some economists think that macroeconomic instability is the result of *coordination failures* that do not permit people to act jointly to determine the optimal level of output, and that the equilibrium in the economy changes as expectations change.

The next question the chapter discusses is: **Does the economy self-correct its macro instability?** The view of new classical economics is that internal mechanisms in the economy allow it to self-correct. The two variants of this new classical perspective are based on *monetarism* and the *rational expectations theory (RET)*. Monetarists think the economy will self-correct to its long-run level of output, although there can be short-run changes in the price level and real output. The rational expectations theory suggests that the self-correction process is quick and does not change the price level or real output, except when there are price-level surprises.

By contrast, mainstream economists contend that the downward inflexibility of wages limits the self-correction mechanisms in the economy. Several explanations are offered for this inflexibility. There can be long-term wage contracts that support wages. Firms also may pay an efficiency wage to encourage work effort, reduce turnover, and prevent shirking. Firms may also be concerned about maintaining the support and teamwork of key workers (insiders), so they do not cut wages even when other workers (outsiders) might be willing to accept a lower wage.

The different perspectives on macro instability and self-correction set the stage for discussion of the third and final question: **Should the macro economy be guided by policy rules or discretion?** To restrict monetary policy, monetarists and rational expectations economists call for a monetary rule that would have monetary authorities allow the money supply to grow in proportion to the long-term growth in the productive capacity of the economy. Both monetarists and rational expectations economists also oppose the use of fiscal policy, and a few call for a balanced budget requirement to limit the use of discretionary fiscal policy.

Mainstream economists see value in discretionary monetary and fiscal policies. They suggest that a monetary rule would be ineffective in achieving growth and would destabilize the economy. A balanced-budget requirement would also have a pro-cyclical effect that would reinforce recessionary or inflationary tendencies in the economy. And since government has taken a more active role in the economy, the historical record shows that discretionary monetary and fiscal actions have reduced macro instability.

As was the case in the past, macroeconomic theory and policy have changed because of the debates among economists. The disputes among mainstream economists, monetarists, rational expectationists, and real-business-cycle theorists have produced new insights about how the macro economy operates. In particular, it is now recognized that "money matters" and that the money supply has a significant effect on the economy. More attention is also being given to the influence of people's expectations on policy and coordination failures in explaining macroeconomic events. The disputes in macroeconomics in the past half-century forced economists to reconsider previous conclusions and led to the incorporation of new ideas about macro theory and policy into mainstream thinking.

■ CHECKLIST

When you have studied this chapter you should be able to

☐ Describe the mainstream view of stability in the macro economy and the two potential sources of instability.

☐ Explain the monetarist view of stability in the macro economy.

☐ Write the equation of exchange and define each of the four terms in the equation.

☐ Explain why monetarists think the velocity of money is relatively stable.

☐ Write a brief scenario that explains what monetarists believe will happen to change the nominal GDP and will happen to ***V*** (velocity of money) when ***M*** (money supply) is increased.
☐ Discuss the monetary causes of instability in the macro economy.
☐ Describe the real-business-cycle view of stability in the macro economy.
☐ Give noneconomic and macroeconomic examples of the coordination failures view of stability in the macro economy.
☐ Use a graph to explain the new classical view of self-correction in the macro economy.
☐ Discuss the differences between the monetarist and rational expectations views on the speed of adjustment for self-correction in the macro economy.
☐ State the two basic assumptions of the rational expectations theory (RET).
☐ Use a graph to explain how RET views unanticipated and fully anticipated changes in the price level.
☐ Describe the mainstream view of self-correction in the macro economy.
☐ Give two reasons why there may be downward wage inflexibility.
☐ State three reasons why a higher wage might result in greater efficiency.
☐ Use ideas from the insider–outsider theory to explain the downward inflexibility of wages.
☐ State why monetarists think there should be a monetary rule, and illustrate the rationale using aggregate demand and aggregate supply models.
☐ Explain why some economists have advocated inflation targeting.
☐ Describe how monetarists and new classical economists view the effectiveness of fiscal policy.
☐ Offer a mainstream defense of a discretionary stabilization policy and a critique of a monetary rule and balanced-budget requirement.
☐ Describe the possible reasons for increased stability in the macro economy in the past half-century.
☐ Summarize the three alternative views on issues affecting the macro economy.
☐ Explain the purpose and components of the Taylor rule (*Last Word*).

■ CHAPTER OUTLINE

1. There are four different views among economists on ***instability*** in the macro economy.

a. The ***mainstream view*** holds that instability in the economy arises from price stickiness and from unexpected shocks to either aggregate demand or aggregate supply. Sticky prices make it difficult for the economy to quickly and fully adjust to economic shocks from unexpected changes in aggregate demand or aggregate supply.

(1) Changes in aggregate demand can arise from a change in any one of the components of aggregate demand (consumption, investment, government, and net export spending). Investment spending is a particularly volatile component of aggregate demand instability.

(2) Adverse aggregate supply shocks which cause cost-push inflation and recession.

b. ***Monetarism*** focuses on the money supply. Monetarists think markets are highly competitive and that government intervention destabilizes the economy.

(1) In monetarism, the **equation of exchange** is $MV = PQ$, where ***M*** is the money supply, ***V*** the ***velocity*** of money, ***P*** the price level, and ***Q*** the quantity of goods and services produced.

(2) Monetarists think that velocity is relatively stable or that the quantity of money demanded is a stable percentage of GDP (GDP/***M*** is constant). If velocity is stable, there is a predictable relationship between ***M*** and nominal GDP (= ***PQ***). An increase in ***M*** will leave firms and households with more money than they wish to have, so they will increase spending and boost aggregate demand. This causes nominal GDP and the amount of money they wish to hold to rise until the demand for money is equal to ***M*** and nominal GDP/***M*** = ***V***.

(3) Monetarists view macroeconomic instability as a result of inappropriate monetary policy. An increase in the money supply will increase aggregate demand, output, and the price level; it will also reduce unemployment. Eventually, nominal wages rise to restore real wages and real output, and the unemployment rate falls back to its natural level at long-run aggregate supply.

c. ***Real-business-cycle theory*** sees macroeconomic instability as being caused by real factors influencing aggregate supply instead of monetary factors causing shifts in aggregate demand. Changes in technology and resources will affect productivity and thus the long-run growth rate of aggregate supply.

d. A fourth view of instability in the macro economy attributes the reasons to ***coordination failures.*** These failures occur when people are not able to coordinate their actions to achieve an optimal equilibrium. A self-fulfilling prophecy can lead to a recession because if households and firms expect it, they individually cut back on spending and employment. If, however, they were to act jointly, they could take actions to counter the recession expectations to achieve an optimal equilibrium.

2. Economists also debate the issue of whether the macro economy self-corrects.

a. ***New classical economics,*** based on monetarism and a rational expectations theory, says the economy may deviate from full-employment output, but it eventually returns to this output level because there are self-corrective mechanisms in the economy.

(1) Graphically, if aggregate demand increases, it temporarily raises real output and the price level. Nominal wages rise and productivity falls, so short-run aggregate supply decreases, thus bringing the economy back to its long-run output level.

(2) There is disagreement about the speed of adjustment. The monetarists adopt the adaptive expectations view that there will be a slower, temporary change in output but that in the long run it will return to its natural level. Other new classical economists adopt the

rational expectations theory *(RET)* view that there will be a rapid adjustment with little or no change in output. RET is based on two assumptions: People understand how the economy works so that they quickly anticipate the effect on the economy of an economic event; and all markets in the economy are so competitive that equilibrium prices and quantities quickly adjust to changes in policy.

(3) In RET, unanticipated price-level changes, called **price-level surprises,** cause short-run changes in real output because they cause misperceptions about the economy among workers and firms.

(4) In RET, fully anticipated price-level changes do not change real output even in the short run because workers and firms anticipate and counteract the effects of the changes.

b. The ***mainstream view*** of self-correction suggests that price and wages may be inflexible downward in the economy.

(1) Graphically, a decrease in aggregate demand will decrease real output but not the price level because nominal wages will not decline and cause the short-run aggregate supply curve to shift right.

(2) Downward wage inflexibility primarily arises because of wage contracts and the legal minimum wage, but they may also occur from efficiency wages and insider–outsider relationships.

(3) An ***efficiency wage*** minimizes the firm's labor cost per unit of output but may be higher than the market wage. This higher wage may result in greater efficiency because it stimulates greater work effort, requires less supervision costs, and reduces job turnover.

(4) ***Insider–outsider theory*** suggests that relationships may also produce downward wage inflexibility. During a recession, outsiders (who are less essential to the firm) may try to bid down wages to try to keep their jobs, but the firm may not lower wages because it does not want to alienate insiders (who are more essential to the firm) and disrupt the cooperative environment in the firm needed for production.

3. The debates over macro policy also focus on the need for ***policy rules or discretion.***

a. Monetarists and new classical economists argue for policy rules to reduce government intervention in the economy. They believe this intervention causes macroeconomic instability.

(1) In regard to monetary policy, monetarists such as Milton Friedman have proposed a ***monetary rule*** that the money supply be increased at the same annual rate as the potential annual rate of increase in the real GDP. A monetary rule would shift aggregate demand rightward to match a shift in the long-run aggregate supply curve that occurs because of economic growth, thus keeping the price level stable over time. More recently, economists have advocated ***inflation targeting*** as an alternative to a Friedman-type monetary rule. Such targeting would involve the Fed specifying a target range for inflation and then using monetary policy tools to help the economy achieve its target.

(2) Monetarists and new classical economists question the value of fiscal policy, and some would like to see a balanced federal budget over time. An expansionist fiscal policy will tend to crowd out investment and cause only a temporary increase in output. RET economists also think that fiscal policy is ineffective and that people will anticipate it and their acts will counteract its intended effects.

b. Mainstream economists think that discretionary fiscal and monetary policy can be effective and are opposed to a monetary rule and a balanced-budget requirement.

(1) They see the velocity of money as relatively unstable and a loose link between changes in the money supply and aggregate demand. This means that a monetary rule might produce too great a shift in aggregate demand (and demand-pull inflation) or too small a shift (and deflation) to match the shift in aggregate supply. Such a rule would contribute to price instability, not price stability.

(2) They support the use of fiscal policy during a recession or to counter growing inflation. Fiscal policy, however, should be reserved for those situations where monetary policy is relatively ineffective. They also oppose a balanced-budget amendment because its effects would be pro-cyclical rather than countercyclical and would reinforce recessionary or inflationary tendencies.

c. Mainstream economists also note that there has been greater stability in the macro economy since 1946, when discretionary monetary and fiscal policies were more actively used to moderate the effects of the business cycle.

4. The ***disputes in macroeconomics*** have led to the incorporation of several ideas from monetarism and rational expectations theories into the mainstream thinking about macroeconomics. First, monetarists have gotten mainstream economists to recognize that changes in the money supply are important in explaining long-lasting and rapid inflation. Second, mainstream economists now recognize that expectations matter because of arguments from the rational expectations theory and theories about coordination failures in the economy. There will be more price stability, full employment, and economic growth if government can create reliable expectations of those outcomes for households and businesses. In short, macroeconomics continues to develop. Table 19.1 summarizes the three alternative views of macroeconomics.

5. (*Last Word*). The Taylor rule specifies what actions the Fed should take in changing the federal funds rate given changes in real GDP and inflation. This monetary rule has three parts: (a) when real GDP equals potential GDP, and inflation is equal to the Fed's 2 percent target for the inflation rate, the federal funds rate should stay at 4 percent, to give a real interest rate of 2 percent; (b) if real GDP rises 1 percent above potential GDP, then the Fed should raise the real federal funds rate .5 percentage points; and (c) if inflation rises by 1 percentage point above its target of 2 percent, then the Fed should raise the real federal funds rate by .5 percentage point.

■ HINTS AND TIPS

1. The chapter may appear complex because many alternative viewpoints are presented. To simplify matters, first focus on the three questions that the chapter addresses: What causes macro instability in the economy? Does the economy self-correct? Should policymakers use rules or discretion? For each question, identify how different types of economists answer each question.

2. Review the discussions of aggregate demand and aggregate supply in Chapters 12 and 18 as preparation for the comparison of alternate views of the macro economy presented in this chapter.

3. Monetarist and mainstream views of the macro economy are two approaches to looking at the same thing. The similarities can best be seen in equations in nominal form. The monetarist equation of exchange is $MV = PQ$. The mainstream equation is $C_a + I_g + X_n + G = GDP$. The MV term is the monetarist expression for the mainstream equilibrium $C_a + I_g + X_n + G$. The PQ term is the monetarist expression for GDP. Monetarists give more emphasis to the role of money and assume that velocity is relatively stable. Mainstream economists give more emphasis to the instability caused by investment spending and to influences on GDP from consumption, net exports, and government spending.

■ IMPORTANT TERMS

monetarism	**new classical economics**
velocity	**price-level surprises**
equation of exchange	**efficiency wage**
real-business-cycle theory	**insider–outsider theory**
coordination failures	**monetary rule**
rational expectations theory	

SELF-TEST

■ FILL-IN QUESTIONS

1. The mainstream view is that instability in the economy arises from price (flexibility, stickiness) ______________ and from shocks to aggregate demand or aggregate supply that are (expected, unexpected) ______________.

2. One of the most volatile components of aggregate demand is (net export, investment) ______________ spending. If it increases too rapidly, then (inflation, recession) ______________ can occur, but if it decreases, then the economy can experience ______________.

3. The economy also is subject to instability from wars or resource shortages that (raise, lower) ______________ per-unit production costs. Such adverse aggregate (demand, supply) ______________ shocks can lead to cost-push inflation and recession.

4. Monetarists argue that capitalism is inherently (stable, unstable) ______________ because most of its markets are (competitive, noncompetitive) ______________. They believe that government intervention in the economy has contributed to macroeconomic (stability, instability) ______________ and has promoted (flexibility, inflexibility) ______________ in wages.

5. The basic equation of the monetarists is ______________ = ______________. Indicate what each of the following four letters in the equation represents:

a. M: ______________

b. V: ______________

c. P: ______________

d. Q: ______________

6. Monetarists believe that V is relatively (stable, unstable) ______________ because people have a ______________ desire to hold money relative to holding other financial and real assets or for making purchases. The amount of money people will want to hold will depend on the level of (real, nominal) ______________ GDP.

7. An increase in M, to the monetarist's way of thinking, will leave the public with (more, less) ______________ money than it wishes to have, inducing the public to (increase, decrease) ______________ its spending for consumer and capital goods, which will result in a(n) ______________ in aggregate demand and nominal GDP until nominal GDP equals MV.

8. Monetarists believe that the most significant cause of macroeconomic instability has been inappropriate (fiscal, monetary) ______________ policy. Too rapid increases in M cause (recession, inflation) ______________; insufficient growth of M causes ______________.

9. The theory that changes in resource availability and technology (real factors), which alter productivity, are the main causes of instability in the macro economy is held by (real-business-cycle, rational expectations) ______________ economists. In this theory, shifts in the economy's long-run aggregate (demand, supply) ______________ curve change real output. As a consequence, money demand and money supply change, shifting the aggregate demand curve in the (opposite, same) ______________ direction as the initial change in long-run aggregate supply. Real output thus can change (with, without) ______________ a change in the price level.

10. A coordination failure is said to occur when people (do, do not) ______________ reach a mutually beneficial equilibrium because they lack some way to jointly coordinate their actions. In this view, there is (are) (one, a number of) ______________ equilibrium position(s) in the economy. Macroeconomic instability is the result of changing (the money supply, expectations) ______________ that result in changing the equilibrium position(s).

11. Monetarists and rational expectations economists view the economy as (capable, incapable) ______________ of self-correction when it deviates from the full-employment level of real output. Monetarists suggest that this adjustment occurs (gradually, rapidly) ______________, while rational expectations economists argue that it occurs ______________.

12. Rational expectations theory assumes that with sufficient information, people's beliefs about future economic outcomes (are, are not) ______________ accurate reflections of the likelihood of the outcomes occurring. It also assumes that markets are highly competitive, meaning that prices and wages are (flexible, inflexible) ______________.

13. In the rational expectations theory, changes in aggregate demand that change the price level and real output are (anticipated, unanticipated) ______________, while changes in aggregate demand that only change the price level and not real output are ______________.

14. The view of mainstream economists is that many prices and wages are (flexible, inflexible) ______________ downward for (short, long) ______________ periods of time. This situation (increases, decreases) ______________ the ability of the economy to automatically self-correct for deviations from full-employment output.

15. A higher wage can result in more efficiency because it results in (greater, less) ______________ work effort, supervision costs that are (lower, higher) ______________, and (more, less) ______________ turnover in jobs. Efficiency wages (increase, decrease) ______________ the downward inflexibility of wages because they make firms more reluctant to cut wages when aggregate demand declines.

16. Monetarists and rational expectations economists support a monetary rule because they believe that discretionary monetary policy tends to (stabilize, destabilize) ______________ the economy. With this rule the money supply would be increased at a rate (greater than, less than, equal to) ______________ the long-run growth of potential GDP; graphically, this can be shown by a shift in aggregate demand that would be ______________ the shift in long-run aggregate supply resulting from economic growth.

17. In recent decades, the call for a monetary rule has faded and has been replaced with a call for (efficiency wages, inflation targeting) ______________. In such an approach, the federal Reserve would specify an acceptable range for (unemployment, inflation) ______________ and use its monetary tools to achieve that objective.

18. Proponents of the rational expectations theory contend that discretionary monetary policy is (effective, ineffective) ______________ and like the monetarists favor (rules, discretion) ______________. When considering discretionary fiscal policy, most monetarists and RET economists (do, do not) ______________ advocate its use.

19. Mainstream economists (support, oppose) ______________ a monetary rule and a balanced-budget requirement. They view discretionary monetary policy as (effective, ineffective) ______________, and think discretionary fiscal policy is ______________ but should be held in reserve when monetary policy works too slowly. They say the use of discretionary monetary and fiscal policies since 1950 has produced (more, less) ______________ stability in the macro economy.

20. Many ideas from alternative views of the macro economy have been absorbed into mainstream thinking about macroeconomics. There is more recognition that excessive growth of the money supply is a major cause of (recession, inflation) ______________, and that expectations and coordination failures are (important, unimportant) ______________ in the formulation of government policies for price stability, unemployment, and economic growth.

■ TRUE–FALSE QUESTIONS

Circle T if the statement is true, F if it is false.

1. The mainstream view is that macro instability arises from price stickiness and unexpected shocks to either aggregate demand or aggregate supply. **T F**

2. Among the components of aggregate expenditures the most volatile is investment spending, which can cause unexpected shifts in the aggregate demand curve. **T F**

3. Monetarists argue that the market system would provide for macroeconomic stability were it not for government interference in the economy. **T F**

4. In the equation of exchange, the left side, ***MV***, represents the total amount received by sellers of output, while the right side, ***PQ***, represents the total amount spent by purchasers of that output. **T F**

5. Monetarists argue that ***V*** in the equation of exchange is relatively stable and that a change in ***M*** will bring about a direct and proportional change in ***PQ***. **T F**

6. Most monetarists believe that an increase in the money supply has no effect on real output and employment in the short run. **T F**

7. In the monetarist view, the only cause of the Great Depression was the decline in investment spending. **T F**

8. Real-business-cycle theory views changes in resource availability and technology, which alter productivity, as the main cause of macroeconomic instability. **T F**

9. In the real-business-cycle theory, real output changes only with a change in the price level. **T F**

10. In real-business-cycle theory, macro instability arises on the aggregate demand side of the economy. **T F**

11. A coordination failure is said to occur when people do not reach a mutually beneficial equilibrium because they lack some way to jointly coordinate their actions to achieve it. **T F**

12. People's expectations have no effect on coordination failures. **T F**

13. New classical economists see the economy as automatically correcting itself when disturbed from its full-employment level of real output. **T F**

14. The rational expectations theory assumes that both product and resource markets are uncompetitive and wages and prices are inflexible. **T F**

15. In rational expectations theory an assumption is made that people adjust their expectations quickly as new developments occur that affect future economic outcomes. **T F**

16. In the rational expectations theory, a fully anticipated price-level change results in a change in real output. **T F**

17. Mainstream economists contend that many wages and prices are inflexible downward. **T F**

18. An efficiency wage is a below-market wage that spurs greater work effort and gives the firm more profits because of lower wage costs. **T F**

19. One reason a higher wage can result in greater economic efficiency is that it lowers supervision costs. **T F**

20. Insider–outsider theory offers one explanation for the downward inflexibility of wages in the economy. **T F**

21. Monetarists believe that a monetary rule would reduce instability in the macro economy. **T F**

22. Rational expectations economists argue that monetary policy should be left to the discretion of government. **T F**

23. Monetarists support the use of fiscal policy, especially as a means of controlling inflation. **T F**

24. Mainstream economists believe that discretionary monetary policy is an effective tool for stabilizing the economy. **T F**

25. The mainstream view of the economy since 1950 believes that the economy has become inherently less stable because of the use of fiscal policy. **T F**

■ MULTIPLE-CHOICE QUESTIONS

Circle the letter that corresponds to the best answer.

1. One of the sources of macro instability in the view of mainstream economists is that
(a) output is fixed in the long run
(b) output is fixed in the short run
(c) prices are sticky in the short run
(d) prices are flexible in the long run

2. From the perspective of mainstream economists, another source of macroeconomic instability is
(a) a velocity of money that is stable
(b) a velocity of money that is unstable
(c) expected shocks to aggregate demand or aggregate supply
(d) unexpected shocks to aggregate demand or aggregate supply

3. The mainstream view of the economy holds that
(a) government intervention in the economy is not desirable
(b) product and labor markets are highly competitive and flexible
(c) changes in investment spending lead to changes in aggregate demand
(d) economic growth is best achieved through implementation of a monetary rule

4. In the monetarist perspective
(a) discretionary monetary policy is the most effective way to moderate swings in the business cycle
(b) government policies have reduced macroeconomic stability
(c) macroeconomic stability results from adverse aggregate supply shocks
(d) markets in a capitalistic economy are largely noncompetitive

5. Which is the equation of exchange?
(a) $PQ/M + V = GDP$
(b) $V = M + PQ$
(c) $MV = PQ$
(d) $V + I_g + M = GDP$

6. In the equation of exchange, if V is stable, an increase in M will necessarily increase
(a) the demand for money
(b) government spending
(c) nominal GDP
(d) velocity

7. When nominal gross domestic product (GDP) is divided by the money supply (M), you will obtain the
(a) velocity of money
(b) monetary multiplier
(c) equation of exchange
(d) monetary rule

8. Monetarists argue that the amount of money the public will want to hold depends primarily on the level of
(a) nominal GDP
(b) investment
(c) taxes
(d) prices

9. Based on the equation of exchange, if nominal GDP is $550 billion and the velocity of money is 5, then the money supply is

(a) $55 billion
(b) $110 billion
(c) $550 billion
(d) $2,750 billion

10. Real-business-cycle theory suggests that

(a) velocity changes gradually and predictably; thus it is able to accommodate the long-run changes in nominal GDP
(b) the volatility of investment is the main cause of the economy's instability
(c) inappropriate monetary policy is the single most important cause of macroeconomic instability
(d) changes in technology and resources affect productivity, and thus the long-run growth of aggregate supply

11. In the real-business-cycle theory, if the long-run aggregate supply increased, then aggregate demand would increase by

(a) an equal amount, so real output and the price level would increase
(b) less than an equal amount, so real output would increase and the price level would decrease
(c) greater than an equal amount, so real output and the price level would increase
(d) an equal amount, so real output would increase and the price level would be unchanged

12. If aggregate demand declined and the economy experienced a recession due to a self-fulfilling prophecy, this would be an example of

(a) real-business-cycle theory
(b) insider–outsider theory
(c) a coordination failure
(d) a change in velocity

13. Which macroeconomic theory would be most closely associated with the concept that the economy can get stuck in less than optimal equilibrium positions because of a lack of consistency in the expectations of businesses and households?

(a) rational expectations
(b) real-business-cycle
(c) coordination failures
(d) monetarism

14. In the new classical view, when the economy diverges from its full-employment output,

(a) internal mechanisms within the economy would automatically return it to its full-employment output
(b) discretionary monetary policy is needed to return it to its full-employment output
(c) discretionary fiscal policy is needed to return it to its full-employment output
(d) the adoption of an efficiency wage in the economy would return it to its full-employment output

15. The views about the speed of adjustment for self-correction in the economy suggest that

(a) monetarists think it would be gradual, and rational expectations economists think it would be quick
(b) monetarists think it would be quick, and rational expectations economists think it would be gradual
(c) monetarists and mainstream economists think it would be quick
(d) real-business-cycle theorists and rational expectations economists think it would be gradual

16. Proponents of the rational expectations theory argue that people

(a) are not as rational as monetarists assume them to be
(b) make forecasts that are based on poor information, causing economic policy to be driven by self-fulfilling prophecy
(c) form beliefs about future economic outcomes that accurately reflect the likelihood that those outcomes will occur
(d) do not respond quickly to changes in wages and prices, causing a misallocation of economic resources in the economy

17. In the rational expectations theory, a temporary change in real output would occur from a

(a) fully anticipated price-level change
(b) downward wage inflexibility
(c) coordination failure
(d) price-level surprise

18. The conclusion mainstream economists draw about the downward price and wage inflexibility is that

(a) the effects can be reversed relatively quickly
(b) efficiency wages do not contribute to the problem
(c) the economy can be mired in recession for long periods
(d) wage and price controls are needed to counteract the situation

19. Which one of the following would be a reason that a higher wage would result in greater efficiency?

(a) lower productivity
(b) reduced job turnover
(c) higher supervision costs
(d) less work effort by employees

20. According to mainstream economists, which of the following contribute to the downward inflexibility of wages?

(a) price-level surprises
(b) insider–outsider relationships
(c) adverse aggregate supply shocks
(d) inadequate investment spending

21. The rule suggested by the monetarists is that the money supply should be increased at the same rate as the

(a) price level
(b) interest rate
(c) velocity of money
(d) potential growth in real GDP

22. To stabilize the economy, monetarist and rational expectations economists advocate

(a) the use of price-level surprises and adoption of an efficiency wage
(b) a monetary rule and a balanced-budget requirement
(c) the use of discretionary fiscal policy instead of discretionary monetary policy
(d) the use of discretionary monetary policy instead of discretionary fiscal policy

23. Proponents of inflation targeting argue that such a policy would
(a) improve productivity and thus increase aggregate supply
(b) make the Fed more accountable by giving it a specific goal
(c) increase the coordination of fiscal and monetary policy to control inflation
(d) give more discretion to monetary policymakers in responding to economic crises

24. Mainstream economists support
(a) increasing the money supply at a constant rate
(b) eliminating insider–outsider relationships in business
(c) the use of discretionary monetary and fiscal policies
(d) a balanced-budget requirement and a monetary rule

25. Which of the following would be an idea from monetarism that has been absorbed into mainstream macroeconomics?
(a) how changes in investment spending change aggregate demand
(b) the importance of money and the money supply in the economy
(c) using discretion rather than rules for guiding economic policy
(d) building the macro foundations for microeconomics

■ PROBLEMS

1. Assume that you are a monetarist in this problem and that ***V*** is stable and equal to 4. In the following table is the aggregate supply schedule: the real output ***Q*** which producers will offer for sale at seven different price levels ***P***.

P	Q	PQ	MV
$1.00	100	$____	$____
2.00	110	____	____
3.00	120	____	____
4.00	130	____	____
5.00	140	____	____
6.00	150	____	____
7.00	160	____	____

a. Compute and enter in the table the seven values of ***PQ***.
b. Assume ***M*** is $90. Enter the values of ***MV*** on each of the seven lines in the table. The equilibrium
(1) nominal domestic output (***PQ*** or ***MV***) is $________.
(2) price level is $________.
(3) real domestic output (***Q***) is $________.
c. When ***M*** increases to $175, ***MV*** at each price level is $________ and the equilibrium
(1) nominal domestic output is $________.
(2) price level is $________.
(3) real domestic output is $________.

2. Indicate what perspective(s) of economics would be most closely associated with each position. Use the following abbreviations: **MAI** (mainstream economics), **MON** (monetarism), **RET** (rational expectations theory), and **RBC** (real-business-cycle theory).
a. macro instability from investment spending ________
b. macro instability from inappropriate monetary policy ________
c. macro instability from changes in resource availability and technology ________
d. equation of exchange ________
e. fiscal policy can be effective ________
f. unanticipated price-level changes ________
g. downward inflexibility of wages and prices ________
h. monetary rule ________
i. neutral fiscal policy ________
j. economy automatically self-corrects ________
k. monetary policy is effective ________

3. Following are price-level (***PL***) and output (***Q***) combinations to describe aggregate demand and aggregate supply curves: (1) ***PL*** and Q_1 is AD_1; (2) ***PL*** and Q_2 is AD_2; (3) ***PL*** and Q_3 is AS_{LR1}; (4) ***PL*** and Q_4 is AS_{LR2}.

PL	Q_1	Q_2	Q_3	Q_4
250	0	200	400	600
200	200	400	400	600
150	400	600	400	600
100	600	800	400	600
50	800	1000	400	600

a. Use the following to graph AD_1, AD_2, AS_{LR1}, and AS_{LR2}. Label the vertical axis as the price level and the horizontal axis as real output (***Q***).

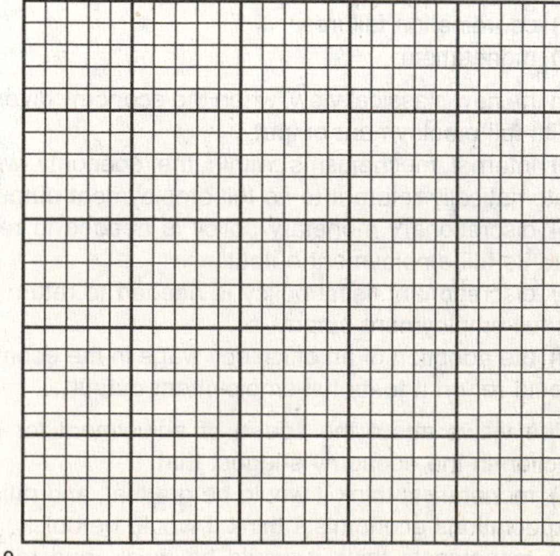

b. If the economy is initially in equilibrium where AD_1 and AS_{LR1} intersect, the price level will be ______ and real output will be ______.
c. If, over time, the economy grows from AS_{LR1} to AS_{LR2}, the equilibrium price level will be ______ and real output will be ______.
d. Assume a monetary rule is adopted that increases the money supply proportionate to the increase in aggregate supply. Aggregate demand will increase from AD_1 to AD_2, making the price level ______ and real output ______.
e. Mainstream economists would argue that velocity is unstable, so a constant increase in the money supply might not shift AD_1 all the way to AD_2. In this case, the price level would fall below the target of ______. It might also be the case that the constant increase in the money supply might shift AD_1 beyond AD_2, so the price level would rise above the target of ______.

■ SHORT ANSWER AND ESSAY QUESTIONS

1. Explain the two sources of macroeconomic instability in the view of mainstream economists.

2. Explain how changes in aggregate demand can produce economic instability.

3. Discuss the role that adverse aggregate supply shocks play in contributing to economic instability.

4. What do monetarists see as the cause of economic instability in the economy? Explain, using the equation of exchange, how a change in the money supply will affect nominal GDP.

5. Why do monetarists argue that the velocity of money is stable? If the money supply increases, how will people respond from a monetarist perspective?

6. Compare and contrast the monetarist and mainstream views on the causes of macroeconomic instability. How do monetarists explain the Great Depression?

7. Explain the real-business-cycle view of macroeconomic instability using an aggregate demand and supply graph.

8. Give a macroeconomic example of how coordination failures cause macroeconomic instability.

9. Explain the new classical view of self-correction in the macro economy. Contrast the monetarist perspective with that of rational expectations in terms of the real output, the price level, and the speed of adjustment.

10. Describe the two assumptions on which rational expectations are based. How realistic is it to expect that people will be able to accurately forecast economic outcomes?

11. Use a graph to illustrate and explain the mainstream view of self-correction in the macro economy.

12. Why would an efficiency wage lead to downward inflexibility in prices?

13. Give an example of insider–outsider relationships and explain how it affects wage flexibility.

14. What is the monetary rule? Why do monetarists suggest this rule to replace discretionary monetary policy?

15. What is the perspective of rational expectations economists on a monetary rule and the conduct of monetary policy?

16. What is the position of some monetarist and rational expectations economists on a requirement for a balanced budget? Why do they adopt such a position?

17. How do mainstream economists defend the use of discretionary monetary policy?

18. What arguments are made by mainstream economists to justify the use of discretionary fiscal policy?

19. What interpretation do mainstream economists make of the historical evidence over the past half century or so on the relationship between macroeconomic policy and stability in the economy?

20. What influences have monetarism and the rational expectations theory had on mainstream macroeconomic theory and policy? Give several examples of ideas that have changed mainstream thinking.

ANSWERS

Chapter 19 Current Issues in Macro Theory and Policy

FILL-IN QUESTIONS

1. stickiness, unexpected
2. investment, inflation, recession
3. raise, supply
4. stable, competitive, instability, inflexibility
5. $MV = PQ$; *a.* the money supply; *b.* the velocity of money; *c.* the average price of each unit of physical output; *d.* the physical volume of goods and services produced
6. stable, stable, nominal
7. more, increase, increase
8. monetary, inflation, recession
9. real-business-cycle, supply, same, without
10. do not, a number of, expectations
11. capable, gradually, rapidly
12. are, flexible
13. unanticipated, anticipated
14. inflexible, long, decreases
15. greater, lower, less, increase
16. destabilize, equal to, equal to
17. inflation targeting, inflation
18. ineffective, rules, do not
19. oppose, effective, effective, more
20. inflation, important

TRUE–FALSE QUESTIONS

1. T, p. 382
2. T, p. 382
3. T, pp. 382–383
4. F, pp. 382–383
5. T, pp. 382–383
6. F, pp. 383–384
7. F, p. 384
8. T, p. 384
9. F, p. 384
10. F, p. 384
11. T, pp. 384–385
12. F, pp. 384–385
13. T, p. 386
14. F, p. 386
15. T, p. 387
16. F, p. 387
17. T, p. 388
18. F, p. 388
19. T, p. 389
20. T, p. 389
21. T, p. 389
22. F, p. 391
23. F, p. 391
24. T, pp. 391–392
25. F, p. 392

MULTIPLE-CHOICE QUESTIONS

1. c, p. 382
2. d, p. 382
3. c, p. 382
4. b, p. 382
5. c, p. 382
6. c, pp. 382–383
7. a, pp. 382–383
8. a, p. 383
9. b, pp. 382–383
10. d, p. 384
11. d, p. 384
12. c, pp. 384–385
13. c, pp. 384–385
14. a, p. 386
15. a, p. 387
16. c, pp. 387–388
17. d, pp. 387–388
18. c, p. 388
19. b, pp. 388–389
20. b, p. 389
21. d, pp. 389–390
22. b, pp.389–390
23. b, p. 391
24. c, pp. 391–392
25. b, p. 392

PROBLEMS

1. *a.* 100, 220, 360, 520, 700, 900, 1120; *b.* 360, 360, 360, 360, 360, 360, 360, (1) 360, (2) 3.00, (3) 120; *c.* 700, (1) 700, (2) 5.00, (3) 140

2. *a.* MAI; *b.* MON, RET; *c.* RBC; *d.* MON; *e.* MAI; *f.* RET; *g.* MAI; *h.* MON, RET; *i.* MON, RET; *j.* MON, RET; *k.* MAI

3. *a.* graph similar to Figure 19.3 in the text; *b.* 150, 400; *c.* 100, 600; *d.* 150, 600; *e.* 150, 150

SHORT ANSWER AND ESSAY QUESTIONS

1. p. 382
2. p. 382
3. pp. 382–383
4. pp. 382–383
5. pp. 382–383
6. pp. 382–383
7. p. 384
8. pp. 384–385
9. pp. 386–387
10. p. 387
11. p. 388
12. pp. 388–389
13. p. 389
14. pp. 389–390
15. pp. 390–391
16. p. 391
17. pp. 391–392
18. p. 392
19. p. 392
20. p. 394

CHAPTER 20

International Trade

After a brief review of the facts of international trade, the text uses the concept of production possibilities that you learned in Chapter 1 to explain why nations trade. Nations specialize in and export those goods and services in the production of which they have a **comparative advantage,** which means the domestic opportunity cost of producing a particular good or service is lower in one nation than in another nation. When nations specialize in those products in which they have a comparative advantage, the world can obtain more goods and services from its resources and each nation enjoys a higher standard of living than it would without trade.

Another question the chapter answers is what determines the equilibrium prices and quantities of the imports and exports resulting from trade. The text uses the **supply and demand analysis,** originally presented in Chapter 3, to explain equilibrium in the world market for a product. A simplified two-nation and one-product model of trade is constructed with export supply curves and import demand curves for each nation. Equilibrium occurs where one nation's export supply curve intersects another nation's import demand curve.

Regardless of the advantages of specialization and trade among nations, people in the United States and throughout the world for well over 200 years have debated the question of whether **free trade or protection** was the better policy for their nation. Economists took part in this debate and, with few exceptions, made a strong case for free trade. They also argued that protectionism in the form of tariffs, import quotas, and other trade barriers prevents or reduces specialization and decreases both a nation's and the world's production and standards of living. Despite these arguments, nations have erected and continue to erect trade barriers using an assortment of protection arguments that have questionable validity.

The latter sections of the chapter address questions related to how to make trade among nations work better and resolve trade disputes. **Multilateral agreements** have been made among nations and **free-trade zones** have been established to reduce trade barriers and increase worldwide trade. The World Trade Organization (WTO) is responsible for multilateral trade negotiations among member nations. The European Union (EU) is a free-trade zone among 27 European nations. The North American Free Trade Agreement (NAFTA) established a free-trade zone for the United States, Canada, and Mexico. The U.S. Congress developed policies to assist U.S. workers hurt by the expansion of trade.

Whether the direction of the trade policy in the United States will be toward freer trade or more protectionism is a question that gets debated as each new trade issue is presented to the U.S. public. The decision on each issue may well depend on your economic understanding of trade and the problems with trade protection.

■ CHECKLIST

When you have studied this chapter you should be able to

☐ Cite some key facts about international trade.
☐ State the three economic circumstances that make it desirable for nations to specialize and trade.
☐ Give examples of labor-intensive, capital-intensive, and land-intensive goods.
☐ Explain the difference between absolute advantage and comparative advantage.
☐ State the three assumptions made about the production possibilities graphs for two products in a two-nation example of trade.
☐ Compute the opportunity-cost ratio of producing the two products in the two-nation example.
☐ Determine which nation has a comparative advantage in the two-nation example.
☐ Calculate the range in which the terms of trade will occur in the two-nation example.
☐ Explain how nations gain from trade and specialization based on the two-nation example.
☐ Discuss how increasing costs affect specialization in the two-nation example.
☐ Restate the general case for free trade.
☐ Construct domestic supply and demand curves for two nations that trade a product.
☐ Construct export supply and import demand curves for two nations that trade a product.
☐ Explain how the equilibrium world prices and quantities of exports and imports are determined for two nations that trade a product.
☐ Define and explain the purpose of tariffs, import quotas, nontariff barriers, voluntary export restraints, and export subsidies.
☐ Explain the economic effects of a protective tariff for a product on consumption, production, imports, revenue, and efficiency.
☐ Analyze the economic effects of an import quota and compare them with a tariff.
☐ Discuss the problems with six major arguments for trade protectionism (self-sufficiency, diversification, infant industry, dumping, employment, and cheap labor).
☐ Describe the purpose and outcomes from the General Agreement on Tariffs and Trade (GATT).

☐ Discuss the purpose and controversies surrounding the World Trade Organization (WTO).
☐ Explain how the European Union (EU) operates as a free-trade zone.
☐ Describe the North American Free Trade Agreement (NAFTA).
☐ Discuss the reasons for the Trade Adjustment Assistance Act of 2002.
☐ Evaluate reasons for and outcomes from offshoring.
☐ Explain how Frédéric Bastiat satirized the proponents of protectionism (*Last Word*).

■ CHAPTER OUTLINE

1. Some key facts on international trade are worth noting.
a. About 13 percent of the total output (GDP) of the United States is accounted for by exports of goods and services. The United States provides about 8.5 percent of the world's exports. The United States also leads the world in the combined volume of exports and imports.
b. The United States has a trade deficit in goods and a trade surplus in services, and overall has a trade deficit in goods and services. The United States has a sizable trade deficit in goods and services with China. Canada is the most important trading partner for the United States in terms of the volume of trade.
c. The major exports of the United States are chemicals, agricultural products, consumer durables, semiconductors, and aircraft. The major imports are petroleum, automobiles, metals, household appliances, and computers. Most of the U.S. trade occurs with other industrially advanced nations and members of OPEC. Canada is the largest trading partner for the United States.
d. The major participants in international trade are the United States, Japan, China, and the nations of Western Europe. Other key participants include the Asian economies of South Korea, Taiwan, and Singapore.
e. International trade links nations and is the focus of economic policy and debate in the United States and other nations.

2. The ***economic basis for trade*** comprises several circumstances. Specialization and trade among nations is advantageous because the world's resources are not evenly distributed and efficient production of different products requires different technologies and combinations of resources. Also, products differ in quality and other attributes, so people might prefer imported to domestic goods in some cases. Some nations have a cost advantage in making ***labor-intensive goods*** such as textiles or toys. Other nations have a cost advantage in producing ***land-intensive goods*** such as beef or vegetables. Industrially advanced economies have a cost advantage in making ***capital-intensive goods*** such as airplanes or chemicals.

3. Specialization and international trade increase the productivity of a nation's resources and allow a nation to obtain greater output than would be the case without trade. A nation has an absolute advantage in the production of a product over another nation if it can produce more of the product with the same amount of resources as the other nation. To specialize and benefit from trade, however, a nation only needs to have a comparative advantage, which means that it produces a product at a lower opportunity cost than another nation.
a. The concept of comparative advantage is presented with an example using two nations (the United States and Mexico) and two products (beef and vegetables). The production possibilities curves are different straight lines because of the assumption of constant opportunity costs, but the curve for each nation is different because of different costs. The United States has an absolute advantage in the production of both beef and vegetables, which means that if all resources were devoted to one product or the other, the United States would produce more of both products (beef: United States 30 tons and Mexico 10 tons; vegetables: United States 30 tons and Mexico 20 tons).
(1) The ***opportunity-cost ratio*** is what one nation has to forgo in the output of one domestic product to produce another domestic product. Using tons as units for beef (B) and vegetables (V), the opportunity-cost ratio for the United States is $1V = 1B$.
(2) The opportunity-cost ratio for Mexico is $2V = 1B$.
(3) If each nation is self-sufficient, they will pick some combination of the two products to produce. Assume this output mix for the United State is $18B$ and $12V$ and for Mexico it is $8B$ and $4V$.
b. ***Comparative advantage*** explains the gains from trade and is directly related to opportunity cost. In essence, a nation has a comparative advantage in the production of a product when it can produce the product at a lower domestic opportunity cost than can a trading partner. A nation will specialize in the production of a product for which it is the low opportunity cost producer and trade for the other products it wants. Although the United States has an absolute advantage in producing both products, it does not have a comparative advantage because of the differences in the domestic opportunity cost of producing the products in both nations. The ***principle of comparative advantage*** says that total output will be greatest when each nation specializes in the production of a product for which it has the lowest domestic opportunity cost.
(1) Returning to the two-nation example, for the United States, $1V = 1B$, but for Mexico, $2V = 1B$. The United States has a lower domestic opportunity cost for beef because for the United States to get $1B$ it gives up only $1V$ whereas for Mexico to get $1B$ it gives up $2V$.
(2) Note that for Mexico, after dividing each side of $2V = 1B$ by 2 it becomes $1V = 0.5B$, Mexico has a lower domestic opportunity cost for vegetables because for Mexico to get $1V$, it gives up only $0.5B$ whereas for the United States to get $1V$ it gives up $1B$.
c. The **terms of trade** or ratio at which one product is traded for another is between the opportunity-cost ratios of the two nations, or between $1V = 1B$ (U.S. costs) and $1V = 2B$ (Mexico's costs).
d. Supposing that the terms of trade are $1V = 1.5B$, it is then possible to show a ***trading possibilities line*** that shifts outward from the original production possibilities line for each nation.
(1) Each nation will be able to achieve a set of beef and vegetable alternatives by specializing in the production of the product for which it has a low opportunity cost

and trading its output of that product for the product for which has a high opportunity cost.

(2) Each nation gains from this trade because specialization permits a greater total output from the same resources and a better allocation of the world's resources. Given the terms of trade (1 *V* = 1.5*B*), if the United States uses all its resources to produce beef (30*B*) and exports 10*B* to Mexico and in return gets 15*V*, it is better off with trade (20*B* and 15*V*) than without trade (18*B* and 12*V*). If Mexico uses all its resources to produce vegetables (20*V*) and exports 15*V* to the United States and in return gets 10*B*, it is better off with trade (10*B* and 5*V*) than without trade (8*B* and 4*V*).

e. If opportunity cost ratios in the two nations are not constant and there are increasing opportunity costs associated with more production of a product, then specialization may not be complete.

f. The basic argument for free trade among nations is that it leads to a better allocation of resources and a higher standard of living in the world because total output will increase from specialization and trade. Several side benefits from trade are that it increases competition and deters monopoly, and offers consumers a wider array of choices. It also links the interests of nations and can reduce the threat of hostilities or war.

4. ***Supply and demand analysis of exports and imports*** can be used to explain how the equilibrium price and quantity for a product (e.g., aluminum) are determined when there is trade between two nations (e.g., the United States and Canada).

a. For the United States, there will be *domestic* supply and demand as well as *export* supply and import demand for aluminum.

(1) The price and quantity of aluminum are determined by the intersection of the domestic demand and supply curves in a world without trade.

(2) In a world with trade, the export supply curve for the United States shows the amount of aluminum that U.S. producers will export at each world price above the domestic equilibrium price. U.S. exports will increase when the world price rises relative to the domestic price.

(3) The import demand curve for the United States shows the amount of aluminum that U.S. citizens will import at each world price below the domestic equilibrium price. U.S. imports will increase when world prices fall relative to the domestic price.

b. For Canada, there will be domestic supply and demand as well as export supply and import demand for aluminum. The description of these supply and demand curves is similar to the account of those of the United States previously described in point **a**.

c. The equilibrium world price and equilibrium world levels of exports and imports can be determined with further supply and demand analysis. The export supply curves of the two nations can be plotted on one graph. The import demand curves of both nations can be plotted on the same graph. In this two-nation model, equilibrium will be achieved when one nation's import demand curve intersects another nation's export supply curve.

5. Nations limit international trade by erecting ***trade barriers,*** which are of several types. ***Tariffs*** are excise taxes or "duties" on value or quantity of imported goods. They can be revenue tariffs, which typically are placed on products that are not domestically produced and whose basic purpose is to raise money for government. There also can be ***protective tariffs,*** which are designed to shield domestic producers from foreign competition by raising the price of imports. ***Import quotas*** are restrictions on the quantity or total value of a product that can be imported from another nation. ***Nontariff barriers*** are burdensome rules, regulations, licensing procedures, standards, or other practices that make it difficult and costly to import a product. A ***voluntary export restraint (VER)*** is an agreement among exporters to voluntarily limit the amount of a product exported to another nation; it has the same effect as an import quota. Governments also interfere with trade by giving a domestic producer an ***export subsidy,*** which is a government payment to a producer that helps the producer sell the product in an export market for a lower price than otherwise would be the case.

a. The imposition of a ***tariff*** on a product has both direct and indirect economic effects.

(1) The direct effects are an increase in the domestic price of the good, less domestic consumption, more domestic production, less foreign production, and a transfer of income from domestic consumers to the government.

(2) The indirect effects are a reduction in the incomes of foreign producers and thus the incomes of foreign nations to purchase products from the nation imposing the tariff, a shift of resources from efficient industries to inefficient industries, and thus less trade and worldwide output.

b. The imposition of a ***quota*** on an imported product has the same direct and indirect effects as that of a tariff on that product, with the exception that a tariff generates revenue for government use whereas an import quota transfers that revenue to foreign producers.

c. Special-interest groups benefit from protection and persuade their nations to erect trade barriers, but the costs of tariffs and quotas to consumers and nations exceed any benefits.

6. The arguments for ***protectionism*** are many, but each one can be challenged for its validity.

a. The military self-sufficiency argument can be challenged because it is difficult to determine which industry is "vital" to national defense and therefore must be protected; it would be more efficient economically to provide a direct subsidy to military producers rather than impose a tariff.

b. Using tariff barriers to permit diversification for stability in the economy is not necessary for advanced economies such as the United States, and there may be great economic costs to diversification in developing nations.

c. It is alleged that infant industries need protection until they are sufficiently large to compete, but the argument may not apply in developed economies: It is difficult to select which industries will prosper; protectionism tends to persist long after it is needed; and direct subsidies may be more economically efficient.

d. Sometimes protection is sought against ***dumping,*** which is the sale of foreign goods on U.S. markets at prices either below the cost of production or below the prices commonly charged in the home nation. Dumping is a legitimate concern and is restricted under U.S. trade law, but to use dumping as an excuse for widespread tariff protection is unjustified, and the number of documented cases is few. If foreign companies are more efficient (low cost) producers, what may appear to be dumping may actually be comparative advantage at work and domestic consumers can benefit from lower prices.

e. Trade barriers do not necessarily increase domestic employment because imports may eliminate some jobs, but create others, so imports may change only the composition of employment, not the overall level of employment. Also, the exports of one nation become the imports of another, so tariff barriers can be viewed as "beggar thy neighbor" policies. In addition, other nations are likely to retaliate against the imposition of trade barriers that will reduce domestic output and employment. The ***Smoot-Hawley Tariff Act*** is an example of legislation passed during the Great Depression that caused a trade war with other nations, thus hurting rather than helping the United States. In the long run, barriers create a less efficient allocation of resources by shielding protected domestic industries from the rigors of competition.

f. Protection is sometimes sought because of the cheap foreign labor argument that low-cost labor in other nations will undercut the wages of workers in the United States, but there are several counterpoints. First, there are mutual gains from trade between rich and poor nations and they lower the cost of production for products. Second, it should be realized that nations gain from trade based on comparative advantage, and by specializing at what each nation does best, the productivity of workers and thus their wages and living standards rise. Third, there is an incorrect focus on labor costs per hour rather than labor cost per unit of production. Labor costs or wages per hour can be higher in one nation than in another because of the higher productivity of workers (and it results in lower labor cost per unit of production).

7. International trade policies have changed over the years with the development of ***multilateral agreements*** and ***free-trade zones.*** They are used to counter the destructive aspects of trade wars that arise when nations impose high tariffs.

a. The ***General Agreement on Tariffs and Trade (GATT)*** that began in 1947 provided equal treatment of all member nations and sought to reduce tariffs and eliminate import quotas by multilateral negotiations. The Uruguay Round of GATT agreements that took effect in 1995 eliminated or reduced tariffs on many products, cut restrictive government rules applying to services, phased out quotas on textiles and apparel, and decreased subsidies for agriculture.

b. The ***World Trade Organization (WTO)*** is an international agency that is the successor to GATT. In 2010, 153 nations were members of the WTO. It is responsible for overseeing trade agreements among nations and rules on trade disputes. The WTO also provides a forum for more trade liberalization negotiations under the ***Doha Development Agenda*** that was begun in Doha, Qatar, in 2001. These negotiations focus on additional reductions in tariffs and quotas and cutbacks in domestic subsidies for agricultural products.

c. The ***European Union (EU)*** is an example of a regional free-trade zone or trade bloc among 27 European nations. The EU abolished tariffs among member nations and developed common policies on various economic issues, such as the tariffs on goods to and from nonmember nations. In 2010, 16 EU nations shared a common currency—the ***euro.*** The chief advantages of such a currency is that it reduces transactions costs for exchanging goods and services in Euro Zone nations and allows consumers and businesses to comparison shop.

d. In 1993, the ***North American Free Trade Agreement (NAFTA)*** created a free-trade zone or trade bloc covering the United States, Mexico, and Canada. Critics of this agreement feared job losses and the potential for abuse by other nations using Mexico as a base for production, but the dire outcomes have not occurred. There has been increased trade among Canada, Mexico, and the United States because of the agreement.

8. Although increased trade and trade liberalization raise total output and income, they also create controversies and calls for assistance. The ***Trade Adjustment Assistance Act*** of 2002 provides support to qualified workers displaced by imports or plant relocations from international trade. It gives cash assistance, education and training benefits, subsides for health care, and wage subsidies (for those aged 50 or older). Critics contend that such dislocations are part of a market economy and workers in the international sector should not get special subsidies for their job losses.

9. The ***offshoring*** of jobs occurs when jobs done by U.S. workers are shifted to foreign workers and locations. While offshoring has long been used in manufacturing, improvements in communication and technology make it possible to do it in services. Although offshoring causes some domestic workers to lose their jobs, it can be beneficial for an economy. It allows an economy to specialize and use its labor resources in high-valued work for which it has a comparative advantage and obtain services for low-valued work that can be done more efficiently by foreign workers. It can increase the demand for complementary jobs in high-valued industries. It allows domestic businesses to reduce production costs, and thus be more competitive in both domestic and international markets.

10. (*Last Word*). Frédéric Bastiat (1801–1850) was a French economist who wrote a satirical letter to counter the proponents of protectionism. His "petition" to the French government called for blocking out the sun because it provided too much competition for domestic candlestick makers, thus illustrating the logical absurdity of protectionist arguments.

■ HINTS AND TIPS

1. In the discussion of **comparative advantage,** the assumption of a constant opportunity-cost ratio means the production possibilities "curves" for each nation can be drawn as straight lines. The slope of the line in each nation is the opportunity cost of one product (beef) in terms of the other product (vegetables). The reciprocal of the slope of each line is the opportunity cost of the other product (vegetables) in terms of the first product (beef).

2. The **export supply and import demand curves** in Figures 20.3 and 20.4 in the text look different from the typical supply and demand curves that you have seen so far, so you should understand how they are constructed. The export supply and import demand curves for a nation do not intersect. Each curve meets at the price point on the *Y* axis showing the equilibrium price for domestic supply and demand. At this point there are no exports or imports.

a. The export supply curve is up-sloping from that point because as world prices rise above the domestic equilibrium price, there will be increasing domestic surpluses produced by a nation that can be exported. The export supply curve reflects the positive relationship between rising world prices (above the domestic equilibrium price) and the increasing quantity of exports.

b. The import demand curve is down-sloping from the domestic equilibrium price because as world prices fall below the domestic equilibrium price, there will be increasing domestic shortages that need to be covered by increasing imports. The import demand curve reflects the inverse relationship between falling world prices (below the domestic price) and the increasing quantity of imports.

3. One of the most interesting sections of the chapter discusses the arguments for and against trade protection. You have probably heard people give one or more of the arguments for trade protection, but now you have a chance to use your economic reasoning to expose the weaknesses in these arguments. Most are half-truths and special pleadings.

■ IMPORTANT TERMS

labor-intensive goods
land-intensive goods
capital-intensive goods
opportunity-cost ratio
comparative advantage
principle of comparative advantage
terms of trade
trading possibilities line
gains from trade
world price
domestic price
export supply curve
import demand curve
equilibrium world price
tariffs
revenue tariff
protective tariff
import quota
nontariff barrier (NTB)
voluntary export restriction (VER)
export subsidy
dumping
Smoot-Hawley Tariff Act
General Agreement on Tariffs and Trade (GATT)
World Trade Organization (WTO)
Doha Development Agenda
European Union (EU)
Euro Zone
North American Free Trade Agreement (NAFTA)
Trade Adjustment Assistance Act
offshoring

SELF-TEST

■ FILL-IN QUESTIONS

1. In the United States, exports of goods and services make up about (13, 26) ______________ percent of total U.S. output. The volume of exports and imports in dollar terms makes the United States the world's (largest, smallest) ______________ trading nation.

2. A trade deficit occurs when exports are (greater than, less than) ______________ imports and a trade surplus occurs when exports are ______________ imports. The United States has a trade deficit in (goods, services) ______________ and a trade surplus in ______________.

3. Nations tend to trade among themselves because the distribution of economic resources among them is (even, uneven) ______________, the efficient production of various goods and services necessitates (the same, different) ______________ technologies or combinations of resources, and people prefer (more, less) ______________ choices in products.

4. The principle of comparative advantage means total world output will be greatest when each good is produced by that nation having the (highest, lowest) ______________ opportunity cost. The nations of the world tend to specialize in the production of those goods in which they (have, do not have) ______________ a comparative advantage and then export them, and they import those goods in which they ______________ a comparative advantage in production.

5. If the cost ratio in country X is 4 Panama hats equal 1 pound of bananas, while in country Y 3 Panama hats equal 1 pound of bananas, then

a. in country X hats are relatively (expensive, inexpensive) ______________ and bananas relatively ______________.

b. in country Y hats are relatively (expensive, inexpensive) ______________ and bananas relatively ______________.

c. X has a comparative advantage and should specialize in the production of (bananas, hats) ______________, and Y has a comparative advantage and should specialize in the production of ______________.

d. When X and Y specialize and trade, the terms of trade will be somewhere between (1, 2, 3, 4) ______________ and ______________ hats for each pound of bananas and will depend on world demand and supply for hats and bananas.

e. When the actual terms of trade turn out to be 3 1/2 hats for 1 pound of bananas, the cost of obtaining
(1) 1 Panama hat has been decreased from (2/7, 1/3) ______ to ______ pounds of bananas in Y.
(2) 1 pound of bananas has been decreased from (3 1/2, 4) ______ to ______ Panama hats in X.
f. International specialization will not be complete if the opportunity cost of producing either good (rises, falls) ______ as a nation produces more of it.

6. The basic argument for free trade based on the principle of (bilateral negotiations, comparative advantage) ______ is that it results in a (more, less) ______ efficient allocation of resources and a (lower, higher) ______ standard of living.

7. The world equilibrium price is determined by the interaction of (domestic, world) ______ supply and demand, while the domestic equilibrium price is determined by ______ supply and demand. When the world price of a good falls relative to the domestic price in a nation, the nation will (increase, decrease) ______ its imports, and when the world price rises relative to the domestic price, the nation will ______ its exports.

8. In a two-nation model for a product, the equilibrium price and quantity of imports and exports occur where one nation's import demand curve intersects another nation's export (supply, demand) ______ curve. In a highly competitive world market, there can be (multiple, only one) ______ price(s) for a standardized product.

9. Excise taxes on imported products are (quotas, tariffs) ______, whereas limits on the maximum amount of a product that can be imported are import ______. Tariffs applied to a product not produced domestically are (protective, revenue) ______ tariffs, but tariffs designed to shield domestic producers from foreign competition are ______ tariffs.

10. There are other types of trade barriers. Imports that are restricted through the use of a licensing requirement or bureaucratic red tape are (tariff, nontariff) ______ barriers. When foreign firms voluntarily limit their exports to another country, it would represent a voluntary (import, export) ______ restraint.

11. Nations erect barriers to international trade to benefit the economic positions of (consumers, domestic producers) ______ even though these barriers (increase, decrease) ______ economic efficiency and trade among nations and the benefits to that nation are (greater, less) ______ than the costs to it.

12. When the United States imposes a tariff on a good that is imported from abroad, the price of that good in the United States will (increase, decrease) ______ and the total purchases of the good in the United States will ______. The output of U.S. producers of the good will (increase, decrease) ______ and the output of foreign producers will ______.

13. When comparing the effects of a tariff with the effects of a quota to restrict the U.S. imports of a product, the basic difference is that with a (tariff, quota) ______ the U.S. government will receive revenue, but with a ______ foreign producers will receive the revenue.

14. There are counterarguments to the six arguments for trade protectionism.
a. The military self-sufficiency argument can be challenged because it is difficult to determine which industry is (essential, unessential) ______ for national defense and must be protected. A direct subsidy to producers would be (more, less) ______ efficient than a tariff.
b. Using trade barriers to permit diversification for stability in an economy is not necessary for (advanced, developing) ______ economies such as in the United States, and there may be great economic costs to forcing diversification in ______ nations.
c. The problem with the infant industry argument is that it is difficult to determine when (a mature, an infant) ______ industry becomes ______ industry.
d. The protection-against-dumping argument does not hold because the lower prices from alleged dumping may be a case of (absolute, comparative) ______ advantage at work and documented cases of dumping are relatively (common, rare) ______.
e. Trade barriers do not necessarily increase domestic employment because imports may change only the (level, composition) ______ of employment, such barriers (increase, decrease) ______ the incomes of trading partners thus hurting an exporting nation and other nations can (dump, retaliate) ______ by imposing their own trade barriers.
f. Proponents of the cheap foreign labor argument tend to focus exclusively on large international differences that exist in labor costs (per unit, per hour) ______ and fail to mention that these differences are mostly

the result of large national differences in productivity that serve to equalize labor costs ______________.

15. The three principles established in the General Agreement on Tariffs and Trade (GATT) of 1947 were

a. ______________________________

b. ______________________________

c. ______________________________

16. The World Trade Organization (WTO) is the successor to GATT and it is responsible for overseeing multilateral trade (barriers, agreements) ______________ and rules on trade (licenses, disputes) ______________. The current round of multilateral trade negotiations is the (Abba, Doha) ______________ Development Agenda that focuses on (increasing, decreasing) ______________ tariffs, import quotas, and agricultural subsidies.

17. An example of a regional free-trade zone is the (Western, European) ______________ Union. It abolished (imports and exports, tariffs and quotas) ______________ among the participating members and established (common, different) ______________ tariffs on goods imported from outside this free-trade zone. The common currency of many of the member nations of the regional free-trade zone is the (peso, euro) ______________.

18. The North American Free Trade Agreement (NAFTA) formed a free-trade (barrier, zone) ______________ among the United States, Canada, and Mexico. This agreement will eliminate (terms of trade, tariffs) ______________ among the nations. Critics in the United States said that it would (increase, decrease) ______________ jobs, but the evidence shows a(n) ______________ in jobs and total output since its passage.

19. The Trade Adjustment Assistance Act of 2002 is designed to help some of the (workers, businesses) ______________ hurt by shifts in international trade patterns. Critics contend that such job losses are a (small, large) ______________ fraction of the total each year and that such a program is another type of special (tariff, subsidy) ______________ that benefits one type of worker over another.

20. The shifting of work previously done by U.S. workers to workers located in other nations is (dumping, offshoring) ______________. It reflects a (growth, decline) ______________ in the specialization and international trade of services. It may (decrease, increase) ______________ some jobs moved to other nations, but also ______________ jobs and productivity in the United States.

■ TRUE–FALSE QUESTIONS

Circle T if the statement is true, F if it is false.

1. The combined volume of exports and imports in the United States as measured in dollars is greater than in any other nation. **T F**

2. A factor that serves as the economic basis for world trade is the even distribution of resources among nations. **T F**

3. People trade because they seek products of different quality and other nonprice attributes. **T F**

4. Examples of capital-intensive goods would be automobiles, machinery, and chemicals. **T F**

5. The relative efficiency with which a nation can produce specific goods is fixed over time. **T F**

6. Mutually advantageous specialization and trade are possible between any two nations if they have the same domestic opportunity-cost ratios for any two products. **T F**

7. The principle of comparative advantage is that total output will be greatest when each good is produced by that nation which has the higher domestic opportunity cost. **T F**

8. By specializing based on comparative advantage, nations can obtain larger outputs with fixed amounts of resources. **T F**

9. The terms of trade determine how the increase in world output resulting from comparative advantage is shared by trading nations. **T F**

10. Increasing opportunity costs tend to prevent specialization among trading nations from being complete. **T F**

11. Trade among nations tends to bring about a more efficient use of the world's resources and a higher level of material well-being. **T F**

12. Free trade among nations tends to increase monopoly and lessen competition in these nations. **T F**

13. A nation will export a particular product if the world price is less than the domestic price. **T F**

14. In a two-country model, equilibrium in world prices and quantities of exports and imports will occur where one nation's export supply curve intersects the other nation's import demand curve. **T F**

15. A tariff on coffee in the United States is an example of a protective tariff. **T F**

16. The imposition of a tariff on a good imported from abroad will reduce the amount of the imported good that is bought. **T F**

17. A cost of tariffs and quotas imposed by the United States is higher prices that U.S. consumers must pay for the protected product. **T F**

18. The major difference between a tariff and a quota on an imported product is that a quota produces revenue for the government. **T F**

19. To advocate tariffs that would protect domestic producers of goods and materials essential to national defense is to substitute a political-military objective for the economic objectives of efficiently allocating resources. **T F**

20. One-crop economies may be able to make themselves more stable and diversified by imposing tariffs on goods imported from abroad, but these tariffs are also apt to lower the standard of living in these economies. **T F**

21. Protection against the "dumping" of foreign goods at low prices on the U.S. market is one good justification for widespread, permanent tariffs. **T F**

22. Tariffs and import quotas meant to increase domestic full employment achieve short-run domestic goals by making trading partners poorer. **T F**

23. The cheap foreign labor argument for protection fails because it focuses on labor costs per hour rather than what really matters, which is labor cost per unit of output. **T F**

24. Most arguments for protection are special interest appeals that, if followed, would provide gains for consumers at the expense of protected industries and their workers. **T F**

25. The General Agreement on Tariffs and Trade sought to reduce tariffs through multilateral negotiations. **T F**

26. The World Trade Organization (WTO) is the world's major advocate for trade protectionism. **T F**

27. The members of the European Union (EU) have experienced freer trade since it was formed. **T F**

28. The 1993 North American Free Trade Agreement (NAFTA) includes all Central American nations. **T F**

29. The Trade Adjustment Assistance Act of 2002 provided compensation to U.S. workers who were displaced by shifts in international trade patterns. **T F**

30. Although offshoring decreases some U.S. jobs, it also lowers production costs, expands sales, and may create other U.S. jobs. **T F**

■ MULTIPLE-CHOICE QUESTIONS

Circle the letter that corresponds to the best answer.

1. Which nation leads the world in the combined volume of exports and imports?
(a) Japan
(b) Germany
(c) United States
(d) United Kingdom

2. Which nation is the most important trading partner for the United States in terms of the percentage of imports and exports?
(a) India
(b) Russia
(c) Canada
(d) Germany

3. Nations engage in trade because
(a) world resources are evenly distributed among nations
(b) world resources are unevenly distributed among nations
(c) all products are produced from the same technology
(d) all products are produced from the same combinations of resources

Use the following tables to answer Questions 4, 5, 6, and 7.

NEPAL PRODUCTION POSSIBILITIES TABLE

	Production alternatives					
Product	**A**	**B**	**C**	**D**	**E**	**F**
Yak fat	0	4	8	12	16	20
Camel hides	40	32	24	16	8	0

KASHMIR PRODUCTION POSSIBILITIES TABLE

	Production alternatives					
Product	**A**	**B**	**C**	**D**	**E**	**F**
Yak fat	0	3	6	9	12	15
Camel hides	60	48	36	24	12	0

4. The data in the tables show that production in
(a) both Nepal and Kashmir is subject to increasing opportunity costs
(b) both Nepal and Kashmir is subject to constant opportunity costs
(c) Nepal is subject to increasing opportunity costs and Kashmir to constant opportunity costs
(d) Kashmir is subject to increasing opportunity costs and Nepal to constant opportunity costs

5. If Nepal and Kashmir engage in trade, the terms of trade will be
(a) between 2 and 4 camel hides for 1 unit of yak fat
(b) between 1/3 and 1/2 units of yak fat for 1 camel hide
(c) between 3 and 4 units of yak fat for 1 camel hide
(d) between 2 and 4 units of yak fat for 1 camel hide

6. Assume that prior to specialization and trade Nepal and Kashmir both choose production possibility C. Now if each specializes according to its comparative advantage, the resulting gains from specialization and trade will be
(a) 6 units of yak fat
(b) 8 units of yak fat
(c) 6 units of yak fat and 8 camel hides
(d) 8 units of yak fat and 6 camel hides

7. Each nation produced only one product in accordance with its comparative advantage, and the terms of trade were set at 3 camel hides for 1 unit of yak fat. In this case, Nepal could obtain a maximum combination of 8 units of yak fat and
(a) 12 camel hides
(b) 24 camel hides
(c) 36 camel hides
(d) 48 camel hides

8. What happens to a nation's imports or exports of a product when the world price of the product rises above the domestic price?

(a) Imports of the product increase.
(b) Imports of the product stay the same.
(c) Exports of the product increase.
(d) Exports of the product decrease.

9. What happens to a nation's imports or exports of a product when the world price of the product falls below the domestic price?

(a) Imports of the product increase.
(b) Imports of the product decrease.
(c) Exports of the product increase.
(d) Exports of the product stay the same.

10. Which one of the following is characteristic of tariffs?

(a) They prevent the importation of goods from abroad.
(b) They specify the maximum amounts of specific commodities that may be imported during a given period of time.
(c) They often protect domestic producers from foreign competition.
(d) They enable nations to reduce their exports and increase their imports during periods of recession.

11. The motive for barriers to the importation of goods and services from abroad is to

(a) improve economic efficiency in that nation
(b) protect and benefit domestic producers of those goods and services
(c) reduce the prices of the goods and services produced in that nation
(d) expand the export of goods and services to foreign nations

12. When a tariff is imposed on a good imported from abroad,

(a) the demand for the good increases
(b) the demand for the good decreases
(c) the supply of the good increases
(d) the supply of the good decreases

Answer Questions 13, 14, 15, 16, and 17 on the basis of the following diagram, where S_d *and* D_d *are the domestic supply and demand for a product and* P_w *is the world price of that product.*

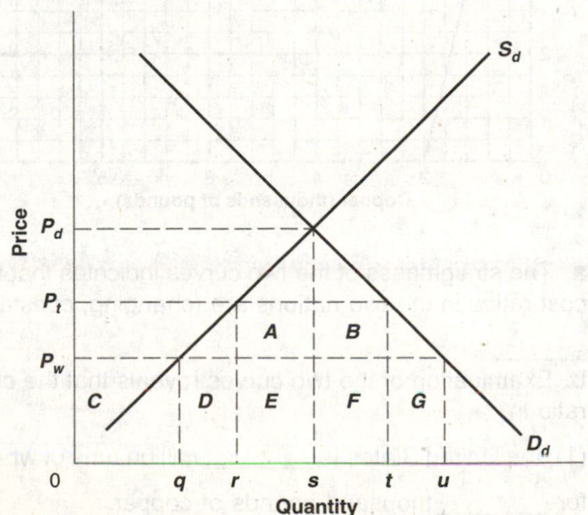

13. In a closed economy (without international trade), the equilibrium price would be

(a) P_d, but in an open economy, the equilibrium price would be P_t
(b) P_d, but in an open economy, the equilibrium price would be P_w
(c) P_w, but in an open economy, the equilibrium price would be P_d
(d) P_w, but in an open economy, the equilibrium price would be P_t

14. If there is free trade in this economy and no tariffs, the total revenue going to the foreign producers is represented by

(a) area ***C***
(b) areas ***A*** and ***B*** combined
(c) areas ***A***, ***B***, ***E***, and ***F*** combined
(d) areas ***D***, ***E***, ***F***, and ***G*** combined

15. If a per-unit tariff was imposed in the amount of P_wP_t then domestic producers would supply

(a) ***q*** units and foreign producers would supply ***qu*** units
(b) ***s*** units and foreign producers would supply ***su*** units
(c) ***r*** units and foreign producers would supply ***rt*** units
(d) ***t*** units and foreign producers would supply ***tu*** units

16. Given a per-unit tariff in the amount of P_wP_t, the amount of the tariff revenue paid by consumers of this product is represented by

(a) area ***A***
(b) area ***B***
(c) areas ***A*** and ***B*** combined
(d) areas ***D***, ***E***, ***F***, and ***G*** combined

17. Assume that an import quota of ***rt*** units is imposed on the foreign nation producing this product. The amount of *total* revenue going to foreign producers is represented by areas

(a) $A + B$
(b) $E + F$
(c) $A + B + E + F$
(d) $D + E + F + G$

18. Tariffs lead to

(a) the contraction of relatively efficient industries
(b) an overallocation of resources to relatively efficient industries
(c) an increase in the foreign demand for domestically produced goods
(d) an underallocation of resources to relatively inefficient industries

19. Tariffs and quotas are costly to consumers because

(a) the price of the imported good rises
(b) the supply of the imported good increases
(c) import competition increases for domestically produced goods
(d) consumers shift purchases away from domestically produced goods

20. The infant industry argument for tariffs

(a) is especially pertinent for the European Union
(b) generally results in tariffs that are removed after the infant industry has matured

(c) makes it rather easy to determine which infant industries will become mature industries with comparative advantages in producing their goods
(d) might better be replaced by an argument for outright subsidies for infant industries

21. Smoot-Hawley Tariff Act resulted in
(a) a significant decline in tariffs
(b) a trade war with other nations
(c) the elimination of import quotas
(d) the imposition of antidumping duties

22. "The nation needs to protect itself from foreign countries that sell their products in our domestic markets at less than the cost of production." This quotation would be most closely associated with which protectionist argument?
(a) diversification for stability
(b) increased domestic employment
(c) protection against dumping
(d) cheap foreign labor

23. Which is a likely result of imposing tariffs to increase domestic employment?
(a) a short-run increase in domestic employment in import industries
(b) a decrease in the tariff rates of foreign nations
(c) a long-run reallocation of workers from export industries to protected domestic industries
(d) a decrease in consumer prices

24. Which is the likely result of the United States using tariffs to protect its high wages and standard of living from cheap foreign labor?
(a) an increase in U.S. exports
(b) a rise in the U.S. real GDP
(c) a decrease in the average productivity of U.S. workers
(d) a decrease in the quantity of labor employed by industries producing the goods on which tariffs have been levied

25. Which of the following is characteristic of the General Agreement on Tariffs and Trade? Nations signing the agreement were committed to
(a) the expansion of import quotas
(b) the establishment of a world customs union
(c) the reciprocal increase in tariffs by negotiation
(d) the nondiscriminatory treatment of all member nations

26. One important outcome from the Uruguay Round of GATT was
(a) an increase in tariff barriers on services
(b) the elimination or reduction of many tariffs
(c) removal of voluntary export restraints in manufacturing
(d) abolishment of patent, copyright, and trademark protection

27. What international agency is currently charged with overseeing multilateral trade negotiations and with resolving trade disputes among nations?
(a) World Bank
(b) United Nations
(c) World Trade Organization
(d) International Monetary Fund

28. One of the major accomplishments of the European Union was
(a) passing the Trade Assistance Act
(b) enacting minimum wage laws
(c) increasing tariffs on U.S. products
(d) establishing the Euro Zone

29. An example of the formation of a regional free-trade zone would be the
(a) Smoot-Hawley Tariff Act
(b) Doha Development Agenda
(c) North American Free Trade Agreement
(d) General Agreement on Tariffs and Trade

30. The Trade Adjustment Assistance Act
(a) increased funding for the World Trade Organization
(b) provided more foreign aid to nations that trade with the United States
(c) extended normal-trade-relations status to more less-developed countries
(d) gave cash assistance to U.S. workers displaced by imports or plant relocations abroad

■ PROBLEMS

1. Shown below and on the next page are the production possibilities curves for two nations: the United States and Chile. Suppose these two nations do not currently engage in international trade or specialization, and suppose that points ***A*** and ***a*** show the combinations of wheat and copper they now produce and consume.

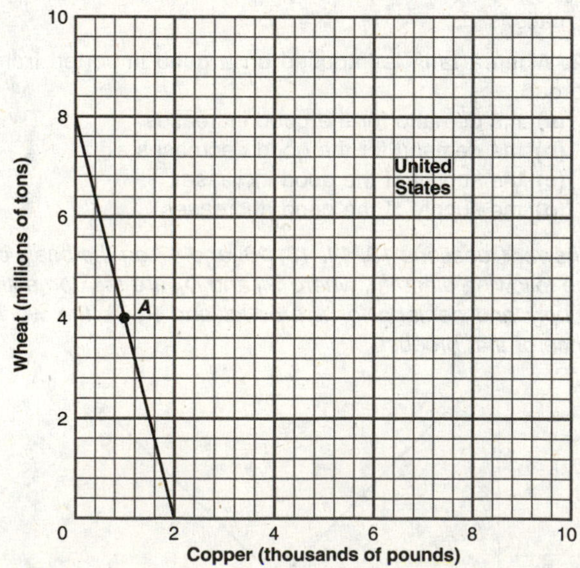

a. The straightness of the two curves indicates that the cost ratios in the two nations are (changing, constant) ________.

b. Examination of the two curves reveals that the cost ratio in

(1) the United States is ________ million tons of wheat for ________ thousand pounds of copper.

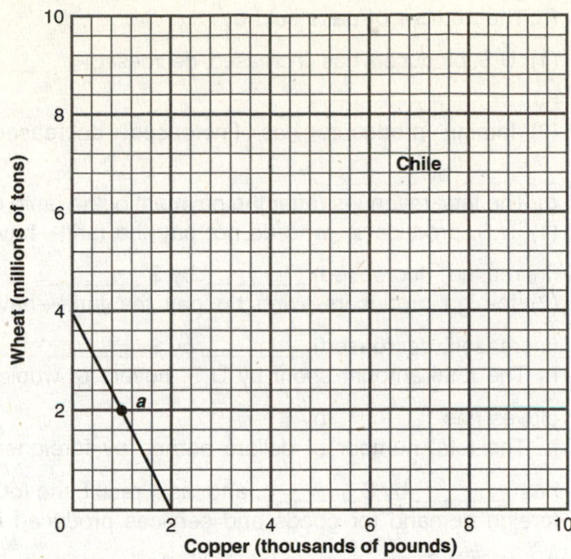

(2) Chile is ________ million tons of wheat for ________ thousand pounds of copper.

c. If these two nations were to specialize and trade wheat for copper,

(1) The United States would specialize in the production of wheat because ________________________.

(2) Chile would specialize in the production of copper because ________________________.

d. The terms of trade, if specialization and trade occur, will be greater than 2 and less than 4 million tons of wheat for 1000 pounds of copper because ________________________.

e. Assume the terms of trade turn out to be 3 million tons of wheat for 1000 pounds of copper. Draw in the trading possibilities curves for the United States and Chile.

f. With these trading possibilities curves, suppose the United States decides to consume 5 million tons of wheat and 1000 pounds of copper while Chile decides to consume 3 million tons of wheat and 1000 pounds of copper. The gains from trade to

(1) the United States are ________ million tons of wheat and ________ thousand pounds of copper.

(2) Chile are ________ million tons of wheat and ________ thousand pounds of copper.

2. Following are tables showing the domestic supply and demand schedules and the export supply and import demand schedules for two nations (**A** and **B**).

NATION A

Price	Q_{dd}	Q_{sd}	Q_{di}	Q_{se}
$3.00	100	300	0	200
2.50	150	250	0	100
2.00	200	200	0	0
1.50	250	150	100	0
1.00	300	100	200	0

a. For nation **A**, the first column of the table is the price of a product. The second column is the quantity demanded domestically (Q_{dd}). The third column is the quantity supplied domestically (Q_{sd}). The fourth column is the quantity demanded for imports (Q_{di}). The fifth column is the quantity of exports supplied (Q_{se}).

(1) At a price of $2.00, there (will, will not) ________ be a surplus or shortage and there ________ be exports or imports.

(2) At a price of $3.00, there will be a domestic (shortage, surplus) ________ of ________ units. This domestic ________ will be eliminated by (exports, imports) ________ of ________ units.

(3) At a price of $1.00, there will be a domestic (shortage, surplus) ________ of ________ units. This domestic ________ will be eliminated by (exports, imports) ________ of ________ units.

NATION B

Price	Q_{dd}	Q_{sd}	Q_{di}	Q_{se}
$2.50	100	300	0	200
2.00	150	250	0	100
1.50	200	200	0	0
1.00	250	150	100	0

b. For nation **B**, the first column is the price of a product. The second column is the quantity demanded domestically (Q_{dd}). The third column is the quantity supplied domestically (Q_{sd}). The fourth column is the quantity demanded for imports (Q_{di}). The fifth column is the quantity of exports supplied (Q_{se}).

(1) At a price of $1.50, there (will, will not) ________ be a surplus or shortage and there ________ be exports or imports.

(2) At a price of $2.50, there will be a domestic (shortage, surplus) ________ of ________ units. This domestic ________ will be eliminated by (exports, imports) ________ of ________ units.

(3) At a price of $1.00, there will be a domestic (shortage, surplus) ________ of ________ units. This domestic ________ will be eliminated by (exports, imports) ________ of ________ units.

c. The following table shows a schedule of the import demand in nation **A** and the export supply in nation **B** at various prices. The first column is the price of the product. The second column is the quantity demanded for imports (Q_{diA}) in nation **A**. The third column is the quantity of exports supplied (Q_{seB}) in nation **B**.

Price	Q_{diA}	Q_{seB}
$2.00	0	100
1.75	50	50
1.50	100	0

(1) If the world price is $2.00, then nation (**A**, **B**) ________ will want to import ________ units and nation ________ will want to export ________ units of the product.
(2) If the world price is $1.75, then nation (**A**, **B**) ________ will want to import ________ units and nation ________ will want to export ________ units of the product.
(3) If the world price is $1.50, then nation (**A**, **B**) ________ will want to import ________ units and nation ________ will want to export ________ units of the product.

3. The following table shows the quantities of woolen gloves demanded (***D***) in the United States at several different prices (***P***). Also shown in the table are the quantities of woolen gloves that would be supplied by U.S. producers (S_a) and the quantities that would be supplied by foreign producers (S_f) at the nine different prices.

P	D	S_a	S_f	S_t	S'_f	S'_t
$2.60	450	275	475	______	______	______
2.40	500	250	450	______	______	______
2.20	550	225	425	______	______	______
2.00	600	200	400	______	______	______
1.80	650	175	375	______	______	______
1.60	700	150	350	______	______	______
1.40	750	125	325	______	______	______
1.20	800	0	300	______	______	______
1.00	850	0	0	______	______	______

a. Compute and enter in the table the total quantities that would be supplied (S_t) by U.S. and foreign producers at each of the prices.
b. If the market for woolen gloves in the United States is a competitive one, the equilibrium price for woolen gloves is $________ and the equilibrium quantity is ________.
c. Suppose now that the United States government imposes an 80 cent ($.80) tariff per pair of gloves on all gloves imported into the United States from abroad. Compute and enter into the table the quantities that would be supplied (S'_f) by foreign producers at the nine different prices. [*Hint:* If foreign producers were willing to supply 300 pairs at a price of $1.20 when there was no tariff, they are now willing to supply 300 pairs at $2.00 (the $.80 per pair tariff plus the $1.20 they will receive for themselves). The quantities supplied at each of the other prices may be found in a similar fashion.]
d. Compute and enter into the table the total quantities that would be supplied (S'_t) by U.S. and foreign producers at each of the nine prices.
e. As a result of the imposition of the tariff the equilibrium price has risen to $________ and the equilibrium quantity has fallen to ________.
f. The number of pairs sold by
(1) U.S. producers has (increased, decreased) ________ by ________.
(2) foreign producers has (increased, decreased) ________ by ________.
g. The total revenues (after the payment of the tariff) of
(1) U.S. producers—who do not pay the tariff—have (increased, decreased) ________ by $________.
(2) foreign producers—who do pay the tariff—have (increased, decreased) ________ by $________.
h. The total amount spent by U.S. buyers of woolen gloves has ________ by $________.
i. The total number of dollars earned by foreigners has ________ by $________, and, as a result, the total foreign demand for goods and services produced in the United States has ________ by $________.
j. The tariff revenue of the United States government has ________ by $________.
k. If an import quota were imposed that had the same effect as the tariff on price and output, the amount of the tariff revenue, $________, would now be received as revenue by ________ producers.

■ SHORT ANSWER AND ESSAY QUESTIONS

1. What is the economic basis for trade? Explain the underlying facts that support free trade and supply examples of three types of goods produced based on resource differences.

2. Explain the difference between absolute advantage and comparative advantage.

3. Provide a two-nation and two-product example that shows the gains from specialization and trade.

4. What is the case for free trade?

5. Explain how the equilibrium prices and quantities of exports and imports are determined. Why will exports in a nation increase when world prices rise relative to domestic prices?

6. What motivates nations to erect barriers to the importation of goods from abroad, and what types of barriers do they erect?

7. Suppose the United States increases the tariff on automobiles imported from Germany (and other foreign countries). What is the effect of this tariff-rate increase on
(a) the price of automobiles in the United States;
(b) the total number of cars sold in the United States during a year;
(c) the number of cars produced by and employment in the German automobile industry;
(d) production by and employment in the U.S. automobile industry;
(e) German income obtained by selling cars in the United States;

(f) the German demand for goods produced in the United States;
(g) the production of and employment in those U.S. industries that now export goods to Germany;
(h) the standards of living in the United States and in Germany;
(i) the allocation of resources in the U.S. economy; and
(j) the allocation of the world's resources?

8. Compare and contrast the economic effects of a tariff with an import quota on a product.

9. Critically evaluate the military self-sufficiency argument for protectionism. What industries should be protected?

10. What is the basis for the diversification-for-stability argument for protectionism? How can it be countered?

11. Explain the arguments and counterarguments for protecting infant industries.

12. Can a strong case for protectionism be made on the basis of defending against the "dumping" of products? How do you determine if a nation is dumping a product? What are the economic effects of dumping on consumers?

13. What are the problems with using trade barriers as a means of increasing domestic employment?

14. Does the economy need to shield domestic workers from competition from "cheap" foreign labor? Explain using comparative advantage, standards of living, productivity, and labor cost per unit of output.

15. What was the purpose of the General Agreement on Tariffs and Trade (GATT), and what did it achieve?

16. Describe the purpose of the World Trade Organization (WTO). Why is it controversial?

17. What is the European Union? What has it achieved?

18. What is the North American Free Trade Agreement (NAFTA)? What do critics and defenders say about the agreement?

19. Discuss the purpose of the Trade Adjustment Assistance Act of 2002 and its advantages and disadvantages.

20. Explain the reasons U.S. businesses have turned to offshoring and evaluate the costs and benefits of such actions.

ANSWERS

Chapter 20 International Trade

FILL-IN QUESTIONS

1. 13, largest
2. less than, greater than, goods, services
3. uneven, different, more
4. lowcost, have, do not have
5. *a.* inexpensive, expensive; *b.* expensive, inexpensive; *c.* hats, bananas; *d.* 3, 4; *e.* (1) 1/3, 2/7, (2) 4, 3 1/2; *f.* rises
6. comparative advantage, more, higher
7. world, domestic, increase, increase
8. supply, only one
9. tariffs, quotas, revenue, protective
10. nontariff, export
11. domestic producers, decrease, less
12. increase, decrease, increase, decrease
13. tariff, quota
14. *a.* essential, more; *b.* advanced, developing; *c.* infant, mature; *d.* comparative, rare; *e.* composition, decrease, retaliate; *f.* per hour, per unit
15. *a.* equal, nondiscriminatory treatment of all member nations; *b.* reduction of tariffs by multilateral negotiations; *c.* elimination of import quotas
16. agreements, disputes, Doha, decreasing
17. European, tariffs and quotas, common, euro
18. zone, tariffs, decrease, increase
19. workers, small, subsidy
20. offshoring, growth, decrease, increase

TRUE–FALSE QUESTIONS

1. T, p. 399	**11.** T, p. 407	**21.** F, pp. 414–415
2. F, p. 400	**12.** F, p. 407	**22.** T, p. 415
3. T, p. 400	**13.** F, pp. 408–411	**23.** T, p. 415–416
4. T, p. 400	**14.** T, pp. 408–411	**24.** F, p. 416
5. F, p. 400	**15.** F, p. 411	**25.** T, p. 417
6. F, p. 402	**16.** T, p. 412	**26.** F, p. 417
7. F, p. 403	**17.** T, p. 413	**27.** T, p. 417
8. T, p. 403	**18.** F, p. 413	**28.** F, p, 418
9. T, p. 404	**19.** T, p. 414	**29.** T, p. 418
10. T, p. 406	**20.** T, p. 414	**30.** T, p. 418–419

MULTIPLE-CHOICE QUESTIONS

1. c, p. 399	**11.** b, p. 411	**21.** b, p. 415
2. c, p. 399	**12.** d, p. 412	**22.** c, pp. 414–415
3. b, p. 400	**13.** b, pp. 412–413	**23.** c, p. 415
4. b, p. 402	**14.** d, pp. 412–413	**24.** c, pp. 415–416
5. a, p. 404	**15.** c, pp. 412–413	**25.** d, p. 417
6. a, pp. 404–406	**16.** c, pp. 412–413	**26.** b, p. 417
7. c, pp. 404–406	**17.** c, p. 413	**27.** c, p. 417
8. c, pp. 408–411	**18.** a, p. 413	**28.** d, p. 418
9. a, pp. 408–411	**19.** a, p. 413	**29.** c, p. 418
10. c, p. 411	**20.** d, p. 414	**30.** d, p. 418

PROBLEMS

1. *a.* constant; *b.* (1) 8, 2, (2) 4, 2; *c.* (1) it has a comparative advantage in producing wheat (its cost of producing wheat is less than Chile's), (2) it has a comparative advantage in producing copper (its cost of producing copper is less than the United States'); *d.* one of the two nations would be unwilling to trade if the terms of trade are outside this range; *f.* (1) 1, 0, (2) 1, 0
2. *a.* (1) will not, will not, (2) surplus, 200, surplus, exports, 200, (3) shortage, 200, shortage, imports, 200; *b.* (1) will not, will not, (2) surplus, 200, surplus, exports, 200, (3) shortage, 100, shortage, imports, 100; *c.* (1) A, 0, B, 100, (2) A, 50, B, 50, (3) A, 100, B, 0
3. *a.* 750, 700, 650, 600, 550, 500, 450, 300, 0; *b.* $2.00, 600; *c.* 375, 350, 325, 300, 0, 0, 0, 0, 0; *d.* 650, 600, 550, 500, 175, 150, 125, 0, 0; *e.* $2.20, 550; *f.* (1) increased, 25, (2) decreased, 75; *g.* (1) increased, $95, (2) decreased, $345; *h.* increased, $10; *i.* decreased, $345, decreased, $345; *j.* increased, $260; *k.* $260, foreign

SHORT ANSWER AND ESSAY QUESTIONS

1. p. 400
2. p. 401
3. pp. 401–407
4. p. 407
5. pp. 408–411
6. p. 411
7. pp. 412–413
8. pp. 413–414
9. p. 414
10. p. 414
11. p. 414
12. pp. 414–415
13. p. 415
14. pp. 415–416
15. p. 417
16. p. 417
17. p. 417–418
18. p. 418
19. p. 418
20. pp. 418–419

CHAPTER 21

The Balance of Payments, Exchange Rates, and Trade Deficits

As you know from Chapter 20, nations buy and sell large quantities of goods and services across national boundaries.The residents of these nations also buy and sell such financial assets as stocks and bonds and such real assets as land and capital goods in other nations, and the governments and individuals in one nation make gifts (or give remittances) to other nations. In Chapter 21 you will learn *how* nations using different currencies are able to make these international financial transactions, the accounting system used to measure them, and what the accounts mean for a nation.

The market in which one currency is sold and is paid for with another currency is the **foreign exchange market.** When the residents of a nation (its consumers, business firms, or governments) buy products or real or financial assets from, make loans or give gifts to, or pay interest and dividends to the residents of other nations, they must *buy* some of the currency used in that nation and pay for it with some of their own currency. And when the residents of a nation sell products or real or financial assets to, receive loans or gifts from, or are paid dividends or interest by the residents of other nations, they *sell* this foreign currency in return for some of their own currency. The price paid (in one currency) for a unit of another currency is called the foreign exchange rate, and like most prices, it is determined by the demand for and the supply of that foreign currency.

At the end of a year, nations summarize their international financial transactions. This summary is called the nation's **balance of payments:** a record of how it obtained foreign currency during the year and what it did with this foreign currency. Of course, all foreign currency obtained was used for some purpose—it did not evaporate—consequently, the balance of payments *always* balances. The balance of payments is an extremely important and useful device for understanding the amounts and kinds of international transactions in which the residents of a nation engage. A balance-of-payments deficit occurs when the foreign currency receipts are less than foreign currency payments and the nation must reduce the **official reserves** of its central bank to balance its payments. Conversely, a balance-of-payments surplus occurs when foreign currency receipts are greater than foreign currency payments, and the nation must expand its official reserves to balance its payments.

How nations correct balance-of-payments deficits or surpluses or adjust trade imbalances often depends on the **exchange-rate systems** used. There are two basic types of such systems—flexible and fixed. In a flexible or floating system, exchange rates are set by the forces of the demand for and supply of a nation's currency relative to the currency of other nations. If the demand for a nation's currency increases, there will be an *appreciation* in its value relative to another currency, and if the demand of a nation's currency declines, there will be a *depreciation* in its value relative to another currency. Fixed-exchange-rate systems have been used by nations to peg or fix a specific amount of one nation's currency that must be exchanged for another nation's currency. Both types of systems have their advantages and disadvantages. Currently, the major trading nations of the world use a **managed float exchange-rate system** that corrects balance-of-payments deficits and surpluses.

The final section of the chapter examines the U.S. **trade deficits** that arise when the value of exports is less than the value of imports. As you will learn, these deficits are the result of several factors such as differences in national growth rates and a declining saving rate that have contributed to imports rising faster than exports. They also have several implications such as increased current consumption at the expense of future consumption and increased U.S. indebtedness to foreigners.

■ CHECKLIST

When you have studied this chapter you should be able to

☐ Describe examples of transactions in international trade and the role that money plays in them.
☐ Explain how money is used for the international buying and selling of real and financial assets.
☐ Give a definition of a nation's balance of payments.
☐ Use the items in the current account to calculate the balance on goods, balance on goods and services, and balance on the current account when given the data.
☐ Describe how balance is achieved in the capital and financial account.
☐ Explain the relationship between the current account and the capital and financial account.
☐ Use a supply and demand graph to illustrate how a flexible-exchange-rate system works to establish the price and quantity of a currency.
☐ Discuss the role of official reserves when there is a balance-of-payments deficit or balance-of-payments surplus.
☐ Describe the depreciation and appreciation of a nation's currency under a flexible-exchange-rate system.
☐ Identify the six principal determinants of the demand for and supply of a particular foreign currency and explain how they alter exchange rates.

☐ Explain how flexible exchange rates eventually eliminate balance-of-payments deficits or surpluses.
☐ Describe three disadvantages of flexible exchange rates.
☐ Use a supply and demand graph to illustrate how a fixed exchange-rate system functions.
☐ Explain how nations use official reserves to maintain a fixed exchange rate.
☐ Describe how trade policies can be used to maintain a fixed exchange rate.
☐ Discuss advantages and disadvantages of using exchange controls to maintain a fixed exchange rate.
☐ Explain what domestic macroeconomic adjustments are needed to maintain a fixed exchange rate.
☐ Identify three different exchange-rate systems used by the world's nations in recent years.
☐ Discuss the pros and cons of the system of managed floating exchange rates.
☐ Describe the causes of recent trade deficits in the United States.
☐ Explain the economic implications of recent trade deficits in the United States.
☐ Assess the role that speculators play in currency markets (*Last Word*).

■ CHAPTER OUTLINE

1. International financial transactions are used for two purposes. First, there is the international trade of goods and services, such as food or insurance, that people buy or sell for money. Second, there is the international exchange of financial assets, such as real estate, stocks, or bonds, that people also buy or sell with money. International trade between nations or the international exchange of assets differs from domestic trade or asset exchanges because the nations use different currencies. This problem is resolved by the existence of foreign exchange markets, in which the currency of one nation can be purchased and paid for with the currency of the other nation.

2. The ***balance of payments*** for a nation is a summary of all the financial transactions with foreign nations; it records all the money payments received from and made to foreign nations. Most of the payments in the balance of payments accounts are for exports or imports of goods and services or for the purchase or sale of real and financial assets. The accounts show the inflows of money to the United States and the outflows of money from the United States. For convenience, both the inflows and outflows are stated in terms of U.S. dollars so they can be easily and consistently measured.

a. The ***current account*** section of a nation's balance of payments records the imports and exports of goods and services. Within this section

(1) the *balance on goods* of the nation is equal to its exports of goods minus its imports of goods;

(2) the *balance on services* of the nation is equal to its exports of services minus its imports of services;

(3) the ***balance on goods and services*** is equal to its exports of goods and services minus its imports of goods and services; and

(4) the ***balance on the current account*** is equal to its balance on goods and services and two other "net" items (which can be positive or negative). First there is net investment income (such as dividends and interest), which is the difference in investment income received from other nations minus any investment income paid to foreigners. Second, there are net private and public transfers, which is the difference between such transfers to other nations minus any transfers from other nations. This balance on the current account may be positive, zero, or negative. In 2009, it was a negative $420 billion.

b. International asset transactions are shown in the ***capital and financial account*** of a nation's balance of payments.

(1) The *capital account* primarily measures debt forgiveness and is a "net" account. If Americans forgave more debt owed to them by foreigners than foreigners forgave debt owed to them by Americans, then the capital account would be entered as a negative (−).

(2) The financial account shows foreign purchases of real and financial assets in the United States. This item brings a flow of money into the United States, so it is entered as a plus (+) in the capital account. U.S. purchases of real and financial assets abroad result in a flow of money from the United States to other nations, so this item is entered as a minus (−) in the capital account. The nation has a surplus in its financial account if foreign purchases of U.S. assets (and its inflow of money) are greater than U.S. purchases of assets abroad (and its outflow of money). The nation has a deficit in its financial account if foreign purchases of U.S. assets are less than U.S. purchases of assets abroad. The ***balance on the capital and financial account*** is the difference between the value of the capital account and the value of the financial account.

c. The balance of payments must always sum to zero. For example, any deficit in the current account would be offset by a surplus in the capital and financial account. The reason that the account balances is that people trade current produced goods and services or preexisting assets. If a nation imports more goods and services than it exports, then the deficit in the current account (and outflow of money) must be offset by sales of real and financial assets to foreigners (and inflow of money).

d. Sometimes economists and government officials refer to ***balance-of-payments deficits or surpluses.*** Whether a nation has a balance-of-payments deficit or surplus depends on what happens to its ***official reserves.*** These reserves are central bank holdings of foreign currencies, reserves at the International Monetary Fund, and stocks of gold.

(1) A nation has a *balance-of-payments deficit* when an imbalance in the combined current account and capital and financial account leads to a decrease in official reserves. These official reserves are an inpayment to the capital and financial account.

(2) A *balance-of-payments surplus* arises when an imbalance in the combined current account and capital and financial account results in an increase in official

reserves. These official reserves become an outpayment from the capital and financial account.

(3) Deficits in the balance-of-payments will happen over time and they are not necessarily bad. What is of concern, however, for any nation is whether the deficits are persistent over time because in that case they require that a nation continually draw down its official reserves. Such official reserves are limited and if they are depleted, a nation will have to adopt tough macroeconomic policies (discussed later in the chapter). In the case of the United States, there are ample official reserves and their depletion is not a major concern.

3. There are two basic types of exchange-rate systems that nations use to correct imbalances in the balance of payments. The first is a ***flexible- or floating-exchange-rate system*** that will be described in this section of the chapter outline. The second is a ***fixed-exchange-rate system*** that will be described in the next section of the chapter outline. If nations use a flexible- or floating-exchange-rate system, the demand for and the supply of foreign currencies determine foreign exchange rates. The exchange rate for any foreign currency is the rate at which the quantity of that currency demanded is equal to the quantity of it supplied.

a. A change in the demand for or the supply of a foreign currency will cause a change in the exchange rate for that currency. When there is an increase in the price paid in dollars for a foreign currency, the dollar has *depreciated* and the foreign currency has *appreciated* in value. Conversely, when there is a decrease in the price paid in dollars for a foreign currency, the dollar has *appreciated* and the foreign currency has *depreciated* in value.

b. Changes in the demand for or supply of a foreign currency are largely the result of changes in the ***determinants of exchange rates*** such as tastes, relative incomes, relative inflation rates, relative interest rates, expected returns, and speculation.

(1) A change in tastes for foreign goods that leads to an increase in demand for those goods will increase the value of the foreign currency and decrease the value of the U.S. currency.

(2) If the growth of U.S. national income is more rapid than other nations', then the value of U.S. currency will depreciate because it will expand its imports over its exports.

(3) ***Purchasing-power-parity theory*** is the idea that exchange rates equate the purchasing power of various currencies. Exchange rates, however, often deviate from this parity. If the inflation rate rises sharply in the United States and it remains constant in another nation, then foreign currency of the other nation will appreciate in value and the U.S. currency will depreciate in value.

(4) Changes in the relative interest rate in two nations may change their exchange rate. If real interest rates rise in the United States relative to another major trading partner, the U.S. dollar will appreciate in value because people will want to invest more money in the United States and the value of the other nation's currency will depreciate.

(5) Changes in the expected returns on stocks, real estate, and production facilities may change the exchange rate. If corporate tax rates are cut in the United States, then such a change would make investing in U.S. stock or production facilities more attractive relative to other nations, so foreigners may demand more U.S. dollars. The U.S. dollar will appreciate in value and the value of the foreigner's currency may depreciate.

(6) If speculators think the U.S. currency will depreciate, they can sell that currency and that act will help depreciate its value.

c. Flexible exchange rates can be used to eliminate a balance-of-payments deficit or surplus.

(1) When a nation has a payment deficit, foreign exchange rates will increase, thus making foreign goods and services more expensive and decreasing imports. These events will make a nation's goods and services less expensive for foreigners to buy, thus increasing exports.

(2) With a payment surplus, the exchange rates will increase, thus making foreign goods and services less expensive and increasing imports. This situation makes a nation's goods and services more expensive for foreigners to buy, thus decreasing exports.

d. Flexible exchange rates have three disadvantages.

(1) Flexible rates can change often so they increase the uncertainties exporters, importers, and investors face when exchanging one nation's currency for another, thus reducing international trade and international purchase and sale of real and financial assets.

(2) This system also changes the terms of trade. A depreciation of the U.S. dollar means that the United States must supply more dollars to the foreign exchange market to obtain the same amount of goods and services it previously obtained. Other nations will be able to purchase more U.S. goods or services because their currencies have appreciated relative to the dollar.

(3) The changes in the value of imports and exports can change the demand for goods and services in export and import industries, thus creating more instability in industrial production and in implementing macroeconomic policy.

4. If nations use a ***fixed-exchange-rate system,*** the nations fix (or peg) a specific exchange rate (for example, $2 will buy one British pound). To maintain this fixed exchange rate, the governments of these nations must intervene in the foreign exchange markets to prevent shortages and surpluses of currencies caused by shifts in demand and supply.

a. One way a nation can stabilize foreign exchange rates is through ***currency interventions.*** In this case, its government sells its reserves of a foreign currency in exchange for its own currency (or gold) when there is a shortage of the foreign currency. Conversely, a government would buy a foreign currency in exchange for its own currency (or gold) when there is a surplus of the foreign currency. The problem with this policy is that it only works when the currency needs are relatively minor and the intervention is of short duration. If there are persistent deficits, currency reserves may be inadequate for sustaining an intervention, so nations may need to use other means to maintain fixed exchange rates.

b. A nation might adopt trade policies that discourage imports and encourage exports. The problem with such policies is that they decrease the volume of international trade and make it less efficient, so that the economic benefits of free trade are diminished.

c. A nation might impose ***exchange controls*** so that all foreign currency is controlled by the government, and then rationed to individuals or businesses in the domestic economy who say they need it for international trade purposes. This policy too has several problems because it distorts trade, leads to government favoritism of specific individuals or businesses, restricts consumer choice of goods and services they can buy, and creates a black market in foreign currencies.

d. Another way a nation can stabilize foreign exchange rates is to use monetary and fiscal policy to reduce its national output and price level and raise its interest rates relative to those in other nations. These events would lead to a decrease in demand for and increase in the supply of different foreign currencies. But such macroeconomic policies would be harsh because they could lead to recession and deflation, and cause civil unrest.

5. In the past, some type of fixed-exchange-rate system was used such as the gold standard or the Bretton Woods system. The exchange-rate system used today is a more flexible one. Under the system of ***managed floating exchange rates,*** exchange rates are allowed to float in the long term to correct balance-of-payments deficits and surpluses, but if necessary there can be short-term interventions by governments to stabilize and manage currencies so they do not cause severe disruptions in international trade and finance. For example, the G8 nations (United States, United Kingdom, Canada, Germany, France, Japan, Russia, and Italy) regularly discuss economic issues and evaluate exchange rates, and at times have coordinated currency interventions to strengthen a nation's currency. This "almost" flexible system is favored by some and criticized by others.

a. Its proponents contend that this system has *not* led to any decrease in world trade, and has enabled the world to adjust to severe economic shocks throughout its history.

b. Its critics argue that it has resulted in volatile exchange rates that can hurt those developing nations that are dependent on exports, has *not* reduced balance-of-payments deficits and surpluses, and is a "nonsystem" that a nation may use to achieve its own domestic economic goals.

6. The United States had large and persistent ***trade deficits*** in the past decade and they are likely to continue.

a. These trade deficits are the result of several factors:

(1) more rapid growth in the domestic economy than in the economies of several major trading partners, which caused imports to rise more than exports;

(2) the emergence of large trade deficits with China and the use of a relatively fixed exchange rate by the Chinese;

(3) a rapid rise in the price of oil that must be imported from oil-producing nations; and

(4) a decline in the rate of saving and a capital account surplus, which allowed U.S. citizens to consume more imported goods.

b. The trade deficits of the United States have had two principal effects.

(1) They increased current domestic consumption beyond what is being produced domestically, which allows the nation to operate outside its production possibilities frontier. This increased current consumption, however, may come at the expense of future consumption.

(2) They increased the indebtedness of U.S. citizens to foreigners. A negative implication of these persistent trade deficits is that they will lead to permanent debt and more foreign ownership of domestic assets, or lead to large sacrifices of future domestic consumption. But if the foreign lending increases the U.S. capital stock, then it can contribute to long-term U.S. economic growth. Thus, trade deficits may be a mixed blessing.

7. (*Last Word*). Speculators buy foreign currency in hopes of reselling it later at a profit. They also sell foreign currency in hopes of rebuying it later when it is cheaper. Although speculators are often accused of creating severe fluctuations in currency markets, that criticism is overstated because economic conditions rather than speculation are typically the chief source of the problem. One positive function of speculators is that they smooth out temporary fluctuations in the value of foreign currencies. Another positive role speculators play in currency markets is that they bear risks that others do not want by delivering the specified amount of foreign exchange at the contract price on the date of delivery.

■ HINTS AND TIPS

1. The chapter is filled with many new terms, some of which are just special words used in international economics to mean things with which you are already familiar. Other terms are entirely new to you, so you must spend time learning them if you are to understand the chapter.

2. The terms **depreciation** and **appreciation** can be confusing when applied to foreign exchange markets. First, know the related terms. "Depreciate" means decrease or fall, whereas "appreciate" means increase or rise. Second, think of depreciation or appreciation in terms of *quantities*: what decreases when the currency of Country A *depreciates* is the quantity of Country B's currency that can be purchased for 1 unit of Country A's currency; what increases when the currency of Country A *appreciates* is the quantity of Country B's currency that can be purchased for 1 unit of Country A's currency. Third, consider the effect of changes in *exchange rates:* when the exchange rate for Country B's currency increases, this means that Country A's currency has *depreciated* in value because 1 unit of Country A's currency will now purchase a smaller quantity of Country B's currency; when the exchange rate for Country B's currency decreases, this means that Country A's currency has *appreciated* in value because 1 unit of

Country A's currency will now purchase a larger quantity of Country B's currency.

3. The meaning of the balance of payments can also be confusing because of the number of accounts in the balance sheet. Remember that the balance of payments must always balance and sum to zero because the current account in the balance of payments can be in deficit, but it will be exactly offset by a surplus in the capital and financial account. When economists speak of a balance-of-payments deficit or surplus, however, they are referring to adding *official reserves* or subtracting *official reserves* from the capital and financial account so that it just equals the current account.

■ IMPORTANT TERMS

balance of payments
current account
balance on goods and services
balance on current account
capital and financial account
balance on the capital and financial account
balance-of-payments deficit
balance-of-payments surplus
official reserves
flexible- or floating-exchange-rate system
fixed-exchange-rate system
purchasing-power-parity theory
currency interventions
exchange controls
managed floating exchange rate
trade deficit
trade surplus

SELF-TEST

■ FILL-IN QUESTIONS

1. The rate of exchange for the European euro is the amount in (euros, dollars) ______________ that a U.S. citizen must pay to obtain 1 (euro, dollar) ______________. The rate of exchange for the U.S. dollar is the amount in (euros, dollars) ______________ that a citizen in the euro zone must pay to obtain 1 (euro, dollar) ______________. If the rate of exchange for the euro is (1.05 euros, $0.95) ______________, the rate of exchange for the U.S. dollar is ______________.

2. The balance of payments of a nation records all payments (domestic, foreign) ______________ residents make to and receive from ______________ residents. Any transaction that *earns* foreign exchange for that nation is a (debit, credit) ______________, and any transaction that *uses up* foreign exchange is a ______________. A debit is shown with a (+, −) ______________ sign, and a credit is shown with a ______________ sign.

3. If a nation has a deficit in its balance of goods, its exports of goods are (greater, less) ______________ than its imports of goods. If a nation has a surplus in its balance of services, its exports of services are (greater, less) ______________ than its imports of services. If a nation has a deficit in its balance on goods and services, its exports of these items are (greater, less) ______________ than its imports of them.

4. The current account is equal to the balance on goods and services (plus, minus) ______________ net investment income and net transfers. When investment income received by U.S. individuals and businesses from foreigners is greater than investment income Americans pay to foreigners, then net investment income is a (negative, positive) ______________ number; when transfer payments from the United States to other nations are greater than transfer payments from other nations to the United States, then net transfers are a ______________ number.

5. The capital account is a net measure of (investment, debt forgiveness) ______________. When Americans forgive more debt owed to them by foreigners than foreigners forgive debt owed to them by Americans, the capital account has a (debit, credit) ______________ that reflects an outpayment of funds.

6. The financial account measures the flow of monetary payments from the sale or purchase of real or financial assets. Foreign purchases of real and financial assets in the United States earn foreign currencies, so they are entered as a (plus, minus) ______________ in the financial account, but U.S. purchases of real and financial assets abroad draw down U.S. holding of foreign currencies, so this item is entered as a ______________.

7. If foreign purchases of U.S. assets are greater than U.S. purchases of assets abroad, the nation has a (surplus, deficit) ______________ in its financial account, but if foreign purchases of U.S. assets are less than U.S. purchases of assets abroad, it has a ______________.

8. A nation may finance a current account deficit by (buying, selling) ______________ real or financial assets and may use a current account surplus to (buy, sell) ______________ real or financial assets.

9. The sum of the current account and the capital and financial accounts must equal (0, 1) ______________ so the balance of payments always balances. When economists or government officials speak of a balance-of-payments deficit or surplus, however, they are referring to the use of official reserves, which are the quantities of (foreign currencies, its own money) ______________ owned by a nation's central bank.

10. If a nation has a balance-of-payments deficit, then its official reserves (increase, decrease) ____________ in the capital and financial account, but with a balance-of-payments surplus its official reserves ____________ in the capital and financial account.

11. If foreign exchange rates float freely and a nation has a balance-of-payments *deficit,* that nation's currency in the foreign exchange markets will (appreciate, depreciate) ____________ and foreign currencies will ____________ compared to it. As a result of these changes in foreign exchange rates, the nation's imports will (increase, decrease) ____________, its exports will ____________, and the size of its deficit will (increase, decrease) ____________.

12. What effect would each of the following have—the appreciation (**A**) or depreciation (**D**) of the euro compared to the U.S. dollar in the foreign exchange market, *ceteris paribus*?

a. The increased preference in the United States for domestic wines over wines produced in Europe: ____

b. A rise in the U.S. national income: ____

c. An increase in the inflation rate in Europe: ____

d. A rise in real interest rates in the United States: ____

e. A large cut in corporate tax rates in Europe: ____

f. The belief of speculators in Europe that the dollar will appreciate in the foreign exchange market: ____

13. There are three disadvantages of freely floating foreign exchange rates: the risks and uncertainties associated with flexible rates tend to (expand, diminish) ____________ trade between nations; when a nation's currency depreciates, its terms of trade with other nations are (worsened, improved) ____________; and fluctuating exports and imports can (stabilize, destabilize) ____________ an economy.

14. To fix or peg the rate of exchange for the Mexican peso when the exchange rate for the peso is rising, the United States would (buy, sell) ____________ pesos in exchange for dollars, and when the exchange rate for the peso is falling, the United States would ____________ pesos in exchange for dollars.

15. Under a fixed-exchange-rate system, a nation with a balance-of-payments deficit might attempt to eliminate the deficit by (taxing, subsidizing) ____________ imports or by ____________ exports. The nation might use exchange controls and ration foreign exchange among those who wish to (export, import) ____________ goods and services and require all those who ____________ goods and services to sell the foreign exchange they earn to the (businesses, government) ____________.

16. If the United States has a payments deficit with Japan and the exchange rate for the Japanese yen is rising, under a fixed-exchange-rate system the United States might adopt (expansionary, contractionary) ____________ fiscal and monetary policies to reduce the demand for the yen, but this would bring about (inflation, recession) ____________ in the United States.

17. The international monetary system has moved to a system of managed (fixed, floating) ____________ exchange rates. This means that exchange rates of nations are (restricted from, free to) ____________ find their equilibrium market levels, but nations may occasionally (leave, intervene in) ____________ the foreign exchange markets to stabilize or alter market exchange rates.

18. The advantages of the current system are that the growth of trade (was, was not) ____________ accommodated and that it has survived much economic (stability, turbulence) ____________. Its disadvantages are its (equilibrium, volatility) ____________ and the lack of guidelines for nations that make it a (bureaucracy, nonsystem) ____________.

19. In recent years, the United States had large trade and current account (surpluses, deficits) ____________. One cause of these deficits was (stronger, weaker) ____________ economic growth in the United States relative to Europe and Japan. Other contributing factors were a (rise, fall) ____________ in trade deficits with China, a ____________ in the price of oil, and a ____________ in the saving rate.

20. One effect of the recent trade deficits of the United States has been a(n) (decrease, increase) ____________ in current domestic consumption that allows the nation to operate outside its production possibility frontier, but may lead to a(n) ____________ in future consumption. Another effect was a (rise, fall) ____________ in the indebtedness of U.S. citizens to foreigners.

■ TRUE–FALSE QUESTIONS

Circle T if the statement is true, F if it is false.

1. The two basic categories of international financial transactions are international trade and international assets. **T F**

2. The balance of payments of the United States records all the payments its residents receive from and make to the residents of foreign nations. **T F**

3. Exports are a debit item and are shown with a minus sign (−), and imports are a credit item and are shown with a plus sign (+) in the balance of payments of a nation. **T F**

4. The current account balance is a nation's export of goods and services minus its imports of goods and services. **T F**

5. The capital account will be a negative number when Americans forgive more debt owed to them by foreigners than the debt foreigners forgive that was owed to them by Americans. **T F**

6. The nation's current account balance and the capital and financial account in any year are always equal to zero. **T F**

7. When a nation must make an inpayment of official reserves to its capital and financial account to balance it with the current account, a balance-of-payments deficit has occurred. **T F**

8. The two "pure" types of exchange-rate systems are flexible (or floating) and fixed. **T F**

9. When the U.S. dollar price of a British pound rises, the dollar has depreciated relative to the pound. **T F**

10. If the supply of a nation's currency increases, that currency will appreciate in value. **T F**

11. The purchasing-power-parity theory basically explains why there is an inverse relationship between the price of dollars and the quantity demanded. **T F**

12. If income growth is robust in Europe, but sluggish in the United States, then the U.S. dollar will appreciate. **T F**

13. If the expected returns on stocks, real estate, or production facilities increased in the United States relative to Japan, the U.S. dollar would depreciate in value relative to the Japanese yen. **T F**

14. The expectations of speculators in the United States that the exchange rate for Japanese yen will fall in the future will increase the supply of yen in the foreign exchange market and decrease the exchange rate for the yen. **T F**

15. If a nation has a balance-of-payments deficit and exchange rates are flexible, the price of that nation's currency in the foreign exchange markets will fall; this will reduce its imports and increase its exports. **T F**

16. Were the United States' terms of trade with Nigeria to worsen, Nigeria would obtain a greater quantity of U.S. goods and services for every barrel of oil it exported to the United States. **T F**

17. If a nation wishes to fix (or peg) the foreign exchange rate for the Swiss franc, it must buy Swiss francs with its own currency when the rate of exchange for the Swiss franc rises. **T F**

18. If exchange rates are stable or fixed and a nation has a balance-of- payments surplus, prices and currency incomes in that nation will tend to rise. **T F**

19. A nation using exchange controls to eliminate a balance-of-payments surplus might depreciate its currency. **T F**

20. Using the managed floating system of exchange rates, a nation with a persistent balance-of-payments surplus should allow the value of its currency in foreign exchange markets to decrease. **T F**

21. Two criticisms of the current managed floating-exchange-rate system are its potential for volatility and its lack of clear policy rules or guidelines for nations to manage exchange rates. **T F**

22. The trade deficits of the United States in recent years were caused by sharp increases in U.S. exports and slight increases in U.S. imports. **T F**

23. Improved economic growth in the economies of the major trading partners of the United States would tend to worsen the trade deficit. **T F**

24. The decline in the saving rate in the United States contributed to the persistent trade deficit of the past decade. **T F**

25. The negative net exports of the United States have increased the indebtedness of U.S. citizens to foreigners. **T F**

■ MULTIPLE-CHOICE QUESTIONS

Circle the letter that corresponds to the best answer.

1. If a U.S. citizen could buy £25,000 for $100,000, the rate of exchange for the pound would be
(a) $40
(b) $25
(c) $4
(d) $.25

2. U.S. residents demand foreign currencies to
(a) produce goods and services exported to foreign countries
(b) pay for goods and services imported from foreign countries
(c) receive interest payments on investments in the United States
(d) have foreigners make real and financial investments in the United States

3. Which of the following would be a credit in the current account?
(a) U.S. imports of goods
(b) U.S. exports of services
(c) U.S. purchases of assets abroad
(d) U.S. interest payments for foreign capital invested in the United States

4. A nation's balance on the current account is equal to its exports less its imports of
(a) goods and services
(b) goods and services, plus U.S. purchases of assets abroad
(c) goods and services, plus net investment income and net transfers
(d) goods and services, minus foreign purchases of assets in the United States

5. The net investment income of the United States in its international balance of payments is the
(a) interest income it receives from foreign residents
(b) value of dividends it receives from foreign residents
(c) excess of interest and dividends it receives from foreign residents over what it paid to them
(d) excess of public and private transfer payments it receives from foreign residents over what it paid to them

Answer Questions 6, 7, and 8 using the following table that contains data for the United States' balance of payments in a prior year. All figures are in billions of dollars.

(1)	U.S. goods exports	$+1149
(2)	U.S. goods imports	−1965
(3)	U.S. service exports	+479
(4)	U.S. service imports	−372
(5)	Net investment income	+74
(6)	Net transfers	−104
(7)	Balance on capital account	−2
(8)	Foreign purchases of U.S. assets	+1905
(9)	U.S. purchases of foreign assets	−1164

6. The balance on goods and services was a deficit of
(a) $107 billion
(b) $709 billion
(c) $816 billion
(d) $935 billion

7. The balance on the current account was a
(a) surplus of $739 billion
(b) deficit of $739 billion
(c) surplus of $816 billion
(d) deficit of $816 billion

8. The balance on the financial account was a
(a) deficit of $372 billion
(b) surplus of $479 billion
(c) deficit of $739 billion
(d) surplus of $741 billion

9. In a flexible- or floating-exchange-rate system, when the U.S. dollar price of a British pound rises, this means that the dollar has
(a) appreciated relative to the pound and the pound has appreciated relative to the dollar
(b) appreciated relative to the pound and the pound has depreciated relative to the dollar
(c) depreciated relative to the pound and the pound has appreciated relative to the dollar
(d) depreciated relative to the pound and the pound has depreciated relative to the dollar

10. Which statement is correct about a factor that causes a nation's currency to appreciate or depreciate in value?
(a) If the supply of a nation's currency decreases, all else equal, that currency will depreciate.
(b) If the supply of a nation's currency increases, all else equal, that currency will depreciate.
(c) If the demand for a nation's currency increases, all else equal, that currency will depreciate.
(d) If the demand for a nation's currency decreases, all else equal, that currency will appreciate.

11. Assuming exchange rates are flexible, which of the following should increase the dollar price of the Swedish krona?
(a) a rate of inflation greater in Sweden than in the United States
(b) real interest rate increases greater in Sweden than in the United States
(c) national income increases greater in Sweden than in the United States
(d) the increased preference of Swedish citizens for U.S. automobiles over Swedish automobiles

12. Under a flexible-exchange-rate system, a nation may be able to correct or eliminate a persistent (long-term) balance-of-payments deficit by
(a) lowering the barriers on imported goods
(b) reducing the international value of its currency
(c) expanding its national income
(d) reducing its official reserves

13. If a nation had a balance-of-payments surplus and exchange rates floated freely, the foreign exchange rate for its currency would
(a) rise, its exports would increase, and its imports would decrease
(b) rise, its exports would decrease, and its imports would increase
(c) fall, its exports would increase, and its imports would decrease
(d) fall, its exports would decrease, and its imports would increase

Answer Questions 14, 15, and 16 using the graph below.

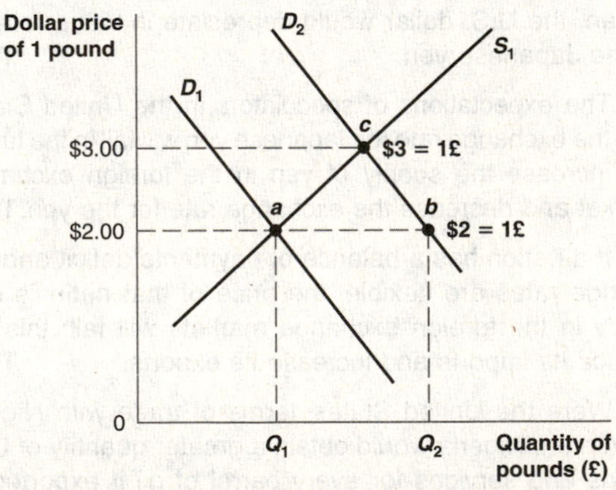

14. If D_1 moves to D_2, the U.S. dollar has
(a) appreciated, and the British pound has depreciated
(b) appreciated, and the British pound has appreciated
(c) depreciated, and the British pound has depreciated
(d) depreciated, and the British pound has appreciated

15. If D_1 moves to D_2, there will be a balance-of-payments
(a) deficit of Q_1
(b) surplus of Q_2
(c) deficit of Q_2 minus Q_1
(d) surplus of Q_2 minus Q_1

16. If D_1 moves to D_2, but the British government seeks to keep the exchange rate at \$2 = 1£, then it can do so through policies that

(a) increase the supply of pounds and decrease the demand for pounds
(b) decrease the supply of pounds and increase the demand for pounds
(c) increase the supply of pounds and increase the demand for pounds
(d) decrease the supply of pounds and decrease the demand for pounds

17. Which would be a result associated with the use of freely floating foreign exchange rates to correct a nation's balance-of-payments surplus?

(a) The nation's terms of trade with other nations would be worsened.
(b) Importers in the nation who had made contracts for the future delivery of goods would find that they had to pay a higher price than expected for the goods.
(c) If the nation were at full employment, the decrease in exports and the increase in imports would be inflationary.
(d) Exporters in the nation would find their sales abroad had decreased.

18. The use of exchange controls to eliminate a nation's balance-of-payments deficit results in decreasing the nation's

(a) imports
(b) exports
(c) price level
(d) income

19. Assume a nation has a balance-of-payments deficit and it seeks to maintain a fixed exchange rate. To eliminate the shortage of foreign currency, it may have to adopt monetary policies that

(a) lower the interest rate
(b) raise the interest rate
(c) reduce the tax rate
(d) increase the tax rate

20. A system of managed floating exchange rates

(a) allows nations to stabilize exchange rates in the short term
(b) requires nations to stabilize exchange rates in the long term
(c) entails stable exchange rates in both the short and long term
(d) fixes exchange rates at market levels

21. Floating exchange rates

(a) tend to correct balance-of-payments imbalances
(b) reduce the uncertainties and risks associated with international trade
(c) increase the world's need for international monetary reserves
(d) tend to have no effect on the volume of trade

22. The trade problem that faced the United States in recent years was a

(a) deficit in its capital account
(b) surplus in its balance on goods
(c) deficit in its current account
(d) surplus in its current account

23. Which was a cause of the growth of U.S. trade deficits in recent years?

(a) protective tariffs imposed by the United States
(b) slower economic growth in the United States
(c) direct foreign investment in the United States
(d) a declining saving rate in the United States

24. What would be the effect on U.S. imports and exports when the United States experiences strong economic growth but its major trading partners experience sluggish economic growth?

(a) U.S. imports will increase more than U.S. exports
(b) U.S. exports will increase more than U.S. imports
(c) U.S. imports will decrease but U.S. exports will increase
(d) there will be no effect on U.S. imports and exports

25. Two major outcomes from the trade deficits of recent years were

(a) decreased domestic consumption and U.S. indebtedness
(b) increased domestic consumption and U.S. indebtedness
(c) increased domestic consumption but decreased U.S. indebtedness
(d) decreased domestic consumption but increased U.S. indebtedness

■ PROBLEMS

1. Assume a U.S. exporter sells \$3 million worth of wheat to an importer in Colombia. If the rate of exchange for the Colombian peso is \$.02 (2 cents), the wheat has a total value of 150 million pesos. There are two ways the importer in Colombia may pay for the wheat.

a. It might write a check for 150 million pesos drawn on its bank in Bogotá and send it to the U.S. exporter. The U.S. exporter would then send the check to its bank in New Orleans and its checking account there would increase by \$________ million. The New Orleans bank would then arrange to have the check converted to U.S. dollars through a correspondent bank (a U.S. commercial bank that keeps an account in the Bogotá bank).

b. The second way for the importer to pay for the wheat is to buy from its bank in Bogotá a draft on a U.S. bank for \$3 million, pay for this draft by writing a check for 150 million pesos drawn on the Bogotá bank, and send the draft to the U.S. exporter. The U.S. exporter would then deposit the draft in its account in the New Orleans bank and its checking account there would increase by \$________ million. The New Orleans bank would then collect the amount of the draft from the U.S. bank on which it is drawn through the Federal Reserve Banks.

2. The following table contains hypothetical balance-of-payments data for the United States. All figures are in billions. Compute with the appropriate sign (+ or −) and enter in the table the six missing items.

Current account		
(1)	U.S. goods exports	$+150
(2)	U.S. goods imports	−200
(3)	*Balance on goods*	____
(4)	U.S. exports of services	+75
(5)	U.S. imports of services	−60
(6)	*Balance on services*	____
(7)	*Balance on goods and services*	____
(8)	Net investment income	+12
(9)	Net transfers	−7
(10)	***Balance on current account***	____
Capital Account and Financial Account		
(11)	Capital Account	−5
Financial Account:		
(12)	Foreign purchases of assets in the U.S.	+90
(13)	U.S. purchases of assets abroad	−55
(14)	*Balance on financial account*	____
(15)	**Balance on capital and financial account**	____
		$ 0

3. The following table shows supply and demand schedules for the British pound.

Quantity of pounds supplied	Price	Quantity of pounds demanded
400	$5.00	100
360	4.50	200
300	4.00	300
286	3.50	400
267	3.00	500
240	2.50	620
200	2.00	788

a. If the exchange rates are flexible

(1) what will be the rate of exchange for the pound? $________

(2) what will be the rate of exchange for the dollar? £________

(3) how many pounds will be purchased in the market? ________

(4) how many dollars will be purchased in the market? ________

b. If the U.S. government wished to fix or peg the price of the pound at $5.00, it would have to (buy, sell) ________ (how many) ________ pounds for $________.

c. And if the British government wished to fix the price of the dollar at £ 2/5, it would have to (buy, sell) ________ (how many) ________ pounds for $________.

■ SHORT ANSWER AND ESSAY QUESTIONS

1. Explain the two basic types of international transactions and give an example of each one.

2. What is meant when it is said that "A nation's exports pay for its imports"? Do nations pay for all their imports with exports? Explain.

3. What is a balance of payments? What are the principal sections in a nation's balance-of-payments, and what are the principal "balances" to be found in it?

4. How can a nation finance a current account deficit? Explain the relationship between the current account and the capital and financial account.

5. Why do the balance-of-payments balance? Explain.

6. What is a balance-of-payments deficit, and what is a balance-of-payments surplus? What role do official reserves play in the matter?

7. Is a balance-of-payments deficit bad or a balance-of-payments surplus good? Explain.

8. Use a supply and demand graph to help describe how exchange rates for a currency appreciate and depreciate.

9. What types of events cause the exchange rate for a foreign currency to appreciate or to depreciate? How will each event affect the exchange rate for a foreign currency and for a nation's own currency?

10. How can flexible foreign exchange rates eliminate balance-of-payments deficits and surpluses?

11. What are the problems associated with flexible-exchange-rate systems for correcting payments imbalances?

12. How may a nation use its international monetary reserves to fix or peg foreign exchange rates? Be precise. How does a nation obtain or acquire these monetary reserves?

13. What kinds of trade policies may nations with payments deficits use to eliminate their deficits?

14. How can foreign exchange controls be used to restore international equilibrium? Why do such exchange controls necessarily involve the rationing of foreign exchange? What effect do these controls have on prices, output, and employment in nations that use them?

15. If foreign exchange rates are fixed, what kind of domestic macroeconomic adjustments are required to eliminate a payments deficit? To eliminate a payments surplus?

16. Explain what is meant by a managed floating system of foreign exchange rates.

17. When are exchange rates managed and when are they allowed to float? What organization is often responsible for currency interventions?

18. Explain the arguments of the proponents and the critics of the managed floating system.

19. What were the causes of the trade deficits of the United States in recent years?

20. What were the effects of the trade deficits of recent years on the U.S. economy?

ANSWERS

Chapter 21 The Balance of Payments, Exchange Rates, and Trade Deficits

FILL-IN QUESTIONS

1. dollars, euro, euros, dollar, $0.95, 1.05 euros
2. domestic, foreign, credit, debit, −, +
3. less, greater, less
4. plus, positive, negative
5. debt forgiveness, debit
6. plus, minus
7. surplus, deficit
8. selling, buy
9. 0, foreign currencies
10. decrease, increase
11. depreciate, appreciate, decrease, increase, decrease
12. *a.* D; *b.* A; *c.* D; *d.* D; *e.* A; *f.* D
13. diminish, worsened, destabilize
14. sell, buy
15. taxing, subsidizing, import, export, government
16. contractionary, recession
17. floating, free to, intervene in
18. was, turbulence, volatility, nonsystem
19. deficits, stronger, rise, rise, fall
20. increase, decrease, rise

TRUE-FALSE QUESTIONS

1. T, p. 425
2. T, p. 426
3. F, p. 426
4. F, pp. 426–427
5. T, p. 427
6. T, p. 428
7. T, pp. 428–429
8. T, p. 429
9. T, pp. 429–430
10. F, pp. 429–430
11. F, p. 431
12. T, p. 431
13. F, p. 431–432
14. T, p. 432
15. T, pp. 432–433
16. T, p. 434
17. F, p. 434–435
18. T, p. 435
19. F, pp. 435–436
20. F, pp. 436–437
21. T, p. 437
22. F, pp. 438–439
23. F, pp. 438–439
24. T, p. 439
25. T, p. 439

MULTIPLE-CHOICE QUESTIONS

1. c, p. 425
2. b, p. 425
3. b, p. 426
4. c, pp. 426–427
5. c, p. 427
6. b, pp. 426–427
7. b, pp. 426–427
8. d, pp. 427–428
9. c, pp. 429–430
10. b, pp. 429–430
11. b, p. 431
12. b, pp. 432–433
13. b, pp. 432–433
14. d, pp. 432–433
15. c, pp. 432–433
16. a, pp. 434–435
17. d, pp. 433–434
18. a, pp. 435–436
19. b, pp. 436
20. a, pp. 436–437
21. a, pp. 436–437
22. c, p. 438
23. d, pp. 438–439
24. a, pp. 438–439
25. b, p. 439

PROBLEMS

1. *a.* 3; *b.* 3
2. −50, +15, −35, −30, +35, +30
3. *a.* (1) 4.00, (2) 1/4, (3) 300, (4) 1200; *b.* buy, 300, 1500; *c.* sell, 380, 950

SHORT ANSWER AND ESSAY QUESTIONS

1. p. 425
2. p. 425
3. pp. 425–428
4. pp. 426–428
5. p. 428
6. pp. 428–429
7. pp. 428–429
8. pp. 429–430
9. pp. 431–432
10. pp. 432–433
11. pp. 433–434
12. pp. 434–435
13. p. 435
14. pp. 435–436
15. p. 436
16. p. 436
17. pp. 436–437
18. p. 437
19. p. 438–439
20. p. 439

CHAPTER 22 Web

The Economics of Developing Countries

Note: The bonus web chapter is available at: **www.mcconnell19e.com.**

This chapter looks at the critical problem of raising the standards of living in **developing countries** (DVCs) of the world. The development problems in these nations, especially the poorest ones, are extensive: low literacy rates, low levels of industrialization, high dependence on agriculture, rapid rates of population growth, and widespread poverty.

There is also a growing income gap between DVCs and **industrially advanced nations** (IACs). To close this gap, there needs to be more economic growth in the DVCs. Achieving that growth requires expansion of economic resources and that these resources be efficiently used. As you will discover from the chapter, DVCs trying to apply these principles face **obstacles** quite different from those that limit growth in the United States and other IACs. DVCs have many problems with natural, human, and capital resources and with technology, all of which combine to hinder economic growth. Certain social, cultural, and institutional factors also create a poor environment for economic development.

These obstacles do not mean that it is impossible to increase the living standards of these DVCs. What they do indicate is that to encourage growth, the DVCs must do things that do not need to be done in the United States or other IACs. Population pressures need to be managed and there needs to be better use of labor resources. Steps must be taken to encourage capital investment. Governments must take an active role in promoting economic growth and limiting the public sector problems for economic development. Dramatic changes in social practices and institutions are required. Without taking these actions, it may not be possible to reduce the major obstacles to growth and break the **vicious circle of poverty** in the DVCs.

No matter how successful the DVCs are in overcoming these obstacles, they still will not be able to grow rapidly without more aid from IACs. This assistance can come in the form of lower trade barriers in IACs that would increase sales of products from DVCs to IACs. There can be more foreign aid in the form of government grants and loans to IACs. The banks, corporations, and other businesses in IACs can provide private capital in the form of loans or direct foreign investment in the building of new factories and businesses.

■ CHECKLIST

When you have studied this chapter you should be able to

☐ Describe the extent of income inequality among nations.

☐ Give examples of industrially advanced nations (IACs) and developing countries (DVCs)

☐ Classify nations based on three levels of income.

☐ Compare the effects of differences in economic growth in IACs and DVCs.

☐ Discuss the human realities of poverty in DVCs.

☐ Identify two basic paths for economic development in DVCs.

☐ Describe natural resource problems in DVCs.

☐ Identify the three problems related to human resources that plague the poorest DVCs.

☐ Explain the difficulties for economic growth that are created by population growth in DVCs.

☐ Discuss how a demographic transition can occur as economic growth takes off.

☐ Describe the conditions of unemployment and underemployment in DVCs.

☐ State reasons for low labor productivity in DVCs.

☐ Give three reasons for the emphasis on capital formation in the DVCs.

☐ Identify obstacles to domestic capital formation through saving.

☐ List obstacles to domestic capital formation through investment.

☐ Explain why it is difficult to transfer technologies from IACs to DVCs.

☐ Identify sociocultural obstacles that can potentially inhibit economic growth.

☐ Describe the institutional obstacles to growth.

☐ Explain why poverty in the poor nations is a vicious circle.

☐ List eight ways that governments in the DVCs can play a positive role in breaking the vicious circle of poverty.

☐ Describe the problems with the public sector in fostering economic development.

☐ Discuss different ways that IACs can help the DVCs foster economic growth.

☐ Explain how reducing international trade barriers in IACs would help DVCs.

☐ Describe the two sources of foreign aid for DVCs.

☐ State three criticisms of foreign aid to DVCs.

☐ Describe the private flow of capital from IACs to DVCs.

☐ Discuss the natural and human causes of persistent famines in some African nations (*Last Word*).

■ CHAPTER OUTLINE

1. There is considerable ***income inequality among nations.*** The richest 20 percent of the world's population

receives more than 80 percent of the world's income; the poorest 20 percent receives less than 2 percent.

a. The World Bank classifies countries into two main groups.

(1) ***Industrially advanced countries (IACs)*** are characterized by well-developed market economies based on large stocks of capital goods, advanced technology for production, and well-educated workers. Among the ***high-income nations*** are the United States, Japan, Canada, Australia, New Zealand, and most of the nations of Western Europe. These countries averaged $37,665 per capita income in 2008.

(2) ***Developing countries (DVCs)*** are a diverse group of middle-income and low-income nations. ***Middle-income nations*** (e.g., Brazil, Iran, Poland, Russia, South Africa, and Thailand) had per capita incomes that range from $925 to $11,906, and average incomes of about $3,251 in 2008.

(3) There are also ***low-income nations*** with per capita incomes of $925 or less, and average incomes of $523 in 2008. This latter group is dominated by most of the sub-Saharan nations of Africa. These nations are not highly industrialized, are dependent on agriculture, and often have high rates of population growth and low rates of literacy. The low-income nations comprise about 15 percent of the world's population.

b. There are major differences between the United States and DVCs. The GDP in the United States is greater than the combined GDPs of all DVCs. The United States produced 25.1 percent of the world's output, but had only 4.5 percent of the world's population in 2008. Per capita GDP in the United States is 150 times greater than per capita GDP in Sierra Leone (one of the poorest nations).

c. There are disparities in the growth rates of nations, resulting in large income gaps. Some DVC nations have been able to improve their economic conditions over time and become IACs. Other DVCs are now showing high rates of economic growth, but still other DVCs have experienced a decline in economic growth and standards of living. If growth rates were the same for high- and low-income nations, the gap in per capita income would widen because the income base is higher in high-income nations.

d. The human realities of extreme poverty are important. Compared with IACs, persons in DVCs have not only lower per capita incomes, but also lower life expectancies, higher infant mortality rates, lower literacy rates, few Internet users, and less per capita energy consumption.

2. The paths to economic development for DVCs require that (1) they use their existing resources more efficiently, and (2) they expand their available supplies of resources. The physical, human, and socioeconomic conditions in these nations are the reasons why DVCs experience different rates of economic growth.

a. Many DVCs possess inadequate ***natural resources.*** This limited resource base is an obstacle to growth. The agricultural products that DVCs typically export are also subject to significant price variations on the world market, creating variations in national income.

b. There are problems with ***human resources*** in DVCs.

(1) DVCs tend to have large populations, high population densities, and higher rates of population growth than IACs. These growing populations reduce the DVCs' capacity to save and invest, and also lower productivity. They also overuse land and natural resources, and the migration of rural workers to cities creates urban problems.

(2) There is a qualification to the traditional view that a high rate of population growth or large population density is a major cause of low incomes in DVCs. Another perspective on the issue holds that a ***demographic transition*** occurs when economic growth creates rising incomes that change the population dynamics and reduce birthrates. From this perspective higher incomes need to be achieved first, and then lower rates of population growth will follow.

(3) DVCs often experience both unemployment, which means that able workers do not have jobs, and ***underemployment,*** which means that able workers are working fewer hours than they want to work. Both conditions waste labor resources.

(4) DVCs have low levels of labor productivity because of insufficient physical capital and lack of investment in human capital. There is also a ***brain drain*** of the more talented and skilled workers migrating from DVCs going to IACs to seek better employment opportunities.

c. DVCs have inadequate amounts of ***capital goods,*** and so find it difficult to accumulate capital.

(1) Domestic capital formation occurs through saving and investing. The potential for saving is low in many DVCs because the nations are too poor to save.

(2) There is a ***capital flight,*** the transfer of private savings from DVCs to more stable IACs.

(3) The investment obstacles include a lack of investors and entrepreneurs and a lack of incentives to invest in DVC economies. The ***infrastructure*** (stock of public capital goods) also is poor in many DVCs.

d. ***Technological advance*** is slow in DVCs. Although these nations might adopt the technologies of industrial nations, these technologies are not always appropriate for the resource endowments of the DVCs, so they must learn to develop and use their own technologies. Some advances can be achieved with ***capital-saving technology*** (that requires less use of other capital goods or resources) rather than ***capital-using technology*** (that requires more use of capital goods).

e. The ***social, cultural, and institutional*** factors in DVCs can be impediments to economic development, and there can be an intangible lack of ***will to develop*** among individuals and leaders.

(1) The sociocultural obstacles to growth include such factors as tribal or ethnic allegiances that reduce national unity, a caste or class system, and a ***capricious universe view*** that sees little correlation between individual actions and outcomes or results.

(2) The institutional obstacles include problems with school systems and public services, weak tax systems, a lack of control over spending by governments, and the need for ***land reform*** to reduce the concentration of land holdings among a few wealthy families.

3. In summary, DVCs face a ***vicious circle of poverty.*** They save little because they are poor, and therefore invest little in real and human capital. And because they do not invest, their outputs per capita remain low and they remain poor. Even if the vicious circle were to be broken, a rapid increase in population would leave the standard of living unchanged.

4. There are differing views about the ***role of government*** in fostering economic growth in the DVCs.

a. The *positive* view holds that in the initial stages of economic development, government action is needed to help overcome major obstacles to growth by:

(1) providing law and order to give political stability;

(2) improving the infrastructure through the provision of public goods that also make the private sector more productive;

(3) embracing globalization by opening economies to trade and establishing realistic policies for exchange rates;

(4) building human capital by providing effective programs that foster literacy, education, and the development of labor market skills;

(5) promoting entrepreneurship to stimulate business formation;

(6) developing policies that strengthen the banking system and make credit more widely available through ***microfinance*** (the offering of small loans to entrepreneurs and business owners);

(7) managing population growth to increase rather than decrease real per capita incomes; and

(8) making peace with neighbors for those nations involved in conflicts.

b. The *negative* view holds that there are problems and difficulties with using the public sector for promoting growth. They include bureaucratic impediments, ***corruption,*** maladministration, and the importance of political objectives over economic goals. Central planning does not work because it restricts competition and individual incentives, which are important ingredients in the growth process.

5. There are several potential ways that ***IACs can help DVCs,*** although each one has its limitations.

a. IACs can expand trade by lowering the ***trade barriers*** that prevent the DVCs from selling their products in the developed countries.

b. IACs can admit more seasonal or temporary workers from DVCs to provide an outlet for surplus labor in DVCs.

c. IACs can discourage the sales of military equipment that can misallocate too many resources to national defense.

d. IACs can provide ***foreign aid*** in the form of public loans and grants to help improve infrastructure or public goods.

(1) This foreign aid can come directly from IAC governments.

(2) The foreign aid can also come from international organizations such as the ***World Bank,*** which makes grants and loans for basic development projects, offers technical assistance, and serves as a lender of last resort to DVCs.

(3) This foreign aid has been criticized because it increases dependency on IACs, expands bureaucracy in DVCs, and encourages corruption.

(4) Although foreign aid declined during the 1990s, it increased from 2000 to 2008 because of greater interest in reducing global poverty and the spending on the war on terrorism.

e. DVCs can also receive flows of private capital from IACs. ***Direct foreign investment*** in new factories and businesses can come from banks, corporations, and financial investment companies, but such investment tends to be highly selective among nations.

6. (*Last Word*). Famines in Africa are due to both natural and human forces. The immediate cause of famine is drought. Other causes are more complex. Civil strife has torn many nations for decades. Population growth outstripped food production in many nations. Ecological degradation has occurred in nations that use marginal land for crop production. There also are poor public policies such as underinvestment in agriculture relative to industrial development and the use of price controls on agricultural commodities that reduces economic incentives. Some nations also have large external debts to service that require cuts in spending for health care, education, and infrastructure.

■ HINTS AND TIPS

1. This chapter offers a comprehensive look at the various factors affecting growth and economic development. Keep in mind that **no one factor** explains why some nations prosper and others remain poor. The chapter should give you insights into how natural, human, and capital resources together with government policies may influence a nation's economic development.

2. Several economic and demographic statistics for comparing rich and poor nations appear in the chapter's tables. You need not memorize the numbers, but you should try to get a sense of the magnitude of the differences between IACs and DVCs on several key indicators. To do this, ask yourself questions calling for **relative comparisons.** For example, how many times larger is average per capita income in IACs than in low-income DVCs? Answer: 72 times greater ($37,665/$523 = 72).

3. The chapter presents some **policies** for increasing economic growth in DVCs, but they may be easy to implement, may be limited in effectiveness, and may be controversial. Be sure to look at these policies from the perspective of both DVCs and IACs. Identify those that you think are most important and explain your reasoning.

■ IMPORTANT TERMS

industrially advanced countries (IACs)
developing countries (DVCs)
demographic transition
underemployment
brain drain
capital flight
infrastructure
capital-saving technology
capital-using technology
will to develop
capricious universe view
land reform
vicious circle of poverty
microfinance
corruption
World Bank
direct foreign investment

SELF-TEST

■ FILL-IN QUESTIONS

1. There is considerable income inequality among nations. The richest 20 percent of the world's population receives more than (40, 80) ______________ percent of the world's income, while the poorest 20 percent of the world's population receives less than (2, 10) ______________ percent of the world's income. The poorest 60 percent of nations receives less than (6, 30) ______________ percent of the world's income.

2. High-income nations can be classified as (industrially advanced, developing) ______________ countries, or (IACs, DVCs) ______________, and the middle- or low-income nations as ______________ countries, or (DVCs, IACs) ______________.

3. IACs have a (higher, lower) ______________ starting base for per capita income than DVCs, so the same percentage growth rate for both IACs and DVCs means (an increase, a decrease) ______________ in the absolute income gap.

4. Low per capita income in DVCs means that there are (lower, higher) ______________ life expectancies, ______________ adult literacy, (lower, higher) ______________ daily calorie supply, ______________ energy consumption, and (lower, higher) ______________ infant mortality.

5. The process for economic growth is the same for IACs and DVCs. It involves (less, more) ______________ efficient use of existing resources and obtaining ______________ productive resources.

6. The distribution of natural resources among DVCs is (even, uneven) ______________; many DVCs lack vital natural resources. Although oil resources have been used for economic growth in (OPEC nations, DVCs) ______________, IACs own or control much of the natural resources in ______________. Also, exports of products from DVCs are subject to (small, large) ______________ price fluctuations in the world market, and that tends to make DVC incomes (more, less) ______________ stable.

7. In terms of human resources,

a. many DVCs are (under, over) ______________ populated and have (higher, lower) ______________ population growth rates than IACs. Rapid population growth can cause per capita income to (increase, decrease) ______________.

b. In DVCs, many people are unable to find jobs, so there is (underemployment, unemployment) ______________, and many people are employed for fewer hours than they desire or work at odd jobs, so there is ______________.

c. In DVCs, labor productivity is very (high, low) ______________, partly because these countries have not been able to invest in (stocks and bonds, human capital) ______________; when the best-trained workers leave DVCs to work in IACs, there is a (demographic transition, brain drain) ______________ that contributes to the decline in skill level and productivity.

8. Capital accumulation is critical to the development of DVCs. If there were more capital goods, this would improve (natural resources, labor productivity) ______________ and help boost per capita output. An increase in capital goods is necessary because the (demand for, supply of) ______________ arable land is limited. The process of capital formation is cumulative, investment increases the (output, natural resources) ______________ of the economy, and this in turn makes it possible for the economy to save more and invest more in capital goods.

9. The formation of domestic capital requires that a nation save and invest.

a. Saving is difficult in DVCs because of (high, low) ______________ per capita income, and investment is difficult because of (many, few) ______________ investors or entrepreneurs, and (strong, weak) ______________ incentives to invest. There is also the problem of private savings being transferred to IACs; this transfer is called (brain drain, capital flight) ______________.

b. Many DVCs do not have the infrastructure or (private, public) ______________ capital goods that are necessary for productive ______________ investment by businesses.

c. Nonfinancial (or in-kind) investment involves the transfer of surplus labor from (agriculture, industry) ______________ to the improvement of agricultural facilities or the infrastructure.

10. The technologies used in IACs might be borrowed by and used in the DVCs, but the technologies used in the IACs are based on a labor force that is (skilled, unskilled) ______________ and capital that is relatively (abundant, scarce) ______________ whereas the technologies required in DVCs tend to be based on a labor force that is (skilled, unskilled) ______________ and capital that is relatively (abundant, scarce) ______________.

11. The technologies used in IACs tend to be capital (-using, -saving) ______________, while the technologies used in

DVCs tend to be capital (-using, -saving) ______________. If technological advances make it possible to replace an inexpensive, but inferior plow with a more expensive but superior plow that has a longer operating life, then the technological advance is capital (-saving, -using) ______________.

12. Other obstacles to economic growth in DVCs include those dealing with problems of national unity, religion, and customs, or (institutional, sociocultural) ______________ problems, and those dealing with such issues as political corruption, poor school systems, and land reform, or ______________ problems.

13. In most DVCs, there is a vicious circle of poverty. Saving is low because the income per capita is (high, low) ______________ and because saving is low, investment in real and human capital is ______________. For this reason the productivity of labor and output (income) per capita remain (high, low) ______________.

14. Government can serve a positive role in fostering economic growth in DVCs, through such policies as improving (the military, infrastructure) ______________, establishing programs that build (arm sales, human capital) ______________, promoting (capital flight, entrepreneurship) ______________, and extending more credit through (macro, micro) ______________ finance.

15. Other ways that DVC governments can encourage economic growth is to (open, close) ______________ their economies to international trade and (encourage, discourage) ______________ direct foreign investment.

16. Government involvement in the economy of DVCs can create public sector problems because government bureaucracy can (foster, impede) ______________ social and economic change, government planners can give too much emphasis to (political, economic) ______________ objectives, and there can be (good, poor) ______________ administration and corruption.

17. Three major ways that IACs can assist in the economic development in DVCs is by (increasing, decreasing) ______________ international trade barriers, ______________ foreign aid, and ______________ the flow of private capital investment.

18. Direct foreign aid for DVCs generally comes from individual nations in the form of (private, public) ______________ loans, grants, and programs. It can also come from the (Bank of America, World Bank), ______________ which is supported by member nations. This organization is a (first, last) ______________ resort lending agency for DVCs and provides (military, technical) ______________ assistance for DVCs.

19. Foreign aid has been criticized in recent years because it may (increase, decrease) ______________ dependency in a nation instead of creating self-sustained growth, may ______________ government bureaucracy and control over a nation's economy, and may ______________ the misuse of funds or corruption.

20. The flow of private capital to DVCs comes in the form of direct foreign (aid, investment) ______________ from IAC firms, individuals and commercial banks, but this flow of private capital to DVCs is (selective, widespread) ______________ among nations and it (increased, decreased) ______________ during the worldwide recession of 2007–2009.

■ TRUE–FALSE QUESTIONS

Circle T if the statement is true, F if it is false.

1. The richest 20 percent of the world's population receives about 50 percent of the world's income while the poorest 20 percent receives only about 20 percent of the world's income. **T F**

2. Low-income developing countries typically have high unemployment, low literacy rates, rapid population growth, and a labor force committed to agricultural production. **T F**

3. The annual sales of the world's largest corporations are greater than the national incomes of many developing countries. **T F**

4. The absolute income gap between DVCs and industrially advanced countries has been declining. **T F**

5. Economic growth in both IACs and DVCs requires using economic resources more efficiently and increasing the supplies of some of these resources. **T F**

6. It is impossible to achieve a high standard of living with a small supply of natural resources. **T F**

7. DVCs have low population densities and low population growth relative to IACs. **T F**

8. A demographic transition in population growth can occur if rising incomes are achieved first because of economic growth, and then followed by slower population. **T F**

9. A major factor contributing to the high unemployment rates in urban areas of DVCs is the fact that the migration from rural areas to cities has greatly exceeded the growth of urban job opportunities. **T F**

10. Saving in DVCs is a smaller percentage of domestic output than in IACs, and this is the chief reason total saving in DVCs is small. **T F**

11. Before private investment can be increased in DVCs, it is necessary to reduce the amount of investment in infrastructure. **T F**

12. Technological advances in DVCs will be made rapidly because the advances do not require pushing forward the frontiers of technological knowledge, and the technologies used in IACs can be easily transferred to all DVCs. **T F**

13. When technological advances are capital-saving, it is possible for an economy to increase its productivity without any *net* investment in capital goods. **T F**

14. A critical, but intangible, ingredient in economic development is the "will to develop." **T F**

15. The capricious universe view is that there is a strong correlation between individual effort and results. **T F**

16. Land reform is one of the institutional obstacles to economic growth in many developing countries. **T F**

17. The situation in which poor nations stay poor because they are poor is a description of the vicious circle of poverty. **T F**

18. The creation of an adequate infrastructure is one important way for government to create a foundation for economic development. **T F**

19. Government programs that encourage literacy, education, and labor market skills enhance economic growth by building human capital. **T F**

20. Governments in most DVCs have avoided the problems of poor public administration of program and corruption. **T F**

21. One effective way that IACs can help DVCs is to raise trade barriers so that DVCs become more self-sufficient. **T F**

22. The World Bank encourages DVCs to go to it first to obtain loans for development projects rather than going to the private sector. **T F**

23. Two reasons why official development assistance from IACs and through the World Bank is viewed as harmful are that it tends to promote dependency and generate government bureaucracy. **T F**

24. An example of direct foreign investment would be the building of an automobile parts factory by Ford in Colombia. **T F**

25. The worldwide recession of 2007–2009 greatly reduced direct investment by IACs in the DVC economies. **T F**

■ MULTIPLE-CHOICE QUESTIONS

Circle the letter that corresponds to the best answer.

1. Data on per capita income from the countries of the world indicate that there is considerable

(a) income equality
(b) income inequality
(c) stability in the income growth
(d) deterioration in incomes for most developing countries

2. Which nation would be considered a developing country?

(a) India
(b) Italy
(c) Japan
(d) New Zealand

3. If the per capita income is $600 a year in a DVC and $12,000 in an IAC, then a 2% growth rate in each nation will increase the absolute income gap by

(a) $120
(b) $228
(c) $240
(d) $252

4. The poorest DVCs would probably exhibit high levels of

(a) literacy
(b) life expectancy
(c) infant mortality
(d) per capita energy consumption

5. The essential paths for economic growth in any nation are expanding the

(a) size of the population and improving agriculture
(b) role of government and providing jobs for the unemployed
(c) supplies of resources and using existing resources more efficiently
(d) amount of tax subsidies to businesses and tax credits for business investment

6. Based on the rule of 70, if the United States has an annual rate of population increase of 1% and a DVC has one of 2%, how many years will it take for the population to double in each nation?

(a) 140 years for the United States and 70 years for the DVC
(b) 35 years for the United States and 70 years for the DVC
(c) 70 years for the United States and 35 years for the DVC
(d) 70 years for the United States and 140 years for the DVC

7. Assume the total real output of a developing country increases from $100 billion to $115.5 billion while its population expands from 200 to 210 million people. Real per capita income has increased by

(a) $50
(b) $100
(c) $150
(d) $200

8. An increase in the total output in a DVC may not increase the average standard of living because it may increase

(a) capital flight
(b) population growth
(c) disguised unemployment
(d) the quality of the labor force

9. Which best describes the unemployment found in DVCs?

(a) the cyclical fluctuations in the nation's economy
(b) the migration of agricultural workers from rural areas to seek jobs in urban areas
(c) workers being laid off by large domestic or multinational corporations during periods of economic instability
(d) the education and training of workers in the wrong types of jobs and for which there is little demand

10. Which is an obstacle to economic growth in DVCs?
(a) the low demand for natural resources
(b) the low supply of capital goods
(c) the decline in demographic transition
(d) a fall in population growth

11. Which is a reason for placing special emphasis on capital accumulation in DVCs?
(a) the flexible supply of arable land in DVCs
(b) the high productivity of workers in DVCs
(c) the high marginal benefits of capital goods
(d) the greater opportunities for capital flight

12. Which is a factor limiting saving in DVCs?
(a) The output of the economy is too low to permit a large volume of saving.
(b) Those who do save make their savings available only to their families.
(c) Governments control the banking system and set low interest rates.
(d) There is an equal distribution of income in most nations.

13. When citizens of developing countries transfer savings to or invest savings in industrially advanced countries, this is referred to as
(a) brain drain
(b) capital flight
(c) savings potential
(d) in-kind investment

14. Which is a major obstacle to capital formation in DVCs?
(a) lack of oil resources
(b) lack of entrepreneurs
(c) lack of government price supports for products
(d) an excess of opportunities for financial investments

15. Which is an example of infrastructure?
(a) a farm
(b) a steel plant
(c) an electric power plant
(d) a deposit in a financial institution

16. If it is cheaper to use a new fertilizer that is better adapted to a nation's topography, this is an example of
(a) a capital-using technology
(b) a capital-saving technology
(c) capital consumption
(d) private capital flows

17. Which seems to be the most acute *institutional* problem that needs to be resolved by many DVCs?
(a) development of strong labor unions
(b) an increase in natural resources
(c) the adoption of birth control
(d) land reform

18. Which is a major positive role for government in economic development?
(a) providing an adequate infrastructure
(b) conducting central economic planning
(c) improving the efficiency of tax collection
(d) creating marketing boards for export products

19. In recent years, many DVCs have come to realize that
(a) there are few disadvantages from government involvement in economic development
(b) entrepreneurship and economic incentives for individuals are necessary for economic development
(c) the World Bank is an institutional barrier to economic growth
(d) private capital is not essential for economic growth

20. Industrially advanced countries can best help DVCs by
(a) lowering international trade barriers
(b) selling more military equipment to them
(c) limiting the admission of temporary workers
(d) increasing control over their capital markets

21. Which is a suggested policy for IACs to adopt to foster economic growth in DVCs?
(a) increased appreciation of their currencies
(b) increased debt relief and forgiveness
(c) elimination of the World Bank
(d) elimination of the International Monetary Fund

22. The major objective of the World Bank is to
(a) maximize its profits for its worldwide shareholders
(b) assist developing countries in achieving economic growth
(c) provide financial backing for the operation of the United Nations
(d) maintain stable exchange rates in the currencies of developing countries

23. A major criticism of foreign aid to developing nations is that it
(a) provides incentives for capital flight
(b) is capital-using rather than capital-saving
(c) encourages growth in government bureaucracy
(d) gives too much power and control to the World Bank

24. Which would be an example of direct foreign investment in DVCs?
(a) a low-interest loan from the U.S. government to Nigeria
(b) a grant from the World Bank to build a dam in Thailand
(c) the purchase of a computer business in Honduras by a U.S. firm
(d) a payment from a worker in the U.S. to a family in Iran

25. Which statement best describes the characteristic of private capital flows to DVCs?
(a) It is less than direct foreign aid from government
(b) It increased during the 2007–2009 recession.
(c) It is mostly directed to low-income DVCs.
(d) It is mostly directed to middle-income DVCs.

■ PROBLEMS

1. Suppose that the real per capita income in the average industrially advanced country is $8000 per year and in the average DVC $500 per year.
a. The gap between their standards of living is $________ per year.
b. If GDP per capita were to grow at a rate of 5% during a year in both the industrially advanced country and the DVC,
(1) the standard of living in the IAC would rise to $________ in a year;

(2) the standard of living in the DVC would rise to $________ in a year; and

(3) the gap between their standards of living would (narrow, widen) ________ to $________ in a year.

2. While economic conditions are not identical in all DVCs, certain conditions are common to or typical of most of them. In the space after each of the following characteristics, indicate briefly the nature of this characteristic in many low-income DVCs.

a. Standard of living (per capita income): ________

b. Average life expectancy: ________

c. Extent of unemployment: ________

d. Literacy: ________

e. Technology: ________

f. Percentage of the population engaged in agriculture: ________

g. Size of the population relative to the land and capital available: ________

h. The birthrates and death rates: ________

i. Quality of the labor force: ________

j. Amount of capital equipment relative to the labor force: ________

k. Level of saving: ________

l. Incentive to invest: ________

m. Amount of infrastructure: ________

n. Extent of industrialization: ________

o. Size and quality of the entrepreneurial class and the supervisory class: ________

p. Per capita public expenditures for education and per capita energy consumption: ________

q. Per capita consumption of food: ________

r. Disease and malnutrition: ________

3. Suppose it takes a minimum of 5 units of food to keep a person alive for a year, the population can double itself every 10 years, and the food supply can increase every 10 years by an amount equal to what it was in the beginning (year 0).

a. Assume that both the population and the food supply grow at these rates. Complete the following table by computing the size of the population and the food supply in years 10 through 60.

Year	Food supply	Population
0	200	20
10	____	____
20	____	____
30	____	____
40	____	____
50	____	____
60	____	____

b. What happens to the relationship between the food supply and the population in the 30th year? ________

c. What would actually prevent the population from growing at this rate following the 30th year? ________

d. Assuming that the actual population growth in the years following the 30th does not outrun the food supply, what would be the size of the population in

(1) Year 40: ________

(2) Year 50: ________

(3) Year 60: ________

e. Explain why the standard of living failed to increase in the years following the 30th even though the food supply increased by 75% between years 30 and 60.

____

■ SHORT ANSWER AND ESSAY QUESTIONS

1. What is the degree of income inequality among nations of the world?

2. How do the overall levels of economic growth per capita and the rates of economic growth compare among rich nations and poor countries? Why does the income gap widen?

3. Describe the basic paths of economic growth. Do these avenues differ for IACs and DVCs?

4. How would you describe the natural resource situation for DVCs? In what ways do price fluctuations affect DVC exports? Is a weak natural resource base an obstacle to economic growth?

5. Describe the implications of the high rate of growth in populations and its effects on the standard of living. Can the standard of living be raised merely by increasing the output of consumer goods in DVCs? What is the meaning of the cliché "the rich get richer and the poor get children," and how does it apply to DVCs?

6. Compare and contrast the traditional view of population and economic growth with the demographic transition view.

7. What is the distinction between unemployment and underemployment? How do these concepts apply to DVCs?

8. What are the reasons for the low level of labor productivity in DVCs?

9. How does the brain drain affect DVCs?

10. What are the reasons for placing special emphasis on capital accumulation as a means of promoting economic growth in DVCs?

11. Why is domestic capital accumulation difficult in DVCs? Answer in terms of both the saving side and the investment side of capital accumulation. Is there capital flight from DVCs?

12. How might the DVCs improve their technology without engaging in slow and expensive research? Why might this be an inappropriate method of improving the technology used in the DVCs?

13. What is meant by the "will to develop"? How is it related to social and institutional change in DVCs?

14. Explain the vicious circle of poverty in the DVCs. How does population growth make an escape from this vicious circle difficult?

15. What are actions and policies that government can take in DVCs to foster economic development?

16. What have been the problems with the involvement of government in economic development?

17. What policies can IACs adopt to foster economic development in DVCs?

18. Discuss the World Bank in terms of its purposes, characteristics, sources of funds, promotion of private capital flows, and success.

19. Discuss three criticisms of foreign aid to DVCs.

20. Describe the role of private capital flows in fostering economic growth in DVCs. Why has this flow been selective?

ANSWERS

Chapter 22 Web The Economics of Developing Countries

FILL-IN QUESTIONS

1. 80, 2, 6
2. industrially advanced, IACs, developing, DVCs
3. higher, an increase
4. lower, lower, lower, lower, higher
5. more, more
6. uneven, OPEC nations, DVCs, large, less
7. *a.* over, higher, decrease; *b.* unemployment, underemployment; *c.* low, human capital, brain drain
8. labor productivity, supply of, output
9. *a.* low, few, weak, capital flight; *b.* public, private; *c.* agriculture
10. skilled, abundant, unskilled, scarce
11. -using, -saving, -saving
12. sociocultural, institutional
13. low, low, low
14. infrastructure, human capital, entrepreneurship, micro
15. open, encourage
16. impede, political, poor
17. decreasing, increasing, increasing
18. public, World Bank, last, technical
19. increase, increase, increase
20. investment, selective, decreased

Note: Page numbers for True–False, Multiple Choice, and Short Answer and Essay Questions refer to Bonus Web Chapter 22.

TRUE–FALSE QUESTIONS

1. F, p. 2
2. T, p. 2
3. T, p. 2
4. F, p. 2
5. T, p. 4
6. F, pp. 4–5
7. F, pp. 5–6
8. T, p. 7
9. T, pp. 7–6
10. F, pp. 8–9
11. F, p. 9
12. F, pp. 9–10
13. T, p. 10
14. T, p. 10
15. F, p. 10
16. T, p. 11
17. T, pp. 11–12
18. T, p. 12
19. T, p. 13
20. F, p. 13
21. T, p. 14
22. F, p. 16
23. T, pp. 17–18
24. T, p. 18
25. T, p. 18

MULTIPLE-CHOICE QUESTIONS

1. b, p. 2
2. a, p. 2
3. b, p. 2
4. c, p. 4
5. c, p. 4
6. c, p. 5
7. a, p. 5
8. b, p. 5
9. b, p. 7
10. b, p. 8
11. c, p. 8
12. a, pp. 8–9
13. b, p. 9
14. b, p. 9
15. c, p. 9
16. b, p. 10
17. d, pp. 10–17
18. a, p. 12
19. b, p. 13
20. a, p. 14
21. b, pp. 15–16
22. c, p. 16
23. c, p. 18
24. c, p. 18
25. b, p. 18

PROBLEMS

1. *a.* 7500; *b.* (1) 8400, (2) 525, (3) widen, 7875
2. *a.* low; *b.* short; *c.* widespread; *d.* low; *e.* primitive; *f.* large; *g.* large; *h.* high; *i.* poor; *j.* small; *k.* low; *l.* absent; *m.* small; *n.* small; *o.* small and poor; *p.* small; *q.* low; *r.* common
3. *a.* Food supply: 400, 600, 800, 1000, 1200, 1400; Population: 40, 80, 160, 320, 640, 1280; *b.* the food supply is just able to support the population; *c.* the inability of the food supply to support a population growing at this rate; *d.* (1) 200, (2) 240, (3) 280; *e.* the population increased as rapidly as the food supply

SHORT ANSWER AND ESSAY QUESTIONS

1. pp. 1–2
2. p. 2
3. p. 4
4. pp. 4–5
5. pp. 5–6
6. p. 7
7. p. 7
8. p. 8
9. p. 8
10. pp. 8–9
11. p. 9
12. pp. 9–10
13. p. 10
14. p. 11
15. pp. 12–13
16. pp. 13–14
17. pp. 14–15
18. pp. 16–17
19. pp. 17–18
20. p. 18

Glossary

Note: Terms set in *italic* type are defined separately in this glossary.

absolute advantage A situation in which a person or country can produce more of a particular product from a specific quantity of resources than some other person or country.

actively managed funds *Mutual funds* that have portfolio managers who constantly buy and sell *assets* in an attempt to generate higher returns that some benchmark rate of return for similar *portfolios.*

actual investment The amount that *firms* invest; equal to *planned investment* plus *unplanned investment.*

actual reserves The funds that a bank has on deposit at the *Federal Reserve Bank* of its district (plus its *vault cash*).

aggregate A collection of specific economic units treated as if they were one. For example, all prices of individual goods and services are combined into a *price level,* or all units of output are aggregated into *gross domestic product.*

aggregate demand A schedule or curve that shows the total quantity of goods and services demanded (purchased) at different *price levels.*

aggregate demand–aggregate supply (AD-AS) model The macroeconomic model that uses *aggregate demand* and *aggregate supply* to determine and explain the *price level* and the real *domestic output.*

aggregate expenditures The total amount spent for final goods and services in an economy.

aggregate expenditures–domestic output approach Determination of the equilibrium *gross domestic product* by finding the real GDP at which *aggregate expenditures* equal *domestic output.*

aggregate expenditures schedule A schedule or curve showing the total amount spent for final goods and services at different levels of *real GDP.*

aggregate supply A schedule or curve showing the total quantity of goods and services supplied (produced) at different *price levels.*

aggregate supply shocks Sudden, large changes in resource costs that shift an economy's aggregate supply curve.

allocative efficiency The apportionment of resources among firms and industries to obtain the production of the products most wanted by society (consumers); the output of each product at which its *marginal cost* and *price* or *marginal benefit* are equal.

anticipated inflation Increases in the price level *(inflation)* that occur at the expected rate.

appreciation (of the dollar) An increase in the value of the dollar relative to the currency of another nation, so a dollar buys a larger amount of the foreign currency and thus of foreign goods.

arbitrage The activity that generates riskless profits by selling one *asset* and buying an identical or nearly identical asset to benefit from temporary differences in prices or rates of return; the practice that equalizes prices or returns on similar financial instruments and thus eliminates further opportunities for riskless financial gains.

asset Anything of monetary value owned by a firm or individual.

asset demand for money The amount of *money* people want to hold as a *store of value;* this amount varies inversely with the *interest rate.*

average expected rate of return The *probability-weighted average* of an investment's possible future returns.

average propensity to consume (APC) Fraction (or percentage) of *disposable income* that households plan to spend for consumer goods and services; consumption divided by *disposable income.*

average propensity to save (APS) Fraction (or percentage) of *disposable income* that households save; *saving* divided by *disposable income.*

average tax rate Total tax paid divided by total *taxable income* or some other base (such as total income) against which to compare the amount of tax paid. Expressed as a percentage.

balance of payments (See *international balance of payments.*)

balance-of-payments deficit The net amount of *official reserves* (mainly foreign currencies) that a nation's treasury or central bank must sell to achieve balance between that nation's *capital and financial account* and its *current account* (in its *balance of payments*).

balance-of-payments surplus The net amount of *official reserves* (mainly foreign currencies) that a nation's treasury or central bank must buy to achieve balance between that nation's *capital and financial account* and its *current account* (in its *balance of payments*).

balance on capital and financial account The sum of the *capital account balance* and the *financial account balance.*

balance on current account The exports of goods and services of a nation less its imports of goods and services plus its *net investment income* and *net transfers* in a year.

balance on goods and services The exports of goods and services of a nation less its imports of goods and services in a year.

balance sheet A statement of the *assets, liabilities,* and *net worth* of a firm or individual at some given time.

bank deposits The deposits that individuals or firms have at banks (or thrifts) or that banks have at the *Federal Reserve Banks.*

bankers' bank A bank that accepts the deposits of and makes loans to *depository institutions;* in the United States, a *Federal Reserve Bank.*

bank reserves The deposits of commercial banks and thrifts at *Federal Reserve Banks* plus bank and thrift *vault cash.*

bankrupt A legal situation in which an individual or *firm* finds that it cannot make timely interest payments on money it has borrowed. In such cases, a bankruptcy judge can order the individual or firm to liquidate (turn into cash) its assets in order to pay lenders at least some portion of the amount they are owed.

barter The exchange of one good or service for another good or service.

base year The year with which other years are compared when an index is constructed; for example, the base year for a *price index.*

beta A relative measure of *nondiversifiable risk* that measures how the nondiversifiable risk of a given *asset* or *portfolio* compares with that of the *market portfolio* (the portfolio that contains every asset available in the financial markets).

Board of Governors The seven-member group that supervises and controls the money and banking system of the United States; the Board of Governors of the *Federal Reserve System;* the Federal Reserve Board.

bond A financial device through which a borrower (a firm or government) is obligated to pay the principal and interest on a loan at a specific date in the future.

break-even income The level of *disposable income* at which *households* plan to consume (spend) all their income and to save none of it.

budget deficit The amount by which the expenditures of the Federal government exceed its revenues in any year.

budget line A line that shows the different combinations of two products a consumer can purchase with a specific money income, given the products' prices.

budget surplus The amount by which the revenues of the Federal government exceed its expenditures in any year.

built-in stabilizer A mechanism that increases government's budget deficit (or reduces its surplus) during a recession and increases government's budget surplus (or reduces its deficit) during an expansion without any action by policymakers. The tax system is one such mechanism.

Bureau of Economic Analysis (BEA) An agency of the U.S. Department of Commerce that compiles the national income and product accounts.

business cycle Recurring increases and decreases in the level of economic activity over periods of years; consists of peak, recession, trough, and expansion phases.

businesses Economic entities (*firms*) that purchase resources and provide goods and services to the economy.

business firm (See *firm.*)

capital Human-made resources (buildings, machinery, and equipment) used to produce goods and services; goods that do not directly satisfy human wants; also called capital goods.

capital and financial account The section of a nation's *international balance of payments* that records (1) debt forgiveness by and to foreigners and (2) foreign purchases of assets in the United States and U.S. purchases of assets abroad.

capital and financial account deficit A negative balance on its *capital and financial account* in a country's *international balance of payments.*

capital and financial account surplus A positive balance on its *capital and financial account* in a country's *international balance of payments.*

capital flight (Web chapter) The transfer of savings from *developing countries* to *industrially advanced countries* to avoid government expropriation, taxation, higher rates of inflation, or simply to realize greater returns on *financial investments.*

capital gain The gain realized when securities or properties are sold for a price greater than the price paid for them.

capital goods (See *capital.*)

capital-intensive goods Products that require relatively large amounts of *capital* to produce.

capitalism An economic system in which property resources are privately owned and markets and prices are used to direct and coordinate economic activities.

capital-saving technology (Web chapter) An improvement in *technology* that permits a greater quantity of a product to be produced with a specific amount of *capital* (or permits the same amount of the product to be produced with a smaller amount of capital).

capital stock The total available *capital* in a nation.

capital-using technology (Web chapter) An improvement in *technology* that requires the use of a greater amount of *capital* to produce a specific quantity of a product.

capricious-universe view (Web chapter) The view held by some people that fate and outside events, rather than hard work and enterprise, will determine their economic destinies.

cartel A formal agreement among firms (or countries) in an industry to set the price of a product and establish the outputs of the individual firms (or countries) or to divide the market for the product geographically.

causation A relationship in which the occurrence of one or more events brings about another event.

CEA (See *Council of Economic Advisers.*)

ceiling price (See *price ceiling.*)

central bank A bank whose chief function is the control of the nation's *money supply;* in the United States, the *Federal Reserve System.*

central economic planning Government determination of the objectives of the economy and how resources will be directed to attain those goals.

***ceteris paribus* assumption** (See *other-things-equal assumption.*)

change in demand A movement of an entire *demand curve* or schedule such that the *quantity demanded* changes at every particular price; caused by a change in one or more of the *determinants of demand.*

change in quantity demanded A change in the *quantity demanded* along a fixed *demand curve* (or within a fixed demand schedule) as a result of a change in the product's price.

change in quantity supplied A change in the *quantity supplied* along a fixed *supply curve* (or within a fixed supply schedule) as a result of a change in the product's price.

change in supply A movement of an entire *supply curve* or schedule such that the *quantity supplied* changes at every particular price; caused by a change in one or more of the *determinants of supply.*

checkable deposit Any deposit in a *commercial bank* or *thrift institution* against which a check may be written.

checkable-deposit multiplier (See *monetary multiplier.*)

check clearing The process by which funds are transferred from the checking accounts of the writers of checks to the checking accounts of the recipients of the checks.

checking account A *checkable deposit* in a *commercial bank* or *thrift institution.*

circular flow diagram An illustration showing the flow of resources from *households* to *firms* and of products from firms to households. These flows are accompanied by reverse flows of money from firms to households and from households to firms.

closed economy An economy that neither exports nor imports goods and services.

Coase theorem The idea, first stated by economist Ronald Coase, that some *externalities* can be resolved through private negotiations of the affected parties.

coincidence of wants A situation in which the good or service that one trader desires to obtain is the same as that which another trader desires to give up and an item that the second trader wishes to acquire is the same as that which the first trader desires to surrender.

COLA (See *cost-of-living adjustment.*)

command system A method of organizing an economy in which property resources are publicly owned and government uses *central economic planning* to direct and coordinate economic activities; command economy; communism.

commercial bank A firm that engages in the business of banking (accepts deposits, offers checking accounts, and makes loans).

commercial banking system All *commercial banks* and *thrift institutions* as a group.

communism (See *command system.*)

comparative advantage A situation in which a person or country can produce a specific product at a lower opportunity cost than some other person or country; the basis for specialization and trade.

compensation to employees *Wages* and salaries plus wage and salary supplements paid by employers to workers.

competition The presence in a market of independent buyers and sellers competing with one another along with the freedom of buyers and sellers to enter and leave the market.

complementary goods Products and services that are used together. When the price of one falls, the demand for the other increases (and conversely).

compound interest The accumulation of money that builds over time in an investment or interest-bearing account as new interest is earned on previous interest that is not withdrawn.

conglomerates Firms that produce goods and services in two or more separate industries.

constant opportunity cost An *opportunity cost* that remains the same for each additional unit as a consumer (or society) shifts purchases (production) from one product to another along a straight-line *budget line* (*production possibilities curve*).

consumer goods Products and services that satisfy human wants directly.

Consumer Price Index (CPI) An index that measures the prices of a fixed "market basket" of some 300 goods and services bought by a "typical" consumer.

consumer sovereignty Determination by consumers of the types and quantities of goods and services that will be produced with the scarce resources of the economy; consumers' direction of production through their *dollar votes.*

consumption of fixed capital An estimate of the amount of *capital* worn out or used up (consumed) in producing the *gross domestic product;* also called depreciation.

consumption schedule A schedule showing the amounts *households* plan to spend for *consumer goods* at different levels of *disposable income.*

contractionary fiscal policy A decrease in *government purchases* of goods and services, an increase in *net taxes,* or some combination of the two, for the purpose of decreasing *aggregate demand* and thus controlling inflation.

coordination failure A situation in which people do not reach a mutually beneficial outcome because they lack some way to jointly coordinate their actions; a possible cause of macroeconomic instability.

core inflation The underlying increases in the *price level* after volatile food and energy prices are removed.

corporate income tax A tax levied on the net income (accounting profit) of corporations.

corporation A legal entity ("person") chartered by a state or the Federal government that is distinct and separate from the individuals who own it.

correlation A systematic and dependable association between two sets of data (two kinds of events); does not necessarily indicate causation.

corruption The misuse of government power, with which one has been entrusted or assigned, to obtain private gain; includes payments from individuals or companies to secure advantages in obtaining government contracts, avoiding government regulations, or obtaining inside knowledge about forthcoming policy changes.

cost-benefit analysis A comparison of the *marginal costs* of a government project or program with the *marginal benefits* to decide whether or not to employ resources in that project or program and to what extent.

cost-of-living adjustment (COLA) An automatic increase in the incomes (wages) of workers when inflation occurs; guaranteed by a collective bargaining contract between firms and workers.

cost-push inflation Increases in the price level (inflation) resulting from an increase in resource costs (for example, raw-material prices) and hence in *per-unit production costs;* inflation caused by reductions in *aggregate supply.*

Council of Economic Advisers (CEA) A group of three persons that advises and assists the president of the United States on economic matters (including the preparation of the annual *Economic Report of the President*).

creative destruction The hypothesis that the creation of new products and production methods simultaneously destroys the market power of existing monopolies.

credit An accounting item that increases the value of an asset (such as the foreign money owned by the residents of a nation).

credit union An association of persons who have a common tie (such as being employees of the same firm or members of the same labor union) that sells shares to (accepts deposits from) its members and makes loans to them.

cross elasticity of demand The ratio of the percentage change in *quantity demanded* of one good to the percentage change in the price of some other good. A positive coefficient indicates the two products are *substitute goods;* a negative coefficient indicates they are *complementary goods.*

crowding-out effect A rise in interest rates and a resulting decrease in *planned investment* caused by the Federal government's increased borrowing to finance budget deficits and refinance debt.

currency Coins and paper money.

currency appreciation (See *exchange-rate appreciation.*)

currency depreciation (See *exchange-rate depreciation.*)

currency intervention A government's buying and selling of its own currency or foreign currencies to alter international exchange rates.

current account The section in a nation's *international balance of payments* that records its exports and imports of goods and services, its net *investment income,* and its *net transfers.*

cyclical asymmetry The idea that *monetary policy* may be more successful in slowing expansions and controlling *inflation* than in extracting the economy from severe recession.

cyclical deficit A Federal *budget deficit* that is caused by a recession and the consequent decline in tax revenues.

cyclically adjusted budget A comparison of the government expenditures and tax collections that would occur if the economy operated at *full employment* throughout the year; the full-employment budget.

cyclical unemployment A type of *unemployment* caused by insufficient total spending (or by insufficient *aggregate demand*).

debit An accounting item that decreases the value of an asset (such as the foreign money owned by the residents of a nation).

defaults Situations in which borrowers stop making loan payments or do not pay back loans that they took out and are now due.

deflating Finding the *real gross domestic product* by decreasing the dollar value of the GDP for a year in which prices were higher than in the *base year.*

deflation A decline in the economy's *price level.*

demand A schedule showing the amounts of a good or service that buyers (or a buyer) wish to purchase at various prices during some time period.

demand curve A curve illustrating *demand.*

demand factor (in growth) The increase in the level of *aggregate demand* that brings about the *economic growth* made possible by an increase in the production potential of the economy.

demand management The use of *fiscal policy* and *monetary policy* to increase or decrease *aggregate demand.*

demand-pull inflation Increases in the price level (inflation) resulting from an excess of demand over output at the existing price level, caused by an increase in *aggregate demand.*

demand schedule (See *demand.*)

demand shocks Sudden, unexpected changes in demand.

demand-side market failures Underallocations of resources that occur when private demand curves understate consumers' full willingness to pay for a good or service.

demographers Scientists who study the characteristics of human populations.

demographic transition (Web chapter) The idea that population growth slows once a developing country achieves higher standards of living because the perceived marginal cost of additional children begins to exceed the perceived marginal benefit.

dependent variable A variable that changes as a consequence of a change in some other (independent) variable; the "effect" or outcome.

depository institutions Firms that accept deposits of *money* from the public (businesses and persons); *commercial banks, savings and loan associations, mutual savings banks,* and *credit unions.*

depreciation (See *consumption of fixed capital.*)

depreciation (of the dollar) A decrease in the value of the dollar relative to another currency, so a dollar buys a smaller amount of the foreign currency and therefore of foreign goods.

derived demand The demand for a resource that depends on the demand for the products it helps to produce.

determinants of aggregate demand Factors such as consumption spending, *investment,* government spending, and *net exports* that, if they change, shift the aggregate demand curve.

determinants of aggregate supply Factors such as input prices, *productivity,* and the legal-institutional environment that, if they change, shift the aggregate supply curve.

determinants of demand Factors other than price that determine the quantities demanded of a good or service.

determinants of supply Factors other than price that determine the quantities supplied of a good or service.

developing countries Many countries of Africa, Asia, and Latin America that are characterized by lack of capital goods, use of nonadvanced technologies, low literacy rates, high unemployment, rapid population growth, and labor forces heavily committed to agriculture.

direct foreign investment (See *foreign direct investment.*)

direct relationship The relationship between two variables that change in the same direction, for example, product price and quantity supplied; positive relationship.

discount rate The interest rate that the *Federal Reserve Banks* charge on the loans they make to *commercial banks* and *thrift institutions.*

discouraged workers Employees who have left the *labor force* because they have not been able to find employment.

discretionary fiscal policy Deliberate changes in taxes (tax rates) and government spending by Congress to promote full employment, price stability, and economic growth.

discrimination The practice of according individuals or groups inferior treatment in hiring, occupational access, education and training, promotion, wage rates, or working conditions even though they have the same abilities, education, skills, and work experience as other workers.

disinflation A reduction in the rate of *inflation.*

disposable income (DI) *Personal income* less personal taxes; income available for *personal consumption expenditures* and *personal saving.*

dissaving Spending for consumer goods and services in excess of *disposable income;* the amount by which *personal consumption expenditures* exceed disposable income.

diversifiable risk Investment *risk* that investors can reduce via *diversification;* also called idiosyncratic risk.

diversification The strategy of investing in a large number of investments in order to reduce the overall risk to an entire investment *portfolio.*

dividends Payments by a corporation of all or part of its profit to its stockholders (the corporate owners).

division of labor The separation of the work required to produce a product into a number of different tasks that are performed by different workers; *specialization* of workers.

Doha Development Agenda The latest, uncompleted (as of mid-2010) sequence of trade negotiations by members of the *World Trade Organization;* named after Doha, Qatar, where the set of negotiations began. Also called the Doha Round.

dollar votes The "votes" that consumers and entrepreneurs cast for the production of consumer and capital goods, respectively, when they purchase those goods in product and resource markets.

domestic capital formation The process of adding to a nation's stock of *capital* by saving and investing part of its own domestic output.

domestic output *Gross* (or net) *domestic product;* the total output of final goods and services produced in the economy.

domestic price The price of a good or service within a country, determined by domestic demand and supply.

dumping The sale of a product in a foreign country at prices either below cost or below the prices commonly charged at home.

durable good A consumer good with an expected life (use) of three or more years.

earnings The money income received by a worker; equal to the *wage* (rate) multiplied by the amount of time worked.

economic cost A payment that must be made to obtain and retain the services of a *resource;* the income a firm must provide to a resource supplier to attract the resource away from an alternative use; equal to the quantity of other products that cannot be produced when resources are instead used to make a particular product.

economic efficiency The use of the minimum necessary resources to obtain the socially optimal amounts of goods and services; entails both *productive efficiency* and *allocative efficiency.*

economic growth (1) An outward shift in the *production possibilities curve* that results from an increase in resource supplies or quality or an improvement in *technology;* (2) an increase of real output *(gross domestic product)* or real output per capita.

economic investment (See *investment.*)

economic law An *economic principle* that has been tested and retested and has stood the test of time.

economic model A simplified picture of economic reality; an abstract generalization.

economic perspective A viewpoint that envisions individuals and institutions making rational decisions by comparing the marginal benefits and marginal costs associated with their actions.

economic policy A course of action intended to correct or avoid a problem.

economic principle A widely accepted generalization about the economic behavior of individuals or institutions.

economic profit The *total revenue* of a firm less its *economic costs* (which include both *explicit costs* and *implicit costs*); also called "pure profit" and "above-normal profit."

economic resources The *land, labor, capital,* and *entrepreneurial ability* that are used in the production of goods and services; productive agents; factors of production.

economics The social science concerned with how individuals, institutions, and society make optimal (best) choices under conditions of scarcity.

economic system A particular set of institutional arrangements and a coordinating mechanism for solving the economizing problem; a method of organizing an economy, of which the *market system* and the *command system* are the two general types.

economic theory A statement of a cause-effect relationship; when accepted by all or nearly all economists, an *economic principle.*

economies of scale Reductions in the *average total cost* of producing a product as the firm expands the size of plant (its output) in the *long run;* the economies of mass production.

economizing problem The choices necessitated because society's economic wants for goods and services are unlimited but the resources available to satisfy these wants are limited (scarce).

efficiency factors (in growth) The capacity of an economy to combine resources effectively to achieve growth of real output that the *supply factors* (of growth) make possible.

efficiency loss Reduction in combined consumer and producer surplus caused by an underallocation or overallocation of resources to the production of a good or service. Also called *deadweight loss.*

efficiency wage A wage that minimizes wage costs per unit of output by encouraging greater effort or reducing turnover.

efficient allocation of resources That allocation of an economy's resources among the production of different products that leads to the maximum satisfaction of consumers' wants, thus producing the socially optimal mix of output with society's scarce resources.

elastic demand Product or resource demand whose *price elasticity* is greater than 1. This means the resulting change in *quantity demanded* is greater than the percentage change in *price.*

elasticity coefficient The number obtained when the percentage change in *quantity demanded* (or supplied) is divided by the percentage change in the *price* of the commodity.

elasticity formula (See *price elasticity of demand.*)

elastic supply Product or resource supply whose price elasticity is greater than 1. This means the resulting change in quantity supplied is greater than the percentage change in price.

electronic payments Purchases made by transferring funds electronically. Examples: Fedwire transfers, automated clearinghouse transactions (ACHs), payments via the PayPal system, and payments made through stored-value cards.

employment rate The percentage of the *labor force* employed at any time.

entrepreneurial ability The human resource that combines the other resources to produce a product, makes nonroutine decisions, innovates, and bears risks.

equation of exchange $MV = PQ$, in which M is the supply of money, V is the *velocity* of money, P is the *price level,* and Q is the physical volume of *final goods and services* produced.

equilibrium GDP (See *equilibrium real domestic output.*)

equilibrium price The *price* in a competitive market at which the *quantity demanded* and the *quantity supplied* are equal, there is neither a shortage nor a surplus, and there is no tendency for price to rise or fall.

equilibrium price level The price level at which the aggregate demand curve intersects the aggregate supply curve.

equilibrium quantity (1) The quantity at which the intentions of buyers and sellers in a particular market match at a particular price such that the *quantity demanded* and the *quantity supplied* are equal; (2) the profit-maximizing output of a firm.

equilibrium real domestic output The *gross domestic product* at which the total quantity of final goods and services purchased *(aggregate expenditures)* is equal to the total quantity of final goods and services produced (the real domestic output); the real domestic output at which the aggregate demand curve intersects the aggregate supply curve.

equilibrium real output (See *equilibrium real domestic output.*)

equilibrium world price The price of an internationally traded product that equates the quantity of the product demanded by importers with the quantity of the product supplied by exporters; the price determined at the intersection of the export supply curve and the import demand curve.

euro The common currency unit used by 16 European nations (as of 2010) in the *Euro Zone,* which consists of Austria, Belgium, Cyprus, Finland, France, Germany, Greece, Ireland, Italy, Luxembourg, Malta, the Netherlands, Portugal, Slovakia, Slovenia, and Spain.

European Union (EU) An association of 27 European nations (as of 2010) that has eliminated tariffs and quotas among them, established common tariffs for imported goods from outside the member nations, eliminated barriers to the free movement of capital, and created other common economic policies.

Euro Zone The 16 nations (as of 2010) of the 25-member (as of 2010) *European Union* that use the *euro* as their common currency. The Euro Zone countries are Austria, Belgium, Cyprus, Finland, France, Germany, Greece, Ireland, Italy, Luxembourg, Malta, the Netherlands, Portugal, Slovakia, Slovenia, and Spain.

excess reserves The amount by which a bank's or thrift's *actual reserves* exceed its *required reserves;* actual reserves minus required reserves.

exchange controls (See *foreign exchange controls.*)

exchange rate The *rate of exchange* of one nation's currency for another nation's currency.

exchange-rate appreciation An increase in the value of a nation's currency in foreign exchange markets; an increase in the *rate of exchange* with foreign currencies.

exchange-rate depreciation A decrease in the value of a nation's currency in foreign exchange markets; a decrease in the *rate of exchange* with foreign currencies.

exchange-rate determinant Any factor other than the *rate of exchange* that determines a currency's demand and supply in the *foreign exchange market.*

excise tax A tax levied on the production of a specific product or on the quantity of the product purchased.

excludability The characteristic of a *private good,* for which the seller can keep nonbuyers from obtaining the good.

exhaustive expenditure An expenditure by government resulting directly in the employment of *economic resources* and in the absorption by government of the goods and services those resources produce; a *government purchase.*

expansion A phase of the *business cycle* in which *real GDP, income,* and employment rise.

expansionary fiscal policy An increase in *government purchases* of goods and services, a decrease in *net taxes,* or some combination of the two for the purpose of increasing *aggregate demand* and expanding real output.

expansionary monetary policy *Federal Reserve System* actions to increase the *money supply,* lower *interest rates,* and expand *real GDP;* an easy money policy.

expectations The anticipations of consumers, firms, and others about future economic conditions.

expected rate of return The increase in profit a firm anticipates it will obtain by purchasing capital (or engaging in research and development); expressed as a percentage of the total cost of the investment (or R&D) activity.

expenditures approach The method that adds all expenditures made for *final goods and services* to measure the *gross domestic product.*

expenditures-output approach (See *aggregate expenditures–domestic output approach.*)

exports Goods and services produced in a nation and sold to buyers in other nations.

export subsidy A government payment to a domestic producer to enable the firm to reduce the price of a good or service to foreign buyers.

export supply curve An upward-sloping curve that shows the amount of a product that domestic firms will export at each *world price* that is above the *domestic price.*

export transaction A sale of a good or service that increases the amount of foreign currency flowing to a nation's citizens, firms, and government.

external benefit (See *positive externality.*)

external cost (See *negative externality.*)

external debt Private or public debt owed to foreign citizens, firms, and institutions.

externality A cost or benefit from production or consumption, accruing without compensation to someone other than the buyers and sellers of the product (see *negative externality* and *positive externality*).

external public debt The portion of the public debt owed to foreign citizens, firms, and institutions.

face value The dollar or cents value placed on a U.S. coin or piece of paper money.

factors of production *Economic resources: land, capital, labor,* and *entrepreneurial ability.*

fallacy of composition The false notion that what is true for the individual (or part) is necessarily true for the group (or whole).

FDIC (See *Federal Deposit Insurance Corporation.*)

Federal Deposit Insurance Corporation (FDIC) The federally chartered corporation that insures deposit liabilities (up to $250,000 per account) of *commercial banks* and *thrift institutions* (excluding *credit unions,* whose deposits are insured by the *National Credit Union Administration*).

Federal funds rate The interest rate banks and other depository institutions charge one another on overnight loans made out of their *excess reserves.*

Federal government The government of the United States, as distinct from the state and local governments.

Federal Open Market Committee (FOMC) The 12-member group that determines the purchase and sale policies of the *Federal Reserve Banks* in the market for U.S. government securities.

Federal Reserve Banks The 12 banks chartered by the U.S. government to control the *money supply* and perform other functions. (See *central bank, quasi-public bank,* and *bankers' bank.*)

Federal Reserve Note Paper money issued by the *Federal Reserve Banks.*

Federal Reserve System The U.S. central bank, consisting of the *Board of Governors* of the Federal Reserve and the 12 *Federal Reserve Banks,* which controls the lending activity of the nation's banks and thrifts and thus the *money supply;* commonly referred to as the "Fed."

fiat money Anything that is *money* because government has decreed it to be money.

final goods Goods that have been purchased for final use and not for resale or further processing or manufacturing.

financial capital (See *money capital.*)

financial investment The purchase of a financial asset (such as a *stock, bond,* or *mutual fund*) or real asset (such as a house, land, or factories) or the building of such assets in the expectation of financial gain.

financial services industry The broad category of firms that provide financial products and services to help households and businesses earn *interest,* receive *dividends,* obtain *capital gains,* insure against losses, and plan for retirement. Includes *commercial banks,* thrifts, insurance companies, mutual fund companies, pension funds, investment banks, and securities firms.

firm An organization that employs resources to produce a good or service for profit and owns and operates one or more *plants.*

fiscal policy Changes in government spending and tax collections designed to achieve a full-employment and noninflationary domestic output; also called *discretionary fiscal policy.*

fixed exchange rate A *rate of exchange* that is set in some way and therefore prevented from rising or falling with changes in currency supply and demand.

fixed resource Any resource whose quantity cannot be changed by a firm in the *short run.*

flexible exchange rate A *rate of exchange* determined by the international demand for and supply of a nation's money; a rate free to rise or fall (to float).

flexible prices Product prices that freely move upward or downward when product demand or supply changes.

floating exchange rate (See *flexible exchange rate.*)

follower countries As it relates to *economic growth,* countries that adopt advanced technologies that previously were developed and used by *leader countries.*

foreign competition (See *import competition.*)

foreign direct investment (Web chapter) Investments made to obtain a lasting interest in firms operating outside of the economy of the investor; may involve purchasing existing assets or building new production facilities.

foreign exchange controls Controls a government may exercise over the quantity of foreign currency demanded by its citizens and firms and over the *rates of exchange* as a way to limit the nation's quantity of *outpayments* relative to its quantity of *inpayments* (to eliminate a *payments deficit*).

foreign exchange market A market in which the money (currency) of one nation can be used to purchase (can be exchanged for) the money of another nation; currency market.

foreign exchange rate (See *rate of exchange*.)

foreign purchase effect The inverse relationship between the *net exports* of an economy and its price level relative to foreign price levels.

45° (degree) line A line along which the value of *GDP* (measured horizontally) is equal to the value of *aggregate expenditures* (measured vertically).

fractional reserve banking system A system in which *commercial banks* and *thrift institutions* hold less than 100 percent of their checkable-deposit liabilities as *required reserves*.

freedom of choice The freedom of owners of property resources to employ or dispose of them as they see fit, of workers to enter any line of work for which they are qualified, and of consumers to spend their incomes in a manner that they think is appropriate.

freedom of enterprise The freedom of *firms* to obtain economic resources, to use those resources to produce products of the firm's own choosing, and to sell their products in markets of their choice.

free-rider problem The inability of potential providers of an economically desirable good or service to obtain payment from those who benefit, because of *nonexcludability*.

free trade The absence of artificial (government-imposed) barriers to trade among individuals and firms in different nations.

frictional unemployment A type of unemployment caused by workers voluntarily changing jobs and by temporary layoffs; unemployed workers between jobs.

full employment (1) The use of all available resources to produce want-satisfying goods and services; (2) the situation in which the *unemployment rate* is equal to the *full-employment rate of unemployment* and where *frictional* and *structural* unemployment occur but not *cyclical unemployment* (and the *real GDP* of the economy equals *potential output*).

full-employment rate of unemployment The *unemployment rate* at which there is no *cyclical unemployment* of the *labor force;* equal to between 4 and 5 percent in the United States because some *frictional* and *structural unemployment* is unavoidable.

functional distribution of income The manner in which *national income* is divided among the functions performed to earn it (or the kinds of resources provided to earn it); the division of national income into wages and salaries, proprietors' income, corporate profits, interest, and rent.

future value The amount to which some current amount of money will grow if the interest earned on the amount is left to compound over time. *See compound interest.*

gains from trade The extra output that trading partners obtain through specialization of production and exchange of goods and services.

GDP (See *gross domestic product*.)

GDP gap Actual *gross domestic product* minus potential output; may be either a positive amount (a *positive GDP gap*) or a negative amount (a *negative GDP gap*).

GDP price index A *price index* for all the goods and services that make up the *gross domestic product;* the price index used to adjust *nominal gross domestic product* to *real gross domestic product*.

G8 nations A group of eight major nations (Canada, France, Germany, Italy, Japan, Russia, United Kingdom, and United States) whose leaders meet regularly to discuss common economic problems and try to coordinate economic policies.

General Agreement on Tariffs and Trade (GATT) The international agreement reached in 1947 in which 23 nations agreed to give equal and nondiscriminatory treatment to one another, to reduce tariff rates by multinational negotiations, and to eliminate *import quotas*. It now includes most nations and has become the *World Trade Organization*.

generalization Statement of the nature of the relationship between two or more sets of facts.

gold standard A historical system of fixed exchange rates in which nations defined their currencies in terms of gold, maintained a fixed relationship between their stocks of gold and their money supplies, and allowed gold to be freely exported and imported.

government purchases (*G*) Expenditures by government for goods and services that government consumes in providing public goods and for public (or social) capital that has a long lifetime; the expenditures of all governments in the economy for those *final goods and services*.

government transfer payment The disbursement of money (or goods and services) by government for which government receives no currently produced good or service in return.

gross domestic product (GDP) The total market value of all *final goods and services* produced annually within the boundaries of the United States, whether by U.S.- or foreign-supplied resources.

gross private domestic investment (I_g) Expenditures for newly produced *capital goods* (such as machinery, equipment, tools, and buildings) and for additions to inventories.

growth accounting The bookkeeping of the supply-side elements such as productivity and labor inputs that contribute to changes in *real GDP* over some specific time period.

guiding function of prices The ability of price changes to bring about changes in the quantities of products and resources demanded and supplied.

horizontal axis The "left-right" or "west-east" measurement line on graph or grid.

households Economic entities (of one or more persons occupying a housing unit) that provide *resources* to the economy and use the *income* received to purchase goods and services that satisfy economic wants.

human capital The knowledge and skills that make a person productive.

human capital investment Any expenditure undertaken to improve the education, skills, health, or mobility of workers, with an expectation of greater productivity and thus a positive return on the investment.

hyperinflation A very rapid rise in the price level; an extremely high rate of inflation.

hypothesis A tentative explanation of cause and effect that requires testing.

IMF (See *International Monetary Fund*.)

immediate short-run aggregate supply curve An aggregate supply curve for which real output, but not the price level, changes when the aggregate demand curves shifts; a horizontal aggregate supply curve that implies an inflexible price level.

import competition The competition that domestic firms encounter from the products and services of foreign producers.

import demand curve A downsloping curve showing the amount of a product that an economy will import at each *world price* below the *domestic price.*

import quota A limit imposed by a nation on the quantity (or total value) of a good that may be imported during some period of time.

imports Spending by individuals, *firms,* and governments for goods and services produced in foreign nations.

import transaction The purchase of a good or service that decreases the amount of foreign money held by citizens, firms, and governments of a nation.

income A flow of dollars (or purchasing power) per unit of time derived from the use of human or property resources.

income approach The method that adds all the income generated by the production of *final goods and services* to measure the *gross domestic product.*

income effect A change in the quantity demanded of a product that results from the change in *real income (purchasing power)* caused by a change in the product's price.

income elasticity of demand The ratio of the percentage change in the *quantity demanded* of a good to a percentage change in consumer income; measures the responsiveness of consumer purchases to income changes.

income inequality The unequal distribution of an economy's total income among households or families.

increase in demand An increase in the *quantity demanded* of a good or service at every price; a shift of the *demand curve* to the right.

increase in supply An increase in the *quantity supplied* of a good or service at every price; a shift of the *supply curve* to the right.

increasing returns An increase in a firm's output by a larger percentage than the percentage increase in its inputs.

independent goods Products or services for which there is little or no relationship between the price of one and the demand for the other. When the price of one rises or falls, the demand for the other tends to remain constant.

independent variable The variable causing a change in some other (dependent) variable.

index funds *Mutual funds* that select stock or bond *portfolios* to exactly match a stock or bond index (a collection of stocks or bonds meant to capture the overall behavior of a particular category of investments) such as the Standard & Poor's 500 Index or the Russell 3000 Index.

individual demand The demand schedule or *demand curve* of a single buyer.

individual supply The supply schedule or *supply curve* of a single seller.

industrially advanced countries High-income countries such as the United States, Canada, Japan, and the nations of western Europe that have highly developed *market economies* based on large stocks of technologically advanced capital goods and skilled labor forces.

industry A group of (one or more) *firms* that produce identical or similar products.

inelastic demand Product or resource demand for which the *elasticity coefficient* for price is less than 1. This means the resulting percentage change in *quantity demanded* is less than the percentage change in *price.*

inelastic supply Product or resource supply for which the price elasticity coefficient is less than 1. The percentage change in *quantity supplied* is less than the percentage change in *price.*

inferior good A good or service whose consumption declines as income rises, prices held constant.

inflating Determining *real gross domestic product* by increasing the dollar value of the *nominal gross domestic product* produced in a year in which prices are lower than those in a *base year.*

inflation A rise in the general level of prices in an economy.

inflationary expectations The belief of workers, firms, and consumers about future rates of inflation.

inflationary expenditure gap The amount by which the *aggregate expenditures schedule* must shift downward to decrease the *nominal GDP* to its full-employment noninflationary level.

inflation premium The component of the *nominal interest rate* that reflects anticipated inflation.

inflation targeting The annual statement by a *central bank* of a goal for a specific range of inflation in a future year, coupled with monetary policy designed to achieve the goal.

inflexible prices Product prices that remain in place (at least for a while) even though supply or demand has changed; stuck prices or sticky prices.

information technology New and more efficient methods of delivering and receiving information through the use of computers, fax machines, wireless phones, and the Internet.

infrastructure The capital goods usually provided by the *public sector* for use by its citizens and firms (for example, highways, bridges, transit systems, wastewater treatment facilities, municipal water systems, and airports).

injection An addition of spending to the income-expenditure stream: *investment, government purchases,* and *net exports.*

innovation The first commercially successful introduction of a new product, the use of a new method of production, or the creation of a new form of business organization.

inpayments The receipts of domestic or foreign money that individuals, firms, and governments of one nation obtain from the sale of goods and services abroad, as investment income and remittances, and from foreign purchases of domestic assets.

insider-outsider theory The hypothesis that nominal wages are inflexible downward because firms are aware that workers ("insiders") who retain employment during recession may refuse to work cooperatively with previously unemployed workers ("outsiders") who offer to work for less than the current wage.

insurable risk An event that would result in a loss but whose frequency of occurrence can be estimated with considerable accuracy. Insurance companies are willing to sell insurance against such losses.

interest The payment made for the use of money (of borrowed funds).

interest income Payments of income to those who supply the economy with *capital.*

interest rate The annual rate at which *interest* is paid; a percentage of the borrowed amount.

interest-rate effect The tendency for increases in the *price level* to increase the demand for money, raise interest rates, and, as a result, reduce total spending and real output in the economy (and the reverse for price-level decreases).

intermediate goods Products that are purchased for resale or further processing or manufacturing.

internally held public debt *Public debt* owed to citizens, firms, and institutions of the same nation that issued the debt.

international balance of payments A summary of all the transactions that took place between the individuals, firms, and government units of one nation and those of all other nations during a year.

international balance-of-payments deficit (See *balance-of-payments deficit.*)

international balance-of-payments surplus (See *balance-of-payments surplus.*)

international gold standard (See *gold standard.*)

International Monetary Fund (IMF) The international association of nations that was formed after the Second World War to make loans of foreign monies to nations with temporary *payments deficits* and, until the early 1970s, to administer the *adjustable pegs.* It now mainly makes loans to nations facing possible defaults on private and government loans.

international monetary reserves The foreign currencies and other assets such as gold that a nation can use to settle a *balance-of-payments deficit.*

international value of the dollar The price that must be paid in foreign currency (money) to obtain one U.S. dollar.

intertemporal choice Choices between benefits obtainable in one time period and benefits achievable in a later time period; comparisons that individuals and society must make between the reductions in current consumption that are necessary to fund current investments and the higher levels of future consumption that those current investments can produce.

intrinsic value The market value of the metal within a coin.

inventories Goods that have been produced but remain unsold.

inverse relationship The relationship between two variables that change in opposite directions, for example, product price and quantity demanded; a negative relationship.

investment In economics, spending for the production and accumulation of *capital* and additions to inventories. (For contrast, see *financial investment.*)

investment banks Firms that help corporations and government raise money by selling stocks and bonds; they also offer advisory services for corporate mergers and acquisitions in addition to providing brokerage services and advice.

investment demand curve A curve that shows the amounts of *investment* demanded by an economy at a series of *real interest rates.*

investment goods Same as *capital* or capital goods.

investment in human capital (See *human capital investment.*)

investment schedule A curve or schedule that shows the amounts firms plan to invest at various possible values of *real gross domestic product.*

"invisible hand" The tendency of firms and resource suppliers that seek to further their own self-interests in competitive markets to also promote the interests of society.

Joint Economic Committee (JEC) Committee of senators and representatives that investigates economic problems of national interest.

labor People's physical and mental talents and efforts that are used to help produce goods and services.

labor force Persons 16 years of age and older who are not in institutions and who are employed or are unemployed and seeking work.

labor-force participation rate The percentage of the working-age population that is actually in the *labor force.*

labor-intensive goods Products requiring relatively large amounts of *labor* to produce.

labor productivity Total output divided by the quantity of labor employed to produce it; the *average product* of labor or output per hour of work.

labor union A group of workers organized to advance the interests of the group (to increase wages, shorten the hours worked, improve working conditions, and so on).

Laffer Curve A curve relating government tax rates and tax revenues and on which a particular tax rate (between zero and 100 percent) maximizes tax revenues.

laissez-faire capitalism (See *capitalism.*)

land Natural resources ("free gifts of nature") used to produce goods and services.

land-intensive goods Products requiring relatively large amounts of *land* to produce.

land reform (Web chapter) A set of policies designed to create more efficient distribution of land ownership in developing countries; policies vary country to country and can involve everything from government purchasing large land estates and dividing the land into smaller farms to consolidating tiny plots of land into larger, more efficient private farms.

law of demand The principle that, other things equal, an increase in a product's price will reduce the quantity of it demanded, and conversely for a decrease in price.

law of increasing opportunity costs The principle that as the production of a good increases, the *opportunity cost* of producing an additional unit rises.

law of supply The principle that, other things equal, an increase in the price of a product will increase the quantity of it supplied, and conversely for a price decrease.

leader countries As it relates to *economic growth,* countries that develop and use advanced technologies, which then become available to *follower countries.*

leakage (1) A withdrawal of potential spending from the income-expenditures stream via *saving,* tax payments, or *imports;* (2) a withdrawal that reduces the lending potential of the banking system.

learning by doing Achieving greater *productivity* and lower *average total cost* through gains in knowledge and skill that accompany repetition of a task; a source of *economies of scale.*

legal tender A nation's official currency (bills and coins). Payment of debts must be accepted in this monetary unit, but creditors can specify the form of payment, for example, "cash only" or "check or credit card only."

lending potential of an individual commercial bank The amount by which a single bank can increase the *money supply* by making new loans to (or buying securities from) the public; equal to the bank's excess reserves.

lending potential of the banking system The amount by which the banking system can increase the *money supply* by making new loans to (or buying securities from) the public; equal to the *excess reserves* of the banking system multiplied by the *monetary multiplier.*

liability A debt with a monetary value; an amount owed by a firm or an individual.

limited liability rule Rule limiting the risks involved in investing in corporations and encouraging investors to invest in stocks by capping their potential losses at the amount that they paid for their shares.

liquidity The ease with which an asset can be converted quickly into cash with little or no loss of purchasing power. Money is said to be perfectly liquid, whereas other assets have a lesser degree of liquidity.

liquidity trap A situation in a severe *recession* in which the Fed's injection of additional reserves into the banking system has little or no additional positive impact on lending, borrowing, *investment,* or *aggregate demand.*

long run (1) In *microeconomics,* a period of time long enough to enable producers of a product to change the quantities of all the resources they employ; period in which all resources and costs are variable and no resources or costs are fixed. (2) In *macroeconomics,* a period sufficiently long for *nominal wages* and other input prices to change in response to a change in a nation's *price level.*

long-run aggregate supply curve The aggregate supply curve associated with a time period in which input prices (especially *nominal wages*) are fully responsive to changes in the *price level.*

long-run competitive equilibrium The price at which firms in *pure competition* neither obtain *economic profit* nor suffer economic losses in the *long run* and in which the total quantity demanded and supplied are equal; a price equal to the *marginal cost* and the minimum long-run *average total cost* of producing the product.

long-run supply curve As it applies to macroeconomics, a supply curve for which price, but not real output, changes when the demand curves shifts; a vertical supply curve that implies fully flexible prices.

long-run vertical Phillips Curve The *Phillips Curve* after all nominal wages have adjusted to changes in the rate of inflation; a line emanating straight upward at the economy's *natural rate of unemployment.*

lump-sum tax A tax that collects a constant amount (the tax revenue of government is the same) at all levels of GDP.

***M*1** The most narrowly defined *money supply,* equal to *currency* in the hands of the public and the *checkable deposits* of commercial banks and thrift institutions.

***M*2** A more broadly defined *money supply,* equal to *M*1 plus *noncheckable savings accounts* (including *money market deposit accounts*), small *time deposits* (deposits of less than $100,000), and individual *money market mutual fund* balances.

macroeconomics The part of economics concerned with the economy as a whole; with such major aggregates as the household, business, and government sectors; and with measures of the total economy.

managed floating exchange rate An *exchange rate* that is allowed to change (float) as a result of changes in currency supply and demand but at times is altered (managed) by governments via their buying and selling of particular currencies.

marginal analysis The comparison of marginal ("extra" or "additional") benefits and marginal costs, usually for decision making.

marginal benefit The extra (additional) benefit of consuming 1 more unit of some good or service; the change in total benefit when 1 more unit is consumed.

marginal cost (MC) The extra (additional) cost of producing 1 more unit of output; equal to the change in *total cost* divided by the change in output (and, in the short run, to the change in total *variable cost* divided by the change in output).

marginal propensity to consume (MPC) The fraction of any change in *disposable income* spent for *consumer goods;* equal to the change in consumption divided by the change in disposable income.

marginal propensity to save (MPS) The fraction of any change in *disposable income* that households save; equal to the change in *saving* divided by the change in disposable income.

marginal tax rate The tax rate paid on an additional dollar of income.

marginal utility The extra *utility* a consumer obtains from the consumption of 1 additional unit of a good or service; equal to the change in total utility divided by the change in the quantity consumed.

market Any institution or mechanism that brings together buyers (demanders) and sellers (suppliers) of a particular good or service.

market demand (See *total demand.*)

market economy An economy in which the private decisions of consumers, resource suppliers, and firms determine how resources are allocated; the *market system.*

market failure The inability of a market to bring about the allocation of resources that best satisfies the wants of society; in particular, the overallocation or underallocation of resources to the production of a particular good or service because of *externalities* or informational problems or because markets do not provide desired *public goods.*

market period A period in which producers of a product are unable to change the quantity produced in response to a change in its price and in which there is a *perfectly inelastic supply.*

market portfolio The portfolio consisting of every financial asset (including every *stock* and *bond*) traded in the financial markets. The market portfolio is used to calculate *beta* (a measure of the degree of riskiness) for specific stocks, bonds, and mutual funds.

market system All the product and resource markets of a *market economy* and the relationships among them; a method that allows the prices determined in those markets to allocate the economy's scarce resources and to communicate and coordinate the decisions made by consumers, firms, and resource suppliers.

Medicaid A Federal program that helps finance the medical expenses of individuals covered by the *Supplemental Security Income (SSI)* and *Temporary Assistance for Needy Families (TANF)* programs.

Medicare A Federal program that is financed by *payroll taxes* and provides for (1) compulsory hospital insurance for senior citizens, (2) low-cost voluntary insurance to help older Americans pay physicians' fees, and (3) subsidized insurance to buy prescription drugs.

medium of exchange Any item sellers generally accept and buyers generally use to pay for a good or service; *money;* a convenient means of exchanging goods and services without engaging in *barter.*

menu costs The reluctance of firms to cut prices during recessions (that they think will be short-lived) because of the costs of altering and communicating their price reductions; named after the cost associated with printing new menus at restaurants.

microeconomics The part of economics concerned with decision making by individual units such as a *household,* a *firm,* or an *industry* and with individual markets, specific goods and services, and product and resource prices.

microfinance (Web chapter) A credit system through which groups of people pool their money and make small loans to budding *entrepreneurs* and owners of small businesses in *developing countries.*

midpoint formula A method for calculating *price elasticity of demand* or *price elasticity of supply* that averages the two prices and two quantities as the reference points for computing percentages.

minimum wage The lowest *wage* that employers may legally pay for an hour of work.

modern economic growth The historically recent phenomenon in which nations for the first time have experienced sustained increases in *real GDP per capita.*

monetarism The macroeconomic view that the main cause of changes in aggregate output and *price level* is fluctuations in the *money supply;* espoused by advocates of a *monetary rule.*

monetary multiplier The multiple of its *excess reserves* by which the banking system can expand *checkable deposits* and thus the *money supply* by making new loans (or buying securities); equal to 1 divided by the *reserve requirement.*

monetary policy A central bank's changing of the *money supply* to influence interest rates and assist the economy in achieving price stability, full employment, and economic growth.

monetary rule The rule suggested by *monetarism.* As traditionally formulated, the rule says that the *money supply* should be expanded each year at the same annual rate as the potential rate of growth of the *real gross domestic product;* the supply of money should be increased steadily between 3 and 5 percent per year. (Also see *Taylor rule.*)

money Any item that is generally acceptable to sellers in exchange for goods and services.

money capital Money available to purchase *capital;* simply *money,* as defined by economists.

money income (See *nominal income.*)

money market The market in which the demand for and the supply of money determine the *interest rate* (or the level of interest rates) in the economy.

money market deposit accounts (MMDAs) Bank- and thrift-provided interest-bearing accounts that contain a variety of short-term securities; such accounts have minimum balance requirements and limits on the frequency of withdrawals.

money market mutual funds (MMMFs) Interest-bearing accounts offered by investment companies, which pool depositors' funds for the purchase of short-term securities. Depositors can write checks in minimum amounts or more against their accounts.

money supply Narrowly defined, *M*1; more broadly defined, *M*2. (See *M*1 and *M*2)

monopoly A market structure in which there is only a single seller of a good, service, or resource. In antitrust law, a dominant firm that accounts for a very high percentage of total sales within a particular market.

monopsony A market structure in which there is only a single buyer of a good, service, or resource.

mortgage-backed securities *Bonds* that represent claims to all or part of the monthly mortgage payments from the pools of mortgage loans made by lenders to borrowers to help them purchase residential property.

mortgage debt crisis The period beginning in late 2007 when thousands of homeowners defaulted on mortgage loans when they experienced a combination of higher mortgage interest rates and falling home prices.

multinational corporations Firms that own production facilities in two or more countries and produce and sell their products globally.

multiple counting Wrongly including the value of *intermediate goods* in the *gross domestic product;* counting the same good or service more than once.

multiplier The ratio of a change in equilibrium GDP to the change in *investment* or in any other component of *aggregate expenditures* or *aggregate demand;* the number by which a change in any such component must be multiplied to find the resulting change in the equilibrium GDP.

multiplier effect The effect on equilibrium GDP of a change in *aggregate expenditures* or *aggregate demand* (caused by a change in the *consumption schedule, investment,* government expenditures, or *net exports*).

mutual funds *Portfolios* of *stocks* and *bonds* selected and purchased by mutual fund companies, which finance the purchases by pooling money from thousands of individual fund investors; includes both *index funds* as well as *actively managed funds.* Fund returns (profits or losses) pass through to the individual fund investors who invest in the funds.

national bank A *commercial bank* authorized to operate by the U.S. government.

National Credit Union Administration (NCUA) The federally chartered agency that insures deposit liabilities (up to $250,000 per account) in *credit unions.*

national income Total income earned by resource suppliers for their contributions to *gross domestic product* plus *taxes on production and imports;* the sum of wages and salaries, *rent, interest, profit, proprietors' income,* and such taxes.

national income accounting The techniques used to measure the overall production of the economy and other related variables for the nation as a whole.

natural monopoly An industry in which *economies of scale* are so great that a single firm can produce the product at a lower average total cost than would be possible if more than one firm produced the product.

natural rate of unemployment (NRU) The *full-employment rate of unemployment;* the unemployment rate occurring when there is no cyclical unemployment and the economy is achieving its potential output; the unemployment rate at which actual inflation equals expected inflation.

near-money Financial assets, the most important of which are *noncheckable savings accounts, time deposits,* and U.S. short-term securities and savings bonds, which are not a medium of exchange but can be readily converted into money.

negative externality A cost imposed without compensation on third parties by the production or consumption of sellers or buyers. Example: A manufacturer dumps toxic chemicals into a river, killing fish prized by sports fishers; an external cost or a spillover cost.

negative GDP gap A situation in which actual *gross domestic product* is less than *potential output.* Also known as a recessionary output gap.

negative relationship (See *inverse relationship.*)

net benefits The total benefits of some activity or policy less the total costs of that activity or policy.

net domestic product (NDP) *Gross domestic product* less the part of the year's output that is needed to replace the *capital goods* worn out in producing the output; the nation's total output available for consumption or additions to the *capital stock.*

net exports (X_n) *Exports* minus *imports.*

net foreign factor income Receipts of resource income from the rest of the world minus payments of resource income to the rest of the world.

net investment income The interest and dividend income received by the residents of a nation from residents of other nations less the interest and dividend payments made by the residents of that nation to the residents of other nations.

net private domestic investment *Gross private domestic investment* less *consumption of fixed capital;* the addition to the nation's stock of *capital* during a year.

net taxes The taxes collected by government less *government transfer payments.*

net transfers The personal and government transfer payments made by one nation to residents of foreign nations less the personal and government transfer payments received from residents of foreign nations.

network effects Increases in the value of a product to each user, including existing users, as the total number of users rises.

net worth The total *assets* less the total *liabilities* of a firm or an individual; for a firm, the claims of the owners against the firm's total assets; for an individual, his or her wealth.

new classical economics The theory that, although unanticipated price-level changes may create macroeconomic instability in the short run, the economy is stable at the full-employment level of domestic output in the long run because prices and wages adjust automatically to correct movements away from the full-employment, noninflationary output.

nominal gross domestic product (GDP) *GDP* measured in terms of the price level at the time of measurement; *GDP* not adjusted for *inflation.*

nominal income number of dollars received by an individual or group for its resources during some period of time.

nominal interest rate The interest rate expressed in terms of annual amounts currently charged for interest and not adjusted for inflation.

nominal wage The amount of money received by a worker per unit of time (hour, day, etc.); money wage.

nondiscretionary fiscal policy (See *built-in stabilizer.*)

nondiversifiable risk Investment *risk* that investors are unable to reduce via *diversification;* also called systemic risk.

nondurable good A *consumer good* with an expected life (use) of less than three years.

nonexcludability The inability to keep nonpayers (free riders) from obtaining benefits from a certain good; a characteristic of a *public good.*

nonexhaustive expenditure An expenditure by government that does not result directly in the use of economic resources or the production of goods and services; see *government transfer payment.*

nonincome determinants of consumption and saving All influences on consumption and saving other than the level of *GDP.*

noninterest determinants of investment All influences on the level of investment spending other than the *interest rate.*

noninvestment transaction An expenditure for stocks, bonds, or secondhand *capital goods.*

nonmarket transactions The value of the goods and services that are not included in the *gross domestic product* because they are not bought and sold.

nonproduction transaction The purchase and sale of any item that is not a currently produced good or service.

nonrivalry The idea that one person's benefit from a certain good does not reduce the benefit available to others; a characteristic of a *public good.*

nontariff barriers (NTBs) All barriers other than *protective tariffs* that nations erect to impede international trade, including *import quotas,* licensing requirements, unreasonable product-quality standards, unnecessary bureaucratic detail in customs procedures, and so on.

normal good A good or service whose consumption increases when income increases and falls when income decreases, price remaining constant.

normal profit The payment made by a firm to obtain and retain *entrepreneurial ability;* the minimum income entrepreneurial ability must receive to induce it to perform entrepreneurial functions for a firm.

normative economics The part of economics involving value judgments about what the economy should be like; focused on which economic goals and policies should be implemented; policy economics.

North American Free Trade Agreement (NAFTA) A 1993 agreement establishing, over a 15-year period, a free-trade zone composed of Canada, Mexico, and the United States.

official reserves Foreign currencies owned by the central bank of a nation.

offshoring The practice of shifting work previously done by American workers to workers located abroad.

Okun's law The generalization that any 1-percentage-point rise in the *unemployment rate* above the *full-employment rate of unemployment* is associated with a rise in the negative *GDP gap* by 2 percent of *potential output* (potential GDP).

OPEC (See *Organization of Petroleum Exporting Countries.*)

open economy An economy that exports and imports goods and services.

open-market operations The buying and selling of U.S. government securities by the *Federal Reserve Banks* for purposes of carrying out *monetary policy.*

opportunity cost The amount of other products that must be forgone or sacrificed to produce a unit of a product.

opportunity-cost ratio An equivalency showing the number of units of two products that can be produced with the same resources; the cost 1 corn ≡ 3 olives shows that the resources required to produce 3 units of olives must be shifted to corn production to produce 1 unit of corn.

optimal reduction of an externality The reduction of a *negative externality* such as pollution to the level at which the *marginal benefit* and *marginal cost* of reduction are equal.

Organization of Petroleum Exporting Countries (OPEC) A cartel of 12 oil-producing countries (Algeria, Angola, Ecuador, Iran, Iraq, Kuwait, Libya, Nigeria, Qatar, Saudi Arabia, Venezuela, and the United Arab Emirates) that attempts to control the quantity and price of crude oil exported by its members and that accounts for a large percentage of the world's export of oil.

other-things-equal assumption The assumption that factors other than those being considered are held constant; *ceteris paribus* assumption.

outpayments The expenditures of domestic or foreign currency that the individuals, firms, and governments of one nation make to purchase goods and services, for remittances, to pay investment income, and for purchases of foreign assets.

output effect The situation in which an increase in the price of one input will increase a firm's production costs and reduce its level of output, thus reducing the demand for other inputs; conversely for a decrease in the price of the input.

paper money Pieces of paper used as a *medium of exchange;* in the United States, *Federal Reserve Notes.*

paradox of thrift The seemingly self-contradictory but nevertheless true statement that increased *saving* can be both good and bad for the economy. It is good in the long run when matched with increased *investment* spending, but bad during a *recession* because it reduces spending, which further reduces output and employment. In fact, attempts by *households* to save more during a recession may simply worsen the recession and result in less saving.

partnership An unincorporated firm owned and operated by two or more persons.

passively managed funds *Mutual funds* whose *portfolios* are not regularly updated by a fund manager attempting to generate high returns. Rather, once an initial portfolio is selected, it is left unchanged so that investors receive whatever return that unchanging portfolio subsequently generates. *Index funds* are a type of passively managed fund.

patent An exclusive right given to inventors to produce and sell a new product or machine for 20 years from the time of patent application.

payments deficit (See *balance-of-payments deficit.*)

payments surplus (See *balance-of-payments surplus.*)

payroll tax A tax levied on employers of labor equal to a percentage of all or part of the wages and salaries paid by them and on employees equal to a percentage of all or part of the wages and salaries received by them.

peak The point in a business cycle at which business activity has reached a temporary maximum; the economy is near or at full employment and the level of real output is at or very close to the economy's capacity.

per capita GDP *Gross domestic product* (GDP) per person; the average GDP of a population.

per capita income A nation's total income per person; the average income of a population.

percentage rate of return The percentage gain or loss, relative to the buying price, of an *economic investment* or *financial investment* over some period of time.

perfectly inelastic demand Product or resource demand in which *price* can be of any amount at a particular quantity of the product or resource demanded; *quantity demanded* does not respond to a change in price; graphs as a vertical *demand curve.*

perfectly inelastic supply Product or resource supply in which *price* can be of any amount at a particular quantity of the product or resource demanded; *quantity supplied* does not respond to a change in price; graphs as a vertical *supply curve.*

personal consumption expenditures (*C*) The expenditures of *households* for *durable* and *nondurable consumer goods* and *services.*

personal distribution of income The manner in which the economy's *personal* or *disposable income* is divided among different income classes or different households or families.

personal income (PI) The earned and unearned income available to resource suppliers and others before the payment of personal taxes.

personal income tax A tax levied on the taxable income of individuals, households, and unincorporated firms.

personal saving The *personal income* of households less personal taxes and *personal consumption expenditures; disposable income* not spent for *consumer goods.*

per-unit production cost The average production cost of a particular level of output; total input cost divided by units of output.

Phillips Curve A curve showing the relationship between the *unemployment rate* (on the horizontal axis) and the annual rate of increase in the *price level* (on the vertical axis).

planned investment The amount that *firms* plan or intend to invest.

plant A physical establishment that performs one or more functions in the production, fabrication, and distribution of goods and services.

policy economics The formulation of courses of action to bring about desired economic outcomes or to prevent undesired occurrences.

political business cycle Fluctuations in the economy caused by the alleged tendency of Congress to destabilize the economy by reducing taxes and increasing government expenditures before elections and to raise taxes and lower expenditures after elections.

Ponzi scheme A financial fraud in which the returns paid to earlier investors come from contributions made by later investors (rather than from the financial investment that the perpetrator of the fraud claims to be making). Named after notorious fraudster Charles Ponzi.

portfolio A specific collection of *stocks, bonds,* or other *financial investments* held by an individual or a *mutual fund.*

positive economics The analysis of facts or data to establish scientific generalizations about economic behavior.

positive externality A benefit obtained without compensation by third parties from the production or consumption of sellers or buyers. Example: A beekeeper benefits when a neighboring farmer plants clover. An *external benefit* or a spillover benefit.

positive GDP gap A situation in which actual *gross domestic product* exceeds *potential output.* Also known as an inflationary output gap.

positive relationship (See *direct relationship.*)

***post hoc, ergo propter hoc* fallacy** The false belief that when one event precedes another, the first event must have caused the second event.

potential output The real output *(GDP)* an economy can produce when it fully employs its available resources.

poverty A situation in which the basic needs of an individual or family exceed the means to satisfy them.

poverty rate The percentage of the population with incomes below the official poverty income levels that are established by the Federal government.

present value Today's value of some amount of money that is to be received sometime in the future.

price The amount of money needed to buy a particular good, service, or resource.

price ceiling A legally established maximum price for a good or service.

price elasticity of demand The ratio of the percentage change in *quantity demanded* of a product or resource to the percentage change in its *price;* a measure of the responsiveness of buyers to a change in the price of a product or resource.

price elasticity of supply The ratio of the percentage change in *quantity supplied* of a product or resource to the percentage change in its *price;* a measure of the responsiveness of producers to a change in the price of a product or resource.

price floor A legally determined minimum price above the *equilibrium price.*

price index An index number that shows how the weighted-average price of a "market basket" of goods changes over time.

price level The weighted average of the prices of all the final goods and services produced in an economy.

price-level stability A steadiness of the price level from one period to the next; zero or low annual inflation; also called "price stability."

price-level surprises Unanticipated changes in the price level.

price war Successive and continued decreases in the prices charged by firms in an oligopolistic industry. Each firm lowers its price below rivals' prices, hoping to increase its sales and revenues at its rivals' expense.

prime interest rate The benchmark *interest rate* that banks use as a reference point for a wide range of loans to businesses and individuals.

principle of comparative advantage The proposition that an individual, region, or nation will benefit if it specializes in producing goods for which its own *opportunity costs* are lower than the opportunity costs of a trading partner, and then exchanging some of the products in which it specializes for other desired products produced by others.

private good A good or service that is individually consumed and that can be profitably provided by privately owned firms because they can exclude nonpayers from receiving the benefits.

private property The right of private persons and firms to obtain, own, control, employ, dispose of, and bequeath *land, capital,* and other property.

private sector The *households* and business *firms* of the economy.

probability-weighted average Each of the possible future rates of return from an investment multiplied by its respective probability (expressed as a decimal) of happening.

producer surplus The difference between the actual price a producer receives (or producers receive) and the minimum acceptable price; the triangular area above the supply curve and below the market price.

production possibilities curve A curve showing the different combinations of two goods or services that can be produced in a *full-employment, full-production* economy where the available supplies of resources and technology are fixed.

productive efficiency The production of a good in the least costly way; occurs when production takes place at the output at which *average total cost* is a minimum and *marginal product* per dollar's worth of input is the same for all inputs.

productivity A measure of average output or real output per unit of input. For example, the productivity of labor is determined by dividing real output by hours of work.

productivity growth The increase in *productivity* from one period to another.

product market A market in which products are sold by *firms* and bought by *households.*

profit The return to the resource *entrepreneurial ability* (see *normal profit*); *total revenue* minus *total cost* (see *economic profit*).

progressive tax A tax whose *average tax rate* increases as the taxpayer's income increases and decreases as the taxpayer's income decreases.

property tax A tax on the value of property (*capital, land, stocks* and *bonds,* and other *assets*) owned by *firms* and *households.*

proportional tax A tax whose *average tax rate* remains constant as the taxpayer's income increases or decreases.

proprietor's income The net income of the owners of unincorporated firms (proprietorships and partnerships).

protective tariff A *tariff* designed to shield domestic producers of a good or service from the competition of foreign producers.

public debt The total amount owed by the Federal government to the owners of government securities; equal to the sum of past government *budget deficits* less government *budget surpluses.*

public good A good or service that is characterized by *nonrivalry* and *nonexcludability;* a good or service with these characteristics provided by government.

public investments Government expenditures on public capital (such as roads, highways, bridges, mass-transit systems, and electric power facilities) and on *human capital* (such as education, training, and health).

public sector The part of the economy that contains all government entities; government.

purchasing power The amount of goods and services that a monetary unit of income can buy.

purchasing power parity The idea that exchange rates between nations equate the purchasing power of various currencies. Exchange rates between any two nations adjust to reflect the price-level differences between the countries.

pure rate of interest An essentially risk-free, long-term interest rate that is free of the influence of market imperfections.

quantity demanded The amount of a good or service that buyers (or a buyer) are willing and able to purchase at a specific price during a specified period of time.

quantity supplied The amount of a good or service that producers (or a producer) are willing and able to make available for sale at a specific price during a specified period of time.

quasi-public bank A bank that is privately owned but governmentally (publicly) controlled; each of the U.S. *Federal Reserve Banks.*

quasi-public good A good or service to which excludability could apply but that has such a large *positive externality* that government sponsors its production to prevent an underallocation of resources.

R&D Research and development activities undertaken to bring about *technological advance.*

rate of exchange The price paid in one's own money to acquire 1 unit of a foreign currency; the rate at which the money of one nation is exchanged for the money of another nation.

rate of return The gain in net revenue divided by the cost of an investment or an *R&D* expenditure; expressed as a percentage.

rational behavior Human behavior based on comparison of marginal costs and marginal benefits; behavior designed to maximize total utility.

rational expectations theory The hypothesis that firms and households expect monetary and fiscal policies to have certain effects on the economy and (in pursuit of their own self-interests) take actions that make these policies ineffective.

rationing function of prices The ability of market forces in competitive markets to equalize *quantity demanded* and *quantity supplied* and to eliminate shortages and surpluses via changes in prices.

real-balances effect The tendency for increases in the *price level* to lower the real value (or purchasing power) of financial assets with fixed money value and, as a result, to reduce total spending and real output, and conversely for decreases in the price level.

real-business-cycle theory A theory that *business cycles* result from changes in technology and resource availability, which affect *productivity* and thus increase or decrease long-run aggregate supply.

real capital (See *capital.*)

real GDP (See *real gross domestic product.*)

real GDP per capita *Inflation*-adjusted output per person; *real GDP*/population.

real gross domestic product (GDP) *Gross domestic product* adjusted for inflation; gross domestic product in a year divided by the GDP *price index* for that year, the index expressed as a decimal.

real income The amount of goods and services that can be purchased with *nominal income* during some period of time; nominal income adjusted for inflation.

real interest rate The interest rate expressed in dollars of constant value (adjusted for *inflation*) and equal to the *nominal interest rate* less the expected rate of inflation.

real wage The amount of goods and services a worker can purchase with his or her *nominal wage;* the purchasing power of the nominal wage.

recession A period of declining real GDP, accompanied by lower real income and higher unemployment.

recessionary expenditure gap The amount by which the *aggregate expenditures schedule* must shift upward to increase the real *GDP* to its full-employment, noninflationary level.

refinancing the public debt Selling new government securities to owners of expiring securities or paying them money gained from the sale of new securities to others.

regressive tax A tax whose *average tax rate* decreases as the taxpayer's income increases and increases as the taxpayer's income decreases.

rental income The payments (income) received by those who supply *land* to the economy.

required reserves The funds that banks and thrifts must deposit with the *Federal Reserve Bank* (or hold as *vault cash*) to meet the legal *reserve requirement;* a fixed percentage of the bank's or thrift's checkable deposits.

reserve ratio The fraction of *checkable deposits* that a bank must hold as reserves in a *Federal Reserve Bank* or in its own bank vault; also called the *reserve requirement.*

reserve requirement The specified minimum percentage of its checkable deposits that a bank or thrift must keep on deposit at the Federal Reserve Bank in its district or hold as *vault cash.*

resource A natural, human, or manufactured item that helps produce goods and services; a productive agent or factor of production.

resource market A market in which *households* sell and *firms* buy resources or the services of resources.

restrictive monetary policy *Federal Reserve System* actions to reduce the *money supply,* increase *interest rates,* and reduce *inflation;* a tight money policy.

revenue tariff A *tariff* designed to produce income for the Federal government.

risk The uncertainty as to the actual future returns of a particular *financial investment* or *economic investment.*

risk-free interest rate The *interest rate* earned on short-term U.S. government bonds.

risk premium The *interest rate* above the *risk-free* interest rate that must be paid and received to compensate a lender or investor for *risk.*

rivalry (1) The characteristic of a *private good,* the consumption of which by one party excludes other parties from obtaining the benefit; (2) the attempt by one firm to gain strategic advantage over another firm to enhance market share or profit.

rule of 70 A method for determining the number of years it will take for some measure to double, given its annual percentage increase. Example: To determine the number of years it will take for the *price level* to double, divide 70 by the annual rate of *inflation.*

sales tax A tax levied on the cost (at retail) of a broad group of products.

saving Disposable income not spent for consumer goods; equal to *disposable income* minus *personal consumption expenditures;* saving is a flow.

savings The accumulation of funds that results when people in an economy spend less (consume less) than their incomes during a given time period; savings are a stock.

savings account A deposit in a *commercial bank* or *thrift institution* on which interest payments are received; generally used for saving rather than daily transactions; a component of the *M2* money supply.

savings and loan association (S&L) A firm that accepts deposits primarily from small individual savers and lends primarily to individuals to finance purchases such as autos and homes; now nearly indistinguishable from a *commercial bank.*

saving schedule A schedule that shows the amounts *households* plan to save (plan not to spend for *consumer goods*), at different levels of *disposable income.*

savings deposit A deposit that is interest-bearing and that the depositor can normally withdraw at any time.

savings institution (See *thrift institution.*)

Say's law The largely discredited macroeconomic generalization that the production of goods and services (supply) creates an equal *demand* for those goods and services.

scarce resources The limited quantities of *land, capital, labor,* and *entrepreneurial ability* that are never sufficient to satisfy people's virtually unlimited economic wants.

scientific method The procedure for the systematic pursuit of knowledge involving the observation of facts and the formulation and testing of hypotheses to obtain theories, principles, and laws.

secular trend A long-term tendency; a change in some variable over a very long period of years.

securitization The process of aggregating many individual financial debts, such as mortgages or student loans, into a pool and then issuing new securities (financial instruments) backed by the pool. The holders of the new securities are entitled to receive the debt payments made on the individual financial debts in the pool.

Security Market Line (SML) A line that shows the average expected rate of return of all financial investments at each level of *nondiversifiable risk,* the latter measured by *beta.*

self-interest That which each firm, property owner, worker, and consumer believes is best for itself and seeks to obtain.

seniority The length of time a worker has been employed absolutely or relative to other workers; may be used to determine which workers will be laid off when there is insufficient work for them all and who will be rehired when more work becomes available.

separation of ownership and control The fact that different groups of people own a *corporation* (the stockholders) and manage it (the directors and officers).

service An (intangible) act or use for which a consumer, firm, or government is willing to pay.

shirking Workers' neglecting or evading work to increase their *utility* or well-being.

shocks Sudden, unexpected changes in *demand* (or *aggregate demand*) or supply (or *aggregate supply*).

shortage The amount by which the *quantity demanded* of a product exceeds the *quantity supplied* at a particular (below-equilibrium) price.

short run (1) In microeconomics, a period of time in which producers are able to change the quantities of some but not all of the resources they employ; a period in which some resources (usually plant) are fixed and some are variable. (2) In macroeconomics, a period in which nominal wages and other input prices do not change in response to a change in the price level.

short-run aggregate supply curve An *aggregate supply* curve relevant to a time period in which input prices (particularly *nominal wages*) do not change in response to changes in the *price level.*

simple multiplier The *multiplier* in any economy in which government collects no *net taxes,* there are no *imports,* and *investment* is independent of the level of income; equal to 1 divided by the *marginal propensity to save.*

simultaneous consumption The same-time derivation of *utility* from some product by a large number of consumers.

slope of a line The ratio of the vertical change (the rise or fall) to the horizontal change (the run) between any two points on a line. The slope of an upward-sloping line is positive, reflecting a direct relationship between two variables; the slope of a downward-sloping line is negative, reflecting an inverse relationship between two variables.

Smoot-Hawley Tariff Act Legislation passed in 1930 that established very high tariffs. Its objective was to reduce imports and stimulate the domestic economy, but it resulted only in retaliatory tariffs by other nations.

Social Security The social insurance program in the United States financed by Federal payroll taxes on employers and employees and designed to replace a portion of the earnings lost when workers become disabled, retire, or die.

Social Security trust fund A Federal fund that saves excessive Social Security tax revenues received in one year to meet Social Security benefit obligations that exceed Social Security tax revenues in some subsequent year.

sole proprietorship An unincorporated *firm* owned and operated by one person.

specialization The use of the resources of an individual, a firm, a region, or a nation to concentrate production on one or a small number of goods and services.

speculation The activity of buying or selling with the motive of later reselling or rebuying for profit.

stagflation Inflation accompanied by stagnation in the rate of growth of output and an increase in unemployment in the economy; simultaneous increases in the *inflation rate* and the *unemployment rate*.

start-up firm A new firm focused on creating and introducing a particular new product or employing a specific new production or distribution method.

state bank A *commercial bank* authorized by a state government to engage in the business of banking.

sticky prices (See *inflexible prices*.)

stock (corporate) An ownership share in a corporation.

store of value An *asset* set aside for future use; one of the three functions of *money*.

structural unemployment Unemployment of workers whose skills are not demanded by employers, who lack sufficient skill to obtain employment, or who cannot easily move to locations where jobs are available.

subprime mortgage loans High-interest rate loans to home buyers with above-average credit risk.

subsidy A payment of funds (or goods and services) by a government, firm, or household for which it receives no good or service in return. When made by a government, it is a *government transfer payment*.

substitute goods Products or services that can be used in place of each other. When the price of one falls, the demand for the other product falls; conversely, when the price of one product rises, the demand for the other product rises.

substitution effect (1) A change in the quantity demanded of a *consumer good* that results from a change in its relative expensiveness caused by a change in the product's price; (2) the effect of a change in the price of a *resource* on the quantity of the resource employed by a firm, assuming no change in its output.

supply A schedule showing the amounts of a good or service that sellers (or a seller) will offer at various prices during some period.

supply curve A curve illustrating *supply*.

supply factor (in growth) An increase in the availability of a resource, an improvement in its quality, or an expansion of technological knowledge that makes it possible for an economy to produce a greater output of goods and services.

supply schedule (See *supply*.)

supply shocks Sudden, unexpected changes in *aggregate supply*.

supply-side economics A view of macroeconomics that emphasizes the role of costs and *aggregate supply* in explaining *inflation, unemployment*, and *economic growth*.

supply-side market failures Overallocations of resources that occur when private supply curves understate the full cost of producing a good or service.

surplus The amount by which the *quantity supplied* of a product exceeds the *quantity demanded* at a specific (above-equilibrium) price.

tariff A tax imposed by a nation on an imported good.

tax An involuntary payment of money (or goods and services) to a government by a *household* or *firm* for which the household or firm receives no good or service directly in return.

taxes on production and imports A *national income accounting* category that includes such taxes as *sales, excise*, business property taxes, and *tariffs* which firms treat as costs of producing a product and pass on (in whole or in part) to buyers by charging a higher price.

tax incidence The degree to which a *tax* falls on a particular person or group.

tax subsidy A grant in the form of reduced taxes through favorable tax treatment. For example, employer-paid health insurance is exempt from Federal income and payroll taxes.

tax-transfer disincentives Decreases in the incentives to work, save, invest, innovate, and take risks that result from high *marginal tax rates* and *transfer payments*.

Taylor rule A modern monetary rule proposed by economist John Taylor that would stipulate exactly how much the Federal Reserve should change real interest rates in response to divergences of real GDP from potential GDP and divergences of actual rates of inflation from a target rate of inflation.

technological advance New and better goods and services and new and better ways of producing or distributing them.

technology The body of knowledge and techniques that can be used to combine *economic resources* to produce goods and services.

Temporary Assistance for Needy Families (TANF) A state-administered and partly federally funded program in the United States that provides financial aid to poor families; the basic welfare program for low-income families in the United States; contains time limits and work requirements.

term auction facility The *monetary policy* procedure used by the Federal Reserve, in which commercial banks anonymously bid to obtain loans being made available by the Fed as a way to expand reserves in the banking system.

terms of trade The rate at which units of one product can be exchanged for units of another product; the price of a good or service; the amount of one good or service that must be given up to obtain 1 unit of another good or service.

theoretical economics The process of deriving and applying economic theories and principles.

thrift institution A *savings and loan association, mutual savings bank*, or *credit union*.

till money (See *vault cash*.)

time deposit An interest-earning deposit in a *commercial bank* or *thrift institution* that the depositor can withdraw without penalty after the end of a specified period.

time preference The human tendency for people, because of impatience, to prefer to spend and consume in the present rather than save and wait to spend and consume in the future; this inclination varies in strength among individuals.

time-value of money The idea that a specific amount of money is more valuable to a person the sooner it is received because the money can be placed in a financial account or investment and earn *compound interest* over time; the *opportunity cost* of receiving a sum of money later rather than earlier.

token money Bills or coins for which the amount printed on the *currency* bears no relationship to the value of the paper or metal embodied within it; for currency still circulating, money for which the face value exceeds the commodity value.

total demand The demand schedule or the *demand curve* of all buyers of a good or service; also called market demand.

total demand for money The sum of the *transactions demand for money* and the *asset demand for money.*

total revenue (TR) The total number of dollars received by a firm (or firms) from the sale of a product; equal to the total expenditures for the product produced by the firm (or firms); equal to the quantity sold (demanded) multiplied by the price at which it is sold.

total-revenue test A test to determine elasticity of *demand* between any two prices: Demand is elastic if *total revenue* moves in the opposite direction from price; it is inelastic when it moves in the same direction as price; and it is of unitary elasticity when it does not change when price changes.

total spending The total amount that buyers of goods and services spend or plan to spend; also called *aggregate expenditures.*

total supply The supply schedule or the *supply curve* of all sellers of a good or service; also called market supply.

Trade Adjustment Assistance Act A U.S. law passed in 2002 that provides cash assistance, education and training benefits, health care subsidies, and wage subsidies (for persons age 50 or older) to workers displaced by imports or relocations of U.S. plants to other countries.

trade balance The export of goods (or goods and services) of a nation less its imports of goods (or goods and services).

trade controls *Tariffs, export subsidies, import quotas,* and other means a nation may employ to reduce *imports* and expand *exports.*

trade deficit The amount by which a nation's *imports* of goods (or goods and services) exceed its *exports* of goods (or goods and services).

trademark A legal protection that gives the originators of a product an exclusive right to use the brand name.

trade-off The sacrifice of some or all of one economic goal, good, or service to achieve some other goal, good, or service.

trade surplus The amount by which a nation's *exports* of goods (or goods and services) exceed its *imports* of goods (or goods and services).

trading possibilities line A line that shows the different combinations of two products that an economy is able to obtain (consume) when it specializes in the production of one product and trades (exports) it to obtain the other product.

transactions demand for money The amount of money people want to hold for use as a *medium of exchange* (to make payments); varies directly with *nominal GDP.*

transfer payment A payment of *money* (or goods and services) by a government to a *household* or *firm* for which the payer receives no good or service directly in return.

Troubled Asset Relief Program (TARP) A 2008 Federal government program that authorized the U.S. Treasury to loan up to $700 billion to critical financial institutions and other U.S. firms that were in extreme financial trouble and therefore at high risk of failure.

trough The point in a *business cycle* at which business activity has reached a temporary minimum; the point at which a *recession* has ended and an expansion (recovery) begins.

unanticipated inflation Increases in the price level (*inflation*) at a rate greater than expected.

underemployment (Web chapter) A situation in which workers are employed in positions requiring less education and skill than they have.

undistributed corporate profits After-tax corporate profits not distributed as dividends to stockholders; corporate or business saving; also called retained earnings.

unemployment The failure to use all available *economic resources* to produce desired goods and services; the failure of the economy to fully employ its *labor force.*

unemployment compensation (See *unemployment insurance*).

unemployment insurance The social insurance program that in the United States is financed by state *payroll taxes* on employers and makes income available to workers who become unemployed and are unable to find jobs.

unemployment rate The percentage of the *labor force* unemployed at any time.

unfulfilled expectations Situations in which households and businesses were expecting one thing to happen but instead find that something else has happened; unrealized anticipations or plans relating to future economic conditions and outcomes.

uninsurable risk An event that would result in a loss and whose occurrence is uncontrollable and unpredictable. Insurance companies are not willing to sell insurance against such a loss.

unit elasticity Demand or supply for which the *elasticity coefficient* is equal to 1; means that the percentage change in the quantity demanded or supplied is equal to the percentage change in price.

unit labor cost Labor cost per unit of output; total labor cost divided by total output; also equal to the *nominal wage* rate divided by the *average product* of labor.

unit of account A standard unit in which prices can be stated and the value of goods and services can be compared; one of the three functions of *money.*

unlimited wants The insatiable desire of consumers for goods and services that will give them satisfaction or *utility.*

unplanned changes in inventories Changes in inventories that firms did not anticipate; changes in inventories that occur because of unexpected increases or decreases of aggregate spending (or of *aggregate expenditures*).

unplanned investment Actual investment less *planned investment;* increases or decreases in the *inventories* of firms resulting from production greater than sales.

Uruguay Round A 1995 trade agreement (fully implemented in 2005) that established the *World Trade Organization (WTO),* liberalized trade in goods and services, provided added protection to intellectual property (for example, *patents* and *copyrights*), and reduced farm subsidies.

U.S. securities U.S. Treasury bills, notes, and bonds used to finance *budget deficits;* the components of the *public debt.*

utility The want-satisfying power of a good or service; the satisfaction or pleasure a consumer obtains from the consumption of a good or service (or from the consumption of a collection of goods and services).

value added The value of the product sold by a *firm* less the value of the products (materials) purchased and used by the firm to produce the product.

value judgment Opinion of what is desirable or undesirable; belief regarding what ought or ought not to be in terms of what is right (or just) and wrong (or unjust).

value of money The quantity of goods and services for which a unit of money (a dollar) can be exchanged; the purchasing power of a unit of money; the reciprocal of the *price index*.

vault cash The *currency* a bank has in its vault and cash drawers.

velocity The number of times per year that the average dollar in the *money supply* is spent for *final goods and services;* nominal GDP divided by the money supply.

venture capital (Web chapter) That part of household saving used to finance high-risk business enterprises in exchange for shares of the profit if the enterprise succeeds.

vertical axis The "up-down" or "north-south" measurement line on a graph or grid.

vertical intercept The point at which a line meets the vertical axis of a graph.

vicious circle of poverty (Web chapter) A problem common in some *developing countries* in which their low *per capita incomes* are an obstacle to realizing the levels of saving and investment needed to achieve rates of growth of output that exceed their rates of population growth.

voluntary export restrictions (VER) Voluntary limitations by countries or firms of their exports to a particular foreign nation to avoid enactment of formal trade barriers by that nation.

wage The price paid for the use or services of *labor* per unit of time (per hour, per day, and so on).

wage rate (See *wage.*)

wages The income of those who supply the economy with *labor*.

Wall Street Reform and Consumer Protection Act of 2010 A law that gave authority to the *Federal Reserve System* to regulate all large financial institutions, created an oversight council to look for growing risk to the financial system, established a process for the Federal government to sell off the assets of large failing financial institutions, provided Federal regulatory oversight of asset-backed securities, and created a financial consumer protection bureau within the Fed.

wealth Anything that has value because it produces income or could produce income. Wealth is a stock; *income* is a flow. Assets less liabilities; net worth.

wealth effect The tendency for people to increase their consumption spending when the value of their financial and real assets rises and to decrease their consumption spending when the value of those assets falls.

will to develop (Web chapter) The state of wanting *economic growth* strongly enough to change from old to new ways of doing things.

World Bank (Web chapter) A bank that lends (and guarantees loans) to developing nations to assist them in increasing their *capital stock* and thus in achieving *economic growth.*

world price The international market price of a good or service, determined by world demand and supply.

World Trade Organization (WTO) An organization of 153 nations (as of mid-2010) that oversees the provisions of the current world trade agreement, resolves trade disputes stemming from it, and holds forums for further rounds of trade negotiations.

WTO (See *World Trade Organization.*)